Natalia Ribas-Mateos

Migration, Welfare, & Borders

The Mediterranean in the Age of Globalization

Transaction Publishers
New Brunswick (U.S.A.) and London (U.K.)

Copyright © 2005 by Transaction Publishers, New Brunswick, New Jersey.
www.transactionpub.com

Library of Congress Catalog Number: 2004051779
ISBN: 0-7658-0257-0
Printed in the United States of America

Library of Congress Cataloging-in-Publication Data

Ribas Mateos, Natalia.
    The Mediterranean in the age of globalization : migration, welfare, and
  borders / Natalia Ribas-Mateos.
        p. cm.
    Includes bibliographical references and index.
    ISBN 0-7658-0257-0 (cloth : alk. paper)
      1. Migration, Internal—Mediterranean Region—Congresses. 2. Mediterranean Region—Economic conditions. 3. Mediterranean Region—
  Social conditions. 4. Europe, Southern—Emigration and immigration. 5.
  Africa, North—Emigration and immigration. 6. Europe, Southern—Social
  policy. 7. Welfare state—Europe, Southern. 8. Marginality, Social—
  Europe, Southern. 9. Globalization—Economic aspects. 10. Globalization—Social aspects. I. Title.

HB2092.7.A3R5 2005
303.48'21822—dc22   2004051779

To Pura, Juan, and Berta

Contents

Tables

x The Mediterranean in the Age of Globalization

Figures

Acknowledgments

I wish to gratefully acknowledge all the people who helped me during my fieldwork. In Algeciras, Mario Arias and Encarni (from Algeciras Acoge); in Athens, Laura Alipranti, Cristini, Balwin-Edwards, Chris Cunion and R. Fakiolas; in Alexandropouli, Dukas Dimostenis; in Barcelona, Estefania, Fabi Díaz, and two researchers who conducted interviews, Teo Mellén and Eduard Solé; in Lisbon, María Baganha, David Justino, Jorge Malheiros, and Margarida Marques; in Durrës, Bajana, Eda, Línia, Vali, and Flora; in Komotini, Maria Petmesidou, Amin, Hristos Pashalakis and the workers of the Kapi center; in Naples, Anna Maria Cirillo and Dora Gambardella; in Tangier, Ahmed, Allal, Aiman, Mercedes, Omar, Rachid, Rhimo, Sami, Sakkat and Taoufik; in Tirana, Berti, Nardi, Olivier and Remzi; in Turin, Chiara Saraceno, Carlo Tagliacozzo, and Giovanna Zincone. My warmest gratitude goes to my adopted families in Durrës and Tangiers.

The origins of the first part of the book were shared with my colleagues—office at the Department of Sociology of the Universitat Autònoma de Barcelona and colleagues from the TMR (Training and Mobility of Researchers) Seminars. Helpful comments in the UK were offered by Richard Black, the members of the Sussex Centre for Migration Research, Nicola Mai, Jenny Money, Miguel Solana, and Mirela Dalipaj (as well as her supervisor Stephanie Schwander-Sievers). Critical remarks were also made by various members of the Maison de la Mediterranée (Aix-en-Provence), Gilles de Rapper, Véronique Manry, Sylvie Mazzella, and Michel Peraldi.

I gratefully acknowledge the helpful comments, critiques, and ideas for revision given by: Elisabet Almeda, Minoun Aziza, Richard Black, José Manuel Díaz, Malcolm Gardner, Ivan Light, Kàtia Lurbe, Mercedes Jiménez, Sarah Moss, Sandra Obiols, Pablo Pumares, Yasmin Rasidgil, Amelia Sáinz, Pierre Sintes, Imma Torres, Chiara Saraceno, Carlota Solé, and Aiman Zoubir.

My special thanks, too, go to the European Commission who helped me find a way into the European Research Space. The work was supported by the EU TMR Programme and two Marie Curie Fellowships. I wish to thank Saskia Sassen for initially encouraging me to write a synthesis of the last eight years of my research life. And I acknowledge the encouragement and enthusiastic support of my editor at Transaction Publishers, Anne Schneider. And, finally, special appreciation goes to three people: Russell King for his belief in the project. Sònia García, as always, supported me from the first until the last day of the book; and Eric gave me his imagination as a present. To all of them, my deepest appreciation.

Introduction

Defining Mediterranean Scales: Globalization and Borders

Time after time migration studies tend to make use of ancient travel myths to recall the living experiences of contemporary migrants, sometimes to highlight an expression of mourning, while others to insist on a venturesome, enterprising nature of modern mobility. Goytisolo (2004) considers that "our civilisation" brings with it two main travel myths: that of Ulysses in the Odyssey and Robinson Crusoe on the Isle of Más a Tierra. The myth is built up around the wanderings of Penelope's husband prior to his return to Ithaca, and those of Daniel Defoe's hero, in the light of the challenge they face in struggling to build up their own world in a hostile environment. Whilst the former acted – consciously or subconsciously – as the seeds for the great travel books, ranging from those by Tangierin Ibn Batuta and Marco Polo to the Pleiades written in recent centuries, for Goytisolo, the Scottish sailor at the centre of Daniel Defoe's novel is not really searching for adventure but survival, and is the victim of his own unfortunate fate. It might be some sort of modern truth in all of those icons, so the tale of this shipwrecked sailor echoes that of millions of women, men and children today as for those who do suffer from not being able to return to Ithaca. We will see them, somehow implicitly, through the space of the book, when we define in this introduction: the Mediterranean Scale (Globalization and its borders), when we identify the sides of the same coin (in the North and in the South of Western Mediterranean), then the Caravanserai will take us to the idea of diverse and intensified circulation (where again the myth persists, the word caravanserai finds its etymology from Persian language, *Karawán saray*, palace of caravans). In fourth place we will detail the itinerary of the book, explaining in how to make a journey by sea calling at a series of ports.

Changes related to globalization and scale cause us to think about new theoretical and methodological questions, and more specifically about the way in which strategic economic and political processes territorialize in the European periphery. Border cities are not in the same hierarchy of power as Sassen's global cities (2001) but they are connected to them, and at the same time they play a role in the old North-South division. Through some sort of binomial relationship, the global city-border city set can now be seen in the context of the triadization[1] of the global economy.

1

If we consider the situation of Western Mediterranean cities today in connection with globalization and triadization we see that none of them are "command villages" in the context of the three powerful world regions, United States, Japan, and Europe. Economic globalization is reshaped by cross-national economic integration of different forms and on different scales, such as those related to the three main axes of the world economies. This process makes us challenge the notion of the globalized world, where North America, Japan, and Europe all have in common the making of fortress regions in the global space. In this geographical clustering, Southern Europe acts as the soft underbelly of Fortress Europe, therefore rescaling the vision of today's Mediterranean world.

Europe is facing a reconstruction of borders, where within we see the new silent borders (such as the Spanish villages facing France) or the emergence of non-prepared borders such as the case of the French-British border where Sangatte (Pas de Calais) became emblematic following the construction of a Red Cross shelter, supposedly to host refugees. Contrary to the institutional project, the refugees showed their determination to reach England. Hence, these new borders require a redefinition of scale. Pumares (2003) establishes a typology of the Spanish territory according to migration: border spaces, agrarian spaces, tourist spaces, and metropolitan spaces. I considered a similar division for the Mediterranean, bearing in mind the different scales of concentration, density, and mobility. According to Pumares, border spaces provide the direct link between international geopolitics and local response. They hold a geo-strategic position that makes them symbolic bridges of mobility. For example, Sebta and Melilla, in northern Morocco, are those spaces par excellence. Twenty thousand people move in and out of these border spaces everyday, which makes them both fortress spaces and defensive spaces for Spain, the Iberian Peninsula, and the whole of Europe. The Canary Islands can also be included here. They are peculiar spaces because entering these areas does not guarantee access to the rest of Spain. They are clearly defined as enclaves that receive immigrants in a space where mobility is restricted, "an open-air prison," and are particularly conflictive due to their supposed first-line defensive role. This is where immigrants are detained and apply for asylum, and where the first migrant minors have been found.

An effort is needed to unpack the forms of cross-border circuits in a context of cross-border systems, which might affect differently specific border cities in the world and different border areas in world regions. It is not so much an issue of comparability among cities but an attempt to identify the role certain cities—affected by the triadization of the global economy—play either as gates of passage or as obstacles of mobility. Border cities are specific places in terms of the way they engage in the new economy, thanks to the manufacturing role they play in helping European service economies. In order to define them I focus on specific processes, which have enabled me to determine the impact of economic globalization in such an analysis: the new relations of work characterized by informalization tendencies, the new patterns of waged labor characterized by export processing zones, and the configuration of households affected by the new patterns of international migration (feminization of labor flows, remittance-dependant economies, and the diversification of the typology of migrants).

One of the most complex consequences of globalization is renewed border restrictions on the movement of people. These restrictions are symbols of a dominant blockade, and they exist in marked contrast to the mobility that people actually desire and to the movement of goods across these borders (as well as being the result of European macro-economic policies). In this way, two Mediterranean port cities, "corners" of Europe—Durrës and Tangier—can be used as strategic locations enabling us to study different forms of mobility in a specific, selected border area. We can analyze what happens on a specific level in these cities which, in themselves, represent physical barriers and areas of control. They allow us to study a "break space" through which we can discern specific changes in the contemporary urban setting, which has been plunged into consumption (with the increasing dominance of images and mass culture) and changes in the mobility—especially in these two cases—of young people. In general, capital, products, and ideas have become more liberated, while certain categories of labor, which are limited by immigration laws, continue to be subject to control, with a penalization of mobility. When we consider the closure of borders (militarization, increase in police contingents, etc.), these types of borders may also be seen as pockets of resistance to globalization.

What Marcus (1998) claims as distinctive of the new anthropology, its multi-sided research imagery, represents an important part of the research for this book. Accordingly, most of the work presented here was also multi-sided in character and kept evolving with the fieldwork. Seen from an empirical research perspective, the city space emerges as a strategic location in the new representation of borders within globalization. As happens with many globalists when they consider that the urban space remains the key to capitalist spatialization, they now believe it integrates now the geographic supranational scales.

These selected border cities represent an area where the north runs directly into the south. Specifically, they are also cities and spaces in the very heart of which a new system of geographies of centrality and marginalization has been created, as well as the emergence of an elite that is connected with the privatization of capital and the sprouting of peripheral neighborhoods deriving from internal migration. Our main argument concerning these border cities defines the question to be analysed, which is how to express the contradictions that arise within a space that is at the same time a place designed to encourage the free circulation of capital and a blockade discouraging human mobility. This dichotomy—on one hand, the closing of borders and on the other, peoples' desire for movement—reveals the two contradictory faces of the global economy: the obstacles encountered by migrants in their search for free circulation are to some extent contradictory to the free market principles of Europe's big cities (which need cheap labor) and to a global capitalist economy (which is attempting to reduce profit borders).

It is quite obvious that the global free market places limitations on workers' freedom through restrictive entry (a situation in which nation-states have the sovereign power to apply such measures), while richer countries (such as those of the European Union) are prepared to defend a global work market for skilled workers. Meanwhile, in spite of the closing of European Union borders, people in many parts of the Mediterranean continue to develop versatile strategies and to plan their lives by using spatial mobility strategies. Fuga relates very accurately how Albania has become a periphery of the European Union, particularly in the way in which the Balkans play a border role in the EU with the arms of Italy and Greece. It is a "periphery" producing cheap, clandestine workers, prostitutes for the unsatisfied libido of rich countries, drug dealers, domestic helpers, children for adoption when fertility rates collapse, hard-working people, and caretakers of the elderly; a periphery that offers its best products to the international market at low prices while Albanians eat EU products past their expiration date; a periphery that, in turn, produces an "under-periphery," namely "the periphery of the periphery"—in other words, the urban world of the peasants, the retired, the gypsies, and the sick (Fuga 2000: 274).

The book is divided into two main parts: one dedicated to Southern Europe, the other to Border Cities. Each part contains two chapters: a corresponding theoretical and an empirical chapter for both investigations.

Sides of the Same Coin

Theories of dualism arose first in the literature on the economy and society of less developed countries and later were adopted in the United States, in the mid-1960s, to account for the situation of black workers in the central cities of the North of the country. These theories would develop even more through research on the dual city concept. However, Berger and Piore (1980), in their analysis of the significance of dualism, used the same frame of reference both for developing and developed societies and were increasingly struck by the similarities between them. The evidence from both types of societies suggests that the process of industrialization and modernization might generate kinds of heterogeneity that would be recast in the old models. Northern and southern cities share common problems, and polarization and dualist dynamics are present in both places. I will attempt to search out these continuities, in the correspondence to their nature and time of occurrence.

In both parts of the book, directly or indirectly, the role of the family is always present. In critical terms, it can be viewed from the progressive family concept (towards a nuclear family, towards a male breadwinner family), or it can be seen in its basic role, replacing caring roles in the complex expansion and weakening of the welfare state. In this sense, migration changes in Southern Europe also respond to a certain household structure and dynamic, as does industry relocation in Mediterranean border cities, which shows that the connection between economic globalization and household dynamics is not obscure. Both parts of the book similarly emphasize the resurgence of reciprocity and solidarity, not only as a result of the development of the various manifestations of welfare capitalism demanding greater flexibility and an expansion of the tertiary sector, but also as a result of the impact of economic globalization and border restriction on countries of the South and the East.

From the heart of the debate on economic sociology, the growing importance of the informal economy is seen not only as a result of the industrialization process of the Southern countries, but as a form "of production and exchange characteristic of industrial capitalism of the nineteenth century, and which persists along its history" (Dore-Cabral 1995: 2). Therefore, in line with Portes (1995, as well as Mingione 1991 and Sassen 2001) the informal economy is seen as a substantial element of the capitalist system and not a residual part of it. Thus, a social agent of the informal economy can be closely involved in the global chain of modern subcontracting through foreign immigration or through export-oriented manufacturing in the production of clothing and textile products.

There is also a feminization of the labor force. This tendency, together with the nimble fingers, servitude, and caring attitudes of women featured consistently in the discourses. Historically, the garment industry has been one of the sectors where capitalism has made the most blatant use of patriarchal structures to connect reproduction and women's reproductive role. Worldwide employment of women in off-shore assembly manufacturing plants has been a subject of considerable interest in labor studies (Fernandez-Kelly 1983). Research conducted on the gendered nature of the internationalization of capital and the implication of women´s wage labor in industrialization processes has highlighted the feminization of female-led- industrialization of the labor force in export zones where production has been relocated. In a study of the clothing industry in Morocco, owners were seen to take advantage of lower female employment costs justifying them on the basis that women were "working for lipstick" (Joekes 1982). A similar justification was used in Hong Kong electronics factories where young, single women were assigned secondary status in the labor market because of their capacity to bear children (Lim 1981, 1990). Other major studies included those on the Bangladesh garment industry (Kabeer 1991), the relocation of international production in Singapore (Heyzer 1988), and the female workers in the Mexican border industries (Fernandez-Kelly 1983; Pearson 1988, quoted in Moser and Peake 1995: 306-307).

While in one part of the world, in tax-free export zones, women are considered a cheap labor force, in another part of the world they have become immigrant labor or the new-sweatshop workers in the garment industries of the global cities (Sassen 1996). These processes have therefore accelerated the international migration of women. In some parts of the world, such as the Caribbean, survival strategies for women include: an increased number in the labor force, particularly in the export processing zones; increased activity in the informal sector; changes in consumer and dietary patterns; and an increase in the predominantly female international migration to the United States. It is through those cases that we see "in both their ideologies and cultural practices people shape and respond to processes of global and domestic economic restructuring in organizing their daily lives" (Feldman 1992: 126). It is important to observe how explanations of women's needlework coincide with those concerning international immigrants' labor in sweatshops: "immigrant skill is more often represented as imported rather than inborn, while immigrant need is usually envisaged as that of the male breadwinner rather than simply extra pin money. Like women, immigrants are described as having a penchant for homework and engaging in informal recruitment patterns. Immigrants, like women, have been described as accepting and even offering derisive prices for their work due to need" (Green 1996: 423-424). The same can also be observed through Sassens' account of post-Fordism, where "women and immigrants" as a category came to replace "women and children" (Sassen 1998). Hence, she shows the substitution from the Fordist topos (of the male breadwinner with the unpaid household work of the woman as wife and mother), to the post-Fordist topos of the flexibilized and casual unvalued service worker.

Beyond the Caravanserai

The search for unity among the Mediterranean societies has always been a constant in historical and anthropological analyses. The idea of convergence is quite well understood by historians, because the Mediterranean was not considered to be a region but rather a series of divergent seas. Much has already been written about the Mediterranean as "common space" where economic and cultural exchanges, as well as violent confrontations, take place. Nowadays, the Mediterranean represents one of the most active friction-planes when considering North-South imbalances in globalized work; it is the setting both for sharp socioeconomic contrasts and for several kinds of migratory phenomena, which derive from global inequality and instability (Ribas-Mateos 2001a: 22). The migration frontier, which during the 1850s and the 1960s ran along the Alps and the Pyrenees, has now changed direction and runs from East to West along the Mediterranean from Istanbul to the Straits of Gibraltar (King 1998).

During the nineteenth century, French geographical and historical tradition used the category of the Mediterranean as a scientific object. The Mediterranean region was also a favorite topic among early anthropologists and sociologists (e.g., Maine, Fustel de Coulanges, Robertson-Smith, Frazer, Durkheim, Westermarck). However, most Mediterranists still used pre-modern research techniques and lacked an overall comparative and historical approach (Davis 1983).

Later, anthropologists continued to refer to the Mediterranean as a universe for internal comparison, in the UK through the research of Pitt-Rivers in Andalusia, the fieldwork of Cambell in Greece and Stirling's work in Turkey. In France, it developed much earlier, in the 1930s with the works of Blok and Parain (Albera and Blok 2001: 16), and through the works of those who used the Mediterranean as an area of cultural mixture particularly in the colonized lands of North Africa (Bromberger 2001). Based on Braudel's work on ecological and historical conditions, where differences and similarities were considered, authors tried to determine the rules of Mediterranean unity and singularity. Efforts were also made to establish the Mediterranean as a regional category of study, as an appropriate tool for analysis. In doing so, it was often constructed as a monothetic category. In general, all those authors shared a common desire to see the Mediterranean as a homogeneous cultural space. Most efforts to delineate a pan-Mediterranean perspective have been made by specialists working on southern Europe (see all authors compiled in Albera and Blok 2001). The focus has been on the unifying themes of honor and shame, hospitality, family friendship, kinship, patronage and the relations of local communities to society at large. Gender and the segregation of women are also often noted, as well as the cultural emphasis on women's virginity and chastity together with their exclusion from public space.

Davis rejected from those dominant works the cultural area approach, like Pitt-Rivers earlier and Gilmore later (Albera and Blok 2001). We will now go on to consider the differences inside the cultural space. Through Wolf's writings, Davis notes how bilateral kinship, the household of the nuclear family, social network and dowry in the Latin countries contrast with agnation, segmentary organization, and the richness of the bride in the Maghreb. He also underlined the contrast between Islamic theocracy and the Christian separation between Church and State. Gellner uses the image of the mirror in order to set up the Christian Church (hierarchical, ritual, meditative, and emotive) and its sects (democratic, puritan, and personal) against Islam (democratic, austere, and personal) and its hierarchical and emotional Orders (Davis 1983: 21). The Mediterranean is often perceived as dialogic space where identities are defined by a mirror game. Relations between communities use both *eros* and *eris*, in the sense used by the French ethnologist Jacques Berque: the crusades, the conquests, and peaceful cohabitation (Bromberger and Durand 2001: 734). On the other hand, influences from North and South are also evident, especially when considering Italy and Spain. In this case, Davis suggests that more than a contraposition of models they can be thought of as contrasting images or reflected images (Davis 1983: 26). Other authors such as Goody (2001) also continue to work on the Mediterranean area trait list by underlining kinship, marriage, and inheritance practices as the main North-South differences, such as the prevalence of patrilineal lineages using ties of agnatic endogamy (meaning preferential marriage to the father's brother's daughter—*bint al am*).

According to Ibert (2003), the Mediterranean discourse has become ideological in the light of the growing awareness of a space filled with values and history. This discourse establishes three types of ideal-typical settings:

1. For Mediterranean archaeologists, it constitutes a classical territory in which the frontiers of a political system and a civilization converge. It also acts as a space for relations and exchange, routes and commercial meeting points. The prime example of this is logically the Roman Empire.[2]
2. It is a setting made up of cultural and political territories, thereby creating a typical-ideal relational system. The prime example of this is the Andalusian model.
3. After Rome and Andalusia, the third ideal-typical setting is that of the port cities, the nineteenth-century city-states that coincide with the invention of modern Greece, the birth of Turkey, and the fall of the eastern empires prior to the birth of the Near East.

Ilbert considers that the Mediterranean model is more than just an ideal type, paradigm or mode; he sees it as a cultural reference that has determined and structured our modern societies—an element of our social representations and collective psychology. This author uses the ideal of the "Mediterranean" as part of a world scale in the sense that Mediterranean formations indicate the successive settings of the universal situation, a scale of orientation in which tiny variations clarify innate—and occasionally radical—mutations.

Nevertheless, the old-fashioned vision of the Mediterranean works only partially in current social sciences. We can distinguish four lines of arguments supporting these criticisms. The first line of argument is related to those who note a growing critical discussion on the very notion of the Mediterranean, often in a postmodern, anti-orientalist mood that questions the "Mediterranist construct" and speaks of failures, shortcomings and ethnocentrism (Albera and Blok 2001). Criticisms are addressed particularly to the "honor and shame complex" in the crisis around the category of the Mediterranean. Tersigni's work (2001) is one of the few contributions that one can find criticizing the supposed code of Mediterranean honor. She alleges that the code of honor has acted as an atemporal means of facing social integration in France. She analyzes different works on the Maghrebi population in France, showing how the obstacles to integration were not due to Islam but to the condition of women at the heart of Mediterranean family ethics, particularly in how the concept of clanic honor based on girls' virginity has been "erected" as the cultural handicap for social integration (Tersigni 2001:57). In line with the critics of the

Mediterranists (Pina-Cabral, Herzfeld, Wikan, Goddart, Lozos and Papataxiarchis, Kressel, Lindisfarne, Passaro, La Cecla), Tersigni explores the counter-arguments based on how Mediterranist anthropology develops an imprecise discourse of a psychological nature and how autochthonous traits emerge as the underlying nature of heterogeneous phenomena (Tersigni 2001: 59).

Another criticism of the broad category of the Mediterranean is focused on the discontinuities in economic and geo-political terms. Dunford and King (2001) see the historical division of the Mediterranean as being the Arab and Muslim world, roughly from Turkey to Morocco; and on the other side, the Western, Christian World from Portugal to Greece. The latter has constantly tried to dominate the rest of the Basin through a combination of political, military, and economic means, following the Western capitalistic commercial model (Braudel 1979 in Dunford and King 2001: 31). Today, the patterns of developed and underdeveloped areas are highly contrasted in terms of the axes of the North-South gap in the Mediterranean GNP; France heads the list with Albania bringing up the rear. Therefore, a clear division can also be seen in HDI (Human Development Index) between Northern and Southern Mediterranean countries. However, for the Southern countries the HDI is worse than their wealth would imply, due to their underperformance on indicators of key human development such as life expectancy, educational attainment, and the low status of women. This can be seen in the case of Morocco, which has the highest illiteracy rates in North Africa, and which are worse in Morocco's northern areas, the borders with Europe and Spain. Other countries, however, show a positive difference in the ratings. These include Albania, which has inherited the communist system's commitment to universal state education and health care, but whose GDP figures have lagged behind in the aftermarth of the Balkan crises (Dunford and King 2001: 37).

A third very interesting criticism is how the concept of the Mediterranean can still remain useful with the Europeanization and globalization of its economy and the restructuring of the state, including the welfare state. Consequently, another point of concern is Europeanization. The North of the Mediterranean has experienced a solid process of Europeanization, particularly from the early 1990s onwards, leading to a gradual distancing from its Southern neighbors. Thus, with time the anthropology of the Mediterranean has given way to the anthropology of Europe. Southern Europe, North Africa, and South Eastern Europe are preferred to the reified concept of the Mediterranean. However, my opinion coincides with that of other authors in that the idea of the Mediterranean is today a means of preventing Euro-centrism: "It destabilises the idea of Europe by reminding us of analogies between cultures inside and outside the continent" (Burke 2001: 99).

A fourth criticism is related to Islamization. In the "new" Muslim politics, "being Muslim" plays an increasingly important role in the way some people see themselves and their society, morality, the rule of law, and the role of religion in their lives. Eickelman specially underlines the role of Muslim politics in the construction of a new moral order and the emergence of a civil society (Eickelman 2001).

The metaphor of the Mediterranean caravanserai or "common space" (Ribas-Mateos 2001a: 24) was used earlier to refer to migrant groups and flows. The way that southern Europe functions as a new reception space for "caravans" or groups of migrants coming from the other side of the Mediterranean or further afield has obvious parallels with this earlier usage. This "Mediterranean effort" attempts to lift the romantic and stereotypical veil that has long covered the Mediterranean region from the perspective of the social sciences. Secondly, it tries to clarify the complexities involved in understanding the Mediterranean area. Thirdly, it is an attempt to understand the traditional vision of the Mediterranean as a space of circulation and a place of exchange in a period of geographical proximity and new communication technologies. Fourth, familism serves as a strategic tool in order to understand the Mediterranean framework of this book.

My interest definitely lies in the possibilities the Mediterranean offers in relating space and globalization. I aim to show, on one hand, how the Mediterranean is a "perfect" illustration of how to view the current day social and political superposition within symbolic borders, and how borders also act as possible negotiation sites. On the other hand, it challenges the Euro-Mediterranean scale, where Europe uses a standard order for the immobility of new migrants (as labor force and as a citizens) as a counterweight to the mobility of capital, goods, and finances. It is also a location from which to observe the impact of Fortress Europe after September 11 and its growing influence on Europeans' vision of the Muslim Mediterranean world. Nevertheless, the general controversy surrounding the Mediterranean space will be considered again as a starting point in chapter 1, when discussing the topic, "Shrinking the Mediterranean: The limits of the Region."

The Itinerary

In this volume, I propose an itinerary on a selected research path of the Mediterranean, that is to say, throughout the whole book, the West Mediterranean up to and including Greece. The book is the result of eight years' research into Mediterranean migration from the perspective of gender, welfare, and border cities. It includes interviews in seven case studies and ethnographies in two border cities. All are narratives of location, where actors, interviewees, and informants give their accounts, a history of social practices. Part 1 (Southern Europe) and Part 2 (Border Cities) intersect as a result of discontinuities in the Mediterranean region that represent a general research site for the analysis of some aspects of the global economy.

Cross-Border Circulation* in Mediterranean Migration: Selected Case Studies

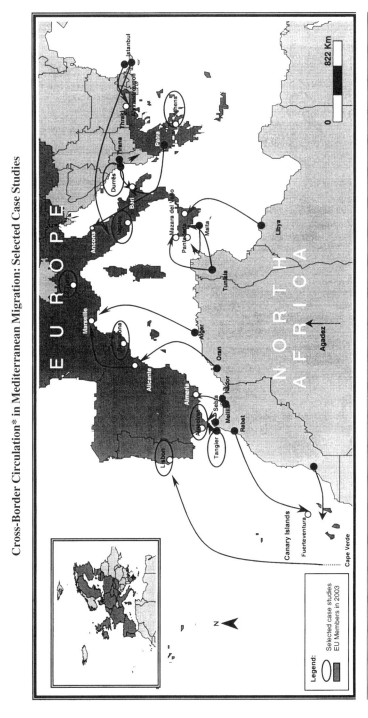

*This map only means to provide an approximate picture of the main flows linking the opposite shores of the Mediterranean.

The book's principal argument is an attempt to articulate a compelling narrative mapping out the Mediterranean as a global place, a place where forces of international and regional hegemonies are intertwined in multiple threads of life and circuits. By conceptualizing global influences (specifically neo-liberal restructuring) I select not only cities on the borders of the global economy but also those on the borders of the Mediterranean space. By looking at major trends we can see how they materialize and impact at the city level. We can find major trends of economic restructuring and local forms that make creative combinations in a socio-cultural locality.

The general aim of the research was to conduct an investigation in the fields of migration and globalization, considering the Mediterranean area. My main objective was always constant but the way of developing the research was continually updated. The work was divided into two main sections: Part 1 analyzes welfare immigration policies in Southern Europe (Greece, Italy, Portugal, and Spain), focusing mainly on the weakening of the welfare state, and Part 2 examines the changes in border cities, the Mediterranean gateways, and deals mainly with the issue of mobility in borderlands. Borders can be thought of as intersections between different spaces, in and out of Schengen Europe.

I seek to explain how economic globalization simultaneously leads to the emergence of new forms of welfare (weakening traditional welfare and creating new combinations under the pressures of neo-liberalism) and new forms of mobility in social relations (weakening traditional forms of migration and creating new categories and forms), where traditional research sites are reshaped by the cross-national economic integration of different forms and scales. This is discussed in more detail using examples of selected city cases. In the Southern European cities the emphasis is on changes in forms of welfare in relation to social services for foreign migrants, using Albanian and Moroccan families as key examples. On the other hand, in the selected cases of the Mediterranean borderlands the emphasis is on changes in the forms of mobility as seen through an analysis of family household strategies.

Part 1 focuses on a final definition of seven case studies in Southern European cities (issues related to immigration and the welfare state), identifying key components of globalization processes—forms of welfare and issues of mobility—in light of the weakening of the European welfare state. To support the argument, the concepts of welfare mix variations will be discussed, including explanations and descriptions of the urban and social differences existing in Southern Europe. Consequently, I direct my attention to an exploration of the frailty of the welfare state in the context of the "new migrations." An explanation is offered as to how economic globalization simultaneously leads to the emergence of new forms of welfare and new forms of mobility in social relations, where traditional research sites are reshaped by a cross-national economic integration of different forms and scales. It describes the framework for analyzing the question of a theoretical convergence in Southern European immigration in terms of an interdisciplinary context located in the labor market (especially in the informal sector), civil society (especially in the role of the family), and the state (stressing the growing importance of local policies). Changes in the market (informalization of the economy, particularly in farming and service sectors) and in the family (in terms of gender and generation structures in relation to the quality of welfare services) are the bases for understanding the situation of foreign immigrants.

Through the logic of comparative analysis, this first part presents the common indicators for the model in Southern Europe. These can be expressed by a triangular context of reception defined by the three previously highlighted variables: a large informal economy, a weak welfare state, and the specific role of the family. However, even though the countries will be used as units of analysis, case studies set in regional and local contexts are deployed to demonstrate the high diversity of welfare mix variations, through the complex system of convergence and divergence. The seven case studies were taken from the southern half of Europe: Turin and Naples in Italy, Barcelona and Algeciras in Spain, Lisbon in Portugal, and Athens and Thrace in Greece.

In Southern Europe, the "migration turnaround" was the statistical product of three distinct, though not entirely unconnected, migration variables: the rapid decline in emigration; the behavior of return migrant flows; and—eventually the most important variable—the rapid and accelerating growth during the 1980s and 1990s of immigration from a remarkable diversity of new source countries. By the 1980s, and earlier in Italian cities, the attainment of "European" standards of prosperity and economic modernization, among other factors, had turned Southern Europe into a major global region of immigration (King and Ribas-Mateos, 2002).

It is in Part 1 that I will develop the thesis on the complexity of the Southern European model of immigration. This line of thinking on the Southern European model brings us to another side of the question: how do we define its border spaces? The answer can be found in tracing the reflection on work of spaces of transit and spaces of settlement, emergency and border restrictions in Southern European cities, towards the Mediterranean border cities to Southern Europe. This aim compelled me to examine the spaces of the global border-site in Part 2, finding its conditions, features, and dynamics, unveiling also how these cities and places have responded to the challenge of global migration, unveiling a wide range of responses at local levels. What is striking, however, is the differences observed in the shaping of welfare provisions, with the organization of multiple systems of divisions, migrants, non-migrants, regular migrants, non-regular migrants, etc. The various cases will reveal how key elements of heterogeneity are present when considering the diversity of the local studies under examination. Differences emerge from the conformation of tendencies in the new welfare mix; these tendencies are forced to cope with the situation of a harsh open dual welfare system.

It is in the first part of the book where I will approach the complexity of the Southern European model of immigration. I will make reference to some common groups of foreigners in the selected case studies. Southern Europe shares interesting commonalities when we refer to groups of migrants, such as Albanian and Moroccans. In this case, if we look, for example, at their representation in prisons and at the weight of non-accompanied minors in Italy and Spain (see Tables I.1, I.2, I.3, I.4 and I.5) we can deduce that they are often trapped in strong processes of stigmatization, which, in turn, poses the question of the integration of lower class groups into these societies.

Table I.1
Foreigners in Italy, Reported, Arrested, and Detained 1999*

Country of origin	Reported to the police		Arrested		Detained	
	N	%	N	%	N	%
Morocco	16,435	17.6	5,857	20.9	3,095	22.0
Albania	15,039	16.1	2,854	10.2	2,104	15.0
Others	62,122	66.3	19,356	68.9	8,851	63.0
TOTAL	**93,596**	**100**	**28,067**	**100**	**14,050**	**100**

* 31/12/1999

Source: Zincone, G. (2001) *Secondo rapporto sull'integrazione degli immigrati in Italia.* Bologna: Il Mulino, 294. Using sources from Ministero della Giustizia.

Table I.2
Foreign Inmates in Spain by Nationality and Sex*

Country	Male	Female
Morocco	2,103	61
Algeria	798	5
Colombia	60	308
Portugal	243	36
TOTAL	**3,204**	**410**

* 1/11/2000

Source: *Ministerio del Interior (2000) Estadística general de población penitenciaria. Administración General y total nacional.* Madrid: Gabinete técnico. Servicio de Planificación y Seguimiento.

Table I.3
Non-Accompanied Minors in Italy Referred to CMS (Foreign Minors
Committee) by Country of Origin

Country of origin	Indications from 1/07/00 to 31/01/02	%
Albania	9,047	57.9
Morocco	1,833	11.3
Romania	1,184	7.3
Others	4,175	23.5
Total	**16,239**	**100**

Source: Data provided by CMS (Comitato per I minori stranieri).

Table I.4
Non-Accompanied Minors Referred to CMS (Foreign Minors Committee) by
Main Italian Regions

Region	Indications from 1/07/00 to 31/01/02	%
Puglia	3,031	18.7
Lombardia	2,416	14.9
Lazio	2,306	14.2
Others	8,486	52.2
Total	**16,239**	**100**

Source: Data provided by CMS (Comitato per I minori stranieri).

What's more, some sub-groups share common regional origins in the Southern European space (specific Chinese origins in Portugal and Spain, specific Peruvian and Rumanian regions in Italy and Spain, Moroccans from Beni Mlal in Italy and Spain). This line of thinking on the Southern Europe model and the importance of neighboring groups such as Albanians and Moroccans will direct the itinerary of the book to another side of the Mediterranean. The effort will be posited then in the concept of border, that of Mediterranean border cities to Southern Europe.

Part 2 deals with "border cities." After conducting the first part of the field-work I realized that the dynamics of the field spoke to the issue of borders located next to the EU more so than the issue of entry dynamics, with which I

Table I.5
Unattended Minors in Spain (place of origin)

Place of origin	N	%
Tangier	455	27.5
Oran and others Algeria	68	4.1
Casablanca	59	3.6
Tetuan	32	1.9
Fes	20	1.2
Rabat	18	1.1
Beni Mellal	17	1
Larache	16	1
Nador	15	0.9
Ar-Rachidia	14	0.8
Ksar el Kbir	12	0.7
Others	200	12.1
Total	926	55.8
No answer	733	44.2
TOTAL	**1,659**	**100**

Source: Capdevila, M: and Ferrer, M. (2003) *Els menors estrangers indocumentats no acompanyats (MEINA)*. Documents de treball. Formació i investigació social i criminològica. Generalitat de Catalunya. Centre d'Estudis Jurídics i Formació Especialitzada, p. 103.

Table I.6
Unattended Minor in Spain (place of departure towards Spain*)

Place of departure	N	%
Tangier	134	51.1
Nador	12	4.6
Casablanca	5	1.9
Annaba/Oran/Beni Saf others Algeria	3	1.1
El Aaiun	2	0.8
Larache	1	0.4
Meknes	1	0.4
Rabat	1	0.4
Tetuan	1	0.4
Ksar el Kbir	1	0.4
Others	6	2.3
Total	167	63.7
No answer	95	36.3
TOTAL	**262**	**100**

Source: Capdevila, M. and Ferrer, M. (2003) *Els menors estrangers indocumentats no acompanyats (MEINA)*. Documents de treball. Formació i investigació social i criminològica. Generalitat de Catalunya. Centre d'Estudis Jurídics i Formació Especialitzada, p. 240.

* The table referes only to Catalonia, but it was the most complete available at the time.

was initially concerned. The issue of borders is particularly prescient for the harmonization of policies (treaty of Amsterdam, trilateral collaboration between Italy, France, and Germany, the Seville summit, etc.). The Commission of the European Communities' Communication on border control (Commission of the EU 2002: 233) set out a number of proposals for developing common control of the EU's external borders. The principal elements of this plan were the creation of a "common unit" of senior border control officials to implement a common border control policy; further exchange of information between a large number of authorities, including Schengen Information System, (the visa information database), police authorities and Europol; and the development of a Common European Border Corps with power to check people at the border, deny them entry, board vessels, and arrest individuals.

The central constituent of my argument in Part 2 is based on the common effects globalization has on border cities in general. Two key components of the globalization processes are identified that specifically affect two tendencies— the weakening of the European welfare state and the relocation and reinforcement of Mediterranean borders. I focus on circulation, such as the circulation of people, commodities, and money, all of which involve processes of the global system. The method used is similar to that of Wallerstein when he focused on the processes in the capitalist world system: " the concept of commodity chain is central to the understanding of the processes of the capitalist world-system...take any consumable product, say clothing. And labor must be recruited either locally or by immigration and must be fed.... We may continue to trace each 'box' further back in terms of its material inputs, machinery, land, labor, the totality constitutes a commodity chain" (Wallerstein 1997: 4, in Marcus 1995: 107). Furthermore, many countries of the Southern Mediterranean basin have had to comply with the programs of structural adjustment imposed by the International Monetary Fund. The consequences have been numerous, especially for the North African countries: reductions in expenditure on health and education, reduced recruitment into public administration, reduced subsidies on food and other essential goods, reductions in development and public enterprises funds (King and Munford 2001: 56).

My aim in this second part is to find a way of constructing a possible border-city model. The concrete objective is to identify the specific role of border cities in the so-called "global assembly line" through exploring two Mediterranean cities. My research on the border city poses the question of whether contradictions related to the free world circulation of capital or to blocked human mobility can be expressed. On the one hand, the closing of European borders and, on the other, the will of people to move, represent two contradictory faces of the global economy. The obstacles that migrants face in the sending countries are partially in contradiction with the principles of a free market and a global capitalist economy. However, the free global market puts limitations on the freedom of workers through restrictive entry, and furthermore, European nation-states have a sovereign right to apply such measures. Nevertheless, the richest countries are quick to defend a global labor market when referring to skilled workers, and yet people continue to develop strategies of mobility. What will be the final definition of these border cities? Are they simply peripheries? Spaces of transit? Or are they places where images play a strong role as in the old quest for *Lamerica* for Albanians and *El Ghorba* for Moroccans?

Notes

1. Meaning how the global economy has developed in a system of geographical clustering. The three main axes are the United States, Japan, and Europe.
2. The *Mare Nostrum* extended from the Bosphorus to Hercules' Columns (The Straits of Gibraltar) and from the other side of the Pontus Euxinus (The Black Sea) as far as the *Mare Exterior* (The Atlantic). The word *mediterraneus* was used in Late Latin, to refer to the central core of inhabitable lands rather than to a specific sea; unlike *maritimus* or open sea (González Calleja 2000: 37).

Part 1
Southern Europe

Introduction to Part 1

This first part of the book searches for a general framework in which to situate common indicators for a general immigration model in Southern Europe. The initial interpretative analysis will focus primarily on convergence logics (conceptual part, chapter 1) rather than on the divergences (case-study analysis, chapter 2).

Considering that Southern Europe is frequently excluded from modelization in comparative research (in relation to the welfare state as well as in relation to modes of migrant incorporation), the main aim of this first part of the book is to study the specificity of the phenomenon of recent immigration in Southern Europe, its social context, and the consequences it poses to society and to foreign immigrants.

This first part includes seven case studies in Southern European cities (on issues related to immigration and the welfare state) that identify key components of globalization processes—forms of welfare and issues of mobility—in light of the weakening of the European welfare state. In order to support the argument, the concepts of welfare mix variations are discussed, including explanations and descriptions of the urban and social differences existing in Southern Europe. Consequently, I focus my attention on an exploration of the reinterpretation of the welfare state in the context of the "new migrations." An explanation is offered as to how economic globalization simultaneously leads to the emergence of new forms of welfare and new forms of mobility in social relations, where traditional research sites are reshaped by cross-national economic integration of different forms and scales. This is discussed in more detail by showing the articulation of the selected city cases. In the Southern European cities the emphasis is placed on changes in forms of welfare in relation to social services to foreign migrants.

The first chapter describes a framework for the analysis of a theoretical convergence in Southern European immigration. This is explained in terms of an interdisciplinary context located in the labor market (especially in the informal sector), civil society (especially in the role of the family) and the state (stressing the growing importance of local policies). Changes in the market (intensification of informal trends of the labor market, particularly in the farming and service sectors, among others) and in the family (in terms of gender and generation structures related to the quality of welfare services) are the pillars for an understanding of the situation of foreign immigrants. The intensification of the already existing informal sector in Southern European cities opens up an interesting labor demand for foreign migrants. However, this labor integration means paying a high cost in welfare terms, when migrants have to face low wages and no protection in contrast with generous welfare coverage in Northern European countries.

At a theoretical level general commonalties are also to be found in relation to global tendencies, the demand for unskilled labor, the reinforcement of gender and ethnic inequalities, strict policies on border restriction, etc. Nevertheless, the empirical findings (fieldwork in Southern European cities) confirm the complexity involved in generalizing about the fragmentation of such Southern European societies—hence the need to focus on locality.

Chapter 1 poses the initial research question following three lines of argument: the recent nature of the immigration phenomenon, its interaction with welfare state dynamics and with a certain type of family structure. Firstly, mass-scale foreign immigration is a new phenomenon if one considers the historical perspective of the region. Labor migrations have arrived in Southern Europe quite suddenly and have brought about substantial changes in these countries. Secondly, the argument is related to the existence of a weak welfare state, in comparison to welfare regimes in Europe. The third line of argument is related to the family context, both in respect to the family system in the host countries and the family structure of foreign migrants, hence the family is conceived here as a "shock absorber."

Chapter 2 analyzes seven case studies from the southern half of Europe: Athens and Thrace in Greece; Naples and Turin in Italy; Lisbon in Portugal; and Barcelona and Algeciras in Spain. The analysis will show how these cities and places have responded to the challenge of global migration, showing a wide range of responses at the local level. What is striking, however, is how differences are observed in the shaping of welfare provisions, with the organization of multiple systems of dual divisions: migrants, non-migrants, regular migrants, non-regular migrants, etc. Development of the welfare mix seems to be at the center of the restructuring of social policy in relation to immigration and seems to respond to the informal welfare needs of immigrants.

The difficulty in considering Southern Europe as an amalgamation of traits, whether they are common to the whole region, or what makes them peculiar in Southern Europe (in considerations such as the Italian North-South disparities, the changing units of analysis from regions to cities, for example) will be seen throughout all of the empirical cases.

1

Southern Europe in a Migratory Context

The Scope of Comparative Research

Classical studies in sociology show a persistent reference to comparative work. Marx studied different societies of the past in order to demonstrate the specific nature of the production relations of modern society. Weber analyzed the relation between material interests and beliefs for different social groups in order to explain the rational type of social organization for modern society (Bendix 1986; in Samuel 1989). Furthermore, both Weber and Marx refer to an interpretative paradigm of socioeconomic change that is capable of accounting for diversity and discontinuity (Mingione 1991:5).

Today, international comparative research is a defined branch of comparative sociology: "The analysis of the distribution of social facts carries explicitly on more than one society. But not necessarily towards the whole society; in fact the most frequent analysis takes into consideration the observance of a social phenomenon well centered round two or more societies" (Samuel 1989: 2). However, the problem of linearity in comparisons as well as the data normally provided limits our analysis of international comparisons. The large amount of historical, macro-economic, and demographic data available on income, productivity, distribution of occupations, demographic movements and so on gives us the derived variables that the various contexts of social relations have included and on occasions "measured" (Mingione 1991:15).

International comparative research focuses on the study of a relation and it can be based, either on the similarities or differences existing between two or more social processes. Several questions arise then when considering the comparative procedure. Why have we chosen those particular countries and why are they relevant to our topic? Which countries in the North are in direct contrast to the reality of Southern Europe? How do we construct the model we are going to explain, by analogy or by dissimilarity? Which units of analysis should we specifically consider: space, nations, regions, cities or population groups? In our case, how do we take care of the variables of time, varying political systems, different immigrant groups, languages and traditions? Can we articulate the macro-level as well as the micro-level in our analysis? How can we situate the control of ethnocentrism in the chosen countries, especially considering that the analytical tools proceed from outside this region, and that an evolutionist approach to societies is often applied?

The Problem of Linearity

The issue of linearity in comparative work has been one of the main problems when dealing with the evolutionary heritage of the social sciences. According to Mingione (1991: 2) this is both a question of changing social reality and of inadequate instruments of interpretation, raising the question as to whether conceptual instruments have been rendered inadequate by a changing reality or whether they have always been so.

Firstly, the idea of linearity is based here on the existence of a fundamental industrializing trend, which itself is built into the main sociological theories. Therefore, unidirectionality is the point of departure; understanding that socioeconomic change moves in a single direction which underlies all the different variants, giving them a more or less standardized form. As Mingione states, "as a result, the changing social picture is composed of features typically found in all industrial societies. In the first place, it is not entirely a platitude to observe that sociological paradigms have developed in parallel with Western industrial societies and have always exhibited a greater capacity to explain these rather than other kinds of societies. The other side of the coin is that sociologists have incorporated the assumption of a 'fundamental industrializing trend' into their theories because, in some cases and for a long historical period, it has constituted an effective way to simplify social complexity" (Mingione, 1991: 5).

Secondly, the idea of linearity can also be applied to the assumed role of the welfare state in the later capitalist era. The modelization of welfare typologies finds its essence in the expansion of the regulatory capacity of the state in capitalist societies that assumes two main forms: the welfare state at the center of the world system (especially Northern Europe and Canada) and the developing state on the periphery and semi-periphery of the world system (in relation with weak democratic systems and different forms of socialization).

The main problem here is that the work attempts to extend comparative sociological tools to other less well researched realities, in our case some countries in the northern Mediterranean; thus, we are constantly forced to deal with the assumed linearity of industrial capitalism. It is a fact that the hegemonic concepts in social sciences have been mostly developed in Northern Europe and in the United States. I have already proved through analysis in the Mediterranean South, especially in the Maghreb region, how difficult it can be to export sociological concepts to other realities.[1] As we will see here the convergence logics we apply are based on the idea that the proximity between different realities can help the discussion more than other comparable societies, which cannot take as axes similarities or open contrasts.

Linearity problems are not only present when taking into account variations in time and space but also when the emphasis is placed on continuity, and which includes the idea of the continuity between the economic, political, and social spheres involved in understanding changes in Southern Europe. Consequently, the very nature of this work is highly interdisciplinary. In a way it creates fuzzy borders between issues often approached from a hermetic sociological perspective: sociology of the family, sociology of migrations, social policy. Moreover, by taking classical forms of invisibility like the gender dimension of the welfare state or the feminization of international migration, the task can become even more arduous.

Logically, social changes bring with them changes in comparative work. For example, in the 1960s comparative research in Europe focused mainly on economic structures. In the 1990s, there was a major debate on the welfare state regimes, while more recently, the social services approach has become more important. According to Antonnen (1998) these changes are related to new demands, new theoretical changes and new political responses.[2]

Apart from the context of social change as a transforming challenge for comparative work, a further issue for review is the way changes and the concepts used to analyze them can actually travel. Consequently, a key point for consideration will be not only to determine if international comparative research can help to develop a tool for social policy—particularly when taking into account quantitative data and the difficulties often found in obtaining them—but if the different concepts, terminology, and categories used can also present a difficulty to assess comparative tools.

Comparative Problems in Migration

We will consider here comparative issues in the light of the main references selected for comparative purposes when considering different migration contexts. Many texts have pointed out the different terms used in national discourses in an attempt to highlight the importance of context and terminology in this kind of work. In this line, Lloyd (1995) indicates that whatever the scope of comparison, one can agree that it involves identifying both universals and differences. The central task for the comparative procedure will be definition, use of concepts, and the identification of variables. In the research agenda on European immigration, two contexts have been established as the main references for comparative work: those of the North American and the Northern European one, modeling how to study other differing realities (see also the identified problem above on linearity in research). Moreover, in welfare typologies the specific context of the studies was often how

Anglo-Saxon countries and the experiences of these countries were interpreted in terms of universals (Sainsbury 1994: 2).

Schnapper (1992) highlights the following as being most important variables for European comparisons in immigration: the national setting, the political tradition, the demographic situation, and economic needs. In our case, when setting the variables for comparison we will have to also add the heterogeneity of immigrant populations (including origins, migratory projects and different chronologies of migratory flows) and the type of rights (from citizenship to social benefits) they benefit from. In all four countries the starting point is an examination of social integration policies. Nevertheless, they cannot be understood without the general framework given by immigration control policies.

Portes (1997) points out that what we have today is an amorphous mass of data on immigration in different countries and a series of concepts whose scope seldom exceeds that of a particular nation-state. In that respect, he stresses the need for comparative projects that focus on research topics at a higher level of abstraction than those guiding policy concerns that employ a common cross-national methodology. Systematic cross-national research can be useful for three purposes: firstly, to examine the extent to which theoretical propositions "travel," that is, are applicable in national context; secondly, to generate typologies of interaction effects specifying the variable influence of causal factors across different national contexts; and thirdly, to produce concepts and propositions of broader scope. Portes (1997) mentions four major issues that he considers appropriate for such comparative analyses: the rise of transnational communities, the adaptation process of the second generation, gender cleavages and household strategies, and the enactment and the enforcement of state immigration laws.

Even though local differentiation is taken into account through the urban setting this is not always the rule in migration research. For example, when considering the case of Thrace (Ribas-Mateos 2000) as a region we are obviously not talking about a city in the sense that we have analyzed the cases of Turin (Caponio et al. 2000), Naples or Athens. If one thinks about population indexes, those in Thrace are not even half of the Athens population. Consequently, research problems are first and foremost linked to the idea of representation, because the geographical unit is not limited to the city alone, but is far more diffuse and extends to the whole of the region, implying a major difficulty in drawing any type of comparison. This will generate future comparative dilemmas such as the dilemmas involved in contrasting this particular case with other European countries. Secondly, there is the assumption of the representation of social actors. For example, in Thrace there are hardly any associations and social workers and mayors are more represented as interviewees.

The comparison of the social realities of different countries implies much more than merely adding statistics that try to display a single photograph, or to offer a single map paralyzed in time. Indeed, if this were the case, we would simply end up reducing reality to stereotypes and essentialisms. Yet what do we mean when we refer to differences? As Geertz (1996) suggests, organizing any analysis around a general contrast is to suspect that the poles selected could have been otherwise, which means that other phenomena would have caught our attention, and consequently, other conclusions would have been drawn. A difference is not the same as a dichotomy; the former implies a comparison and a relationship, while the latter is an assertion, which is isolating. Along these lines, I propose looking for the differences, which can be mutually reflected, reciprocally structured at the country level. Therefore, it is only by doing so that we can contrast cases in a Southern European setting.

Shrinking the Mediterranean: The Limits of the Region

From the studies on the Mediterranean area one can see the skeleton of universality and diversity that can be applied to this region. Key elements such as religion (monotheism and manifold secularization processes), family (kinship and gender roles), and migration (understood within the de-ruralization processes) can be set out as a preliminary outline.

As mentioned in the introduction, the search for the unity of Mediterranean societies has always been a constant in historical and anthropological analyses. The idea of convergence is quite well understood by historians, because the Mediterranean was not a region but a universe, a planet. However, it has not been seen as a single (convergent) sea but rather as a series of seas (divergences). History shows this persistence in the idea of unity and coherence of the Mediterranean region, as Braudel puts it, "I retain the firm conviction that the Turkish Mediterranean breathed with the same rhythms as the Christian, that the whole sea shared a common destiny, a heavy one indeed, with identical problems and general trends if not identical consequences" (Braudel 1976: 14). Hence, the ideal meeting point of the Mediterranean elicits the image of a place where everything is mixed and reconstructed as a coherent unit. The idea of constant migrations in the region[3] can be a common factor; the idea of a similar kinship structure has also been considered a common factor in history.

The Mediterranean can also be a stereotype, where no precise boundaries can be traced. Inside it, there are many "fuzzy zones," between the North and the South of Europe, between Asia Minor and the rest of Asia, between North Africa and Sub-Saharan Africa. These fuzzy zones reveal the dilemma of the presence of commonalities as well as the regional divergences that explain contrasts inside the Mediterranean as it is taken as a heuristic concept.

As regards labor migration, the 1950s and 1960s had shown the same Mediterranean strategy; at the beginning men departed alone, sending money back for their families; but after their spouses joined them, thereby often completing the break with the country of origin, it often meant that the village of origin would eventually fall into total abandon and ruin. As regards the family, the patriarchal family model has been common in the whole of the Mediterranean.[4] Anthropologists have shown that the degree of integration of women in the various types of families and the reflection of this integration in the intensity of their identification was their husband's honor. This was a Mediterranean-wide issue.

Nevertheless, if the field of classical anthropology had tried to analyze the mosaic of cultures along with the idea of unity (the idea of honor and kinship structure and the birth of the monotheist religions), it seems that today such inter-culturality gives rise to many open questions. The North-South rupture (especially between the North of the sea and their Maghrebian neighbors), the integration of Southern Europe into the EU, and the collapse of eastern Mediterranean socialism (with particular reference to the Balkan instability and the Kurdish question and their European integration), are elements that help us to understand the new migrations of the eighties. Curiously enough, the question of the social integration of Muslim communities in the North Mediterranean has once again raised the issue of the ancient Christian-Muslim division of the Mediterranean.

Today, the South European region (considered here to be Portugal, Spain, Italy, and Greece) is clearly understood within the limits of the European integration. Nevertheless, the Mediterranean aspects are emphasized where cooperation and commercial partnership are concerned (through the Euro-Mediterranean discourse, present from the time of the 1995 Barcelona conference). From the standpoint of the European Union, the classical "blue banana" would be the most dynamic partition for the different regionalizations, delimited by the Paris-London-Amsterdam triangle. In 1992, the European Union (DG XVII) established the following development areas in Europe: Eastern Europe, Scandinavia, the Southern Rim, new German states, the South and East of the Mediterranean, the Atlantic Rim, the Central Mediterranean, the Continental Diagonal, the Alpine Rim, and the Latin Rim. Within these development areas, we could then highlight the least developed regions of the EU: the Northern Aegean, Madeira, Azores, and Alentejo.

For some authors (see Roque 1999), the Western Mediterranean area would emerge from this symbolic representation as a second development axis that would extend across the north of Italy as far as the dynamic zones of southern France and the Spanish *Levante*. This axis is called the "Latin arch." This European space would be constructed from five perspectives: landscape, demography, business dynamics, life-styles, and regional synergies. According to this study, the results of the survey identify the "Latin Rim" as sharing the following common elements: geographical proximity, dynamic regions, a business tradition, Latin-based languages, and a Catholic culture.

Petmesidou (1996) describes another partition on the Eastern side of the Mediterranean, this time represented by the shape of a nutshell, using West-

East coordinates, where she considers the difference of the Eastern Mediterranean societies, especially by applying socioeconomic concepts and social policy development for Greece and Turkey, as will be seen later.

Looking for Common Indicators

When generalizing, international comparative research gives us the possibility to construct and draw up classifications, ideal types, and models. It helps us to identify and understand the exceptions to those models, and it also constitutes a way for the development and enrichment of theoretical concepts (Berthoin-Antal 1987: 499; in Samuel 1989: 5).

Nevertheless, only a small amount of literature has looked into the question of immigration or the welfare state in Southern Europe as a unified region. Most research concerning immigration has been country specific, on localities or individual migrant groups. If they refer to Southern Europe, they only underline their "unpreparedness." Most research concerning welfare state regimes has either failed to include Southern Europe or has not provided an in-depth analysis, and if they are alluded to, only their rudimentary and familist residual character is highlighted.

Some authors point out only the common historical conditions. Isolating the particular features of each major Mediterranean city causes serious difficulties in making comparisons and generalizations and even the best of typologies are doomed to be deficient. Yet as far back as the seventeenth century, and when considering a single country, historians made the distinction between bureaucratic, commercial, industrial, military, artisanal, and agricultural cities, and even those dedicated to wool farming. Although these inherited circumstances vary in intensity in accordance with the population group, city or metropolis, together they represent a highly specific whole within Southern Europe (Giner 1994: 22). Ibn Khaldun, who possessed a profound knowledge of Andalusian and Maghrebi cities, was one of the first social theorists to point out the importance of the gap existing between intramural and extramural life. He did not believe that they were merely two antagonistic and opposing worlds. He considered them to be complementary universes, alternative conceptions of life, each with its own dignity and mutual dependence. Convinced that they were intrinsically distinct, even the city populace felt arrogantly superior to the country people, convinced that they were intrinsically different. Up until recently, the poorest city dweller has scorned the countryman, the *contadino*, the *pagès* (Giner 1994: 26). According to this author, from the time of the French Revolution onwards, the history of the Mediterranean countries has had a greater sense of coherence than may appear at first sight: the economic peripherization[5] of the South, cities dominated by the political classes, metropolitan polarity, and national and state development. Some cities even played out the proverbial "tale of two cities." This is why Spain and Italy can be considered bicephalous countries, whose metropolises Milan and Barcelona, Rome and Madrid became paradigmatic examples of industry and bourgeois society on the one hand, and political and administrative power on the other (Giner 1994: 37). Giner also considers that the discontinuities between east and west in Mediterranean countries have on occasion been as deep as those existing between its northern and southern coasts (for example during the Balkan Wars from 1991 to 1994). Besides, some of the cities display certain similarities with North African or Latin American urban agglomerations, while naturally retaining the structure of the Western European city. (Giner 1994: 56)

Nevertheless, the most significant factors for this analysis are those classical historical conditions that have helped the construction of the welfare state. All four countries have lived through long dictatorships, with the exception of Italy, where the totalitarian regime was in power for a much shorter time. Until very recently, Southern Europe seemed to be stranded half way between "advanced societies" and other "less advanced" parts of the world. The confrontation of diverse forces (tradition/modernity, less advanced capitalism/capitalism, religiosity/rationality) in the North shore of the Mediterranean and successive antidemocratic solutions—in spite of internal variations—constitute a considerable unity and even a common entity in the European process (Giner 1995:13). Therefore, despite the wide heterogeneity existing within this region and the existence of a marked diversity within the different countries, a general outline does exist. Those general features are related to the types of political domination, to its form and to its rhythm of economic development (or stagnation), and to the system of class relations.

Leaving aside the historical conditions, let us now revise the migration background. According to Portes, immigration as a data-driven field of study has had no need for wide generalizations based on highly abstract theorizing. Indeed, the general tendency has been quite the opposite, that is, toward ground-level studies of particular migrant groups or analysis of official migration policies (Portes 1997: 799). It is for this reason that rather than providing major generalized theories, immigration studies have consistently yielded conditionals constrained to a single time and place. The continuing growth of immigration and asylum issues and the emergence of dilemmas in immigration models across the whole of Southern Europe are raising a series of issues in national and European Union institutions. In the "old countries of immigration" rather distinct models of immigrant incorporation have been developed over the past twenty years. Despite all that has been achieved, these differences raise awkward problems for the harmonization and coordination of national polices at a European level. However, the coordination problems these discussions pose for European policymakers are even more difficult when considering the complexity of the situation in Southern Europe due to the fact that this is a recent phenomenon in this region.

Table 1.1
Foreign immigrants in Southern Europe

All figures '000 unless otherwise stated	Portugal	Spain	Italy	Greece
Total population (million)	10.0	39.1	57.0	10.3
Immigrants with permits	190	900	1,25	450
of whom, EU nationals	50	380	150	200
Irregular immigrants (average estimation)	100	350	260	420
Total of immigrants (estimated)	290	1,25	1,51	870
of whom, non-EU	240	800	1,33	600
All immigrants as % total population	2.9	3.2	2.7	8.4
Non-EU as % total population	2.4	2.0	2.3	5.8

Source: King and Ribas-Mateos (2004), based on Baldwin-Edwards (2002: 29)

However, the coordination problems these discussions pose for European policymakers are even more difficult when considering the complexity of the situation in Southern Europe due to the fact that this is a recent phenomenon in this region.

One of the first references to the Southern European immigration is the book by Simon (1987), which studies the geodynamics of international migrations. In the history of human migrations, Southern Europe is, together with China, one of the cradles of the world Diaspora. In the space of fifteen years (1970-1985), the intensity and direction of emigration flows from this region to the industrialized North, where major changes have led to a massive decrease in permanent emigration flows, a sharp drop in Greek, Spanish, and Italian emigration and the diffusion of Portuguese emigration in France and the neighboring countries.[6]

We should start by trying to examine commonalties in order to identify a model. Many scholars have been searching for a suitable model in which we can take account of this immigration phenomenon (Arbaci 2000; Baldwin-Edwards 1997; Malheiros and Ribas-Mateos 2002; King 1997; Pugliese 1997; Reyneri 2001; Ribas-Mateos 2001, etc.), with a particular focus on the characteristics of heterogeneity which can be defined by a multiplicity of nationalities and types of migrants (from rural and urban origin) and a gender asymmetry depending on the origin. In spite of strict border controls, in all four countries, each of which have a considerable informal economy, there are a large number of irregular immigrants that make up a considerable percentage of the labor force in certain sectors (services, agriculture, and construction). However, differences within the four cases will also be taken into consideration. The North-

South regional gap,[7] which is obvious in most of these countries together with as their respective historical conditions (such as the ex-colonial PALOP[8] migrants in Portugal and the status of the ethnic Greeks in Greece), are two appropriate examples of this diversity.

Using 1991 sources (in Werth and Körner 1991: 48), King et al. (1997a: 7) detail the following types of immigration flows in Southern Europe: (1) a high status immigration from Northern Europe and North America (mainly professionals, business-owners, and retired migrants), (2) migrations inside the region (e.g., Portuguese to Spain, Cypriots to Greece), (3) immigration from former colonies (e.g., from Brazil and Cape Verde to Portugal, Argentina to Spain), (4) immigrations from within the Mediterranean Basin (e.g., Tunisians to Sicily, Egyptians to Greece, Moroccans to Spain), (5) immigrants from other "Third World" countries: a diverse range of long-distance migrants (India, the Philippines, Senegal etc.), and (6) Eastern European immigrants, notably Poles and Yugoslavs. Under (3) we would also include the intensified Latin American and Moroccan flows into Spain; and under (6) the prominence of Albanian flows into Greece.

Apart from the description of flows, other important characteristics of the migratory reception contexts should be taken into account, such as political factors and labor market conditions. Our considerations here will be limited to the former only, as labor market conditions will be discussed in the next section. The political factors involved can be divided into restricted-control borders and a lack of social integration policies for immigrants in a weak welfare state context. If we compare immigration policies, it is evident that Greek immigration policies are some way behind those of other southern EU member states. This becomes clear simply by looking at the chronologies of the various regularization processes that have taken place in each of the four southern countries: Italy (1986, 1990, 1995, 1998, 1999, etc.), Spain (1986, 1991, 1996, 2000, 2001, etc., plus additional minor regularizations through the quota system from 1993 until 1997, and from 1997 until 1999), Portugal (the first ones were in 1992, 1996, 1997), and Greece (the first one was in 1998).

Along these lines, immigration policies, either through the quota system (the case of Spain) or through the regularization process, make up the structure that shapes labor niches. Those niches are mainly identified through the substitution of the autochthonous labor force. Consequently, if the countries of Northern Europe had once opted for the "return logic" (excluding the family dimension), we can observe that thirty years later, the countries of Southern Europe opt for a mere "mercantile logic" in immigration flows. We understand here the concept of mercantile as opposed to that of reproduction, according to Mingione's division (1995).

Italy is probably the best representative of the "clientelist model" in the welfare typology, as its features have been more often analyzed. Besides, Italy is probably the best representative in the Southern European immigration pattern. Italy is the country that experiences the quickest decrease of the emigration flows (whereas Portugal presents a more isolated case in that respect) and the first immigration settlements in the region. Therefore, we could suggest that Italy is probably the most paradigmatic type of the Southern European model.

Arbaci (2002) links urban development, time of arrival of migration, and housing insertion to a welfare system related to late industrialism in Southern Europe. According to this author, comparative research in several European cities reveals some fundamental aspects. These include the absence of a single ethnic spatial organization model among European cities or among ethnics groups, and therefore, the absence of a European model of ethnic segregation. Secondly, the coexistence of parallel patterns: of ethnic concentration and ethnic dispersal city and increasing socio-spatial segregation, processes of spatial de-segregation, and middle-class dispersal within the same city. Thirdly, the increasing success of ethnic entrepreneurship in areas of ethnic concentration reveals—within the traditional patterns of segregation—the active and relevant role played by ethnic cluster dynamics and by the development of local survival strategies beyond the orthodox market paradigms (Mingione 1999; Kloosterman et al. 1999; Kesteloot and Meert 2000, quoted by Arbaci 2002: 85).

Using the type of corporatist and rudimentary welfare cities, Arbarci characterizes a greater vertical socio-spatial segregation and patterns of class co-habitation. This is due to the architectonic reproduction of particular typologies of dwellings, which historically have been designed for this kind of cohabitation, as the example of the Haussman-Mansarde model exported into the continental capitals from the nineteenth century onwards, and which are variants of the mercantile model that flourished especially in the South-European historical port cities, such as Lisbon, Barcelona, Marseilles, Genoa, and Naples (Arbaci 2002: 90).

The Research Questions

Here I will address the questions directing the research through three lines of arguments that articulate the scope of comparative research: the novelty of the immigration phenomenon, its interaction with a weak welfare state, and its interaction with a certain type of family structure. These research questions will serve as an outline for how to understand the next section, which will define Southern Europe as a migratory context of reception.

The Weakness of the Welfare State

I will start by approaching welfare state clusters based on the grounds of the development of welfare state typologies, which has been a constant in comparative social research since the 1960s. The formation of groups according to defined geographical areas is the result of political ideologies combined with other social criteria, such as those seen through the explanations of Esping-Andersen reproducing Titmuss' work (1974; Abrahamson 1995).

In accordance with the frequently referred to Esping-Andersen typology (1990)[9], we can identify four welfare regimes in Europe: social democratic (Scandinavia), conservative (continental Europe), liberal/social democratic (UK), and that of Southern Europe. Going further, Ferrera (1995) identifies some of the common traits to be found in the welfare states of Greece, Italy, Portugal, and Spain, namely low coverage of the population; high differentiation of benefits; a massive asymmetry of expenditure together with underdeveloped unemployment benefits and inadequate universalistic national systems. It is within this framework that the South European regime has experienced a considerable turnaround, made up of societies that have gone from being countries of emigration to countries of immigration.

The Southern European model has not been discussed in literature dealing with comparative welfare regimes, except in the case of Italy (Ferrera 1995: 85). Where it has been included, the general features relate to its "rudimentary character," combined with the Catholic influence of the designed programs and a context where the traditional family still plays an important role.[10] However, according to Ferrera, this "rudimentary character" cannot always be generalized and the strength of the leftist tradition[11] must also be considered. In this model, welfare services are dependent on workers' contributions; therefore the dual labor market system also reproduces a dual welfare system. In this context, an important indicator in the analysis of new immigration flows is the presence of low coverage for workers belonging to the irregular or non-institutional sector of the labor market. According to Ferrera (1995), the best illustration of the clientelistic market of the welfare state is the Italian case.[12]

Abrahamson (1995) shows the different typologies of welfare states not only by using different ideologies (Esping-Andersen) and geo-political criteria (Konosen) as a support, but also different organizational principles.[13] Within those different axes, he establishes the following models: conservative, liberal, and Catholic. Following this typology, the core of the last model is the individual; but when he/she fails to take care of himself/herself, the resources will be found first through the nuclear family, then the extended family, and thirdly through local communities, which include the Church, civil organizations, and informal neighborhood networks (we will have to see the extent to which this is applicable to modern forms of welfare mix). The model assumes a clientelist and "patronage" structure, which in a way has been eroded by the development of labor market structures of late capitalism and political and social rights.

According to Rodríguez Cabrero (1998), the Spanish and Italian cases are specific instances of growing universalistic models and private spaces of welfare production, with strong financial tensions and public control in social protection and the social services. He offers an even more precise definition of the Spanish case, adding the following elements: political and administrative decentralization, selective privatization of the welfare state (along EU lines), and the crucial role of the family (placing greater responsibility on the family and on the reproductive and caring role of women) (Rodríguez Cabrero 1998: 136-141). Some approaches emphasize historical influences (path-dependency) as a restrictive factor for public policies. In the Spanish case, the "franquismo" (Francoism) situated policies in the country a long way from the coordinates of a Keynesian welfare state. The practically nonexistent public services had little or no relation with the European models of universalistic public assistance (Subirats 1998: 15). Consequently, we can distinguish two different tendencies existing today in Spain: (1) a rupturist line: for example, the fiscal model, a universalistic and decentralized health system, a territorial outline for public policies and the new linguistic regime for the different nationalities, and (2) a continuity line (or of historical dependence): for example, a professional based tax system, the familist approach in the design of social services (idem).

As mentioned earlier, Petmesidou (1996) goes beyond the so-called "Latin Rim model," while the socio-cultural characteristics of the Balkan countries (the role of the Orthodox Church and stronger forms of statist and paternalist social organization) have so far been neglected in comparative social policy studies. She highlights the differences between the various regions of southern Europe, illustrating dissimilarities through north-west to the south-east differences, "the nutshell form," based on differences in the structure of economy, the state/civil society relationship and the strength of the civil society vis-à-vis state authority and interventionism. In the tradition of contractual relations, collective solidarity and an active civil society is weakest, such as in the Southeast, Greece, and the other Balkan countries, as well as Turkey. As regards the role of the church in the Latin Rim, Catholicism has strongly supported subsidiarity in welfare services, which enhanced the role of the family in welfare delivery and the institutionalization of large-scale voluntary action in social protection. In contrast, in countries like Greece, the Orthodox Church has never been involved in social assistance in the way that the Catholic Church has.

With regard to the issue of gender, various clusters of countries have also been drawn up. Lewis (1993) divides the welfare states into strong, modified, and weak "male breadwinner models." In the breadwinner type, the labor market is built up around this figure, while wives and family members depend on derived rather than personal social rights; therefore, through a familistic view, social insurance-based social policies tend to produce a division between those on the inside and those on the outside of the labor market.

Countries that correspond to the strong male breadwinner model are the Netherlands, Germany, Switzerland, Austria, Greece, Spain, Portugal, Great Britain, and Ireland. Sweden and Denmark belong to the weak breadwinner type. However, Lewis' model does not take into account the care provided in the home, which can also be paid. In that respect, Sainsbury's model (1994) would be more accurate. Sainsbury sees the limits of Lewis' typology because it is based exclusively on a single underlying dimension: the strength of the male breadwinner model in terms of the traditional division of labor between the sexes and its implications for social entitlements. Mainstream typologies have often distinguished three bases of entitlement: need, market work performance, and citizenship. According to Sainsbury (1994: 167) in the traditional family model two further bases of entitlement are central: the principles of both maintenance and care. This model allows her to pinpoint variations between welfare states that mainstream typologies have not revealed. Consequently, gendering welfare states require that women's entitlements be conceived not only from being *wives* and *workers* but also as *mothers* and *citizens*, a perspective that should also be built into the analytical framework and investigated as cross-national variations (idem: 69).

Other comparisons could also be taken into account, including the contrast between family structures and the labor market in different countries, encompassing a bond between strong family structures and a weak professionalization of women (e.g., Spain and Ireland) or between disintegrated families and part-time female work (e.g., Sweden and Denmark) (Commaille 1993). This differentiation also opens up the debate of the holistic approach (e.g., Norway) and the dualistic approach (e.g,. Sweden). The former is based on cash benefits that enable women to stay at home and look after their children, while the latter is based on offering women the freedom to choose between staying at home or going out to work, or alternatively a combination of both.

For the purposes of our work, another major contribution elaborated by Sainsbury is the identification of a major gap in mainstream research into the care and the human service sector, in contrast to a traditional comparative analysis, which concentrated on social insurance schemes and income maintenance policies, or to a gender analysis that concentrated on the state-market nexus with reference to gender, without including the state-market-family relationships. Social services indicators are not only useful for analyzing the gendering of the welfare state but could also be seen as the matrix of the linkage of immigration, the welfare state, and the family. In a privatized conception of services, along the lines of the native family's strategy for care, the double-earner household could be playing a reproductive role on the demand side. On the other hand, immigrant women (who are also involved in transnational family strategies) could be seen as playing an important role on the supply side. Accordingly, gendered family strategies and a sexual division of labor can constitute the grounds for the ethnic gendered conception of care.

Last but not least, we should consider here the identification of the Southern European gender order. How can we identify it by encompassing change and continuity? How can we understand the changes in the breadwinner-female care giver model of family and the need for reconciliation of employment and family life? González et al. (1999) examine the transition toward a new gender role by considering the following factors:

1. the weakening of the figure of the male provider. The role of breadwinners (a full-time and lifelong, stable occupational career) is no longer guaranteed
2. the improving of women´s occupations and their attachment to the labor force. This means implications for highly educated women in having less time for procreation and a reduction of family size. Hence, controlling fertility to a low level seems to be a strategy for women to reconcile with paid work and family life.
3. the gradual inclusion of gender equity principles and the expansion of the welfare state. Including progressive individualization of social rights[14] and including maternity policies as part of the expansion of the welfare state.
4. the relaxation of traditional family hierarchies. Thanks to higher levels of financial independence (in the case of wives) or higher levels of cultural and symbolic power (in the case of adult children). The increase of extra-marital births is a sign of the increasing de-institutionalization of the traditional model of the family.

On the other hand, the same authors show the legacies of the traditional gender role through the following factors: (1) the inflexibility of male roles (no sharing of family and domestic tasks), (2) female dependency on father´s and husband´s income (with significant regional differences as regards the level of female active participation in the labor market), (3) "women-unfriendly" welfare states, which display many deficits in services, such as childcare and assistance for the elderly. There are also great regional variations, since the poorest regions offer less childcare services.

The Family Parameter

The second line of argument is related to the family context, both with regard to the family system in the host countries and the family structure of immigrants. The family, conceived here as the "shock absorber," is seen from two perspectives: first, from the familist character of the host societies (especially considering gender in middle-class household strategies), and second, from the family formation of immigrants (especially considering gender in family reunion processes).

The object of this study is based on two valuable general contexts "inspired" by two questions surrounding migration issues in Europe and established by Bastenier and Dassetto (1990: 56-57). These two major contexts are defined as:

1. "Ethnicity," which seems to contradict the dynamics of the growing individualism in society. In this context the welfare state plays an important

role in terms of the nationalism that defines who is entitled to benefits in the welfare state. However, it can be added here that the welfare state may stress ethnicity, in so far as it grants benefits only to nationals, or as in the case of Belgium and the Netherlands when it uses ethnic/cultural pillars to provide benefits. Or it may contrast/weaken ethnicity in so far as it grants benefits on the basis of legal residence, not on the basis of group membership.[15]

2. The ethnic-based communitarian organization has the family unit at its core, which needs to be looked at in closer detail. The behavior of migrants is often analyzed as individual behavior (for example, that of the young), which has to be completed in the context of the family substratum. In this context we should also bear in mind the role of Islam as a form of cohesion for these new identities.

One of the main objectives is to establish an analysis that allows for a framework of comparative instruments on the one hand, and on the other to look for the different functioning of immigration policies capable of defining the type of impact on immigrants and their families. When examining social integration, it is essential to consider these policies on a local as well as on a national level. In order to do so we will have to look at the changing role of the welfare state and the effects of the welfare mix. The target population here is immigrants and their families with a particular emphasis on the role of women in the migratory process.

From the first perspective, familism means that families should be responsible for the well-being of their members in a context of weak decommodification. Decommodification follows here the reasoning of immigrant labor, that shown in private caring services. This context of familism is marked by weak family policies as well as by other indirect policies, which reflect very different data for southern Europe when one considers various activity rates according to sex, fertility rates, single-person households, marriage, separation and divorce rates, etc. However, if public welfare is nowadays under stress we should also consider the degree to which family welfare in Southern Europe is also affected. We consider the role of women as caretakers and informal givers, highlighting the relevance of welfare insufficiency and its response through a commodified form by the recruitment of immigrants. From the immigrant's family perspective, their role as the community pillar and as a base for an economic network is granted particular consideration. Here, relevance is given to welfare insufficiency related to social policy addressed to migrants, and its response through welfare mix arrangements.

What is interesting when establishing the differences between these two types of families is that their strategies are connected: namely, one household spending some of its time to ensure the survival of another; they therefore belong to the reproduction pattern of the receiver rather than the provider, often a foreign immigrant. Secondly, the relevance of the role of gender in the family structure is here preponderant, from the perspective of both the native and the immigrant family.

Migration Context and Welfare Conditions: A Difficult Relationship

From a historical perspective, foreign immigration is a new phenomenon. This is the third line of argument, how labor migrations have undergone a substantial transformation. The situation today is quite different from that of the European labor migrations of the 1950s and 1960s, when the countries of Southern Europe offered a migrant labor force for their economically advanced neighbors. This change implies that if the general socio-historic map of the European South is different from that of central and northern Europe in many ways (for example, democratization paths, European integration processes, socioeconomic development, and welfare trends), it has been extended in terms of migration patterns. Hence, in the case of the role of immigration in Europe, our map of the south seems also to be structured differently. Besides, the socioeconomic transformation of the region with regard to post-Fordist structures (tertiarization, flexibilization and informalization of the market affecting above all women and youngsters) has paralleled the chronology of the migratory changes.

Therefore, this social context is quite different from the European migrations of the past during the 1950s and 1960s, when these countries were still labor exporters. This scene, which is often referred to by King´s writings as a "migration turn-around," is characterized by a series of fundamental elements (with their own variations based in country and regions), including the heterogeneity of the origin of the migratory flows (especially in the case of Italy and Spain), the marked female representations of the flows, the dynamic role of the informal economy, and a high concentration of migrants in the tertiary sector.

Simultaneous processes, such as the entrance of migratory flows (accompanied by the presence of large quantities of irregulars), weak immigration policies (in terms of both effective controls and social integration measures), and the informality of the labor market, could be included in the contexts of reception. However, many of those areas have become reception contexts for agricultural labor (like Southern Italy, parts of Greece, and parts of Spain), while others, some of the old industrial contexts—former receptors of internal migrations—have become destinations for foreign labor force in the service sector, especially in big cities. To a certain extent this forms part of a reproduction of the various internal migration patterns of the 1960s: the powerful interregional currents of rural-urban migration from the Italian South to the northern Industrial Triangle, from southern Spain to Catalonia, Madrid, and the Basque region, from rural Portugal to the Lisbon metropolitan area, and from rural Greece to the Athens conurbation (King 2000: 5).

In general terms, the scope of the discussion here deals with the key social divisions of class, "race" (as defined in common Anglo-Saxon literature), and gender. In other words, those divisions form the basis for tracking down the different position of groups in relation to the welfare state. Other major social divisions such as age, sexual orientation, and national identity also exist. According to Ginsburg (1992: 2-3) the importance of this triad is largely dictated by contemporary politics of the welfare states and social science data. Taking these divisions in a national case study approach, it could be claimed that the United States is the only country where there has been extensive data collection regarding "race" and welfare needs and provisions.

Very rarely have these three key social divisions been considered together in relation to the welfare state. Even Wilson (1989) who tries to elucidate an integrated approach of these divisions in British society is eventually forced to examine each division separately, without adopting an integrated approach. Nevertheless, he shows how the state can model intervention towards the benefits of the working classes as well as accepting a welfare state pattern within a specific conception of the family and the nation (which, of course, affects foreigners and ethnic minorities). According to Wilson (1989) and to Ginsburg (1992), those divisions of social structure are the result of a patriarchal and racially structured capitalism. Together with these social divisions, the status of the foreigner should also be revised, which cuts another division locating people outside of the welfare system as a result of their legal status. Citizenship enables the recognition of legal and political rights, which are important aspects in relation to welfare. Yasemin Soysal's approach to these issues placed a stronger emphasis on the limits of citizenship (1994), as does the work of Bäubock (1998). The nation-states, by applying national restrictive laws also limit social policy dealing with these aspects. Therefore, the nation-state is responsible for saving social policies towards foreigners as well as directing them towards the familist approaches of the welfare state.

Social policy is intimately linked with the analysis of social structure, because it is understood that it has to be thought of as a means of bridging the gaps in the social structure. It is at once a reflection and a reproduction of it. In immigration policies it is what I refer to as the "policy mirror mechanism" (Caponio et al. 2000). The welfare state institutionalizes class, gender, and ethnic divisions inequalities.[16] Hence, the welfare state would reproduce those divisions: (1) through the amelioration of women's lives but also reinforcing female dependency and the sexual division of labor, and (2) through institutionalized racism, by denial of access, second-class provision, reproduction of "racial" divisions, and the maintenance of immigration controls.

Defining a Context of Reception

As a starting point, we will here readapt the classical concept or the reception context in migration studies used by Portes and Rumbaut (1990) for our case of the Mediterranean. According to these authors, the main elements of analysis for such a context are: the policies of the receiving government, the conditions of the host labor market, and the characteristics of ethnic communities. We will here focus on the conditions of the labor market (highly informalized economy), the type of welfare (and its connections to deregulated immigration policies), and the changes in the family structure. In this third element we will also take into account the family base for the formation of ethnic communities.

The transfer from private duty to public responsibility for care (e.g., public childcare and parental leave), which has been typical of Scandinavian countries or the so-called "women-friendly states," has not occurred in Southern Europe. If different mixes can be found between family-market-state in different countries, in the South European breadwinner model the sphere of care is primarily private. This importance on the private as a welfare provider eventually leads to an over-valuation of the role of the family, although this situation can be seen also in relation to social classes: the inclusion of the middle class in relation to welfare, typical of the social democratic welfare state variety can not be found. The lack of services for these families forces them to pay for external workers, which in many urban settings are foreign women. As a result, women provide reproduction functions for middle-upper-class women, but at the same time, in some sectors, foreign women also compete in the production function with working-class autochthonous women. All these issues show the complexity of social stratification in connecting the variables of gender, class, and ethnicity.

On the other hand, migration is also seen as a family and community strategy of households headed by immigrant women. I therefore believe that it is essential to note that in Southern Europe, the role of female immigration seems to perpetuate indirectly dependence on the family (this is especially true of urban Italy), considering the reluctance of the state to develop schemes such as personal assistance. Therefore, the work of immigrant women seems to be embedded in important changes occurring in the countries of origin (the role of transnational families) and in receiving countries, the new immigration countries, Southern Europe (see Ribas-Mateos 1999a).

This chapter poses the question of convergence in terms of the interdisciplinary context located in the labor market (especially the informal sector), civil society (especially, the family), and the state (highlighting the growing importance of local policies). Changes in the market (informalization of the economy) and in the family (in terms of gender and generation structures in relation with the quality of welfare services) are the basis for the reproductive effect on the situation of foreign immigrants. The lack of citizenship rights and the different conditions for welfare benefits for this type of population questions not only the base of democracy but it also reveals the rigid boundaries of the welfare state.

So where does convergence lie? As already mentioned, common indicators for the model could be expressed by a triangular context defined by three variables: an important informal economy, recent foreign immigration, and a weak welfare state. This study, using the logic of comparative analysis, will be addressing also differences through local case studies.

Looking at Changes from a Multilevel Perspective

One of the main challenges in studying immigration in late capitalism is the speed with which changes affect all spheres of social life. Our time is characterized by a period of very fast changes and that can be seen as a highly entangled reality for a social scientist: for example, de-industrialization and tertiarization processes, the emergence of foreign immigration, the reformulation of social services in the questioning of the welfare state, the "municipalization" of social policies, the demographic trends and the future problem of the "ultra-elderly." All these problems can be seen as a wide scenario for changes in Southern Europe. Nevertheless, pointing out these changes is not so simple as it first appears, due not always to their innovative nature, but due also to the speed at which they occur. In this respect, Mingione (1991: 33) considers,

> The point is that, to a certain degree, the passing of time always brings about change in the nature of social formations. Such change is not linear or evolutionary and cannot often be defined as revolutionary. Social change in the industrial age is intense; that is to say, significant social transformation takes place within a shorter time-span than in pre-industrial societies. Re-state provocatively, the "post" societies or "service" societies or "disorganised capitalism" can be said to be unconvincing as explanatory terms because they describe real changes which are not, however, particularly significant relative to the dominant characteristics of contemporary societies" (Migione 1991: 33).

For the purposes of our study, one of the main changes to be seen here is in relation to international migration flows. Today, in all regions of the world there is a continuous growth of international flows of people covering the traditional but also the new migratory routes. Within them one can also differentiate additional new features: the increase of female migration, globalization—where more countries are involved—acceleration and differentiation of flows (introducing diverse categories: temporary workers, family reunion, etc.) (Castles and Miller 1998: 8). We could also add the progressive blurring of the differences between emigration zones and immigration zones, as the traditional developed-developing country division is created as distinct pockets within both types of countries.

Furthermore, compared to other fields of research, immigration studies have traditionally used an interdisciplinary perspective. In that respect, my interest here lies in relating the new immigration flows into Southern Europe with other current changes that are taking place in industrialized countries. Those migratory contexts, located in Southern Europe, are also related to the recent attention given by social scientists to the changes in family patterns and to the diffusion of informal activities, together with recent debates on the role of the welfare state.

However, if immigration changes are taken as the key variable, those are also analyzed through other types of changes. Hence, the first and general aim of this work is to identify changes through an interdependent perspective. Immigration issues are here related to three scientific concerns that had emerged in the 1980s: (1) changes in the employment structure related to the informalization of the labor market, especially focused in main cities and in the service economy, (2) the conceptualization of the family in a context that takes into account the "two-fold presence" of women's work, leading to a complex and often confused combination of productive and reproductive roles, and (3) the controversial role of the state in shaping economic and social relations (cuts in the provision of social services, together with other tendencies related to neo-liberal restructuring), particularly in defining the policy networks in multilevel governments and in welfare mix arrangements.[17] Within the first and second concern, I also include the traditionally gendered conception of caring,[18] which also raises important and challenging theoretical questions in the relationship between state provision, the market, the families, and the relative merits of each system.[19]

My efforts here will be addressed to an interpretation of the different meanings of these changes in the context of a diversity of patterns, times, and local conditions. The size and quality of social changes are different over time and space, so those generalizations are rather dangerous. In this respect, Mingione (1996a) points out how the transition from large to smaller family units generates different times and rhythms in different regions, assuming that in some areas, such as the rural regions of the northern Mediterranean, this is not yet complete.

My perspective here intends to fill two gaps that exist in social research: one is new immigration flows into Southern Europe; and the other is related to comparative studies on welfare, considering the relation of inequality and migration in the context of the welfare state. One of the main reasons for choosing Southern Europe for the purpose of studying policies towards migrants is that little research has been done on immigration policies in this region, the so-called "new immigration countries." The primary reason for this choice is that, in my view, this region provides an excellent setting for a new study of migration due to the great variety and entanglement of the migratory phenomenon in the area. At the same time, the analysis of new immigration flows demonstrates that they constitute one of the clearest expressions of social inequality in the context of the European Union. This is particularly true in the case of Greece. There, the non-European migrant population has less access to welfare than in any other member country, especially when considering the great number of immigrants with an irregular status. In short, welfare policies do not only produce, but they also reproduce the inequality of the immigrants' status and gender in the social structure.

In a broader sense, trying to synthesize the interaction between these changing phenomena as underlined by our triangular setting—immigration, the welfare state, and the family—is a complex and a highly ambitious task. Many social processes may lie embedded in such a complex network. Indeed, it is precisely this very intermixed nature of elements, an endless circle of processes that makes pinpointing the boundaries extremely complex. It has been possible to speak of a globalization process in Southern Europe since the 1990s, especially with regard to the way in which capital flows and new patterns of international competition have affected the restructuring and relocalization of the labor force, especially having an impact on the weaker labor force and social polices in these countries. Even if Southern European countries are affected by globalization and European integration trends, processes in Southern Europe are also the result of the way in which these countries have been positioned towards them, for example, in the different ways they react to migratory history or differences in their welfare evolution and development.

Hence, those factors have been taken from three different spheres: the market, the family, and the welfare state,[20] corresponding to the three lines of argument addressed in the research questions. However, it is also difficult to separate dimensions,[21] as Carrasco notes in the activities in the domestic-family sphere: from cooking to shopping (consumption) or in mediating between the household and the state (the use of public services) (Carrasco 1991). Apart from the typical considerations of the nuclear family of the 1960s, this family unit can no longer be considered in a closed spatial dimension but in a mobile setting, which can also cover kinship structures, as anthropology has always done.

In addition to global changes, we have to deal with assuming time-space differences in local, regional, and global processes, at the same time that these processes become more diffuse in public-private dynamics (welfare mix models). Apart from global changes, local processes are one of the main contexts in which to consider further research into the problem of divergences. When considering the localization of immigrants in the living space, the same circumstances apply as those noted by many authors with regard to the question of poverty in the United States, which is concentrated in the central parts of the large older metropolises and in the small towns and above all in rural areas. Degraded jobs on the labor market correspond here to degraded housing. Martínez Veiga (1999) has applied this theory to the case of Spain, with particular reference to the central parts of Madrid and Barcelona (as transition areas according to the literature of the Chicago School of sociology) and to the rural areas of the Western province of Almeria (Torre Pacheco, Roquetas de Mar, El Ejido, which are the main destinations for men who enter the Moroccan-Spanish border without documents), locations with a strong rural component. The same can be said for other areas of the cities in Southern Europe where I have conducted research: Omonia in Athens, Porta Palazzo in Turin, and Stazione Centrale in Naples. However, in the case of Lisbon the situation is quite different, where spontaneous constructions have appeared on the periphery.

Elements of the Host Labor Market

Together with the "clientelist" (patronage) or "rudimentary" typology of the welfare state and the typology of "new immigration countries," we can also add to this model of countries the adjective "late developers" of European capitalism (Mingione 1995). This model can be defined by obsolete economic structures (except in some regions), a modernization from rural to urban service-based economic and social structure, a gender asymmetry in sectorial employment changes and an important role of a dynamic informal sector. The model is typical of late-coming economies where family enterprises and self-employment are resisting capitalist concentration. More than elsewhere in Europe, in the Southern European countries the unofficial economy comprises a vast and complex area centered on micro-enterprises in the traditional service industry and tourism, in semi-autonomous jobs, which vary greatly in innovation and transformation.

Apart from the lack of national policies towards migration, according to Simon (1987: 287, quoted by King 1997), the key characteristics of the "new immigration" in Southern Europe are their often clandestine nature, the wide variety of migrant nationalities, and the fundamental role of the "new underground economy." Reyneri has calculated from a variety of sources the following weight of the underground economy in selected European countries in terms of average GNP estimates: Greece 29.4 percent, Italy 17.4 percent, Spain 11,1 percent, The Netherlands 9.6 percent, Germany 8.7 percent, and the United Kingdom 6.8 percent (Reyneri 2001: 22).

In addition to the "push factors" in the sending countries, immigration flows in the region respond to a demand for certain types of jobs (which are low-status, low-wage activities, primarily in these expanding informal economies) often filled by immigrants from "Third World" countries. On the other hand, in correspondence to the dualization of the labor market, another type of demand is found, namely a professional demand mostly covered by immigrants from the "First World"[22].

The existence of a demand for low-status jobs has to be understood in the context of the socioeconomic formation of Southern Europe. King et al. (1997: 9) indicate the key features of this formation as processes of modernization, urbanization, and tertiarization, the dynamism of the informal sector, the importance of small-scale enterprises, an enhanced level of education for most young people leading to the rejection of manual work, and a sharply defined conception of social and family prestige reflected in attitudes towards "acceptable" and "unacceptable" types of work. One can also introduce here the concept of degraded jobs, those that are mostly taken by the newcomers. Sassen (1995) defined the concepts of a "degrading manufacturing sector" and the growing demand in the service sector in "global cities," which have been useful for the analysis of immigrant employment insertion. The arrival of migrants has a lot to do not only with segmentation tendencies but also with other characteristics of those markets: high unemployment rates, a major presence of autonomous and irregular jobs, and the dynamism of small-scale enterprises, especially in the case of Veneto in Italy.

Irregular work is particularly concentrated in the agriculture sectors of less developed regions, in the construction sectors, local manufacturers, and services for individuals and families, which highly coincides with the labor demand for foreign immigrants. In Europe, this type of work is particular to the South of Italy, Spain, Greece, Ireland, and some areas of Southern France (Mingione et al. 1990: 5). In general terms, this specific model of labor is also related to low levels of female participation and low fertility rates (Solsona, et al. 1999). Facing this demand attraction in the informal labor sector, the classical analysis by Piore on the dual market, labor flexibility, and the reserve army function of the immigrants serves as a suitable application for the case of Southern Europe. To these mainly irregular and underground types of employment other "irregularities" have to be added, in particular those that refer to the legal status of migrants.

Consequently, the context of high unemployment and the crisis and revision of the welfare state favors the debate on the perception of foreign immigrants as a problem for society, even though there is a specific demand for their work. In this region, the formation of a specific demand for foreign immigrants can be appreciated through the interrelation of different factors: improvements in the living conditions of the autochthonous population, the increase in educational achievements, and the expectations and presence of the family net for the native population, which can be also understood in connection with the absence of family policies. Therefore, from this cross-section we can identify how the host society identifies the location of the contradiction of immigrant perception: between the devil and the deep blue sea, between the crisis and revision of the welfare state and the re-emergence of the underground economy. In Southern Europe, the decline of the work-force in the agricultural sector, the progressive tertiarization, and the development of the so-called atypical jobs (temporary and part-time jobs, which mainly affect newcomers to the labor market, young people, and women) are problems that are clearly reflected in the occupational structure of the foreign labor force.

Together with Southern Europe, other places like the southern border states in the United States show a similar pattern in immigration reception contexts. This is especially true when considering the entrance of foreign domestic work, in contrast to other countries where co-resident, full-time domestic help has disappeared and where entrance to the country is more restricted. In line with Mingione (1991: 280), these kinds of live-in domestic workers are increasingly being adopted by migrants from underdeveloped countries. Another characteristic of these immigrant reception contexts is that the situation comes about when the employer wishes to save on social security payments, and in some cases also on wages, while the employee saves on social security contributions and income tax, yet may still be covered by the social insurance of his/her spouse or that of a first job. A further area of informal employment in the service sector is connected with the different background of welfare programs in each country. Irregular forms of employment become more diffuse in social contexts where the welfare state has developed in a less efficient and comprehensive form.

Immigration Patterns and Policy Elements

According to Portes, as immigration is a data-driven field of study, it has not had to deal with broad generalizations for highly abstract theorizing. On the contrary, the bias has run in the opposite direction, namely towards ground-level studies of particular migrant groups or analysis of official migration policies (Portes 1997: 799). It is for this reason that studies in immigration not only provide important theoretical statements but they have also constantly yielded conditionals constrained to a particular time and place.

We should begin examining commonalties in order to identify a model. Many scholars have been searching for a suitable model in which we can take account of this immigration phenomenon, focusing particularly on the characteristics of heterogeneity and defined by the following factors: a multiplicity of nationalities and types of migrants (from both rural and urban origins), and a gender asymmetry depending on origins. In spite of stringent border controls, in all four countries, each with a large informal economy, there are a large number of irregular immigrants with a high representation of this labor force in certain sectors. We can also find an ethnic and gender stratification within these markets: Albanian men in Greek agriculture, Moroccans and Western Africans in Spain and Italy, Filipina women in caring and domestic services in Southern European capitals such as Athens and Barcelona, with the exception of Lisbon.

With the exception of Portugal, the origin of the immigration flows from particular Southern Mediterranean countries seems to be an important factor for most of the selected countries. As noted in the introduction, it is important here to underline the weight of the Moroccan community in Spain and Italy and the presence of the Albanian flows in Greece and Italy. As regards Portugal, the migrants' origins are mostly represented by their colonial links, most obviously through the importance of the Cape Verdian community in the Lisbon metropolitan area.[23]

However, differences within these countries will also be taken into consideration. The North-South regional gap which is obvious in most of these countries as well as their respective historical conditions (such us the ex-colonial PALOP countries in Portugal and the status of the ethnic Greeks in Greece) are two illustrative examples of this diversity. The historical past also plays a significant role in marking privileged relationships between the exporter and the importer labor force: the Latin-American colonies and the Moroccan protectorate for Spain, the Greek diaspora abroad, Brazil and Portuguese-speaking Africa for Portugal or the Somalian and Ethiopian flows towards Italy.

Apart from the SOPEMI reports on migration trends (conducted by the OECD—Organization for Economic Cooperation and Development) and Eurostat figures, little data is to be found regarding comparative statistics for migration. Even if we take into account the traditional immigration countries in Europe we find highly varied material, which makes comparisons difficult. Some include ethnic monitoring while others do not, some use population census and others labor force surveys. They have no consistent definitions of the target groups and there are considerable differences in legal frameworks for foreigners. Southern Europe also presents the following obstacles: a number of difficulties surrounding accuracy of estimates regarding immigration trends due to poor statistical recording systems, the undocumented status of large numbers of immigrants, the diversity of nationalities and migrant types and the high degree of spatial mobility of migrants, both between and within countries (King 2000: 11). According to this author the important clandestine element encourages us to raise estimates by three million or even as much as three and half million. Nevertheless, although this is a new phenomenon and the lack of literature and experience in the field does not help, the figures are still small in comparison with other European countries, and they are also insignificant when considering nationalization.

In addition to the description of migrant flows, other important characteristics of the migratory context should be taken into account, such as migrant-related social policies. It must be assumed that immigration policies in Southern Europe can be seen as related on the one hand to restricted border controls and on the other to the lack of integration policies for immigrants in the context of a weak welfare state.

In general terms, the speed of these changes, combined with inexperience in the issue of foreign immigration, has taken the countries of Mediterranean Europe by surprise. To this we have to add the marked contradiction between the policies of flow control and the policies of social integration, linked to new questioning of the welfare state. Furthermore, in the last twenty years, the integration of migrants in EU countries has emerged as an important area of public policy.[24] Even though European integration has meant that doors have been shut, Southern Europe seems to represent the place where the borders of Schengen space are the most permeable. On the Greek coast and in the Southern regions of Italy and Spain there are the three principal gateways that isolate the countries of the South and the countries of the east. In general, these gateways may be more permeable than others, but they reinforce public order and national security measures in dealing with of foreign migration.

What conditions the first level of this immigration pattern in the first place, together with entry-restriction policies in line with the EU demands embodied in the Schengen provisions are the almost nonexistent social integration policies. Let's take as an example the quota policy, which is applied in some countries like Spain. The poor functioning of these quotas illustrates clearly the inadequacy of immigration policies in its broadest sense. In this line, immigration policies—either through the quota system (Spanish case) or through regularization processes—are the structures that shape labor niches. Those niches are mainly identified through the substitution of the native labor force.

Welfare Elements and the Family Shock Absorber

Having addressed the Southern European welfare state typology we will now go on to consider the welfare mix dynamics of this study. In the framework of this analysis, changes in the welfare state are seen under the light of the shrinking borders between private and public spheres in organizing innovative welfare arrangements. In this context, we can distinguish two dimensions of the welfare mix for our proposal: (1) where particularistic forms of solidarity have been placed, excluding immigrants. Social benefits are lower for excluded groups, such as single mothers, the poor elderly, etc., in Southern European countries. However, single mothers are not always excluded—in Italy their poverty rate is lower than that of intact families—and, in fact, they are often the specific target of income support policies in a country that has no general income support measure for the poor; (2) where the division of care labor, meaning costs are shared between the family, the market, the state and the voluntary/community sectors are located. However, also in the corporatist welfare state, caring is shared between the state, the family, and third sector/volunteer agencies, but in our case more stress is put on the last two.

The weight of the welfare mix analysis, which especially reflects upon the empirical case studies I use, responds to the continuity of spheres and resources. A distinction should be made here between "internal" resources, which are contributed to by the state, as well as the community, charities, friends, and kinship networks. According to Mingione (1991: 83), this distinction is not always sufficiently clear but it is useful in order to highlight the importance of social factors and socialization mixes.

Traditional social policy ideologies (as Keynesianism and ultra-liberalism) are being abandoned and replaced by the welfare mix, underlining the idea of sharing responsibilities (often in the form of the partnership). The three classical poles of the welfare triangle can be seen through the interaction of the market, the public sector, and civil society. Through applying three distinctions: public/private, formal/informal, profit/nonprofit we can distinguish the so-called third sector—the NGOs (nonprofit, private, and formal) and the welfare mixes, which are the areas where the co-responsibilities and cooperation between agents of different spheres take place (Abrahamson 1995:139). This construction of welfare mixes within the Southern European model will be an important focus of this study in order to prove heterogeneity within a general model; in other words, how the welfare mix is constructed in different settings.

Apart from the welfare mix focus of the study, another important point is the question of social citizenship for foreign immigrants, which has generated so much debate in Europe over the last years. Marshal distinguished between three types of citizenship: civil, political, and social. Social citizenship includes the right to live according to society's standards, and to have guaranteed minimum material rights in relation to citizenship status. Hence, inequality can be expressed as the absence of civil rights (not to be entitled to express one's differences), the absence of political rights (not to be entitled to vote or to have access to public jobs), and, lastly, the absence of social rights (not to be entitled to be a customer or a beneficiary of social services). However, even though we have tried to determine "the birth of welfare mix" we should add that it is probably when considering this phenomenon that the differences within Southern Europe are most exaggerated. We can find a clear-cut distinction, which shows polarization even inside countries: for example, Turin and Barcelona on the more developed side, and Athens, Naples, Thrace, and Algeciras on the weaker side.

Introducing changes in the family cannot be considered in isolation from family policies—which can be implicit in all social policies—and, consequently, cannot be treated separately. Therefore, the issue of family changes is interdependent with the changes in the welfare state and the efforts in searching for welfare typologies, as mentioned before.

As shown by many historical and sociological studies, the Southern European family displays several distinctive features according to structure, behavior, and attitude. Among these characteristics, it is interesting to note the different conceptions of kinship, family networks, and the high institutionalization of marriage. Under these conditions, multigenerational households (with two adult generations) are common, often composed of young descendents who are reluctant to abandon the parental home, and to whom familial responsibilities carry great weight in constructing their life narrative. Notwithstanding, these family strategies have to be seen in terms of family net function in interaction with other spheres, for instance the labor market: in relation to high unemployment (acting as a safety net) or in relation to the family business, the "family business net" (especially seen in the case of Greece).

The family is supposed to assume the function of shock absorber in case of a member's unemployment and for the high index of late marriages. This context also explains the multiple generational households and the low fertility rates (with some autonomous regions like Catalonia showing the lowest rates ever in recorded world history). Another important sphere of interaction is to be found with family policies and the pension system, where we can point out widespread home ownership as a primitive form of insurance against social risks and the relative generosity of the side-track contributory pension schemes; these strategies can be understood in a semi-extended family strategy, where families gather a diverse combination of incomes.

It is in this context that Trifiletti´s work is of considerable interest because it goes beyond the classic stereotypes of the "rudimentary cluster," trying to look past the cluster explanation. According to Trifiletti (1998), this accumulation takes place within the family and highlights the function of the family, which is very different from the classic model of the male breadwinner, typical of the nuclear family. Although, most interpretative models refer to the traditional role of the family and to the "insufficient" family policies, Trifiletti uncovers a new type of function of the family as regards its relations with the welfare regime and the carrying out of joint strategies in this field. She points out that decommodification is a gendered notion of independence: to be rendered independent of the market may result, for a woman, in compulsory care work for another family member who is at work. Hence, the hypothesis that Southern European social policies function alike provides little information as to the gendering of the welfare state. Generally speaking, the only easily discernible feature shared by Southern European countries is their scarcity of resources to subsidize social policies. This is often explained due to their late and rapid economic development and the classical reference to a leapfrog nature of social change.

Compared to the rest of Europe, in most Southern European countries (Italy, Spain, and Greece—Portugal is always an exception in these gender trends), a smaller proportion of women work outside the home (mainly full-time, and very often not for reasons of independence, but for family reasons). Only in this case, through their worker status, can they get benefits and have access to social services. Portugal seems always to be the exception (even in terms of the migration turnaround) in the varying insertion of women in the labor market, namely due to the Portuguese women's high activity ratio. In 1993, Denmark, Finland, and Sweden were the European countries with the highest female activity rate (between ages of 25 and 49), followed by France, Portugal, and the United Kingdom. In contrast, Ireland, Spain, Italy, and Greece showed the lowest rates. Compared to men, women's rate of unemployment was the highest in Greece, Portugal, and Spain (Flaquer and Brullet 1998). What all countries of Southern Europe have in common with regard to women's participation in the labor market is that the proportion of active women who work part-time is far lower than in the rest of the countries of the European Union. For Trifiletti (1998), the case of single mothers can function as a corollary in trying to go beyond the classical breadwinner model typology.[25] She applies the following proposed typology for the case of single mothers: (1) breadwinner regimes protect them precisely because they lack a breadwinner, (2) Mediterranean welfare regimes have no special reason to protect them, (3) universalist welfare regimes protect single mothers because they have to cope with difficulties in at least one of their roles, (4) liberal welfare regimes protect single mothers because they have no access to the labor market. By this typology, she demonstrates that the Mediterranean welfare regimes are not in the early stage of a development model, rather they are in the midst of a different type of model. They do not correspond exactly to the male-breadwinner model, and this is not so much due to a phase of imperfect implementation, but due to a sort of middle way of decommodification and gendering.

The work of Flaquer and Brullet (1998) gives us an in-depth analysis for the characteristics of family policies in Southern European countries by painting a picture of Catalan reality. The lack of family policies even at welfare mix level in the Catalan context structures a different view of the family, in contrast to the Northern European countries where care for parents is understood as a moral obligation, and also operates differently according to gender and generations, because it is mainly women who care for parents and also for their partners. Therefore, family policies that have to deal with the combination of market and family spheres[26] (the classical Laura Balbo women's "double presence") should include not only measures for children but also for the dependent elderly. However, policies that can balance labor market and families include, in a more broader sense, measures in relation to the labor market, maternal and parental leave, services for children, measures related to the times of the city as well as measures that balance the work at home between family members. The policies analyzed at the Catalan level (see conclusions of Flaquer and Brullet's work) cannot be considered universalistic because they cover only a few target families. In the absence of universal measures that include all children and that are to be found in most European countries, the only income is that produced by the labor market, causing birth rates to be dependent on the state of the labor market. The difficulties that this pattern implies for the conciliation of the labor market and the family, especially for women, leave dependence on the family and demand for personal services in the market as alternative ways of care, which often include the use of native but also foreign women for these tasks.

Finally, growing privatization of the welfare state and weakening universalistic measures challenge the understanding of reciprocity structures; it is in this respect that the family is once again taking on a leading character role. Besides, foreign immigrants, when arriving in hostile reception contexts, have to reconstruct reciprocity structures in order to deal with the new situation, either the family, the community networks, the immigrant's businesses, or the mixes between the private and the public sector. Other authors, such as Mingione (1991: 41) in the case of the United States, have underlined the persistent importance of a diversified range of ethnic minorities using a dualistic organization of survival that is not supported by a extensive welfare state. In contrast to the "minorities," the white majority—increasingly involved in the associative forms of socialization—has been able to rely on private services offered on the market because they receive relatively high wages, which leads to the high cost of labor, while the diverse minorities have relied on various kinds of reciprocal arrangements. Firstly, the family as the "shock absorber" is here considered from two aspects: on the one hand, the familism context, which characterizes these countries, and on the other, the context of immigrant families. When establishing the differences between these two types of families it is interesting to note that their strategies are connected. As Mingione points out (1991: 41), reciprocal and supportive activities involve one household spending some of its time to ensure the survival of another; they therefore belong to the reproduction pattern of the receiver rather than the provider. Secondly, the relevance of the role of gender in the family structure is here preponderant, taking into consideration two perspectives: (1) from the native family side, we consider the role of women as caretakers and informal givers. Here we give relevance to welfare insufficiency and its response through a merchandised form by the recruitment of immigrants; (2) from the immigrant's family side, especially taking into account their role as the community pillar and as the base of an economic network as well as the caregivers of the family members. Here we highlight the insufficiency of welfare social policy as addressed to migrants and its answer through welfare mix arrangements.

Convergence and Divergence through Local Case Studies

The Seven Differences

Where does convergence lie? As already mentioned, the common indicators for the model are expressed by a context of reception defined by three variables: a large informal economy, a weak welfare state, and the specific role of the family. We have concentrated mainly on how this is comparable in Southern European societies. In contrast, we will discover indicators, discourses, and realities that make us aware of the contradictions that exist between the assumed commonalities. A good perspective from which to observe this is from extreme cases within a single country.

Our research, based on the logic of comparative analysis, uses a model of countries set in commonalties, but which also addresses differences through case studies, especially by looking at welfare mixes. In that respect, many problems have to be considered, for example, by choosing a model of similar countries we run the risk of over-focusing on the specificity of those countries.

Even though the countries are used as units of analysis, case studies set in a local context can show a diversity of welfare mix variations.

The cases are mainly represented by cities, as these provide the most interesting illustrations concerning local changes (local market, local welfare) and migrations from a perspective of international comparison. Nevertheless, in Thrace we are not talking about cities in the same way as I have examined the other fieldworks. With Thrace there is a problem of representativity, because we are dealing with the far more diffuse unit of a region rather than a city. In the case of Portugal, we have only considered the case of Lisbon in the empirical examples.

The significance of dualism is not that a society is divided into two autonomous and discontinuous segments but that a society is divided segmentally rather than continuously (Berger and Piore 1989). Authors such as Mingione (in many of his writings) underline the social and economic dualism between North and South as an important point of departure for addressing some of the unresolved problems of the Italian Mezzogiorno. An illustration of this dualism can be seen in Mingione's (1996) analysis of the relationship between youth unemployment, featuring high youth unemployment, and informal work in the Southern European countries of Greece, Italy, Portugal, and Spain, drawing on 1995 Eurobarometer data. He confirms how a Southern European model of migration/employment emerges in the post-industrial age.

It is important to take into account the scientific tradition of each country when conducting comparative work. There is a clear lack of comparative research for Italy in relation to Southern Europe. Most of the research into immigration in Italy has been conducted taking the case of Italy and the old immigration countries, logically because those countries have a few lessons that are of use to the situation existing in Italy, but also another reason could be that Italian researchers take their socioeconomic system as being nearer to the North instead of the "backward countries" in Europe. Another common feature of research done in Italy is that much of it is connected to deviance and criminality; one explanation could be due to its long-standing tradition in the sociology of law and in the political climate of the country, together with the fact that this kind of stereotype probably spreads faster among public opinion. As in Greece, the subject of the criminalization of foreigners is also present; while in Greece it is associated with Albanians, in Italy it is associated with Moroccans (meaning all people from Maghreb countries) and secondly with Albanians. This type of research has often produced a general conception that treats migration exclusively as a matter of public order, a perception that has also been reflected in the media (Quazzoli 2004).

In order to interpret the Italian case in the Southern European model I put forward the hypothesis of how a sharply contrasting socioeconomic regional frame leads to the polarization of social policies addressed to immigrants. The socioeconomic dualism related to the growth in the service sector and the informalization of the labor market can also be related to population changes, like the decrease in the birth rate, the growing elderly population, the reduction in internal migration and immigration from Third World countries. I use as an example the immigration policies towards immigrants as a result of this dualization: the different structure of the labor demand, the different welfare services available for Italians and for foreigners reproduces a polarization in the welfare mix policies that deal with immigration issues. In the South of Italy, the relative ease with which immigrants can live, find housing or precarious employment, and the difficulties which they encounter in terms of a real insertion—above all for family groups—explain the arrival of working immigrants to the South of Italy, as well as their exodus. In the Naples region, a significant component of immigrant's work constitutes domestic work or family assistance in diverse forms.

In Spain, differences that exist due to divisions throughout the national territory must be noted. Despite the fact that Catalonia, together with the autonomous community of Madrid and Andalusia, is one of the places with the highest concentration of immigrants, the sectors of activities of foreigners, their origins, the quality of social services, etc., differ enormously from one place to another. Divisions in the national context are especially pronounced in Italy: the changing role from emigration to immigration, the North-South dualism, the South as the first gateway for migrants are major factors. This contrast can also be seen in Spain (with Barcelona as a main urban reception context, Algeciras as the main door for "illegal" flows).

As already mentioned, the three classical poles of the welfare triangle can be seen by applying three distinctions—public/private, formal/informal, profit/nonprofit—we can also distinguish the so-called third sector—the NGOs (nonprofit, private, and formal) and the welfare mixes. This construction of welfare mixes within the South European model unveils how the welfare mix is constructed heterogenically in different settings. Furthermore, in order to understand the Southern European specificity we have considered its contrast with the rest of the EU countries, and we have seen a framework for national differences inside Southern Europe from the historical context and the making of the national identity (e.g., Greek nationality and the social construction of the foreigner; Spain as the Latin-American "motherland"; Portugal and the linguistic affiliation in Africa).

Historical determining factors are also diverse. For example, the facility for communication through the use of a common language and cultural proximity were factors that attracted African immigrants to Portugal. In contrast to other countries of the South, the settlement of African communities took place earlier, and was even started during colonization. Other historic determining factors can be noted in the case of Greece. Ancient communities and new communities with historic ties in Greece, such as the Pontian Greeks, have acquired special relevance in regard to policies of immigration, a situation which no other country in the south of Europe shares. A case similar to that of the Greeks who were coming from Asia Minor to Greece can be found in the Portuguese *retornados* (returnees) from the decolonization processes in Africa in the mid-1970s.

Lastly, coincidences can be found also depending on the sector of policy that we look at. For example, similarities are shown when we consider Portugal and Greece in terms of education (the situation of Cape Verdians in Lisbon and Pontios in Thrace who do not finish their compulsory basic education until 14 years of age), housing (Pontios in Thrace and the PER program in the Lisbon metropolitan areas) or citizenship (the political use of Cape Verdians and Pontios as electoral voters).

The Italian North-South

In our European Mediterranean model, Italy appears to represent the most suitable case for analysis, and it is also where the methodological contrast of cases is most appropriate, as well as other marks related to the chronology of changes or to the tradition of assistance, mainly of a Catholic nature.

The cases of Turin and Naples seem to structure two distinct models of integration, the former being more well disposed towards immigrant associations and cultural groups, the multicultural type (Caponio 2000), whereas the latter has not yet found a background agenda for the social integration of migrants. By choosing these two cities we approach two different models which conform Italian society, while also dealing with two differing societies in terms of internal migration, the traditional immigration city (Turin), and the traditional emigration city (Naples). However, today's foreign immigration varies from the old internal flows for a number of reasons: (1) it is not only a phenomenon of large cities as was previously the case, especially in the triangle Turin-Milan-Genoa, and (2) it is diffuse in the North where it affects the medium-small-sized cities of Emilia Romagna, Lombardia, and Veneto, regions that show a higher increase in the small business sector.

Much research has already underlined how, from a comparative perspective, the Italian case reveals a high polarization of areas, from high industrial transformed areas like the Northwest triangle to other decadent traditional sectors in the South, in the Northwest, and also in the Center of the country. However, this polarization has had a different effect on these last two regions of the country. The theory of the three Italies can be used from the criteria of different macro-economic models but also from a sociological perspective (Bagnasco 1977). It supposes that regional imbalances do not represent a regional problem in the strictest sense but that the three Italies are integrated in different forms in a unified model of national growth. However, even considering the triple division, we can usually distinguish two general socioeconomic formations. For example, taking into account the diffuse industrialization based on small- and medium-sized manufacturing industries, this has been a typical characteristic of the far northern and central areas of the country. Nevertheless, even Bagnasco himself would argue that the three Italies model does not hold any longer. Territorial differences in services in Italy are based not only on unequal economic development but also on the decentralized responsibility for most social services since the institutionalization of regions in 1978. Other differences in social protection derive from the fewer job positions in the South, which are covered by the standard protections.

It is likely that Italy is the most paradigmatic case for Southern Europe in the immigration phenomenon as well as in the welfare mix approaches. Besides being examples of dualism, Turin and Naples have also been chosen as emblematic of other North-South contrasts within the country: today Italy is witness to the re-emergence of old Gramsci *Questione meridionale* (1952). The dual character of this society is probably much more accentuated than in any other European country; this polarized dualism is marked by the combination of two different economic and social systems. Furthermore, in the Italian case, "the concentration effect" of the underclass indicated by Wilson (1993) is that of the North-South division, as poverty is concentrated in socioeconomically disadvantaged areas of the Italian Mezzogiorno (Morlichio 1996a). As other researchers such as Negri and Saraceno have already pointed out: "in Italy the mechanisms of economic poverty are mainly due to territorial dualism" (idem: 118). We can also speak of a Southern/Northern labor division and a Southern/Northern family division. In other words, diverse services such as school dining facilities, home help for the elderly, services for the disabled, and services for drug addicts are considerably less available in the South than in the Center and the North. As a result, individuals are more dependent on their direct family and often relatives to meet their needs. Consequently, even though Italy remains a centralized and not a federal nation, the place of residence leads to considerable inequalities not only in terms of labor market opportunities, but also in terms of the acknowledgement of and access to social rights. This does not imply that such differences and inequalities remain unaltered in time, nor that the general regional divisions used in the standard presentation of national data (North, Center and South, or Northwest, Northeast, Center, South and Islands) are internally homogeneous.

Hence, as also occurs with research into poverty and social exclusion in Italy, immigration studies cannot elude the territorial dualism of the country. In the South, immigrants face a different type of labor market, a much weaker welfare system, and also different attitudes from the population. Here I take as an example the discourse on immigration policies towards immigrants as a result of this dualization. The different structure of the labor demand, the varying welfare, reproduces a welfare mix polarization. Through fieldwork (interviews with key informants) patterns have constantly emerged, namely polarization in the role of the municipalities, in the varying reactions of the traditional left, in the varying roles of the Church, and in the different role of women's groups.

Such a hypothesis is based on Mingione's work on the South of Italy in order to illustrate a case study of "fragmented societies." From his work I relate the concept of the fragmented society in relation to welfare, the labor market, and the family. However, Mingione, in his framework, does give special consideration to the role of immigration. From his point of view, the cleavages in the Italian polarization are based on two premises (Mingione 1993: 421) related to industrial development: (1) the center-periphery divisions, and (2) the divisions rooted in historical traditions, cultural differences, mainly religious, national and ethnic, which play an important role in the structuring of social relations.

The persistent deficit in the system of social protection stimulates the development of irregular work in two important forms: a peculiar symbiosis between the private and the public sphere (predicting the privatization tendency) and the responsibilities of families and kinship structures. In the South of Italy we can speak of a double repercussion of the weak welfare policies in relation to the cash benefits addressed to needy families and the direct or indirect production of services. On the one hand, this affects a large number of people, because it operates towards the growth of the informal economy (where foreign immigrants are also included) in combination with the strategies of families. On the other hand, it affects a minority of people (urban middle and upper classes), who by using private care services demand foreign female work. Poor workers and poor unemployed are two social categories that portray many areas of the Mezzogiorno. These phenomena are closely linked to low rates of employment in this region. In demographic terms, Southern Italy is the single, largest backward area in an industrialized country. According to Mingione (1998: 33), it is more appropriate to speak not of a "Southern question" but of a number of different questions. Some agricultural areas remain characterized by backward, fragmentary, and subsidized productive structures, while others have benefited from extensive processes of agricultural modernization. The South of Italy is probably the largest and most populated underdeveloped region (weak industrialization and weak social services) in an industrialized country (Mingione 1993: 470).

Finally, the relation between immigration and criminality has also been constructed differently in relation to the North-South axis. According to Zincone, one of the differences between the North-South immigrants' insertion into criminality is that in the South migrants encounter a strong and capillary organization where they are potentially the weak subjects, whereas in the North, as in Turin and Genoa, migrants can easily find their own market for drug trafficking (Zincone 2001).

In Italy, the political left wing, among other sectors, has played a major role in the organization of the *comitati per la sicurezza* (security committees organized at neighborhood level) in the country's northern and central suburbs, which explains the gradual degradation of these suburbs based on the formation of *kasbahs* (Barbagli 1998:57). These are based on a discourse that claims that the appearance of foreigners in small-time drug dealing and street prostitution, which has led people to believe that immigration is the principal cause for the rise in urban crime rates. This issue has always contained an underlying ideological question for those who see the binomial immigration-criminality from a demagogically over-simplified stance, yet also for those adopting a more right-wing posture. Barbagli believes there are two reasons for the host community's hostile reaction. The first is the rise in the crime rate, leading to a greater sense of fear and insecurity among the population, although this fails to convince as this lack of security was already present prior to the arrival of the immigration phenomenon. The second is that as people are more afraid, there is a demand for stricter laws, an opinion that the author considers to be ungrounded.

Turin. "There does not exist in any other Italian city such a reception and social aid network comparable to the one in turn. Not even in Emilia, not even in the almost perfect Reggio, where the whole community gets involved in managing the different centers. In turn they are able to do the work even in a flexible way, for irregular minors" (IRES Morosini 1997: 3).

We can distinguish different levels of analysis in the examination of social integration policies. At the national level, according to Bolaffi (1996), Italian immigration policies share two common failures: inefficiency when dealing with clandestine immigration and the failure to reach an acceptable model for the access of citizenship (which peaked during the months of December 1997 and January 1998 with the arrival of Kurds in Southern Italy, and their impact on the deterioration of German-Italian relations). The result of these failures is consistently negative, both for the image of the immigrants, as public opinion is influenced by the attention given to the most marginalized groups, but also as an easy topic for xenophobic and conservative politics, creating a conflictive atmosphere of political collusion and electoral propaganda (Bolaffi 1996: 51).

It was in 1986 that the government first considered social integration through free Italian language courses, despite the fact that no public funding had been set aside for these initiatives. The aim of the act was to legalize and regulate the situation of immigrants and to prevent future irregular immigration (Zincone 1994b: 130). In order to achieve those objectives, two committees were created: one for consultative functions (attached to the Ministry of Employment and Social Security, composed of six representatives appointed by the main non-EU immigrant organizations; four from the trade unions; and three from the employers' associations and also representatives of other ministries), and a second committee for the purpose of regulating migrant flows. Two main axes articulated these discussions that would become central to the future debate in Italian society: the link between irregular immigration and the underground economy (although no serious efforts were made in this direction) and the competition between national and foreign workers. In 1997, two specific reactions of the Italian government can be given as an example of the endurance of the politics of immigration control: the massive repatriation of Albanians[27] and Kurds and the various negotiations with other countries in the Mediterranean area through treaties of readmission.

The politics of immigration in Turin have long been characterized by emergency measures, especially addressed to "primary attention." Legislation at a regional level has been especially defined by the tendency to give priority to the problems of social assistance and public order. Local administrations have been able to activate, directly or indirectly, a series of initiatives directed at immigrants: social assistance, *centri di prima acoglienza*, and initiatives to support voluntary action and immigrant associations and housing policies. Because the right to vote on a local level has as yet not been given, local consultations are the tool by which to achieve better social integration of migrants.

On a local level, we can underline three main characteristics of the situation in Turin: (1) the existence of numerous well established Catholic organizations specializing in social intervention,[28] (2) the trade unions' tradition and the social intervention of the left, and (3) the relative weakness of local policies (IRES 1994:32). How does the Turin model play a role in the various discourses of the interviews? In the case of Turin, there is clearly a considerable amount of interaction between all of the social actors who work to provide services for immigrants to a greater or a lesser extent. The type of integration model required was more a subject for debate among nongovernment organizations than the administration itself. The case of Turin was a prime example in Italy of the way in which the network of actors operated in order to cover migration needs. It also revealed a dense migrant concentration in city centers. Paradoxically, this concentration also recalls the ancient migration of the "Meridionali" migrants.

Social actors in both Northern and Southern Italy agree on the need to find a common formula that will enable them to manage the migratory phenomenon more effectively. They also agree that, like other selected cities, they are fairly unprepared to receive migrants, and that they are faced with a phenomenon for which no provision has been made. In the case of Italy, this lack of provision has resulted in its so-called emergency policy. Therefore, and in view of the fact that the situation already existed and required urgent measures, the solution at the time was to capitalize on their presence in the labor market.

Naples. Naples probably bears the greatest resemblance to Greece in terms of welfare services and also when considering the functioning of the so-called *economia del vicolo* (alley's economy or lane's economy), related to precarious and low-skilled jobs in the urban area and seen as a means of survival.

This case study has been selected because in its immigration policy related to a family and welfare model, provides a distinct contrast with the North of Italy. Within this polarity, Naples is the second city chosen as an emblematic example of these contrasts. Like Turin, its polarized dualism is characterized by the combination of two different economic and social systems.

In the Italian case, "the concentration effect" of the underclass, the mechanisms of economic poverty are due mainly to "territorial dualism." The main labor market indicators (occupational rate, labor force participation rate, structure and sectorial composition of occupation) are presented in drastically different ways in the North and in the South (Morlichio 1996a: 13). Besides, the gaps between both situations are widening with time, especially as far as the unemployed are concerned—young people who have no access to unemployment benefits in the same extended way as in other countries. Therefore, the unemployment model here contrasts with the male adult breadwinner model present in Northern Europe (Morlichio 1996a: 65).

Therefore, choosing Naples was a way of getting closer to the Southern reality, and to the main urban context when describing (as others have done before in other contexts, taking as an example the big city of the South) the Italian model of poverty (Mingione 1996), and the attributes of the local social services. In the South, large families with small children are one of the main "victims" of poverty. However, the growing tendency of this poverty among families is present not only in the South but also in certain areas of the North and Center of the country.

In the mid-1980s, the first concentration of immigrants in the Mezzogiorno, started in Villa Literno, in the province of Caserta. Together with some areas of Puglia and some Sicilian localities, it became a pole attracting immigrants in the agricultural sector (Pugliese 1996: 7). In opposition to this traditional male labor force, women from various nationalities would be recruited in the domestic sector. One of the important consequences of the regularization effect was that it stimulated labor movement from different regions in terms of the ease or difficulty in obtaining a labor contract.

Within the context of the city, I have given special consideration to the old historical quarter, because of the higher concentration of immigrants to be found there rather than in other areas defined by particular urban conditions, and where fewer social services are available. Those conditions are repeated on the outskirts of the city where the old housing estates are located, which together with other better-off areas, constitute the Neapolitan metropolitan belt.

In studying the poverty and social exclusion in Naples, one cannot exclude the extreme fragmentation and pulverization of socio-assistential services. In this sense, Naples is an emblematic example of the Mezzogiorno (Amaturo et al. 1998) and the specificity of the South in an urban context, which, on the one hand, is heavily representative of the poverty of the Italian model as well as the weakness of the local social services on the other hand. It therefore combines a labor market with narrow opportunities and a lack of social policies, making it difficult for immigrants to escape from such a vicious circle. Large families within this population are considered at risk in the context of high unemployment and a widespread informal economy. This is why most of the municipal budget for social assistance is addressed to children, who are the target of the most important innovations in the structure of the current local administration. Particular attention is given to the situation of MIT (*minore in transito*—minors in transit), for example *nomadi* and migrant children, which are considered a separate category.

In Naples, family networks are supposed to replace the action of the state. However, it has been proven that those networks are highly ambivalent; on the one hand, they are supportive, but, as other studies have shown (Amaturo et al. 1998), they do not really function as a means of escaping from social exclusion. Also connected with the weakness of the family is the so-called "partner-effect," where one member of a couple is more likely to be out of work if his/her partner is also unemployed (Morlichio 1996: 40).

The situation of the social services in Naples is completely different from that of Turin. According to De Filippo and Morniroli (1998), in Naples *prima accoglienza* services (first reception services) do not even exist. The lack of services is a consequence of the absence of an institutional response to the insertion strategies of the community. As for the actors who are working for immigrant services, we can highlight the *Servizio sanitario immigrati*, ISI (Health Service for Immigrants). In the *Comune* (municipality) there is also the *Asessorato alla Dignità* (Municipal Department for the promotion of Dignity). We can also distinguish a number of quasi-institutional actors where Caritas Migrante plays the central role (Centro Ascolto Immigrati della Caritas Diocesana di Napoli [Caritas Center in Naples]). Regarding associations focused on immigration, the Forum antirazzista della Campania was set up in 1994 as a centralized service for organizations working with migrants.

How does the model of Naples play a role in the different discourses of the interviews? The arrival of the boats bringing the Kurds to Italy during the first half of the 1990s had such a traumatic effect on the border issue that calls were made to deploy the army along the frontiers. In addition, this phenomenon coincided with the impact that the rising immigrant crime rate was having on public opinion. The enormity of the problem, which has dominated Italy's immigration policy, has led to the majority of services being directed at primary reception measures, although it must be said that these measures have failed to produce an effective solution to the problem. Associating Naples with a border or gateway city gives it a transitory character, a point on a route leading to other destinations where, in theory at least, other types of labor opportunities exist, together with increased prospects for job stability. Another factor related to geographical contrasts is that lower levels of development in the South of Italy favor a transitory nature of immigration in this area.

However, this vision of Naples as a place of transit depends not only on the labor situation in the North of the country, but also on the patterns established by immigration regulations. The spatial distribution of the population of Naples, as the largest city in Southern Italy, according to social class is highly irregular, as are the types of services available.

Naples is different from Turin not only because its social services are less developed, but also because Neapolitans have a greater dependence on extended family networks. At the time of our fieldwork, Naples was undergoing radical changes in terms of the philosophy of its social service structure in that there was a shift from a transfer-based model towards a truly modern system of social services. The Neapolitan context is characterized by large pockets of poverty, in a setting totally unlike that of Turin. In Naples, immigrants are faced with social exclusion trends in which the informal economy and family networks are total different from those of the North. In urban terms, these forms of participation are subject to strict divisions between Neapolitans and migrants.

Catalonia and the Southern Spanish Border

As referred to in the introduction, Pumares (2003) provides us with a classification of the different spaces of migration in the Spanish territory. The border spaces come first: Sebta, Melilla, the Canary Islands, and Algeciras, albeit to a lesser extent. Algeciras posed a differential component with respect to the other territories because it is not an enclave space, and therefore does not have an accumulative effect typical of the other cases. Once detained and attended, migrants are returned (especially Moroccans) or are freed with orders of expulsion, and those who are not repatriated have the freedom of movement in order to reach their proposed destinations (Pumares 2003: 189). Algeciras and Tarifa are still important in terms of the numbers of *pateras* and dinghies arriving via the Straits of Gibraltar (in 2000, 40 percent of the vessels were confiscated here) (idem). Agrarian spaces are second in Pumares' typology, represented as the threshold insertion onto a labor market with pre-industrial features (e.g., places such as El Ejido in Andalusia). Thirdly, there are the tourist spaces, where the labor market of the hotel and catering industries is linked to the necessary flexibility of the building sector. And fourth are metropolitan spaces built around large cities, especially Madrid and Barcelona, which bring together the highest concentrations of foreign population facing a highly diverse incorporation into the labor market.

In broad terms, the Spanish immigration spatial pattern shows a focused concentration in the areas of the Mediterranean coast, Madrid and archipelagos, occupational over-specialization and a high labor discrimination and unequal access to the property market (in prices, landlords' attitudes and conditions), as provincial concentration with respect to the total provincial population number is particularly noteworthy in the Balearic Islands, Santa Cruz (Tenerife), Malaga, Las Palmas, Girona, and Almeria.

In overall terms, the general picture can be synthesized in the following manner:

1. A highly concentrated spatial distribution: Madrid, the Mediterranean Coast, and the Canary and Balearic Islands;
2. An over-specialization in the occupational structure: in the service sector (especially domestic service and catering industries), the intensive agriculture sector, and the building sector.

Direct discrimination operates as a consequence of the Alien Act, and indirect discrimination is found within social stereotypes and the unequal access foreign immigrants have to the labor and housing markets.

The example of Catalonia (and more specifically Barcelona's metropolitan area) within the Spanish case offers us an intermediate model of the Spanish immigration reception context: the two main tendencies affecting immigrants are the concentration of foreigners in teritary occupations and their influx into the sector of intensive agriculture. Together with the strong presence of service employment in the Spanish labor market, it should be noted that tertiarization of the foreign population is even higher than that of the native population. The high rate of women in-flows in the population is also clearly evident, above all in Madrid and Catalonia, which host the two largest concentrations of immigrants.

The differences between Barcelona and Algeciras reflect to a considerable degree many of the contrasts already noted in the polarization of Turin and Naples. It has traditionally been claimed that social resources differ widely in the North and South of Spain, both in terms of public and voluntary aid. In the case of Barcelona, urban decay and urban renewal play an important role in relation to the urban insertion of migrants.

One of the new demands in social services is clearly the result of the rise in foreign immigration, especially in those boroughs where the number of foreign workers is higher than the average in other European countries with a long-standing tradition of importing foreign labor. When examining this new demand, an analysis of the discourses reveals a fundamental change, and the beginning of a new phase in immigration history in Spain, which, in turn, implies the existence of another, earlier stage. The first phase was characterized mainly by the initial influx of foreigners in the late 1980s, set against the context of the first Alien's Act with its more restrictive base and by the voicing of early concerns regarding immigrant settlement, with particular reference to the procurement of residence and work permits. At the same time, this initial phase of migratory flows coincided with a period of consolidation of Spanish social services (although we must take into consideration the sharp contrasts existing between the various autonomous regions). The second phase—which, despite having been conceived earlier, was not put into practice until the year 2000—highlighted immigrant-related problems that went beyond the traditional concept of the immigrant-worker, namely that of the worker who merely had to legalize his/her situation. This second phase involved the period of time during which families settled down and became established in the area, as well as issues such as school integration. Apart from the second Immigration Act, this phase was also distiguished by a number of other features; these include increased coverage of the immigration issue in the media, open conflict in relations with other residents and the routinization of racial attacks, which would ultimately lead to including the immigration issue in political agendas.

Barcelona. If we look at the case of Spain through our interviews, the contrasts between North and South are similar to those of Italy in that they may be defined according to multiple socioeconomic criteria. Despite the fact that Catalonia has some of the highest percentages of immigrants in Spain, there are considerable variations in the areas of activity in which migrants work, and, to a certain extent, in the organization of social services. This inequality would appear to be the result of the functional nature of space in migratory projects; in other words, whether they act more as a gateway than as a metropolitan settlement area.

For example, in metropolitan cities, female migrant labor has to be seen in terms of the demand for jobs relating to domestic service, health care, and leisure. In Barcelona and Madrid, migrant women usually fill jobs rejected by local Spanish women, for instance in the extended system of live-in domestic services. The data available for Barcelona, for example, indicate that 50 percent of all foreign immigrants in the city are women; in Madrid that figure rises to 53 percent (Ribas-Mateos 2002b: 55).

The growing number of immigrants in the cities of Barcelona and Mataró (the focal points for immigrants in each of the administrative divisions they represent) has led to an increased demand for resources. Although this demand seems to have found a more coordinated response in the case of Mataró, the same cannot be said for Barcelona. The paradigmatic new user of social services (as well as the complications these imply) is increasingly represented by the irregular immigrant in Catalonia. The attention given to the foreign immigrant represents the counterpoint of the classic conception of social citizenship, tied to the acquisition of nationality, and in a more diluted way, to the linking of residence and work permits.

Universalizing the mechanisms of public welfare (basically through pensions and unemployment subsidies) for the provision of goods and services (above all in the area of health and education) must be viewed against a background of the exclusion of irregular immigrants from the welfare system. In other words, the foundations of the welfare systems fail when the case of the irregular immigrant comes into question. This new challenge for social citizenship is put into perspective especially through the comments of interviewees in Barcelona, when we consider those social policies that make up the core of the welfare state, such as health care and education (the schooling of children and adult occupational training). The situation of irregular minors, as well as that of health care, are that most extreme examples defining the character of social exclusion of irregulars. In the case of irregular minors we see a more serious contradiction in the role of the state between the policies of immigration control and those of welfare policies (social integration), that is to say, between the means of controlling the population flows and the welfare policies related to social integration.

Our case in Catalonia focuses on two large urban nuclei in the province of Barcelona: the cities of Barcelona and Mataró. The reception context to be found in Barcelona is characterized by immigrant economic activity similar to that found in other large Southern European cities, and practically the same as that of Madrid, where immigrants play a large role in the service and construction sectors. In the case of Mataró however, this context is characterized mainly by immigrants' participation in the agricultural and textile sectors, and in addition it is dominated by nationalities other than those found in Barcelona, mainly Gambians and Moroccans. Together with Barcelona, Mataró has been one of the principal areas for settlement chosen by Moroccans in Catalonia and Spain in general, and it has large numbers of Sub-Saharan immigrants, particularly from the Gambia. Both of these cities represent the two *comarques* (Catalan districts) where immigrant family settlement has the longest-standing tradition: el Barcelonès and el Maresme. Furthermore, and as we shall see later, the case of Mataró is based on a heavy dependence on the charity work of the Cáritas organization for migrants, which is made up of seven parishes and a single social center.

Apart from the specific difficulties involved in renting accommodation, the problem of housing affects other issues in relations between migrants and natives. These include the impact of the spatial concentration of foreign migrants and the way in which this occasionally leads to a process of classic degradation and causes natives to move to other parts of the city:

> Obviously, the immigrants end up living in worse conditions for financial reasons, and this explains why immigrants tend to concentrate in certain areas. The autochthonous population also tends to move away from these areas, it's the same with the schools, people who had known one another all their lives or the traditional shops disappear and are replaced by immigrants and businesses run by them. This is one of the causes of racism. This is where the public powers should be investing, in order to ensure that the influx of immigrants doesn't bring with it the social degradation of the district. (BM6)

We could point to a kind of philosophy created by the respondents regarding the issue of immigrant concentration, in other words, a common discourse in which the concerns expressed by the native population hinge on the problem of *ghettos*. Furthermore, some believe it necessary to consider whether the creation of ghettos is a freely chosen process or whether this process acts as a reinforcement for existing intra-community networks. In the interviews conducted, we focused on an issue frequently raised by the interviewees themselves: the tremendous difficulties encountered by immigrants in finding housing. Other related issues also addressed were the changes in spatial concentration, gentrification, and the urban renovation tasks taking place in the historical center of cities such as Barcelona:

> *Ciutat Vella* has had the PERIs—the urban renovation plan-, which has meant that many of the houses have been demolished. What's happened as a result of the PERI is that the people who have been able to prove that a few years ago they were living in a apartment that has been demolished are now entitled to another apartment, regardless of whether or not they are migrants. So the housing problem not only affects migrants. There's a boy from one of the associations who always says to me, *a housing policy for immigrants? No, a housing policy for whoever needs it. What's the idea? To lump all migrants together?* (B9)

Algeciras. The community of the Campo de Gibraltar area represents a complex network of relations between Morocco, Gibraltar, and the city of Cadiz. The Straits of Gibraltar lead from the Atlantic to the Mediterranean and link Africa and Europe by means of a maritime border between Spain and Morocco. Algeciras, an area of strategic border importance for the European Union, is a city lying on Europe's southernmost border and is considered one of those Mediterranean gateways. Thus, it is used as a base for industrial delocalization and movement across the Straits. It is a key area for policing of illegal operations such as people trafficking as well as drugs trafficking and money laundering. The Spanish Civil Guard carries out strict controls throughout the region. Its location also makes it an area of vital importance for relations between Spain and Morocco; an example of this is the fact that Spanish vessels fish in Moroccan waters.

While Campo de Gibraltar is an area of considerable industrial activity, the Bay of Cadiz, as far as industry is concerned and despite its undisputed geographical and strategic value, is practically paralyzed. Consequently, although in many aspects this region may be considered underprivileged (communication difficulties create added problems), its industrial sector is currently the object of major financial investment, and the area is experiencing a population boom. However, although Algeciras is located in an area of economic development, thanks to its port activity, the city continues to suffer high levels of unemployment and low wages.

Interest shown by researchers in this area is due to the fact that many of its beaches have become "corpse-collection points," and the issue of irregular immigrants trying to reach the shores of Spain in small boats has been widely covered both in the local,[29] national, and international press. Algeciras has become a crossroads for both national, regular and irregular immigrants, and Cadiz heads the list of Spanish cities in terms of the number of illegal immigrants arrested in 1996. The province of Cadiz encompasses has the highest rate of unemployment in Spain. Because of this, immigrants have been discouraged from settling in this province, which corresponds to low immigration quotas, and the reason given has always been precisely the few market opportunities in the region, although perhaps an underlying explanation could be an attempt to prevent immigrants from settling in a border region.

Algeciras stands out due to its strategic geographical situation. As a border port with regular connections to Morocco it plays a special role as a gateway for irregular immigrants heading for the province of Almería. They are drawn by the rapid economic development that has taken place in this region over the last few decades, following the creation of greenhouses on the farming land. The so-called *plastic culture* has resulted in intense migratory flows, attracted by the agro-business boom, which has positioned the province of Almería as Spain's principal fruit and vegetable producer. This reception context is characterized by a demand for unskilled workers in the agricultural sector, together with considerable development in the service sector in this area. It is for this reason that Algeciras is viewed by the new migrant as a place of transit, one that holds no attraction in terms of labor opportunities. Worth highlighting here is the fact that conditions in this city also offer little advantages to local young people and women.

Algeciras is also an example of the contradictions to be found in government policies. Although border controls are implemented, a contraposition arises with the reality that is experienced just 14 kilometers away in Morocco, where measures are desperately needed to effectively channel social and economic development. Due to its border location, this area is particularly sensitive to Morocco's social problems, particularly among those inhabitants that have suffered most severely from the effects of social exclusion in recent years, namely women and children, and who have become the most vulnerable actors in any attempts to cross the Straits. This contradiction is also in evidence in the destinations, where control and repression models are applied, and where there is direct opposition to any measures designed to promote social integration.

A considerable imbalance of social resources exists in comparison to other areas of Spain such as Barcelona. Policies consider the figure of the immigrant as temporary, more of a person "in transit" than a migrant. For this reason, social policies are divided into three areas: specific services, where the immigrant is considered a temporary, non-resident figure; specific services designed for immigrants who have settled in the area; and general services, also directed at settled migrants.

The Portuguese Litoralization

Coastal areas of the Mediterranean have been amply documented, based on the fact that the majority of large towns, tourist areas, industrial areas, and transport axes are concentrated along the coast (Dundford and King 2001: 39).

In regard to the urbanization processes in Portugal, we should point out the large concentration of the population in the metropolitan areas of Lisbon and Porto as well as some diffuse urbanization in other areas of the country. Even though the space is highly differentiated in terms of socioeconomic criteria, how can we properly divide the country for a case study? In spatial terms, the sharpest contrast in Portugal lies between its inland and coastal regions. These differences are not only demographic (the most densely populated areas are to be found on the coast), but also socioeconomic and cultural. However, another traditional contrast to be considered is the North-South axis. In this sense, historically, Southern Portugal has been less Catholic, more industrial, and politically more left wing. In the case of Portugal, we have chosen the metropolitan area as the unit of analysis since focusing exclusively on the city center itself could possibly restrict our results, due to the fact that in Lisbon, immigrants tend to concentrate around the periphery of the city. Furthermore, we must also consider, despite it being a later phenomenon, the fact that in the case of Lisbon, the implementation of policies designed to renovate the historic center coincided with the arrival of considerable flows of foreign migrants.

We focus mainly on the process of the geographical litoralization and urbanization of the population, the desertification of the interior (especially the Alentejo, as despite major changes in the socioeconomic interior, the Alentejo seems to be the most complex region in terms of socioeconomic structuring), the crossed directional migration flows—internal and external—the ageing structure of the population, the strong growth of female presence in the professional sphere and in the educational system, the tertiarization of work, and the emergence of the extension of the new middle classes (Machado and Firmino 1998). Nevertheless, Portugal still has the lowest educational levels of all the EU member states, despite the progress made over the last decades.

The number of professionals in Portuguese society also remains lower than that of other European countries, a fact that highlights one of the aspects related to the coexistence of dynamics that indicate an unfinished process of modernization (Machado and Firmino 1998: 8). The growth of this "new middle class" is linked not only to the urbanization, tertiarization, and professionalization of the population but also to the construction of the welfare state. Compared with other countries during the same period of economic growth, Portugal displays a tremendous incidence of poverty, the highest rate of "poverty extension" in the EU, which as a dual characteristic of this economic growth could be the result of its resistance to modernization. This double-faced modernization results in a dualization of society marked by the existence of well-defined poverty groups. Furthermore, the extension of the informal economy has contradictory effects on the population: a deregulated job is a deregulated welfare (in terms of unemployment, illness, and old age). Families combine the income of the informal economy with other sources such as pensions and remittances from emigration. These practices for family and community help substitutive services in the area of social reproduction; they constitute a "civil society" that some actors call "providence" (Sousa Santos 1987).

Portugal has also been known for its semi-peripheral nature, which has distinguished it from other European locations. In addition to this, our study draws attention to the specific articulation existing between emigration and immigration—far more in evidence than in the case of Greece—as well as to the concept of mixed race groups, Africanism, and links with the PALOPs.

Feminization and tertiarization processes were clearly in evidence from 1991 onwards as the proportion of women in the workforce rose above the average for the EU. However, the countries most similar to Portugal in terms of cultural background or social structure (Spain, Italy, Greece, and Ireland), curiously enough, showed far lower female activity rates. The tertiarization process was lowest in countries like Greece and Portugal, while unlike other Southern European countries the weight in the agricultural sector seems in this case to be a symptom of less developed structures.

When comparing European data the situation of Portuguese women appears, paradoxically, to be in sharp contrast with the rest of the Southern European countries. Data show a low political but a high economic participation for women in Portuguese society. Nevertheless, this high economic activity rate must be viewed within the context of long working hours and fewer part-time jobs than their European counterparts, combined with a lack of family services, a weak urbanization rate, and high poverty among families (Ferreira 1999: 201).[30] This high rate of female activity is also closely connected with women's occupations in the agricultural sector. In addition, the expansion of public services and the growth of an underground economy are also associated with the presence of women in the labor market.

Over the last ten years, Portugal has registered the highest activity rate of professional occupations in the European Union. Furthermore, compared with other European countries, more Portuguese women between 20 and 39 are in full-time work than in any other EU country (Nunes de Almeida et al. 1998: 57). This specificity of the Portuguese society is explained by a diversity of factors related to family ties and solidarities.

In terms of its migratory role and in contrast to its European neighbors, Portugal can be seen as a kind of launching pad or turntable terrace for international migratory movements (Baganha and Peixoto 1996). Therefore, and with reference to the classical central-periphery model of the world system theory, it is possible that Portugal functions as a kind of turntable, receiving unskilled foreign labor while also exporting its own unskilled national workforce. As Portugal is unable to absorb an immigrant workforce, it replaces emigrating nationals with foreign immigrants.

A second distinguishing feature of immigration in Portugal is the strong presence of the PALOP.[31] Despite their dominant presence in Portuguese immigration, in recent years, a certain heterogeneity has been detected in their flows, as in the case of the Senegalese or Moroccans, and particularly in the increased number of Ukrainians, which is leading to a slight shift away from the predominance of migrants from Portuguese-speaking countries. It can also be deduced that although the first communities were made up chiefly of Africans from PALOP states, in recent years there has been an increase in flows from countries bordering PALOP states, as is the case of Senegal.

The integration of Portugal into the European Community in 1986 opened up the opportunity for civil work and enterprises to compete on an European level, which led to the "subcontracting model"—which has been operating for the last decade in Portugal—as well as the move of Portuguese construction workers to other countries, such as Germany. At the same time a large percentage of European structural funds would also be used for that sector (Baganha and Góis 1999: 247). The labor market, characterized by the overwhelming presence of immigrants in the construction sector, is composed of a highly informal sector demanding long working hours (night shifts, etc.). Working conditions in the construction area are extremely poor. Another feature of the labor market is the considerable presence of Cape Verdian women working in domestic service. In the case of Portugal, it is important to understand the dynamics of the labor structure in relation to the recruitment of the labor force. First, there are occupations suitable for skilled migrants often attracted by foreign investment and the salaries offered by large multinationals. Secondly, there is migration abroad, Portuguese emigrants working in other European countries (e.g., Luxembourg), who are attracted by the higher wages, particularly in the construction sector. Thirdly, we find the foreign immigrant workers, attracted, in turn, by the wages offered in Portugal, yet who suffer a reduction in their status in terms of their qualifications, while a further group is made up of unskilled workers who occupy the posts left unfilled by Portuguese workers.

As far as the migratory chronology is concerned, we can establish the traditional division between the first generation that arrived during the period of the *retornados portugueses*, many of whom were able to obtain Portuguese nationality. These included soldiers who fought on the Portuguese side. Interestingly, these retornados Portugueses also settled in the outskirts of the city, as occurred with the Greeks from Smirna (today part of Turkey), who settled in what would later become known as Nea Smirna. In both cases this "return" would lead to a settling process similar to the internal migrations to large cities, even though they took place at different times. In the case of Lisbon, the phases of internal migration and the arrival of the retornados were followed by the foreign migratory phases.

In the case of Portugal, immigration policies clearly belong within social exclusion programs and the fight against poverty. The model adopted by Portugal was that of the Dutch social policies, where analysis is based particularly on the risk groups classified as a target population, rather than on social divisions according to communities.

With regard to the management of social services, both Portugal and Greece offer a state-centralized model, unlike Italy and Spain, where these services are decentralized and are left in the hands of autonomous regions and communities. However, all these services have benefited strongly from various European Union programs and funds. The Cohesion Funds reflect the structural nature of these changes, which have had a direct impact on foreign immigration in a number of ways, including the increasing number of professional women and the gradual, albeit slow, setting up of measures aimed at reconciling work and family life, thereby creating ideal conditions for the entry and settlement of foreign women.

Lisbon. The case of Lisbon is characterized by a number of highly unusual historical features. Two major factors contributed to shaping the history of Portugal and the city during the 1960s: the colonial wars and emigration. It is essential to consider the loss of the colonies in order to obtain a clear understanding of the current sense of Portuguese identity. The Portuguese Empire was the first to reach and colonize Africa and the last to bring the decolonizing process to a close. This extended period of colonialism has meant that the migratory processes today possess a very special postcolonial character. A further fact to keep in mind is that emigration, as well as immigration, continues to form a part of Portuguese life today.

For Lisbon, the principal area of policy action in terms of immigration is related to problems of social exclusion, and in particular to the urgent need to resolve the question of shantytowns. Various courses of action exist in order to solve this issue, both in legislative and in practical terms, yet both depend on the role played by the local authorities.

Various studies have been carried out in regard to the poverty areas existing in Lisbon's degraded districts, as a result of European programs aimed at combating social exclusion and poverty (here we are referring in particular to the European Union's URBAN[32] programs in Amadora and Oeiras). These two districts are excellent examples of urban metropolitization and outward expansion towards the areas surrounding Lisbon. This peripheral area around Lisbon,[33] which includes Cascais, Oeiras, Amadora, Vila Franco de Xira, Alcochete, Almada, Barreiro, Moita, Montijo, and Setúbal, has been highly affected by the rural exodus, as well as the migratory flows caused by the decolonization process and current migratory trends. This urban growth, based on major spatial distinctions, leads us to look closely at the concept of the degraded district.

In the Lisbon metropolitan area I have selected the cases of Amadora and Oeiras to observe how the results of local strategies can vary considerably depending on the type of immigration policy adopted. Both of these Lisbon-based examples represent the success and failure of these stereotyped actions—

the former overseen by a right-wing government and the latter by a left-wing authority, upon which additional urban pressure is also placed. The discourse coming out of the borough of Oeiras indicates an absence of *Conselhos* or links with immigrant associations in the borough, and therefore the immigrant residents enjoy better living conditions, while in the case of Amadora[34] precisely the opposite is true.

The logic behind the major re-housing projects today is subject to criticism. Attempting to solve the housing problem by building large apartment blocks, which are then occupied by families grateful to have a roof over their heads, does not constitute a resolution to the difficulties. As this re-housing is often carried out on a large scale, the problems (drug dependency, unemployment, etc.), and the social tensions existing in the slums are merely transferred to the new areas. This, however, does not appear to be the case of Oieras. The cost of building land and the need for space is forcing these *bairros sociais* to the outskirts of the city, thereby reinforcing the sense of marginality, and of being in the city without really belonging to it. The PER program is important because for the first time foreign immigrants are entitled to subsidized housing. The spatial concentration may be an unwise policy, but it may also constitute a natural tendency of a group of people wishing to live together as a community.

In this case the complex urban planning situation is a vital factor in understanding foreign immigration, and, within this context, the problems caused by the shantytowns. The apartment blocks inhabited by the Portuguese stand side-by-side with the so-called concrete "clandestine homes." The streets run between these homes in labyrinth-style passageways. This disorganized distribution favors the appearance of clandestine bars and cafés, as well as clandestine textile workshops, which can be found even inside the homes themselves. The precarious construction, the result of a lack of urban planning means that one of the city's largest Cape Verdian associations continues to be housed in a prefabricated building. The clandestine[35] districts that sprang up in the 1960s would spread and become consolidated over the following decade, which was also marked by a process of residential transition whereby they gradually became Africanized. Today, immigrants live mainly in degraded districts and dormitory towns. Despite the frequent fines imposed, shantytowns have been springing up in the span of a weekend ever since the period of the *retornados*.

As far as the identity of these districts is concerned, there is a general identity problem affecting the second generation. It is important to mention here the question of ethnic identity, which, in the case of the youth, is closely linked to Afro-American trends and rap music. Another important factor is the traditional distinction made between the first generation and the Portuguese retornados. Indeed, the situation of the retornados is reminiscent of that of the Algerian *pied noirs* in Marseilles, or the Greek *Nea Smirna* arriving in Athens from Asia Minor.

The Greek Specificity

Greece can be characterized precisely by its lack of state organization—despite harsher attitudes adopted by the police and the army—which, in addition to its greater flexibility within a context of closed borders, makes the country an attractive destination for immigrants, particularly for the migrant population traveling from eastern countries. It is worth mentioning here that all those interviewed believed that the Greek borders were more accessible than others due to their geographical locations in close proximity to the Eastern countries, whose inhabitants today are in need of labor opportunities.

Many assumptions prevail that Greece, the most underdeveloped economy in the EU, has the highest percentage of foreigners among southern European countries (see, among others, Papantoniou et al. 1996). It is estimated that immigrants—either regular or irregular—make up 4.5 percent of Greece's total population (Linardos-Rylmon 1994, quoted by Pteroudis 1996). The analysis of new immigration flows to Greece illusstrates one of the clearest expressions of social inequality within the context of the European Union. These immigrants seem to have less access to welfare than any other non-European migrant in the member states, if we consider the high number of immigrants that do not hold a regular status (a number of sources point to a figure of somewhere around 500,000).

Perhaps more than in any southern European country, the significant role played by Greece's external relations is one of the main characteristics featured in foreign immigration. Furthermore, according to Baldwin-Edwards (1997), the particular mix of institutional, internal dynamics and external relations distinguishes Greek policy from the rest of Southern Europe. The country's geographical position as the southeastern gateway of the European Union—bordering on the former communist countries (Albania, the Former Yugoslav Republic of Macedonia, and Bulgaria) and Turkey (the Mediterranean passage from Asia and North East Africa, especially from Eritrea and Kenya)—makes Greece the country chosen by potential Third World migrants. In order to undertake a more in-depth study, each of the following geographical axes should be examined: (1) East-South and the Mediterranean, (2) South-North gap, (3) the Middle East and the Gulf War, (4) the Kurdish issue (Kurds from Turkey, Iran, and Iraq)—Greece is considered the first gateway for the Kurdish conflict—and (5) the collapse of communism, Eastern Europe—Rumania, Bulgaria, Ukraine, FYROM—and the former Soviet Union. Given the geographical location of Greece, today's conflicts in the Middle East are central to an understanding of the situation of refugees, and, as has been noted earlier, who are living the life of irregular immigrants, and sometimes experience even greater difficulties (victims of torture etc.).

The creation of the kingdom of Greece at the beginning of the last century and its expansion in 1947 into its current configuration with the construction of the nation-state, did not take into account the dispersion of the Greek populations in the East Mediterranean, in the ancient lands of the Ottoman Empire. Therefore, once again, this Balkan-European region, like all its neighbors, has to deal with unsolved problems from its past.

The traditional idea of space is still considerably relevant in the establishment of today's settlements and migrant networks. Greece's neighbors have a strong representation of migrants distributed throughout the country. The best demonstration of how international events can have an impact on immigration can be seen most clearly in the case of Albania. The number of Albanian deportations in Greece rises and falls according to the state of relations between the two countries and according to the treatment the Greek minority receives from the Albanian government. As Karidis (1993) suggests, migrants are taken as a political enterprise in the Greek-Albanian relations. In August 1994, Greece intensified its deportations (about 50,000 "illegal" Albanians were deported in one month) after five Albanian citizens of Greek origin were arrested when they tried to annex the southern part of Albania (Northern Epirus) to Greece, with the knowledge and collaboration of the Greek government. On the other hand, the Greek government insisted on vetoing financial assistance to Albania by the EU if the situation of the Greek minority in that country did not improve (Fakiolas 1994). The 1975/1991 Aliens Law reinforced the policies of deportation and border controls on illegal entry and also tightened the criteria for residence and work permits.

In relation to the labor market, most researchers have explored the competition that supposedly exists between national and foreign labor forces, albeit often considered from purely economic approaches. An example of this is the study of "illegal immigration in the case of northern Greece" (Lianos et al. 1996) during a period of slow economic growth and rising unemployment. Many years ago, Nikolinakos (1973; quoted by Fakiolas and King 1996) suggested that "the import of Africans" was a response to the structural labor shortages experienced by certain sectors of the Greek labor market in the 1960s and early 1970s as a result of mass emigration over the previous two decades. Fakiolas and King (1996) note that two major factors, uneven regional development (60 percent of the industrial development is concentrated in the Greater Athens area), and stunted industrial development is what pushed Greek emigrants before, and is once again responsible for the reduced number of job opportunities in the economic integration of returnee emigrants. Regular immigrants have been contracted from the countries of origin, applying first for a visa and later for a work permit (taking into account the lack of Greek manpower in certain sectors of the economy).

The selection of Thrace also helps in illustrating the contrast between a high immigration pole (Athens, Attiki region), and a low immigration pole (Thrace), between a big metropolitan area and a more depopulated and rural one, and between regions with very different levels of social services. Thus, there emerges a clear division between Athens and the Salonica area on the one hand, and, Thrace and some of the more isolated areas on the other. The same could be said of the European programs: the least favored areas do not have access to the kind of qualified staff so necessary for the programs, which, in turn, reflects the general lack of trained personnel in the Thracian occupational structure.

Athens. Several factors need to be taken into account when considering the relationship of non-citizens with the welfare system in this city. First of all, in relation to the labor market, if immigrants are really taking so many benefits, there is enough evidence to say that they occupy jobs in the most segmented sectors. Secondly, there are the demographic reasons, as the descendants of immigrants are potential taxpayers for European elderly people. Finally, while in an expanding economy, migrants were welcomed to the extensive welfare system thirty years ago, nowadays with the fiscal crisis and the welfare reform, unskilled labor is mostly unwelcome. As Baldwin-Edwards (1998) points out, the cause of this change is mainly economic, although the question of policy options remains open and is largely ignored with respect to migrants.

Our objective is to look for policies explicitly addressed to immigrants and their families as well as the social policies that specifically include institutional regulations on those same immigrants and their families in this city. Regular immigrants have access to social services, with the exception of unemployment benefits. As far as pensions are concerned, they depend on bilateral agreements. According to the Aliens Act of 1975/91, any kind of social services provided for foreigners is penalized, with the exception of emergency health situations, but in reality these measures have not been put into practice.

Athens is the only place in Greece where a number of changes have been implemented recently; these include the acceptance of foreign children in kindergartens (in 1995, the Ministry of Education allowed foreign children to be enrolled in schools, regardless of their status) and the opening of a Health Center. Because of the difficulties the majority of immigrants in Greece experience in benefiting from welfare rights (naturally due to their irregular status), a new framework had to be constructed in order to look at the alternative benefits that the immigrants would be able to enjoy. The general context that arises for the examination of immigration policies presents, on the one hand, rapid social changes in immigration policies, and on the other, a reluctance or a lack of reaction on the part of the Greek government when faced with the social reality, which results in a system of unpredictable policies.

In addition to the feeling of a lack of planning in the light of the situation that was developing, the respondents, including members of the trade unions, mentioned to me that they felt overwhelmed by the migrant[36] population ratios in Greece, and particularly by the number of Albanians migrants, who are largely responsible for the existing sense of social alarm. Another feature of the case of Athens is the amount of red tape and bureaucratic procedures involved in immigration, which contrasts directly with the dynamic nature of the private sector, particularly of small business. In addition to an inefficient bureaucratic system, immigrants in Athens also complain that the security forces are guilty of a certain abuse of power.

The most critical Athens-based associations claim that Greece has consistently attempted to block immigration, even more so than the Italian and Spanish governments. In Greece, immigration is a complex problem that goes hand-in-hand with other issues related to the labor market and European integration. As far as the identities are concerned, the Balkan element is a key feature, together with the Christian-orthodox identity and the foundations of a nationalist policy that rejects the ethnic mix. The question of Hellenism is constantly brought up when discussing immigration and the treatment each of the various immigrant groups should receive. Generally speaking, there is a considerable awareness of the presence of the worldwide Greek diaspora among all respondents.

The analysis of the presence of the new and old communities in the Thracian region, brought about by the disintegration of the Ottoman Empire, is informed by the notions of Diaspora and minorities, and provides us with very interesting empirical information about how to work simultaneously with commonalties and divergences in a context of comparative analysis of Southern Europe. This case shows how differences can be perceived by looking at the national level (here, Greece) through a bipartite case study, which by emphasizing socioeconomic differences reveals quite a lot of information about the differentiation of reception contexts where migrants arrive. In terms of commonalties, we should say that in this case some characteristics of the Southern European model are perhaps exaggerated, such as the clientelistic and family-based system, the very low level of social services, and lack of alternative actors to the institutional ones in the development of social policies.

With regard to the role of immigration in Southern Europe, restrictive borders and inexperienced immigration policies can be noted, whereas gender asymmetries seem to play a very different role in a rural setting (in contrast with the urbanized and tertiarized Athenian economy). In the urban setting, the need for family care seems to fit in far better with the new female flows; the gender nexus between the demand side—urban middle class family—and the supply side—foreign women—is, therefore, not present. Furthermore, irregular immigration is characterized by the presence of Albanians in the rest of Greece and seems to be quite different in this region, where all communities we focus on benefit from citizenship rights.

Thrace and the Greek paradox.[37] This case looks at a Greek region bordering on Turkey and Bulgaria. Thrace also represents a direct contrast in terms of the concentration of Greek and foreign populations. This case considers an integrated focus in which two types of policies—social policies affecting the minorities and those designed for Pontian immigrants—reveal the paradoxical strategies involved in the official Greek concept of "difference." Three different themes are taken into consideration: new immigration, new minorities, and old minorities.

This case puts forward an unusually integrated approach for viewing the interaction of new immigration and old communities in the new reality of Thrace. *Old communities* here refer to the different communities that have been living in Thrace for many years, and the newly arrived immigrants called Pontians from the former Soviet republics that are also ancient Greek communities. Possibly the main reason for the uniqueness of the Greek case is the fact that the Balkan scenario plays an important role in immigration issues. An important aspect of the Thracian region is that it has been the main point of arrival and settlement for the Pontians (ethnic Greeks from the former Soviet republics) in Greece. In terms of the *old minorities*, the aim is to show how the intricate problem of mixed communities and the impossibility of drawing ethnic boundaries in the Eastern Mediterranean area are of immediate relevance. The Muslim community (Turks, Pomaks, Roma) in Western Thrace illustrates clearly the problems of trying to differentiate between groups for whom Turkey represents a kin-state. The Greek government recognizes only one minority, the "Muslim" minority, living in Thrace and protected under the 1923 Treaty of Lausanne.[38] However, most Muslims identify themselves as Turks, regardless of their ethnic origin (Turkish, Roma, or Pomak). The case of the Turkish and Muslim minority in Thrace reveals a minority linked in terms of education and culture to Turkey.

In the context of Thrace, the urban-rural cleavage neatly reflects the socio-economic exclusion of Pomaks and Turks, both of which enjoy generally poorer living conditions. The urban-rural cleavage also reflects the division between urban and rural occupations, where the vast majority is in the hands of Muslim families. Other divisions can also be found: for example, the Turks work in the weekly open-air markets, while Greeks own the most modern and expensive fashion shops.

First, from the historical perspective, we will argue that current immigration policies are in part a continuation of the demographic policies carried out by the Ottoman Empire. Furthermore, it is common knowledge that Pontios communities were made to settle in this specific area in order to balance the presence of the Turkish/Muslim community, given the government concern about the growing birth rate of the latter.

Secondly, in terms of the historical background we should point out that when mentioning today to the different communities we should first refer to the prevailing organization of confessional communities during the Ottoman Empire. In this sense, Greeks who lived in the space of today's Turkey, Pontios (originally from certain areas of the Black Sea) from the former Soviet Union, Pomaks, the Turkish population, and gypsies all follow the legacy of the Ottoman system in mode of the division of communities, although, inserted today in the context of the construction of the young Greek nation-state.

Immigration policies cannot be detached from the socioeconomic situation of the different communities already living there. Furthermore, the concept of the Greek diaspora becomes essential not only for understanding the idea of Greek national construction but also for understanding better the outline of immigration policies aimed especially at the Pontios. The notion of diaspora is powerful in providing a sense of common identity. This Greek word, meaning "dispersion," has been used generally to recall the forced Jewish dispersion during ancient times. The notion of diaspora is linked to a strong identity awareness that a minority group uses as a reference even when the minority is settled in different territories. This identity consciousness uses the existence of an organization structured along political, religious, or cultural lines. The Pontios affirmation of identity is more clearly witnessed from the 1970s onwards in the form of cultural and religious identity, where identity is inherited mainly through an extended family system. The memory of this diaspora is based on the loss of an original territory, which for the Pontios is often dramatically evoked by memories of the genocide suffered at the hands of the Turks.

There are two premises that articulate well this last case. Firstly, both Greek and Turkish nationalism has used the issue of demography as a way to legitimize their policies. The program for the settlement of Pontios would appear to be in response to a demographic rationale.[39] In fact, we wish to argue that immigration policies towards Pontios pursue a change in the demographic population balance.

Secondly, dialogues of homogenization and nationalism are employed by the Greek nation-state. The word *omogueneis* (those who belong to the nation, in contrast to those who do not belong, *allogeneis*) is widely used for Greek immigration policies directed at the Pontios, despite the fact that Greece was always a mosaic of different origins. The model chosen so far is based on that of an ethnically homogenous society, with common traits not only of language and culture but also of a generalized myth of being descendents of an old civilization, in this case, Ancient Hellenism.

Notes

1. Examples of this include the problems involved in exporting the feminist theory to Third World countries (for examples, see Ribas-Mateos 1999b)

2. Within the new demands she distinguishes: the growth of elderly populations and the need for care, changes in the family pattern, in the women's labor market participation, increasing unemployment, economic changes (forcing inexpensive solutions), European integration (divergence or convergence?), changes in the political climate (neo-liberalism, communitarianism). Within the new theoretical changes she distinguishes: feminist work on the welfare state, women's social rights and the reconciling of work and family, communitarianism and neo-Aristotelism (less state, more communities, civil responsibilities), neo-liberalism, neo-conservatism (less state, more families) and new languages for social policy (the welfare mix debate). And finally, as far as political responses are concerned she distinguishes: the care of

the elderly and disabled members of society, children´s day care (different arrange-ments), the debate between cash benefits or services, children's active citizenship and care services, and the decreasing importance of the national state (Antonnen 1998).

3.   The mix of populations has always been a constant for this region. Yet the coexist-ence of ethnic groups was not always easy. All dominators left their trace on it, even though it has been bedeviled. The "Turkish Youth" neglected the Armenian geno-cide; twice the Spanish Castilla had applied the "cleansing by bloodshed," first with the Jews in the late fifteenth century and 100 years later with the *moriscos.*

4.   Traditionally, the extended family system, however, was not common to all these societies. It can be distinguished among North African families (especially Berber, who have mixed their own traditions with those of Islam, Greece, Serbia, and the Balkans in general.) We could also include Sardinia, Corsica, and the South of Italy, which are not fully characterized by an extended family system, but where one can distinguish strong links of moral solidarity. Within the extended family we should also consider the endogenous family preference among Muslim societies through parallel-cousin marriages; this system is reinforced by Koranic law, which attributes to daughters one-half of the son's share.

5.   The political development of patrimonial authority in Southern Europe is based on the concept of delayed development and the associated theory of dependent develop-ment. A corollary of patrimonial authority is patron-client politics. A patrimonial state can be seen as an immense pyramid of patron-client chains, culminating in the top patron, the patrimonial ruler. During the mid-1980s, Wallerstein proposed the con-cept of "semi-periphery" and its relevance to an analysis of the political economy of Southern Europe. The notion of semi-periphery is often used as an in-between category, but he finds it particularly relevant as an "indicator of certain political processes" (Wallerstein 1985: 34).

6.   We are referring in particular to certain emigration areas within the countries: the North of Portugal, Galicia and Andalusia in Spain, the Italian Mezzogiorno, and Macedonia and Thrace in Greece.

7.   However, they are "mobile divisions," which vary according to the different coun-tries. In Greece, the Attika region is here opposed to the islands, Epiros and Thrace, but not to Macedonia, which is in the North. In Portugal, the poor Alentejo is next to the touristy Algarve, but they are both in the South. I would say that the North-South dualism is more transparent in the case of Italy. The regional gaps also work quite differently according to the centralization-decentralization criteria. The two most clearly extreme examples would be the case of Greece and that of Spain; the Spanish "*comunidades autónomas*" in contrast to the "Greek *peripheria*," a regional arm of the central government, although now going through a shy transition.

8.   African countries with Portuguese as an official language.

9.   His analysis goes beyond the theoretical framework of the social democratic model. It proposes differences in cross-national comparisons as a variation in the quality of social rights, in the resulting patterns of stratification, and in the way in which state, market, and family are interrelated. However, the gender structure that underlies the relationship of these three institutions was not explicitly addressed, a situation which he would attempt to redress several years later.

10.   The family is a co-protagonist of social policies in Italy, together with other features of the Italian welfare system (based on measures that are added to income more than offering services, disparity of benefits and measures for social assistance, regional and even provincial disparity) (Saraceno 1995: 271). The family is a socioeconomic unit with "dependents" (children, women who do not work, and adults with special needs) and "household heads" who redistribute the income. It is also a unit for the

care of people, also with "dependents" and individuals (mostly, wives and elder daughters) who redistribute care services (Saraceno 1995: 262). These family responsibilities (strongly related to gender and generation differences) have much to do with the design of policies by southern welfare regimes, but they also play an important role in the analysis of immigration flows. Immigrant women are supposed to not only complement uncovered welfare services but also to replace autochthonous female roles within the reproduction of a specific family model.

11. According to Sarasa (1995) the traditional monopoly of the Catholic Church has been the cause for the clerical and anticlerical division of (some) Mediterranean societies. Even if these features have been watered down, the consequences are still quite visible in the symbolic meaning of private welfare provisions. On the other hand, Sarasa (as Ferrera does for the case of Italy) also stresses the influence of the leftist tradition in the view of social services (Sarasa 1995: 182).

12. The establishment of a regime of fragmented negotiations between central and local authorities leads to "clientelist chains" (Zincone 1992), which have influenced public administration and the public world, as clientelist mediation is the most direct form of obtaining public benefits (Ranci 1998: 191).

13. Like Titmuss, as indicated by Bismarck and Beveridge, and of general use by the European Commission. Even if we consider the interaction of actors in this field, we will have to differentiate the leading role in each situation (EU, central government, etc.). Another important question which must not be overlooked is the classical idea of power: "Any aim of using public policies as a form of knowledge or real government mechanisms risks becoming marginal if it does not face the issue of power" (Regonini 1995: 21; quoted in Subirats and Gomà 1998: 22).

14. They refer here to the individualization of social rights in the following way: "women will have to acquire direct entitlement to current social security benefits through a universal social security system covering all citizens independently of the nature of work (paid or unpaid), working time (part-time or full-time) and type of contract (short-term or long-term) (González et al. 1999: 31).

15. I would like to thank Chiara Saraceno for this clarification.

16. These processes cannot by any means be explained solely in terms of explicit racism in legislation (e.g., immigration laws) (…) nor can they just be explained satisfactorily in terms of the structural, socioeconomic requirements of capital (…) The term "institutional racism" is useful in identifying policy and administrative processes in the welfare states, which result in relatively adverse treatment of ethnic minorities. Institutional racism takes many forms such as stereotyping ethnic minority clients, failing to recognize their particular welfare needs or to consider them legitimate, and accommodating overt racist pressures in the wider community. The impact of contemporary social policy on racial inequalities is quite different in each welfare state, but in all of them social welfare has both mitigated and reinforced racial inequalities and institutional racism (Ginsburg 1992: 5).

17. In this framework of analysis the welfare state changes are seen from the perspective of the dissolving borders between the private and the public spheres in organizing innovative welfare arrangements. In this context we can distinguish two dimensions of the welfare mix for our purpose: (1) where particularistic forms of solidarity are in place, which serve to exclude outsiders of the system, including part of the recently arrived immigrants, (2) where the division of care labor and costs between the family, the market, the state, and the voluntary/community sectors can be located.

18. The concept of care traces its roots to the day-to-day reproductive work of household and the material significance of women's domestic labor. It was initially conceived of in terms of the unpaid domestic and personal services provided through the social

relations of marriage and kinship. Lewis (1999) suggests a heuristic category of "social care" in order to capture the political economy of the concept and the role of the state in the following dimensions: (1) conditions under which such work is carried out, where the role of the welfare state is indispensable, (2) the normative framework of obligations and responsibilities, (3) an activity with costs, both financial and emotional, that extends across public/private boundaries. She also stresses the fragmented conceptualization of care due to the formal/informal dichotomy and the separation of the care of children from that of dependent adults.

19. This gender reproduction can also be seen in the feminized work of immigrant women; as Lewis indicates, it is a reproduction that affects all women: "An examination of the nature of sexual divisions relate to a more complicated set of structures than men, because of their role within the family...This is important because it is possible for policies to give greater equality in one aspect of women's lives, yet it also helps to maintain or actually to reinforce traditional sexual divisions in another. Changes in policy must therefore be considered with regard to their effect on the totality of women's experience (Lewis 1983: 2). From the labor market point of view, caring is also now revised through the new strong demand for personal services. As Torns (1995: 7) indicates: they are services addressed to cover the needs of people and their families, present in everyday life of Western societies. They are characterized by their servile and unqualified nature and become especially useful for the urban middle classes. In this process the "personal services" have become a go-between for production and reproduction activities.

20. Millet had observed this complex relationship in the family sphere long ago: the family not only induces its members to adapt to society, but also facilitates the government of the patriarchal state, which directs its citizens through the household heads. Even in those patriarchal societies, which give them legal citizenship, only on limited occasions do women establish contacts with the state apart from the family (Millet 1970: 44).

21. The re-emergence of those links cannot only be understood within cultural variables (the familism, characteristic of Mediterranean countries), but it responds to the impact of social policies: in a context of privatization and market deregularization, reinforcing family links is a way of fighting uncertainty (SAPS 1998: 8).

22. Most of the studies of this dualization are to be found in the case of Portugal.

23. However, the statistical situation is evolving fast in the different countries. The Portuguese example illustrates this perfectly. A new Portuguese regularization was conducted in 2001 that revealed startling information about the scale of hitherto clandestine migration from Eastern Europe, especially from Ukraine and Moldova. Quite apart from the doubling of the total legal immigrant population in Portugal, Ukrainians emerge as the largest national group, followed by Brazilians and Cape Verdeans (King and Ribas-Mateos 2004).

24. It is the old division between old immigration countries and new immigration countries. However, even in the old immigration countries' policies vary widely: the British and Dutch model traditionally focused on communitarianism, the division of groups that share a common public space, the German model based on the idea of the guestworker (*gastarbaiter*), with highly restricted access to the acquisition of nationality and voting rights. And thirdly, the French assimilation model was legitimated for a universalism applied equally both to men and women, nationals and foreigners. The main topics of concern for local policies have been exclusion, understood in the context of urban marginality and unemployment; the second is political (political representation of foreigners at the local level), and third is cultural (Ribas-Mateos 1998).

25. This analysis has also been developed by other authors, Lewis and Hobson (1997) on the case of Lone Mothers in European Welfare Regimes, and Almeda (2002) for the case of Catalonia in Spain. However, Trifiletti´s interpretation is interesting but debatable. In Italy, there are specific provisions for unwed single mothers. They also come first in childcare services, precisely because they are perceived as a family at risk. Moreover, in some Scandinavian states there is no special protection for single mothers as such (a difference from the UK, France, and Germany). They receive the same kind of protection as anybody else (e.g., income support if they are poor and out of work). It is the generosity of the welfare state in general, together with a strong orientation towards a conception of citizens as workers that allows them to set up their own household without having to depend on a husband. I thank here Chiara Saraceno for this clarification on single (lone) mothers in Italy.

26. Three situations are the main challenge for family policies in Europe today: the weak fertility rate, the impoverishment of families, and the conciliation between market and family spheres (Gauthier 1998; Dandurand and Pitrou 1996; Schulteis 1998; quoted by Flaquer and Brullet 1998).

27. Two historic moments of Albanian migration into Italy, 1991 and 1997, are relevant when examining the way in which politicians and the press have covered the issue of asylum seekers. In contrast with Spain and probably closer to French migration dynamics, the debate on immigration is clearly introduced earlier into political discourse and the subject is also mediatized much sooner. After the crisis in Albania (October 1990-March 1991), in the former-Yugoslavia (autumn 1991), and in Somalia (September 1992), a new status, asylum for humanitarian reasons, was created. Notwithstanding, recognition of this status for categories and groups depends on the government and can be given and taken away at will (Zincone 1994: 134).

28. Many of them are only local (Salesiani di Don Bosco, Camiliani, Figlie della Carità di San Vincenzo de Paoli, Suore de Santo Natale, Suore Vicenzine di Maria Immacolata and the Suore del Formulato Cristiano and the Congregrazione di San Giuseppe). The rest are non-local organizations such as the Ciscat and Caritas (from 1980), Gruppo Abele, and Sermig.

29. The issue of these small boats and their attempts to cross the Straits are reported on a daily basis in local newspapers such as *Europa Sur.*

30. There is a lack of support structures related to the provision of care services for dependents; in this context women's wages are often those that cover similar services in the private market. Even though in Portugal there is an increase in the number of women in more professional categories, they continue to be a majority within the least qualified professional categories and most affected by precarious jobs, subcontracting, and unemployment.

31. People generally consider PALOPs as those who possess a colonial connection. PALOP would appear to synthesize the idea of the post-colonial black population.

32. Part of the Community Initiative Program developed within the framework of the European Community Structural Funds for urban areas.

33. The Lisbon metropolitan area is made up of eighteen districts.

34. The Seis de Maio district defines the communists' lack of efficiency in the following way: "The communists never adopt any kinds of policies; they leave everything up to central powers." (interviewee n. 7, Lisbon)

35. My visit to the *Moinho de Juventude* area during the course of my fieldwork made a major impression on me. Here we found living conditions and the use of space on a par with that in the outskirts of a number of Sub-Saharan cities.

36. For migrants they use the Greek word *metanastes,* for refugees they use *profuges*, while in Albanian it is the word *refugiat* that is used for migrants.

37. There is a more extended version of this case in the article "Old Communities, Excluded Women and Change in Western Thrace," Ribas-Mateos 2000.
38. The Treaty of Lausanne is the main legal framework protecting the Muslim community living in Thrace. The Lausanne Treaty of July 24, 1923 laid down further guarantees concerning the rights of minorities, and used the term "Muslims of Greece." The treaty put an end to the Greco-Turkish War, secured Turkey's present borders, and obliged both countries to respect the rights of the Greek minority in Istanbul and of the Turkish minority in Thrace concerning religious practice, the use of language, including in primary schools, and control over religious affairs.

    In January 1923, Greece and Turkey signed the Convention Concerning the Exchange of Greek and Turkish Populations. Turkey demanded the repatriation of ethnic Greeks residing in the Anatolian areas of the former Ottoman Empire in exchange for the return of the ethnic Turks living in the Kingdom of Greece. For its part, Turkey allowed those ethnic Greeks residing in Istanbul before (HRW 1998: 7).
39. By analyzing the historical legacy left by the Ottoman Empire in order to understand today's Balkan mosaic of communities, I was able to find in the works of Courbage and Fargues (1992) two central points in order to locate these demographic questions: (1) Contrary to what is often thought about polygamy in its Muslim-Arabic form, it is effectively a moderating influence on fertility. Hence, contrary to today's tendency that associates Islam and demographic explosion, evidence suggests that in the Ottoman times fertility rates were low among Muslim women when repudiation tended to mean the end of a woman's reproductive life. However, during the first centuries of Muslim domination, together with conversions, demography always played a role in favor of Muslims due to the effects of inter-community marriages. (2) Demographic change formed part of the strategy of the Ottoman Empire. One of the basic tools for this was the *sürgun*, the transfer of entire populations by administrative decisions. It was meant to revive devastated populations, especially in Istanbul. It tended to mix populations, both rich and poor, with the policies adopted not only limited to Turks and Muslims. Indeed, Greeks and other Christians were also authorized, and even encouraged to settle in the city.

2

Understanding Welfare Mix Variations

Approaching the Case Studies

This chapter is a response to those comparative studies that adopt the nation-state as the unit of analysis. Rather than applying an interpretative logic articulated by national regimes, and organizing the cases according to countries, on the contrary our study begins with the cases of the various cities. The comparison of the particular cases has not been based on a set of consistently homogeneous criteria that are traditionally found in comparative studies, considering that the relevance of certain criteria varies from country to country in the understanding of the migration narrative. For instance, while in the case of Italy the need for a methodology of opposing cases is clear, this is not so obvious in the case of other countries such as Greece and Portugal. Consequently, our starting point in this analysis has been the selection of a series of cities rather than the application of an interpretative logic based on regimes and which makes use of the national scope rather than a local one, namely the city.

In all of the contemplated cases, specific historical events are also of major importance in analyzing the existing differences. For example, the relevance of African groups in Portugal is therefore extremely preponderant. Indeed, the position of immigrants from Portuguese-speaking countries residing in Portugal is somewhat reminiscent of the situation of immigrants and ethnic minorities from the Commonwealth states, who generally benefit from increased guarantees and certain privileges to which immigrants from other countries do not have access.

This chapter is also a response to ethnocentrism, which has consistently characterized sociological comparative studies on Southern Europe: this has resulted in an evident lack of interest in the reality existing in this area in contrast to other European regions. Indeed, until recently, any research in the social sciences into Western Europe would in all likelihood fail to include countries such as Portugal or Spain. Furthermore, the theoretical models used have always been taken from "other Western realities," different from those existing in the South and which even go so far as to presuppose a certain evolutionism within societies. Yet despite this, Southern European countries have gradually become one of the preferred contexts for study in the field of social sciences. Many arguments defend the idea of the Southern European axis as a single welfare regime despite what we consider to be major differences: the obvious weakness of the Welfare State and, in comparison with other European countries, the much later commencement of consolidating migratory flows. I will therefore make use of the framework offered by both axes in order to interpret our interviews.

I will later carry out a double analysis of the discourse presented here that will combine (1) a macro approach based on the study of services directed at individuals, from family-based gender inequalities; and (2) an analysis of the cases, focusing on social services for immigrants based on the dynamics of the welfare mix. The analysis of interviews is based on the one hand on criteria of communality and generality of the discourse that occurs in various places and is produced by varying social actors, and on the other hand emerges from the identification of contrasts and differences between the cases analyzed, according to the seven Southern European fieldwork locations. Finally, and within the context of interactions within the welfare mix, we will be able to find a considerable polarization. On one hand, those places where associations really do play a major role, and on the other, those characterized by a weak associationism, as is the case of Algeciras, Athens, Naples, and Thrace. Interpretation of the cases begins with those models that are supposedly more developed in terms of the chronology of foreign migration, namely Italy and Spain. The interpretation is followed by Portugal, and lastly by Greece, a country with features that in many aspects can be considered different from those shown in the preceding patterns.

For a graphic display of all the interviews, see Table 2.1. Quotations in the text are followed by the city initial and interviewee number. The discourses comprise a broad spectrum of communications, such as statements by practitioners and civic society spokespersons. In each place, institutional actors (from regions and municipalities), semi-institutional actors (trade unions, religious organizations), and non-institutional actors (associations) were interviewed.

Discourses on Immigration Policies

The emergency measures implemented in Southern Europe will undoubtedly remind us of many of the features included in the classic concept of the guestworker, which, according to Soysal (1994: 123), implies: "When the guestworker programs first began, migrants were conceived as temporary, and their existence was defined by constraints of economic cycles. Guestworkers were denied many of the basic civil rights, such as family reunion, freedom of assembly and association, and freedom of movement."

Table 2.1

An Overview of the Case Studies: Convergence and Divergence in Southern Europe

CASE STUDY	FOCUS OF EMPIRICAL	MAIN FEATURES ENQUIRY	POINT OF CONVERGENCE
ALGECIRAS (AL) February 2000 Interviews: 13. Municipality, NGOs, trade unions	• Border context • Network analysis • Privatisation of social services • Black market • Low immigration area in contrast with Barcelona	• Weak immigrant settlement • Border closure • Emergency policies	• Restricted borders and relative non-regulation of immigration policies. • Port of entry: transitory immigrant categories • Informal economy • High unemployment amongst women and youth. • Irregular immigration • Local chains of clientelist welfare state • Strong North-South contrast (Barcelona)
ATHENS (AT) June-September 1997 Interviews: 20 All social actors	• Novelty and unpreparedness of foreign immigration policies	• No integration policies • Weak welfare system of alternative channels to welfare benefits. Low associationism • Emergency policies	• Deregulated policies. • Recent regularisation

Table 2.1 (cont.)

CASE STUDY	FOCUS OF EMPIRICAL	MAIN FEATURES ENQUIRY	POINT OF CONVERGENCE
BARCELONA (B) MATARÓ (BM) Barcelona and Mataró January 2000 Interviews: 20 All local level actors (no central and autonomous administration)	• Debate general-specific services • Modes of specific attention for irregular immigrants at municipal level	• Transversality of municipal services for immigrants • Lack of welfare for irregulars and welfare mix strategies based on human rights legislation • Welfare mix: important role of Caritas. • Social racism based on welfare comparisons • Health and education, paradigmatic cases of attention for irregulars • Fight for immigrants' voting rights • Social racism based on welfare comparisons	• Welfare mix development in the immigration area (like Turin)
LISBON (L) Specially focused on 2 municipalities of the metropolitan area: Oeiras and Amadora. July-October 1999. Interviews: 18 All actors except trade unions	• Big poverty bags. Of poverty. Strong dualisation of economic growth • Relevance related to families and social exclusion. • Housing. PER programme • Urban programme (EU)	• Housing. Urban segregation. Periphery • Very marked results of immigration policies according to different municipal teams. • High female participation in the labour market, different labour supply for immigrant women in contrast with other SE countries.	• Importance of building sector in urban labour market. • Historical particularities • High concentration of immigrants in metropolitan areas

Table 2.1 (cont.)

CASE STUDY	FOCUS OF EMPIRICAL	MAIN FEATURES ENQUIRY	POINT OF CONVERGENCE
NAPLES (N) June-July 1998 Interviews: 13 All actors	• Families and social exclusion • Regional exclusion • Low immigration area in contrast with Turin.	• Lack of family policies, extended social exclusion • High segmented labour market and weak welfare. • Different attitudes towards immigration from local population	• High segmented labour market. Informal market (black market and "vicolo" economy, based on survival strategies) • Weak welfare state. • Fragmentation of welfare provision of services. • Strong North-South contrast (with Turin) • High segmented labour market. • High unemployment women and youth • Port of entry to the North of the country. Transit.

Table 2.1 (cont.)

CASE STUDY	FOCUS OF EMPIRICAL	MAIN FEATURES ENQUIRY	POINT OF COVERAGENCE
THRACE (T) Komotini, Alexandropouli, Sappes, Theró. December 98-January 99 Interviews:13 Local authorities and associations	• Low immigration area (in contrast with Athens) • Historical context, regional exclusion. • Old communities and new migrations. • Balkan context	• Border significance • Historical context. • Relevance of international relations and demographic interests in immigration policies	• Historical differences • Social exclusion • Deregulated policies
TURIN (TU) December 97-March 98 Interviews: 12 All actors	• Debate general-specific services • Network analysis	• Specific and *ad hoc* approach for social services (contrast with Barcelona). Especially sectors: health, children and women. • Welfare mix. • Important role of Caritas and women's associations. • Hostile environment and organisation of anti-immigrant local committees.	• Developed welfare mix: alternative channels for services. • Gender asymmetry • Care services needed

In Southern Europe, the implementation of immigration policies has traditionally been based mainly on the French model; in other words, local authorities have generally assumed the model of France's Public Administration. In revising the immigration models we will consider a series of national and urban variables, in accordance with the tertiary sector tradition and the type of immigrant reception, as well as the predominant immigrant groups (according to project, temporality, and legal status).

As far as immigration policies are concerned, the discourse makes constant reference to the impact and consequences of immigration regularization processes, the problems associated with family reunion, as well as gender implications. These policies tend to contemplate the existence of a dominant migrant group for each of the cases studied: Moroccans in Turin, Barcelona and Algeciras, the Albanians in Athens, the Pontians in Thrace, and Cape Verdians in Lisbon. As far as common elements are concerned, we underline a Southern European model based on ideal typical cases that fit into the various areas of migration management, and that are more clearly in evidence in certain cases than in others.

In general terms, immigration policies in Southern Europe are distinguished by a continued and contradictory connection between entry control measures and the need for social services (designed to bring about social integration). This is combined with continuity between irregular (and clandestine) entries and market irregularity (and casual work). The following interview extract clearly reveals the generalized opinion that immigration presents a tremendous challenge for Italy, and even leads to the questioning of the bureaucratic nature of the state:

> Italy is a southern country and therefore some of its features are similar to the Third World…in this country bureaucracy is very extreme and strongly limits the flexibility of state organization. In the last twenty years Italy had to face a new challenge, immigration. Our state is very old, democratic and therefore unable to respond timely to the transformations taking place in the world and in the country itself. (N2)

In general terms, Italian immigration policies are based on a specific model that sets them apart from those of other Southern European countries, as shown below:

> The Italian model is characterized by a specific policy as it is linked to a fragmented legislative framework, which has been going on for hundreds of years. Our legislative approach paralyzes an otherwise dynamic system, which is why many problems are still not being addressed. Unfortunately, our legislation functions in a fragmented way, each problem is left isolated, as a case on its own, when many issues could be dealt with. (N2)

Throughout Southern Europe, a key problem facing immigration policies is the need to deal with the paradigmatic situation existing between irregular status—the problem is further complicated by the fact that their status frequently oscillates between regular and irregular—and the informal labor market, which has a highly negative and damaging effect on working conditions: "This underground economy is very well adapted to the immigration reality. This immigration policy is intertwined with this irregularity of the labor force. It is a question of dignity, of working conditions, more than of jobs" (TU5).

In Italy, the mentality of emergency was clearly manifested by the 1990 Martelli Act (February 28, 1990), created without the basis of any kind of model whatsoever. During the 1990s, the integration philosophy in Italy continued to be the subject of open debate, as expressed by the Turin City Council. In the opinion of a Turin City Council expert on immigration, stricter entry controls and the lack of a regularization provision will inevitably lead to irregularity:

> Of course, because they say "stop regularizations and let's expel the irregulars." It depends also, on how expulsions work. Therefore, like in other European countries there is the closure of labor migrations with very small quotas for employment, so the irregular entrance will be the only solution left. And asylum is very limited in Italy, so it always continues the *primissima accoglienza* for this category of people. (TU10)

The most critical sectors among the respondents in Turin reported the nonexistence of a clear means of entrance; regular immigrants are not considered citizens and over time a deep division has been drawn between regular and irregular migrants:

> They have not found a system of practical legal entrance, and from my point of view this is not a coincidence. Secondly, they had not been able to give citizenship rights to those who are already regulars. They have tried in every way to discriminate between the good—the regular—and the bad—the irregular. The good ones are always under control and from one day to another they can change their situation. (TU4)

The result has been the criminalization of irregular migrants, combined with the idea that a regular migrant must have a stable job and must never be tempted by any form of illegal activity. It is a reproduction of the long tradition of the idea of the passive and poor immigrant grateful for assimilation. Indeed, the most critical voices among respondents in Naples and Turin refer to the dominant situation of strict police controls, demanding standards of migrants that they would not demand of native residents. The image of non-European migrants is often reproduced in the different discourses through the *extracomunitari* adjective. For Colombo, "this visibility is not due to colour or culture, but due to their position in the urban imaginary of migrants as the new dangerous class" (Colombo 1998: 229).

In the first place, the question of the impact of regularization processes was a constant feature in the interviews, albeit particularly so in the case of those held in Italy, Barcelona (due to the fact that they coincided with the regularization process of the year 2000), and Athens (where the fieldwork coincided with the first regularization process held in 1997). In the case of Italy, this consistently recurring issue is the result of the emergent nature of migratory flows; immigration is perceived as a temporary problem, and not as the questioning or call for the rights of non-EU immigrants. It is important to take into consideration here the fact that Italian immigration policy merely mirrors the contradictions of the country's social policies:

> When a right is given then it should also be guaranteed. Maybe over here we are very welcoming, but then many services are not actually working. Thus, we are very good legislators but not good implementers…even social legislation from the 1970s on has never been implemented, whether it was health or family legislation. And I guess it is going to be even more difficult with non-citizens. Maybe the declarations of principle are very good, the Italian constitution is very good. It guarantees, acknowledges, but it is not really implemented. Let us remember that in Italy bureaucracy is still a big power in the hands of those who manage it. (N2)

The Aliens Act passed in Spain in the year 2000 aimed to set up a series of consensus-based devices allowing for the application of badly needed welfare policies; in other words, to use the law as the framework for a public policy that included the social integration of immigrants. This act represented a clear, albeit limited attempt to bring immigrant rights in line with those of Spanish citizens. It was a broad comparison for regular immigrants, while for registered undocumented migrants it was based on a minimum equivalence of a clearly guarantist and social nature. Indeed, it is within just such a guarantist framework for protection in health and education that most of the discourse of respondents interviewed in Catalonia was positioned:

> I suppose with the new immigration law that acknowledges everyone's right to health and education services, things will change because those were the problems up until now. I mean the public institutions had to provide services that were not legally recognized and this affects the levels of transfer, resources and many others. (B5)

The 2000 immigration law also contemplated the Spanish 2000 regularization process. During this process, trade unions and NGOs played a major role in informing the various migrant communities. Yet these organizations frequently complained that the information was not always sent in the fastest and most efficient manner. Several respondents (members of NGOs) complained of the difficulties involved in the regularization process, particularly with reference to the low levels of attention given to immigrants, forced to queue for long periods of time outside the Spanish Civilian Government Offices:

> Yesterday, which was really the limit, I went to the government offices to deal with some paperwork and stuff, and they give you a piece of paper and say regularization: wait and see, this is great. They say this or that regularization and look out in the media or the NGOs or trade unions for further details, you see what I mean (…) The information should be available there and then, just like when you go to the Social Security

> Offices and there's a bit of a line, but it goes down quickly and they tell you where you have to go and who you have to ask for, I mean the line's not that much of a problem, it's faster, they need more staff, and a faster information service. (BM1)

Secondly, and related to the impact of regularization we locate the discourse based on border restrictions. Algeciras is the perfect example of a restrictive policy caused by the establishment of a quota system. This contrasts with other areas in Spain, where government policy actually acts in this case as an impediment for migrant settlement:

> The excessively low quotas are due above all to government efforts to prevent settlement by limiting the quotas for the province of Cadiz. But in the long run what all these low quotas will do is to create large pockets of irregular immigrants (…) In the case of El Ejido the problem is that a policy of quota concentration has been applied. It should be more widely distributed on a regional level. If you look at the Spanish Official Gazette, you'll see that in Almeria the quotas became more flexible. They include all the irregulars. (AL8)

When discussing models to implement, other European references are constant. The Portuguese government has traditionally shown a certain inclination for the Dutch model of community insertion for two main reasons: (1) the application of particularist logic of insertion, and (2) an attempt to formalize associations, although this fails to correspond to the current situation existing in Portuguese society, as immigrants do not demonstrate a strong tendency towards associationism. This latter point once again highlights the impossibility of obtaining positive results through the transfer of a model that has been successful in one society to another entirely different one. As for Greece, the severe exclusion suffered by migrants is particularly evident when the respondents compare immigrant status with that existing in traditional immigration countries:

> In the immigration department there are police officers who only take orders and they don't care what happens and they don't make rational decisions...here nothing can change. If you are in France, even though we say France has a difficult system for migrants, at least they let you stay for a number of years; if you meet the immigration requirements you will be legalized. Forget the mass legalization process. However, here in Greece when you apply for citizenship they look for you, arrest you and deport you without compromise. Furthermore, a child born in this country has no legal documents. The child remains illegal and the parents remain illegal, there are no social benefits. (AT6)

> If you want to control your borders, if you want to have a clear policy, you have to decide not only the way you will legalize the immigrants... you have to be clear, you either want the immigrants or you don't. Because other countries are very clear, they don't want them, or they want some… (AT1)

Immigration policies cannot be detached from the socioeconomic situation of the different communities already living in the region of Thrace. Furthermore, the concept of the Greek Diaspora becomes essential not only in order to understand the idea of Greek national construction but also in order to fully comprehend the outline of immigration policies specifically aimed at the Pontians migrants from the former Soviet republics. The notion of Diaspora has been considered as powerful in giving a sense of a common identity. As seen throughout the interviews, the idea of Diaspora is mixed in with the issue of immigration and with the construction of national identity. The host society lacks social integration policies, only offers assimilation ones, that is, specific policies that deal exclusively with Pontians. Nevertheless, it is not only the Greek government that has no experience in the field of social integration policies for immigrants; it was not until 1997 that even the international institutions like the International Migration Organization in Greece tried to set up a program aimed at the cultural aspects of the social integration of migrants. Furthermore, the Greek government has used religion to distinguish Greeks from Turks, even though minorities (Turkish, Pomaks, Roma) have chosen to define themselves as Turkish. Ethnic Turks have lived in the region since at least the fourteenth century and they are Greek citizens, protected by the Treaty of Lausanne[1] (as regards religion, languages, culture, and equality), and, as Greek citizens, they also enjoy the protection of Greek law and the European Convention of Human Rights.

Here we can distinguish clearly two types of discourses that back immigration policies: the demographic hypothesis and the dialogue based on homogenization and nationalism. Firstly, from the historical perspective, I shall argue that current immigration policies are in part a continuation of the demographic policies carried out by the Ottoman Empire. Furthermore, it is common knowledge that Pontian communities were made to settle in this specific area in order to balance the presence of the Turkish/Muslim community, given government concerns about the growing birth rates among the latter. Both Greek and Turkish nationalism have used the issue of demography as a political weapon. In the case of Greece, the program for the settlement of the Pontians would appear to obey demographic reasons. My argument is that immigration policies towards the Pontians pursue a change in the demographic population balance, especially when considering: (1) the supposedly high birth rates of the Muslim community, (2) the control of political votes in the region, and (3) the "Christian representation" of the population bordering with Turkey. Secondly, we consider the term *omogueneis* (those who belong to the nation, in contrast to those who do not belong, *allogeneis*), which is very much used for Greek immigration policies directed at the Pontians, despite the fact that Greece was always a mix of different origins. Notwithstanding the construction of the modern nation states, Hellenism as an ethnocultural entity has survived for centuries, as can be seen, for example, in the case of the "Ethnic Greeks" abroad. The Pontians have always been recognized as an integrated part of Hellenism, as the most Greek of the Greeks, *trandellines* (Greek three times over), considering Greece as their *patrida*, the land of their ancestors:

> We did not think it would be so difficult to integrate into Greek society. This is our motherland and we have more rights than other migrants, we are refugees from the Turkish genocide.... What are we supposed to do? Where are we supposed go? The only place where people cannot tell you to go away from is Greece. Even if it is difficult here, it is our motherland, and that is why we have more rights than the rest. On the other hand, if you compare our situation with that of the locals, we should say that the Turkish at least have land, but none of us do. It is something! (T4)

Therefore, the historical context plays a large part in understanding the organization of the different communities today. We should first go back to the time when Smirni was burned to the ground, Asia Minor was all but destroyed, and the region of Thrace began to take in refugees and offer them hospitality as they fled Kemal's forces. These events have had a strong historical impact, and became commonly known as the "Asia Minor catastrophe." This issue is very much related to the so-called *Megali Idea,*[2] the idea of Ancient Greece, which would include those territories in Asia Minor with ancient Greek settlements in what is today part of Turkey.

Through the demography hypothesis, the discourse on ethnic homogenization, and the construct of nationalism I have been able to examine the core of the discourse on immigration policies in Thrace. The Thracian case is difficult to solve within the Greek context, because it directly addresses the very issue of the "Greek paradox." It recognizes difference in a complex way (through a historical treaty) and promotes assimilation through a badly planned policy based (for the Pontians) on short-term goals that expect urban people to settle in a rural and still economically marginalized area. The "Greek paradox" can here be discerned, on the one hand, as the way in which a hard-line assimilation strategy is pursued in order to redistribute populations and voters (complex assimilation strategies that in one way are explicitly addressed to the Pontians, although, implicitly, are aimed at Pomaks and Gypsies). On the other hand, there is heavy reluctance to recognize "new" cultural cleavages, which would be perceived as a threat to a solid Hellenic equilibrium. Furthermore, the construction of each of the identities of all these communities is still based on religion and not only on ethnicity, as was the case of the old criterion for determining who was a Turk and who was a Greek. Embedded within identity, family systems and gender relations also seem to play an important role in the construction of "new and old" communities.

To a certain extent, Greek immigration looks back at its own history, at the ruins of the Ottoman Empire, and at Soviet socialism. After the 1990 disturbances in Komotini, driven by inter-communal conflicts in Western Thrace, there was a change in governmental policies that focused on greater economic development for the region and the settlement of Pontic Greeks arriving from the Soviet Union, the elimination of some of the more petty examples of long-standing discrimination, and the encouragement of division among the Muslim community (Turks, Pomaks, and Muslim Roma) (Poulton 1997b: 87). The long period of Ottoman rule and the *millet system*[3] nurtured a strong sense of belonging, which was determined exclusively by religion. In this context, the cohesive nature of Islam as a social force emphasizing the notion of a universal Islamic community or *umma* reinforced this.

The Regularization Axis

The topic of regularizing foreigners is present in all discourses on immigration, and harsh criticisms are expressed regarding the efficiency of such policies. For instance, all of the respondents interviewed in Barcelona during the course of the regularization process carried out in the year 2000 indicate that the available resources still appear to be considerably limited:

> The resources should be extended and increased. Sometimes the answer is really simple but it just doesn't happen. That's just what happened with those lines outside the—Government Offices. They solved the problem simply by setting up various places where you can go and sort out your paperwork. It wouldn't have been so difficult to have thought about it beforehand. Besides, there was also the question of the way you were dealt with and the suspicions; by suspicions I mean that sometimes you were given some papers, you went back to Morocco to get your visa and then they told you that those papers were no good and you couldn't go back. (B2)

According to the immigrant associations we contacted in Lisbon, the 1996 regularization process led to a strengthening of these associations, as they were directly involved in the processing of applications. Nevertheless, they are also of the opinion that this process had a number of negative effects:

> The situation created by the regularization process in '96 and the police activity has always been interpreted in different ways. There were two phases in the 1996 regularization: during the first, the aim was to legalize as many as possible, and the second, to put a stop to this favorable moment. The entry of almost 4,000 Pakistani, Indian, and Chinese immigrants became complicated, which meant that the regularization process didn't work properly, as those groups had no representation in the associations. (L3)

A particular feature of this process was the fact that priority was given to those immigrants from countries where Portuguese was the official language. It was not until the final article of this act that the process was extended to citizens from other countries. From this time on, and based on the results of the regularization process, it became clear that the number of immigrants of other nationalities was on the increase, particularly Senegalese and Moroccan immigrants, revealing for the first time the priority existing in the concept of "lusophones only."

My stay in Athens coincided with the regularization process, which opened up a heated debate also regarding the role the government should play, and in particular regarding its lack of experience. Immigrant support associations also expressed the apparent fears of the trade unions in the light of this process, fears which became evident following the publication of a series of trade union circulars expressing highly focalized interests on the labor market, and claiming to be against the process due to potential labor competition. The start of the first regularization in Greece generated considerable doubts and debate regarding the way in which it should be carried out:

> The problems that will be created from this legalization make the government think, because they consider that they might not legalize 500,000 foreigners. It's a very big number, and it seems that a big part of this will be legalized. However, they have different positions with ministers that were also a problem. As far as I know, the Minister of Public Order was more reluctant. The Ministry of Labour is very open for the legalization. The Ministry of Economy is against it; it has created many problems. In addition, there are problems with the ministry. There were also different positions from the trade unions and the associations. The General Confederation of Workers (IESSE), and the Labour Center of Athens, changed their initial position concerning legalization. They have accepted the proposal of the Coordination for Antiracist organizations…. They have accepted the proposals of the migrants, they accepted that the legalization must extend to all migrants, and has to be as open as possible. (AT9)

Implementing the process during the tumultuous summer of 1997 proved no easy task. Indeed, the so-called "legalization process" was interrupted several times through the application of "presidential decrees." Several respondents saw economic motives as the reason for this:

> Because the ministers are not convinced, and they are afraid of the problems that legalization is going to create. However, generally, in the political way you can say that legalization means that the comparative advantages of the migrant worker will be cancelled, namely that the migrant is cheaper. And this is why it's something very convenient for an economy in difficulty. (AT9)

At the time the fieldwork was carried out, immigrants were still waiting to discover the full implications of the country's first regularization process and the consequent reduction in the threat of expulsion:

> The Government gives papers to the migrants but there is no security that papers will be renewed, and possibility of deportation is still there after the renewal date of papers. No solution has been found for undocumented immigrants, or new arrivals. The government must help to improve our lives. (AT7)

The Different Migrant Groups

In each of the chosen countries the weight of the predominant immigrant groups varies, as does their articulation on the labor market, their own social networks and sense of self-perception, and their group relations. In Italy, for example, there is an overriding heterogeneity of the varying communities, while in Greece greater relevance is given to groups of Albanian immigrants, compared with the importance of Morocco and Latin America in Spain and the PALOPs in Portugal. We will now look at how the varying discourses raise the hierarchical and discriminatory scales according to national origin and gender.

In each of the countries, stereotyped images form the social construction that exists for each type of immigrant according to nationality. Interestingly, many of these stereotypes function according to group visibility (either due to their actual number, or due to their presence in the media) based on their weight and influence as neighbors or alternatively as a result of historical ties. These are constructions of a solely local nature, and which are generally based on labor and criminological profiles. As shown by earlier research (Ribas-Mateos 1999a), the economic sectors and the gender- and ethnic-based division of occupations is closely linked to the new precarious nature of the labor market and to restrictive immigration policies. These findings are backed by the majority of the respondents, as for example, in reference to the farming sector and the racist events that occurred in El Ejido in the year 2000, directed particularly against the Moroccan community:

> In El Ejido, Moroccans were being exploited on the labor market because they had no bargaining power, no recognized labor rights. (B3)

Another interesting factor is the way in which a series of scales has been created within this range of stereotypes:

> There is a hierarchy between them; before the Polish were the source of cheap labor, now it's the Albanians, where before, it was the Polish, and before them, the Romanians, because they had more freedom to cross the borders. (AT11)

Firstly, we can therefore speak of a division of groups based on the degree of stigmatization they face from the receiving society. The Albanian and Moroccan communities appear to suffer the effects of a heavily stereotyped image in all Southern European countries apart from Portugal, although this depends to a considerable extent on the level of their presence in the country. In addition to the heavy criminalization of the Albanians in Italy, their image in Greece is also linked to the stereotypical connotation of being "backward," as they are associated with the figure of the peasant:

> Because they were people used to living in cities, but the Albanians... The Romanians, the Poles, they came from the cities, from industrialized countries, but the Albanians were farmers and lived in the countryside, so they have no sense of this urban culture. That's the difference that explains why the Albanians are so closely observed. (AT11)

In Athens, most respondents refer to the impressions they had of Albanians prior to their arrival in the city in 1991, following the opening of the borders:

> When they first arrived they came *en masse*. They went to the center of the village in the mornings and waited, and then the employers would come.... Later we had problems with a kind of mafia, there is say, the boss of a troupe, who has contacts with the Greek establishment or the Police (...) there are exceptional cases in which people would give money to the leader of the group in order to find a job, like an agency. (AT10)

References to the specific characteristics of Albanians consistently allude to the image of a backward, predominantly agricultural nation and to people whose work ethics remain rooted in an old-fashioned communist system:

> The person who comes from Morocco, they know what it means to work by now, they know what we call here the profitability of the firm, they know how a firm operates to maximize profits or to sell to the market. The person who comes from Albania used to work for the state, and probably used to go to work for 8 or 10 hours, but he could be working 2 or 3 hours, and this is the mentality, his idea, his work ethic. (AT10)

Furthermore, on the labor market, Albanians are the ideal representation of the flexible workforce that is essential for the Greek economy:

> What they do is they work part time, they work on the farms for a few months, then they go to work in construction. They harvest tobacco for ten days, then they go to cotton, in the meantime they do building work or clean gardens, or make a roof. Then in the winter they go to the olives, then they go to the tourist industry which everyone is preparing, construction, tourism, they clean up and do the washing-up in the bars. They take the money to their country and come back. They are everywhere, they leave their money, they come back and start again. (AT10)

Continuing with the stereotypes in Greece, we also find comments that further the idea that Polish immigrants are the workers employers prefer the most as in Greece the Poles are represented as the antithesis of the Albanians in the ethnic division of labor:

> In the agricultural sector the most productive workers are the Poles, irrespective of the fact that they are legal or illegal. The person from Poland gets more money because he's more productive in farming. They get the same money as Greeks, probably more in the construction industry because they are highly skilled, for instance they make good roofs. The same with farmers, some of them were using agricultural machinery which we used here before, so a farmer would give a Pole the use of a tractor or farm machinery, but he would not give it to an Albanian, because Albanian agriculture was not mechanized." (AT10)

Secondly, immigrant groups are linked to each of the historical processes and specific phases of the migration. Indeed, their representation mirrors the history of foreign immigration. For instance, we can establish a traditional divide between the before and after of first-generation African immigration in Portugal, which coincided with the period of the Portuguese retornados, when many managed to obtain Portuguese nationality, as is the case with the soldiers that fought with the Portuguese colonial troops. Curiously enough the Portuguese retornados also settled on the city peripheries, as occurred with the Greeks arriving from Smirna who settled in an area of Athens, which would later be called Nea Smirna. In both cases, this kind of "return" was to have a settlement process parallel to the internal migratory flows towards the large cities, albeit at different periods.

In the case of Lisbon, the period of international migration and the retornados, produced by the decolonization processes, was followed by a period of foreign immigration. Today, and as one of our respondents (L2) indicated, second generations live in a state of evident contradiction on the periphery of Lisbon. They fail to identify with either their parents' culture or that of Portugal. Indeed, the resurgence of the black African cultural models on the outskirts of Lisbon can clearly be seen. Although the early immigrant communities were made up mainly of Africans from PALOP nations, the late 1990s experienced diversity. In this sense, it is interesting to note how global migrations increase the range of immigrant origins, revealing new places that exceed the classical ties between countries that maintained the migratory links. This absence of traditional links is also in evidence in other Southern European regions, including the presence of Gambians in Catalonia. It is important to emphasize the increase of the new flows from countries outside the PALOP countries, such as Chinese and Senegalese migrants. These new flows show us how today's migration has gone beyond the post-colonial situation, following the closure of Northern European gateways, and the way in which the flows head for certain countries such as Portugal, where the increase in the number of Ukrainians since the late 1990s shapes a new geography of origins.

The Cape Verdian community, which is also present in Italy and certain areas of Spain, although to a lesser extent, is one of the communities that has integrated most easily into Portuguese mainstream society. Indeed, Portugal, followed by the Netherlands, is the principal European destination for Cape Verdian immigrants. There are also small communities in Italy (women employed in domestic service), France, and Germany. However, main destinations for Cape Verdian immigrants on a worldwide scale are the United States, Senegal, Argentina, and Brazil. Cape Verdian emigration to Portugal began in the 1950s, while the area was still a Portuguese colony, followed by further large waves of immigrants during the 1960s and 1970s, which interestingly enough coincided with the period during which Portugal was sending large numbers of workers to France. Initially, this immigration was mainly male dominated, although today it is of a markedly familial nature. The early Cape Verdian immigrants settled in Portugal in order to do the work the Portuguese were reluctant to do, particularly in the construction and agricultural sectors.

From 1975 onwards, following the decolonization process, they began their return. It is precisely this long-standing immigratory tradition that distinguishes the Cape Verdian community from other PALOPs, both in terms of their relations with Portugal and other countries, such as the United States and the Netherlands. Today, groups of second-generation youths are beginning to emerge among the Cape Verdian population, creating a new series of challenges for migrant support groups in terms of the type of activities, the question of identity, and the paralyzing of remittances to the countries of origin. In the 1990s, the majority of foreign migrants living in Portugal were from Cape Verde. On the associations level, they are far better organized than the other immigrants. Indeed, unlike other African nations, the Cape Verdian government itself maintains the state through its emigrants, as can be seen from the following quote:

> In the sixties only young men would come here to work, and then the migratory chains; they were farm workers and asked for letters of recommendation for themselves, their children and their neighbors and developed work the very next day. The PALOP Cape Verdians had the best economic indicators; the other PALOPs weren't so willing. Today, the Cape Verdians have become small-scale labor contractors. (L6)

Attempts to find specific characteristics in order to explain the government links with Cape Verdian associations, as well as the bilateral programs existing between countries, is a constant feature of the Lisbon-based discourse:

> Cape Verdians enjoy a privileged position among the institutions. Yet there are various reasons for this. They are the oldest community, and have been in the country for 30 years. They were the first to be brought here to work in construction and what have they done with them? Thirty years on and they're still in working in the construction sector, in the same way that some people have been living in shantytowns for 30 years. Well, getting back to the reasons that explain those privileges. They've been here the longest, they're the poorest, and generally speaking they have more agreements and treaties with Portugal. (L22)

Thirdly, we can speak of the types of competition established between the various national groups. The long-standing tradition of Cape Verdians in Portuguese society is precisely one of the factors that has enabled them to enjoy certain privileges in comparison with other communities, as referred to above. The Cape Verdian association itself admits:

> The Cape Verdian community enjoys the greatest privileges for two reasons: firstly, it is the most numerous, and, secondly, it is the most integrated in Portuguese society. (L6)

This privileged situation generates a certain sense of competition with other immigrant communities, particularly the Angolans. All of the discourse reflects the classical divide that distinguishes the PALOPs from migrants from third countries.

Fourthly, a further element for discussion is the fact that in addition to nationality, gender also represents a considerable element of distortion in terms of the representation of the various groups, as seen by this comment in the case of Athens:

> Yes, the labor market is important; it's mainly the women who work in domestic service in private homes. African and Philippine women have the best reputation. But the Albanians are murderers, drugs traffickers, thieves, it's true. The Greeks are afraid of the Albanians. (AT16)

When considering the gender variable, key differences arise within the same group. As occurs in the case of Spain, Filipino women were the first to be noticed, due to their numbers in the migratory flows from the Philippines. It must also be noted that the fact that they are highly valued in the domestic service sector acts as an added attraction for potential female emigrants:

> Filipino women were the first to arrive and work as maids and are in very high demand from families belonging to high social strata. (N6)

> There are more foreigners looking after the elderly than looking after children. In the case of domestic service they prefer certain nationalities. We sometimes get a call from Sotogrande asking for a Philippine woman because of her status and English. (AL7)

The servile stereotypical image of Philippine immigrants in Athens and their knowledge of English are the main factors that determine the preference for Philippine women in domestic service.

> They have become synonymous as domestic helpers; we see that also as racist, you know. They think of us as being very submissive.... Most of the people who are diplomats have a Philippine, it has become part of the diplomatic status. There is one Philippine, her employer is the second most important person at one foreign embassy, and this girl has no papers. Therefore, although the employer wants her to be legalized, we try to enquire at the Greek ministry how to do it, and if she goes back to the Philippines, if she could still come. But the answer is negative, they refused to give her a visa. (...) They are often left alone, taking care of the houses, because the employers go away on holiday; they also go to the islands with them. I know one that has been working for 23 years and she gets 120 dollars a month. She feels like part of the family that is why she stays with them. Sometimes it is not really a patronizing relationship, because they don't get medical care from them, or they don't want them anymore when they get sick. (AT5)

The stereotypical image of the Philippine woman in Greece, as in Spain and Italy, coincides with this idea of the submissive woman. Therefore, the ethnostratification of personal services becomes a preferential system, highly influenced by the stereotypes of the migrant groups.

As mentioned earlier, the beginnings of Cape Verdian immigration in Portugal were predominantly male. In some cases, they received support from religious institutions in order to enable them to make the journey between the islands and Europe. One such organization, which was involved in finding work for Cape Verdian women in private European homes during the 1960s, particularly in Italy, was the Lisbon-based Obra de Santa Zita, directed by Italian Capuchin monks. For Cape Verdian women today, cleaning jobs are the alternative for the female breadwinner, and for live-in workers it implies a breakaway from their networks of social relations. On the other hand, birth rates among Cape Verdian women are far higher than those of their Portuguese counterparts. Indeed, the number of pregnancies in the Amadora districts inhabited by Cape Verdian women is extremely high, with most women having their first child before the age of 18, and the percentage of women with two children stands at more than 80 percent.

In a fifth instance, another question regarding the differences between migrant groups is the significance of these profiles and stereotypes for the social services. One of the changes that took place in Turin with regard to immigration from the 1980s until the mid-1990s led to the creation of a new scenario following the rapid transformation of all the variables involved in the immigration process: the change in migrant groups and the different demands they made. In the case of Catalonian municipal services, constant references are made to the different nationalities of migrant groups. In this sense, a further issue to be noted from differing nationalities is that user percentages of these services fail to coincide with immigrant population percentages existing within the borough. Indeed, a paradigmatic case is that of the Chinese community that fails to make use of the institutional networks or its contacts with NGOs. However, demand for these services is on the increase among other communities, particularly those arriving from Eastern bloc countries in Italy.

Naturally, differing demands for services also reveal contrasts, which are determined by the size of the various communities within a borough: in Barcelona, the Filipinos are the most solidly established community, while in Madrid it is the Dominicans, and in the Maresme and certain provinces bordering on Girona, the Sub-Saharans (particularly Serahule Gambians). Their needs also vary considerably depending upon the length of time they have been living in the district, whether they are recent arrivals, as in the case of those coming from Sebta or Melilla, or if they have been settled for some time. A further difference that tends to depend on migrant origin is the degree of organization and politicization among the communities (weaker, for example, in the case of the Moroccans and stronger among the Latin Americans), as well as the strength of the solidarity networks they establish, which are of great importance to the Filipinos, as can be seen from the following quotes:

> The South Americans have more associations, they are also more politicized. The same cannot be said, for example, of Moroccans. (B2)

> In Barcelona, for instance, the Filipinos organize themselves extremely well and they also provide services for their own community. They're an example of a group that's considerably different from the Maghrebis, for example. Their associations are different, acting as a channel for protests rather than for services for their own community. (B3)

Although in administrative terms Naples has a regional and provincial framework, social policies are considered above all on a local scale, with the local municipal authority acting as their origin. This enables these policies to be applied to different groups existing in different areas. Indeed, the study of our chosen cases has revealed highly diverse migrant origins and considerable territorial contrasts. In Turin, for example, Moroccans form the predominant community while in Naples the largest immigrant group is of Sri Lankan origin. Furthermore, and despite the larger numbers of immigrants belonging to a particular group, differences in the spatial distribution of immigrant communities also exist within each particular city. According to data obtained from three immigrant offices located in different areas of Naples, each has a predominant user type: Albanians, Moroccans, and Central Africans. In Naples, each of the communities is determined according to a series of factors such as size, the length of time of the community, and the roles played by their leaders:

> I don't have many relations with the Filipino community, I know they are linked to some priests in the historical center...near Piazza del Gesù; they meet on Sundays at the church and organize social activities. While the Sri Lanka community tries to resolve real social problems. Marco Antonio acts as a mediator and probably is the only one playing this role in Naples. Another community that is quite active and contested is the Somali one, which promotes projects such a training courses in agronomy for those who return home. It is a very well organized community; they also work on accommodation, in other cities as well, in Milan, for instance. Then there is the Eritrean community, in the *Quartiere Spagnolo*; it is quite small, 150 people, but it used to be the strongest community before, as they were linked to the Front for the Liberation of Eritrea. (N7)

A final reference must be made to a highly complex factor involved in the differences existing between immigrant groups, namely the *sui generis* case of Thrace. Constant references are made to ethnic Greeks in the differences established in Greek integration policies, a fact which is particularly evident in the case of the Pontians in Thrace. In general terms, the idea of ethnic Greek is closely linked to the historical concept of Hellenism:

> Greece doesn't consider the ethnic Greeks as immigrants. They're not like the Albanians or the Africans; they're a class apart because they are *ethnic Greeks.* They arrive under the protection of the Church and the Ministry of Foreign Affairs. For example,

> Greece has a Turkish minority in Thraki, when they arrived from the Soviet Union they sent them there, to alter the population balance. (AT9)

> The Pontians are covered by their organizations here; their organizations give them protection and promote their legalization by saying that they are really Greeks. In addition, there are the embassies. For example, they know from the country they come if they are Greeks or not and they give them visas, saying *he is a Greek.* Also the motherland, the state in the motherland gives them passports saying *grej.* The Pontians have it written on their passport, and the Greeks from Albania have an identity card. Nevertheless, it is not always accepted by the Greek authorities. Moreover, the new ones no longer make this distinction, they are not recognized as a minority. Today, it's recognized but it's not written down. The minority category used to be included on Soviet Union passports. (AT9)

The Pomaks, living in the mountainous Cold War boundary between Bulgaria and Greece have created a separate identity. The Pomaks of the southern Rhodope Mountains have tended to live in areas where freedom of movement is restricted, marked by the border, which represented the NATO/Warsaw Pact confrontation. Islamized slaves of the Rhodope Mountains, Pomaks are mainly concentrated in rural areas near the Bulgarian border. They do not want to be considered Bulgarians, nor do they feel like Greeks because of the Greekphobia towards Muslims. However, since they do not have a written language, they use the Turkish schools and end up defining themselves as Turkish as a reaction to the hostility shown towards Muslims by the orthodox community. They now have EU programs directed at their needs, but these programs use the Greek alphabet. In Bulgaria on the other hand, they are officially known as the Bulgarian Muhammadians or Bulgarian Muslims, a confessional minority of 220,000 people. Pomak villages are organized around a tightly knit kinship structure that works in a peasant economy. They live in a socioeconomic context of non-mechanized tobacco production, which demands a large workforce. All the members of the family are involved, and the farming tasks are divided according to gender. However, the tobacco industry is losing ground to new forms of employment. This has led to an increase of women engaged in tasks that were previously performed by men (Vernier 1981: 146), which has led, in turn, to an overall reinforcement of women's inferior status, a status intensified in their comparison with Greek women. (Vernier 1981: 141).

However, the problem of terminology centers on how to assign names to the different communities living in Thrace and has caused an open controversy on all sides. The different possibilities are presented here according to the distinct type of criteria: (1) religion rather than ethnicity would be the criterion used to define who is a Turk and who is Greek. It is also interesting to see how in border territories identities become specifically religious, such as the case of Sebta and Melilla, the Spanish territories in North Africa, where local population makes the distinction between "Musulmanes and Cristianos" (Muslims and Christians); (2) as a result of a state-sponsored policy of assimilating the

Pomaks into the Turkish population, particularly through the introduction of compulsory schooling in Turkish (and subsequently, using Turkey as a kin-state), and (3) the self-definition of communities. The issue of the terminology used to refer to the different groups is the subject of frequent discussion among the various groups of respondents:

> When we were in the Soviet Union we always called ourselves Romei, we did not know about this term Pontians until we came here. It is a question of identity. Then here, we made our own Pontian associations. We used to call each other Romei there. Everywhere they used to call us *Greki*, but here they call us Russian-Pontians. (T4).

Gender Differences

As mentioned earlier, throughout Southern Europe a regular feature of the discourse is a clear gender division based on the national origin of immigrant groups. The growing number of women in the migratory flows heading for urban areas can be seen in all the cities studied, not only in terms of statistical percentages but also through the constant references to women in the various voices:

> Do you know that most of those who arrive are women? Forty-seven percent women against 53 percent men. Female occupations are: working as a maid or assisting elderly people, as is the case with other communities: Somali, Moroccan, Egyptian, from the Ivory Coast, South America. (N6)

Furthermore, all the associations are aware of the greater or lesser level of predominance of male and female flows:

> From some countries we have a lot of women, for example, from the Philippines, it's 90 percent. From ex-communist, ex-socialist countries, we have a lot of women and from Poland a lot. (AT9)

A common problem encountered throughout the Southern European countries has been women's dependence on the granting of residence permits to men:

> The situation of wives in Greece is that the husband can have a resident's permit. She could apply for a permit if the husband had one, if they wanted to accept it but they do not, they do not accept applications from women. That is what you call 100 percent racism. Putting the women down or suppressing marriage. (AT6)

In Turin, from the late 1990s onwards, the increased demand for places in public shelters revealed the arrival of new female flows that were no longer using the traditional immigration processes of family reunion:

> In the last few years, there has been a change, the figure of the lone women out of the family reunion projects or women out of traditional projects arranged as live-in do-

mestic helpers. They are mainly Romanian, Albanian, and Somalian. Therefore, they have opened another dorm but only for women. It was for foreign women, but it does not mean that they would not accept an Italian woman. (TU10).

A major feature of the large numbers of females migrating to Turin is the fact that the majority of the women are considered skilled professionals in their countries of origin. It is above all the discourse of Italian respondents that points to the commonly held belief that the rise in female immigrants in Italy since the 1980s is largely a response to the changes that have occurred within the traditional Italian family.

> The majority of women working in Italy as domestic helpers, they are actually taking care of elderly people and this reflects social change in Italy. Nowadays many elderly people need assistance and in the family nobody wants to take care of them, but somebody has to. The traditional family, whereby the whole patriarchal structure would live under the same roof no longer exists. Now there is the nuclear family, which is formed by three people, two parents and a child, therefore there is a need for labor. (N6)

The Italian cities were also the first to reveal the existing coincidences between the ageing of the population, the lack of care services available, and the need of foreign workers, particularly female. However, when considering the issue of gender in the various countries, it is interesting to note that the Italian model is far more feminized than the Portuguese model. While in Italy female migrants arrived mainly in order to work in domestic service, in the case of Portugal they had a more family-oriented objective, namely the reunion of families of men who had initially arrived to work in the construction sector. The question of stereotypes is also a recurrent theme in the recruitment of female domestic service workers. In both Spain and Italy, Caritas plays a central role in this process, acting as a mediator. This became clear through the analysis of the discourse produced in Caritas regarding the type of female employers that use this organization. Furthermore, there is a continuous use of ethnic and gender stereotypes in adapting the recruitment to the type of job offered:

> Sometimes it seems like they talk about machines, Peruvian, Somali, Filipino.... Sometimes they even indicate how dark-skinned they want them. I would like to clarify that foreign women do not come to steal existing jobs away from Italian women. It is a role Italian women don't want anymore and that is why there is a market for these jobs. Among men there is more unemployment, for instance. Once they asked me to find a Somali woman who would wear her traditional clothes, evidently they appreciated Somali culture, they wanted her to be dark. I remembered when Italians went to Ethiopia, in Mussolini's times...and I would have liked to remind that family that they were still living in the past. (N6)

The question of migrant women's work has led some militant feminists to question the type of emancipation these women experience and the one predominant today in Southern Europe, specifically in Italy:

It is with pain that I remember how among migrant women there still is that strong feeling of submission, of the lack of a deep sense of freedom in relation to their men. This has surely got something to do with structural factors linked to the household income. Domestic helpers are already more emancipated as they have their own job, but it is still difficult being a woman. Nowadays Italian women are still addressing the issue of their emancipation, which is still far from being over. (N2)

While ethnic and gender stereotypes play an essentially selective role in analyzing demand, it is unquestionably the reproduction strategies that are at work in determining the supply strategies of working women. As a result, migrant women in Naples apply a range of insertion tactics, many of which are based on temporary migratory projects. In the long term and once the migrant woman has assumed a reproduction project, she encounters problems similar to those experienced by working class Neapolitan women:

Migrant women in Naples are very differentiated. Polish women are usually young and in most cases they were unable to register at the university at home, they come here to save the money for their fees. They don't stay much in Italy, some stay longer because they don't only save, they spend as well, being young and then they start relationships and things like that. There were more Somali women earlier. In general they want to go back home, although some have returned here. Sri Lankan women are usually with their husbands and therefore they often settle down here. The most recent group are Ukrainian women. Usually they are adult women who stay in Italy for two, three years, to save up some money for their families. In the end, migrant and Italian women face the same problems. I mean, women who work and have kids don't know what to do and therefore have to leave their kids with their neighbor, to an elderly person. Or they leave them with nuns, who offer cheaper rates. (N13)

As occurred in the case of Naples, the question of women's condition also appeared during the course of the interviews held in Algeciras, although on this occasion linked to a strong feeling of social exclusion. Respondents made frequent references to the issue of prostitution, although they made a distinction between two different types: (1) low level prostitution, organized in low-priced hotels situated in the area surrounding the city's food market, and practiced by Spanish and Moroccan women, and (2) prostitution in clubs, where each establishment would have more than twenty Latin American workers. Women working in this profession tend to concentrate in the areas known as Bajadilla and Saladillo. Organizations and institutions working with migrants in Algeciras describe their suspicions regarding the links with prostitution in the following way:

The thing is that many lone women live in rented flats and don't want live-in domestic work. They only want to work in the mornings or by the hour. We suspect that they're working as prostitutes and are trying to combine this activity with other jobs. (AL10)

In Thrace, the social exclusion of women acquires a fairly unusual character. In terms of the status of Turkish women in Thrace, it became apparent in various interviews that education creates divisions in terms of gender and community issues:

> I think the main difference between women's roles in the different communities comes down to education. Turkish women are more reserved than Greek women; they also tend to do most of the agricultural work, in the fields with the tobacco crops and cotton. The whole family works on the land. (T7)

In terms of family law, the *Charia* is combined with Greek law, depending on the case. Family formation is here a good indicator of the complex social relations between communities. Mixed marriages are still unheard of in Thrace, at least for partners belonging to different religions. We see how cultural differences and also differences in family structures lead to different demands on social services. The programs for Pontians are defined around a family-orientated approach where housing is its only expression. Even if the family is always the basic unit of the targeted program, there is never any special attention to women's issues. However, there is a special concern for the cases of single-parent family units with small children. According to the social workers of the programs, the persistence of single-parent families is very high among Pontians.

In the case of Greece we see how, as a result of modernization, traditional forms of family solidarity and paternalistic structures decline without being replaced by alternative forms of social protection and by a weak development of social policy. This implies a high risk of marginalization for a number of social groups. Family networks for finding jobs and supporting the unemployed are in this respect important, although they differ according to the community in question. The traditional regulation of communities such as those related to social control and *tiní* (honor) are still very important in rural Greece for both women and men. The code of honor is one of the foundations for a highly cohesive community, not only for Greeks but also for Turks, Pomaks and Pontians, and is a means of keeping and expressing their own identity. Seen mainly as traditional communities, they also practice arranged early-age marriages. Furthermore, "traditional Pontians," as we mentioned, are thought to be the "true Greeks," like the Greeks who emigrated to the United States, or those from the island of Crete. For Pontians, family cohesion seems to be the basis of their identity.

Most of the respondents in Thrace specifically mentioned gender issues, particularly the division of the cultural elements based on stereotypes related to the family structure and the organization of gender roles. It was from this contrast of gender roles that the idea of the Greek community and the Turkish community has been constructed. The latter would be defined by its relegation of the female presence to the status of a typical feature of Muslim-dominated societies. On the other hand, the Muslim and Turkish family can also be understood in terms of a model of cohesion and as the basis for the construction of social networks, especially effective in searching for jobs. In terms of the model of the urban Greek family, it is commonly assumed to be a very united model of family, based on small entrepreneurial activities and aspiring to urban middle-class lifestyle and values. From the Greek point of view, it is often gender inequality that stands out in their discourse on "Muslim communities."

In terms of the labor market, Pontian women seem to perform the traditional female tasks of private cleaning services and looking after children that Albanian women tend to assume in the rest of Greece. However, they carry out these tasks only in the most urbanized areas. Thus, in rural and semi-urban settings the cleavage of genderized occupations for migrants seems to have a different function. The Pontian men, although quite well qualified, work mainly in the building sector as plumbers or electricians. The situation in Thrace is by no means comparable to the situation in Athens, where one can find a clear distinction between foreigners and nationals. In regard to the status of Pomak women, gender discrimination seems to be double that suffered by Greek women. In this region where tobacco is still cultivated in the traditional manner, with the work is organized into household units, gender divisions are also seen in agricultural tasks as well as in family roles.

Gender differences are also crucial when discussing discourses on gender and family reunion processes. The matters related to the formation of families are vital issues linked to problems involved in entering the country and obtaining the corresponding work and resident permits. The right to family reunion, which has experienced increased demand in recent years, is one of the most controversial modifications to Spain's new Immigration Act (the February 2000 Act, its reform and counter-reform). It is therefore the state that decides which types of families may enter the country and the nature of their dependency, particularly if we consider the regulatory differences involved in the fact that non-working dependent spouses hold neither residence nor work permits.

Nevertheless, as we have indicated, the question of the availability of migration documents is essential in order to understand any type of situation experienced by immigrants. Consequently, legislation regarding family reunion forms the axis for family construction, as well as for the settlement of migrant populations and their social integration. The lack of such legislation is indicative of governments' poor support for immigrant permanence and stability. The fact of the matter is that family reunion processes are one of the most controversial aspects of immigration laws, particularly due to the long waiting periods involved and the breakdown of family networks. In the case of Spain, if we add the weak family policies to the legal difficulties involved, the context of family reception can be considered extremely weak. Indeed, family policies are fragmented even for the autochthonous population, depending on the one hand on the type of actor (children, women, the young, the elderly), and on the other hand, on the combination of a series of differing and separate benefits covering various aspects such as housing, the labor market, and taxation. However, the fragility of family policies is not only noticeable in terms of the type of actor or sphere, but also due to the fact that other positive action policies—which could aid the family context—are noticeably lacking.

Take another example in the case of Portugal. This county witnessed the start of family reunion processes in the mid-1970s. The eldest son was generally the first migrant to arrive, due to the relative ease with which these family members could find employment. He was followed by the women and the younger members of the family. This led to the appearance of the first districts populated mainly by migrants. The first districts to appear were Venda Nova and Pedreira dos Húngaros, although the largest were to be found in Amadora—Alto de Cova da Moura, Barrio de Santa Filomena, Venda Nova—and in Oeiras—Pedreira dos Húngaros, Alto de Santa Catarina. It is important to consider that the regulations restricted the family reunion to kin and did not include those of the extended relatives, whom it must be noted are included in the traditional African concept of the family. Indeed, the vast majority of female migration to Portugal is the result of family reunion processes. Nevertheless, a growing number of migrants are opting to travel of their own free will, displaying a high degree of associationism and mobility, a result of the fact that these associations provided them with help and support following their arrival in the country, as shown in the following interview excerpt:

> Some of them were reunited with the help of relatives, but there are also single girls who come to try and find a living. The women who used to come were those left alone at home, and who had relatives so they didn't need accommodation. From then on the women started working for themselves in cleaning services, as bosses in the construction sector and later to hire women for cleaning. They used the local associations in their districts to set up the *créches.* The women work in companies; they're really well organized in the districts. I think that the women are so well organized because they received help from the local associations. (L6)

Doors of the Labor Market

Since the 1980s, economic policies in Southern countries have failed to establish a successful long-term strategy. This becomes particularly clear if we consider the role played by foreign immigration in labor market transformations:

> The attempt to control migration flows is linked to the fact that Italy is not able to develop a long-term economic policy and therefore an analysis of the real demands of the labor market is lacking. In this way Italian institutions are unable to calculate how many jobs are actually available to Italians, since they did not implement a policy aimed at developing new profiles and occupations, or those available to migrants. These are left to their own devices and end up doing those jobs Italians do not accept any longer, in agriculture, as maids or assisting elderly people. This situation is also influenced by the fact that nowadays articulated families do not exist anymore, there are only nuclear families who have to resort to the black market for their needs. (N2)

This market is characterized above all by its low capacity for a wide insertion. Throughout Southern Europe, the non-EU migrant is faced with extremely limited opportunities as to the range of available occupations. The problem is that the only opportunity they have for entering the labor market is by starting off on the lowest rungs of the social ladder:

> It is good to give some posts to qualified migrants. In Italy you can only be a servant or do manual work. But who says so? It is not written anywhere that people can only be integrated into the lower levels of society. (TU5)

Nevertheless, the Italian discourse seems to display the greatest awareness of the relation between the fact that immigrants are overqualified for the positions open to the difficulties they encounter in accessing the labor market.

> There was a slight *overqualification* in Italian emigration abroad or in internal emigration. Therefore, it is not new as you say, but it is more accentuated. At least for the majority of the flows. However, it also depends on the time; illiteracy levels were high among early Senegalese immigration. But now the situation has changed. (TU5)

Not all immigrants consider themselves to be equal in labor market insertion. Consequently, in Greece, the immigrant labor force also experiences a segmentation process based on their cost and professional skills:

> Skills first and then labor costs, so it's true, Albanians are at the bottom, and if I had to choose a certain category to put at the top it would be the Polish. Albanians are the least skilled and therefore they are paid the least. (AT2)

It should be stressed that the key to the analysis of Southern European labor markets in the case of foreign immigration is the question of regulation levels, as discussed below in the case of Greece:

> Since the vast majority of these people do not have a work permit, they have no proper rights. There is no minimum wage for them... the agreement is between the employer and the employee, they just talk. They are not paid a lot of money, they are not insured. (AT10)

Relations with the autochthonous population take on a special significance in the identification of the means for labor insertion. Hence, the importance of the hypothesis of complementarity and substitution in the labor market is of considerable relevance in terms of the construction of immigration discourse for the majority of respondents:

> The majority are Moroccans or from Western Africa. Many come with a visa valid for a few days, in order to work for a few days, and then they opt to stay, while others are directly illegal, with no papers at all, and there are also others who have permits which they renew; it varies. Many work without any papers and earn 300 pesetas an hour

(less than 3). This means that the demand for this kind of worker is always on the increase. (BM8)

The question of migrants acting as a complement or competitor for autochthonous workers has been a constant issue in the creation of a Southern European model of immigration, as shown in the case of Turin. This competition is also reflected in the tension that exists between migrants and the native labor force.

> When we speak about immigration we must consider all of the components, so that, somebody who has a degree in medicine may also wash cars for a while, but we should try and acknowledge that title and to put it to some use at some stage. The problem is that there are many unemployed Italian doctors, it is not an easy situation. Of course, this person could start as a paramedic and then we would see. There are training courses for these people, I think they are the only possibility to find a real job in the future. (TU3)

> And so these immigrants are seen as competitors or as future competitors. This is the basis, which has led to non-acceptance and rejection. Moreover, if you add the fact that immigrants are connected with drug dealing or other criminals, an explosive mix is formed. (TU4)

In Naples, one of the consequences of this competition on the labor market was that the first incidents of racial conflict were associated with the crisis in agricultural work, particularly in the drop in demand for tomato pickers:

> Saying that we are facing these problems because of the migrants is not fair. Perhaps we might say that migrants exacerbated the preexisting situation and not so much as far as work is concerned. If you think that in Naples there are more than 43,000 resident migrants, you have to consider that there are 13,000 people working in domestic occupations, where there are the greatest possibilities. Once there used to be the gathering of the so-called "red gold," the tomatoes, which used to employ many migrants and then there was an epidemic and the whole economy went into decline. However, the labor used to be almost exclusively migrant. When the tomato economy declined many people were left unemployed and it was then that the problems of co-existence between the immigrants and the Italians began. (N8)

What is quite certain is that agricultural areas were the first to experience racial conflict in the Catalonian province of Lleida and the Campania region in the province of Naples. In Greece, these conflicts were sparked by the arrival of Albanians who came to work in farming, due to the fact that they were competing directly with the local community.

> The conflict occurred during the first years between Albanians and gypsies. Before the appearance from Eastern Europe of cheap labor, cheap labor in Greece came from the gypsies...they were paid less, they were uninsured, and we had fights between gypsies and Albanians in the early years. But now the gypsies are moving to other sectors, they sell fruit in the street. (AT10)

As a result, in these contexts the question of competition is often a catalyst for racist attitudes:

> A small percentage of the Greek unemployed feel a sense of bitterness or exasperation about the fact that immigrants have jobs, but you cannot generalize about that, it's a minor problem. (AT2)

The seasonal nature of the agricultural sector is another factor that has led to the creation or intensification of the competition existing in the agricultural sector in southern areas of Italy, Spain—specifically in Andalusia—and Greece:

> Compared with other countries, Greek agriculture has never had permanent farm workers. It is exceptional to have a farm in Greece to be big enough to employ a full-time worker, because the farms are small, or products produced are seasonal, which demands seasonal labor, unlike livestock farming. (AT10)

In the case of agriculture, the fact that immigrants are a cheaper workforce than autochthonous workers also facilitates their access to this kind of seasonal work:

> We do not have a minimum wage for farm workers, we have never had one, but don't forget that the minimum wage in Greece is very low, it can't be more than 7,000 drachmas a day. So if you are an unskilled worker from Greece you get about 7,000 a day, if the Albanian gets about 5,000 it's not a huge difference; no Greek will be prepared to work for that money. However, it has no basis because most of the work is temporary work, picking fruit, which is paid not by the day but by the kilo, by the quantity. When you pick fruit, you are paid by the kilo. If you clean something, you are paid by the day. By the day we will have a minimum wage, by the kilo… those who work well get a good wage, those who work less get less. (AT10)

The classic reaction of all respondents concerning the question of competition and substitution, regardless of where the fieldwork is carried out, is that "migrants do the jobs nobody else wants," and they use this hypothesis to argue the absence of conflict:

> Albanians do not do skilled work, they carry stones, they do the dirty, unskilled jobs, and so the skilled worker has no problems with Albanians. (AT10)

Interestingly, the arrival of the Albanians in Greek farming areas has even been a kind of ecological blessing:

> In Greece we used to have a lot of problems with weed killers, we used a lot of chemicals to kill the weeds before the Albanians came. Now many farmers joke that instead of using such and such a weedkiller we use "Alba mix" which means that the Albanian goes there and picks the weeds by hand, so the farms are cleaner because it's cheaper to use labor than to use chemicals, so it's ecological. (AT10)

Yet the Albanians not only fill these job vacancies, but they also carry out the temporary and seasonal work available from the subcontractors. In the case of Greece, the idea of labor competition resulting in migrant workers replacing natives is shared by both the administration and trade unions, but not by migrant support associations, as the following respondent indicates:

> The Ministry of Public Order said that they wanted to become heavily involved in the issuing of green cards; the view of most of us who were there was that if the migrant had to go to the police he would be afraid. The Minister of Labor and the trade unions believe that these immigrants replace Greek workers. The trade unions were strongly against the bi-lateral agreements. They believe that the migrants substitute Greek labor, I don't agree…they don't do the same jobs, they generate income. (AT9)

Secondly, the lack of opportunities for labor insertion becomes even more evident if we consider the limited options available to women. The relation between inclusion in domestic service and training in such tasks offered by the associations is practically automatic in the case of Northern Italy. Yet there are critical voices that speak out against this view, claiming that they look for other options such as the care for the elderly. It is also thought that this sector is opening up professional options and possible competition with Italian workers. A number of associations also search for opportunities outside this sector, opening up routes to access the textile, catering, and industrial cleaning sectors. In general, the question of competition and substitution should also be analyzed from those sectors on the labor market that have already been feminized, as well as from the specific context of the local labor market:

> Immigrants here have very little formal professional training. The maximum level of education is *graduado escolar* (compulsory education up to the age of sixteen). Apart from that, they have to compete with the local population, who don't have much training either, and they are limited to domestic service. There aren't many opportunities in the catering industry; it's not like the Costa del Sol. Professional opportunities for women are very limited, and there isn't any agriculture here either (…) There's no competition as you can see, they take what the others don't want. It's not a question of discrimination, there's no competition for people who aren't trained, because there isn't any for the local population either. (AL7)

Native labor force demands better wages and working conditions than migrant labor force does, not only in agriculture as we have seen, but also in domestic service in urban areas:

> Women usually find a small job as servants and contribute to the household economy, but there is crisis in this sector, too, now, because of immigrants. They are real competitors because their labor is cheaper. For 600,000 Lire per month you can have a Filipino working all day for you, an Italian asks for more. That is also because usually immigrants stay in your place night and day while an Italian wants to go back to her place to sleep. (N3)

Finally, when analyzing our hypothesis in the case of Portugal, various authors have spotlighted the understanding of the occupational structure dynamics in relation to the recruitment of the workforce. Firstly, qualified, skilled immigrants are frequently attracted by foreign investments and the salaries offered by major multinational organizations. Secondly, Portuguese emigrants who have moved to other European countries are, in turn, attracted by the higher wages available, particularly in the construction sector. Thirdly, although foreign immigrant workers are attracted by the wages available in Portugal, they are forced to accept a process of disqualification of their initial skills. We therefore find a sub-group made up of overqualified workers occupying posts left vacant by Portuguese workers. It is precisely the question of the dynamics of the occupational structure that opens up the question of complementarity—in the case of skilled workers— and substitution—in the case of the non-skilled ones—of the workforce. It is therefore in Portugal where the complementarity-substitution hypothesis is of greatest interest. As with Naples and the question of social exclusion, we could here claim that many Portuguese workers constitute an underclass. As far as the question of competition is concerned, future conflicts may arise among qualified workers, as the level of training among Portuguese workers is constantly increasing. What will happen, when they see that vacancies are being occupied by Spanish doctors? When looking into the question of substitution according to sectors, it would appear to exist in the construction sector, while in other sectors requiring higher levels of qualification and skills a situation of complementarity exists instead. In Portugal, the issue of immigration is particularly complex due to the large numbers of former emigrants returning to Portugal: Within this "migratory platform" represented by Portugal in terms of working class flows (Baganha and Peixoto, 1996), of particular relevance is the concentration of immigrants in Lisbon's periphery, that like the Portuguese themselves, have been forced out of the central districts of the city as a result of the revaluation of these areas. The concept of irregularity goes hand-in-hand with the need for greater flexibility in the workforce, as has occurred in the case of Mediterranean agriculture. Furthermore, it fits in with the entry strategies of irregular immigrants. In the short term, however, this leads to problems of social integration—including difficulties experienced in such apparently simple actions as renting accommodation—and high accident rates in the workplace. Moreover, the saturation of the labor market, either by unskilled workers—as in the case of Moroccan farm laborers in El Ejido in Spain—or by highly qualified ones—such as Spanish doctors working in the border regions between Portugal and Spain—tends to intensify the conflict.

The Peculiarities of the Informal Market

Firstly, the frequently referred to *lavoro nero* (literally translated as "black work") in Italy seems to be the principal attraction that draws workers to Italy and Southern Europe. Consequently, in Naples, respondents speak of "a capacity to absorb the black market" unlike any to be found in Northern Europe and one which favors the non-regulated entry of immigrants. This occurs precisely because the local context of reception is characterized by an informal system:

> In Naples working "in black" is a regular feature for many firms. One might think that many people actually have a regular contract as they are receiving a regular pay slip, but the wage they actually get is different from that indicated on the slip. Non-EU migrants with a regular permit to stay usually earn between 30 and 35,000 Lire per day, in black. (N9)

As far as labor rights are concerned, the situation of migrants in Southern Europe is inevitably linked to regularization policies and the general framework of the labor market. This indicates an evidently low level of syndicalization:

> The level of immigrant participation in politics and trade unionism is low. Very few are involved in the trade unions. On the one hand, many are in an unstable personal, professional, and family situation; thereby making it difficult for them to join a trade union or to belong to any type of groups or associations. Today they're working here, but in three months' time they may or may not still be here. (BM9)

The hypothesis of competition or substitution referred to earlier is also often linked to the structure of the informal market. Furthermore, the degree of competition, or at least the generally perceived idea, depends largely on the type of context being referred to. In the case of Naples, it must be seen within the context of the informal economy on a local scale:

> It is partly so because they are exploited by the Camorra. There are Chinese people who work for 18 hours a day and get 600,000 Lire a month, an Italian would never accept a job like that. That is why it is partly true what they say, that their presence lowered the cost of labor. Of course, they are employed in humble occupations; when you went to the railway station you must have noticed how many immigrants there were, when you arrive there you almost feel like you are in Africa! (N3)

Within the system of the underground economy, the native Neapolitan also has access to unemployment benefits, thereby acquiring a privilege beyond the reach of migrants:

> A Neapolitan working "in black" does not pay taxes, remains officially registered in the unemployment lists and still benefits of all of the relative concessions. So while the Italian citizen can somehow survive, the foreign one can't. Working as a street peddler is more tolerated by Italians; they don't see it as competition as they sell products that are produced locally and therefore they are seen as contributing to local production. (N13)

In the opinion of various respondents, this local insertion concept, where new arrivals have access to informal work, the network used by the local mafia (the *Camorra Napoletana*) would play a vital role:

The south is poor in social resources and those available are not being used properly. Moreover, an Italian citizen finding himself in financial difficulties feels as if he was deprived of the possibility of receiving social assistance and sees the immigrant as an unfair rival. Personally, I came to the conclusion that this invasion of people looking for a more dignified life is the responsibility of the false promises spread by the local mafia, promising people that they will find work and peace of mind in Italy. Otherwise many of them would not leave in such precarious conditions. I think this is a serious international problem, the lack of knowledge on migration and on organized crime, which must be eliminated. (…) This is because they see Italian civilization as a myth, a dream. (N2)

In the case of the Catalonian Maresme, as well as the predominantly male-oriented agricultural and construction sectors, the market offers women the possibility of entering one of the region's traditional occupations: the underground clothing industry.

Most of the women who work do so in the textile industry; a few work in the cleaning sector, but the majority are in the textile business. They don't have a contract, of course; if the people from around here don't have a contract then they're not going to have one either. (BM8)

The informal sector in Athens is characterized not only by the fact that it employs undocumented workers, but also by the fact that these people have no form of protection or coverage whatsoever:

Sometimes, she works but is not paid the pre-arranged amount, sometimes nothing at all. She has no fixed wage, and is often exploited. She has no contract and is unable to do anything about such professional abuse. She believes that her case is typical. There is no protection for immigrants. (AT7)

A series of circumstances surrounds this irregular situation, and the preferred sanction is that of expulsion, although no sanctions are imposed on those contracting these workers. This informal economy is not always associated with illegal products, but there are frequent coincidences between informality and illegality:

There are those who control the traffic of prostitutes, those who do the taxi driving for them, those who control the telephones. All those who live an easy system of illegal activities and who also show off (gold, cellular phones, cars.). It is a whole system of illegality based on exploitation. But these systems have always been present in all big cities, like the Italians in Chicago in the thirties. (TU4)

Dissertations on the informal market in Southern Europe are consistently interspersed with discourse referring to criminalization. We are referring specifically to those arguments put forward regarding occupations that have been used as the basis for the criminalization of foreign immigrants. Special mention must be made of immigrant insertion into local mafias—as in the case of the Neapolitan group and its micro-criminalistic structure—into prostitution networks—as in the case of Nigerian women in Turin and the Dominiziana area of Naples—and into hashish smuggling and the activities of young people in Algeciras who work in immigrant trafficking. When discussing the creation of these networks initial references mention the immigrant trafficking networks, and also the way in which they are developed, as can be seen from discourse produced in Athens regarding the networks of trafficking clandestine female immigrants:

> We had problems with a kind of mafia. There is say the boss of a troupe, who has contacts with the Greek establishment or the police. There are exceptional cases in which people would give money to the leader of the group in order to find a job, like an agency; this agency works very well for people who come from India and Pakistan with a Pakistani and Indian agency. In order for a Pakistani to find a job in the greenhouses, he must have a contact with a Pakistani boss to whom he pays money. This is very strong with Pakistanis and Indians, but it is not as strong for Egyptians who have a tendency to work in fishing, on the fishing boats. (AT10)

In Algecíras, a prime border area, criminalization discourses include constant references to those transporting migrants:

> The question of the *borregueros* (local transporters of migrants) is having a major social impact. I'm really concerned about all this. Motorbikes and mobiles…there's a lot of it about. Unemployment rates among the young are fairly high and they're not well trained. And they're used to living like that, living with risks and drugs too. There are also families who take in immigrants for money. (AL2)

Secondly, the particular features of the informal market cannot be understood without looking at the varying dynamics to be found in each sector. Insertion in Mediterranean agriculture is one of the most common features of our Southern Mediterranean immigration model (except in the case of Portugal). As a result, temporary agricultural work in Greece displays the same labor insertion conditions as those to be found in the Spanish Mediterranean. The seasonal nature of Mediterranean agriculture has brought with it added complexities for regularization processes:

> Some keep on working in agriculture, but it is very difficult to regularize them as they work 7-8 days and then they leave. They are the only ones who work and go around all Italy according to the different harvesting and picking times. I'm am telling you, the first to pick tomatoes were students working during summer, but with the shifts in the way people think from 1985 to the present day I believe no student would now accept a job "for a foreign migrant." (N9)

The Greek case is interesting in terms of the energy that migrants give to transforming the local context. As referred to earlier, the arrival of the Albanians led to the rapid revitalization of traditional farming methods. Furthermore, this revitalization has also extended to other economic sectors that interact with the rural context:

> The rural areas, in the places where people sell cement and materials for construction, paint for houses etc., are flourishing because there is a demand for these jobs. People are painting their houses, which they have not done for 20 years because they could not afford to employ anyone. So the house would stand there practically in ruins because the owner could not afford to pay a Greek, but now they are being done up. (AT10)

Employing immigrants enables either the farmer or his family to take on better-paid work. This cheap labor force may be used by the Greek farmer to adapt to the dynamics of intensive farming, thereby increasing production levels and boosting both his economy and that of the area. Today, immigrants occupy the position traditionally held by women in tobacco, fruit, and cotton picking. Indeed, the Greek Farming Association has indicated, "without the immigrants, Greek agriculture would have collapsed." Yet it would also have collapsed if the immigrants had been paid the same as their Greek counterparts. The fact of the matter is that Albanians are responsible for the revival of Greek agriculture.

A look at more male-dominated urban occupations, such as the construction sector, once again leads us to the conclusion that migrants tend to join the more flexible labor sectors, those with low levels of trade unionism and which are strongest in the informal sector. A prototype case is that of the construction sector in Lisbon. Sectors such as the construction industry are also responsible for making the stability of the immigrant considerably more complex:

> Construction work is temporary: you start and finish various buildings. They change workers whenever they get the chance. (L6)

In Algeciras, there are also a considerable number of migrants working in the construction area, which is characterized by large numbers of informal contracts and long working hours (night shifts, etc.). It must also be said that working conditions in the construction sector are generally extremely poor. Yet it is not only in the construction field that such irregularities exist. The temporary nature of certain contracts in the industrial sector in Northern Italy also lead to the employment of non-EU workers, which is also the sector that most frequently resorts to subcontracting:

> At first people like the Ghanaians were taken on by Fiat as soon as they had arrived, doing jobs that the Italians did not want to do: work for six months, or work subbing for people off sick or on maternity leave. In the building sector, there is always subcontracting to small business and co-operatives. Therefore, the contracts are temporary. (TU5)

Feminization and Internationalization in Domestic Service

Such tendencies can be found in all case studies. However, Turin is the city where the internationalization of personal services has developed the most. Personal services in Turin depend almost exclusively on the foreign workforce. A number of associations that criticize this process refer to the way that it has contributed to retaining the traditional family model:

> In places like that you cannot say that there is competition; you should say the migrants make the development of economic activities possible that could not be developed otherwise. We talk about the assistance for the elderly. This kind of job can also mean a return to traditional ideas; I mean to a revaluing of the idea of domestic work. In reality without migrants assistance for the elderly in the city of Turin we could not go on. (TU5)

In this instance, we are faced with a process whereby workers with regular contracts are substituted in the care of the elderly, thereby confirming the vital importance of the family context,

> The foreign woman is the alternative to homes for the elderly. The foreign woman is the alternative to the civil death of the family. It is the new resource in the country and is cheaper than a hospital or any other institution. (TU8)

The emancipation of native women, combined with new and existing family demands, have created a major source of employment for foreign women in Italy:

> There is perhaps more demand for assistants for elderly people. There was a change in the last three years and this has got something to do with the fact that women have different priorities now. Two years ago, domestic workers would have worked night and day, but now they want to work half a day or with no lunch-break because they are married or they have a family. I see an emancipatory aspect in this. (N6)

It is important to bear in mind the fact that the Italian labor market fails to make use of immigrants' skills and training, and instead channels them almost exclusively towards domestic help, as the following respondent points out:

> I agree with the necessity to consider and value the cultural level of immigrants; that is what happened in France and Germany, I think. But creating illusions by telling these people that if they have a degree in engineering, they will put it to some use here would be a big mistake. In Naples, and I guess the same is true for the rest of Italy, it is domestic jobs which are available to them and I think it will still be so for the next 20 years. (N13)

More specifically, we are faced with entry flows of domestic workers, which were originally set up by the Catholic Church and which now have been further developed and consolidated by ethnic and mixed networks:

The first recruitment from Sri Lanka was in 1970, through the Catholic Church in Naples, Rome, Milan. Before the Catholic Church was the main link...now it is through relatives and friends. (N5)

During the 1990s, all cities experienced the arrival of large numbers of migrant women into domestic service, which would appear to be peculiar to Southern Europe. Only in the cases of Algeciras and Lisbon does the situation vary slightly. In Algeciras, domestic help is centered in a residential area on the outskirts of the city called Sotogrande. The low number of middle-class residents means that the demand for personal services is restricted to families with serious problems, such as relatives suffering from Alzheimer's. The second exception is Lisbon. This close connection between the large number of migrant females and the internationalization of domestic service brings us to discuss a major factor determining the nature of the migratory flows, which as yet has not been found in all of the countries studied. In the case of Portugal, the discourse on the construction of male or female niches in the labor market is not so much in evidence. The majority of foreign women in Portugal, most of whom originate from Cape Verde, work in the catering and restaurant industry, particularly in the kitchens and in cleaning, occupying most of the unskilled jobs in the sector. Studying the records of mothers whose children attend district non-profit associations of the Lisbon periphery, revealed that the majority of Cape Verdian women work in large cleaning companies, and a few more slightly skilled women work providing home support. It would appear that live-in domestic service in Portugal is a residual occupation for live-in domestic workers. Indeed, we found that of all the foreign female workers, only Cape Verdian women carry out this type of work. In our study, Portuguese cities are the only places where live-in domestic work is not the principal labor niche for immigrant female workers. The tolerance threshold here is lower due to the live-in workforce offered by the workforce from the provinces. Notwithstanding, the main source of employment for immigrants in Lisbon is in the construction area—it is interesting to note that Portuguese emigrants in Germany also work in construction—and the women tend to work in the catering industry or as external cleaners. Native cleaning workers in Portugal earn 900 escudos an hour, while African women earn 600 escudos an hour. Some clients have indicated that they prefer to contract non-African women for domestic service because they do not approve of African women's hygiene standards. In the case of transformation industries such as the textile and electricity sectors, the level of female presence is fairly high.

We can highlight other processes linked to migrant women and this internationalizing of domestic service. It is undoubtedly true that the question of gender relations between the various communities and migrant groups comes up constantly and the same is true of women's implication in sex work:

...then you have another group of families consisting of unmarried women, and who are also working in bars. Not all of them. I think the *bailarinas* came first, and then the Pontians. I think that the women who work in a bar aren't real Pontians, perhaps their father was Russian, Armenian or Bielorussian, and they are freer. They're different, blonde and more attractive. The Pontians are small and dark; women like that are no good in the bars. (T3)

In an area inhabited by such a large number of distinct communities as is the case in Thrace, the concept of the woman and the framework for her rights has become an identity icon. Differentiation corresponds to women's role within the Pomak, Turkish, Pontian or Greek family:

Greeks says that Turkish men are very bad, because they keep the women at home, make them wear the *chador*, and refuse to allow them to go out, and then they go with the Russian prostitutes. However, I think that the *chador* is not so repressive, the fact is that inside the houses the women always have the power. (T7)

The Paradigmatic Case of the Irregulars

Irregulars are a typical example not only for analyzing the labor market, but also in view of the particular features of their rights and the social services to which they may or may not be entitled. The initial problems arising from irregular immigrant status are easily detected in border cities, where the entry of irregulars forces associations, and taxi drivers, among others, to become accomplices in fooling the systems of control.

In the early nineties everything was more covered up. For instance, when we—in this association—had to buy a ticket for someone, we had to put it in our name and we couldn't use the real names. That doesn't happen anymore, as even though the money comes from public funds we can do it now, even when the person doesn't have any papers. (AL3)

Taxi drivers in Tarifa and Algeciras also refer to constant trips to Spain's Poniente region, the preferred area chosen by the most fortunate irregulars looking for work as low cost laborers. This network of individual assistance in the border areas was common practice up until 1997:

During 1997 and the beginning of 1998, things changed considerably, as the people who helped those who came over in the boats started to get arrested. But everyone knew what was happening, like in the case of Father X or the association Algeciras Acoge. It wasn't a matter of just one case being discovered, everyone knew that this was going on every day, and the *Guardia Civil* knew it too. Things didn't change until it started appearing in the press; it happens a lot this way with the topic of immigration." (AL3)

In Algeciras, accusations surrounding this informal set up eventually led to serious problems of legal prosecution:

> As for those arrested for helping the immigrants, the people who fed them and gave them a place to sleep were providing emergency support, to the extent that they knew they could get into trouble over it. That's what made people stop in the end. (AL3)

This led to a debate among the various associations (including here all types of associations working with and for migrant's issues) in Algeciras, who were divided as to whether the irregulars should be reported:

> Unlike *Algeciras Acoge*, we don't report the immigrant networks. We don't think that solves anything; if you report one person, then another one will appear and so on. The problem is rooted in the actual existence of the Alien's Law. (AL12)

The following quote summarizes the way in which irregulars embody all the paradoxes within the context of Southern Europe's immigration factors, family reunion processes, the blocking of universal health care, etc.

> There is an accumulation of irregulars for each new regularization. The irregulars make life impossible for any organized structure. They cannot have a regular job; their children can only go to school with those special measures related to the Turin case. It is a difficult subject for health services; there are those *Sportello* ISI[4] where they do not ask for documentation. Therefore, in this case there is a way of access. (TU5)

The most urgent issue that needs to be addressed regarding the irregulars' situation is that of health benefits; their state of health acts as a barometer or indicator that often implies emergency policies:

> Unfortunately these people arrive here in healthy conditions and get ill here because of stress, lack of hygiene, precarious housing conditions. The most incredible thing is that nobody told documented migrants that they are entitled to health assistance, with the result that only 50 percent of documented migrants are registered with the national health service. There is a dramatic lack of information. I think that at the moment these people arrive they should be given a paper saying that they should register with the nearest health center to receive the services they are entitled to. The result is that we end up by working in a situation of emergency…also with regular citizens, because they are not aware of these things. (N2)

Secondly, irregulars not only represent the paradoxes in all possible phases of social integration, but they are also emblematic figures for repressive measures by law enforcement agencies:

> Irregular immigrants make life impossible for the two types of institutions, regardless of whether they are welfare institutions or repression institutions, like the Questura (police headquarters). This irregular fact—more common in Italy than in the North of Europe—is an important distinction in immigration. The real problem of irregularity is born in the irregular form of the Italian labor market. More than a quarter of the total number of job vacancies in Italy are irregular. (TU5)

> I agree with the need to carry out controls in bigger and smaller towns alike; it is fair enough. What I don't accept is the way they treat us: handcuffs, rude manners, as if we really did something wrong…this is indeed racism. We don't even know why they always check us. (N4)

As to the challenges facing the health system, those individuals and institutions interviewed believe that Turin's ISI, the Health Information Center for Immigrants, is the most effective in comprehensive health rights:

> I think that the ISI is the only service in Italy to be based on the idea of universality. I can have two options if I have a problem and I am irregular; I can either go to the *Pronto Soccorso,* which is for everyone, or to the ISI, which is specific, it is a way of avoiding Italian bureaucracy. Maybe if I lose my documents as an Italian, it would be more practical for me to go to the ISI and to say that I was a Kurd. (TU5)

Despite the problems facing the welfare state caused by irregulars, frequent references are made to the fact that irregulars can resort to international legislation for protection. The case of Athens once again reveals how an irregular can access basic humanitarian aid through international organizations such as the United Nations:

> Yes they have to go to the police first, and then they come here to ask for help. We also have people from Albania, when we don't have many refugees, to give them food; our catering program addresses everyone. The school program is for children and adults. They have to show us their appointment with the UN and the birth certificate of their children; it doesn't matter if they don't have it. It's our priority to help refugees, only political refugees, but we can also help immigrants, but not as a priority. (AT13)

Dual Welfare

The basic issue in understanding the various aspects of welfare involves, on the one hand, the debates on the specific-general social services dilemma and, on the other hand, the question of assistentialism and self-management, as seen in the various applied philosophies at the local level:

> We try not to fall into assistentialism. We aim to promote, train and guide migrants. Here everyone says "*poor things.*" But if you remember that they have come over on a boat, then they're brave. Besides, they know how to cry, they know the game of charity, and they know that if they tell you a certain story they'll touch a soft spot in you. They know the network well. They know that if we won't help them, they can go to the community worker, or the parish. They really know how the network works. (AL10)

We are faced here with a double standard of welfare. This means that dual standards exist with different services for different social groups. One aspect is related to the urban middle classes and their needs in terms of family services, and the other relates to urban social exclusion in regard to social welfare for migrants. At this point it is worth emphasizing that the concept of social welfare is understood in a wide sense (Montagut, 1994). This dual welfare would appear to correspond to the changing social situation in Southern European societies: namely changes within gender relations in the family; the recent and rapid settlement of foreign immigrants; and the shift towards new forms of social welfare, even before the previous ones had been fully consolidated. However, although the urban middle classes frequently recruit foreigners to provide private social services, this is not always the case. The exception is due mainly to two reasons: (1) in many cases, foreign women tend to work in domestic service, although this is not the case in Lisbon, where the local labor force is still available for this kind of work; (2) domestic work paid by the hour appears to be a resource used by both foreign and native women who find themselves standing side-by-side. However, in the case of Lisbon such positions are almost always filled by migrant and ethnic minority women.

The Welfare Mix options open to Southern European migrants tend to vary considerably from one geographical area to another. This diversity is due to a number of factors: (1) the fact that migration occurs at different stages in varying countries, regions and cities; (2) the diverse traditional role of the Church as an administrator and provider of social services; (3) the socioeconomic level of the area under consideration, together with the contrast between strong and weak industrialization; and (4) the diverse traditional role played by the trade unions in defending workers, specifically foreign workers. Moreover, this idea of dual welfare can be considered from two points of view: the first, combining two future trends, the development of private services and the transfer of responsibilities traditionally accepted by the state onto civil society organizations; and the second with regard to the labor market, which reproduces this dualization based on gender differences and ethnic crosses. This inequality is also spatial in terms of regional differences, with the cities constituting the maximum realization of inequality. In addition, this dual welfare system eventually translates into the social structure of two emerging worlds: that of the urban middle class—particularly in relation to professional women—and that of new migrations in the process of social exclusion in relation to power and domination.

General or Specific Services?

In recent years there has been a general debate in Europe as to whether services for foreign migrants should consist of general services, in other words standardized services, in which no differentiation is made according to population, or whether in view of the fact that certain sectors of the population possess different characteristics, assistance should be offered through different services, specific services. Between these two extremes we can observe a continuum of variations, which are not as simple as they may at first appear. By looking at the structure of the supply according to sectors we may observe specific situations, but at the same time there may also be general resources. Health services constitute one of those areas that have opted to provide specific services, particularly as a result of the migrant's irregular status.

In addition to the traditional topics included in the debate—whether these services should be general or specific, whether they should be based on a transversal or targeted focus, whether on the promotion or rejection of positive action— other characteristics should be considered in the analysis of the social service offered. Namely, the type of treatment being offered and the way relations with users are conceived. This has been a long-standing issue in terms of social welfare when evaluating the excessive assistentialism resulting from social policies. Here we will look at three possible perspectives: assistentialism, the paternalistic attitude of organizations towards users, both of which are fairly closely connected, and promoting participation. This latter aspect includes a wide number of considerations ranging from the use of social services—where migrants adopt a more autonomous approach—to a means of creating incentive, namely ways of encouraging greater participation and involvement among immigrants in improving their living conditions in the country in which they settle. In other words, promoting associationism among immigrants requires their active participation in formulating demands on the administration and its policies.

In the opinion of many respondents, avoiding specificity is the key to preventing any sense of unfair comparisons among the population. This would justify the arguments of those who prefer a general approach to policies designed to combat social exclusion because otherwise, specificity would merely fuel the stereotypical attitudes already present among the native population in cities such as Barcelona:

> If for example you give school benefits to gypsy children in order to ensure they attend school, society will say *they come to school dirty and goodness knows what else, and on top of it all they receive aid*. This is the reaction of non-gypsies in a neighbourhood like La Mina. The scale for benefits should be based on financial need. (B7)

It is in this context that since the mid-1990s, immigration in Barcelona (and in its provinces, such as Mataró) has been subjected to a transversal policy rather than a specific approach:

> We also had an *ethnic minority commission* at the City Council, but I don't know if it still exists because the commission was constantly being transferred from one department to another. It used to be part of Social Services, but now it probably depends on a newly created department for transversal issues: inequality, gender, multiculturality. We don't design social service programs specifically for immigrants. We have programs designed for everyone, which the immigrants can also benefit from, because the needs they may have are the same as those of any vulnerable group. (BM4)

Yet in practice this desired transversality is more complex than it sounds, due to the particular characteristics of the associations and organizations working with immigrants. While the Barcelona-based CITE[5] talked of an integrated approach to workers' problems, in Mataró their vision was restricted to purely labor aspects. However, the Mataró Town Council indicated that these centers were responsible for applying an integrated user approach, based on the concept of the citizen:

> The legal advice provided by the AMIC and CITE trade unions is comparable with the work we do, although only at this level. We also have the municipal dimension which provides far greater information. This means that we can deal with foreign workers and autochthonous individuals. We don't direct our services at workers, but rather at citizens in general, whatever their personal situation may be. (BM7)

Associations working with migrants in Barcelona and Mataró are faced with similar problems, as indicated in various municipal reports drawn up in Mataró. Common concerns include literacy courses that inevitably cause the service to become specific, or particular concerns regarding legal issues that demand urgent attention. One of the main handicaps is the differential nature of the Immigration Act, plus insufficient knowledge of the languages in use:

> In Can Torner for instance—this a civic adult training center—we have literacy courses, as well as job training schemes, but they are open to everyone. It's true that they are more aimed at immigrants, but that's because their personal situation means that they have a greater need for these services. (BM4)

Generally speaking, the majority of actors in Spain, both in Algeciras and Barcelona, believe that general services form the ideal context and that specific services can only lead to a form of discrimination:

> They handle the social services and the administration's specific policies very well. Specific models eventually insert migrants in the special resources, resources that produce differentiation. That eventually leads to marginality. We should be concentrating on inserting them in generalized resources, ones that already exist. The purpose of a specific project is to obtain a subsidy. Fine, but you have to try and include it into the general services. Besides, it's hard for the general public to understand the specific services. (AL8)

The quest for generality or universality is made even more complex by an additional factor, namely the duplicity of services and the patching functions that are frequently put forward by NGOs.

> We believe that the services should be general. The role of the NGOs is to patch up situations. The idea is to have a generalized service open to everybody, otherwise we would be creating ghettos. (AL10)

As far as the Italian cases are concerned, mention must be made of the fact that the specific nature of the services was due mainly to the *Martelli Law*. During the early stages of social services in Italy there were no specific recipient services and no specific structures were set up; they did not begin to appear until the second regularization process was underway:

> The first services were general, the migrants used to use the classical dorms. However, in the second regularization the need for a structure of *prima accoglienza* (first reception) was included. There were the budgets for that. I think that specific services make sense when they are highly justified by the diverse original situation of the population. And even now, today, each time that a service is to be constituted one thing is checked, if there is really a diverse situation from the general population; if that is not the case, general services are constituted. (TU10)

Nevertheless, specific programs have appeared over the years, partly fomented by EU programs:

> But on the other hand, for many years, we have had specific training programs for immigrants. If you consider the budget for these purposes from the EU, one of the objective categories is always immigrants, as a separate category, together with handicapped, etc. The specificity of a service is needed when the situation is justified for giving equal opportunity. It's fair that those services exist. (TU10)

Emergency measures,[6] the philosophy behind the suggested responses and the outbreaks of racism they caused, are important elements for consideration in the debate surrounding general or specific services in Turin,

> There were some public dormitories that were only for migrants in order to separate them from marginal people. You cannot put a foreigner with a drug addict, an alcoholic; he is not in that category, he does not have a health problem, and he doesn't want to mix with those people, because they are difficult people. The best thing was to give him a post in a dorm as a passage to a house, but for Italians a post in a dorm is not a passage to a house but a passage to the street. I also received many criticisms because of this partition. As regards the number of beds, I always thought that the maximum amount would be 50 people, but it was difficult to find these small places. We always had problems with the population, not at the very beginning but from 1994 onwards. For the last four years there have been constant complaints from the population regarding all aspects of immigration. But it is not a spontaneous reaction, it is an organized movement, or the Lega, or the *Alleanza Nazionale* or the so-called Comitato Spontaneo. (TU8)

The general debate originates from the question of general (universal) or specific services, a legacy from the universalist and republican traditions, and therefore closer to the French Jacobin model. However, the lack of a legally established framework results in unclear practices:

> The services can be general for everyone, but these generalities can include different paths inside these services. For example, if there are associations that start working only with Peruvians or only with Philippines it is understandable that there will be a

higher concentration of these communities. I think that this problem may exist more in the future than now. For the time being, to say that public policies are addressed mainly to the community is more an image than a reality. (TU5)

In the city of Turin, as in Barcelona, the mid-1990s saw an attempt to adapt to a transversal service approach, as explained by the *Centro Interculturale*:

> They were specific at the beginning because there was an emergency. The change from multicultural to intercultural has been the policy of this center, which was born from a political decision from the *Giunta Comunale*. Our goal is for the policies to become intercultural, not to maintain the existence on the territory of diverse cultures that do not speak to each other, but to encourage people to start communicating regardless of their origins. In that sense, there is a political aim, so they can talk to each other, also at a community level, and at the level of the different associations. It is a transversal approach, with all of them, to try to get them to interact. (TU11)

There appears to be a need for specific services in certain contexts, particularly in education. In any event, the multi-dimensional nature of the immigration phenomenon makes it difficult to separate the interventions, in other words, services created specifically to tackle a certain problem. The Spanish and Italian debate can also be transferred to Portugal. Here social services are becoming increasingly dualized; on the one hand we find those offering services to individuals, and on the other hand those who restrict offering services specifically to immigrants. We must consider that the impact caused by the change from dictatorship to democracy through a revolutionary movement, and the effect this has had in terms of organizations is responsible for the philosophy behind social services is concerned. The Carnation Revolution was essential to establishing of democracy in Portugal; it created new forms of administration that would continue into the future, such as the social housing co-operatives. A legacy of a certain amount of radicalism in dealing with social issues was therefore handed down that was to have no equal in Spain. Yet one highly common aspect shared by various Southern European contexts is a rejection of positive discrimination, which is expressed by all actors:

> Here we have set up a program to fight poverty that includes gypsies and non-gypsies, and it has worked well, involving everyone. We have to mobilize local members as much as possible. It has to include everyone in order to stop people from coming out with typical remarks like "it's for the gypsies," etc. Popular awareness is highly sensitive to the question of equality. Popular awareness isn't ready to cope with positive discrimination. (L11)

A further aspect for consideration in the debate on general and specific services is whether the chosen model requires a mediator. Opposing opinions are almost always concomitant with the division over the need for general or specific services. Many respondents are aware of the complexities embodied in the use of a mediator, yet also accept that he/she is a necessary figure. The interviews carried out in Turin and Barcelona[7] expressed the debate regarding the use of the social mediator in a most direct and explicit manner:

> Even now in Turin this is the subject of a major debate. It's even linked to the stages of immigration. In the first phase, from the 1980s until the 1990s, emergency was used as an interface. Now things are changing, there is all this discourse of stabilization, so the discourse is more difficult. Novella (from the Barcelona municipality) says that we have to put an end to the figure of the mediator. Well, I think that in some respects, they can still be useful; in some cases, they are only useful for linguistic mediation, that's all. (T10)

The role of the mediator oscillates between a cultural or intercultural figure—capable of working with one or various cultures—and translator or interpreter—dealing particularly with health matters. However, despite Northern Italy's frequent recourse to mediators, there is a great deal of controversy surrounding the actual role this agent should play: "They want to make mediators the scapegoat, but they should only act as a bridge; the mediator cannot be made responsible for all the problems. Normally, the institution does not understand the foreigner. And lastly, the service is unidirectional. I think the mediator is a very ambiguous figure, at least in terms of what the institution is asking of them" (BU4). The harshest criticisms of the controversial function of the mediator claim that these agents prevent migrants from being considered as users of social services in their own right—in other words as citizens—not as consumers. In Italy, mediators are found particularly in actions carried out by social co-operatives.

Welfare comparisons. Any analysis of attempts to alleviate tensions that result from a comparison of the benefits and services available to the native and immigrant populations has to be understood as a complex vicious circle. On the one hand, the actors involved endeavor to avoid specificity by not revealing the full extent of the services designed for immigrants, mainly in order to prevent tension; while at the same time they attempt to continue to provide support for immigrants, maintaining them as marginalized population in order to avoid a potential source of considerable stress generated from a sense of marginality as well as to prevent their rejection by the autochthounous population, as shown in the following quotes:

> This means that other types of immigration will appear, not just economic; there will be other types of demand, more social and perhaps more diverse. And this means that at a time when all the Welfare State can talk about is social cohesion, the needs of the autochthonous population may increase and diversify. The immigrant population also has new social needs, this could lead to some real trouble, as it could be the source of possible outbreaks of xenophobia and racism.... I often talk to the gypsies and the other day they were complaining about migrant street sellers. Or the tramps in the *soup kitchens* who complain that the *moros* (pejorative for Moroccans) take all the food. (B8)

In Spain, from early 2000 onwards, the question of unequal treatment was not limited exclusively to social benefits, or social rights, but also extended to the obligations of the immigrants. Failure of immigrants to comply with these obligations is often justified by the fact that their sense of civic or democratic culture is not sufficiently developed due to the poor democratic tradition in their countries of origin:

> This is a democratic country, and therefore everyone should be able to express their thoughts and views, but many of these people don't have that democratic background; they come from countries where democracy doesn't exist, so their way of doing things isn't democratic, sometimes even the leaders (…) you have to understand that there are certain standards necessary for a peaceful co-existence, of living in a community that everyone respects, so you have to respect them, too, and that discourse still hasn't been produced. (B8)

Compliance with rights or obligations frequently affects the rights of Muslims in Spain, upon whom assimilationist practices are frequently imposed, even by those working with them:

> I think that the general trend is based on an attempt at respect, but maintaining certain minimum principles. At least that's the philosophy I think should be applied. It's hard, because trying to preserve, understand and respect another culture requires a knowledge of it, but you also come up against a number of points where you want to maintain certain basic rights that are guaranteed here, but which in other cultures still remain undefined. I think that we're also making too much use of stereotyped images, as important changes have occurred, particularly among the people of Morocco. The thing is that in Cáritas we sometimes unwittingly apply assimilationist actions. Without realizing it. You have to keep up to date, keeping a careful watch on yourself as to where you're going and what you're doing. (B7)

As in the case of Barcelona, racism in Algeciras is based on comparative differences existing in the benefits provided by the welfare state:

> *Pateras* (boats) are arriving here everyday, but only those who arrived before are eligible for the regularization process. People are against the new Act. People are really angry, especially at the comments made by the Social Security; they say it's all wrong. They say *there's no money for pensions but they provide migrants with social insurance?* That's what everybody says. (AL7)

It is in the provision of personal services where racism is most frequently and openly expressed, where civilizational values infringe on private spaces:

> I don't think there is a thread behind the preference for different nationalities, maybe it is the mass media which create prejudices, the level of ignorance is crazy. A lady once told me that she did not want an Albanian maid as she claimed that they had invaded the Italian coasts and that she did not want them to invade her place too! Incredible! But I think they have a point when they prefer a white woman as an assistant for an elderly

person; I can understand this. Elderly people find it more difficult to live through changes and sometimes they don't accept transformations. (N6).

Lastly, as we have mentioned on several occasions, and as far as benefiting from public services is concerned, renting accommodation is one of the most difficult racist hurdles :

> Things are really bad here; people are extremely reluctant to rent out houses. Most of the residents' associations are made up of elderly people, lots of retired people whose actions are guided by the interests of their own districts. They're very frightened. They are obsessed by two things: that they're going to take their jobs away from them, and that they will bring crime and drugs with them. They all, each and every one of them, say the same thing. Except for one association that has Senegalese members, who are always accepted better than the Moroccans. The president says that the Senegalese are very well integrated, and they go to the adult education center. But in the other district they say that the Moroccan immigrants isolate themselves. (AL4)

Which Social Polices?

The complex nature of the immigration phenomenon in Southern Europe requires the consideration of a large number of aspects in order to be able to grasp the management of services. Migrant services cover wide areas of demand, yet almost always begin with demands regarding documentation, before moving onto basic demands, similar to those expressed by the autochthonous population:

> The most important thing for them is work, followed by education, housing and health; those are immigrants' basic needs. (B8)

Naturally, processing applications for migrants' permits is not considered a social service, yet the fact that it is a *sine qua non* requirement for any further process can be considered an essential condition prior to the standardization of any type of social benefit management. As a result, many of the actors involved in immigrant services have been obliged to offer legal advice regarding Alien's legislation, even though it lies outside their particular field of knowledge. Occasionally, this service may practically be covered by the objectives of the actor in question as in the case of the CITE:

> Here we mostly give information, particularly written information about how to go about obtaining a work and residence permit. (BM3)

However, two major elements mentioned by all respondents in reference to changing social service demands should be highlighted here, which are related to two recent phenomena: the high number of women in the migratory flows and the established ways of family reunion, and the arrival of unaccompanied minors. In recent year, Algeciras, due to its strategic position as a southern border, has seen a rise in the number of clandestine immigrants in a highly vulnerable condition:

> There are children who come across in lorries and boats; there are also those who come in small motor launches. They know they're not going to be arrested for having committed an offense but will be sent to the reform schools run by the Autonomous Government of Andalusia. (AL2)

It is worth highlighting here the fact that Turin was the first in Southern Europe to set up initiatives designed for dealing with minors:

> With the children who have special permits we have done something new now, that when they are 18 years old they can ask for another type of permit: work, research-work of professional training. In this project for small children we are involved with the school, Caritas, and the *Tribunale dei Minori.* (TU4)

I will now proceed to examine in detail the complexity of some social policies, such as those related to education (in connection with the National State and identity issues) and health (as one of the most vulnerable policies in relation to migrant). Finally, city planning management and its relation to migrants and housing are essential in the assessment of both the type of welfare state existing in a country and of the way in which migration flows are managed, as well as immigrants' quality of life. In the case of housing we will focus principally on the actions carried out in Portugal in recent years and, in the following section, on the case of Pontian resettlement in Thrace.

Educational Challenges. When analyzing immigrants' living conditions, educational aspects appear to fall within a wide context encompassing a large number of diverse factors, such as the right to education in equal conditions, access to educational resources, the problems involved in validating foreign qualifications, the battle between private and state schools, foreign children dispersion policies in schools, the right of irregular minors to education, etc. The question of education is addressed here in terms of the nature of the offer, which is basically related to the children's needs.

Other issues reported by representatives from nongovernment organizations mention the lack of efficient schooling support for immigrant children and the excessive emphasis placed on the cultural issue, centered on religious differentialism. There are also constant references to the fact that immigrant children tend to be concentrated in certain schools and to the pressure for educational dispersion and the factors involved, particularly in terms of the clash between state and private education. Indeed, the public sector in Catalonia, Spain, has criticized the lack of interest shown by the private sector in incorporating immigrants:

> It's a complex issue. By saying, *let the parents choose the school* we imply *let's allow the existence of ghettos*. It's a delicate issue, the thing is it does no good; I think that

concentrating them isn't a good idea because that's not the way society is organized…the world of education is rather perverse; private or subsidized schools won't take children they consider to have problems and the state schools are suffering; you can have teachers from schools here in the Old City who have up to 37 different ethnic groups in one class. The teacher is bound to have problems. That's the reality, and it's pretty frightening. (B7)

A certain amount of confusion often arises in Catalonia regarding exactly who is responsible for what, as in the case of linguistic integration. With regard to the issue of Spanish and Catalan language classes, doubts have been expressed as to whether the administration is organizing the courses correctly, in other words whether or not the community centers are the ideal setting for these classes:

Most of the immigrants have received no education, and education, as the *Intermón* slogan says, breaks the binds of poverty. That's why this issue needs to be looked at closely. This is not a role for the civic centers. Although if the administration thinks it is because there's nobody on the council who is prepared to take on this responsibility at a given time, then perhaps it should be assumed by the civic centers, but it's not really their job. (BM9)

In direct contrast to the type of debate existing in Barcelona, in Algeciras the general tendency is to address the question of immigration as an emergency, as the dramatic situation of the irregulars, and as a result of this framing the cultural issue is overlooked. Despite its proximity with Morocco, no cultural exchange programs exist on either side of the Strait.

There is a constant concern regarding educational failure in all the sites of the study, particularly among children of Cape Verdian origin living in Lisbon. This is mainly the result of the fact that the parents work and are therefore unable to help their children with their school homework. Certain associations, such as Moínho da Juventude are attempting to address these issues. Vocational training initiatives are partly a continuation of other child support programs for street children and young offenders. These programs have enabled associations to discover that the root of the problem lies in the fact that the children are left alone for long periods of time, due to the hours their parents worked. In addition these children tend to leave school from the age of ten onwards, thus between the ages of ten and sixteen they are therefore isolated from both the educational and the labor systems.

At the time when my fieldwork was carried out, the question of interculturality had not yet become an issue for debate or an objective of the Greek educational system. It is important to mention that in terms of cultural heritage, the Ottoman influence does not play a major role. Nevertheless, despite the emphasis on cultural homogeneity, the Balkanic component in Greece has been portrayed by the coexistence of multiple communities, as in the case of the Arbanites in Greece, whose mother tongue is Greek. The model chosen so far for Thrace is based on a representation of an ethnically homogenous society, with common traits not only in language and culture but also from a generalized imaginary of being descendants of an ancient civilization, in this case, Ancient Greece. This is partly what typifies the model of a closed society based on the Greek ethnos (defined by orthodox religion, national spirit, and Greek language) and on a Gastarbeiter regime (understood by accepting immigrants on a temporary basis). In short, a restrictive approach which does not leave enough space for cultural differences, either in schools (where secularism does not exist) or in religious practice (where mosques are officially forbidden as is the case in the city of Athens).

The health gap. The question of health is one of the principal causes for concern, and one that has most clearly revealed the lack of compatibility between migrant legal procedures and the international treaties protecting universal rights. This is due to the seriousness of the fact that a line is drawn between those who are entitled to medical attention through the standard channels, and those who encounter difficulties in receiving medical attention in certain centers—which also depends on the cases. We will see how this latter aspect depends on a whole series of conditions, namely whether the need for attention is urgent or regular; whether the individual has chosen the right center; on the attitude of the health care and administrative workers responsible for the service at that time, etc. The principal issue for debate is therefore the universality of medical care, in other words who is entitled to what:

> As far as benefits are concerned, if you're an immigrant with a work permit but don't have a legal contract, you don't pay social security. On the other hand if you're a Moroccan, you aren't entitled to medical attention, but if you're Chilean or German you are, OK? (B7)

> Most immigrants, 70 percent of immigrants cannot receive medical attention. There is an act written in the constitution that states that no attention should be given to any illegal immigrant except...when the immigrant is almost dead. They can receive him and put him in the mortuary. It is absurd; it is an abuse of human rights. Have you ever heard of a country deporting an AIDS patient? It only happens in Greece. (AT6)

According to the SOS Racisme Report (2001), complaints regarding lack of medical attention for immigrants by INSALUD[8] in 1999 were the focus of a debate regarding medical attention for migrants, and formed the basis for discussions regarding extending the rights to medical services during the drawing up of the new Spanish Immigration Act. Discrimination in terms of access to medical services occurs mainly among irregular and under-age immigrants. In theory, the August/2000 Act contemplated medical coverage for those registered on the census, and those who were not registered remained entitled to emergency and maternity care. Apart from the key debate concerning the universality of medical care, the health care issue also reveals the differences existing between the responsibilities of the various administrations, in other words, with whom the ultimate responsibility lies and how far actions by the local administration can go in this area:

> Maximum responsibility lies with the Autonomous Government. If you talk to someone from the Autonomous Government they'll tell you that everyone receives attention, but if you talk to the immigrants, and the people who work with the immigrants they tell you *of course there are people who are left unattended....* I also think something should be said in favor of the majority of the doctors who deal with this—there may be the odd racist among them—but they know that what they have to do is to attend to the individual and nothing else. (B7)

Lisbon has also been forced to come up with a series of alternatives to compensate for the lack of medical coverage for irregulars. It has done so by establishing contacts with the association *Sanité* in the peripheral district associations. Initially, children born to irregular migrants encountered serious difficulties in obtaining medical attention. Later, and according to respondent L6, a solution was found for these difficulties. The law states that they are entitled to go to a public hospital in the event of a medical emergency. Immigrants are no longer refused medical care, but there are ways of reducing that care to a minimum. Another measure designed to fill the gap in medical coverage are the mobile units, which can be seen in certain districts in Lisbon:

> We go from house to house in order to get to know the families and we discover that they don't have a general practitioner or medical card, and that they don't go to the surgery, and we find people suffering from tuberculosis. We know which families don't have a medical card and we take the people to the vans for their vaccinations. (L16)

The problems surrounding health care were a recurrent issue among respondents in Athens, particularly with regard to the lack of medical cover for irregulars:

> The second biggest problem is health. Even now, we have more than three Ethiopians in the hospital. They are not required to pay for this hospitalization. Sometimes the Church will only support these patients in cases where they don't have health insurance or they can't get good treatment. (AT4)

In contrast to the situation in Athens, the creation of the ISI in Turin is the most effective response to date in meeting irregular immigrants' demands for health care:

> In 1992 we activated the *Sportello ISI*, for migrant's health. We signed a contract with a *cooperativa* sociale, which now holds an office (counselling, interpretation, organization of medical visits and delegation to other services) six times a week.... The number is very high; for example, in 1997 we had 2,000 new patients to be added to the 3,000 from the previous years, 80 percent of the users of this office are irregulars. (TU7)

The case of the ISI in Turin is paradigmatic in that it attempts to resolve the question of the rights of irregulars to medical care:

> The ISI was created for the irregulars. In order to have a health book you need to be a resident.... And in order to have a residence permit you have to show your rent contract, the house where you live. Everyone knows that migrants do not have a rent contract even when they are paying rent, money that even the Italians would not pay. (TU1)

The ISI is also one of the most innovative experiences, as it extends to mental health issues and a series of services for women and irregular migrants.

> Of the 2,000 users attended last year, 1,300 were women. One of the reasons could be that they find it more difficult to get information elsewhere about abortion, like in the Catholic associations, so they come here. The majority are Peruvian and Nigerian, and lately there has been an increase in the number of women from Eastern Europe, particularly from Albania and Romania. There are not particular situations or pathologies; they are all common to the Italian poor. (TU7)

Urban Segregation and the PER Program. Ethnic segregation, especially in U.S. research, has been found to be one of the main structural features of the perpetuation of urban poverty and racial inequality. Whereas in Europe, the contrast between Northern and Southern Europe in terms of housing rights clearly accentuates the differences in migrant lifestyles,

> In Coventry, for instance, some of the working class areas have better facilities than the middle class areas. When you see those low-rise houses with a garden, and with central heating too, for us the Portuguese, that's a dream. The English are amazed when they see the photographs of the *favelas* here, they can't believe things like that still exist in Europe, they thought they were only in Brazil. The poor are worse off every day and things will get worse unless they have access to education; they will be stuck in these pockets of poverty and the gap will continue to grow wider. (L8)

In Lisbon, as far as immigrant associations are concerned, we find the classic division between those representing immigrant communities that are closer to the population and those that are more removed. As elsewhere, the gateways to the city were also often the historical centers, as in the case of the Cape Verdians that arrived in the neighborhood of San Bento. According to Lisbon's commissioner for ethnic minorities, the only way to combat the concentration of immigrants on the periphery of Lisbon is to activate policies in the historical quarters; that combined with active housing policies aimed at promoting a social mix. This would mean that the high rents in the city center and the irregularity of the land on the peripheral belt would provide immigrants with the opportunity to settle in the peripheral districts. Another important factor for consideration is the type of immigrant occupation; the fact that the majority of immigrants work in the construction industry made it possible for the shantytowns to spring up in places in which they were working.

Since the 1960s, a series of urban projects have been designed for Lisbon, yet they have never been implemented. The projects aimed at rehousing the inhabitants of the shantytowns in flats were planned until 2001. These measures, all part of Portugal's *National Plan for the Fight Against Poverty*, aim to eradicate once and for all the shantytowns of Lisbon and Porto in order to offer the local authorities and social solidarity institutions an extensive social insertion program for the communities involved, fighting against criminality, prostitution, and drug dependency. Responsibility for this project falls upon the Portuguese state and the local authorities.

The PER[9] is a local urban planning program designed for the cities of Porto and Lisbon—where the main concentrations of immigrants are to be found—whereby the Councils assume responsibility for managing the available resources and for deciding where to build. Basically, the key issues behind this urban planning program are the following: concerns regarding the spread of shantytowns; the destruction of clandestine areas; rehousing; and lastly the creation of a working class district. One of the features of the PER programs is the high percentage of foreign immigrants involved. In theory, according to Act 797/96, the right to subsidized housing is restricted to Portuguese nationals, although many local authorities such as those of Lisbon, Amadora, and Oerias have overcome this legislation by implementing the PER. The logic behind these major rehousing projects has been criticized on various fronts. Solving the housing problem by opting for an extensive monoculture consisting of the construction of blocks of flats that are then occupied by families grateful for a roof over their heads does not mean an end to the problems. In some cases, large-scale rehousing through the PER merely means that the problems and tensions that existed in the shantytowns (such as unemployment or drug addiction) are transferred to the new areas. The cost of building land and the need for space has pushed the *bairros sociais* (housing state neighborhoods) towards the periphery of the city, thereby adding to the feelings of marginalization, in other words of being in the city but not forming a part of it.

The boroughs of Amadora, Lisbon, and Oeiras have generated the greatest amount of controversy regarding the administration and management of the various PERs. Clear differences exist in the way Oeiras and Amadora have tackled the construction and administration of subsidized housing. Oeiras has always had a housing policy, unlike Amadora, which two decades ago formed part of Oeiras, and whose local authority had never accepted the responsibility for urban planning and housing or the management of migratory flows.

Oeiras is a borough with approximately 180,000 inhabitants, and is practically a dormitory town of Lisbon. Its local authority currently includes a housing department known as *Acção Social,* and constitutes a key element of local government policy. The PER-related housing policy is considered to be exemplary in Portugal; however, Oeiras is surrounded by Socialist Party controlled boroughs, which are proving to be far slower in implementing rehousing policies. Yet action in Oeiras is not restricted exclusively to the management of "an exemplary rehousing policy." The rehousing process implemented in Oeiras initially included a dispersion policy involving the various communities within the borough. A number of factors were taken into consideration: the social networks (ethnic and interethnic); family networks; family type (nuclear, extended, single-headed households); and adjustment mechanisms (the simultaneity of the PER and the family reunion process). A year prior to the implementation of the PER, a survey was conducted in order to assess family rehousing selection and relations among residents. This allowed for the definition of the predominant type of family member and the network of relations. The aim was to eliminate all those solidarity networks that the local authorities considered as having a negative impact.

As far as the rehousing mechanisms themselves are concerned, one of the respondents (L8) pinpoints two key elements: (1) The importance of the family, as households are counted by families. Moreover, several of the affected families were involved in family reunion processes at the time. The Oeiras Local Authority respected the nuclei and family links in its rehousing policy, but also applied (2) dispersion policies. The Council was convinced of the need to prevent conflictive atmospheres from being reproduced, and of the need to establish a new one.

As a result, one of the basic objectives of the PER rehousing process was to do away with the stigmatized perception of the shantytowns, and therefore of the immigrants themselves: "People maintain their solidarity micro-networks but we get rid of the identity, the stigma" (L8). However, despite all the efforts made, the rehousing strategy and construction of new districts through the PER program has resulted in the creation of disconnected spaces, even between spaces with short distances. A considerable amount of work also remains to be done in these districts in order to establish a sense of identity:

> The feeling is one of being nowhere. You're not in the center, or in a village, you're not even really on the outskirts. Besides, those vast distances between small nuclei are what really make you feel completely isolated. It doesn't surprise me that they say the people in the PERs have no sense of being part of an area; that's the way anyone would feel. (L10)

> *Urban segregation and the EIYAPOE program.*
> I've noticed that the programs are always referring to the family, to *Ikogenia*, why is that? Why is the unit always the family? Because I think that's what it's really about, about families. *Ikogenia* means house, it means money for a house. *Ikogenia*, means that the program is only going to build a house and nothing else. (T3)

During 1988 and 1989, the need to implement a specific refugee policy for the Pontians became apparent to the Greek government. As part of the policy, an agency IAPOE[10] (known by its short name, *Idrima*, meaning "foundation") was set up in December 1990 to pursue a strategy of territorial implantation in the marginal areas of Northern Greece, which basically corresponded to the policy of hellenization of Macedonia and Thrace. This agency is here used in the text by the abbreviation EIYAPOE (*Ethnikó Idrima Epodohis Apodimon & Palinosteton Omogenou Elinon*, National Foundation for the Reception of Expatriated Greeks). Housing policy has been the main goal of the EIYAPOE program, and a key issue for the social integration of the Pontians. The housing program started with the reception centers; and was followed by prefabricated buildings, and finally purchased houses, though often using models of spatial segregation.

The program covers all the stages, from the first reception center (only present in Thrace), where the immigrants first arrive from their countries of origin, to their definitive settlement. The EU and the Greek government co-finance the measures. The program used to include sub-programs such as the teaching of the Greek language and a program for promoting entrepreneurship, although, subsequently, only housing benefit was provided. The Ministry of Foreign Affairs has overseas delegations in the former Soviet republics (and also in Northern Epiros in Albania) to recruit those persons to be located in the main reception and settlement program in Thrace (with its main delegation in Komotini). The main settlement centers are based in Kabala, Xanthi, Rodopi (settlements of Komotini and Sappes), and Evros (settlement areas of Alexandropouli, Orestiada, and Tiheró).

The program consists of five different phases: information centers, reception centers (short stays), reception for settlement, rented housing, and purchased houses. In phase two, health services and the teaching of the Greek language are also considered, while in phase three, the immigrants are housed in pre-fabricated homes. In phase four, they are entitled to cash or vouchers as well as to some specific medical assistance. In this phase, family issues related to children's education (with no extra budget allocation) are dealt with, and access to social workers and contacts with other services of the agency are also established. However, the main problems observed with this program are: (1) the lack of concern for labor market insertion (with the result being that the Pontians do not wish to go to Thrace, preferring instead the big urban centers like Athens and Salonika), (2) the lack of prevision for rotating migrations, and (3) the lack of a wider approach based on social integration (which is also related to the mismanagement of public funds).

The only specific service for a target group in Greece is through EIYAPOE, while all other communities must make do with general services, apart from primary education and issues concerning family law. Within the Pontian groups differences exist in the level of services provided for the flows of migrants that arrived at the very beginning of the 1990s and those that arrived in the late 1990s, while the same differences also occur across different nationalities (for example, in the case of Georgians and Armenians, various migrant networks are constructed, with a high degree of solidarity, especially present among Armenians). Receiving some social services like those related to health can be difficult given the lack of nurses that speak Russian. However, an alternative option, that of the informal help of the members of the community, seems to be frequently available. Another problematic matter is that the financing of Greek language classes has been halted. Thus, all services have been cut except those related to housing, the final goal of which is the provision of permanent accommodation and settlement. However, the main problems observed with this program are those concerning the labor market, emigration of the Pontians to larger urban areas, and the lack of a wider social integration approach. With regard to insertion onto the local labor market, certain issues should be considered especially problematic. In an area characterized by its agrarian economic structure, there is little call for a skilled industrial labor force and much less for those specializing in heavy industry. In addition, unlike the Attiki region, in a rural family setting there is little need for a female labor force as either family helpers or domestic cleaners. In the opinion of the Pontians, the problems associated with the lack of insertion on the labor market are the clearest evidence of the failure of the settlement programs:

> We had a dream to come to Greece, to leave for Greece and work, but we did not think it would be so difficult to relate to Greek society, to integrate. (T4)

The key obstacle for Pontian integration in Greece is that they constitute target of geographical-spatial control by the state, exerted through the housing policy, and which excludes the essential profile of the Russian-Pontian population, which is essentially urban and with a previous work experience in factories:

> The problem was that the people who came from Russia were people who worked in cities and as you see here we have small cities, and most of the people here have land or animals.... The government put them into small houses. Very small, very cold in the winter and very hot in the summer. And life in Greece is difficult if you don't work, if you don't have the language, because in the USSR, most of them did not know the Greek language, they knew Russian because they were living there, or Georgian, or else, the Uzbekistan language. (T11)

Essentially, the instrumentalization of housing for Pontians responds in political terms to the desire for a return to the demographic balance, a wish that is openly expressed by the various respondents:

> That's because they wanted to bring Christians here, that's why they've developed this programme here and not in Macedonia. The programme says: "if you want to come to Thrace, you will own a house, but if you don't want to, then go wherever you please but you won't get a house." But of course, people prefer to find a job rather than

> somewhere to live, work is the most important goal and housing comes next. That's why they go to Salonika. But, of course, it's easier for them to give them a house than a job. There is no work around here, not even for those who were born here. There aren't any factories, they're all a long way from the center. (T3)

At the end of the day, the instrumentalization of the settlements responds mainly to the context of a border area:

> Maybe because many of us have taken part in many different local wars in the former Soviet Union, we have skilled soldiers, all of us are in some part soldiers here. When we are living on the borders, because of demographic reasons, we become soldiers. (T4)

Welfare Mix Dynamics

Since the 1990s, and corresponding to the height of changes in migratory processes in Southern Europe, a debate has emerged on the form the new style of cooperation between local authorities and the nonprofitmaking sector should take. This new approach is based on the positive assessment of the growing initiative being taken by NGOs in a number of fields including community work, health education, on-going training and social services, and others that have traditionally been dealt with by social policies. Relations between nongovernment organizations and trade unions and the different administrations are often based on informative and advisory tasks, as well as the delegation, or derivation towards other services.

Concerns about the intervention of the nonprofitmaking sector have coincided with demands from those sectors of the population that suffer most from social exclusion—the very poor, convicts, and the migrant population. However, these trends also imply other hazards, namely delegating too many services to the NGOs. These hazards are particularly evident in the critical discourses produced by respondents in Turin, with particular reference to the Catholic voluntary workers, the largest group of its type in the city:

> But we have to say that in the 1990s there have been some demands, which asked the public institution not to delegate services, and also to other bodies like the *Questura* and the *Prefettura*. They were accused of getting rid of the problem instead of taking on a responsibility role. The *volontariato* is open to collaboration but does not want a delegation of services. Until the end of the eighties, there was an important delegation in this city, above all for Caritas and the rest of the Catholic volunteers, nearly an absolute delegation of services. Another characteristic of the Turin case is that there is a strong tradition of *volontariato cattolico* (Catholic voluntary institutions), but not only from Caritas. (TU10)

During the 1990s, the decision to opt for a type of welfare mix system became the basis for standard discourse in the majority of Southern European cities. Despite this defense of the welfare mix philosophy, welfare mix practices are now irreversible, closely linked to the socioeconomic trends of the 1990s.

Nevertheless, these practices are the object of harsh criticism from some, especially in sectors from the Italian left, who are working as social volunteers. One such volunteer is the following respondent, who is in favor of taking on greater public responsibility in the management of social services:

> There is a huge gap between a society that defends acknowledged rights and ours, which still moves along the concept of charity. Private initiatives of social intervention, which emerged as voluntary associations through the real participation of citizens to the political and social life of the country, are present in all of Europe, but arrived here much later in the form of working opportunities "in black" for young people…. I don't mean to deprive the state of its functions and to subcontract them to a private sector which will not be controllable. There is a very big difference between the spontaneous movements advocating for human rights in the 1970s and the way young people are today, without any ideology or beliefs. (N2)

Nongovernment organizations can offer support and facilitate processes of social integration for immigrants, but the lack of labor stability they frequently suffer, and their lack of access to formal alternatives, such as applying for a bank loan, makes things extremely difficult for them:

> They are given an offer, a firm commitment that when they have…they can start work, and that can involve a wait of up to six and seven months, and just how are they going to be able to survive all that time? Can they ask the bank for a loan? Of course not. They can ask their friends, but not the bank. And that's the difference between us and them. (BM3)

The Welfare Mix Philosophy

The debate surrounding the construction of a welfare mix is based on the distinction between public and private and the privatization of public services. As the Immigration Commission in Lisbon informed us, the administration rejects the possibility of full privatization, as it believes this is the co-responsibility of public and private resources and that the best option for the future is for the efforts of both sides to be combined. Nevertheless, the somewhat unusual situation existing in the countries of Southern Europe, where the welfare state is still considerably underdeveloped—due to the historical and political circumstances of recent years—means that attempts are being made to implement a welfare mix before the welfare state has become firmly established. Government response tends to be an indirect appeal to the traditional strength of family ties and informal connections (friends and neighbors). This is particularly true of Southeastern Europe and the cities of Naples, Algeciras, and Thrace. The lack of services and associationism are therefore compensated by solidarity networks,[11] an element they believe needs to be promoted.

Generally speaking, the welfare mix receives the support of all the local authorities, a support which is openly expressed in the discourse produced in

Barcelona and Algeciras. On the other hand, the most vociferous critics of the welfare mix have been the Italian associations. We have observed that a frequent tactic employed in the welfare mix debate has been to appeal to the need to end charitable actions and work toward enabling the immigrant communities to defend their own interests:

> I believe the most important thing is to put an end to charity and to continue to look for a means of working *with* the communities rather than for them. (AL10)

Petmesidou et al. (1994, 1996) underline the divergent transition paths across Europe according to historical trends of socio-structural patterns, the patterns of conflicts and contradictions related to the variations of welfare capitalism in North-West Europe, and the State/paternalistic structures in the South. Within Southern Europe, traveling along a path from the Northwest to the Southeast, significant differences are observed as to the economic structure, the state-civil society relationship, and, particularly, to the strength of civil society vis-à-vis state authority and interventionism. In the case of Greece, the rapid change from agrarian structures to a service-oriented society has led to weaker collective forms of solidarity and universalism in welfare provision than in the rest of Southern Europe. In the South-East (Greece and other Balkan countries) the traditions of contractual relations, collective solidarity, and active civil society are weakest. Hence, statism and clientelistic forms of social organization typical of Southern Europe are, according to the author, accentuated as one goes further south and southeast. As noted in chapter 1, in contrast with the role of the Church in the countries of the Latin Rim, where Catholicism has strongly supported subsidiarity in the provision of welfare services, which, in turn, enhances the role of the family in welfare delivery as well as promoting voluntary action in social protection, Greece suffers from a lack of voluntary religious institutions acting as providers of welfare.

> The Church in Greece, compared to that of Italy, is weakly developed in terms of social welfare. Besides, the political relation is not the same; here the Church is very conservative and does not have such a political role. (T2).

A Network of Actors?

In the case of Turin, most of the respondents reiterated the existence of a "network of actors" whereby the local authorities provide the funding while the organization and management of the services is left up to the voluntary workers. The need for a network is not only the option preferred by the various workers, but it is also a response to the strategy whereby all aspects of this multi-dimensional phenomenon can be included. In the opinion of some respondents, the fact that the actors form part of an extensive network is simply a means of tackling the multi-dimensionality of the services demanded. The network system existing among the various members that interact in Turin has allowed systems to be set up to prevent users from requesting the same services twice. Relations between them are informal, rather than institutional.

Identifying the various administrative actors in Barcelona and Algeciras reveals an idea shared by many respondents: in order to understand relations between administrations it is necessary to first identify the responsibilities. The actors state that the central government should play the key role in immigration in terms of entry regulations, permits and regularization processes. The Autonomous Government of Catalonia should play a major role in terms of education—although responsibility for providing financial aid for aspects such as school meals would fall to the local authorities—and in the case of the Courts, the role should be carried out by the Autonomous Department of Justice.

As far as new arrivals are concerned, migrants in Barcelona have access to municipal shelters—where the number of days they are allowed to stay is limited. This, however, is an alternative resource for immigrants, in the event that the contact with their network should not yield successful benefits. Support from the various networks depends on the degree of settlement, cohesion, and solidarity that the immigrant enjoys:

> The way the immigration law works now means that not many slip through without any form of control; those traveling with a tourist visa have to give the address of the person they're staying with and who will take responsibility for them, so they already have an address prepared when they arrive. But of course, many have to put people up in their apartments and that's not easy, but we divide them up, that's the way our Gambian culture works; if there are twenty, then we share ten each, trying to help the others to get started, that's the way we think. (BM2)

An important factor for consideration is the degree of immigrant socialization when making use of a social service system. According to a respondent from Cáritas, the Latin Americans are the group most familiar with these systems, while the Moroccans are the least familiar with them:

> It depends on the country; for instance, socially, these structures don't exist in Morocco. You talk about social services and appear with a social worker and they look at you as though you were talking double Dutch. The social worker doesn't exist there. The Latin Americans though, are fully aware that it is a profession that exists within a specific structure. (B7)

In Algeciras, the local authority's social service department not only provides assistance, but also tackles social policy issues through its Immigrant Co-ordination Committee. Early initiatives included meetings with migrant support associations, and a series of workshops were organized. Later the Immigrant Co-ordination Committee was set up,[12] the first and only initiative of this kind to exist for some time in Andalusia, although Cadiz also saw the creation of an Immigration Platform. The solidarity network created in Algeciras has no formal organization, relying instead on those persons that pick up newly arrived migrants on the road and offer them shelter, food, and dry clothing. Yet the recent stepping up of police controls and fines for those offering these services has generated a certain amount of fear. This type of solidarity is completely removed from all forms of organized aid. It is a spontaneous attitude of solidarity, similar to that shown by the *Puglieses*, in Southern Italy, following the arrival of the Albanians by sea.[13]

During the course of our fieldwork, we frequently encountered difficulty in ascertaining whether or not these assistance networks were at work in Lisbon. The Portuguese High Commissioner for Immigration holds a privileged relationship with the oldest immigrant association, the Cape Verdian association, and which is precisely the community that made the greatest contribution to his appointment.

> The High Commissioner should report on the projects, and he meddles in immigration affairs as if he were the boss. The associations in the city are linked to the powers; if you go out to these districts just see how many computers you'll actually find…the Portuguese government has to decide how it wishes to deal with immigration, a decision it hasn't taken so far. (L6)

With regard to the immigrant population in Portugal, the institutions demonstrate a positive discrimination towards those countries linked historically to the country, through the application of reciprocal rights, as in the case of voting rights, and rights to medical care. As referred, the Dutch model has acted as a permanent reference for the Portuguese model, particularly as a model for adaptation based on the firm establishment of immigrant associations, combined with a state social service model of a universalist nature, similar to the French model. Yet the details of these models remain unclear; associationism in Portugal is not yet ready for a project in which associations form the basis of the migratory integration policy. Moreover, the question of foreign immigration is interlinked with other essential issues, such as rehousing projects that require action mainly from the local authorities. The shantytowns are the spatial representation of the labor niches in the construction sector. This is a major problem which, according to a representative of the Oeiras Local Authority, has provoked three differing types of reaction and action: those local authorities—including Oeiras—that have successfully dealt with the problem; those that are gradually overcoming the problem—like the socialists in Lisbon; and those communist-controlled councils that have been left behind due to their reluctance to accept the PER.

Type of actors. In Portugal, only two types of institutional actors exist: the state and the private social solidarity institutions (IPSS), which are gradually becoming more firmly established among all levels of the population. In the case of immigration, these institutions take the form of district associations.

The fact that there are only two types of institutional actors is due to the low levels of regionalization in the Portuguese governmental system—administrative and political autonomy exists in the Azors and in Madeira—as well as the restricted powers of the local authorities in social affairs.

Despite the major role played by Cáritas, which in the majority of cases studied is considered a semi-institutional actor, the specific nature of Algeciras as a border and transit city has positioned the Red Cross as the key figure for migrant support and services:

> In Algeciras the Red Cross is more important than Cáritas. Here the role played by Cáritas is weak. (AL10).

Cáritas and the Muslim associations stand out as the main religious-based semi-institutional actors. In some cases, reference is also made to the legitimate role of the Imams in managing services as in Turin:

> But over here the Imams are people who took the Koran in their hands and started preaching. The are self-nominated and pretend to guide people through prayer, but I think they only represent themselves and I don't accept that they ask for things, as there is no real unity among Muslims. I remember that when Italians living in Algeria wanted to pray, they went to the only church, which was available. There were not enough churches for the Christians, the Algerians, and all others.... They ask for a Koranic school for their children, but here the school is state run. They are asking for something completely new! Because they are semi-illiterate. However, the Imams over here were not elected by people or sent by their countries and as such I don't consider them. (TU2)

In the case of Greece, the associations and the Church—in this instance the Ethiopian Orthodox Church—are forced to intervene in various issues that are not covered by non-institutional applications, such as housing. In the Greek context in general, and in the specific case of Athens, the role of the Orthodox Church is one of the most distinct factors in comparison to the welfare mix experiences referred to in other cases:

> If you compare it with Italy, here the Church has not developed very much in the social field. They finance a few residences for the chronically ill and for the elderly—more have been set up over the last few years. The connections between politics and the Church are not like in Italy. Here they are more conservative, they don't have so much political weight. Only rarely does the Church get involved in any political activity. (T2)

ASSOCIATIONS AS THE CENTER OF THE WELFARE MIX. In our analysis of the welfare mix space we have studied the discourse of the various actors involved in some form or another in local immigration policies. Yet it is particularly the discourse generated from within the associations working in the area of immigration that has afforded us a privileged insight into the welfare mix space. These associations have often anticipated the work of the institutions, and have also had the greatest impact on the construction of immigrant networks.

The case of Lisbon provides us with a clear example of this centrality. In Portugal, and since the 1996 regularization process, the associations have played a major role, both in terms of disseminating information and orienting and managing the regularization process itself. Indeed, it is during this time that the associations initiate a period of mobilization. Yet the degree of mobilization varies according to the associations, which opt to operate in varying ways. For example, when organizing the regularization process, *La Casa de Brasil* focused principally on its own community in order to guarantee sufficient infrastructure—access to the Internet and its recourses, such as mailings. It was not until the 1990s that the associations started to establish political relations, specifically as a result of the 1993 and 1996 regularization processes. There also exist some cases of organizations that adopted a legal format other than that of the association, the IPSSs (Private Social Solidarity Institutions), governed by Legal Decree 111/93 dated February 25. These IPSSs may assume the format of Social Solidarity Associations, thereby entitling them to benefit from favorable conditions when entering into contracts with the state and the local power. Other associations also choose to carry out more globally oriented actions, such as the Lisbon-based Associação Cavo-Verdiana (Cape Verdian Association), or collaborate with other local associations that represent the daily life of these geographical groups. Their working methods also vary considerably. Cape Verdian associations are mainly concerned with questions of literacy and, more recently, with women´s issues and vocational training courses for the young. However, the locally based associations opt instead for activities that are closer to the immigrant's daily lifestyle, where soccer is of major importance.

The rise in associationism can be partly explained by the need for solidarity among the immigrants themselves and the defense of their rights. Indeed, despite not having the appropriate structures, the associations play an essential role in acting as mediators between migrants and the administration. Their workers are mainly returning migrants from the former colonies. The strength of the Cape Verdian community in comparison with other communities is to a large extent the result of not only the fact that it is the longest-standing group in Portugal, but also because its members are present in all sectors of society, from the ministries right down to the construction sector, and for this reason they have been able to exert the pressure necessary in order to obtain the greatest number of benefits. The other associations do not share these advantages. An example of this type of association is the Guinean Bissau association, a far more recent arrival in Portugal in comparison with other communities from Cape Verde and Angola, attracted by the available opportunities existing at the time in the construction sector. The Cape Verdian community, on the other hand, is present in more skilled labor market sectors. Today the Guinean association[14] occupies a central position in the search for alternative welfare, capable of exerting a considerable amount of pressure in order to obtain immigrant rights, although it tends to focus more specifically on the rights of the Guinean community. It is extremely active as an interlocutor with the government. Furthermore, this association has greater influence than others in questions of social intervention, unlike the Cape Verdian association, which is far more cultural in nature, and is involved in vocational training, providing support for families in need—food parcels, document organization, services for foreigners—exerting pressure in order to obtain permits—and family reunion. Another interesting aspect is its work in health issues and in the legal field, by means of agreements with lawyers whereby they receive quotas in exchange for dealing with the most difficult cases.

Firstly, it is necessary to draw attention to the way in which associations play a key role in welfare mix processes. One of the reasons for this is that they were the first to address the issue. This can be seen in the network analyzed in Mataró, which naturally is far smaller than that of Barcelona and where relations could be considered far more personalized. Consequently, and unlike Barcelona, which is often the center for provincial associations, there are only a few immigrant associations, and the interlocutors are always clear. In Mataró, this is the case of Jama Kafo,[15] an association formed by Gambian and Senegalese immigrants that has set up a series of health care projects in conjunction with the local authority, targeting both the Gambian population in Mataró and cooperation projects in the Gambia (with a hospital and female agricultural workers). In spite of the difficulties they encountered, it must be said that many of these associations laid the foundations for the task institutions. This association once again serves as an example, as it began working in the Maresme region without the support of any form of infrastructure or organization:

> At first, this association was the meeting place for all the migrants in the city of Mataró. It later lost much of its influence following the creation of a large number of smaller associations such as the Mali Immigrants Association, or the Maresme Senegalese Association, etc. However, these associations only have around twenty members. Their main goal is to set up a stand at one of the multicultural fairs organized from time to time by the Council or a residents' association. It's headed by a well-off Gambian family with political connections. Today this association doesn't attract as many people as it used to. (BM7)

Associations are a key element of welfare mix dynamics because they are often the only possible option available. In the case of Turin, it can be observed how associationism is the last resort used by immigrants in demanding assistance, after having probably first appealed unsuccessfully to their own networks and to the formalized social services:

> Foreigners come here when they have already been around the services of the whole
> city. Therefore, you have to work with very complicated situations. So, it is difficult to
> give them an answer, or at least to give them the answer they are expecting. (TU1)

Once they have applied to the two levels mentioned above, namely migrant
networks and formalized services, what factors then determine the migrant's
choice of a particular association? It would appear that vital factors in this
choice include the networks themselves and the external symbols of the association:

> To be frank, the foreigner moves from his/her needs; there is not so much an ideology
> of where to go, and the ideology comes afterwards. We are talking here about more
> specific demands: housing and work. For example, Somalian people go all to the
> Caritas, either the one for males or the one for females, to ask for jobs and a house—
> they do everything there. But there are so many foreigners who come from countries
> in which services are completely different; they do not have this domesticity, this
> relation with this type of structure. However, Caritas gives them this feeling; even if it
> is big, it gives them security. Because when a Muslim woman goes to Caritas all
> covered up... I mean, what the foreigner sees is the efficiency of the response. (TU1)

It is interesting to observe the way in which the selection is made from the
range of service options available. In addition to Turin, we have also observed
the way in which these choices are made in Barcelona. The NGOs also admit
that the migrants prefer them to institutional actors, as they inspire a greater
sense of trust. Variations in these preferences occur according to geographical
origin; the Ecuadorians, for example, prefer Cáritas due to its dependence on
the Catholic Church:

> If you don't have a job or papers then you will tend to go more to these organizations.
> All Ecuadorians come to Cáritas, because they are involved in and have close cultural
> links with the Church, so as a Church organization they see us as being fairly close to
> them, while they see the administration as the lion's den. (B4).

Consequently, it can be seen that in addition to the characteristics referred to
above, and which influence the specific features of the demand, the self-help
migrant networks play a major role in promoting the use of these channels
rather than the more institutionalized ones. In Barcelona, the Chinese and
Filipino communities rely most heavily on their own networks, as well as the
Pakistanis, unlike the Moroccans, who tend to make greater use of the SAIER
(Servei d'Atenció a Immigrants, Estrangers i Refugiats. Migrants and Refugees Welfare Service) or OPAS:[16]

> Because regardless of whether they're good or bad, the Filipinos and Chinese have
> self-help networks, which in the case of the Filipinos are really effective: they know
> when they're arriving, they are there to receive them, and they've got a job and
> accommodation waiting for them.... If instead of being a Philippine you're a Pakistani

woman, then it's not the same…because the Pakistanis have their own special character-istics. But if you're Moroccan then there are other difficulties involved because the group isn't organized: they come here, they're completely lost and when they need an organization they go to the SAIER or the OPAS and they enter an administrative support system, but that's not the case with many other communities. (B10)

In the case of Nuova Famiglia[17] in Turin, the integration of the welfare mix can be clearly observed, making this association a highly original initiative, a private structure working in a private way. On the other hand, the Turin-based Alma Mater is another integrated example that enjoys a privileged position within the borough in terms of its financial management, which resulted in a series of political problems:

> The Alma Mater is in part sustained by the Cooperativa La Talea but also by the Comune of Turin. It has been an attempt to get closer to women in difficulties. It still maintains this strong discrimination as a Center for women. However, from my point of view that makes no sense in a multicultural society, because it emphasizes the difference. But the positive thing is that the budget for immigration from the Comune has been very strong, which provoked strong attacks from the opposition, and elec-toral campaigns from the right. (TU1).

Despite the role assigned to immigrant associations as actors in the welfare mix, in practice a series of impediments exist due to the fact that these associa-tions are still in their early stages. As a result, and as in other countries such as Italy where similar situations exist, the development of immigrant associa-tions in Barcelona has recently encountered several obstacles. This is basi-cally due to the lack of institutional support and the precarious socioeconomic position of the various communities, as well as internal difficulties, which prevent them from consolidating their representations. The lack of internal cohesion and the need for strong leadership in immigrant associations are frequent complaints among the majority of actors, as expressed by an expert from the Barcelona City Council in reference to the divergent opinions ex-pressed by immigrants regarding the fight to obtain the right to vote:

> Today there's a fair amount of distrust and disagreement among immigrants. For instance, if you ask them whether they are interested in fighting for the right to vote, you find some who are and some who aren't, who say that putting food on their plate is the most important thing, and that it's a political instrumentalization. (B8).

One of the principal problems in Turin in terms of actor intervention has been the excessive role conferred upon the organizations, despite the fact that they are still in the early stages of development:

> On the other hand, migrant associations like the Filipinos and the Egyptians have always been very weak. They have always been coordinated by the *Comune*, other-wise they just wouldn't work. Considering the weakness of the associations, the

Comune has always had a problem of representativeness, and the Consulta was chosen, in order to provide a classical instrument of representativeness. Even though you cannot say that the associations do not exist, they do, but we expect them to have a greater presence in the future or to have a propositive role, political representation. I realize that once their personal problems have been solved, their attention turns to the demands of everyday life. (TU10)

Secondly, when defining welfare mix dynamics it is also necessary to determine exactly which type of NGOs we are referring to, as they are not all equal in strength. For example, migrant associations in Spain today are still lacking the force and representativeness necessary to tackle the responsability frequently demanded of them by the various administrations. It is important to mention that the centrality of associations in welfare mix processes varies depending on the country, and particularly emphasizes the contrasts already discussed: the North-South contrast and the difference with the border areas. Unlike the rest of Southern Europe, in Italy the emphasis is placed on the creation of cooperatives for research into services as well as training and management. In the case of the Naples-based Dédalus we can also see how relations with the various associations depend on the type of community.

The associations do not agree with suggestions to raise the ratio of immigration in Mezzogiorno, as there is only a weak social awareness among citizens and an as yet nonexistent welfare mix. One of the principal problems of the representativeness of associations on a local scale, particularly evident in the Mezzogiorno cities, was that the immigrant communities were still unprepared for the Consulta Municipale (Municipal Consultancy Service).

In Italy, social cooperatives fill a large gap left by local authority action to a far greater extent than in other Southern European countries. These types of foundations are also to be found in Barcelona, an example of which is SODEPAU (Solidaritat per el Desenvolupament i la Pau [Association for Development and Peace]), whose achievements include having popularized participative action techniques. In the case of the NGOs, cases of discrimination in renting accommodations to immigrants are becoming far more transparent, as indicated by SODEPAU in the studies carried out in the Old City as part of the Xenofilia project:

We have two programs, an accommodation rental service and a mediation service.... For one of the studies we diagnosed the accommodation situation in Barcelona's Ciutat Vella (Old City), we noticed that discrimination existed in the rents, in the APIs.[18] And not only that, but there was also a lot of precarious accommodation at really exorbitant prices, and a lot of mistrust. (B2).

In the case of Algeciras and Naples, the most surprising aspect is that unlike Barcelona and Turin, the associative structure simply does not exist. Furthermore, Algeciras suffers also from problems experienced by other border areas and sites such as Sebta, and the associations, in particular Algeciras Acoge, are forced to cope with all the front line situations that exist in border areas, which are also areas of transition and often conflict:

> At Algeciras Acoge we indirectly get many of the problems of Sebta and the reception program. The numbers of people waiting in Sebta are growing all the time. The first to arrive are waiting at the wall, but behind them are the ones in Camp Calamocarro. There must be around 5,000 waiting now. (AL3)

Today, the general tendency is for associations to work in specific fields, with the exception of Algeciras Acoge,[19] which acts as a key pivot for all immigrant-related matters in Algeciras. This association appears as a privileged actor, not only because of the extent of its scope but also due to its excellent relations with the local authority.

In Algeciras we also find the action of the Asociación Pro-derechos Humanos de Andalucía (Andalusian Pro-Human Rights Association). Its philosophy is based on the need to open up all frontiers. They work somewhat sporadically in the area surrounding the Straits of Gibraltar, helping immigrants on the road and providing them with shelter in private homes, which has led them to be heavily sanctioned. It is also important to mention the task of the FAVA,[20] which reveals how the question of the immigrant depends on the types of need and group.

Thirdly, we must consider the various types of associations. It is difficult to determine exactly the influence associations have on the welfare mix process due to the differences existing between them and the varying functions they perform and the activities they provide. Here we have opted to consider a wide range of associations. They can be classified according to whether they are (1) associations made up exclusively of autochthonous members, and therefore considered to be support associations, which includes the social cooperatives; (2) associations with an ethnic or national base—for example, the case of the Kurds; (3) mixed associations made up of members of various national origins; (4) associations with a religious basis; (5) mixed women's associations; (6) professional associations, such as groups of lawyers; and (7) international support associations. Associations vary both in formation and size. Associations made up of only a few members and of a semi-family atmosphere are often criticized strongly by those interviewed. In addition, the nature of the various associations obviously varies according to the type of actions they carry out, including sports and cultural services, etc. The better-organized groups are those that benefit the most from the "pseudo welfare" systems. However, in the case of other associations, such as those whose objectives are culturally oriented, their goals tended not to include legal services. In these cases, the solution lay in delegating these matters to other social actors, or alternatively in resorting to the use of external lawyers or even individuals who sympathize with the objectives of the association.

The traditional problem suffered by associations with regard to welfare mix processes is that they have been characterized by an exaggerated interest in cultural activities. This has been particularly true in those areas where associationism is least developed, as in Greece. In Athens, immigrant associations have mainly been of a cultural nature. They have also undergone a major transformation process since their prohibition to the current fight in favor of immigrant rights. Despite attempts in the late 1990s to set up a network (*Dyktio*), which was the sole immigrant experience at the time the fieldwork was carried out, it was harshly criticized for its radical political nature and for the ineffectiveness of the measures adopted, as described by the association.

Cultural motives also dominated the associations set up in Thrace. The perspective used in this case, based on the division of communities, shows how even if two communities are made up of Greek citizens their demands are placed on very different levels. While Pontian associations deal mostly with cultural activities and display an eagerness to preserve their traditional folklore, in the case of the Turkish associations their strategy is mainly political, and they use a politicized discourse critical of the Greek administration and its opaque conception of diversity. Although they address cultural issues, their greatest demand is for rights and services. As a result, one of the bases for action from associations and also a point of reference between them is the call for immigrant rights. Consequently, the issue goes far beyond an attempt to provide socioeconomic resources and to preserve the culture of the country of origin, and extends to a search for means of becoming full citizens, as also indicated by SOS Racisme and CITE in Barcelona.

The ASGI,[21] an association of lawyers, stands out in Turin as a major actor in dealing with migration and rights. The question of rights also extends to issues such as migrant's involvement in politics at a local level, a goal that has been particularly addressed in Italy. Although the Consulta is merely a consultative body, it is made up of representatives chosen by foreign immigrants in Turin,[22] The locally organized Consultas in Italy attempted to provide foreign immigrants with a greater degree of representation. The idea was for the Consulta to function as an effective form of mediation between immigrant associations and the general community. In practice it encountered grave difficulties in terms of both representativeness and operability. The alternatives and capacity of the Consulta were restricted following the introduction of a geographic quota, in other words, the larger the number of residents the greater the representation on the Consulta. Eventually, this led to a situation whereby the Moroccans voted exclusively for the Moroccans, thereby producing a perverse effect on the results.

What the associations ultimately offer is services, and this is their major contribution to the welfare mix. They supplement issues related to immigrant family policies, for example, by providing nursery services. These services are clearly in evidence in the associations of the districts of Lisbon,[23] which, with the exception of Athens, is unlike other cases. Curiously enough, and despite the low level of associationism in Athens, both the Filipino and Pan-African nursery services are well developed.

In the case of Lisbon, the associations have received considerable support from the European Union's URBAN[24] project. This is especially true of the 6 de Maio district, where the district associations are even referred to as the "new nuns." The greatest problem facing these associations is training for males, as they tend to prefer immediate labor insertion in the construction industry. There are services also related to the young. A good example of these associations at a district level is the Moîhno da Juventude Cultural Association in the Venda Nova district. This association was set up in 1984 and was directed principally at women and children, although over the years, the association has become a kind of training center. It currently works with children of various ages. The most recent project set up by this association was to create a laundry for young, irregular eighteen- and nineteen-year-old Cape Verdians. Today they have a greater dependence on the European Institute programs. With regard to this type of services it must be said that relations between associations in Portugal appear to be very fluid, despite natural differences in criteria existing between religious and lay associations. On a cultural level, a number of associations in Lisbon are heavily criticized for their socio-cultural integration models, due partly to the fact that Portugal has still not fully engaged a post-colonial period. This leads to a reluctance to abandon the former traditional hierarchies regarding the superiority of the colonist. Critics also claim that Portugal has no immigration policy and that the idea that young Luso-Africans lack a sense of identity is untrue.

Space, Welfare, and Racism

It is the urban space that provides us with the physical manifestation of racism in the city and that reflects the racial conflicts based on a clearly spatial formation. The city of Turin serves to illustrate this through the special public dormitories it created, concentrating its immigrants in certain degraded areas in the quarters of San Salvario and Porta Palazzo, which provoked reactions from the native population. Generally speaking, the problems are here related to conflicts arising from the manner in which urban space is divided.

In the 1960s, the cities of Northern Italy organized committees to fight for housing, education, and social services, which were structured along territorial lines. The 1980s saw the introduction of environmentalist committees. As for security committees,[25] these began to appear in the late 1980s, making use of the same territorial-based formula and incorporating some of the discourses initially produced in the 1960s regarding urban degradation and lack of services. This threatening discourse was one way of reacting to the social changes and crises of recent years. The crisis in terms of financial and individual resources experienced in the late 1980s, plus the attack on the system of social policy guarantees—linked to the Fordist productive system—and the crisis of the political representation and social mediation channels—with the consequent lack of resources—all constituted intertwined factors related to the difficulties involved in urban life. All of this explains the background against which a growing sense of insecurity was beginning to be felt among the population, which, in turn, provides an explanation for the creation of these new urban committees. The central discursive element of the idea of a threat therefore acquires a double meaning. On the one hand, it is seen as a series of specific episodes that act as reasons behind the protests. On the other hand, it also acquires the character of a rumor that is typical of these episodes: the location of the threat, a sense of continued unease, which points to the association with an underlying, non-rationalized insecurity. Nor can we overlook the fact that the protests of these committees are also associated with other changes taking place in the urban space, such as the gentrification or rehabilitation of working-class urban areas, converting them into middle-class areas. This is taking place in several urban areas in Northern Italy—some of which have been the scene of major demonstrations, such as the historical center of Genoa, Corso Buenos Aires, and Milan's Directional Center.

Two parallel trends have played a part in the development of committees during the 1990s. The first is the result of the action of specific groups led by individuals who consider themselves to be apolitical, despite the fact that several of them have admitted to having been politically active in the past. The second constitutes a group of certain local politicians that defend tighter restrictions on foreign immigration. In general terms, two different types of committees can also be distinguished: those in favor of applying restrictive measures on immigration and on other areas that they claim generate a lack of security; and those less influential committees, whose activity is limited to engaging a spirit of protest. The committees have increased their capacity for organization, albeit intermittently so, depending on their communicative resources and their relational ability for making themselves heard among the influential spheres of local society. The harshest forms of protest, accompanied by street blockades and organized community watch groups are now also combined with, and on occasion even replaced by, other measures aimed at putting up a "gentler" fight against social exclusion, based on mediating with local institutions.

Generally speaking, relations between the committees and the forces of order have a three-fold effect, which has a considerable impact on the social formation of the deviant-migrant and, consequently, on the nature of local information. Firstly, by constantly emphasizing the presence of drug trafficking, transvestites and black prostitutes, illegal camps, etc.—always through the media—there has been increased ad hoc intervention by the police on numerous occasions, which has intensified the repression of a specific category of migrant. Secondly, it is highly conceivable that the media and initiatives of the committees have exerted considerable influence on the way in which the security forces operate. Finally, the committees also exert a certain amount of pressure in relation to the security forces, in the transferring opinions from the former to the latter.[26] This third factor reveals how sound and prudent judgment can put an end to the viewing of the migrant as deviant or abnormal, by communicating common sense to the "citizen"—and the media—and to the police.

There have also been instances of conflict over space in Catalonia. One of the most controversial issues during the period of our interviews was that of racial conflicts sparked by events such as those in Premià de Mar,[27] which had a direct impact on the region. Respondents were faced with a media blitz on racist issues following similar events in Terrassa, Girona, Banyoles, and El Ejido.[28] As a result of these tragic episodes, issues of prevention are discussed far more openly than before, which is a logical consequence of events of this nature that occurred because of a lack of foresight on the part of local authorities, who should be more aware of the problems and tensions existing in everyday life. This issue has become a topic for reactive reflection; where the practice of everyday life has created reflection:

> Provision must continue to be made, but at the same time action must also be taken in those places where conflict has broken out: the events in Mataró, Banyoles, and Martorell all indicate that it's too late for prevention, and what's needed now is direct intervention. (B3)

> I think that the advantage in Barcelona is that since the early eighties a lot of work has been done on prevention culture and policies. And this is having an effect in both the political and technical spheres: the question of prevention, of working without conflicts. (B9)

There appears to be a desire to encourage a sense of preventative logic in regard to community race relations, especially in working with the indigenous population. Frequently, it is the native population that complains not only about the dangers in the street—during the summer of 2000 Catalonia witnessed the formation of citizen defense patrols in Barcelona's Old City— but also about the unequal distribution of welfare and social benefits. The rejection of migrants partly mirrors the rejection of the gypsies, specifically in terms of the problems that affect both groups. It is interesting to note how some local authorities have failed to resolve the settlement problems concerning the extremely poor living conditions and the serious difficulties of the itinerant population in accessing medical care. Complaints by local residents against gypsy families are based on their lack of hygiene, high noise levels, and the supposedly preferential treatment they receive in terms of social benefits. Conflicts normally arise following a specific crime against residents and these conflicts have come to symbolize the so-called social racism in Spain. Problems occur following flare-ups between residents, which then lead to racist comments and insults. Local community work would appear to be the most effective antidote for these conflicts and the way to achieve resident integration:

> In Santa Caterina—a central area of Barcelona—when there was the case of that migrant who had committed various thefts and rapes—the first to react were the local immigrant organizations, the residents' associations, etc., who said, "Don't get it wrong, this is not typical of the whole group." For instance, there's some excellent community work being done in Ciutat Vella, and lots of experts are working really hard and there are really good relations with the organizations, and this helps to prevent more conflicts from breaking out, but this is a social question. (B8)

In Thrace, on the plains to the south of Xanthi, Komotini, and Sappes one can find Turkish Muslim villages, while the Pomaks live in the mountainous north. Christian settlements are distributed primarily along the coastal zone of these prefectures; the prefecture of Evros is almost exclusively made up of Christian settlements. In Komitini, the neighborhoods are highly segregated and it is not difficult to differentiate between Greek middle-class areas, Turkish working-class areas, and new areas of Pontian settlements. In addition to the spatial segregation, differences in the types of construction are also in evidence: the Turks, for example, build low, white houses with small windows, often with satellite TV discs on the roofs. The gypsies are found on the outskirts of Komotini, in an area with muddy roads where small children of the neighborhood seem to be the guardians of the area. The Turkish-Greek divide of the city represents two different societies with weak or nonexistent personal relationships between the two. In Sappes, the division of space is also quite marked, with the Turks on one side, the Greeks on another, the Pontians on yet another, in addition to the military sector. The spatial organization of the different communities is really very illustrative of their socioeconomic conditions. Now all groups also have access to satellite TV, except the Pontians, who are currently trying to organize a system in order to receive Russian TV. Paradoxically, the settlement policies administered from Athens and shaped in Sappes have led to forms of spatial segregation rather than forms of spatial cohesion:

> Its a crime that the houses were built over there because, they are separate, they speak Russian and the Uzbekistan language. Yes, it is a ghetto, a ghetto. A lot of people don't come to the center of Sappes, they just stay there, they are watching the Russian channel and they have been here for almost five years and they don't know how to speak Greek; how will we communicate? And now the mayor got the OK from the central city of Athens and from the government, so that he can build about sixty houses between Sappes and the small city, the ghetto, so the city of Sappes can finally get together. (T11)

It is also important to stress the fact that in addition to racial problems that occur due to spatial conditions, the discourse on racist issues range from the historical characteristics of the receiving areas to the distinctive forms of national identity. In Greece, for instance, the harshest criticisms link classical xenophobia and the concept of national identity with the context of modern-day immigration:

> Here in Greece, racism isn't the same, it's different; it's not just a question of color, it's foreigners in general. Greek people have always been afraid of foreigners and that's why racism and nationalism get mixed up together. Here, nationalism and foreigners is the same thing. That's why you see the question of Greek identity in Europe. The Orthodox religion is linked to the idea of what's "Greek" and the sense of national identity. A good Greek has to be orthodox. (AT16)

On the other hand, the discourse in Lisbon centers around values related to tolerance and a spirit of mixing—the notion of a creole Lisbon—as well as the traditional flexibility of Southern Italians:

> In Naples there is more tolerance. Naples is almost not a racist city as we are used to mixing. (N9)

Interestingly, in Portugal, a country of "gentle customs," we also encounter signs of racism. Despite these "gentle customs" and despite the fact that Portugal declares itself non-racist and non-xenophobic, Portuguese society does display various indications of crypto-discrimination. The clearest example of this is the stigmatized image of black Africans as unskilled workers who are channeled towards the construction and cleaning sectors. On the other side of the social ladder, there is a general hostility towards anything Spanish,[29] which today manifests itself in an antagonistic reaction against the massive influx of Spanish products. However, the context of Portuguese society is similar to that of Spain, in that both are structured around rigid class systems and have experienced a rapid growth of the middle classes, thereby creating a specific setting for the reception of foreigners. In contrast to the Portuguese miscegenation, the supposedly tolerant Andalusia is now beginning to reveal its darker side:

> It must be admitted that there is no long-standing tradition of immigration in Andalusia. In El Ejido it has only been going on for seven years. There hasn't been any integration, and that's been a bit of a shock for the newcomers. Besides, bad stories about the Moroccans have been passed down from parents to their children and grandchildren. (AL9).

Therefore, in the Andalusian city of Algeciras, foreign immigrants are now the scapegoats of racism:

> In the stores of the Algeciras bazaars around the markets there's a considerable amount of bad feeling. The quality stores have gradually moved further up. The gypsies used

to be blamed for everything that went on in the center, but now the blame is being put on the Moroccans. The bazaars have gradually closed down; they used to act as wholesalers, for fake Adidas tracksuits. (AL9)

Finally, racism takes on its most virulent expression in the areas of irregularity and delinquency:

It's not only the children that are affected by this reality that mixes irregularity and delinquency, but also the adults, whom many conceive as the *minority of troublemakers*, and the cause of distorted generalizations that eventually become the basis for racist conflicts among residents, a phenomenon that has recently been termed social racism. (BM2)

From the Southern European Model to Its Borders

In order to see the elements common to Southern Europe we have previously defined a migratory context of reception. Three lines of arguments supported this approach: the novelty of the immigration, its interaction with a weak welfare state, and its interaction with a certain type of family structure (a conception of welfare based on the family structure). As far as the shared elements are concerned, we underlined a Southern European model based on ideal typical cases that fit into the various areas of migration management, and which are more clearly in evidence in certain cases than in others.

The case-focused research revealed the processes observed in the cities and brought about by migratory flows: (1) the spatial segmentation or fragmentation of production and (2) the re-localization of economic activities, namely the processes of economic centralization and decentralization. Marginality frequently tends to be associated with dualist theses regarding the existence of two segments within the economy and society (the developed center versus the poor, exploited, and underdeveloped periphery). In this sense, the social polarization model is here of increasing relevance, as it is inextricably linked to the new emerging social structure of immigration.

The first set of common elements to be found through the case studies is as follows:

1. Border restrictions and the relative non-regulation of immigration policies, the configuration of specific ports of entry where immigrant categories are of a more clearly transitory nature. The principal areas of geographical transit studied are Algeciras and Naples, and partially Thrace.
2. Emergency policies, considered particularly from the comments of Italian respondents located both in the north and the south of the country.
3. The lack of regulation of immigration policies and the impact of recent regularization processes. Of particular relevance here is the late development of immigration policies in the city of Athens.
4. The fairly original development of a locally administered welfare mix process for immigration, particularly in the cases of Turin and Barcelona.

Secondly, regarding labor market insertion, distinctions can be made between the particular features existing on the informal market in each of the fieldwork sites. Nevertheless, in general terms, the labor market is highly segmented, and has been developed within the context of a dominant informal sector, as can be seen from the survival strategies of Neapolitan families. The following are the principal common elements of the labor market: (1) communalities on the labor market and the importance of the construction sector for the local labor market, particularly in the case of Lisbon; the relevance of female migrants and an internationalization of domestic service in major Southern European cities; and (2) a strong gender segmentation that leads to a gender-segmented demand in the more developed service economies such as Turin, Barcelona, and Athens.

Thirdly, with the reference to the discourse on present development of the welfare state, we could pinpoint the following: (1) a confusion regarding the definition of models based on the generality or specificity of social services; (2) the relevance and impact of specific historical events on the city and country with regard to the administration of social services; (3) the relevance of the category of irregular immigrant as a paradigmatic case in the lack of social cover for immigrants and in their lack of human rights; and (4) a social racism based on welfare comparisons and on the divisions of the urban space.

An analysis of interviews was not only articulated through the common themes of the discourse that occurred in various places and was produced by diverse social actors, but particularly through the identification of contrasts and differences between the cases. A first major differentiating factor between these sites was identifying them as either Mediterranean European areas of transit or of settlement. This also highlights the radical opposition to the degree of socioeconomic development regarding the configuration of the urban labor market and the maturity or lack of maturity of the associations working with immigrants or the overall extent of urban associationism.

A second differentiating factor was produced when looking at changes from a multi-level perspective. Efforts have been addressed to allow an interpretation of changes in the context of diversity of patterns, times, and local conditions. As far as immigration policies are concerned, the discourse makes constant references to the impact and consequences of immigration regularization processes, the problems associated with family reunion, as well as gender implications (in the welfare mix dynamics).

Regarding gender implications, we highlighted how reciprocal and supportive activities involve one household spending some of its time to ensure the survival of another (Mingione 1991), thus, creating a space for the analyses of dual welfare processes: welfare for migrants and welfare for natives, in different contexts of welfare development. As we shall see, considering family reciprocity will also be a key for understanding changes when dealing with the second part of the book on border ethnographies.

A third differentiating factor was that immigration policies tend to contemplate the existence of a dominant migrant group for each of the cases studied: Moroccans in Turin, Barcelona, and Algeciras; Albanians in Athens; Pontians in Thrace; and Cape Verdians in Lisbon.

A fourth differentiating factor was space. Meanwhile, ethnic segregation, especially in U.S. research, has been found to be one of the main structural features for the perpetuation of urban poverty and racial inequality; however, it shows a different pattern for the case of Europe. This issue also addresses the problem of linearity in comparative work, which has been one of the main problems when dealing with evolutionary heritage in the social sciences. In addition to it, most of the patterns in the development of the global economy express themselves in terms of territory. In Europe, spatial contrasts are important to consider, for example in regard to housing conditions not only for foreigners but also for natives. The issue of spatiality highlights the broader picture of regional segregation and concentration issues in relation to migration.

In effect, most of the conceptual categories used in this part regarding globalization, the informal economy, subcontracting, feminization of migrants flows will be found again in the second part of the book. Moreover, the welfare mix dynamics have some interesting parallels with the patchwork economy of the border ethnographies. There are also resonances between the problems of health as the most exaggerated lack of universal migrants' rights and the commodification of the body in border areas as an allegory of extreme vulnerability provoked by global capitalism. Finally, in reflecting on the work of spaces of transit and settlement, emergency and border restrictions in Southern European cities, the narrative moves on to the concept of border, Mediterranean border cities of Southern Europe.

Notes

1. This treaty has already been discussed in the introductory section dealing with the case of Thrace. (endnote 38, chapter 1)
2. Greek nationalism (which had its golden period at the beginning of the twentieth century) was founded on the "Megali Idea (the Big Idea)"; the dream that placed Greece in two continents—Europe and Asia—with five seas—Aegean, Ionian, Black Sea, Marmara, and Crete Sea, with Constantinople (today's Istanbul) as its capital. It was President Venizelos who called on the Greeks to fight for the "Magna Greece"; after occupying Western Anatolia, their mission was to free their "repressed brothers." The second historical chains of events are those surrounding the more recent invasion of Cyprus in 1973 by Turkey. Secondly, the process of nation-state building and the definition of the foreigner leave no space for potential local social-policy dynamics. When delineating ways of accommodating minorities, two poles can be distinguished: an assimilationist and paternalistic policy of promoting the settlement of the Pontians and a communitarian policy based on the Treaty of Lausanne (and on the state of the Greek-Turkish relations).
3. The basis of religious institutions under the Ottoman Empire is the millet system. Under the millet, each religious group was allowed limited independence in running

its own community, under a recognized leader who represented the community. Matters of law related to personal status were also left to the community control.

4. Informazione Salute per Immigrati (Health Information Center for Immigrants).

5. Center d´ Informació per a Treballadors Estrangers (Foreign Workers' Information Center [office of the Trade Union]).

6. In the case of Turin, it is mainly church volunteers who deal with emergency related matters.

7. In other places, however, this figure does not exist: "The issue of family educators here isn't like in Catalonia. There aren't any cultural mediators working here, although there has been a course on it." (AL4)

8. The Spanish Institute of Health.

9. Special Reform Plan.

10. EIYAPOE (Ethnikó Idrima Epodhis Apodimon & Palinosteton Omogenou Einon), in other words, Foundation for Pontios Settlement, or the National Foundation for Greeks of the Diaspora.

11. It is true that in moments of need both the family and neighborhood networks constitute a major resource (consider Portuguese emigrants to Switzerland in the 1960s or the survival strategies often researched in the city Naples).

12. The Immigrant Co-ordination Committee was made up of the Algeciras Local Authority Social Welfare Department, Algeciras Acoge, the Immigrant Women Group from the Victoria Kent Association, the Red Cross, CITE (CCOO), FAVA (Federation of Andalusian Residents' Associations), UGT, the Immigrant Service Office, AME (Association for Marginalized Persons and Foreigners). It did not include the Local Authorities of La Línea de la Concepción, Tarifa or Los Barrios.

13. For more details on the workings of these solidarity networks, see Beatu Leuthardt (2002) *Aux marges de l'Europe*, particularly the chapters that refer to the province of Algeciras and the Pugliese region.

14. The characteristics of this association include the following: it is integrated into the district; it has a large number of members; it has religious links; great emphasis is placed on health issues; political contacts in Guinea are maintained and the refugee problem is tackled.

15. Appearing in the late 1970s-early 1980s, it is a good example of the vicissitudes encountered by ethnic-based immigrant associations in Catalonia.

16. Oficina Permanent d´Atenció Social (Social Service Office).

17. This association operates as a meeting and information point for mixed couples, particularly for the purposes of resolving legal issues such as the consent from the embassies for marriages between non-Muslim women and Muslim men, or in the event that the Law refuses to allow the marriage between an Italian national and an irregular migrant, or advice on international adoption procedures. At the time of the interview, this association was made up of twenty-five mixed couples.

18. Agents de la Propietat Immobiliària, Estate Agents.

19. The Algeciras Acoge association was set up in 1990, while immigrant aid from UGT (Trade Union) began in 1991. Initially, therefore, the only association in existence was Algeciras Acoge, which was later followed by others such as *Victoria Kent* and the Red Cross that focused on offering aid for the sick and homeless. All the *Acoge* associations in Andalusia belong to a large nongovernmental organization and are part of FAIN (the Federation of Pro-Immigrant Associations). This association deals with various aspects related to the quality of immigrants' lives, and offers legal advice as well as working on issues related to education and training.

20. Federation of Residents' Associations.

21. Associazione per le Studi Giuridici della Immigrazione (Association for Immigration Legal Studies).

22. The Consulta is normally made up of 21 members: 3 Moroccans; 1 Ecuadorian; 1 Jordanian; 1 Palestinian; 1 Nigerian; 2 Congolese; 1 Albanian; 2 Roma (from the former Yusgolavia); 1 Brazilian; 1 Chinese; 1 Egyptian; 1 Iranian; 1 Filipino; 1 Peruvian; 1 Somalian; 1 Tunisian.

23. Associative action in these districts is also combined with institutional support from the IAC (Instituto Apoio a Crianza—the Child Support Institute), particularly in the form of programs for children who do not receive sufficient attention from working parents.

24.. Part of the Community Initiative Program developed as part of the activity in urban areas and financed by European Union Structural Funds.

25. The term security committees (in Italian *comitati di sicurezza*) refers to those district committees set up in the late 1980s to protest against insecurity and the social and material degradation of the city, and which is normally attributed to the presence of immigrants or nomads. These committees represent a new type of actor that has been an almost constant presence in Italy's national and local press. The first significant event, which linked them with the relations between the native and immigrant populations, was a protest against the setting up of a nomad camp on the outskirts of Rome in 1987. Since then, a growing number of demonstrations have occurred in practically all central and northern cities, and which have been widely echoed in the media.

26. For example, the telephone number 113 is not merely a channel for communicating security requests to the police, but it is also an instrument for determining exactly which crimes constitute a real cause for concern among citizens.

27. The incident in Premià de Mar (in the province of Barcelona) began when a Moroccan assaulted a Spaniard over a debt related to the sale of drugs. The victim's family and friends turned this incident into a racist battle. They organized protests against Moroccans and distributed fascist pamphlets claiming that "the *moros* come here to steal and abuse the social services." The case received wide media coverage (especially in the local newspaper *El Punt*), and sparked rumors that skinheads from outside the area would attend the demonstrations to show their support. A counter-demonstration was organized to coincide with the protest.

28. The racial conflict, which was aimed particularly against the Moroccans and which occurred in El Ejido, in the province of Almeria in early February 2000, had a major impact on Spanish public opinion and also received international attention. Thus, El Ejido represents a before and after in migration studies and in public opinion in Spain. As the most extreme example of racial conflict in the country to date, it is an excellent example in the analysis of social conflict on a spatial level.

29. As the saying goes, "De Espahna ni bon vento ni bon casamento" (No good wind or marriage ever comes from Spain).

Part 2
Border Cities

Introduction to Part 2

This second part involves a conceptual and empirical development of the border city model. In chapter 3, I will develop the border, global, conceptual framework and method—as well as their elements—in order to integrate the city component, the border city to be described in chapter 4. All these elements are present in the city and we will see to what extent it enables and creates them. Chapter 3 explores those impacts provoked by economic globalization and international migration at an analytic stage. Hopefully, this exploration will enable me to place the details contributed by ethnographic research within the framework of the transformation of border cities.

The research methodology is articulated through an in-depth ethnography of two cities. Therefore, the research is multi-sited, although originally movement was seen only from the place of departure of migration flows. However, that movement is viewed neither while the migrants are actually on the move, nor from the perspective of the migrants' adaptation strategies in the receiving societies. My focus is on how mobilities are revealed in the definite locality of the household. After focusing on the general theoretical context I will next review the concepts needed to discuss the ethnographic work: the household strategy, the patchwork economy and the informal work.

In chapter 4, I use two borderland and harbor cities—Tangier in Morocco and Durrës in Albania—as strategic sites from which to examine the symbolic new borders of the European South. In these Mediterranean borderlands, one might hope to capture new movements based on transience, channeling, and control, as well as on the impact of globalization at the household level, by sorting through aspects of the "patchwork economy" (as we will discuss later). Even if treated as ethnographic pairs, (a) Durrës-Tirana and (b) Tangier, they are presented in a varied, different manner. For example, the ethnography on Durrës is slightly longer than that of Tangier. This is explained by how I have presented the ethnographies; the second ethnography tries to catch up with some interesting resemblances and contradictions of interplay with the ethnography developed earlier, bringing to light a topography with the border as the organizing trope.

Finally, following ethnographies (a) and (b) is a short, pertinent section matching the conceptual and empirical chapters of Part 2 as well as showing some interesting reflections that will be taken up again in the conclusions.

3

Border Cities in a Global Perspective

The Global Focus

The social sciences are only now starting to systematize explanations of the changes towards a global society. Most authors refer to a global organization of production and finances—a non-regulated world of transactions—with a visible impact on the internationalization of the state, as well as to an acceleration of interdependence, distant action, time–space compression, transregionalism, interconnection, intensification and acceleration of global interactions (Held and McGrew, 2000). They refer to objects, ideas, and people on the move thanks to new technologies, to mobile capital flows outside national borders.[1] However, the social sciences have not yet systematized the heterogeneous impact of economic globalization on different areas of the world.

The impacts of globalization are understood in view of the restriction of borders, in stark contrast with mobilities of people, and other movements in the Western Mediterranean region. Therefore, the emphasis is on mobilities in selected borderlands, in specific cities, with the city emerging as a strategic site for the creation of new representations of borders. These are cities and spaces where North meets South, such as King's "Rio Grande" (King 1998) or the Moroccan-Spanish and Albanian-Italian borders with Europe. They are spaces where the new constitution of the geographies of centrality and marginality can be portrayed.

Firstly, I was stimulated by Sassen´s literature on the methodological questions involved in finding the strategic sites where current processes of globalization can be studied, especially understanding the strategic discontinuities these processes imply. It is what Sassen refers to as spaces of intersection, by calling them analytic borderlands, spaces of power, of meaning, constituted in discontinuities rather than being reduced to a dividing line.

Secondly, I was motivated by the reassurance, through migration research, that many of the answers to my questions could be found in the household dynamics, especially when focusing on gender and migration and in relation to the formation of transnational families (Ribas-Mateos, 1999b and 2001b).

Thirdly, I was also stimulated by the debate on "work" and "employment," and "formal" and "informal" activities in household strategies (see Anderson et al. 1994a; Mingione 1991) in Third World cities and how we can understand them in the light of today's globalization impact. Since Keith Hart's (1957) research in Accra, and the work of Portes (1995) and many others in Latin America, such cities have been the elucidated in regard to the core dynamics of the informal economy. Later research would turn to cities of the capitalist center as well as to examining immigration in developed countries. However, if issues of international immigration and the informal economy in advanced economies were developed, such a relationship was hardly ever studied in cities of the periphery (Dunay et al. 1995).[2]

Fourthly, as literary research progressed, it became obvious that the issue of "making a living" belonged to a much broader analytical framework, where structure and agency (at the household level and at the migration project level), the individual and the community, the fixed and the mobile, the place-boundedness and the deterritorialization of social interaction, were complex categories to be considered. Hence, I wondered about the relationship between individual agency and structure in the areas of globalization and migration, looking at how people make choices in household economic behavior, going beyond the classic atomized and undersocialized conception of social action (Anderson et al. 1994a: 7).

Therefore, I have tried to pinpoint questions revolving around the diverse organizational forms and relations that structure and are structured by the choices people make in response to changing socioeconomic circumstances. The precise research question thus emerges as the following: How do household members, in specific borderlands contexts, through their ideologies and cultural practices, respond to processes of global (and domestic) economic restructuring in organizing their survival strategies?

The processes that have enabled me to determine the impact of economic globalization in such an analysis are those of the new relations of work characterized by informalization tendencies, the new patterns of waged labor characterized by export processing zones, and the configuration of households affected by the new patterns of international migration (women in the labor migration flows,[3] remittance-dependent economies, diversification in the types of migrants). In other words, all of these issues raised one general question, which has motivated the research, that is, how is household pooling organized under the impact of economic globalization and international migration?

The Global-Local Frame

The general framework of this second part of the book is generally situated in the context of globalization. Although acknowledging economical, political, and cultural processes within globalization, the emphasis will be placed on the framework of economic globalization. Although a variety of interpretations may be distinguished, authors generally refer to a global organization of production and finances, harbored by the new technologies and having a visible impact on the internationalization of the state and on the intensification of word-wide social relationships. They refer to objects, ideas, and people on the move thanks to information technologies, to flows, which escape the traditional boundaries of the nation-state. However, they do refer especially to processes of transformation in the spatial organization of social relations, in terms of their extension and intensity (Held and McGrew, 2000: 55).

The notion of a global economy is increasingly used to distinguish the particular phase of world economy that began to emerge in the 1970s. This phase is now featured by a rapid growth of transactions and institutions that pass over the older framework of inner-state relations. We first need to identify older phases in the recent history of world economy in order to focus on the elaboration of categories at this moment.[4]

This stage, driven by the internationalization of production, finance, banking, and services, coupled with cheap labor, takes full advantage of information technology and weakens the role of the state in decisions on where to locate production plants. In many parts of the world, this location has been a female-led industrialization in export processing zones, particularly in countries like Bangladesh, Morocco, Mexico, and Singapore. Nevertheless, these processes of industrial delocalization and the emergence of export zones were particularly intensified in certain regions of the world, namely South-East Asia, Latin America, and the Caribbean. It was what some authors have labeled as "the global assembly line."

Economic globalization allows companies to adopt decisions of an international nature that are adjusted to national regulations and standards instead of international ones. This converts the multinationals into the leading players on the global scene, and explains the claims of social dumping, in the sense that the companies invest and disinvest—thereby creating and destroying employment—in certain countries, benefiting from the diverse legislation existing, particularly in those countries offering the lowest levels of social protection such as Morocco and Albania. Economic globalization also has an impact on business strategies, on their investment decisions and recruitment policies. This affects employment both in quantitative terms (volume of employment) and qualitative working methods, labor links, training, job requirements, etc. It also has an impact on the countries themselves and their state policies (Alós et al. 2001: 19).

The ethnography here does not merely imply the comparision of two sites that create the local and global framework but also the application of my perspective that looks at the global within the local. Therefore, the global can be understood by a thorough examination of the local. There is an everyday life of global finance and global production just as there are various everyday life-lived experiences. Here the ethnography moves from its conventional single-site location, contextualized by the macro-construction of a larger social order, such as global capitalism, to two main sites of observation and participation. Marcus would describe this as cross-cutting the local and the global: "comparisons reenter the very act of ethnographic specification by a research design of juxtapositions in which the global is collapsed into and made integral part of it, in the form of juxtapositions of phenomena that conventionally have appeared to be (or conceptually have been kept) "worlds apart"(Marcus 1995: 95-96).

Globalization remains more a phenomenon to be understood than a research paradigm but, it is critical to introduce it because of the challenge it poses to past theories and their underlying assumptions. Sassen (2000, 2001, 2002b) refers to how the emphasis shifts today to the practices that constitute what we call economic globalization and global control: the work of producing and reproducing the organization and the management of a global production system and a global market place for finance. In our case studies, recapturing the geography of places in specific borderlands involved in globalization allows us to recapture people, workers, and communities in the context of international migrations.

At the end of the twentieth century, globalization, as a key concept in the social sciences and in the political debate, indicated a general shift in the relation between the social and the spatial. At the same time in migration studies, and as a central field for studying this ongoing reconfiguration of social and spatial relations, the focus of transnationalism became important. It considers transnational social spaces as a key concept for understanding the dynamics of international migration as well as new arrangements of the social and the spatial in human life in general. Guarnizo and Smith (1998) have revealed in particular how transnational practices associated with migratory processes are a case in point of the so-called grassroots globalization. Although on the one hand transnational capital weakens the role of the nation-state and strengthens transnational political authority, it is also perceived as the driving force for cultural homogeneization. Nevertheless, these processes and practices in varying parts of the world reveal a range of diverse effects in terms of the acceptance and reaction to this power, expressed through various forms of local resistance. These are forms of transnationalism "seen from below" that emphasize the way in which the nation-state becomes weakened by the informal economy, ethnic nationalism, and grassroots activism (Guarnizo and Smith 1998: 3). In the opinion of these authors, deconstructing transnationalism "from below" involves highlighting the asymmetries of domination, inequality, racism, sexism, class conflict, and unequal development that restricts and even perpetuates the processes of transnational practices.

The emphasis put on these processes allows us to discover interesting illustrations for the purpose of our research: the importance of migratory networks and survival strategies, the role of migrants as entrepreneurs responding to the structural conditions of labor migrations, the role of transmigrant investors through their remittances and their social development in the countries of origin, and new forms of migrants' political deterritorialization. These types of new mobilities can be related to today's conceptions of transnational communities. They represent a non-hegemonic form of globalization and may be thought of as agents of the transformation of places, and they can be characterized by: (1) movements, the intensity of circulation, (2) an active migration culture, (3) dual or multiple involvement of societies, and (4) a conscience identity in diaspora belonging (Malheiros 2001: 73, 96).

Only two sites are selected for this global focus, which I thought would enable me to see better the general framework of economic globalization. According to Marcus (1995), ethnography has moved from its conventional single-site location, contextualized by macro-constructions of a larger social order, such as the capitalist world system, to multiple sites of observation and participation that cross-cut dichotomies such as the "local" and the "global." This challenge in designing research acknowledges macro-theoretical concepts and narratives of the world system, but is not constrained by them for their contextualization. The object of study is in many ways mobile and multi-situated. This is the reason why Marcus underlines the idea of circulation through different contexts, such as commodities, gifts, and money, as the most common approach to the ethnographic study of processes in the world system—in other words, the analysis of commodity chains.

At a second level, the research analysis works outwards from the domestic instead of inwards from the public, from the perspective of the household level. Therefore, the main focus of analysis is the household: "It is precisely the permeability of the household, the absence of a wall separating it from a putative 'wider economy' that has led us to treat the product of domestic labor as commensurate with the product of all other social relations of production. In other words, domestic labor, as well as other forms of non-wage-labor, are linked in our model to commodity chains which are themselves created and recreated by processes of the world economy" (Wallerstein and Smith 1992: 271).

The household is a locus of residence, the place of practice of everyday life, while families in an anthropological sense are a locus of meaning and relationships, the symbolic terrain of kinship. As Benería and Feldman (1992) point out, the household can be the contested terrain of contradictory interests and can emphasize the space where women negotiate labor and wage employments. The Marxist and socialist-feminist conceptualization of the household is understood as a unit that functions as a kin-based group operating as a unit of reproduction of the larger structural relations of production and consumption, including particular attention on the intrahousehold division of labor: "Capitalism involves commodification...only partial commodification. The description of the secular process of the commodification of everyday life has comprised a large part of social sciences efforts for two centuries.... In the meantime, it is translated into household structures whose internal dynamics have been, and are increasingly, commodified, from the preparation of food, to cleaning and repair...to emotional repair. With the increasing commodification of everyday life there has been a decline in co-residence and kinship as determinative for the boundaries. However, I do not see the end point of this secure pressure as being the 'individual,' or the 'nuclear family,' but a unit whose cohesiveness is increasingly predicated on the income-pooling function it performs" (Wallerstein 1984: 21).

Hence, the household can here be understood as a co-residential unit where survival resources are organized and brought together. However, it is often a subject of debate with those authors on the one hand who see the household as a site of harmony and solidarity, and those on the other who perceive it as a contested terrain of contradictory interests. Instead of having the household site as a unit of analysis, the key objective will be to look instead at household strategies. However, these objectives will enhance a complex task, since strategies are always being reviewed and amended in light of subsequent events. Human beings appear only to have difficulty in coming to terms with the changes and inconsistencies in their apparently firm and rational plans when they happen to be looking at them as social scientists (Anderson et al. 1994b: 66).

The Border Frame

The concept of border is today one of the most frequently used terms, not only in the main debates of the social sciences, as the metaphors that refer, for example, to cities as the new borders of citizenship, but also in philosophy and in the arts. On the one hand, the border is seen as a limit or even a barrier (behind which as yet undiscovered space still remains to be "enlightened" and conquered), such as in the Balkan region during the 1990s, but also as a concept which sees especially all the aspects of exchange, a zone of contacts, mixing, encounter, meeting and, above all, cultural mix, such as in some areas of Mexican-American cultures or in the surviving image of nostalgic cities such as Tangier. Critical accounts of cultural borders also often narrativize the conflicts emerging along and between cultural boundaries.

The theme of "borders" in the Balkan region has been symbolically strong, as it has been the most direct representation of the opening of the last post-communist country of the Balkans. This notion of border is here seen after a time of seclusion, isolation, and exposure to the dramatic consequences of a political crisis, all of which have opened up the country to Europe and the global context. Furthermore, in Albanian history, there is a strong feeling today of living in a period of transition, in a historical stage between the communist past and the uncertain capitalist future. The Albanian words *kufi* and *sinor* have a territorial sense of border. Kufi derives from the Italian *confine*, from the Latin *confinis*. In Romanic languages, words derived from confinis where substituted in the sixteenth century by *frontier* (in Spanish, *frontera*), with a military sense (De Rapper 1998: 476). In classical Arabic, the word *alhudud*,[5] deriving from the verb *Hadda*, means "to stop." In the Moroccan dialect they use the words *lhadada* or *diwana* to refer to the frontier. Tangerines use the Spanish word *frontera* and *diwana* (the word translates as customs).

What is the mental framework of the border? Borders have always been seen as the limit of any concept, from the philosophical period of Averroes to borders of the "single Europe" and the extra-European thought of Nietzsche. The limits and frontiers have always had a strong capacity for resistance. Braudel takes the word frontier from its adjective *frontero* (meaning opposite, facing, having a position on the other), etymologically meaning that there is an adversary and a dividing line. This word has had to compete for a long time with other words of Latin origin such as confines (limit, boundary, edges), *metae* (finishing line). According to Braudel, since then, borders have been designed to refer to the exterior limits of a territorial state. They relate to verbs like to delimit, to enclose, to be at home, to fortify. States obstinately search for such security, where the complex of the Great Wall of China fascinates and obsesses everyone. Fortification is not only a result of fear, restlessness, and prudence but also a product of wealth and strength. History makes borders take roots and permits them to become natural features incorporated into space, difficult to displace (Braudel 1993: 302-303). The French historian Pierre Vilar indicates that from borders "the history of the world is best observed" (in Sahlins 1989: xv). Historically, the concept of border city was particularly developed in the case of the Iberian Peninsula and in the United States. In those two countries it characterized by a shifting, permeable border zone.

Contemporary borders are also questioned within the framework of economic globalization, especially in terms of their relation to the nation-state: "...pay particular attention to the borders, for it is in these uncertain regions where the landscape of politics is most susceptible to sudden change and reversal. Indeed, it is within this landscape that the nation can reappear with sublime force" (Castronovo 1997: 217).

Staud (1998: 15) applies five cases for the identification of five state-centric contexts: (1) transition toward market economy (post-communist states), (2) welfare state economy (Great Britain), community dependence, (3) amid poverty, partial welfare and widespread immigration (U.S.), (4) uneven regional development, amid partial welfare (Italy, Spain), and (5) uneven regional development without welfare (Mexico). Staud attempts to explain in the case of the U.S. city of El Paso how at least one-third of the households, on both sides of the border, participate in informal work. She attempts to consider the borderline as a space over which people cross to generate informal income. For Staud, the general context is set by "late twentieth-century capitalism's globalized economy of the porous borders, and the free informalization, which itself recalls some of the earliest observations of southern countries, income generating and income-stretching practices that fall through the cracks of modern surveillance" (Staud 1998: 59). Tijuana offers one of the common and most prevalent images of border cities: those images of a casino city, a city of free perimeters, a city of border processes, a cosmopolitan city; these are all heuristic illustrations in the representation of Tijuana.

Border relations have been particularly noted in the U.S.-Mexico border-lands as using four different types of relations: alienated borderlands, coexist-ent borderland, interdependent borderlands, and integrated borderlands. The American border region represents here a lack of integration between different border cities and the phenomenon of peripherical urban development. The only relation between these border cities is the economic dependence of the population in binational pairs of adjacent cities—such us the case of Tijuana and San Diego—which is one of the principal factors in the economic interde-pendence of territorial borders (three generations of Maquila in Cuidad Juárez and Tijuana have already existed). The U.S.-Mexico border region is here a case-in-point that represents the paradigmatic example of border crossing, types of circulation, material mixing and the different forms of resistance (see the case of Ciudad Juárez[6] in Vila 2003b). However, from the perspective of North American cultural studies, the work on borders has failed partly because of its excessive metaphorical notion of border, focusing on border crossing and the hybridization of cultures. As Vila puts it, current border studies suffer from two contradictory and equally problematic tendencies. The first essentializes the differences it finds in any border encounter, and the second ignores such differences (Vila 2003c: 213).

This kind of literature sees the border frame within the parameters of cul-tural representations. As Vila states, "border studies thus takes as its own object of inquiry any physical or psychic space about which it is possible to address problems of boundaries: borders among different countries, borders among ethnicities within the United States, borders between genders, borders among disciplines and the like. Borderlands and border crossing seem to have become ubiquitous terms to represent the experience of (some) people in a postmodern world described as fragmented and continually producing new borders that must again be crossed" (Vila 2003b: 308). At the same time, Barrera (1995; quoted in Vila 2003b: 310) stresses that both borders and migrants are used as mere topos to illustrate processes of identity differentia-tion and deterritorialization, where the migrants become mere carriers of cul-tural codes crossing abstract frontiers between territories that are only semiotic spaces. The economic migrant becomes the *demiurgic* (craftsperson) nomad and the border dwellers in essence become the border crossers. Therefore, the migrant becomes a strategic subject for mainstream border studies. The exemplary "border crosser" is one who is completely bilingual (in order to take full advantage of being "in between"), while many Mexican immigrants are Spanish monolingual or have low English proficiency" (Vila 2003b).

Finally, beyond the cultural, crossing the border can also be seen as the ideal scenario for conflict, or as a potential militarized conflict. Here the regulation of borders takes on a very prominent physical form. One of the most important aspects of this border frame is the impact of border control. In this way Eschbach et al. (1999) focus the debate of the United States border control policies on undocumented migration by estimating the number, causes and location of migrant deaths on the southwest border of the United States between 1993 and 1997. Official deaths from hyperthermia, hypothermia, and dehydration increased sharply from 1993 to 1997 as intensified border enforcement redirected undocumented migration flows from urban crossing points to more remote crossing areas where the migrants are exposed to a greater risk of death. However, the data are not an accurate reflection of the real situation due to the fact that some deaths may never have been registered because the bodies were never officially found; an uncertain number of would-be migrants die at the northern border of Mexico, some by drowning in the Río Bravo (Río Grande). Amid the discussion of the increasing mobility of labor and capital in globalization, people are dying on the world´s borders.

The Context of International Migration and Circularity

…but the hobo in this account was a worker who wandered, whose number at times when work was plenty and development wide-ranging must have exceeded two hundred thousand. This was the urgently needed labor force of the frontier. Indeed, he was a creature of the frontier, and he moved into history with the frontier. (Anderson 1975: ix)

Much of the international migration scholarship has taken the nation-state as a given context within which to examine the issues at hand. The approach of the relationship between the countries of origin and the countries of destination has been a major and necessary contribution to the understanding of migration dynamics. But now, when considering the impact of globalization on international migrations, it becomes important also to subject these analyzes to further examination. The crucial theme of the nature of mobilities has prompted me to review the classic Marxist analysis of migration related to the international movement of the labor force. It is adequate but insufficient to explain international migrations within the bipolarity origin-destination, at a time of economic crisis and restrictions to spatial mobility.

Notwithstanding, Tapinos (2000), putting forward the question of the globalization of migration flows, rejects the widespread conception of a globalization of international flows. Using statistical data, it is shown that migration flows have not accelerated over the past three decades at a pace comparable to those in capital flows and trade in goods and services. Although countries have implemented policies to trade and capital flows, they have reinforced their control over the migration of movements. However, if Tapinos found that it is not possible to talk of a globalization of migration, it is agreed that the increasing interdependence of sending and host countries, the diversity of migrants' nationalities, and the migration channels used, as well as the growing proportion of movements of temporary and skilled workers in total migration flows, do show that migration is now taking place in the context of economic globalization—or at least, more strongly tied to economic globalization, and radically different from Fordist migration models. Therefore, it is the underlying context and not the superficial reality (obtained through data collection) that has radically changed.

From the viewpoint of the sending countries, with the intensification of economic informalization tendencies, the neighborhood and the household re-emerge as strategic localizations of economic activity of people, migrants and non-migrants, often operating in spatial and temporary organizations, and often of a circular nature. Many of these new questions are a product of feminist scholarship on female migrants, focused on how international migration alters gender patterns and how the formation of transnational households can empower women. All these issues have taken on an added complexity, that of many migrants living their lives and planning their futures within the parameters of transnational circuits. It is within this matrix that we understand the complexities surrounding the different types of migration in our selected households, due to processes of internal, return, and temporary migration.

There is a growing tendency to analyze socioeconomic transformations in the context of the erosion of the diverse forms of identity offered by local societies. Such studies open up new questions for the examination of social structures within the axes of new space–time geographies. In this respect, this section addresses the challenge to conceptualize the migrant in an age of globalization, trying to give an operational definition that is better adapted to the new mobilities of the circular migration, transnational networks, and return migration that are nowadays characteristic of the dynamics of human mobility in the Mediterranean region. Therefore, they move beyond the assumptions of the nation-state. The forms of today's diverse mobilities underline how the resource of mobility can be seen as an important tool for people's strategies in a global economy.

Most of these complexities have been inspired by Tarrius' work on Mediterranean mobilities. He is able to elucidate, through his own research, that migrant identities are not reaffirmed as characteristically stable but through populations characterized by their movements; they function through a combination of territory and movements. Tarrius mints the term "circular territories" to refer to certain population groups who are hallmarked by movements, the coming and going, the type of entry and exit between worlds designed as different (Tarrius 2000: 8).[7] Studies like the one developed by Tarrius enable us to address critical questions on the study of the social structure of migration along the line of the time-space geographies beyond the limits of the national space. Notwithstanding, those circularities can be expressed not only by the actual physical mobility of the people themselves, but also by the circuits of information that bound transnational communities, flows of information with the help of today's technologies, and bound people's social lives between those border cities and the migrants' dispersal over the globe. Therefore, the notion of territorial circularities will be underlined in order to give relevance to groups of population for whom movement is an essential characteristic: the coming and going, the entrance and exit of worlds represented as different. These mobilities will be located at the case-study level when considering such categories in borderland settings, how people express them and how people consider them in managing their strategies of survival.

These types of mobilities have been largely considered in the context of the Euro-Mediterranean space. Research conducted by Peraldi (2001) and Tarrius shows us the urban spacialization of migrant entrepreneurs. Far from constituting "villages" or ethnic enclaves, they construct "territorial circles," participating in the organization of an economic transnational space searching for new forms of business in the post-Fordist era, presenting new forms of production from previous socio-spatial forms of Fordist manufacturing. A case in point is Marseilles, border city and harbor city, and its "marche aux Puces" entrepreneurs,[8] where far from responding to the dynamics of the ethnic business, family and community networks are widened to extra-communitarian relations (such as peer group), combining transborder mobility, flexibility, and relational competences. Goods come from all over the place, but it is interesting to note how they combine the productions of Southern Europe with the Algerian and Moroccan markets (Peraldi 2001: 16). Peraldi refers here to an "économie de bazar," the "bazaar" as the place where the different stages of the economic market can be found, the place of equilibrium between the logic of economic rationalization of exchange and the logic of the different social orders.

Migration as a Contradiction of Globalization

In the preceding sections we have seen how the impact of the internationalization of capital has contributed to the configuration of a different articulation of mobility of people in regional, national, and transnational circuits. In her book, *The Mobility of Labor and Capital*, Sassen (1988) emphasizes the correlation between foreign investment and emigration. In that respect, she goes beyond the explanatory reasons, which normally frame international migration on the grounds of demographic explosion, poverty, and economic stagnation. Historical relations, whether they be military, political, or economic form *invisible bridges* that remain long after the macro-relations have dissolved across places to which people will migrate. This study helped me to bring into focus the relationship between the global capital and migration flows, but further reading allowed me to also see the contradictory aspects.

I refer in particular to the contradictory tendencies of globalization underlined by academics such as Mittleman[9] (see Mittleman 2000). One of the contradictions he points out is the creation of economic ties with Africa and the simultaneous attempt by nation-states to restrict labor migration and economic refugees. Authors such as Mittleman draw attention to the contradictory trends of globalization, revealing how cross-border flows of undocumented workers and instant telecommunications are positioned outside the effective control of state regulatory bodies. In keeping with this perspective, globalization also represents a dialectical set of continuities and discontinuities, an intensification of previously established models, as well as new features of a system that is lacking in effective regulatory measures. It is the varied nature of modern interdependence and the surprising challenge facing the global government. Mittleman perceives globalization as a series of interrelated processes, a functional integration of various activities at an international level. From this perspective, the analysis involves discovering the transcription of these processes in space, both in terms of deterritorialization and reterritorialization. Forms of deterritorialization that accompany processes of localization; in other words, the repositioning on various spatial levels of social relations, as well as action and social activities. It consists of discovering the way in which we articulate a universal thought and a territorialized thought, bearing in mind the changes of scale and the parameters for analysis.

My argument poses the question of whether those contradictions can be expressed on the one hand by the closing of borders and on the other through the will of people to move, as they would be represented by two contradictory faces of the global economy. The obstacles that migrants face in the sending countries are partially in contradiction with the principles of a free market and a global capitalist economy. On the one hand, the free global market puts limitations on the freedom of workers through restrictive entries, and furthermore, nation-states have a sovereign right to apply such measures. Nevertheless, the richest countries defend a global labor market when they refer to skilled workers. On the other hand, people continue to develop strategies of mobility.

Generally, capital, products, and ideas have become more mobile, while certain categories of labor, constrained by immigration laws, continue under the control and penalization of mobility. Considering the closing of borders (militarization, etc.), these types of borderlands can be thought of as sites of resistance to globalization. Can one call it an act of resistance? Can it be called forms of circumvented states' reactions to globalization, such as the stopping of human transborder flows?

The contradictory nature of borders acquires meanings, which can be given two faces, one driven by a neo-liberal logic and the other one driven by a neo-conservative or territorial logic:

1. *The open face.* Borders that mean the actual path for crossing them, the historical place of encounter (between nationalities, cultures, ethnicities, and the like), where identity can become a metaphor of communalities (the Al-Andalus in Spain, the Muslims in Europe, the Arbanites in Greece, for example). Also meaning the path where the migrant is placed as a privileged actor of global process in a "third space" or an "in-between place" in the sense noted by Vila (2001). The open face of capital can also be seen as a destination for foreign Southern European investment, seen for example through the Spanish mobile telephone companies in Morocco or the Italian ones in Albania.

2. *The closed face* of territorial logics. Confirming borders as the place for reinforcing restrictive policies, borders as physical fences that mark the political-administrative borders of Spain or Greece. This closed face explains why they are a waiting place for internal migrants, such a Sub-Saharan waiting place in Tangier, or until recently the Middle Eastern waiting place in Durrës. However, these borders are continuously questioned by ordinary people and by those who think that their lives have a continuum in the transnational processes. It is through the articulation of this pattern of contractions that we will see in the next chapter how the two border cities emerge.

Border Cities to Southern Europe

We will continue by identifying the border frame in the Western Mediterranean Region. Considering the above-mentioned contradictions, one could easily think that those borders are simply the allegory of a clash, at a time when historical borders have moved on from the Iron Curtain, which formerly excluded socialist countries; when the free mobility of people in the European Union has become the motto of regional cohesion; when the domestic-foreign and external-internal divisions no longer wholly explain the movement of flows. Among globalists, especially those who believe in hypermobilty, images repeat themselves in relation to the neutralization of place and distance, and they often argue that place no longer matters (Ribas-Mateos 2002a). On the contrary, our emphasis on border cities suggests a recuperation of material places, that which in Sassen's terminology is the recuperation of production sites and place-boundedness that are also part of economic globalization.

Border cities are here to be found in relation to the limits of Southern Europe (as one of the main closing doors of the intensified Fortress Europe,[10] the borders of the Schengen construction). Notwithstanding, the concept of border can be seen in a much more complex way. From the philosophical border to the limit of any concept, to the social anthropological borders of ethnic groups, to border dynamics—its myths and border practices, to the mental divisorial line within people.

On the other hand, when we refer to borderland or border cities, borders not only distinguish social, cultural, economic, and political systems but also determine zones where those systems interact in specific ways. Those zones can be wider than the border site; it is in this way that we refer to border cities. Border cities have been a center of interest for historians, especially those dedicated to the history of the Iberian Peninsula and that of the United States. Anywhere else in history, the border has not had such importance. Those borders have been moving and permeable. For example, in Europe, they were thought of in this way: "Border cities—except those which are temporary borders—appear not only to be random centers, located at the edge of two political dominations or at the limits of two civilizations. They constitute a particular type of agglomeration within the network organized progressively in tremendous urban development started in the XI century in Western Europe...maritime cities in which the harbour plays the role of port of entry for the cities located in the hinterland" (Menjot 1996: 6).

In our case, the Mediterranean can be thought of as the space for those locations of border cities in Southern Europe (see for further discussion, "The Mediterranean Caravanserai" in Ribas-Mateos 2001a). The old channel between Spain and Northern Africa or the Braudelian river is not so much of a natural border. Especially, when we remember that at the beginning of the sixteenth century the Strait of Gibraltar became a political border for the first time in history; subsequently, the degree of permeability of this border has been variable since then, marking today a political, economical, and possibly ideological border.[11] For me, Tangier becomes in this context the most suitable selected site "built under the protection of the hills and facing Europe: Tangier was always the port of entry of foreign influence in Morocco. Turned into a symbol of foreign domination, the city was known by the rest of the country as l'kelba (the bitch)" (Driessen 1994: 61).

Economic globalization simultaneously leads to a reshaping of cross-national economic integration on different scales, such as transnational development areas or new forms of regionalization that challenge the classical divisions of the Mediterranean. Here I concentrate on the borderland sites of Southern European migration. Globalization features are here seen to bring into focus the reinforcement of national borders from two specific sites in the North–South Mediterranean divide. Most cities are not at the world command level; indeed, they occupy a variety of niches in the capitalist network economy, especially when one considers border regions. Much study has been developed on the Mexican–American border region when dealing with regionalization, migration, social development and industrial relocation, but little has been done on the so-called "Mediterranean Rio Grande economies."

I focus here on borderlands as research sites, encompassing the very specific friction in places of globalization processes. These sites offer the possibility of exploring the globalization process in great detail, within a bounded setting and with its contradictory features. Simply put, global economic activities such as the mobility peculiar to the export processing zones, can also be very embedded in place. It is where global processes become structured by the local constraints of border cities (especially those that restrict mobilities to some nationals by the states and their policing powers) as well as by their own characteristics that define the heterogeneous forces. However, it is important to recognize that borderlands are not the rule for all socioeconomic processes in the countries under study. Globalization tendencies such as the development of export industries are not to be seen for the whole of the country but it becomes clearer when one selects those that are the nodes of the privatization processes.

Consequently, the selected unit of analysis has been the transfrontier city. This has been mainly inspired by U.S. migration literature, particularly that surrounding the topics of the international boundary in the Mexican-American region: immigration, production plants (*maquiladoras*), environment, and areas of urban growth. It is in these borderland areas that one locates places like Tijuana or even, Marseilles. Tijuana recalls images of a casino city, a city of free perimeters, a city of border processes, cosmopolitan cities, an imaginary city as an heurisitic illustration that guides ideas, concepts, and structures. Marseilles, as we have seen, recalls the images of Cliffords´ bazaar economy, seen through the pull of the small business. Especially in the case of the Maghrebians in the neighborhood of Belsunce, in Marseilles, the bazaar economy is identified as a form of social mobilization existing in all European cities but that can be better understood in the context of border towns like Marseilles.

Here I introduce some analytical distinctions to the various cases mentioned and then focus comparatively on the two selected borderland cities, Tangier and Durrës. I argue that these borderlands are cities of transition. Not only geographically but also historically, cities like Tangier and Durrës can be thought of as sites of transition, experiencing changes from the socialist model or representing the transformation of Muslim societies. I employ the notion of borderland to refer to certain cities instead of referring to frontier, which often denotes a physical division. I refer to it as placing these cities in a broader context, in the ways in which Tangier and Durrës share experiences found in borderlands in general, specifically, or borderlands strictly separated instead of having an integrated interaction.

Finally, another concept important to consider in this border frame is the concept of peripheral city. The study of peripheral urbanization starts from the axiom that Third World development is constrained by and interacts with the global political economy, influencing not only social organization but also local culture. Walton (1982) provides a full account of how the physical form and spatial organization of the peripheral city reflects and reciprocally recreates the urban economy. The process can be summarized as follows.

First, rapid urbanization of the Third World is caused by the expansion and penetration of the global economy in the form of commercialized agriculture for export, the destruction of traditional rural social organization, urban (push) migration, the exploitation of new urban markets of labor and import consumption, and the reorientation of the urban economy toward export production and trade. As a consequence of this impact, industrial employment does not expand at the same rate as the population and export trade because foreign manufacturing firms establish themselves on the national market through wholly owned subsidiaries, joint ventures, or companies capitalized completely from local sources while controlled from abroad. The diverse strategies to reduce costs have an impact on the casualization of work that can go from vending, petty and personal services, artisan or low-paid traditional manufacture, and sundry clandestine (e.g., household production avoiding tax and labor codes), or illegal economic activities.

Secondly, the local urban society responds with new initiatives. The construction industry is a prototype. It both absorbs large quantities of labor and stimulates a variety of local industries less easily penetrated by foreign capital (e.g., cement, wood, construction materials, and furnishings). Thirdly, it affects culture even if broader cultural traditions are also alive.

The Context of Globalization and Household Practices

The notion that work and family life are distinct and separate spheres has been well documented but has also been shown to be problematic in social science (Ram et al., 2001). Transnational practices related to migratory processes and economic and political expansion across national spaces tend to focus on the three axes where most scholars center their discussions of grassroots transnationalism. Common perspectives on transnationalism have been seen through: migratory networks and survival strategies, the role of ethnic or immigrant business, the role of transnational business activity and its impact on remittances, and new forms of political deterritorialization of migrants.

The first reference we can find in our bid to connect global processes and household units is the work by Joan Smith and Immanuel Wallerstein (1992), where the household is seen as performing the function of an income-pooling unit and representing an institution of the world economy. It is suggested that households are socially constituted entities subject to pressures deriving from the cyclical rhythms of the world market and from the state machineries. One can even find an exact relation between global constraints and household functions: "typically, stagnations in the world economy create pressures on small household structures to enlarge boundaries and to self-exploit more…relocation of industries from one zone to another. They are moving primarily to reduce wage costs, and they can do this because of the household structures prevalent in the zone into which they are relocating." The impact on households can also be seen in the alteration of their composition and perhaps their mode of functioning and internal decision making as well as the multiple levels and forms of state machinery: laws and policies that determine composition, requirements of co-residence; financial and legal possibilities; fiscal obligations, right to physical movement, etc. (idem: 17).

Therefore, the core-periphery relationship can also be seen through the household as a main unit of analysis, the household as an institution of the world economy. In this sense, for Wallerstein and Smith, the general pattern for understanding household dynamics is not the combination of wages and subsistence, but the combination of wages and petty market operations. For these authors, household dynamics can be understood in relation to the desperate need for cash, precisely because the process of peripheralization is undermining, reducing, sometimes even destroying totally the possibility of obtaining resources out of traditional subsistence activities (idem: 257).

I consider two central issues when breaking down globalization to its impact on border cities. First, at the meso level, I consider the situation of the individual city in the globalized economy, general trends of foreign capital flows, IMF relations, industrial relocation, and border status. Secondly, at the neighborhood level, I consider the patchwork economy, or how to bring together and share disparate resources, which conveys the often uneven and unplanned quality of members' contributions to the household economy, both in substance and in timing.

First, at the meso level, neo-liberal policies (International Development policies, International Monetary Fund policies) can be seen through policies of deflation, devaluation de-control and privatization. Those neo-liberal policies can be seen better through studies that center their interest on the impact of structural adjustment policies in Third World countries, in the distribution of resources, and on living standards of different classes of urban households. Specific aid and trade regimes dependent on financial resources from the World Bank and bilateral lending institutions have brought demands for economic restructuring and a decline in public expenditure. Households sharing limited resources tend to respond to economic crises with a protective strategy that increases intra-household dependence (Feldman 1992). At the same time, low wages have made those employed in the formal sectors particularly vulnerable to declines in real wages, to inflation and currency devaluation, forcing people to move to an expanding informal labor market.

Secondly, there is a micro level, where processes are to be seen from the household angle. In other words there are two intertwined processes at work, the homogeneization forces of globalization and the heterogeneization forces. Those can be underlined from the perspective of the household as the site of workforce reproduction (the raising of children, the caring for family members) as the unit where the biological community is regulated by cultural norms of endogamy and inheritance laws.

Finally, single mothers are particularly affected by the difficulties imposed. In 1996, the GNP per capita in U.S. dollars was 820 for Albania and 1,290 for Morocco. Urban population was 34 percent for Albania and 42 percent for Morocco (World Bank 2000c: 132) In all countries the percentage of female-headed households below the poverty line was important, but it was of particular relevance in Latin American countries.

After focusing on the general theoretical context we will next review the concepts needed to articulate the ethnographic quest: the household strategy, the patchwork economy, and the informal work.

Articulating Concepts for an Ethnography at the Border

Some British sociologists such as Gershuny and Pahl (1979) have related the provision of goods and services in middle-income families of developed economies as being an answer to the maximization of time and quality of consumption. Others like Mingione (1991) and Pardo (1996) focus on survival strategies in Italian *mezzogiorno* families. In Pardo's Naples, the diverse work activities of the local people belong to ordered but multifaceted processes which develop and have significance well beyond formal employment and unemployment. These activities may even be the expression of an entrepreneurial spirit and a cooperative attitude (Pardo 1996: 11), and beg the question as to how people negotiate between their normative and their instrumental values. Pardo´s example in the center of Naples shows us how the "*popolino*" goes beyond the classification of colorful examples of *arte di arrangiarsi* (art of living by one's wits, as the French *se débrouiller*[12] or the Spanish *buscarse la vida*).

Many scholars find in the extended family system in developing countries, as well as in migrants' adaptation strategies in receiving countries, an explanation of household survival dynamics. Often household extensions are seen as the result of a combination of economic, demographic, and cultural factors. The extension mechanism can help to alleviate poverty, or at least provide households with greater flexibility in allocating market and domestic roles among members. Granovetter uses the term "embeddedness" to refer to the idea that the last resource against corruption is the mutual trust of people who belong to a same group (Granovetter 1992). Within this framework, he stresses the tendency to develop Polanyi's reciprocal behavior in kinship and neighborhood networks with regard to specific relationships limited in space and time.[13] In contrast to the utilitarian tradition based on the undersocialized Hobbesian conception of man that emphasizes the rational and self-interested behavior, where social relations hardly intervene and economic action would result from rational calculation and individual gain, we can also distinguish the oversocialized conception of man in modern sociology as guiding survival strategies. Thus, I underline here a notion of trust as a pattern of behavior linked to strategies of survival.

In theory those strategies can be understood depending on the social class of the individual or the labor market sector to which they belong, afterwards, everything then would be automatic. Piore (see in Granovetter 1992) argues that members of each of the labor markets (from the labor market segmentation theory) are characterized by different styles of decision making. The making of decisions by rational choice, custom, or command in upper-primary, lower-primary, and secondary labor markets respectively corresponds to the origins of workers in middle, working, and lower-class subcultures (today it could also be thought of in the logics of the commodified relations in the terms of the circulation of global capital). Others would understand those strategies viewing culture as an ongoing process, continuously constructed and reconstructed during interaction, not only shaping its members but also being shaped by them, in part for their own strategic reasons (Granovetter 1992. 57).

Under the family strategies examination, the embeddedness argument stresses the role of concrete personal relations and structures (or "networks") of such relations in generating trust and discouraging malfeasance. The embeddedness position is associated with the "subtantivist" school in anthropology, identified especially with Polanyi and with the idea of "moral economy" in history and political science, and it has also some relation to Marxist thought. In that respect, Granovetter's view is that the level of embeddeness of economic behavior is lower in nonmarket societies than is claimed by substantivist and development theorists, and it has changed less with "modernization" than people believe. However, he also mentions that this level has always been and continues to be more substantial than is allowed for by formalists and economists. Granovetter thinks that social relations, rather than institutional arrangements or generalized morality, are mainly responsible for the production of trust in economic life (Granovetter 1992: 61). Therefore, the embeddness approach to the problem of trust and order in economic life, threads its way between the oversocialized approach of generalized morality and the undersocialized one of the impersonal, institutional arrangements by following and analyzing concrete patterns of social relations. Unlike the Hobbesian conception, it makes no sweeping predictions of universal order or disorder but rather assumes that the details of social structure will determine that which is found (Granovetter 1992: 63), therefore, relating to the Weberian category of social action but adding the insights of modern structural sociology.

The rationality or non-rationality of family strategies also have been examined in the field of international migrations. Firstly, in relation to globalization, migrants have also been selected as main actors of a global space articulated by networks (Malheiros 2001), not only by their vertical networks (country of origin-country of destination) but also by their horizontal networks (between different communities). This approach is also related to the reorganization of spatial economy articulated by urban networks. Secondly, we can also find in the sociology of migration reference to the adaptive role of immigrants' ties and institutions through extended families. In that respect, one finds the discovery and even the celebration of the strength and resilience of immigrant institutions, and their roles in facilitating the economic survival and adaptation of their members in a new society (Kibria, 1993: 18). The emphasis on adaptation also pretends to counterbalance the assimilation models on the view of the passive immigrant. A revival has been seen also in the extended living arrangements as a help to buffer the effects of labor market disadvantages faced by minority household heads. Ronald and Tienda (1982) refer to this demographic mechanism as a compensatory strategy for supplementing the temporary or chronically low earnings of those heads. In their research, the extended family household refers specifically to the actual living arrangements of relatives (family or residence). Furthermore, among immigrants, the need to rely on relatives may be particularly great because of the ability of those who have migrated earlier to cushion the potentially disorganizing consequences of internal migration for new arrivals (idem: 1363). These extended, reciprocal, kin-based exchanges can be found in aspects such as residential proximity, type of interaction, measures of familism, value transmission, and affectional bonds (Troll, quoted in Ronald and Tienda, 1982). The central issue here is that of resurgence reciprocity, or social economic action, which has become one of today's most acclaimed elements of economic sociology.

For all these factors, the kin-based system is relevant to the research. In Moroccan society, the extended family system has long been thought of as one of the foundations of traditional society, whereas in the Eastern Adriatic region of the Mediterranean, Albanians have shared, with the Serbs and the Montenegrins, the distinction of an extended patrilineal kin-group organization.

The Concept of Strategy

The concept of strategy has become a critical issue in economic sociology. One of the central points of the debate is whether strategy can be considered as a topic of analysis or as an analytical tool in household examination. For Feldman (1992) the debate develops from the view of those who consider survival strategies as a process of negotiation over a diverse set of social and technical resources, to that of those who examine survival strategies as an outcome of individual or household behavior. Hence, the use of the term strategy is the result of a form of behavior embracing neither negotiation nor choice. As such, the term strategy meets the actual processes involved in choosing from a range of possible options that a household or individual might use in the face of changing employment circumstances.

The emphasis on strategy is normally a result of the growing importance given to social agency. Benería (1992) shows how in Mexico households sharing limited resources tend to respond to economic crisis with a protective strategy that increases intra-household dependence. The emphasis here is on the creative mechanisms employed by households and household members to generate alternative production and consumption patterns to ensure survival. "These mechanisms include new patterns of community organizing inter- and intra-household patterns of support as well as processes of family and household dissolution. They also include new relations of work; new patterns of integration among wages, exchange and domestic labor; new configurations of household membership; and new patterns of migration" (Feldman 1992: 11).

When referring to the patchwork economy we need to underline operational concepts that have played a pivotal role in the economic sociology debate. We refer to the concept of strategy and especially the concept of "household strategy" that has proved to be theoretically and empirically problematic (Anderson et al. 1994; Bourdieu 2000; Stame 1990, among others), and has reflected a major debate in the bridge between structure and agency. The problem particularly involves the medium or long-term perspective of the goals and the consciousness of action in order to be able to consider it a household strategy. It becomes of practical use when referring to a roughly interlinked set of practices. Accepted subconscious strategies can be part of accepted practices, others can be changed and continuously reinvented due to changes in light of events. This is more applicable to our case when considering how families have to change their strategies in relation to changing circumstances such as variations in migration policies.

For example, we can consider also under these circumstances, the marriage strategy in border contexts. Bourdieu has especially considered marriage strategies in his ethnographic works. One wonders if it is the same with individuals, if households can make rational choices as individuals can. The term strategy is used to refer to a type of behavior embracing neither negotiation nor choice when there is no change of possible options that a household might use. According to Bourdieu, the conditions involved in choosing a marriage partner are so numerous and complex that they exceed the awareness of the agents. Family strategies are the product of the *habitus*, the practical form of a reduced number of principles. This habitus includes the principles for the solutions that may be adopted: restrictions on the number of births, the emigration or celibacy of the young, depending on their position on the social scale, their ranking in the family and gender. Purely marital strategies cannot be separated without the abstraction of succession and fertility strategies, or pedagogical strategies. In other words, it includes all the biological reproduction, cultural, and social strategies applied by any group in the transmission, maintenance or increase of the powers and privileges it has adopted from one generation to another (Bourdieu 1972: 1124-1225).

One can see that to underline the use of household strategy is not only to find a way to complement a rigorous interpretation of structuralism but also to avoid falling into extreme voluntarism, which in the end leads us to the classical debate on structure and action. It is a way of separating the interpretation of action from rational choice theories, which would say that households are just individuals, also acting rationally, who would act to optimize their quality of life by a rational distribution of their resources. In contrast, other scholars would point out that people cope with the exigencies of day-to-day life in many ways, and that in "getting by," much more is involved than purely rational action (Anderson et al., 1994b: 60).

Much of this debate reflects the division between, on the one hand, utilitarian tradition, including classical and neoclassical economics, which assume that rational, self-interested behavior is affected minimally by social relations, and, on the other, what Granovetter calls embeddedness (1992: 53): "behaviour and institutions are so constrained by ongoing social relations that to construe them as independent is a grievous misunderstanding"; embeddedness relates therefore to economic action as a category of social action. However, neither does Granovetter devolve into determinism because he offers contextualized agency by avoiding the trappings of both extremes.

The main debate here is whether strategies are seen neither as behaviors nor practices but systems of rationally grounded decisions leading towards a desired medium, to long-term goals, or whether people are or are not conscious—in terms that Bourdieu refers to as the subconciousness in traditional societies. In that respect other authors also add the ethnic category as a characteristic of household strategies, be it the migrants' adaptation strategies or be it their adaptation to urban life, as in the case of the Rifians in Tangier. Such an example of the Rifian community in Tangier was already documented in the 1950s by the anthropologist David M. Hart (1957), who related the adaptation of the community to an urban environment.

The Notion of Patchwork Economy[14]

Many scholars have shown how the pooling of resources and networks is a common response to conditions of scarcity and uncertainty, and that the expansion of household boundaries to include more members, as well as such cooperative kin-based economic practices as pooling, are both responses to conditions of economic deprivation. However, for Kibria, whereas pooling refers to the sharing of income and finances, one can also include other assets such as information, services and education; patchworking conveys the merging of many kinds of resources, similar to the way disparate resources meet in risky economic contexts in developing social countries (Kibria 1993: 77). Patchworking also conveys the often uneven and unplanned quality of members' contributions to the household economy, supported on the collective ideology of (in her case) Vietnamese Americans, both in substance and in tempo.

Polanyi originally distinguished between three forms of exchange: reciprocity (the reciprocal flow of goods and services persists beyond a single transaction), redistribution, and market exchange (Lomnitz 1977b: 189). However, his critics think that this model implies a judgment, a preference for reciprocity (based on generosity and social solidarity) over market exchange. Lomnitz answers to it and affirms that in her study "the use of reciprocity is a result of need rather than social idealism.... Instead it represents an economic lifestyle for an increasingly large sector of the population" (Lomnitz 1997b: 203). However, as Granovetter points out, the suggestion that sociology is about how people do not have any choices to make reflects then an "oversocialized conception of mán" (Anderson, et al. 1994), and roots trace to structural determinism.

Lomnitz (1977b) researched a shantytown on the outskirts of Mexico City. The only resource available to families was of a social nature, kinship and friendship ties that generate social solidarity. For her, the intensive use of unpaid family labor could be seen as an integral part of the informal economy system based on reciprocal exchange networks. A large family was seen to be an advantage due to the use of unpaid child labor (permanently available with no cost and flexible in the use of space and leftovers) and the use of relatives for emergency assistance during periods when there was no work (Lomnitz 1977b: 67).

Ronald and Tienda (1982) investigate the extent to which extended living arrangements help buffer the effects of labor market disadvantages faced by minority household heads in the United States. They mention (according to Troll´s categories) diverse aspects of kinship exchange: residential propinquity, type and frequency of interaction, economic interdependence or mutual aid and varied qualitative measures of familism, value transmission, and bonds of affection. Through their research they highlight how in black and Hispanic households non-nuclear members contribute significantly to total household income, although their relative contributions are approximately similar for poor and non-poor households. In contrast, non-nuclear members in non-Hispanic white households appear not to participate significantly in the generation of household income. Therefore, they show how the extension mechanism of reciprocity may help to alleviate poverty, or at least provide households with greater flexibility in allocating market and domestic roles among members, especially used among minority households and those headed by single women.

For Kibria's research, the social networks of the patchwork economy revolved around kinship and neighborhood ties, but also around age, gender, and social class background. From her perspective, cooperative household and economic practices such as patchworking are seen as negotiated processes generated and supported by specific structural and ideological contexts and not as natural outcomes, as seen in the idea of the reciprocal household, the answer to the consensual unity of the household (idem: 99).

Research that treats the behavior of immigrant families as central to the explanation of income-generating strategies and migration itself has been examined as a powerful determinant of internal and international migration behavior. As already mentioned, the notion that work and family life are distinct and separate is problematic. This is increasingly evident in the literature on "family business," where both family and business systems are so intertwined that they cannot be disentangled from one another. On this subject, Ram et al. (2001) show the links between household dynamics and ethnic minority business in the UK.

We consider here two types of pooling tools for the ethnography: remittances and factory work. Remittances here meaning an indicator of the internationalization of household reproduction and, through the receipt of remittances, as a way of protecting household members at the migrants' place of origin from economic pitfalls. Remittances will vary not only according to the number of years spent abroad or the country the migrant is in (e.g., a Gulf state or a European country) but also according to gender. Families might opt to maximize income if it is a woman who leaves, where women are often preferred as migrants over males because they tend to remit more regularly than their male counterparts.

Secondly, we can consider factory work. As indicated earlier, the globalization of production and its impact on the employment of women in many Third World industrialization processes has been the subject of a prolific literature. This literature has documented a high concentration of women workers in the more traditional "female industries" such as the clothing and textile industries, as well as in the newer industries such as the manufacture of electronics and toys, often geared toward the global market. In the garment industry, many manufacturers have established highly dispersed and complex production systems by subcontracting in low-wage cities and nations. This has been promoted by the lowering of tariffs through world trade agreements made by actors such as the World Trade Organization.

Fernández-Kelly (1983) focuses her research on offshore production along the Mexican-American border in the expansion of multinational industrialization and the incorporation of large numbers of women into direct production. She uses the case of Ciudad Juárez as a good illustration of the results of the implementation of the Border Industrialization Program (since 1965), enabling the penetration of international capital into local economies. She divides the female labor force into sectors: the electric/electronic sector and the garment manufacturing sector. In the first sector, they are mainly urban single women who contribute more than half their weekly earnings to their families. In the second sector, they tend to be older, less educated, and recently arrived in the city. One out of three of these women provide the only means of support for their family, and tend to support their children rather than their parents or siblings. In sum, this is a gender structure in consonance with the requirements of capital accumulation at a global scale.

The Informal Economy: Context of the Pooling Tool

Can the informal economy be an expression of global chains? The problem of informality can be traced back to the studies of Keith Hart (1973) in Accra, Ghana, and finds its most developed work today in the American structuralist school. According to Portes (1995), most of the scholars interested in that field underline the economic action of the small business and those centered on the reproduction of the household as a space of survival. A key point in Portes' analysis is that informality is a part of the modern economy and not a backward indicator. Economic informal activities are not simply the result of Third World industrialization, but forms of production and exchange typical of the capitalist system of the nineteenth century and which are reproduced along with its history. The informal economy is to be thought of as a major structural feature of society, both in industrialized and in less-industrialized countries. It is this framework, which allows us to see the selected families not as poor families fighting poverty through informality (separated from the modern economy) but, on the contrary, as families who are part of the most modern and complex network of global capitalism.[15] According to Portes (1995: 221), the universal character of the informality phenomenon reflects the great capacity for the resistance of most societies to override the exercise of state power.

However, the informal economy is not a euphemism for poverty, a set of survival activities by people on the margins of society, but a specific form of the relations of production, while poverty is an attribute linked to the process of distribution. Its central characteristic is that it is unregulated by the institutions of society, in a legal and social environment in which similar activities are regulated (Castells and Portes 1989: 12). The authors differentiate it from criminal activities only in that the poor specialize in the production of goods and services socially defined as illicit (idem: 15).

The results of the research on the informal economy edited by Castells and Portes show how different cases of informality in different places share many structural characteristics—small scale, avoidance of state regulations, flexible sites, use of family labor among others—and that they could have different meanings and functions depending on the character of the overarching "formal" economy (1989: 2). The informal economy simultaneously encompasses flexibility and exploitation, productivity and abuse, aggressive entrepreneurs and defenseless workers, libertarianism and greediness. And above all, there is the disenfranchisement of the institutionalized power conquered by labor (1989: 11). There are a few themes that can be seen as causes of informalization: (1) the reaction by both firms and individual workers to the power of organized labor; (2) the reaction against the state's regulation of the economy, in taxes and social legislation; (3) the impact of international competition on all countries, affecting in particular labor-intensive industries; (4) the process of industrialization in Third World countries, such as the runaway U.S. industries, or *maquiladoras*, in the Mexican–American border region; and (5) the global recession and the austerity policies promoted by international financial institutions, particularly in the countries of the periphery (Castells and Portes 1989: 29).

In respect to gender we can add how women negotiate the demands of their private contribution to household work in the form of unpaid family labor and unwaged commodity production, with their public contribution through informal sector activities and formal sector employment. This emphasis draws attention to changes in men's behavior in that they are more willing to accept women's increased control of their own wages but less willing to share household labor.

The context of a border zone creates peculiar conditions for the examination of the informal economy as a pooling tool. Border smuggling—the term *trabendo* is often used in Algeria (from the Spanish *contrabando*)—is a common coin in the Mahgrebian borders, such us the case of Uxda with the Algerian border or the case of the Sebta and Melilla border, Spanish enclaves in Northern Morocco that represent one of the main places for circulation of Spanish products, and involves a great number of the population, emerging in forms of everyday smuggling often called *matuteras* (trans-border women carrying suitcases). Are those acts of resistance by people? In a way, they can be considered acts of resistance against a global context, or part and parcel of the informalization of the economy in accordance with globalization.

The Characteristics of the Ethnography

These ethnographies of border cities that I now present are framed within a common context, the fact that they all suffer—at first hand—from the closure of what has come to be called "Fortress Europe," which has led to the growth of different forms of irregularity and illegality in borderlands. As a consequence, different kinds of mobility are reinvented where certain cities become crossing places for north-south migrations, specific locations that shape the transience points for international migration projects in the Mediterranean. The case of the Sub-Saharan migrants in Tangier or the Moldavians in Durrës are two perfect examples. These cities exist as connecting points, not only for the trade of goods but also as extremely significant sites for industrial relocalization from the North (especially textiles and services) to the South, and the resulting high rate of female labor force in the labor market.

As often occurs, adaptation of the theory and its concepts onto the subsequent work itself tends to complicate initial perceptions, as well as adding new information that did not exist within the scope of the original framework. In spite of this, I do not believe in this second part of the book that very much has altered with respect to the initial broad approach that helped me to define the two contexts. This is, on one hand, the context of economic globalization, considering both the forces of homogeneization and heterogeneization in the border cities, while on the other, it is the analysis of the global impact on household strategies through the patchwork perspective. What has really changed are the ways of focusing on what we are searching for, by combining the statistical data, which provide us with the objective traits of the border city, with the ethnographic focus that reveals how people experience border characteristics in their social relationships.

The theoretical work is a study that was, to a great extent, fixed at a certain time by gathering and reprocessing bibliographical information. In contrast, the empirical material collected in Tangier and in Durrës was only relatively static, given that to a certain degree, consistency can only be achieved once the researcher physically leaves the field of study, when the researcher disembeds him/herself. Even so, people's migratory stories do not allow the researcher to be limited to the perspective of a single site; this is seen in the way that monitoring some of the Tangier emigrants' stories led me on to different places, and to different kinds of problems.

The initial theoretical focus—and in particular the visualization of an a priori established conceptual map—turned out to be rather inflexible for the applied research. This initial focus was an attempt to discover a way of articulating the notion of the border city in such a manner that it would provide me with a definite site where I could examine the framework of migrations and the family strategies as conditioned by economic globalization. In this sense, in the case of Tangier, one of the most important contributions to the ethnographic study is definitely the connection between survival strategies and the types of informal practices within the global economy.

Many of the theoretical traits that I had included for an analysis of Tangier as a border city bring together ingredients I had considered when approaching the question of family economic strategies. However, I was aware that many border traits could also be viewed as being folklorist and widely publicized, details such as the image of the Africans who are waiting for the chance to start their journey through the Strait of Gibraltar, the *pateras* and the role of hashish smugglers. In the case of Durrës, the most highly publicized topics often concern the trafficking of women.

These multi-sited ethnographies were carried out by the researcher during two periods: in Tangier (Morocco) from April to September 2002, and in Durrës-Tirana (Albania) from December 2002 to May 2003. In both places, two families were selected as the basis for the ethnographic study, in order to analyze strategies within the domestic space: Ihsan's family in Tangier and Nora's in Durrës. These families were selected because they fulfilled the criteria of my research question and methodology on the transformations I planned to analyze in selected frontier sites, though also because they offered me full accessibility to their homes and lives. Incidentally, the names of the families, the different informants, the associations and the factories that appear in the text have all been modified. I will follow two different transliteration systems in these ethnographies, one Albanian and the other Arabic.[16]

These two ethnographies are conceived as an association or connection between two sites that define the main argument of the ethnography, their roles here as border places. However, I do not "follow the people" of the research; it is not a case of the researcher being on the move. I have analyzed movement from my own fixed postions in those two specific places.

The Ethnography in Tangier

The predominant focus of the ethnography carried out in Tangier was based on visits with families. It was through the family lens that I observed the structural impact of the peculiarities of a border city based upon everyday life. The Tangier study was based essentially on two main families, within which one person played the role of liaison. These two liaisons were chosen for linguistic reasons, as both spoke Spanish well, thus, their role was not only an introductory one, they were also my interpreters.

As for defining the chief features of the border city, I should emphasize that in the case of Tangier it was extremely difficult, owing to a lack of available data on all levels, especially when it came to reflecting socioeconomic indicators on an urban scale. The data gathered refer mainly to the national scale, and consequently, the information has not always allowed me to discover as much as I would have liked about the urban picture.

Apart from the families and the purely statistical data, I should also mention other kinds of informants or key contacts that I made during the fieldwork. I am referring to foreigners who did not speak Arabic and had no interest in learning it—the typical insular Europeans who live in African countries, after having successfully exported their mother culture. These tend to be middle-class people who have escaped from the West to lead a life of luxury, the supposedly "easy life" that Europeans from the beat generation had also discovered in Tangier in the 1970s. In such countries they can have the servants that they could not afford in their home countries. In addition, as they commonly believe Moroccans to be culturally inferior, any information they provided should often be treated with reservation during the interpretation.

Each of the informants furnished information on different topics, which challenged me to adapt and constantly control the initial points of departure. Thus, to get me into the factories and workshops, one of my informants introduced me as a potential client who was interested in the products being manufactured, which meant that I had to spend time comparing fabrics, talking about them, and handling them. This "customer role" strategy was the best way to get them to give me their time and to explain all the work and everything it involved. The informants were always willing to cooperate with the researcher, showing enthusiasm and sharing complicity. Even so this mixture of means and methods also established different interpretations and levels of debate.

One of the main difficulties of ethnography is how to compare the collected information. Naturally, the informant cannot always be right, and in the role of researcher one must double-check everything he/she is told. In addition, sometimes significant discrepancies can occur, for instance, one of my informants told me that I would not be able to grasp Moroccan society because I was a foreigner. The idea of centrality and periphery (as stated in De Sousa Santos 1995) refers to the difficulty of viewing a subject clearly when looking from the actual center, and this was the argument I used to counteract his idea. The importance of the informant also involved having a reflective attitude to his/her society, an awareness of his/her position, together with a critical viewpoint, when possible. Some people turned out to be excellent informants: Hanif (a student of French literature) showed me around in the city, and his synthetic vision of Tangier later helped enormously when I appropriated it for my own interests. Malak tried to build a bond between myself and the female workers to make my fieldwork easier, but he was only partially successful because his contacts let him down; however, he did help me to make several discoveries. Rawi explained the historical context to me, from beginning to end, while Hijra told me about women's lives, and opened my eyes to the great social inequality within the city. Mahdi showed me the importance of peer groups, within which gender, age, religion and neighborhood of origin were of key importance in the formulation of migration and marriage projects. Chafik taught me that international co-operation can be like a marriage strategy when it comes to emigration. In addition, all my relations with the informants and their families took place within an atmosphere of reciprocity and friendliness. It is also interesting to note how we impose objectification onto our informants. Take the case of Rawi, who had never been aware that he had a migratory experience until I asked him to make a genogram of his family.

Some relationships with informants developed accidentally, such as with the merchants in the Casbah. It was simply passing by every so often and talking to the shopkeepers that resulted in meeting other people, such as Rawi. In no case did a relationship exist where they where trying to take advantage of the foreigner. Admittedly, none of these people were really laboratory objects/subjects, although inter-subjective relationships often create a distinct bias in ethnography. In fact, many of my informants and relationships during the fieldwork were based on a buffer zone between Moroccan and Spanish societies.

Both in ethnographic work and in real life, many chance events often occur, and this also applies to choosing informants. During the fieldwork I attempted to maintain a fairly participatory approach, not like interviewers who are only prepared to offer people an hour or two of their time. The term that I use to refer to people in the fieldwork is not that of "natives," but "actors" or "insiders" (obviously, with respect to me, the "outsider"). My field notes are very much located within a particular place and a precise context, allowing me to observe conclusions locally; they concern Tangier, and thus are much more limited to an even more specific context, that of the Medina and the Casbah neighborhoods in Tangier.

The Ethnography in Durrës

From a sociological perspective, Albania could be said to represent an ideal social laboratory, owing to the mixture that exists there between the context of post-Communism and that of neo-liberal capitalism. The blank slate of the last ten years has led to a scenario where the country seems to have started from zero. The country has evolved from the strictest form of impregnable communism to rampant capitalism, and from a community morality to the ethics of individualism. In this transition period, international migration represents—for many people—a way of searching for freedom, and paints an excellent portrait of the changes that have come about—almost as if people could now opt for an exile to which they were not previously entitled. In addition, mass media (particularly television) act as an enlarging mirror for people's desire for capitalism.

As Fuga (2000) points out when discussing the concept of "periphery," the Balkan countries lie on the border of the European Union. This is a border that is making an effort towards integration and modernization, but which also contains a social periphery that is chaotic, de-structured, poverty-stricken and often lawless, and which represents a major factor that helps in maintaining the delicate central equilibrium. It is a peripheral area that is a source of irregular labor, prostitution, drug trafficking, domestic workers, and adopted children. Within this periphery, Fuga also describes an infra-periphery, to which the urban world banishes various groups from its social periphery—groups such as those involved in the rural exodus, the elderly, Gypsies, and the sick (Fuga 2000: 275, 277; also quoted in the introduction of this book). This is the way in which Albania has entered the global labor market and has taken on forms of pan-European homogenization: this is globalization within a country that has been historically excluded from Europe, and which now raises serious questions on global transformations. In short, this involves a number of challenges to an understanding of "this difficult country," as Ismail Kadaré calls it.

The method I employed for my fieldwork in Albania was established through two NGOs: Créche International (Tirana) and the Social Services Association (Durrës). The first organization took me to visit different Roma families in a neighborhood on the outskirts of Tirana, while the latter association enabled me to make the necessary contacts in order to visit a family in Porto Romano (Durrës), as well as offering me the chance to visit a factory. I used these two associations as a basis for an understanding of the dynamics related to family strategies, while in the interviews, the key informants helped me to discover all the attributes that I had been searching for, and which eventually configured the definition of the border-city. In addition, I also made visits to textile and footwear factories.

Under communism, families had completely different jobs compared to their present ones; they have experienced a sudden change in their working lives. No one has had a fixed job in all of their working lives. In spite of the changes, one needs to have contacts to get a job nowadays. Ira (from Créche International) says that she had a better life in the time of communism, as her father was the head of the sector for the party; however, now she has no contacts anymore and has to get by on her own.

All of the families I visited not only experienced a rupture following the change in the system, they also experienced a before and an after as a result of the 1997 financial crisis, when it is estimated that 70 percent of Albanians invested in financial pyramid schemes that were fraudulently backed by the government. As a result, in 1997, there was great social unrest, which led to widespread destruction. During this time, people began to attack every possible place, to force the government to give them back their investments. Thus, capitalism was as big a change as the fall of the state. During that time one major disturbance took place at the port of Durrës, where people attacked the ships, even the ones awaiting repair. The Albanians remember the importance of television in what happened, and they are still perplexed by the effect that the illusory image of capitalism had on them. They also believe that the pyramid schemes of 1997 were a good lesson for the Albanians, which taught them that under capitalism everyone has to work for what they have. Before 1997, they were living relatively well, and they were shocked by the looting of that year, when the people rebelled and began to destroy everything. Many are still astonished by the memory of the collective madness that took place.

The Ethnographic Contrast

Gathering Information

Though I was familiar with research conditions in Morocco, the situation in Albania was completely new to me. For foreigners, Albania has become a kind of social laboratory in which they attempt to search for strategies to promote civil society, to fight against the trafficking of goods and human beings and against corruption, or to return unaccompanied minors to their families, as well as the women victims of trafficking who have been living abroad.

I approached my fieldwork in Albania differently to the line of observation I adopted in Tangier, both in the way that I gained access to my sources of information and to the types of access. In Morocco, the degree of trust that I was given and the suspicious attitude of the government and public information offices were much more complex. The legacy of the *maghzen* reproduced and fostered by the King Hassan II dictatorship and the lack of democracy in the country have all created an atmosphere of greater suspicion towards researchers—and especially towards foreigners—although in general, they treat you in a friendly manner. In contrast, Albanian society is renowned for having endured what was one of the strictest-ever communist secret police forces—the *segurime*; but despite this, people seem to have lost any fears they had about providing information. This could also be seen in the freedom of the press. Therefore, when we refer to the process of democratization, or the way civil society operates, we are talking about completely different worlds. The lack of trust towards the foreigner was heavily accentuated during the days of Communism, but today these states are at the mercy of foreign aid and investments; transition therefore once again swings from one extreme to the other, to the satanized West during decades of placing reliance on it. Uncle Sam substitutes Uncle Enver. However the identity of the fortress, erected against foreigners, seems to persist in present day Albania. It has even been claimed that Albania will become a type of Israel in Europe, sustained by the United States and surrounded by enemies (Ditchev 1996: 30).

In Albania, I met many different kinds of people who were always willing to help me with my research. It was also very easy for me to ask people questions, even those from the poorer classes. It was as if, from the very start, everyone saw the act of giving information as something that was positive and beneficial. In contrast to the situation in Morocco, where there is much greater control, people were more trusting in Albania, and as a result fewer research permits were required. Even within Albania's dictatorial past, you could move freely as a researcher; however, later you would find that the great difficulty was in getting precisely the information you were searching for. Thus, for example, while I was in Albania I found it impossible to obtain any economic data on Greek presence in the country, or any kind of information on the companies that administer remittances. Thus, economic data was the most difficult to find, and the typical reply I received from commercial offices was: "You can't count businesses as if they were schools; business are constantly being born, and then they die."

I had no official connection or links in either of the two research sites; I merely introduced myself as an independent individual working for a British university. This meant I had to be very persistent when trying to open doors, and I was even accused by a Moroccan local newspaper of being a spy, along with some other foreigners.

During my fieldwork in Durrës and Tirana, I tended to use the interviews as a base for the field diary more than in Tangier. This enabled me to see how the interviews defined the ethnographic study in a more articulated manner. I managed to base my work on systematized meetings in the form of interviews, combined with a form that analyzed the family system in a way similar to that of Tangier, with genograms included. In Tangier, meanwhile, my visits to the families were much lengthier and more intense. In Tangier, I used different forms of participant observation, which ranged from examining the family structure through repeated viewings of videos of family events (daughters' weddings, a grandson's circumcision, and grandchildren's birthdays) as well as a joint visit to relatives with problems (such as visiting a brother in prison).

The Socio-Historical Contexts

There are an endless number of geographical definitions we could employ; in the Arab world, Morocco means *Maghreb*, or the West. Morocco is Spain's semi-exotic neighbor, though the Spanish know little about Morocco—that land with its French and Spanish colonial past, the inland area of which was historically prohibited to foreigners. In contrast, Albania is in the center of Europe. But, at what point exactly does the East begin?

Muka (2002) notes how by opening the borders, Albanians sailed in search of the new God (*Perëndi*): the West (*Perëndim*). Albania has been stereotyped as a country that no one knows anything about except the Albanians: an unknown, faraway land, a region that is cut off and of no importance in Western European eyes. It is a country that is hardly featured on the map owing to its notoriety as a primitive European or mythical Balkan area, mainly referred to as a *terra icognita*, and also as the opaque and impenetrable communist Albania. It has been the terra incognita of the Balkans, characterized by a fundamentalist Stalinism (Combe 1996). Until the fall of the communist regime, it had come to represent not only a border that was closed to Europe and the Mediterranean, but also isolated from the rest of the world, a country where the free mobility of people was prohibited. Nowadays, Europeans see Albania as a borderland, almost like an under-age country that has to be watched over carefully by international institutions, driven by the European Union policies, and even watched over by a kind of European protectorate.

In these two places I have selected, the influence and nature of historical perspective is radically different: while colonialism plays a fundamental role in Morocco, in Albania (apart from its own particular colonialism) it is the fifty years of communism that have marked the country's particular socio-historical context. In the case of Morocco, the dictatorship was a long-lasting one that has often perpetuated the characteristics of an extremely archaic society. The Albanians, meanwhile, want to get rid of all traces of the past, and to start again with a blank slate. Albania's opening up culturally to the world outside is exemplified by the existence of Anglo-Albanian schools, while Morocco still has those classic private French schools, aimed especially at children from the elite families.

Cultural processes and consumer practices within a post-socialist context are extremely complex. These representations should be linked to an analysis of global and local relations in cultural processes. To a certain extent, in Albania, the best way to sell Western and consumer culture is to package it as Italian or Greek. In turn, in Morocco quality products are sold as French or Spanish. These are good examples of localism within globalization. This phenomenon is also present in the marketing of foodstuffs (in Albania, everything that is bottled is Italian; in the north of Morocco it is always Spanish), as well as in soccer coverage: in Albania they follow the Italian teams, while in Morocco they support Spanish clubs. It is very strange to see how some young people have an idea of Europe that is based on what make of car people drive in each country and on football teams. This type of perception is also visible in Morocco. Another factor I would consider a common trait is the young people's desire for mobility, that form of cross-border mobility that simultaneously intermixes many different places.

A second contextual difference is the fact that the Balkans is a very conservative region, which helps to explain the lack of any protest there against the war in Iraq, as well as an absence of criticism about the repatriation of unaccompanied minors. As a consequence, the NGOs that work in migration-related areas are less critical than in Morocco. It is probably due to the same mentality as that of creating a post-communist nation.

A third stream of differences in the localization of the two ethnographies derives from Albania's peripheral position, or rather in the way the country is excluded from the European Union. This exclusion from Europe is patently a more urgent situation for Morocco than for Albania. Though both countries are excluded from Schengen territory in all senses, Albania is different in terms of its geography, as it is considered part of the European continent. What's more, Albania has already overcome the first obstacle to joining the EU, and is now one of the countries in the "waiting room" of candidates for European integration. The role of the European Union with regard to Morocco is completely different from that in respect to Albania. These divergences in the location of the two ethnographies represent the differences of the role of the European Union, which, though it might be opening up towards the east, has sealed off its doors to the south.

However, similarities do exist between these two border ethnographies. One point the two border areas have in common is the role of internal migrations. These play a crucial part in both urban transformation and foreign emigration from border areas. Within the context of these changes, a stereotype of the internal migrant has become strongly established, a person who gets the blame for everything bad that happens in these border cities. In addition to being labeled as ill-mannered, uncivilized people, these immigrants are also stereotypically mountain people—the *Jibli* in Morocco and the *Malok* in Albania. In Tangier, they still yearn for their lost international period and despise the newcomers, while in Durrës they simply feel overwhelmed by the rural exodus. In Tangier they dream of the city's past, while in Durrës they want to rid themselves of the taint of arid communism and to dream up a better future for themselves, one in which no one will be without water or electricity. Durrës, that old city-bunker of a communist fortress, is the country's main port, the Adriatic port which leads to Italy—that country which everyone has seen on television. In this world of internal migrations, border cities perfectly combine spatial marginalization (i.e., all manner of poverty-stricken habitats) and the upsurge of the underground economy, even in areas of extreme toxicity (jobs such as gathering lindane, and Chromium VI in the Porto Romano area in Durrës, an area that has been dubbed the "Chernobyl of the Balkans"). Citizens often complain of groups of outsiders "flooding" the urban area: in Tangier, they complain about the mountain people (the *Jebalis* from Bir Chifa who have settled in Tangier) and their lack of civic education, while in Durrës they criticize the ancestral societies of exogenous patriarchal families from the north of the country, who have reintroduced the harshest *Kanun* laws. In Tangier, the people of the north speak disparagingly about those from the south, because as far as they are concerned these newcomers only bring problems to the city. It was they who began stowing away on lorries to get into Spain (the aforementioned immigrant children). Curiously, the complaints made about these rural exodus populations in Durrës and in Tangier all concern issues regarding mentality and civic education, complaints that are not so very different to the attitudes some Southern Europeans have about foreign immigrants.

These internal migrations summon up the mental image of a revolving door through which some people come in while others go out, to travel and live abroad. In Tangier, many people live as if they were permanently on the verge of leaving, and feel as if they were in transition to somewhere. There are the Sub-Saharans who use the hostels in the Tangier Casbah like a waiting room, and the young people from Tangier NGOs who leave as soon as they get their chance. In Durrës—just as in the rest of Albania—people are repeatedly told that theirs is an economy in transition. Youngsters long to go and live abroad, just like any other people of their age would like to leave and live in a capital city somewhere else in the world, but for many of them migration restrictions mean they have to resign themselves to a decadent social and economic situation. In addition, there are people who live daily the experience of migration as an integral part of their family's relationships, as well as their friends and other people for whom mobility is seen as a regulating factor in their lives.

Not all neighborhoods are the same in terms of international migration. The *Banque Populaire* in Morocco clarified this assertion by providing us with a map showing family dependence on remittances in specific neighborhoods. Western Union offices made available to us the same kind of map for Albania (their offices are located in around thirty-five towns and cities, which represents a particularly wide dispersion). Oddly enough, the dismembering of the Albanian state and its financial de-legitimization in the eyes of the population have made the country a paradise for *Western Union.*

Paradoxically, Durrës is also known to the inhabitants of Tirana for its patriarchal mentality, and because everything that everyone says and does in Durrës is still under observation. This is also the case, with a few differences, in Tangier (open and closed); both cities are transit areas, passing places and circulation zones, though they are also renowned for their narrow-mindedness. In contrast, what is dying out in one city (Tangier) is just appearing in the other: it is surprising to see the big hotels sprouting up on the beach at Durrës, while the hotels in Tangier had become increasingly empty during the 1990s.

A second point these cities have in common is the feminization of the labor force. In both places I witnessed (explicitly in Tangier and implicitly in Durrës) the role played by women in the industrialization of textile production (which in Albania has led to a second wave of industrialization, after the first one that came in with communism). Though this feminization is the tip of the iceberg with regard to the changes taking place in the globalization of production, it is expressed differently in Tangier and Durrës. In the former, textile production plays a fundamental role in the way the city's labor market functions. In Durrës, meanwhile, it is more of a concealed phenomenon, though it is also important in terms of numbers and in proportion to urban employment. There are also significant differences inside the factories: both the intensity of work and the tension shown by the workers seem to be less in Durrës, and the machinery is more out-dated.

A third point these border areas have in common is the fact that they are key geographical nodes for smuggling illegal drugs into the European Union.

Hashish is produced and marketed from Morocco, while heroin is distributed from Albania. Therefore, Albanian drug smugglers receive harsher sentences than do Moroccans, as heroin smuggling is more strictly penalized. Thus, the penalization for drugs is contemporary with the processes of the racialization of criminality in Europe.

A fourth trait that border spaces share is the fact that they effectively form migratory destinations with certain common peculiarities. Thus, Spain (for neighboring Morocco) and Greece (for neighboring Albania) represent the first "shock absorbers" for the migratory flows on each side of the Mediterranean. They also represent the first exit routes, the most permeable borders, the easiest places in which to find agricultural work, and the first jumping-off point to Schengen-Europe or—in the case of Greece—the route to the UK. In addition, on the subject of international migration, both places are affected (both by land and sea) by the large-scale homeward flows of summer emigrants, who either cross the Strait of Gibraltar from Andalusia or pass through the border at Kakavia, in the south of Albania.

Another feature these cities share is the importance of family ideology in shaping survival strategies, as well as the way that migratory networks operate. Therefore, comparisons between family ideologies in Morocco and in Albania are also influential in terms of both understanding the forms of survival within border economies as well as the construction of migratory networks within emigration. Even so, some patent differences come to light when we dissect these family systems, as can be seen below:

1. At weddings in Morocco, spaces are segregated according to gender (except in the case of more modern families or if they are not from the north of the country). There is also a division between the two families of the couple, which celebrate at different parties and receive separate presents. Very often, middle-class families relax the rules of virilocality and they opt for a nuclear family household, even more frequently than in Albania. Finally, Albanian families tend to have much lower levels of education, though having said that, one of Morocco's most pressing problems is its high illiteracy rate.
2. Weddings in Albania contain spaces that are segregated, though not according to gender, but to how the spouse's family have divided the wedding feast. The groom and bride celebrate separately at different parties. What is most striking is the way in which the persistent rule of patrilocality has been maintained. In addition, the number of children per mother is much lower here than in Morocco. Thus, they fulfill the typical idiosyncrasy of a nuclear family more according to the size of their homes than to the type of established family relationships.

Marriage plays a significant role in the construction of social networks within emigration. Choosing to marry an emigrant is a common option for women's social mobility strategies. A mixed marriage with a foreigner is also a possible alternative, both as a form of mobility and as an expression of freedom for women faced with the decision of marrying an Albanian or a Moroccan man, and who believe they will reach modernity or freedom with the type of man they think will be more supportive. Thus, there are women who opt for mixed marriage as a way to free themselves from traditional roles and relations.

Family bindings are a key word for entering these societies. Let's recall that in ancient Albania the youngest brother was called by the name "youngerbrother" and the only child was called by the name "onlychild" (Kadaré 2001: 78). Whereas in Morocco there is still a difference between each degree of family member, as for example, in the North, the aunt on the maternal side is called *halty*.

Ultimately, in both places, old residual codes persist that govern relationships among families: the old *vendetta* systems that still exist in Rif (Morocco) and the *Kanun* law from northwest Albania.

Co-ordinating Migration

The Strait of Gibraltar and the Strait of Otranto in the Adriatic are currently the scenario for large movements of people in the Mediterranean; during the 1990s, both witnessed tragic waves of migration. During the last decade of the twentieth century, most of the Albanian and Moroccan population that are now living and working in southern European countries passed through these two ports. These two ports function as checkpoints for Fortress Europe, and are now part of a complex system that is comprised of border administration, the fight against illegal immigration, and social and economic development, such as the case of northern Morocco. In spite of the great geographical distance between them and the fact that one belongs to Europe and the other to Africa, these cities do have common traits, particularly their function as the gates into Fortress Europe, seen as a result of EU policy in the region, as we can see in Table 3.1.

Meanwhile, overseas, Europe intensified its visa policies, and on a national level, Morocco was transforming politically (in terms of government and civil action) and Albania started its transition period. In addition, on an urban level, new neighborhoods were created, which were the product of the complex dynamics of internal migration and rural exodus. In terms of the global economy, neo-liberal capital encouraged production, the growth of tax-free zones, and the delocalization of telephony and textile industries. At the same time, consumption encouraged the spread of smuggling in border regions.

The lack of coordination of Albanian emigration abroad is not paralleled in Morocco, since to a great extent it is the Moroccan government that channels the flows and the remittances. This difference is owed to a number of causes, such as the fact that Albania is a country new to emigration, while Morocco

Table 3.1
EU Migration Policy towards Albania and Morocco

Type of action/country	Albania	Morocco
Migration Management	*Border management*:Integrated project for the management of external borders, emphasizing the systems that control trafficking in Albanian territorial waters. Location: East-West corridor branch of the Pan-European Corridor VIII leading to Greece, North-South corridor leading to Greece, and Durrës as main port of the Pan-European Corridor VIII leading into Albania. *Asylum and migration*: information on best (police) practice, reinforcing the capacity of police forces and the courts to deal with migratory flows, improving the capacity for receiving illegal migrants and asylum seekers. *Border control*:ICMPD (International Center for Migration Policy Development). Upgrading border control system of Albania along European standards. *Combating illegal migration*:MARRI (Migration, Asylum, Refugees Regional Initiative). To combat illegal migration and to promote the orderly and free movement of persons. *Asylum*: UNHCR. Development of the asylum system in Albania. Under the Stability Pact for South Eastern Europe.	*Organization of legal emigration via creation of a migration center*:Fighting illegal immigration. CGEP-DPG (Spain): technical equipment and training for border control, fighting illegal immigration and detection of falsified documents. AFD (France): Development of the country of origin by Moroccans residing in France and through rural tourism and the creation of SME. *Migration management* (Netherlands): support to entrepreneurs of Moroccan origin residing in Europe in setting up economic activities. *Fighting Illegal immigration*: French Mol/National police: financial and technical assistance for combating illegal migration. Moroccan migrant in Italy as an agent of cooperation and development.
Social Development	Civil society and political cooperation	Support for economic development of regions with high emigration such as Province du Nord, support for reintegration.

Source: Mainly notes from European Commission of the European Communities, 2002.

has had a long history of international migration, especially to Northern Europe. Albanian migrations have only been taking place for the last decade. If one compares Tangier and Durrës as geo-strategic locations, the Strait of Gibraltar is probably a more dangerous crossing-point owing to climatic factors, as it is the point where the Mediterranean meets the Atlantic. The Adriatic, in contrast, is a calm and fairly predictable sea. The port is a material feature for both cities, and not only for the city itself, but also for the relationship that it has with its hinterland. Most incoming cargoes at the port of Durrës come from Italy. If you compare what the two cities represent in terms of routes, Durrës is just another channel for the flow of goods into the European Union, while in Tangier traffic seems to be much more concentrated around this point in the Mediterranean.

Tangier and Durrës are subject to the same policies restricting people's freedom of movement. Even so, at present no one knows exactly how long this policy of closure against Albania will last, since it will depend on the state of the country's relations with the European Union, as well as on international regulations. From the viewpoint of the various institutions that are investigating this subject, it is becoming clear that if Albanians continue to meet border standards, eventually they will be rewarded with free circulation. One significant and distinct factor in the case of Albania is that it is often assumed that Albania derives from the same historical context as Western Europe; mention is often made of how the country's geography legitimizes this—the fact that it is part of the European continent—and that the current situation leaves Greece cut off from Europe.

Tangier and Durrës are currently experiencing one of the most complicated impacts of globalization, reflected in renewed border restrictions on people's movement; these restrictions are symbols of a dominant blockade, in marked contrast to the free mobility of people and movement of goods across borders (as well as being the result of European macro-economic policies). In this way, these "corners" of Europe—these two Mediterranean port cities, Durrës and Tangier—can be used as strategic sites that enable us to study different forms of mobility in a distinct, selected border area, within the physical territory of economic globalization. These cities represent spaces that allow us to analyze what happens on a specific level in such places that in themselves represent physical barriers and areas of control. They enable us to examine a "break space" through which we can discern specific changes in a contemporary urban setting that has been plunged into consumerism (with the increasing dominance of images and mass culture) and in the mobility of young people, especially in these two cases. In general, capital, products, and ideas have become more mobile, while certain categories of labor, which are limited by immigration laws, continue to be subject to control and are criminalized by the penalization of mobility. When we consider the closure of borders (militarization, the increase in police contingents, etc.), these types of borders can also be seen as pockets of resistance to globalization within Mediterranean mobilities.

Tangier and Durrës reveal the typical dynamic of revolving doors. For example, in Albania during the 1990s, emigrants traveled from Albania to Greece, and then after a couple of months they returned to Albania, brought back by smugglers. This "revolving door" system can also be seen in Tangier; it has created a parallel circulation that has been established upon an absurd system (according to UNHCR [United Nations High Committe for Refugees] in Albania) that disregards the protection of people's human rights, both in the Strait of Otranto and in the Strait of Gibraltar. Nevertheless, people disappear or die much more frequently in the latter channel, owing to its rough waters, and as this area is much more thoroughly policed, the routes the boats are forced to take are more dangerous.

Tangier and Durrës are also waiting areas: for internal immigrants, such as the Jebala on the outskirts of Tangier and the people from Kukës on the edge of Durrës. This "waiting room" also includes other nationalities: Tangier is also a waiting place for Sub-Saharan people on their way to Spain, while in Albania Durrës has become a transit area for immigrants traveling on routes from eastern countries. Thus, we can see that in spite of the intensification of controls and closures, these borders are continually challenged by people who actively desire freedom of mobility, and who believe their lives to be structured on a continuum within the context of transnational processes.

Many young people in these border cities are waiting for the chance to leave. In Nora's family in Albania, Elvis, her son, is waiting to leave his country so he can chase his dreams (interestingly enough, I found the same attitude in Tangier, in the case of Mohamed Ad-dubbu). Many of the things that Elvis told me about his life and his friends' lives reminded me of the young Moroccans: the way they go out for a drive in their free time, their criticism of the clientelism of the NGOs, the scarcity of available opportunities, the problem of only working part-time, and their dependence on co-operation projects.

In my search for border attributes, as I have already mentioned, Albania happens to be an ideal social laboratory because, like Morocco, the familist ideology explains and provides the perfect interpretative tool for understanding the migration project, which is common to so many other places, but particularly visible in Mediterranean countries. Thus, it is not a question of an immutable code of honor that unites the Mediterranean, or the portrayal of a reality as intangible and out of sync as the Mediterranean when compared to an emergent European identity; rather it is a question of appreciating the importance of the familist ideology that underlies the migration projects and impacts the ways in which immigrants are received in the south of Europe.

Definition of Circuits

I am particularly interested in examining in-depth the circuits that can be identified in the Mediterranean region, as well as—the other side of the coin—

considering the policies of border restriction. Such restrictions can be proved through the amount of funds that are invested in border control and the fight against undocumented migration from Albania and Morocco. In Albania, these policies are based on border control and police administration, whereas in Morocco they display a wider range of action, since the country has also implemented projects related to business promotion in the development of the northern provinces.

The very conceptualization of the border as a point of closure and control is part of what I consider in my ethnographic study to be circuits of control. Thus, I was quick to perceive the relative permeability of Durrës' port border. This permeability and the lack of control in terms of manpower management cannot be simply compared with the sealing-off of the European-African route.

With respect to the international circuits, it is relevant to see how the process of the internationalization of NGOs ultimately goes hand-in-hand with the role of foreign capital in the flow of manufacturing jobs. Something similar occurred in one NGO in Tangier, where women were being trained in clothes-making. Very gradually, I began to realize that the topic of the sweatshops was important. Everybody knows that it goes on, but nobody talks about it. The whole subject of industrial outsourcing across borders is much more widespread than it appears to be, as there is an active process of informal, invisible industrial relocalization in progress. In a broader scope this clothing circuit covers foreign-led firms, full-package manufacturers, joint ventures/U.S. subsidiaries, assembly plants, subcontractors, manufacturers (Bair and Jereffi 2001).

Other types of circuits include those connected with smuggling. An analysis of these circuits leads us to a controversial conception of the problem of legality and illegality in Albania, as this issue has been problematized in the context of a de-structured society. For example, the television companies buy DVDs in Italy and broadcast them directly, which is effectively the same as smuggling, in that they violate copyrights laws. In real terms, they act as if borders did not exist. All these circuits are more hyped by the media in the case of Albania, since television news is much more modern and transparent than the news programs broadcast in Morocco. Within the context of analysis, there are also other elements that take place in a much more exaggerated way in Albania than in Morocco. Namely, these are the constant fronts that are based around the fight against smuggling, anti-corruption advertisements, and anti-trafficking policies.

Another type of circuit is connected to what I call the "vulnerable actors." In these peripheral Mediterranean spaces selected for the study, certain processes affect the most vulnerable people in the circulation of transnational flows, which include movements within the formal as well as the informal economy. I refer specifically to the processes concerning women's roles of survival. The concept of feminization of survival refers to the way in which homes and communities are increasingly dependent on the social resources provided by women (Sassen 2000c). Three examples of such circuits are the increase in trafficking by prostitution networks, the growing demand in the European labor market for domestic workers and services connected with the care of the elderly, and a general increase in remittance-generating activities driven by emigrant women.

The high number of women involved in survival strategies clarifies the existing link between the increase in survival circuits and the pressures that economic globalization imposes on southern countries and countries in transition. To be more precise, the impact of economic globalization on these economies is intertwined with some very tangible factors: an increase in foreign debt (particularly to the World Bank and the IMF programs), cuts in social benefits, and the disappearance of traditional businesses (organized for local markets) in the wake of burgeoning export industries.

This brings us to the issue that not only migratory strategies but also the delocalization of European industrial production (which is much less apparent in Durrës owing to the peculiarities of Albania's transition economy) have constructed a labor market framework in which women emerge as the key workers in the market's search for cheap labor (which is then provided by internal migration). These vulnerable actors include women used as cheap labor in small-scale clothing factories (especially for the Spanish market) in Tangier and, to a lesser extent, in the foreign-run factories (especially Italian) in Durrës.

With respect to migration into southern Europe, a process of commodification has taken the place of everything related to migration, from documents to human beings, and which especially involves women and children. As shown in the introduction, in Italy and Greece, most unaccompanied children are Albanians. Moroccan children are the second most prominent group of unaccompanied minors in Italy, and the first in Spain. We can illustrate this phenomenon by cross-categorizing for nationality, as well as for sex, age, and ethnic origin of unaccompanied minors in Italy. Such a cross-categorization reveals the absence of any Moroccan girls, the difference between the ages of adolescence and childhood, the proportion of gypsies among Albanian emigrants, as well as the distinction between the phenomena of trafficking,[17] Mafia and the existence of isolated networks among peer groups. Moroccan minors arrive at younger ages than their Albanian counterparts, and most of these Moroccans come from one precise region: Beni Melall. In contrast, Albanian children come from all over the country. This information on the two most prominent groups of unaccompanied minors—the Albanians and the Moroccans in Italy—confirms for me the importance of these two emigration countries on one side of the ocean, and of the Southern European border and peripheral areas on the other side. In turn, particular feminization processes arise either through industrial relocalization (in Tangier), or as a result of the commodification of women and children, as in the case of Albania. Underage children become outstanding actors on the border circuits, circuits that tend to suck in the most vulnerable actors. As far as USAID (The United States Agency for International Development) and the U.S. government are concerned, the fight against the trafficking of human beings in Albania and abroad is the main objective of their policies.

According to the Terre des hommes report (2003: 8), a trafficked child is moved from one place to another, legally or illegally, within his or her country across borders, and this often takes place without the child's consent. Often, if not always, a third person is involved as an intermediary and the transaction is carried out in an organized fashion. At his or her destination, the child is exploited through work or involved in unlawful or illicit activities, through force or deception. The child may also be sold for adoption. The principal aim of child trafficking is profit. In most cases, child trafficking involves additional criminal activities. Other reasons for trafficking children involve: exploitation through work, including slavery and forced labor, sexual exploitation, including prostitution and pornography, illegal activities, including begging, theft, drug trafficking, commercially motivated adoption schemes, traffic in organs. The three principal criteria for identifying child trafficking are: (1) geographical displacement. The child's place of residence is moved (within a country or beyond its borders); (2) coercion (including the use of deception, threats or force); and (3) a profit-making motive for the benefit of a third person.

However, the main focus of this commodification of human beings is the globalization of the sex industry, together with other similar ways of commercializing people. Italy has become the number one destination for Albania-based networks of trafficking in women that sprang up in the 1990s; these networks buy and sell not only Albanian women, but also women from other countries such as Moldavia, the most impoverished country in Eastern Europe. The introduction of global chains for the illegal movement of bodies implies here an effort to include issues related to commercializing sex and the female body and the idea of its lucrative returns across borders. The impact of the global landscape in relation to the commodification of the body is here understood how not only it produces commodification and commercialization of diverse forms of culture and ideologies but also of individual bodies (Bauman 1998).

Firstly, the examples of this commodification of the body are normally related to the global traffic in human organs, tissues, and body parts due to the capitalist expansion and the spread of biotechnology in medical and surgical techniques.

Secondly, examples can be related to the new practices of arranged marriages in the mail-order bride market. A key factor of the women's interest may be the economic condition of the groom, but her foreign male counterpart's interest may lie in her ability to provide a caring function, very often for the elderly.

Thirdly, examples related to human trafficking can cover the act of migration from one country to another and trafficking for prostitution purposes. The key objects of this exchange on this global market are most often women and children. Therefore, apart from the economic conditions that instigate this type of trafficking, there is also a critical reading on gender and child-adult differences between "objects" and buyers, as well as for goods regarding traffickers and clients. Under this type of trafficking, the debate is often formulated from the paradigmatic abstractions of the notions of free choice and true consent in examining the possibility of the women's agency when analyzing forced and voluntary prostitution.

Focusing on sexual work among borders also implies recognizing a new geography of sexual work, where not only North-South but East-West differences serve as a structural explanation. Therefore, they can be underlined as a paradigmatic example of a cross-border labor market. Within these routes, even European countries such as Italy have become areas of transit as well as the destinations of sex work clients. For example, from Nigeria (and to a lesser extent from Ghana and Cameroon) women arrive with tourist visas obtained through Paris, via Marseilles and head for Turin, as a distribution center for Northern Italy. Some even reach Belgium and the United Kingdom (Zincone 2001: 629, using sources from *Associazione Parsec* and *Dipartimento Pari opportunità*).

Different types of prostitution can be established that vary according to the degree of choice, from freely chosen, to semi-chosen, to trafficked prostitution. Those types can be recognized by the individual's awareness of being a sex worker or being a victim of trafficking. In the case of Italy, Carchedi et al. (2000) distinguishes four types according to origin: Albanian (dominated by coercion), Nigerian (dominated by persuasion), Eastern Europe (dominated by the voluntary type), and Latin American (dominated by the voluntary type with some instances of coercion). (Carchedi et al., 2000, in the panel "Combating the Exploitation of Undocumented Migrants," Sixth International Metropolis Conference, Rotterdam, November 26-30). Those types are also intertwined with the classical three phases of trafficking—exit from the country of origin, the type of transfer, and finally settlement in Europe—when trafficked women are used as high value commodities that are supposed to be highly mobile within the European space.

Morality and ethical arguments are frequently used in examining the in-between gray areas of the two poles mentioned. The nature of this market can also include consumer-related aspects linked to the use, sexualization, and exoticization of the female body as well as the historical perspective, referring back to the representation of slaves within the colonial discourses (when owning a body meant reducing it to the status of a commodity).

The Difficulty of Selecting a Border-City

At these strategic locations we can observe a concentration of the trends associated with the globalization of production (i.e., factories subject to special taxes) and consumption (i.e., remittance payments from immigrants to remittance-dependent economies). These border cities are characterized by the following specific features: firstly, owing to their front-line location, they are the first to suffer from the closure of Fortress Europe (a closure which encourages illegal activity and reinvents various forms of mobility); secondly, they represent passing places on the south-north migration route, as well as being temporary stop-off points for certain migratory projects. These cities are also important in terms of the goods trade, being key sites of industrial relocalization from northern countries (especially textile and service industries) and the resulting increase in female workers.

In this global market, a reassessment of spatial scales is taking place in regard to the places where the heart of the new economy (i.e., production, consumption and circulation and their components—capital, workforce, products, management, information, technology, and markets) is organized on a global scale. On an economic level, this type of global economy has led to the restructuring of companies (for example, the outsourcing of Spanish textile factories in Tangiers) and financial markets (the fall of the financial pyramid groups in Albania in 1997 is a good example) as well as the subsequent expansion of information technologies. On a political level, this is as much a result of the application of the governmental policies of a neo-liberal court (which have been fully introduced following the political transition of Morocco's King Mohammed VI) as of the privatization programs of the Albanian economic transition.

In the case of Albania, selecting border features caused me great difficulty from the very start. I was not at all sure about these chief border features because I was well aware that what seemed to be complex, identifiable Mediterranean border marks in Tangier appeared in a much more diluted form in Durrës. Therefore, it was immediately clear that the border checkpoint of Durrës had nothing at all in common with the hustle and bustle of Tangier. In the port of Durrës, there is no preliminary passport control point, nor children waiting to jump onto lorries, nor people attempting to jump the queues.

In considering the context of international migration, I would emphasize the migrants' role as strategic actors within current mobilities and, consequently, it is these migrants who can best help us comprehend these border-spaces in an explanatory effort of what "global" actually means. Secondly, I should also mention the fact that these border spaces enabled me to establish strategically (using Robert Merton's conception of strategic location, see in Portes 1997), and to elucidate more clearly, the specific materialization processes taking place in a space within the global scenario. These two ethnographic case studies allow us to confront one of the largest-scale fractures to appear on the regionalized scenario of globalization. In turn, we must also question whether these two cases are truly indicative of global fractures; that is to say, judged from a quantitative perspective, whether when we contrast the Italian-Greek GDP with that of Albania, and examine the Spanish GDP against that of Morocco, we see that some are more significant than others. Essentially, it is question of asking why we were guided by these points of polarization and not others, as there are many regions like the Mediterranean in the world and a great many borders. All in all, why have we picked these particular ones?

In terms of "border features," Durrës is the embodiment of a trading place, for goods and for passengers. Even so, the nodes of globalization are located in Tirana, since it is there that the Bretton Woods institutions are based. In this context, one must also consider the triangular effect created by the poles of Tirana, Durrës, and Vlorë, the same as Sebta's effect within the western Mediterranean borderlands. Albania's geographical division contains two cities that have their gaze set on Italy, Durrës and Vlorë. Before I arrived at the latter, there were several marks that attracted me to Vlorë as a possible case of a border city. These features included the presence of the Scabolini Italian kitchen factory (the Italians' favorite kitchen), the ongoing construction of a military airport, the work of the OSCE (Organization for Security and Cooperation in Europe), the Vlorë Women's Hearth and their work against trafficking in women, and the fact that Vlorë represents a strategic point for the traffic of mobility and for crossings by *gommone*.[18] Unquestionably, Vlorë stands out as the capital for the trafficking of illegal immigrants into Italy. It also was once the old capital of Albania, and it still has strong cultural ties with Italy. However, when I reached Vlorë, I saw that it was very different in terms of everything that I had initially thought characterized it as a border city. It could only be described as such in terms of its closure and its blockades—a closure to all types of trafficking, which is the result of anti-trafficking policies, as a result of an anti-trafficking drive throughout Albania, and the firm decision by foreign countries to put an end to all this.

During the first stage of my fieldwork in Albania, the determination of case suitability progressed very slowly. This involved breaking down the peculiarities that defined each city as a border city: (1) Tangier: internal and international migration circuit, industrial outsourcing, creation of free-trade area, remittance-dependent neighborhoods, and waiting areas for Sub-Saharan peoples; (2) Vlorë: trafficking capital, small city (100,000 inhabitants), difficult access to families, the historical perspective of a place of transit (the events of 1997 and a main objective in the fight against trafficking), the commodification of bodies in border spaces (a key point in the trade of women); (3) Durrës: a larger port, with more intense trade, greater transit of documented and undocumented migrants and probably with a higher presence of smuggling than in Vlorë. It is also one of the most substantial reception cities in the country for the rural exodus. Moreover, it is the main center for the in-flow of manufacturing jobs that the country is experiencing—one significant example being the *Shoelace* Italian shoe factory. Durrës is also an important location for NGOs.

We can also analyze the contrasts between Durrës and Vlorë as border cities. Vlorë has always had a closer relationship to Italy, in terms of both civilization and culture. Historically, this is the site that has greater Italian presence. As for Durrës, it is a focus area for internal migration, and is also relevant for the volume and speed of trafficking that evolves there. This city is both a point of transit and of origin of migrations. However, the situation has now changed to a great extent owing to two factors: (1) the cooperation between Italian and Albanian police, and (2) the fight against illegal networks that operate both internally and internationally. Solving these two problems are sine qua non conditions for joining Europe. Currently, people emigrate much less by sea, and furthermore, during the 1990s, Vlorë was the symbol par excellence of irregular immigration—the slowcoach of the Adriatic—though the city later lost its influence in terms of circulation and border economy. This was the influence that I was looking for, and which I had previously found in Tangier.

The Researcher's Place

In my view, in the context of fieldwork, an analysis of the power structure should be based on the socioeconomic division existing between the researcher (salary type, social status, belonging to the middle class) in contrast to the people with whom the researcher spends his/her time during the fieldwork. This division highlights a significant difference in terms of purchasing capacity, lifestyle (freedom to go to restaurants or to travel), prestige, and especially the fact of being foreign European and having the ability to move freely across borders. These divisions are of fundamental importance when we consider the differences that exist between the researcher and the researched field. Nonetheless, we should also bear in mind all the distinct relationships involving dominance that are affected by the fact of the researcher being a woman, a foreigner, Spanish, and having a salary that is out of proportion within a context of "poverty" such as in a city like Tangier and, more specifically, in certain neighborhoods that have experienced a significant decline.

These socioeconomic differences were also brought to the fore with several people I met in Albania; Bart[19] is currently looking for work. He told me that all the associations arrived in 1998, with the Kosovo crisis, and he complained that they were all about to leave. Through the conversations I had with Elvis, Bart, and Julio (a student in mechanical energy) I realized the great difference that exists between them and me, and that a certain polarized power relationship exists, even though I am a woman. When I think of this person's opportunities as a social worker and I compare them to mine, it also reminds me of the difficulties in finding work experienced by Berty, the sociologist in Durrës who is a friend of Julio's. First he worked as a substitute teacher, teaching sociology in a school, and then he started work in a cyber-cafe, which has since then closed.

As in ethnography, relations between interviewer and respondent reproduce the image of the respondent as localized between two extremes: that of the guest-sociologist and the intruder-sociologist. The limit lies between the Western guest and his/her host within the framework of Moroccan hospitality, and the Western intruder, whose curiosity is such that it can be seen as a threat. The discourse is located in a context of evident domination, particularly in the case of rural settings and with uneducated respondents or informants. As Said's prodigious definition states (in his classic work, *Orientalism*, 1995), the perceptions of the "other" take place within the context of a dominant and conquering West. The imbalance in perceptions and a lack of knowledge of the so-called Orient (languages, customs, etc.) means that the only advantage held by the Western interviewer is the opportunity to benefit from a distanced analysis, thereby approaching the objectivization of the target of his/her study (Ribas-Mateos 1999b).

In addressing participant observation, the researcher's starting point should be presented from the position of power and responsibility he/she enjoys with respect to the different actors. In principle, the power differences should be balanced out, and when one considers involvement in the participatory research, the fieldwork should be interactive, communal, and participatory, but its objectivity becomes doubtful. In this ethnography, no research-action was established beforehand, rather a relationship of interaction was created, a reciprocity relationship established by doing people favors during the various field trips and spending time with families during the course of their everyday lives. Other differences within this power structure in the research environment derive from the problem of not being able to speak the local languages (in these cases Moroccan Arabic and Albanian) and being forced to translate via other languages, such as Spanish, French, Italian, and English.

As Rabinow points out, "participation does not prevent you from continuing to be both a foreigner and an observer" (1977: 77). Most of the people in my fieldwork in Tangier considered me to be the prototype of a European. It is this point that often leads to the creation of a rupture between "us" and "the Europeans." Apart from seeing me as a Spaniard, the Tangerines also saw me as a Christian or *nasrania* (literally, nazarene). Rosander, through her research on identity of Muslim women living in the village of Sebta, shows how modernity is expressed by the women as *hayat nasaraniyen* (Spanish things)—but implied as having a second-rate morality (Evers Rosander 1991: 7) The idea of the nasrani also implies the constant dialectic of here and there, the so-called *otro lado* ("the other side"—the term used by Mexicans to refer to the United States, "them and us" or "the others").

In the case of Spaniards, and in particular Spanish researchers, relations between researcher and informer have to endure added stereotypes, such as that of the Spanish people's ambivalent historical image of the Moroccan, be it through *maurofilia* (the Moroccan as the friend, the friendliness of the Moroccan) or be it through *maurofobia* (the Moroccan as the traitor, the villain). Martín Corrales (2002) goes through an in-depth observation of this stereotype using a graphic collection, where the historical background of five centuries of Spanish-Moroccan relations sets the scenario of the contemporary anthropologic discourse. It starts with the conquest of Melilla in 1497 (launching the so-called Spanish African policy). It continues through the African war (1859-1860) and the orientalization of Morocco, the period of warmongering escalation (1909-1927), the colonial domination (the Spanish protectorate in Northern Morocco and the Sahara), the period of Moroccans soldiers in the Spanish Civil War (1936-1939), the war Ifni-Sahara (1958-1959), the frustrated decolonization of the Sahara and the Green March (1975); they all set up the chronological steps by which to understand changes in the polarized image of Moroccans in contemporary Spanish minds.

Thus, although they respect me, they are also convinced that Islam is the greatest religion and, deep down, many of them would like me to convert to their faith. On the other hand, they admit that people from "Christian countries" always have a better standard of living and are better educated, because "they are the ones that rule the world." Hijra's comments always brought that perception home to me very clearly. I imagine that time played an important part in my role within my relationships and my integration into the community, since my stay was quite a long one, and people began to forget about my initial "foreignness." Europeans share at the same time a positive and a negative image; the positive is related to formal education, resources, and opportunities, the negative is related to their moral, religious, and community conceptions.

As for my version of my own role during the time spent in Tangier, I always perceived it to be a very slow, laborious, fragmentary process. Partly (and the same happened to Rabinow), I was fighting to avoid the synthesis of my field material and the search for specific questions and their answers. It was hard to give a structure to all my notes because, as Rabinow points out (paraphrasing Lévi-Strauss), "if ethnology is an adventure, the ethnologist is the bureaucrat of that adventure" (1977: 113).

I have frequently considered my image and stereotype as a foreigner, and especially as a foreign woman, though not so much as a Spaniard. Tangerines also have distinct stereotypical images of Spaniards as being people who are more open, and they suppose that a friendship exists between the two peoples of both sides of the Mediterranean based on a closeness and certain friendliness, paradoxically enough, without sharing the stereotypical flamenco images that other foreigners embrace. I suppose that on the negative side they are also aware of Spanish racism regarding the *moros*[20] (Moors), and that they see the Spanish as backward compared to the French, for example, or that they even recycle the stereotypes that the French have about the Spaniards. Other stereotypes held concern social class, as most Tangier inhabitants believe that foreigners come from a superior social class. However, other stereotypes exist that are possibly more liberating, such as that of the social scientist who is really more independent than a foreigner working in international cooperation or a journalist.

As in Morocco, in Albania the perception of a foreigner is shown within the rules of hospitality. But in general, it is easier for a foreigner to pass unnoticed in Albania than in Morocco. However, De Rapper (1998) works on the place of the foreigner in a Southern Albanian village, indicates how the place of the foreigner (*jabanxhi*) is problematized, because people cannot locate you genealogically, as they do with the rest. Unlike in Morocco, Albanians never call me *nasranía*, they always call me by my name. However, for centuries, the stereotype of the Albanian in Western travel literature was that of a wild and warmongering individual. In 1573, a Piamontese describes the Albanian as being "straight from hell, proud and frightening to look at." Byron was fascinated by the warrior temperament of the Albanians in a period when they still acted as guardians of the Balkans (Morozzo della Rocca 1997: 8).

In Tangier, the segregation of the sexes is so extreme that it has created two separate, isolated worlds, which meet openly only within the sphere of family relationships. This context creates forms of communication that are very different to those of people accustomed to mixed settings. What are the consequences of working in a masculine space? In what sense does a foreign woman "become" a man in a segregated space? Does she end up with a male view of the research site? How do relationships embed themselves when there is a constant shuffling of fixed stereotypes? These are all questions that are difficult to answer. What they often really expect from me is to behave like a man, to be present in the public space, be strong, be driven, etc., and they also expect everything one can expect from a woman in the private space. In Albania, meanwhile, it is interesting to note how the explicit gender discrimination that you live and breathe in the streets of Morocco simply does not exist. It is difficult to even describe the differences in the Albanian case. All I can say is that I hardly ever saw a woman driving a car, and that when we went out into the field, women would speak first to the man I was with, instead of to me. These are just a few of the ways that sexism manifests itself in the Albanian research.

The subject of hospitality has always represented an analytical difficulty during the fieldwork. It has put all my conceptual illustrations of social and cultural categories to the test. Such open displays of hospitality and generosity simply offer you no alternative, and it is impossible to refuse. As a result, it is often best not to expose yourself to these displays, and it is better to avoid them if you do not have either the time or the energy to respond suitably to people's offers of hospitality. The role of the host is very important in Moroccan society; as Rabinow points out (1997: 54), the host is judged by his/her generosity throughout the Arab world. It is the expression of *Karim*, meaning "magnificently generous," or "the generous one." Rabinow also goes on to explain that essentially it is a way of ensuring that one maintains unfailing bonds with Allah, the origin of all wealth. However, when you begin to accept the rules of Moroccan hospitality (apart from what this can mean for the fieldwork) you may also find yourself—as Rabinow also suggests (1997: 54)—involved in a relationship of dominance. When they say to you "*Kul!*" (Eat!) and you do what you are asked, you have ended up accepting the rules of the game for Moroccan hospitality and thus, what Rabinow calls a relationship of dominance has now been established. For ethnographers or researchers, the chance to participate in this game provides one of the best possible contexts for embedding oneself in ethnographic work. Accepting food signifies (as Rabinow explains) "recognizing the host's power." This is one reason why they do everything they can to be able to display their full hospitality. In a very different context, such as in the context of immigration, hospitality rules will often be present in the countries of Southern European immigration; when co-nationals open their doors to the recently arrived migrants, it represents an important ingredient for the reciprocity networks.

In both field studies, I have frequently experienced the expression of generosity from families. Sometimes it makes me feel distinctly uncomfortable, as it seems to me that they are giving me too much for what I am giving them in return, while also being aware that I will be making use of this very generosity in my work, because after all I am with them because they fall within my "family profile." Thus, the subject of hospitality and the ethical problems that arise with families has been a key point in my relationships with the families, and in my approach to participation observation. Very often they express generosity to an exaggerated degree, and they will offer you accommodation as well as food if you let them. In Albania, the welcome is also always hospitable, they invite you to take sweets and a drink (compulsory elements of Albanian hospitality), and they even tell you that you do not have to take off your shoes when all the rest of the family does.

The subject of hospitality leads me to think about the forms of exchange that need to be established. The families express their hospitality and the researchers use it to their advantage for their studies. Often the researcher is unsure as to whether they are overdoing their hospitality, whether they want something in exchange, or whether it is simply a result of their overvaluation of the person's "foreignness." As Ihsan said, "If the pills come from Spain, they must be better," and the same goes for anything that comes from that country, whether it be a product or a person, again another sign of the legacy of the colonial mind. Therefore, during the fieldwork, it is important to carry out a detailed deconstruction of any hospitality that is offered as a basis of exchange, or of the labeling of that exchange between the researcher and others. Here the different strategy of interests between subject and the supposed objects of the research can be clearly seen.

The researcher's position has implied a certain embeddedness in order to understand what underlines peoples' actions. For instance, without it one cannot understand the feeling nor the extent of the risk that children take when crossing the border hidden in a lorry. Nevertheless, after this embeddedness period, one finally has to separate herself/himself in order to reflect and write. Therefore, in the next chapter I will attempt to tangle and disentangle the discourses and actions from each one of my informants and interviewees. However, the difficulty will always remain, as it is not always easy to approach the multiple discourses of social reality present in both these cities.

Notes

1. The debate on globalization can distinguish the arguments of skeptics and globalists from an interdisciplinary perspective. The debate employs a series of analytical axes related to concepts (internationalization versus globalization), power (the influence of the nation-state), culture (nationalism versus hybridization), economics (economic triadization versus transnational economics), inequality (the traditional North-South division versus the new hierarchies), and order (international society versus global governance) (Ribas-Mateos 2001a).

2. The study on the informal economy conducted by Dunay et al., (1995) was the only one I could find on the subject. It underlines the link between international migration by undocumented Dominicans in Puerto Rico, waiting to make their way to the United States. This situation could be analogous to that of Sub-Saharan migrants in Tangier waiting to cross to Spain.

3. Sassen used the concept of the counter-geographies of globalization to refer to circuits directly or indirectly associated to programs and conditions that structure the hard nucleus of the global economy but that are not normally represented as part of it (Sassen 2000: 523). In that respect, when referring to the international migration of women, I put it as one of the forms that the feminization of survival takes in different parts of the world, that is, how households and communities tend to depend more on women for their survival (Ribas-Mateos 2001b).

4. Yue-Man Yeung (1995: 191) uses the three major reorganizations of the world economy. The first involved the incorporation of colonial regions as new material suppliers and consumers for industrializing European economies (NIDL1). The second witnessed the industrialization of developing countries through the efforts of indigenous or foreign enterprises, or both in partnership (NIDL2). The third is the current process of globally integrated production and transnational corporation (NIDL3). The three-phase distinction is useful to see how some developing regions might not take full advantage of the globalization process but they are still participants in the global economy. In this base, some regions of developing countries become more important actors of global manufacturing, making more complex the traditional division of center and periphery in the long popular World System Analysis.

5. Alhudud also has a religious meaning. In the Koran there is a sentence saying "Man taada hudud Allah lan yadlima ila nafsah," that who transgresses Allah's rules will hurt himself/herself. (I offer thanks here to Aiman Zoubir for this search.)

6. The work on ethnographies at the border has been especially prolific in the case of Ciudad Juárez (see the collection of works in Vila 2003a). In the same introduction, Vila quotes García Canclini (1990) on this notion of strategic laboratory: "is only partially true for U.S.-Mexico border inhabitants, living as they are in the so-called living laboratory of postmodernity" (Vila 2003b: 33).

7. According to Tarrius, these movements are highlighted by "stage systems," which are articulated by diversities in micro-places within the unity of circular territories, marking the modalities of mobile populations (idem: 244).

8. For a detailed account of the market dynamics see Manry (2001). Sellers are always searching for the best price, the most successful article, the jackpot of the business. Although some aspects of social success are articulated in long term-strategies, towards a more settled installation of their business, they participate in an economy based on opportunities and business practices that can be related to an act of performance. Actors' situations are contextualized by opportunities or constraints in different spheres, personal (changes in the family situation), political (open or closed borders), economic (closing of economic spaces). The choice of individuals is related also to other individuals, to the nature of social relations in their network. Actors of transactions use trust on one's words to establish forms of control and social regulation, which can guarantee the morality of the interlocutor. We can refer here to the *nisba* in the Arab *medinas,* which marks the relation of a person to an idea, a place; it is the "name of the type of relation."

9. Mittleman looks at globalization from the cross-border involvement of the flows of capital (capital which applies highly selective forms), knowledge, information, and consumer products. His vision also includes the mass population movements between and within countries, and democratic demands for a global division of labor. He aims to go beyond the teleological analyses of globalization and delve into a perspective that not only analyzes the structures behind the "global society" but also provides a perspective for social action that goes beyond those structures and the corresponding historical circumstances.

10. The EU financial resources program for external aid 2000-2006 linked to the migration issue provides a key importance to the management of migration flows. We can quickly deduce it through the following broken-down budget: management of borders, 321,971760 €, combating illegal immigration, 65,042526, and management of flows, 51,367336) and to development (sources of emigration, 71,569477) (Commission of the European Communities 2002: 51).

11. The political division is widely described by historians, especially in the history of the nation-state, as Braudel puts it: "In the last instance, it substitutes, and from then it primarily designs the extended limits of each territorial state.... To delimit, to surround, to be at home, states obstinately search this sense of security. The complex of the Chinese wall fascinates them, all of them are obsessed by it.... The fortification is not only a response to fear, to anxieties, to the good judgement, but also a proof of richness, of strength.... It is in this way that history allows borders to put out roots as if they were natural accidents, inserted in the space and difficult to displace." (Braudel 1993: 303).

12. Bouillon refers to the "se débrouiller," as the capacity of individuals to use their ingenuity in the combination of activities in the heart of the relational world, she specifically refers to the case of Bosnian-gypsy women selling flowers in Marseilles (Bouillon 2001).

13. In the same framework of analysis as Granovetter, I find particularly relevant to my work that of Geertz on the bazaar economy in Sefrou (Morocco) during the 1970s: "It is a distinctive system of social relationships centering around the production and consumption of goods and services.... Bazaar, the Persian word of uncertain origin

which has come to stand in English for the oriental market, becomes, like the word market itself, as much an analytic idea as the name of an institution, and the study of it, like that of the market, as much a theoretical as a descriptive enterprise.… Considered as a variety of economic system, the bazaar shows a number of distinctive characteristics. Its distinction lies less in the processes which operate and more in the way those processes are shaped into a coherent form. The usual maxims apply here as elsewhere: sellers seek maximum profit, consumers maximum utility, price relates supply and demand; factor proportions reflect factor costs..."

"The institutional peculiarities of the bazaar thus seem less like mere accidents of custom and more like connected elements of a system. An extreme division of labor and localization of markets, heterogeneity of products and intensive price bargaining, fractionalization of transactions and stable clientship ties between buyers and sellers, itinerant trading and extensive traditionalization of occupation in ascriptive terms, these things do not just co-occur, they imply one another" (Geertz 1992: 266-7).

14. Patchwork has also been used at a micro-level to refer to how people combine self-help elements in the changes of the welfare mix, to how women's lives can be expressed by a patchwork of work (continuing education, family obligations etc.), or to how the Balkans are a patchwork of ethnicities.

15. This idea of a global communality can also be seen through issues addressed by other authors, as for example Seabrook (1996: 299) who indicates contemporary changes in the city of the South, which no longer merely evoke half-effaced historical memories of Western society in the nineteenth century, but correspond to a converging contemporary reality. In other words, with these descriptions of today´s urban poor in the cities of the South and in places like London, Los Angeles, and New York, we see in today's interdependence on the globalization impact on people. For him it is represented by the impoverishment of people in all cities of the world, by saying that we are all in the same boat.

16. For Albanian transcription in English I use the phonetic Albanian transcription suggested to me by the ethnologist Gilles de Rapper; for Arabic transcription in English I use the IJES system of transliteration.

17. Article 3 of the Palermo protocol defines human trafficking as: "the recruitment, transfer, harboring or lodging of human beings by either threat of force or by force itself, or other forms of coercion, by kidnapping, fraud, deceit, abuse of authority or of a situation of vulnerability or by the offer or acceptance of payments or advantages to obtain the consent of a person having authority over another, for the purpose of exploitation. Exploitation includes, as a minimum, exploitation through the prostitution of others, or other forms of sexual exploitation, forced labor or service, slavery or practices equivalent to slavery, servitude or the removal of organs."

18. Fast, inflatable motor dinghy.

19. Bart is a friend of Elvis; they are both social workers.

20. In Rosander´s research (1991) in a border town of Sebta, identity of Muslim women was expressed through a belonging to the same family, the same gender, the same social age group and the same ethnic and religious group in relation to Spanish women and men and to "Christian" cultural values. In this village, for the Muslims, tradition is much more than a symbol of religion, it is also language, ethnicity, and regional belonging. In the increased polarization of communities, religious practices are for Muslims a way to assert their identity. In this polarization, the relations between Spanish people and *moros* (the Spanish word for Arabs in general and Moroccans and Sebta Muslims in particular) resemble the relations and behavior of Muslim men to Muslim women. For Spaniards, Muslims have low status and are subordinated politically and economically, just as Muslim men experience a superior position in relation to their wives and family women (Rosander 1991: 12).

4

Border Ethnographies

Tangier

The Socio-Historical Context

Northern Morocco is comprised of the provinces that constituted of the old Spanish protectorate, and which were made independent in 1956. It is an area that has been traditionally marginalized from the rest of Morocco—that is to say, ignored by a Frenchified South that had no interest in the linguistic and cultural peculiarities of the North (Ribas-Mateos 1999b: 133). Throughout this section on Tangier an effort will be made not to neutralize this historical background of the ethnography.

While in Albania, I used the setting of communism to contextualize my fieldwork; in Morocco I used the country's colonial legacy. Even though—within the context of the qualities of border cities—I tended to prioritize the interpretation focused on movement and transition, and the concept of a passing place, this space also exercises a form of closure. The classic protection against "European colonists"—the prohibition of non-Muslim foreigners from entering mosques—still exists, though it was the Marshal Liautey who established this prohibition in the time of the French protectorate. Jacques Berque (Rabinow: 1988: 37) noted, "the language, the women and the religion are like three areas of freedom that North Africans have defended ferociously against European transgression." Thus, once European economic dominance and land confiscation had taken place, all the metaphorical and symbolic representations of the Moroccan people's cultural integrity and identity were concentrated inside protected areas. Rabinow believes that the fact that Moroccans learned the French language could also be seen as a kind of defensive mechanism, as it effectively prevented the French from using Arabic.

Why can the colonial legacy be so important here? Because, in various discourses, be they with the selected families and informants in Tangiers, or within the immigration societies (Ribas-Mateos 1998), the effect of the symbolic capital on the main anti-colonial and nationalistic ideologies will often be used in referring to the construction of an identity based on higher moral values than those of the "West."

The city. Tangier is today the main urban center in Northern Morocco. After the second regionalization process conducted in October 1997, Tangier became the capital of the region Tangier-Tetouan, a region comprised of two prefectures and two provinces: the prefectures of Tangier-Asilah, El Fahs Beni Makada and Tetouan, and the two provinces of Laraix and Xauen. While the wilaya[1] of Tangier-Asilah comprises two urban communities and twelve rural communities.

According to the last census (1994), the population of Tangier stood at 497,000 inhabitants. By calculating with a growth rate of 4 percent, it is estimated that by 2002 the population will have risen to 700,000 inhabitants. The great impact this will have on Tangier and the fact that the city is not prepared for such a large influx of people is reflected in contrasting data. In 1971, the city contained 155,000 inhabitants, a figure which rose to around 600,000 by the year 2000. Divided into areas, the figures read thus: Beni Makada: 144,154; Charf: 214,000; and Tangier: 134,000. We have to note here that the last administrative remodeling created in Tangier three urban communities or municipalities which were segregated into: Tangier-Medina, Tangier-Charf, and Beni Makada.

Localities are constructed from historical contingency. Until now the city of the Strait was a "city of passage and clientele of passage" (Martin-Hilali, 1996). The city began to develop its cosmopolitan character[2] at the dawn of Tangier's international age (1923-1956). It was then that all of the city's unique-ness appeared, qualities and features that have made it unlike any other city in Morocco. International Tangier was organized around a highly original gov-erning administration that took the form of a legislative assembly with twenty-six members, all designated by the consuls or by the *mendoub*[3] in the case of Muslims and Jews. There was also a controlling committee of diplomats who nominated the city's *administrateur* (governor), who was the actual head of the area. This governor had two assistants, one French and the other British. On a judicial level, Tangier possessed a mixed court comprised of French, British, and Spanish magistrates for foreign subjects from the signatory coun-tries of the Treaty of Algeciras—with the exception of North American citi-zens. In addition, a city police force and a *Gendarmerie* for the area replaced the old French and Spanish *tabores* (platoons), which had existed since 1906. The 1924 statute saw the beginning of French political control of the institu-tions in Tangier, and that date also witnessed the urban development plan devised by the French architect Henry Prost, known for his plan to isolate the *Medinas*, while working under Liautey. In spite of this plan, the city was already going through a phase of growth, characterized by an overcrowded *Medina*, an urban belt that had completely surrounded the old city, with its radial roads emerging from the huge *souk* (market) and the enormous amount of building in the Hasnona and Marxan area. I believe that all these distinctions have given Tangier and other North Moroccan cities a different kind of spatial organization. Thus, for example, as Abu-Lughod points out (1980), in spite of his best intentions, Liautey created a system of cultural and religious apartheid, confining the Moroccans to the old city, which was to be left untouched as far as possible. This is corroborated by the following fragment of a speech by Liautey, quoted by Abu-Lughod:

> You know how jealous the Muslim is of the integrity of his private life: you are familiar with the narrow streets, the façades without opening behind which hides the whole of life, the terraces upon which the life of the family spreads out and which must therefore remain sheltered from indiscreet looks. But the European house, with its superimposed stories, the modern skyscraper which reaches ever higher, is the death of the terrace; it is an attack upon the traditional lifestyle. (Abu-Lughod, 1980)

According to Abu-Lughod's thesis, the period of the protectorate created substantial ruptures in the structure of Moroccan cities, which have led to a number of divisions according to social class. She was referring to a struggle between classes that were separated by spatial segregation as a legacy of the colonial era, and who were engaged in a growing competition in their search for building land. Rabat is a suitable case for this analysis: a space where you can discern the division of the Moroccan Medina and the complete separation of the natives from the concentration of Europeans. Generally speaking, an international approach was used in urban planning, and thus Tangier's Medina was one of the first in Morocco to show signs of European influence, in addition to the outskirts. The real driving force for the construction of Tangier was the vitality of its economy and the fact that the real estate market was steeped in the commercial rules of the game, which gave the city an advantage in respect to all the other cities in northern Morocco (Bravo Nieto 2000: 127).

Mediterranean port cities have often been considered foci of cosmopolitanism, such as the case of Alexandria in Egypt. According to Bravo Nieto, Tangier's cosmopolitan outlook can be seen as a fundamental, defining trait of colonial Tangier, and that it is most important to point out that—in spite of specific legislation and the high degree of French and British diplomatic influence— much of its architecture and urban planning originated from and developed under the Spaniards (Bravo Nieto 2000:121).

It is this historical substratum that makes the Tangierines feel that they are different, and, in fact, even other Moroccans consider them as "children of the Spaniards." Thus, a mish-mash of cultures developed within the city's everyday life, "and you could hear the call to prayer sung in mosques at the same time as you heard the bells from an Italian church." A historical link makes Tangierines feel closer to the Spaniards, and this explains why people today follow Spanish soccer teams and watch Spanish television channels. This socialization of youngsters in information about Spanish soccer—and the European leagues—will also continue with the emigration of young Tangierines.

When you mention the old days, Tangierines tend to feel nostalgic: a taxi driver told me: "We were like brothers to the Spanish and the Jews. My mother gave birth in front of Spanish people. Before, the Tangierines used to be very good people, but when people started arriving from Casablanca, everything changed." People called the city "the bitch"—especially people from outside, because they said they felt as if the city had been forced into prostitution. Or as if the city was not anybody's in particular, it was everybody's. Those same foreigners who saw Tangier as the country's most Europeanized city were responsible for it being called "*le chien*." The city of Tangier had been very small until the nineteenth century when it became Morocco's most European city. However, at that time Muslims were unable to buy land because it was difficult for them to compete with the established power of the consuls.

The people of old Tangier, those from the city's international age, remember an area of coexistence that could not be found anywhere else in Morocco: "You could sit down in the cafes with foreigners, and go wherever you wanted," unlike the *Medina* in Rabat at that time. And in fact, the concept of cohabitation is commonly used when referring to the old Tangier, implying that people felt that the situation was more one of coexistence than one of dominance, a place where people lived under the protection of a foreign consul.

Features that comprise the image of a city include roads, axes and neighborhoods. This type of analytical model can be clearly identified in the study of a border city such as Tangier, which is, at the same time, a passing place (the gateway of Africa), a place with a cultural mix that is still nostalgic for the international Tangier, but which has instead become a place of waiting and certain isolation. During the 1960s, Tangier attracted people from all over the world in search of exoticism and freedom; this is a point that has been mentioned by various writers, such as Choukri, Ben Jelloun, and Serhane. However, at the same time as this legend was beginning to decline and disappear, the city's border marks were becoming more pronounced.

It is difficult to achieve one single view of the city of Tangier because the city really exists in multiple forms; in the same way that many other cities are characterized by some huge contrasts, by their forms of polarization, which are clearly visible. In the case of Tangier, this can be observed through the acute differences in people's lives in places such as the Medina, the port area, and Beni Makada. And this is, in fact, what makes it difficult to capture the essence of the city. In addition, bearing in mind the historical perspective, it is impossible to find a parallel with any other city—which makes Tangier a unique case. Those who are fascinated with the old Tangier keep harking back to that racial mixture that existed in the city, when people were a little Muslim, a little Christian, and a little Jewish, and they stress the way that coexistence and cohabitation sprang from the tolerance that was shown between the different communities. For those lovers of Tangier, all these elements were significant, yet they tend to forget about present-day Tangier in their nostalgic monologues.

In the late 1950s, an industrial free trade area was created in the city, which led to Tangier becoming home to the country's third most developed textile industry, after Casablanca and Fes. This industrial center led, in turn, to the development of new construction on the outskirts of Tangier that often (and especially during the 1970s) required a certain tolerance on the part of society towards the erection of shantytowns. The evolution of the population showed a significant demographic increase (and again, particularly during the 1970s), which was partly the result of natural growth, but was also the consequence of the migratory influx, mostly concentrated in the municipalities of Beni-Makada and Charf. In the 1940s, the city received a wave of immigration comprised mainly of Rifian people. This was the period when an industrial policy had been initiated in Mediterranean Morocco—that former Spanish protectorate enclave that had been written off as worthless—and an underground economy had developed, based around smuggling hashish into Sebta because the cannabis from the Jebala mountains had become commercialized.

In the 1990s, the city was the location for a complex system of migratory roles: it was the destination for the rural exodus, as well as for inter-urban migration from the north of Morocco and places in the south. However, Tangier also became a great exit point for emigration to Europe, particularly to Belgium, the Netherlands, Spain, France, the UK, and Germany. Construction of new neighborhoods usually resulted from land speculation, often financed by the work of emigrants abroad.

Tangier's Medina is a place of trade and commerce; it is the home of haggling over all the perennial products; it is the *souk* that does not move on every week. However, when I went to Bir Chifa and saw the enormous dynamism of the *souk* and how active it was, I realized how the commerce of the Medina had been surpassed by these outlying neighborhoods. The Medina cannot be understood independent of the port. In addition, this Medina has nothing in common with other Moroccan Medinas that have no port, such as Fes. The commercial and trade role of the port is significant to our understanding of its border character. Both the rich and the poor once inhabited the Tangier Medina, all living together; in fact, "Medina" literally means "city." Gradually, however, the wealthier inhabitants settled in villas in the surrounding mountains. Nowadays, the windows of the houses in the Medina are still small, to keep out the heat, to make them more difficult to see into, and to protect the women inside from prying eyes. In the old European-style houses, even part of the first floor windows had now been walled up.

Features of a Border City

Rabinow (1997) notes that fieldwork tends to be characterized by a reflection and a critique that shakes up all of the researcher's theoretical assumptions including the initial empirical applications considered. When I arrived at a particular field of study, I was unable to clearly distinguish the features of the border city, and everything that had led me to that point suddenly seemed to dissolve into mere fanciful research. I did not get the impression that I was in a place of circulation, a space between two places, a point of transition, nor did it remind me of anything I had seen—very fleetingly—in Tijuana.

In general terms, it is a question of whether—from a theoretical-conceptual perspective, an historical perspective, and a present-day perspective—Tangier can be described as a border city. Firstly, Tangier is a border in the geographical sense, and it may also be a border as a civilizational boundary. From a historical perspective, studies of the city's architectural evolution have shown that a multiplicity of communities have lived in these border spaces, leading to cultural hybridity. Secondly, we should ask ourselves whether Tangier is a gateway onto European influence, and if it also functions as a conduit in the opposite direction. Thirdly, considering that we now have a whole series of defining slogans for Moroccan cities, such as Ouxda, "the border city," and Tetouan, "the white dove" (literally, a meaning translated from Berber ethimology), Tangier has now become known as *Bab Europa* (the door to Europe). It is interesting to note that during the 1980s Moroccans who traveled to Tangier used to say, "I have been to Spain."

This border space contains a whole range of diverse images and definitions: for Westerners it is their first sight of the East, for Moroccans it is the city that leads to foreign European countries, while the Tangierines—thanks to what they see on their television screens—feel as if they already live in Europe. Even so, a key question should be addressed at this point: whether they themselves think of it as a border city or not. More than anything else, it is a border city for the Moroccans, and a border with a symbolic quality, both for the country's exterior and its inland areas.

Hence, in recent decades, northern Morocco has become a real border area with Europe. Within the Maghreb, Tangier historically had always been a port, and it is a border as much as any port can be one. Even so, the physical and terrestrial nature of the harshness of the border is represented by the seven kilometres of border with Sebta, an area that the people of Sebta view as a real scenario for human dramas. Pepe (an archivist in Sebta) is of the opinion that Tangier can be considered a border city, "because there is always something floating around there, something in movement, just like there is in all the borders in the world. And also, it is the door to Europe." Many people see it as the gateway to Europe, in spite of the fact that most of the young Tangierines have never set foot on the Old Continent.

From the perspective of international migrations, the city's cosmopolitanism is a legacy that prepares people for mobility; the historical legacy and the languages, to some extent, are potential instruments of the people. However, the command of foreign languages has decreased among urban youngsters, even those with university degrees, due to the arabization policies.

At present, the physical location of the city of Tangier encourages this kind of pre-project, the sense that people are always about to take the plunge and cross the water. And Spain is clearly visible from Tangier—this is view for those young Moroccans who are constantly looking off in another direction.

From the perspective of free circulation, it is the north-south flows of capital that are significant, as a result of large-scale projects such as the installation of the Tangier Free Zone. However, these are also flows producing little trade and consumption, and which highlight alternative circuits—such as the smuggled goods passing through Sebta. In terms of free circulation, the city represents a key site from which to cross the Strait, but it also represents a European blockade for others. With respect to internal migration, the flourishing textile industry attracts a flow of unskilled female workers. In addition, the boom in foreign telephone investment attracts "modern" young people to this hub of delocalized services. But beyond this structural scenario that the border city offers, families formulate their own strategies, differentiated by social class, gender and their position within the international and internal migration projects.

The transit marked by the Sub-Saharans. Not only for Moroccans but also for migrants and refugees from Sub-Saharan Africa, Tangier is the emblematic city of transit, border-crossing, and a waiting place for European migration projects. The role of the city of Tangier as part of an itinerary was confirmed during the 1990s, when the whole Maghreb region became a large area of transit. Tangier, and the binome Tangier-Sebta is a key point on the waiting route towards the southern border of Europe (the so-called *Frontera Sur*, Andalusia). However, there are other points on the waiting route such as Rabat and Agadez in Niger.

Sub-Saharan migrants travel complicated routes through Niger to Algeria. Very often, the Moroccan government sends them back to Algeria. During 2001, many of them were caught in Tangier, and many of those who were in the north were sent to Rabat. In Tangier the Sub-Saharans are mainly English speakers (coming from Nigeria and Sierra Leone), while in Rabat there are more French speakers. Many Sub-Saharans see Morocco as a highly developed country.

Once Sub-Saharans get to Morocco, after crossing diverse territorial borders, they are ready for the first time to cross sea borders via the Straits of Gibraltar or via the Canary Islands, in an attempt to slip by the controls of the Frontera Sur. Tangier's position as a waiting place is a result of European border closures during the 1990s, but today it is Spanish immigration policies that mark Tangier or Morocco as waiting places. The reasons for this are threefold: (1) Spain cannot repatriate Sub-Saharan migrants as easily as Moroccan citizens;[4] (2) Sub-Saharans have more difficulty than other migrant groups such as Latin Americans in obtaining tourist visas; (3) implementation of the GRECO Plan measures (2000) regarding border control, which includes improvements to the material management of borders (including the so-called

SIVE [*Sistema Integrado de Vigilancia Exterior*] system), better trained border staff managers, the creation of special units called UCRIF (Unidad Contra Redes de immigraión y falsificación. Unity Against Migration and Fraud Networks) (specialized in forging documents) and police cooperation with Morocco; all are part of the infrastructure of the sealing off of borders. The SIVE is an operational system created to fight drug traffickers and irregular immigration and to improve Spanish and European security through the use of new technologies. It is based in Algeciras and covers the Andalusian coast and the Canary archipelago. It has three stations equipped with sensor radar (of 10 km), video cameras, infrared cameras (covering low light conditions), and a telecommunication aerial, in short, a military surveillance of the border. Furthermore, this detailed operation of border control has been developed in the context of a bad relationship between the Moroccan and the Spanish government over different international discrepancies, including migration issues. Rabat made the Moroccan ambassador in Rabat leave in October 2001.

Tangier is one of the spaces where Sub-Saharans structure their short- term and long-term projects of transition. In these projects, mobility is the main factor of social resource, where migration is seen as a tool of enterprise and where the danger of the border-crossing is assumed as inevitable. Let's remember that Sub-Saharans present one of the highest mobility indexes in the world, particularly Nigerians.

The Medina of Tangier functions here as a tampon, resulting from the closure of borders, which has creates a severe situation of marginalization and a concentration of population ready to cross, especially Sub-Saharans (mainly from Nigeria, Ghana, Sierra Leone, Liberia, Cameroon, Mali, Congo, Senegal). However, not only in the Medina of Tangier but also in that of Rabat, Nigerians tend to be the dominant group. In 1997, according to data from the migrant reception center in the city of Sebta, there were 2,828 migrants of twenty-seven different nationalities, with the largest groups being from Nigeria, Sierra Leone, and Liberia and representing one-third of the total. In number they are followed by nationals from Mali and Congo (Lahlou 2002: 19).

For Sub-Saharans, Tangier has epitomized the space of the old center, the *Souk el Dahel* (the interior market), the Medina and the limits of the city, the over-peripheries in the space of rural areas such as the Mesnana area. In both cases, mobility and hidden strategies respond to invisibility: in the old, beautiful but run-down *pensiones* (hostels) of the center they hide in the terraces, away from people and from the police; in the periphery, they use forests and village outskirts. Those pensiones are even comprised of little shops selling drinks, shampoo or even a walkman. They are also a space of violence (where migrants come up against Moroccan racism and informal prostitution, and fights often take place). A need-hate relationship evolves between neighborhood dwellers and Sub-Saharan "stopovers." Furthermore, the local mafias operate fully with migrants in transit and contact through mobile phones is always active. Outside in the streets those who dare to walk freely beg around the city and use the Western Union office to receive economic support from home.

The Sub-Saharans in the Medina asked me for help, complaining that they were short of everything—clothes and food—because none of them could find a job. They also asked me for information about deportation from Spain to Nigeria. One Sub-Saharan, who came from Sierra Leone had been deported from Fuerteventura in the Canary Islands to Nigeria; he explained how conditions were bad in Nigeria because there was not even a welfare office where they lived, and now he was back in Tangier. His most serious problem was the fact that he did not even have his Sierra Leone documents, because his entire street had been completely destroyed. They place their hopes on the migrants' reception center at Tarifa and especially on finding out how the center can help them. Hence, the question of the documents helps to understand the image of the border city as the site for administrative assistance also.

Looking off over the flat rooftops of Tangier's Medina, you can see many Sub-Saharans sitting around, waiting. They say that this is where they are safest from the police. On another rooftop there were some Moroccans who had also come to the hostels to wait until they could leave for Spain. People from the neighborhood say that everybody here has the same "sickness." The Sub-Saharan migrants don't like going to the boulevard, the commercial heart of the city, as they risk being stopped by the police. They complain about the police harassment to which they are subjected, as well as the robberies and violence inflicted upon them by the Moroccan population.

I saw Oliver and his wife, both Nigerians, throughout the summer. They were in the old pensiones of the Medina, waiting for their chance for getting to Spain. A friend of Oliver's is looking for a way to join his wife, who is in Tarifa. He was deported to Nigeria via the Canary Islands. He has two small children, one born in Morocco and the other born in Spain. When I ask them if they want to go to Europe or Spain, they answer *Spain* without hesitation. Through my conversations with them, Oliver has explained his situation very clearly: he and his wife want to go to Tarifa as soon as possible, as their baby is there, and they want to know how they can get help. They are a couple with only one aim: to go and live in Spain, and they are prepared to do anything to get there. They do not care about the anxiety they might feel, or the fact they may have to wait for two to nine months to leave. Meanwhile, Oliver is being sent money by his father, a technical engineer. Oliver's wife is depressed; all she can think about is seeing her baby son. When I suggest that they could do some work while they are shut away like this, for instance, sell something, they reply that they are not interested in working in this country, and they repeat, once again, that their immediate plan is to get to Spain. After four months, Oliver and his wife finally managed to cross the Strait and see their baby again, who was being cared for by a friend. Once in Spain, they had another baby and they decided to name him after the person who had helped them reach Spain. One year later, Morocco passed its first immigration law.

Forms of polarization. If we look at polarization through the colonial eye, French urban colonialism in Moroccan cities followed Prost's division between the native city and the European city; it aimed at avoiding the loss of the Medina identity and that of its inhabitants. This form of segregation ended up creating a dual socioeconomic and cultural reality, being in the European city where industrial activities were to be developed (Bravo Nieto 2000).

During the 1980s urban problems took center stage in Morocco's political arena. After the 1981 urban riots, the urban question played a more prominent role in government discourse. During the 1990s, the *quartiers populaires* polarized the attention of the administrative power. Living in the limits of the city and isolated from all the elements of urban life, inhabitants of these neighborhoods scrutinized even the simplest of state actions, where an electric cable on a fountain could be interpreted as the administration's recognition of the neighborhood, an initial step towards integration into the city (Abouhani 1999: 355).

In Morocco, in 1983, there were already many inhabitants living in the "clandestine" neighborhoods; they represented 13 percent of the country's population, which accounted for variations according to different cities (Salé: 140,000 people, 45 percent of the urban population; Ouxda: 90,000 and 35 percent; Fes: 120,000 and 26 percent; Tetouan: 51,000 and 25 percent; Meknes: 35,000, 11 percent; and Tangier: 34,000, 11 percent) (Signoles et al. 1999b: 15). Due to the mobilization of large amounts of capital, non-regulated urbanization has been the most dynamic process structuring the urban space, using savings from all social categories (from official circuits as well as from non-official ones). The terminology used to define which mode of urbanization is "spontaneous," "anarchical," "illegal" has been the object of severe criticism. Some authors (Signoles 1999: 223) search for a less neutral term, one less charged with ideology or moral connotation, namely non-regulated urbanization (*urbanisation non réglementaire*), or even suggest the expression of contested settlements. Signoles et al. (1999a) are critical of the writings on the non-regulated settlements in the Arab urban world. They argue that rules do exist; it is not left to the invasion of the space, those settlements function inside the rules of the market for people who do not have the resources to be integrated in official circuits. The price of land in such areas is often more expensive than in other neighborhoods, but the land tends to be smaller than in regulated neighborhoods. Furthermore, they pinpoint that they are far from being clandestine as they have been built under the eyes of the urban authorities.

In Tangier, polarization trends tend to reproduce a domination system marked in terms of hierarchical mobilities. Those people who recall the sweet and sour nostalgia of the belle époque of international Tangier remember it as a gateway defined by a cosmopolitan entrance. Meanwhile it now attracts other Moroccans while in the past it used to pull Spaniards, British and European Jews, among others. Many of those new migrants of this border city see Tangier as a factual place of passage more than of settlement, they have transformed the city into a sort of Mediterranean caravanserai. The forms of polarization in Tangier city originated from the changes in internal migrations. The Medina and the bulevar area are images of centrality for the city, with the center being the symbol of space in the city, the place of memories, of identification with urbanization and the urban civilization. However, part of the population has contributed more to its rurality than to its urbanity (Martin-Hilali 1996: 49).

The arrival of the rural migrants to the cities, leads to a division between different models of consumption, and to a "composite" division of the population of the urban area. On the one hand, in Tangier, exclusive neighborhoods with villas and high-quality housing exist, and on the other hand there are the more traditional neighborhoods, such as Bir Chifa. As the city was completely unprepared for this influx of people, all the problems typical to a saturation of urban development and shantytown construction took place right in the center of the city.

Tangier and its metropolitan area are now polarized by two forms of dwelling concentrations, another expression of the divided city: a horizonal axis along the coast—the old Tangier and the modern apartments—and a vertical axis heading towards the south and depicted by blocks of apartments referred to by the Tangierines as the *chaabi* type (literally, popular type). Three forms of spatial distinction exist in three zones: (1) in the Medina (the neighborhoods of Emsallah and Dradeb, created by the rural exodus during the international period); (2) in the specific shantytowns (Beni Ourigahel, Saddam, El Hafa); (3) in the non-regularized neighborhoods (in the municipality of Beni Makada, especially the neighborhoods of Bendibane and Bir Chifa [PNUD 1999]). One distinguishing factor of these polarization trends is the emergence of what has been called "illegal neighborhoods." They are even present in the city center. Al-filu (an urban planner for the municipality) notes that the neighborhood of Hafa is an illegal neighborhood, as is Sidi Bouknadel, in the Kasbah. When I compared parts of these "illegal neighborhoods," I found that Sidi Bouknadel is in the most precarious state, because its houses are built on sand.

Since the 1970s in Tangier—as well as in other Moroccan cities—inhabitants have shown disdain towards these shantytowns, which have spread steadily spread towards the outskirts of the cities. In the 1970s, the population underwent significant demographic growth, partly as the result of natural growth, but also due to the incoming migratory flow, particularly in the municipalities of Beni-Makada and Charf. Starting in the 1980s, following the creation of the neighborhoods of Satvillage, Casabarata, El Boughaz, AH. Khatour, Ben Dibane, Ahlen, Beni Makada, and Ingetex, the city of Tangier began to spread southward. At the same time, industry expanded towards the south and southeast of the city. The new industrial areas included Oued Moghohga, Mouley Ismail, Route de Rabat, Route de l'Aviation and Bahrein (in the countryside). This industrialization drew on labor from the rural exodus, as well as on speculation, which was often financed and reproduced by the work of emigrants abroad. Therefore, these new neighborhoods developed thanks to the money generated by international migration. The subject of housing is also essential for international migration, as it means also a new urban design, Moroccan families living abroad (who are traditionally accustomed to living in a horizontal space) have to adapt to a vertical space, especially in the French HLM (Habitations à Loyer Modéré. Low Rent Housing) apartment blocks.

Data on schooling and illiteracy rates reveal the plight of the Beni-Makda people (especially those who live in Bir-Chifa), and show how little access these people have to education. Over 52 percent of the population over ten years of age (and 66 percent of the female population) are illiterate, and the schooling indicators are the lowest in Tangier (Abdelhak and El Kaomouni 2001: 46). Bir Chifa is the poorest neighborhood in Tangier, which is why it is considered the ideal location for anti-poverty programs. The entire neighborhood was built illegally; it looks like an isolated mountain, and some people from the center even call it Kabul. Hence, Bir Chifa shows the worst socioeconomic indicators in Tangier (see Table 4.1 in contrast with Tangier-Medina), and the neighborhood plays the same role as a bridge for internal and international migrations as other shantytown neighborhoods such as Guadalupe (in Keleton, Larache).

Another neighborhood that displays these same instances of polarization is Idrissia, which is a typical MRE (*Marocains Résident à l'Étranger*) neighborhood. Here, all the young men have either gone to Europe or are about to leave. In Idrissia, Rifians live alongside Tangierines and others who have arrived from outside. Abdelfatah, who is now in Catalonia, believes that he is typical of many young men who leave Morocco, as he has finished his secondary school studies and speaks Arabic, English, and French. His mother is divorced and works as a maid in a house in Vilanova i la Geltrú (province of Barcelona). First he worked for the *Wilaya* (an organ of the provincial administration) of Tangier, but it did not pay very well, only 700 dirhams a month, considering that one needs 3,500 dirhams to get a visa. Since arriving in Vilanova i la Geltrú four years ago, he has worked in the catering industry; he arrived without any documents, and began washing dishes for twelve hours a day, though later he got a steady job as a waiter. During the week, his mother sleeps at the house where she works as a domestic helper, but she spends the weekends with her family. Idrissia in

Table 4.1
Comparative Table of Socioeconomic Indicators between
Bir Chifa and Tangier Medina

Indicators	BIR CHIFA			MEDINA		
	MASC.%	FEM. %	TOTAL %	MASC.%	FEM.%	TOTAL %
Population	49	51	19,840	49.4	50.6	18,560
Size of housing			5.9			4.3
Members under age 15			46.8			28
15-59 years			50.8			74.4
Over age 60			2.4			7.6
School age population (6-14)			31.6			17
Single population over age 15	40.4	31.5	35.9	54.6	37.2	45.7
Married population over age 15	58.6	59.7	59.2	42.4	43.6	43
Separated population over age 15	1	8.8	4.9	3	19.2	11.3
Age at first marriage	26.1	23.3	24.5	30.9	27.7	29.3
Fertility index		5.8			1.9	
Illiteracy of the over age 10	46	77.8	62.6	20.6	47.4	34.2
Schooling among age 8-13	75.2	46.6	59.5	88.7	85.6	87.1
GDP	51.7	16.5	33.8	60.9	30.9	45.7
Unemployment rate	16.3	32.3	20.3	23.5	35.5	27.6
Self-employed. Active population			15.5			23.4
Dependent workers. Active population			77.6			72.3
Active population with family aid			0.7			17.7
Entrepreneurs and apprentices in active population			5.7			2.4
Type of dwelling: apartment			0.3			6.7
Installations: sanitary			94.9			94.7

Source: PNUD 1999:11.

Tangier, as well as other neighborhoods such as Lazare in Ouxda, contains many empty houses owned by emigrants living abroad (Ribas-Mateos 1999b).

Migrations

Experiences of mobility. People in the North of the country are accustomed to commuting. An agreement of free circulation exists between Sebta and Melilla and the provinces of Tetouan and Nador, which generates a daily flow of some 30,000-40,000 people.

During my fieldwork, the question often arose as to whether the obtaining of a nationality and the consequent freedom of mobility were really legitimate desires for any human being. People such as Emir (an emigrant from Tetouan living in Spain) talked about this potential for mobility, the idea of having proper documents so he could come and go as he pleased. The emigrants who go back and forth from Morocco, like Emir, talk about possessing permanent, valid documents so they can move freely between Tetouan and Spain. For many young men this freedom of movement represents a very modern way of life, and Emir thinks of himself as belonging to one of these modern mobility groups, involved in constant transit from one country to another, which means the construction of a circular life cycle. In Emir's eyes, "Spain and Morocco are the same; the only difference is the standard of living." Abu, an emigrant living in Barcelona, seems to be another of these young men who is searching for new forms of mobility. He told me about a friend of his who chose to move from Barcelona to Andalusia so that he could travel more easily between Spain and Morocco. The subject of these young men's travel abilities is significantly similar to the lifestyles of many European young people; the difference here is in the various scales of that mobility. That is to say, for an inhabitant of Tangier, the idea of going to Seville must be like someone from Girona moving to Barcelona, even if in the case of Tangier it represents a cross-border perspective. Therefore, if we fail to understand this perspective of mobility, we will not understand the new migration projects, and our interpretation of international mobility will be reduced to the classic view that has been traditionally centered on shaping the direction between the points of origin and destination in human migration. Reciprocity in the context of chain migration to Southern Europe plays an important role within this mobility construction. To be embededded in social networks means to work in diverse rings of social relations, their range can go from people of common neighborhood to, even, the relation with specific foreigners who can work as contacts in reciprocity relations.

The mobility experience also affects the middle class, especially the bilingual young who use the expression *travel* as a synonym for *work*. Society fails to provide its young with a career opportunity, access to modern consumption, and the possibility of "modern" and gendered mixed leisure activities. This last factor, together with the difficulties of arranging a marriage, partly explains why prostitution can be so common among the city's young (it is the lack of affective and sexual relations out of wedlock that make young men look for commodified sex). The experiences of people on the move are a constant as in the case of those children who adopt migratory projects as if they were pseudo-adults, especially children from Bir Chifa and Char Bendibane, in the municipality of Beni Makada. They end up looking like heroes in the eyes of their peer groups and families, as if mobility lent them the ingredient of adventurousness.

For many women mobility means a great change in the challenging of gender relations, when it is often noted that a woman's place is in the home, and a good woman should remain *jalisa* (literally seated, meaning inside the home, outside of the public space). For some families, especially lower class families with traditional education, the movement of young women is heavily constrained. However, it is difficult to reach a conclusion on these issues, as often middle-class women are more submissive to their husbands' decisions, in order to obtain a higher status among their kin and better living conditions.

Through international migration strategies, women now appropiate the public space, the space of international migration, due to their awareness of the shrinking socioeconomic conditions of their state and that of their families. Nevertheless, contradictions facing women´s appropiate behavior coded within a system of Muslim morality is always present: between the "good Muslim woman" and the diverse interpretations of her moral transgressions (often in light of the opposition of the *haram*—non-allowed—*halal*—allowed—division). Nervertheless, the different views that present an account of the "good, or true Muslim" are quite complex, having often a new reinterpretation in Europe.

In Tangier, people say that everyone in Morocco is infected with the "European virus" (in a way, tied in the colonial experience) and especially so in Tangier. In a parallel sense, you can see how the other virus—racism—spreads across Europe. The difference (the Tangierines point out) between the migrations of the 1960s and the current ones is that nowadays even the skilled population talks about leaving the country. Everybody wants to leave, to change their lives, because salaries are considered to be very low. Encarnación, a secretary at the Spanish consulate in Tangier, told me that it is not unusual for a policeman in the city, who earns 2,000 dirhams monthly, to be prepared to emigrate to pick strawberries, and to earn more than his original wage. "A street sweeper in Spain earns the same as a bank manager here. The rich want to leave, too, but what they want is to live half their time in Spain and half in Morocco." But what is Tangier's role amidst all these changes? "Tangier is constantly looking into the shop window of Europe," Encarnación replies.

The Exit towards Europe. By analyzing the migrations from Tangier as a border city we obtain an overall understanding of the forms of emigration,[5] as well as of the different ways of leaving the country. Deconstructing migration projects within the context of my family visits—whether they be past, present, or future migration projects—reveals the complexity of the ancient forms that are expressed in the sociology of migration for the classic reasons for departure. In view of the complexity of migration projects, the context of the family unit—nuclear or extended—is reflected by an examination of the genograms, projects that readapt the family ideology to the changing times.

Visits to families, plus the genograms, have also highlighted the influence of support networks among neighbors and peer groups (Ribas-Mateos 2003), since the creation and strengthening of these networks is an organizational constant for Tangierine migrations. The survival strategies and the ways of encouraging people to leave and adapt to the new country, all serve to set up and reconstruct the most suitable networks. Within this context, foreigners are often evaluated as to possible contacts they might have in their place of origin, as well as to ways of obtaining a visa and finding a job and a work contract at the point of destination.

Emigration then takes a diverse form; even if the family context is often important for it, it can be an individual decision, a decision by other members of the family, or a family decision, or else it can be the result of the action of the peer group. It is often through those peer groups that youngsters exchange images of European countries, help each other in getting traveling documents, find ways to offer the first job abroad, share aspirations and leisure tastes, etc. By peer groups we can understand those group of individuals who share common features, like age and origin, job occupation or other criteria. They do identify themselves and they are identified by the rest of society as a socially distinct community (Colombo 1998: 137). The same author distinguishes different types of peer group bonds in the case of young Algerians involved in micro-criminal activities in the city of Milano: the first bond is based on friendship, coming from school days, common neighborhood; the second bond is based on being a fellow countryman or countrywoman, compatriot, when they are met in the county of destination; they can also be people who share the same life style or the same problems; the third bond is based on a feeling of sharing a common experience, such as the experience of immigration or the conditions of marginality (Colombo 1998: 104).

The Tangierines who were the first to leave for Belgium were generally skilled workers. On the one hand, we find the sedentary tendencies of migration to Northern Europe, especially to Belgium, as well as the new tendencies of connections between old and new diasporas through family links. An urbanist of the city recalls how these first emigrants were searching for "the Tangier they were losing"; in addition, they would not work for the government because they had no desire to work for someone from the South. This is why they say that "the Tangierines have suffered a lot." For the nostalgic, the Tangierines used to be very different, and now they are even losing their specific dialect, the Tangierine *Darija*. The main destination for migrations by Tangierines in the 1960s was Brussels. As they took place so long ago, these migrations represent the largest settlement and the greatest solidity with respect to the installation of family nuclei. Malak's family is typical of the old Tangierine migrations, which were almost always directed towards Belgium, and more specifically to Brussels, where they settled in specific neighborhoods. Thanks to his brothers' and sisters' work in Brussels during those years, Malak was able to pursue his studies, and his family in Tangier could not only survive day to day but were also able to afford to purchase several apartments in the city. Malak told me that he is virtually the only one of his generation who did not want to emigrate, because he could not leave his mother alone (she died a year later). Prior to this situation, when his father was alive, he could not even dare to think of traveling abroad, because he was taking care of his parents. Out of 1,000 people he knew as a student at the university, he calculates that only about thirty have remained in Morocco.

According to my informants, for a person in this country, wanting to go abroad is the most logical goal to accomplish, and every day this migration culture can be better understood as an increasing trend. During the period of my fieldwork in Tangier, the forms of migration and the wide range of types of mobility accessible were constant features. These subjects are part of daily life: from the *pater*[6] (Oliver), to the purchasing of documents (Chafik, a member of an association), to marriage (Mohammed, his cousin), enrollment in French universities, and beginning an internship in Germany (Ihram, textile engineer). One of Mohammed Ad-dubbu's uncles, who is now in Madrid, was a guide and because of his profession he met foreign people whom he used to invite home to his family. This latter case, who has worked for Bless in Tangier, corroborates very well Sassen's thesis that revealed that the greater the economic and relational contact with a country, the stronger the migratory links become. He feels fed up with associationism, since he has spent six years of his life working as an unpaid volunteer. Chafik keeps thinking about applying for a Schengen visa so he can attend all the international conferences to which he is invited. Long-term migration projects may yield varying results, but Sassen´s thesis in "The mobility of labor and capital" (1988) reveals a pattern showing that the greater the relationship between countries, the more the population develops links with the other country.

Other people I met in the field are still waiting to leave as well. In Family 1, Iddah, who is divorced, no longer works because she is hoping to settle in Spain one day. Meanwhile, her sister Sara works in a factory and is also hoping to go to Spain. In the end, there are multiple migration projects, each one related to the specific category of the person: some have visas, others do not, some are planning to study, others to work and earn quick money.

Hijra is divorced and mother of three children. She appears be over fifty years old. She works as a secretary in an association, but she constantly complains of her low pay, and complains that it is not enough—not only to provide her children with a decent future but also to send them to private professional training schools in Morocco. Hijra confessed to me that she was very unhappy in her country; she had a great many problems at work and if she left she would never return. The truth is that when any obstacle or problem arises, people often think of leaving the country. Hijira told me that working in Morocco meant not only a low wage, her working was also riddled with sexual harassment, clientism, and corruption. Curiously, while she was talking to me, she never mentioned other factors such as stress at work or motivation, elements focused about the individual.

For a long time (around 1975) Hijra worked on a ship that sailed between Tangier and Sète (France). She also worked as a secretary for a Jewish gentleman who was a rabbi in an office near her home. In Casablanca, she worked for Seaman and in other factories. She has a long and varied working history behind her. Nevertheless, her problem now is not just that she does not earn much, but that she has to live with the uncertainty of not knowing how long her contract will last. Hijra's aim is to be able to give her children a decent education and to get them good jobs; that is why she is planning her own migration project. She told me that she has no friends because she found that women in Tangier were not as open-minded as the women in Rabat and Casablanca. In contrast, she views herself as different. For example, she does not want to live in the Medina with the *chaabi* (common) people, and when she talks about Moroccans she emphasizes that she is different, because she is very open, because she likes to lead the conversation, and because other people spend all day involved in a form of social control in which they keep accusing each other of *chuma* (shame).

Hijra has decided to go and live in Spain at all costs, and this is where I can play an explicit role. She would like to leave and work in someone's home, possibly as a "housekeeper." She thinks that a house in Spain will provide her with everything she needs, which is (1) to get out of Tangier, this city that so many Tangierines remember nostalgically (hence the importance of the historical perspective); (2) to settle somewhere in Spain where she will automatically be offered her food and lodging; and (3) to send money back periodically to Tangier, thus enabling her to pay for her two children's education.

Internal migration. Tangier's position in the context of Moroccan geography makes it the main urban reference axis in the north of the country; it is a point that exerts an attraction across the whole northern area of the country, where a wide series of features connected with the magnitude of the city, the socioeconomic context and its geo-strategic position are all interwoven. Since the 1960s, the city has acted like a magnet, and this attraction intensified once the city chose the liberal path. In spite of this, the effects of liberalism have been increasing within the dynamics of social polarization in the city. A frequent subject that comes up in conversations with the Tangierines about the urban perspective of the people is the divisions between the neighborhoods and the idea that there are urbanized as well as "un-urbanized" people. Finally, we should also mention here the subject of cultural diversity.[7] In Tangier, many cultures coexist, such as Jebala, Rifian, Arubia, and thus many ways of speaking the Moroccan dialect—not to mention Berber—coexist within the city.

Certainly, internal migrations are significant for an understanding of migrations abroad. Whether you are in Spain or Italy, you hear the same arguments about migrations abroad in Europe, over and over. Understanding the national population dynamics is of key importance to achieving a clear picture of international dynamics—whether it be in Morocco or in Tangier—as a bridge and periphery for international migrations. Settlements of interior migrations are also important if we wish to understand the current socioeconomic dynamics of urban spaces, which are subject to a mixture of influences such as political and economic interests. As a last resort, these dynamics represent the dividing framework as breaking up the different classifiable groups within the city's population. These include *arubi* (peasants, except for those from the north) and *harraga* (in a way, emigrants, but the term is also used for immigrants who have already settled there, also *hagara* in Tunis for undocumented migrants). It is, in fact, these populational classifications that have led many Tangierines to develop the basis of their argument on Tangier's decadence.

Within this transformation, the Tangierines also mention the city's spectacular demographic evolution, which is basically due to Tangier's geo-strategic position. They refer to the city's four factors of attraction for the deprived population from other parts of Morocco: (1) its industry; (2) its access to mobility, which provides the opportunity to cross the Strait; (3) the chance the city offers of opening a trade route with Sebta; and (4) the income that hashish production can generate here. These are the factors of attraction, but paradoxically they have also created a certain social tension between different populations. The "deprived" population of Morocco (which is, for the most part, illiterate) travels north[8]—on a route that passes through the worst neighborhoods of Larache and Asilah—until they reach Tangier, the gateway to Europe.

Notwithstanding, the Tangierines who hark back to Tangier's past tend to underestimate the significant influence of the interior migrations. When they are questioned on this point, they usually fall back on arguments concerning the civic-urban imbalance; "what should happen is that all the Tangierines who have come from the country should give up their rural approach to life and become urbanized," a well-known historian stated. Internal migrations are also the reason why Tangier has lost its own character, its specificity. "Tourism has finally moved southward, and people here are placing their hopes in the factories. All the construction that is going on in the city is just a political decision which has led to a specific demographic change." Furthermore, Mohammed An-nasru (a bank manager) blames everything that has happened to the city on the proliferation of factories. He argues that their increased numbers has attracted a cheap labor force that is unskilled and illiterate, at the same time as it has boosted the real estate sector. The boom in the construction sector had attracted, in turn, the arrival of Saharan labor in the time before the Green March. Saharans are preferred because they are considered good workers in that sector, they can withstand the heat, and can live on the building sites. In addition, there was the Rifian emigration of the 1940s and 1950s. It is these people to whom Mohammed Choukri refers in his book, *For Bread Alone* (2000), as well as Hart (1957) in an anthropological article.

Remittance-dependent neighborhoods. Monetary remittances are one of the most visible forms of global migration trends. Formal and informal remittances measure the internationalization of the household reproduction. Migration dependency has been crucial for the city of Tangier, especially some of its neighborhoods,[9] in showing how society has developed and how the economy has shaped the urban market, making it permanently dependent on a external orientation, either from the export of goods or labor. On the one side, there is an economic benefit; the remittance mechanism serves as a survival strategy for families, enabling them to be self-sufficient in terms of their social development. On the other hand, this dependency is also inserted into a migration ideology; therefore going abroad is a part of their career, their social mobility plan, their initial insertion onto the labor market, their first chance to access a formal contract.

Furthermore, the neighborhood networks, for most of Tangier's working classes are considered practically a kind of extended family, and they play a key role as a form of social capital in the chain formation of the migratory projects.

In July and August, everything changes in the north of Morocco, as many more migrants travel through the harbors of Sebta and Tangier. The traffic changes, and the roads begin to fill up with large numbers of Belgian, Dutch, German, and French cars (see Table 4.2 for Moroccans abroad) . Only from late July onward do Spanish vehicles begin to appear. The volume of people in the streets also swells, and multiple, temporary street markets spring up. Prices go up, the tourist complexes in the region of Tangier and Tetouan fill up, and the number of weddings also increases. All of this leads to a summer saturation, which is intermingled with internal tourism.

In Morocco, emigration has been one of the mechanisms the government has used as a way of stabilizing certain regions, especially the Rif area. The government's plan during the 1970s also included temporary emigration abroad as one of the release valves for its demographic policy, while from

Table 4.2
Moroccan Immigrants by Main Host Countries*

FRANCE	888,007
NETHERLANDS	258,292
BELGIUM	200,941
SPAIN	180,857
ITALY	171,460

*(Estimation 1999. In thousands of persons)

Source: Khatibi, 2001:157

1988-1992 a support fund was created for emigrant workers, as well as a social rehabilitation plan for volunteers on their return. Then later, a ministry for the members of the Moroccan community residing abroad was also set up (Ribas-Mateos 1999: 183). Morocco began a strategy to develop emigration as a measure to encourage the country's socioeconomic progress, based on the interchange between development and emigration. Thus, the Moroccan government established itself as a mediator for relations between capital and the migrant work force. However, what began as a temporary measure ended up becoming an integral part of the system (idem: 117). Nowadays, in this interchange between international migration and development, greater emphasis is being placed on co-development practices, particularly that of rural tourism. The investments needed are not very large, and the aid for MREs comes from self-financing, from the European Union and from banks, while it is also calculated that 50 percent of emigrants are living in European Union countries. The government also wants to intertwine development with a strategic, high-priority development of the provinces in the north of the country, specifically the creation of new industrial areas, as it is calculated that 24 percent of MREs (Moroccans residing abroad) are from the north.

Using data that I received from the Bank Chaabi (and, where possible, from Western Union), I would like to demonstrate the existence of remittance-dependent societies, and particularly certain neighborhoods in the city. The banks in the city of Tangier have verified the changes that have taken place in the way MREs send money home. The first generation used the old system, but the second is much more modern in their approach. Because they are now much better informed, they use the bank systems and their information networks, and they now know that changing foreign currency on the black market is no longer such an attractive option. Before they used to bring cash back and change it in Morocco, but now they prefer to use the much safer system of sending remittances via bank transfers, which shows how greatly MRE habits have changed. There is a whole series of remittances that are now visible (Table 4.3 details these findings) though another series are still invisible: money brought in by immigrants, compensation payments and objects. As a result, we can never achieve complete statistical reliability. Property is always the emigrant's main investment, and this serves to boost the economy, though there are other sectors that also need to be promoted.

Table 4.3
Development of MRE Remittances by Main Country of Origin

	1995	1996	1997	1998	1999
FRANCE	1,019.42	1,052.81	946.81	978.55	962.84
ITALY	68.37	156.58	164.17	180.75	192.79
BELGIUM & LUXEMBOURG	136.5	143.41	128.9	119.22	101.45
NETHERLANDS	89.95	94.87	81.09	124.02	100.51
GERMANY	93.1	94.01	88.57	100.93	90.53
SPAIN	22.17	44.43	58.24	74.24	54.74
UNITED ARAB EMIRATES	40.8	47.61	57.75	49.8	48.72
GREAT BRITAIN	18.15	24.44	32.88	37.04	45.93
SAUDI ARABIA	26.72	34.97	42.09	41.3	40.77
SWITZERLAND	22.31	21.37	23.77	30.57	32.46
OTHER	49.29	66.04	77.02	85.41	121.86
TOTAL	1,586.79	1,780.55	1,701.27	1,821.79	1,792.6

Source: Office des charges, in Khatibi (2001: 219).

In fact, it was the remittances sent back by the emigrants in Belgium and the Netherlands that funded the construction of the new neighborhoods, especially Rifian emigrants who were more interested in buying property in Tangier than in the Rif mountains. Thus, the first neighborhood was built thanks to emigrants' remittances, and the same happened in Hawmat Belgica, the so-called Belgian quarter because they were migrants in Belgium. Neighborhoods were constructed, benefiting from land speculation of the 1950s, where for Tangierines the housing sectors seem to have been the only welcoming investment. The case in point is Hawmat Belgica.

With respect to the data on remittances, the bank that negotiates most of them provided me with a detailed analysis which considers the factors that influence their evolution. For instance, the peaks in the colder months of the year and in summer correspond to the fact that the end of the year is when people in Europe receive their Christmas bonuses, while summer is when the migrants go to Morocco on holiday. Sometimes banks do not know exactly where the money fluctuation comes from. I believe that part of the summer money might also be connected with the weddings that are held at that time. In any case, with respect to the data from the *Banque Populaire*, we must bear in mind that: the data are cumulative, starting from January 1, and they do not differentiate between data from Tangier or from Tetouan. The figures were not broken down, instead they covered the whole region. I managed to obtain data regarding neighborhoods, but not regarding country of origin. Thus, I cannot be sure whether Belgium is the dominant country in Tangier's dependence on foreign countries. Even so, when analyzing whether a neighborhood is remittance-dependent, we should consider the bias represented by the number of offices per location in Morocco and in the destination. Another serious bias for the correct representation of data is the amount of informal remittances, and whether there are other data from other banks to consider. However, it is important to emphasize that the *Banque Populaire* channels 60 percent of bank remittances. In Tangier, Beni Makada is the main remittance municipality, especially Moulay Slimane and Idrissia. We also have to note that for migrants, gifts have always existed; nowadays, the commodification of gifts and visas can be clearly seen for example in temporary markets such as the local one in Idrissia during the summer.

Forms of Control

Checking visas is the most obvious method used in border policies and at border check-point controls. The Spanish consulate in Tangier offers Moroccan citizens two types of visas: (1) Schengen visas, which are determined by the applicant's economic situation, the labor situation, and the object of the trip. Eligibility depends upon the estimation that the applicant does not represent a high risk. In principle, they prefer people who are firmly rooted in Morocco. Naturally, this type of visa is aimed at the wealthier social classes. (2) The Sebta visa, which is especially designed for people who do business with the goods that come in from Sebta. A holder of this visa is not allowed to spend the night in Sebta. The visa can have a duration of thirty days or of one year.

The figures for the evolution of visas are difficult to interpret since their variations involve many factors. Firstly, the number of visas issued is an expression of the relation between the existing visa policies of the two countries; using those sources, people find out if new channels have opened up, and word gets around. Secondly, the number of visas is also relative, because it includes the migrants when they come back to Morocco. This implies that migrants had previously left irregularly, and return to apply for residence visas. A study of the evolution of visas demonstrates how much stricter the controls in the Strait have become (see Table 4.4). The number of applicants refused in August 2001 was 274. In general, visa applications increase in summer. One example is the case of the Moroccan teachers who go abroad to pick tomatoes in summer, or those who give classes to Muslim groups, though they are working irregularly. According to information from the Spanish consulate in Tangier, people who want to travel to Spain have a different profile than earlier generations, given that now the demand originates from all the social classes. "After the death of King Hassan II, everybody thought about getting out in some way." They mention the case of a person who had a bakery in the city, just to demonstrate that even people as settled as this baker were thinking about leaving. However, mobility rights are not the same to all Moroccans; there are acute differences in visa requirements that make mobility disproportionally easier for the elite.

While the choice of Tangier as a border city represented—within the port of Tangier—the most obvious form of control within the context of economic globalization in this part of the Mediterranean, I should also explain why I did not select other sites. I am specifically referring to the examples of the border at Sebta, the border at Tarajal, and the border crossing at Bel Yunech, also in Sebta. In Sebta, the Tarajal border is the only existing border with Morocco, and all trade with Morocco passes through this point/border. The town's geographical position is represented in the constellation of the Bel Yunech border, which is characterized by the existence of border workers and the shady deals that take place there, and also by education and the media. This is an Arabic-speaking town, though many people here speak better Spanish than they can write in Arabic. They use Sebta as a consumer area and as a place where they can obtain public services. It is slightly similar to the case of Souza, as described in Eva Evers Rosander's book (1991), because on one hand they have Sebta as a point of reference for work and consumption, while on the other, they maintain their family values as Muslim identity.

Of course, the border pass at Bel Yunench is the scenario for daily conflicts, including confrontations with the Spanish *Guardia Civil*, who fire at merchants with rubber bullets. This border pass did not previously exist; it was set up only a few years ago, when the whole question of strengthening borders was first being addressed by the Spanish state. Later, a wire fence was built across the side of the mountain. However, the strongest border is clearly the one between Nador and Melilla, especially since a double wall was built there a few years ago.

From the hill of Sebta one can enjoy a perfect view of the small town of Bel Yunech, which has grown in recent years. Illumination is provided by a large spotlight that lights up the border checkpoint, the wall, and the sea. Below this, there are two Spanish *Guardia Civil* policemen. The border pass closes at ten o'clock at night (Spanish time) and on weekends. At the end of the day, there is a build-up of people on the Spanish side carrying goods wrapped in plastic. In contrast, some people swim from the Spanish side to the Moroccan shore together with their goods.

Bel Yunech is vitally important for its strategic position as the gateway to Sebta. In the town, I learned that 80 percent of the population comes from other parts of Morocco. It made sense for them to settle there and become

Table 4.4
Evolution of Issued Visas to Spain in Tangier

YEAR	UNIFORM	SEBTA/MELILLA	Resid/Natio.	'94	'95	'97	'98	'99	TEMP.	VTL	TOTAL
1990	396	0	174	0	0	0	0	0	0	0	570
1991	5,263	15,960	260	0	0	0	0	0	0	0	21,483
1992	6,070	24,770	189	0	0	0	0	0	0	0	31,029
1993	7,399	28,342	431	0	0	0	0	0	0	0	36,172
1994	6,819	29,906	519	0	0	0	0	0	0	0	37,244
1995	12,898	10,450	761	974	0	0	0	0	0	0	25,083
1996	8,612	10,375	0	44	1,071	0	0	0	0	0	20,102
1997	5,939	6,897	1,015	0	0	98	0	0	0	0	13,949
1998	5,590	5,891	677	0	0	435	884	0	0	0	13,477
1999	6,649	7,475	854	0	0	0	64	908	0	3	15,953
2000	7,364	6,727	1,493	0	0	0	0	156	139	25	15,904
2001	7,808	5,934	1,989	0	0	0	0	0	507	0	16,238
TOTAL	80,807	152,727	8,362	1,018	1,071	533	948	1,064	646	28	247,204

Source: Data provided by the Spanish Consulate of Tangier. Only for visas issued in Tangier, 2002.

residents of the town, as in this way they are entitled to benefit from a special statute which gives them free use of the Bel Yunech-Sebta border passage. At the end of the town lies the border pass into Sebta, and people who carry Bel Yunech residence cards can pass through freely. The inhabitants of this town are perfect examples of typical cross-border workers; they catch a bus that runs between Sebta and Bel Yunech to go to work every day. From what I can gather, the women work solely in the domestic sector: they clean, cook, and look after children for the "Christian *patrones*" of Sebta.

This all goes to show that Bel Yunech is a micro-example of how borders are being strengthened. Firstly, it represents an attractive area for people from other parts of Morocco to settle in and make a living. Secondly, there is the border's purely physical appearance: the wire fence and the wall—signs that are not present in Tangier's parameter as a border city. In addition, there are the contrasts that the concept of border creates: the socioeconomical (the people from outside Sebta) and the cultural (the inhabitants of Sebta). Thirdly, another consequential factor is the concept of the counter-border through the development of the circuits that justify the wall's very existence, which is the actual nature of the border: the "illegal" crossing of people and the authorized crossing of small goods. Fourthly, there is the concept of the border as a control area *par excellence* and, in consequence, violence often erupts in this boundary space.

Definition of Circuits

The question of whether internationalized economic circuits exist for the city of Tangier can be examined through a number of factors:

Table 4.5
Indicators of Clandestine Moroccan Immigration in Spain

	1991	1992	1993	1994	1995	1996	1997	1998
REJECTIONS	1,558	2,131	609	17,263	17,751	25,748	22,829	0
EXPULSIONS	1,497	971	1,040	3,548	3,398	3,327	5,058	0
DETAINED IN SMALL BOATS (PATERAS)	477	616	1,925	513	1,257	1,573	887	2,995
SMALL BOATS (PATERAS) INTERCEPTED	4	15	33	34	130	339	399	557

Source: Khatibi, 2001:156

1. The influence of the distribution of Tangierine migrants throughout European countries; data concerning migrants distributed in Belgium, the Netherlands, Germany, France and Spain.
2. The influence of the European country of origin on the distribution of remittances.
3. The origin of direct investment capital, according to foreign country (Alós et al. 2001).
4. The origin of imports by country or origin.
5. The type of transnational associationism: Muslim/local, European cooperation (especially Spanish and French) Med programs, etc. These types of associations point out that not only is production heavily globalized but the way in which the local civil society operates is also.

One aspect that should be considered as a form of internationalization is the way in which associationism has flourished in recent years. In Tangier, there has been a sharp increase in the number of associations, whether linked or not to international networks. The change took place mainly after Mohammed VI came to power.

Another distinguishing mark in this description of circuits is the prominent role that the most vulnerable ones play, particularly through the quantitative and qualitative importance of unaccompanied minors, as well as the *harraga*—the undocumented emigrants. However, some researchers claim that children who emigrate are not street children. Mawla (a Spanish anthropologist) states that they have all tried it two or three times. This is exemplified by the case of the younger brother of a boy from one association, who was one of these emigrant children. He reached Sebta, and stayed there in a center for minors; from there he traveled to Spain, where he went to Seville; and then ended up in Barcelona. His friends in the neighborhood regard him as a hero. This itinerary is frequently repeated: Tangier-Seville-Barcelona. I was told also about the wide variety of ways of entering Spain, such as stowing away in a lorry or a bus. A new scheme has recently been devised that involves stringing a hammock under a bus, which adds greater risk and danger to physically crossing the border.

The border economy. The connotation of a border economy usually suggests illegal, informal aspects. Thus, Hussein (an urban planner in the Wilaya) points out that border cities create an element of erosion that results in poor housing and the upsurge of sporadic work. In places such as these, a certain bias exists among the population as people try to find ways of readapting themselves to the changing social situation. This border economy explains how the network for goods coming in from Sebta functions. Sebta is a free port, and Moroccan production cannot compete with Sebta's prices. This sphere of competition with Sebta has been gradually increasing and, particularly during the last ten years, has expanded southward. According to the urban planning department of the Wilaya, this seriously harms the Moroccan economy and weakens it in terms of the purchasing of foreign currencies. Smuggled goods reach as far as Casablanca, and it should be noted that two television factories in that city have closed down due to this illegal competition, which is a testament to the scale of illegal trade. Smuggling activities are especially present in border cities such of Tangier, Ouxda and Nador. During the 1970s, Tangier's economic development was exploited by its link to smuggling activities.

People in Tangier often prefer Spanish products to those from inland Morocco. People's great desire for Spanish products, as well as for Spanish media, such as television, is significant to our understanding of the tradition of smuggling through Sebta. But once they arrive to Spain they tend to focus more on the satellite television; for example, during Ramadan 2003, families in a neighborhood of Barcelona were breaking the fast by using Arabic satellite channels as the real vehicle of the modern *umma*.

Men and women who live in border areas usually deal in smuggling. In the Oued Marsa area, heading towards the border pass of Bel Yunech, I had already seen that many towns derive their income from the production of hashish and smuggling. Given their suitable geographical location, many men choose to work in smuggling. In the case of Spain, the informal routes must be more developed, owing to the geographical proximity of Sebta and Melilla, which creates more population flows, people who live out their lives in the to-ing and fro-ing of mobility. Al-Sayrafi, who is a smuggler with years of experience on the Sebta border, confided some the tricks of the trade, and the main characteristics of the smuggling markets. To get through customs, you first need to make specific contacts with the Moroccan policemen who work there, so as to facilitate the process. This system of contacts with policemen works through knowing people: the policemen know you, you pay them a certain sum of money, and then bring back from Fndek what the policemen ask for as "a gift." The most common "gifts" are items for the home and babies' nappies, though they sometimes ask for a music system or a television set. These gifts are dependent on the type and cost of the goods. For example, clothes and electrical goods tend to be more expensive, and as a result the men who work in customs usually ask for a cash commission.

One important peculiarity of smuggling is that merchants do not work in a group; they work alone. In contrast, women work in groups, mainly to ensure that they are protected from the policemen. They organize a system among themselves in order to collect the money necessary to get them through customs. As for profits, the women make more than men, according to Al-Sayrafi,[10] because they use their feminine charms when making their purchases in Fndek, and as a result they can beat the prices down. The same applies to means of transportation: in buses or in taxis, female smugglers manage to negotiate a lower fare. Thus, women are better able to compete in the final market—the Casablanca market. This is a new version of the feminization of the economy.

As for products, fabrics are deemed to be the most profitable goods, because they sell well throughout the whole year. With respect to the sale of fabrics for the textile factories in Tangier, I was told that they do purchase in this alternative way, but they only have a deal if they place a large order. The goods are transported on mules over the mountains. If the amount of goods is particularly large, it is transported by a group of about twenty men who carry the packages on their backs.

The main markets are those of Castillejos and Nador, located parallel to Sebta and Melilla, respectively. The first market for smuggled goods exists at the very point where the products are distributed, once they have passed through the border. The second market takes the form of a network of strategic points, where there is always a great demand to be met. Ksar el Kbir in the north of Morocco is a perfect example of this situation. These points are selected according to their geographical location (situated at the crossroads of several

Table 4.6
Distribution of Companies with Foreign Capital in the Moroccan Textile
Industry by Main Country of Origin

COUNTRY	CLOTHING & TEXTILE INDUSTRY in %
CANADA	95
GREAT BRITAIN	83
SIRIA	68
BELGIUM	63
GERMANY	40
SPAIN	35
U.S.A.	34
ITALY	28
SWITZERLAND	15
NETHERLANDS	15

Source: Alós et al. 2001:68.

routes within Morocco) and due to their role as intermediate points and intermediate cities. These market places can be reached from Casablanca in only one day, so merchants can get there easily. At these final points the price is a little higher than at the aforementioned distribution markets; there are large amounts of products and a wide range. What struck me most at Ksar el Kbir was the amount of trade that was going on with products from Sebta, much more even than at El Fondak in Tangier. Thus, this trade route confirms the importance of Ksar el Kbir. There was a wide selection of goods on offer, typical items ranging from cleaning products to bars of chocolate. Most of the brands were Spanish, and most items had been labeled in Sebta's industrial estate. The most crucial selling points for the Moroccan consumer are a good price and the type of foreign packaging—in this case, Spanish. The third market takes place in the main destination cities, such as Casablanca.

Smuggling is a "formula" which is so widespread that it becomes a normality, and everyone views it as such. Therefore, given these structures of informality, the concept of legality is a very complicated one. It is the same as saying that the whole Bir Chifa neighborhood is illegal, when "illegality" is something of a norm there.

Other examples show us how we face a peculiar labor market. I realized that working in factories (in which it is said that you need to have completed secondary education to be offered a job), working in Amigo (the Spanish telephone company), and engaging in migration projects are the three main sources of income for many of the young men that I met, such as Emir, Zaqqum from the Kasbah, and Mahdi's friends. These three options, together with family strategies, seem to be central to an understanding of young people's projects in a border city. In addition, they are very significant in all the processes of femininization of the labor force.

Mohammed Ad-dubbu has not yet completed his *bacaloria* (secondary school studies), but he assured me that in Morocco everything gets sorted out through contacts—the *marifa*. People constantly refer to this system, which is the form that clientism manifests in Morocco. It is the key to finding work; for instance, in the event that your prospective employer asks for your *bacaloria* and you still have one year of studying left, the *marifa* can solve your problem. This is how it worked for Abdou, his stepfather, and they expect the same for Mohammed Ad-dubbu. At our first meeting, he informed me that he was unemployed, but later he admitted that he works sometimes as an electrician or an aerial installer, and sells soccer tickets. Previously, he was working in a factory producing electric cables for the car industry. He had to work long hours, and only earned 2,000 dirhams a month. To make matters worse, some chemical used in the manufacturing process had affected his throat, and he had to spend 900 dirhams on doctors, as he was not covered by Social Security. In light of this, he says that "working in this country is just a joke," as you earn very little money for working hard in bad conditions. His father has advised him not to work, and that he ought to get ready to do some real work when he goes to Belgium. One year later, Mohammed Ad-dubbu settled in Madrid.

Ostman arrived in Tangier and started work in McDonald's, where he worked ten to twelve hours a day and earned 2,000 dirhams a month. This was not even enough to rent an apartment, and so he is now living at a friend's house. He compared his salary with that of people who work in Amigo, and he realized that he was earning very little. He chose to come to Tangier because it is a place where he could find a job quickly, not as in Ksar el Kbir. Even so, he also complained about working in McDonald's, because he had to wait for two hours until the customers arrived. After a while, he gave up this job and went to work in a Pizza Hut near the boulevard, but he was still dissatisfied with the work, and wanted to go and work abroad. Ostman had not come to Tangier for money; he came because "there is really nothing for me in Ksar el Kbir." This is what many other people have done, and all his friends agree. Consequently, they all come to Tangier, which they consider to be an "open" city in the north of Morocco. Casablanca often holds the same image for those from the south. His immediate plan is to go back to Ksar el Kbir in a little while, live with his family, and wait for two opportunities he has got coming up; the first is a contract to work on a cruiser. He is very surprised that I have not heard of this type of contract, as they have been advertised often on television and in the press. He explained that they are European cruise ships and they need to recruit about 30,000 Moroccans. He paid 50,000 dirhams (1€ = 10 dh) in Casablanca to get into this program, but then a few months later it was revealed in the press that the program had been a complete fraud, and that the Moroccan government was going to accept part of the responsibility for reimbursing thousands of people. The second option he has with respect to his future is to try and obtain false documents in Modena, Italy, through the help of a friend. One year later, Ostman settled in Modena.

In summary, the different working lives of the people I met during my fieldwork constantly emphasize the fact that employment is the main problem. Many people are dissatisfied with their work, and they have put all their hopes into setting up projects that will provide them with a minimally decent existence.

Children's circuits. Minors[11] in Morocco are seen not only as vulnerable actors of the detailed border circuits but as representing a new stage in Moroccan international migration. This encompasses the fourth period of Moroccan migrations towards Europe, when, as of the end of the 1990s, Spain and Italy emerged as new migratory destinations. A first period of "male emigration" was followed by a second period of family reunion (plus, at the end of the 1970s the classical emigration areas such as the Sus Region and the Eastern Rif diversified, affecting the whole country), then a third period of increased female emigration, and lastly the fourth period. For Jiménez (2003), this last period represents the importance of unattended minors as migrants. They started to emigrate in the mid-1990s, first to Belgium and France, and then, from the end of the 1990s, to Spain and Italy. They originated from various zones of the country. Research work shows a predominance of the urban over the rural areas (Jiménez 2003), but what is interesting to note here is the strong evidence of Tangier, our selected border city, being the main origin of these minors. They travel hidden in lorries or as stowaways on ferries. It was not until the end of 2002 that minors started using *pateras* as a means of transportation—about the same time that routes took on a more dangerous aspect due to the SIVE control.

In the Spanish enclaves in North Africa, the cities of Sebta and Melilla, because of their geographic location, have become for Moroccans the main entry gates to Europe. It is particularly important in this context to underline the irregular expulsion of children of Moroccan origin from both of these cities. According to information received from Human Rights organizations working in the area, children in Sebta are arrested in the center of the city and taken into custody in police vans. They are often harassed during detention and some have suffered several types of abuses. Deportations are often carried out without the child having a hearing, since they have access neither to the help of an interpreter nor to legal assistance. They suffer abuses from police on both sides of the borders (the Spanish Guardia Civil and the *Mehani*, Moroccan border police,) and even sexual assaults. According to the Asociación Pro Derechos de la Infancia (on defense of children's rights) (2002), most of the children are teenagers, and are themselves from border areas. Some have escaped from difficult situations with their families, others have been abandoned when the father marries a second wife. They all come from poor families. Most of the expelled children attempt to return again to the border after an average period of five days. Their lives are perfect examples of mobility circuits in Europe. Moroccan children use these routes in order to get to Spain, as well as the Tanger-Algeciras connection or other connections with Spain. The transport system they use involves high risk. Once in Spain they use Andalusia as an entrance to move on towards Madrid and Barcelona in the search for big cities. However, some of them prefer to stay in agricultural zones. From Barcelona they tend to head towards the south of France, especially Marseilles; and from there to Northern Italy, Belgium, and the Netherlands, following the routes of the settlements of Moroccan emigration in Europe. It is interesting to establish a proper categorization of minors who emigrate in those circuits. Minors who have arrived in Sebta and Melilla to settle tend to be the ones who have made street life their own way of life. Only some of those are involved in seeking passage to the Iberian peninsula.

Much participatory research on this issue or other colateral issues has already developed among Tangier-based NGO's (Darna, Don Bosco, Paideia, etc.); this includes observations about the different neighborhoods in Tangier, but especially about the increasing number of groups of children and teenagers that hang around Tangiers' harbor. Many questions have been posed when working with the children: Who is supporting the migration strategy? Is it the minor's decision or is it a family strategy? Is the family really aware that the minor cannot be expelled from abroad as the adult can? According to Jiménez (2003), four different typologies relating these questions can be distinguished: a family situation where minors attend school and enjoy a stable family situation (10 percent); children who attend school irregularly and have had working experience and enjoy a stable family situation but with poor economic resources; children who are often in the street but live at home (40 percent); thirdly, children with a unstable family situation and with very poor economic resources. (The family is not together due to diverse reasons, sickness, divorce, second marriage, bad relations among children, violence and abuse) (35 percent); and fourthly, a group of children who live in the streets and do not keep any kind of family ties (15 percent).

The new challenge now is how to monitor this type of circuit as border crossing in wooden boats becomes the new variant of movement towards the peninsula. These are children, teenagers, and youngsters under eighteen who wish to start a new life in Europe by irregularly crossing borders. Notwithstanding, even if the legal framework does not allow unwarranted repatriation in the case of minors, cases do exist; for example, at the Setbta and Algeciras borders, as well as from the Autonomous Communities of Madrid, Catalonia and Andalusia. In October 2003, the Spanish government made repatriation possible within 48 hours for youngsters over sixteen.

Relocalization: textile and telecom circuits. There is a flexible specialization in this city: decentralized companies put out work to either independent contractors or to relatively autonomous units or the whole factory is relocated, for example from a Catalan town to Tangier. The commodity chain model is very useful in identifying strategic sites of employment and to see how the global economy moves diverse circuits that overshoot geographical boundaries. The phenomenon of outsourcing across borders through textiles occurs in many Third World countries, but it is especially significant in Morocco because industry is based on the large Spanish textile brands. Spain is the main country for outsourcing textiles in Tangier (they are mainly multinational companies present in Spain that are working for Spanish brands and retailers; Table 4.7 provides a regional distribution by Spanish social capital) and after Casablanca, Tangier is the largest textile center in Morocco. Generally speaking, off-shore production tends to result in various forms of exploitation: poor working conditions, non-unionized workers and the great inequality between the situation of women and men.

Peraldi often refers to the "colonial straightjacket," for example when referring to the grassroots circuits built up by the commercial routes from Algeria

Table 4.7
Regional Distribution of Companies and Jobs by Percentage of
Spanish Social Capital

MOROCCAN REGION	<50% SPANISH CAP.		SPAN.CAP.DOMINANT		100%SPANISH CAP.	
	COMPANIES	JOBS	COMPANIES	JOBS	COMPANIES	JOBS
CASABLANCA CONURBATION	25	1,673	29	3,586	15	1,415
NORTH-WEST	14	1,517	18	599	39	2,352
NORTH-EAST	5	657	13	414	5	41
OTHER CITIES	3	571	7	616	2	21
SOUTH	7	199	8	231	3	31
TOTAL	54	4,617	75	5,446	64	3,860

Source: Alós et al. 2001:76

to Istanbul. This colonial straightjacket is also reproduced in the textile circuits by the attitudes and discourses of foreign entrepreneurs in North Africa, which Peraldi clearly expresses:

> When he resettles in Morocco and in Tunisia, the French, Italian or German businessman dreams at once of changing his behavior. He loves them from a far, as if anchored in childhood, the sun, the peppers, the mildness of the day, and the smell of cumin, but he is convinced that they think only of stealing from him and he wishes nothing else than changing those who work for him, to teach them everything, they who know nothing. (Peraldi 2003: 26)

This can be also easily transported to other places such as Ciudad Juárez (Vila 2003c: 317), by claiming that many Anglos cross borders but do not become hybrids, showing as example the American *maquiladora* managers in Juárez who work in a U.S.-like setting in Mexico, without ever learning to speak Spanish. However, Vila also points out that on the other hand, there are many Chicanos who do not speak Spanish, and that there are thousands of Mexican immigrants living a Mexican lifestyle in El Paso without ever having learned English.

In Tangier, some people are well aware of the implications of industrial relocalization and its impact. They know that the unions are helpless to react, and industrial development is usually justified with the argument that it guarantees socioeconomic progress and acts as a buffer to unemployment. This type of argument is also used when a hypermarket is opened on the outskirts of the city: the staff tends to defend the system with arguments about rationalization and economic progress. Since the hypermarkets have opened on the outskirts of Tangier, the same justification is always used: they are clean, organized, efficient, and they create new jobs. In some ways it is like a typical developmentalist discourse from the 1960s that transposes the dichotomous perceptions of tradition and modernity onto the world of production, distribution, and consumer habits. Against this, there is another line of argument that complains that globalization imposes one single model of development, one homogenized model that stifles the creation of the area's own, local forms. This global model imposes itself easily onto places with scarce technology, such as Morocco. Thus these countries represent an "end of line" in all senses, from the delocalization of industry to the delocalization of agricultural production. Does this mean it is better to grow strawberries in Lukus than in Huelva?

In Tangier, there are hundreds of sweatshops in the basements of multiple buildings. Although the workers are exploited, they also know (thanks to television) that many people enjoy better labor conditions than they do. It is the mass media that makes them aware of their situation, and this is where a bank clerks' whole argument on the problems of democratization begins. In his view, the process of industrial delocalization is at odds with the process of democratization. Meanwhile, the major Spanish representatives in Tangier deny that Spaniards have set up any illegal sweatshops. The situation of the vulnerable groups inserted inside the commodity chains of the textile industry have opened up the debate on consumer ethics and as well as the ethical ways of sourcing from the producers' perspective.

The first textile visit I made in Tangier was to a factory that produces textile products for pregnant women. They were just completing an order of 12,000 items, 8,000 of which had already been sent. They were manufacturing these goods for two nationalities: Spaniards and Germans. In my conversations with the men in charge, they often spoke about the importance of the nationality of their clients, their preferences and their quality requirements. In this factory, there were almost 200 workers, nearly all men. Ihram (a textile engineer) explains that this is because the boss is from a very religious family. The first floor is where the clothing patterns are made. The machines are quite simple, and the work is fairly manual. The main conclusion of this visit was to verify whether an accentuated process of victimization was being unleashed among the textile workers—a situation where the "Europeans" make use of traditional *machismo* to turn it into something that is industrially exploitable.

Abu-talib is a sweatshop located in the Char Djedid neighborhood, in the proximity of Casa Barata. It is much smaller than the former one, more oppressive in terms of space, and with generally more unstructured labor lines. In contrast, the atmosphere inside is pleasant, as it is more communal with music playing. Its clients are French and Spanish, the latter basically consisting of the minipremium in Seville. Most of the women working in this workshop are young, though some are middle-aged. There are a few boys, but not children, like the ones I saw on my first visit. The sweatshop has only been open for a year. It can produce forty skirts and sixty-five pairs of trousers in an hour. There are two production lines, one making black skirts and the other manufacturing deep-red ones. The female laborers' working day ends at six o'clock in the evening, and they are usually free for the whole weekend, or sometimes only on Sundays.

Tangertem is a factory comprised of four production lines, three of which are not complete, and a total of a hundred and thirty workers. Their working hours are from eight o'clock in the morning to six in the evening (a ten-hour day), with one hour for lunch. They sometimes work up to two hours overtime daily, if there is an urgent job to finish. Most of the laborers are young girls, who regard the new visitors with suspicion.

The port area of Tangier includes the shipping companies and the manufacturing premises. The women working in this area are very different in their manner from the women in the other factories I have visited, as they seem much more professional. The most prominent feature in this free-trade area is the materialization of so many different mobilities: the outgoing textile industry, the incoming and outgoing MREs, the organization of *harraga* (undocumented emigrants), the children waiting by the walls to cross the sea, and the incoming and outgoing flows of tourists.

One afternoon we went to meet some factory girls at the main gate of the port. They work in the Papagayo factory in the free-trade area. However, they are not ordinary workers, they are production line supervisors. Fatiha has been working in the factory for ten years. She is entitled to a month's holiday every year, divided into two fortnight periods, one in April and another in September. These holiday slots are compulsory, and workers have no choice in the matter. Last week, Fatiha had to work on Saturday, and was not notified until the day before. However, in spite of all the disadvantages, they do have the opportunity of setting up an association that aims to provide a children's nursery, cultural activities and trips, as well as training and sensitization activities. Setting up this association represents the women's attempt to somehow break out of the closed environment of reducing their lives to traveling between home and the factory.

The second relocalization process I looked at is that of the telecom circuits. Amigo is a branch of the Spanish company Telefónica based in Morocco and in fourteen other countries, mainly in Latin America. The branch in Tangier is an interesting case, since it represents a way of delocalizing services in addition to all the industrial delocalization trope present in the city. Mohammed Al-batriqu is one of the young men I met who worked in Amigo. He speaks perfect Spanish, without any accent, and uses quite a few colloquial expressions. He informed me that there were around 600 people working there; 80 percent were from Tetouan; half of them were women, and ranged in age from twenty to twenty-four. So many of them are from Tetouan because there is a university there with a Spanish philology faculty, although I also believe that it is because people from Tetouan have been historically more exposed to the Spanish language. The company's basic profile or criterion for recruiting employees is their accent. Some have learned the language in their Spanish philology studies, while others have learned it from watching Spanish television. In the corridors, the workers greet each other in a friendly manner, "Hola ¿qué tal?" Nowadays in Tangier, people have learned Spanish from television, but in earlier times it was different, they had learned it because communities were simply living together.

Mohammed Al-batriqu is very happy with his job at Amigo, because he feels that the workers are all treated equally; they all have the same status. They work from five o'clock in the evening to one in the morning—eight hours straight, answering the telephone, with only a half-hour break for coffee. The contract they are offered depends on the number of hours they work. All the workers have been given Spanish names, and they also attend seminars to improve their accents. I was told that the most important trait is to be able to speak the language, but it was also vitally important to become familiar with the cultural context—for example, understanding the jokes and the different turns of phrase. For him, the contextual aspect of Spanish is fundamental for the job. The Instituto Cervantes has become very involved in these types of seminars—and here a clear link can be distinguished between cultural coop-eration and foreign capital. It was interesting to meet all these young people, because they are, in a way, the modern face of Morocco. You can see it from their lifestyles: they go to fashionable clubs to dance Salsa, or meet up to watch commercial video films (mostly American). Though some of them feel fortunate to work in a company such as this, others complain about the total exploitation that Amigo represents. While clothesmaking is a more explicit kind of exploitation, this is a more concealed form. I use the term "exploita-tion" in view of the fact that costs here are a third of what they would be in Spain. This phenomenon has also spread to other sectors, such as Tele-sales companies. One year later, Amigo made a large number of its personnel redundant.

The Family's World

This ethnography used the space of the family as a main vehicular refer-ence. Getting closer to their everyday life was a way to discover a family's own rhythms, its different centers in the city, around the market and the promenade (not so much the mosque, for Moroccan women). It was also a way to observe the social practices within the space of the family, and within the home. Time observance was built up by a reciprocal process of getting to know each other. The discourses around the family's world, be it in Tangier or in Durrës, are based on the reconstruction and interpreting of events from the family's own description and interpretation. Families were selected in relation to the ques-tions put by the initial research on the study of migrations and female labor in the textile factories.

As part of my follow up with the chosen families, I constructed some family trees, which produced information which revealed work life and emigration cycles. This ethnographic method was very suitable for the relational system that was established in catching up on families lives, and tended to apply better than in-depth interviews. Thus, I used the system of repeated visits to families, as well as selecting and working with informants within the household context. Access to these families generally took place randomly; I would just walk down the street and talk to people, making spontaneous contacts. The system I devised for the families in Tangier was to pay somewhat spontaneous, irregular visits to the homes. I selected a series of families from the Casbah, and thanks to them I was able to perceive the family structure through their genograms.

The genograms were organized according to different types of categories of migration history: (1) the returning migrant—Mohammed the trader; (2) immigration in Belgium—Malak; (3) internal immigration—Rajah; (4) the potential immigrant—Hijra; (5) the Belgium-Madrid migration connection—Mohammed Ad-dubbu, Family 2; and (6) the female potential migrants—Ihsan's daughters, Family 1.

The space of the family represents four main features: (a) a security belt in the uncertain process of economic crisis (considering the solidarity of the family network as a crucial resource as well as a notion of loyalty to the family); (2) support of the migratory project; (3) a basic form of social control for young Moroccans; and (5) a social control based on the gendered honor of the family.

However, not everyone I met had an experience with mobility—quite the opposite, in fact—and I realized that categories I had excluded from this mobility should also be considered. I needed to define correctly the different categories of people in accordance with their experiences and relations to mobility. In this sense, it is interesting that I managed to select a group of people who, since they first settled in Tangier, had always lived there and had never left the country. It was also interesting to see how these people viewed all the others who live their lives in an itinerant manner. Although in principle my main area of research was focused on the family environment, through the changes in this exploration I ascertained that my perspective was based more on the contextual features of this city, which enabled me to refer back to the role of the border city. As this analytical perspective became progressively transformed, I also found greater dangers of dispersion in relation to the topic of the condition of women in factories in the context of the research.

The house is the symbol of the moral order of the family. The *horma* is the sacred space that symbolizes the home, and it is characterized by its inviolability. The protection of *horma* is such that research on it (for example, in relation to data on divorces, non-recognized children, etc.) is often avoided to protect its intimacy. This inviolability of *horma* is also expressed in traditional homes by leaving the women out of the male visitors' view. However, in the case that the researcher is a woman those spatial codes do not apply in that way. There is a traditional tendency towards a bipartite organization of the house, between the public side for visitors (marked by the male spaces) and the side that corresponds to women's rooms and the kitchen. This division is made among families in which the household head remains attached to a traditional vision of the extended family and to the strict segregation between male and female use of space.

The plan of the house is more inspired by the conception of family relations than vice versa (Boughali 1974). It is interesting to note that the home is not only the core space for nuclear and extended family relations but also for some of the neighbors. These common visitors do not share any blood ties, only neighboring relations (*aj-joura*). It is interesting to note that houses that seem to be impervious to external contact, have on the inside communicating doors; those who can trespass those doors are long-term neighbors (Boughali 1974: 65).

In some peripheral areas, there are the European-style villas that are inhabited by one single, nuclear family. In contrast, the extended family uses a spatial structure that is organized in a horizontal manner, and to which people who are not part of the nuclear family can more easily adapt. On the other hand, those who live in detached houses spend their money on ostentatious consumer goods and lead a European lifestyle. Among middle-class families there is evidence of a tendency toward the individualization of space, particularly with students in the family, which results in the specialization of various rooms as opposed to the traditional multi-purposed rooms.

Figure 4.1
Structure of a Home in Tangier's Medina

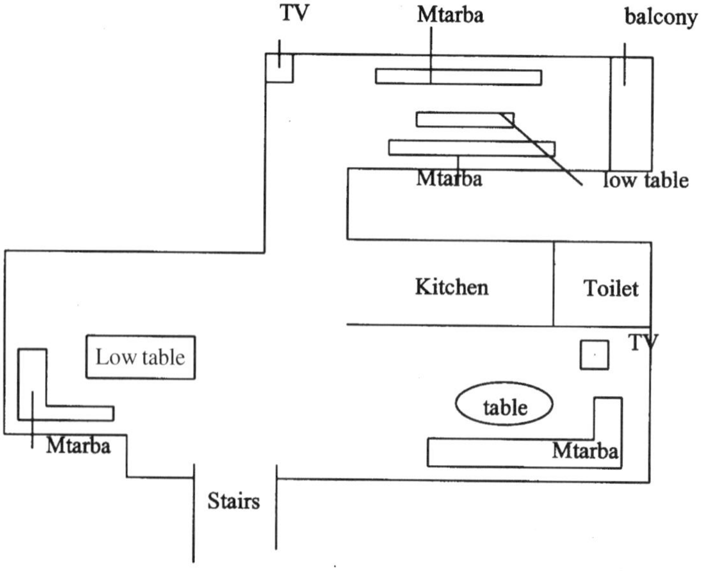

Sometimes it is, in fact, the people who co-exist between the aforementioned villas and the dwellings of the common people that are best able to fulfill the role of intermediaries between the ethnologist and society. Very often, the images of the houses coincide with the images of the families. For example, the huge *mtarbas* (Moroccan-style sofas), which have room for the whole community, are focused around the television as the family center (I am referring specifically to the dining room of Family 1; see Figure 4.1). The television set inevitably plays an essential role: it is always switched on, showing all those television and video images of consumerism, the attributes of the modern Egyptian lifestyle (Egypt being the country that produces most of the Arab cinema and television). Egypt, considered the core of the Arab culture, is now the one to transmit the image of a fantasized Arab middle class in Moroccan homes. TV plays a significant role in socializing families to modern values. Romantic love, beautiful women who dance and sing, big homes and cars are part or the repertoire in the process of homogenization of mass consumption products.

On my first visit, Hijra warned me that hers was a poor people's house. Now she is divorced and her husband's family lives in the city of Sale as well as in Belgium, France, and Spain. In the old days, whole families would live in one single house in the Medina, but in recent years many couples have separated (see in Table 4.8 the base of the nuclear household size). In fact, there are some houses that are only occupied by girls from outside Tangier who work in the textile industry, and some in local prostitution. Some of them are also wives in nuclear families.

Table 4.8
Household Size in Tangier

Size. Number of persons by household	%
1	2.5
2	9.07
3	13.26
4	16.95
5	18.26
6	14.63
7	10.82
8	6.63
9 or more	7.88
Total	**100**

Source: Plan d'aménagement de la Commune Urbaine de Tánger. Rapport enqûete ménages (January 1999). Commune Urbaine de Tanger, 1999: 31.

Ihsan, from Family 1, was a perfect informant and her family was ideal because it combined many of the features of a border city which I was looking for: some members of her family are employed in textile factories, she works as a cleaner at a hostel where Sub-Saharan migrants live, her son used to be involved in smuggling activities in Sebta, and two of her daughters wanted to emigrate abroad. Furthermore, she is a Tangierine whose biographical past is intertwined with the historical memory of the city, as she used to work for Spaniards living in the Medina (see Figure 4.2. Genogram Ihsan to identify this family).

Ihsan had been working for about six years in a well-known, emblematic hotel in the center of Tangier. She only worked there in summer, and this is why she needed a change; she wanted a job all year round, which she has now at the hostel. However, she is not covered by social security there, either. As regards international migrations, part of her family lives in London, Belgium, France, and Spain. Among other difficulties she experiences, her family has constant problems with the law, as well as problems related to maintenance money for the grandchildren, which is not paid by the fathers. Consequently, she is fed up with the children, and with the responsibility of supporting so many people at home. A noteworthy peculiarity is that Ihsan has always had to support family members, and now even more so, since two of her daughters are divorced from their husbands. At present, her daughter Iddah is jobless, because she is waiting to go to Spain; Sara, another daughter, currently employed in a textile factory, is also waiting to go to Spain. Iddah was divorced from an immigrant in Italy—originally from Uxda—who turned out to have been married to another Moroccan woman who was living in Italy, but Iddah did not know. She wanted to marry him to get her documents so she could go and live in Italy. One year later, Iddah opened a hairdressers' parlor, only to close it again when she married a Tangierine doctor.

While married, Ihsan worked for a Spanish woman. Her mother had also worked for Spaniards, and that is why she can speak Spanish, though not as well as her mother did. Ihsan separated from her husband ten years ago, and she always complains that men do not bring money into the home. Her daughter Sara worked in Mgougha, the largest industrial area in Tangier. Laila also worked there, but what I did not know was that Fatima—her sister-in-law—worked there, too. Meanwhile, her husband Mohammed was still unemployed. One year later Fatima had her first baby. Laila worked in Dewhirst Ladieswear Trousers, SARL, in the final audit section. This company has about 1,000 workers, and Laila has a fixed shift, from 6 a.m. to 2 p.m. There are two additional shifts: from 2 p.m. to 10 p.m. and from 10 p.m. to 6 a.m. They have the same shifts at Abanderado, but her shift keeps changing. Dewhirst is composed of three sections: steams, ironing, and final audit. This last section is also in charge of packaging and preparing the items for the depot.

Figure 4.2
Genograme Ihsan

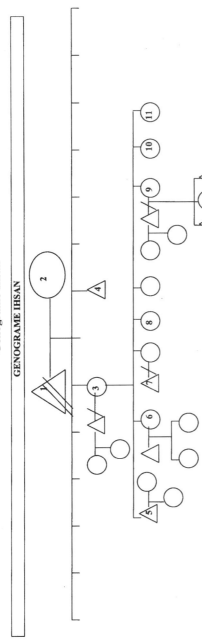

GENOGRAME IHSAN

1: **MAN:** Deceased.
2: **WOMAN:** Cleaner in the shops of the Medina. She used to work for the Spanish.
3: **IHSAN:** Cleaner in a *pension* in the Medina. She used to work for the Spanish. She is divorced. Her ex-husband is married and has a child aged 1.
4: **Man:** At present in prison, smuggler of migrants.
5: **Man:** Jobless. He used to smuggle goods from Sebta.
6: **Woman:** Worker in the textile industry. Lives in the Marxan.
7: **Woman:** Waiting for her documents to go to Spain. Ex husband from Uxda living in Italy. Married in April 2001. Wishes to marry a Spanish man.
8: **Woman:** Works in the textile industry. Candidate to emigration towards Spain.
9: **Woman:** Her ex husband is from The Rif, from Alhucemas. .
10: **Woman:** Aged 19. Lives with her maternal aunt in the neighbourhood of California looking after her cousins
11: **Woman:** Aged 12. Goes to a school in the Kasbah. Has difficulties with her studies.

It is now from these families' worlds that we will discern key aspects of analysis: the patchwork economy, family and marriage strategies, and the factory-emigration hypothesis.

The patchwork economy for female-headed families. The 2000-2004 Development Plan for Morocco was focused on the improvement of education, a wider access to health services, and to general measures related to the eradication of poverty. Family, women, children, and the elderly are the targeted population for such policies. Within the plan it is relevant to note the data concerning female-headed household units. The 1995 Moroccan family inquiry showed that 20 percent of urban women (rising to 23 percent in 1997) and 27 of rural women were declared economically active in the formal economy. In 1995, inquiry results pointed to a total of 15 percent of women as household heads. Widowhood and divorce are the variables explaining most of the figures. Furthermore, in the case of divorced women with children; they were the ones to win custody of their descendents (Ministère de la Prévision Economique et du Plan 2000).

Patchwork here can refer to many different ways of using all the available opportunities to be found by families. In the immigration society, they can also continue this available patchwork by combining labor market income, welfare, welfare mix (see chapters 1 and 2 for its understanding), and community resources (lending, remittances from other countries, etc.). In our case, family members combine incomes from formal and informal resources as well with occasional jobs. Those strategies are to be seen as an intensification of labor exploitations facing economic crisis (Dunay et al. 1995). Patchwork strategies for single (lone) mothers are constantly present when considering saving and consumption strategies. It is mostly the case with women who are able to work in precarious jobs (textile factory workers, cleaners, prostitutes), but they become unprotected from the income of family work. Therefore in these cases, both conditions, "not having a man at home" and the incidence of women in low status and low pay jobs, are present.[12]

In regard to the administration of the family economy, I discovered that the subject was more complicated than I thought. The lower you descend on the social scale, the more likely it is that the head of the family will be a woman, usually corresponding to the profile of illiterate, divorced, or widowed (CERED 1992: 58 in Ribas-Mateos 1999: 217). With regard to the problems facing single mothers in Morocco, it is very interesting to hear about the true cases of children related by Aïcha Ech-Channa (2000). Those stories underline the social phenomenon of what it means in Morocco to be a child born out-of-wedlock, normally regarded as a dishonor for everyone. Single mothers who have children tend to feel forced to abandon their children without registering their birth with the authorities. Abandoned baby girls eventually become "petites bonnes" (young servants), who are often subjected to severe physical abuse.

The case of Ihsan's family illustrates—within one single home—all the existing problems regarding the social vulnerability of a woman who is socially detached from a man in Morocco. Hence, this is the reason why the mother of the family keeps saying, "the fact is, men are very bad." She now feels responsible for all those useless marriages, in the face of the difficult task of being a mother to seven daughters, many of which were already divorced as young girls. In fact, one of her daughters has been forced to go back to her mother's house because her husband had taken a second wife, and now he refuses to pay her any income support. This man from the Rif mountains simply will not pay up, which is just what happened with Ihsan's husband. Two months later, Ihsan told me that she had chased her daughter's husband through Tangier, and in the end she had managed to take him to the police. "Even though that didn't solve anything, either, because you know, the Moroccan police always want money." As far as she is concerned, it was all just a typical man's dirty trick, and that's why she thinks all men are bad. There are repeated cases of vulnerability that result from the behavior of the husband, who uses the law's patriarchal bias (the legislation of the *Mudawana*, the personal and family law) to defend himself. On the other hand, one common denominator of these families is that they are homes run by women who play strong leader roles, and who are always prepared to fight for their survival. It is no coincidence that these are, in fact, the homes that have been identified as suffering from greater social vulnerability in the anti-poverty programs. There is also the case of Hijra: according to her, she was abandoned by her husband and he would not pay her any income support either.

As regards the Mudawana, I should point out that finally, in 2003, amendments were brought to the family law (Mudawana, which regulates marriage and divorce following an interpretation of the Sharia). Women's groups had

Table 4.9
Demographic Structure of the Family Head in Tangier by Sex and Age

AGE GROUPS	MALE	FEMALE	BOTH
15-24	1.31	2.28	1.44
25-34	8.09	7.76	8.04
35-44	29.97	17.35	27.56
45-54	24.56	26.48	24.8
55-64	18.8	27.87	20.77
65+	17.27	18.26	17.39
TOTAL	**100**	**100**	**100**

Source: Plan d'aménagement de la Commune Urbaine de Tanger. Rapport enqûete ménages (January 1999). Commune Urbaine de Tanger, 1999: 36

feared that reforms, first promised when King Mohammed VI succeeded his father, Hassan II, in 1999, would never happen after protests from Islamist groups. The reforms cover various family-related issues such as marriage, divorce, domestic violence, and child custody. Marriage age has been raised from 16 to 18 years, inheritance measures have been also modified in order to protect women, and polygamy has been restricted, repudiation has been cancelled, and only judiciary divorce shall be valid and child custody will be retained even if the woman remarries (www.arabicnews.com).

Understanding the system of pooling earnings was of key importance in my ethnographic work. Undoubtedly, there was a huge difference between my situation and that of my informants, for instance, when I imagined how many hours Ihsan had to work as a cleaner just to be able to afford the food for the whole family. The crux of many questions in my family visits in Morocco was—"Shal?" (literally, "How much?"), which sometimes posed difficulties for me. It embarrassed me so much when Ihsan asked me how much I paid for my rent that I answered that I would tell her later, but I never did.

In any case, people do talk about poverty concerns and the difficulties involved in this whole world of "maxakil" (problems), though poverty does not seem to have such a strong stigma as it can have in other societies, or in the experience of emigration abroad. In addition, people do not always conceptualize their situation in terms of social class; the poor are considered unfortunate within a world of moral scales, but deep down, what really matters to them is whether or not someone has a "white heart" (is a good person).

The topic of family income has always been difficult to discern in the ethnographic daily routine, as I saw from my various visits to Family 1. The man from the Rif mountains, Ihsan's former son-in-law, had been working as a bricklayer in Tangier. He was repairing their house when he fell in love with the daughter of the family; as I was told he then married her, divorced her, remarried, and now he no longer sends them any money. Mohammed, the son, worked buying and selling goods from Sebta. At present, the house only has two sources of direct earnings: Ihsan's, from cleaning the hostel and Sara's, from working in the factory.

Family strategies. In border cities, dichotomous analyses of social classes can be observed very clearly, in accordance with Sassen's theories on social polarization on an urban scale. Foreign capital also plays a part in this polarization, and thus the delocalization of telecommunication services helps, for example, as an strategy to swell the ranks of the urban middle class. The upper middle classes use the route of the private school to support themselves and to reproduce socially. Thus, Hijra's twin objectives of giving her children a decent education (private schools) and "getting them settled" explains and justifies her migration project.

For certain types of lower middle-class families, emigration represents a strong investment in education, and is the most suitable strategy for social mobility. I imagine that people in Morocco have been combining two types of strategies in recent years: on one hand, the emigrant worker uses the migration project as a key strategy for social mobility, while, on the other, the lower middle-class family attempts to focus it on university studies for the few family members who can afford to study.

As I have mentioned, the concept of social class in Tangier is not a subject with which people are commonly concerned. They tend to talk about the difference between educated people and those with little education, which is, in fact, a euphemistic way of talking about social classes. The concept of "educated" and "uneducated" is revealed in various ways. For instance, in the social class that a person shows when speaking, whether or not a boy tends to sexually harass girls in the street or not, whether they speak any foreign languages (language establishes forms of social prestige—from the use of French to the use of *darija*, the Moroccan dialect, while speaking Spanish seems to have a more popular connotation), and whether they can understand other people's way of thinking, other types of mentality. There is also the tendency to speak about "us," the "*umma*" (the community of Islamic believers), and the idea that all Muslims are the same, that Islam blurs social class differences. By contrast and, surprisingly, in Morocco there are sharp differences in social class within one single extended family (Ribas-Mateos 1999). This is due, in a large extent, to the contexts of colonization and international migrations (derived from the purchasing power of MREs and the power of international strategies)—these are just part of the explanation for this disparity.

As in any other peripheral urban area, the houses of the upper classes face away from the majority of the Moroccan population, the common people (the *Chaabi*). The former social class usually adopts Spanish or French lifestyles, and tends to live their lives with one eye fixed on Spain, either taking a trip there for a long weekend, or going to the sales, etc. Consequently, they tend to create completely isolated worlds, which can be described as islands of well-being. They are even educated differently, mainly in Spanish and French. In this way, the language used by certain people becomes yet another barrier between social class boundaries.

People from Tangier province are highly mobile: this is not exactly nomadic movement, but rather a constant commuting, which represents a form of geographical mobility for the purpose of attaining any kind of upward social mobility. It is also linked to the culture of "making quick money," which is necessary when people are lacking either a support infrastructure or capital with which to set their strategies in motion. In poorer contexts, emblematic of the weakness of dominant social networks and low salaries, the temptation to earn high wages is considerable, and includes taking jobs within the informal economy. A good illustration of this is a lady that lives in the Kasbah in Tangier and who brings in fabrics every day from the border market of Castillejos in a "*grand taxi*."

For Hijra, who is faced with what she sees as an outlook of poverty and closed opportunities for a single woman, working as a domestic helper in a house in Spain has to be—and must be—a better option. In Morocco, divorced women are seen as women who have dropped in their social status. Her migration project would involve working as a domestic helper in Spain, after which she would bring across her two children—who are in full agreement with her future plans. Hence, this is the only way she can envisage a kind of social mobility that will provide her with something specific, so that she does not have to continue to suffer so much hardship. Because, as she always says, she is a single woman, a lone mother, a family without a man. I think that, in general, the ideas of Ramírez (1998) on the structure of connection and non-connection to a man in migration typologies would be very suitable for some interesting operative categories of analysis, particularly in how divorced, repudiated, and widows are common categories in autonomously led migration.

In Tangier, transnational migratory projects are revealed as a perspective of social mobility that is created within spatial mobility, especially beyond national borders, and with a wide range of destinations. In this sense, it is particularly useful to analyze family strategies as they connect with migratory strategies in accordance with the multiple criteria that operate in this context, such as the cost of marriage, the cost of documents, and the context of relations within the extended family.

In Tangier, apart from the conditions of migratory contexts of departure (which are very well known thanks to the classic studies on emigration), it seems crucial to stress that Shenghen has also led to a sense of people feeling as if they are being held back—a certain kind of imprisonment. With this in mind, the subject of border features currently comprises the creation of migration projects, whether by paying and buying their journey on the market, or by carrying out a reconstruction of the traditional community networks, which are made more flexible due to the imperatives of European immigration policies. And here we have, as a good demonstration, the key element of family strategies. That is to say, examining how families make use of the network systems that have been traditionally used, and reinterpreting them within the framework of a restrictive immigration policy. Furthermore, this is a policy that also determines the constitution of the family: the accepted family structure and the way in which the family of origin depends on the reuniting of immigrants in Europe. At the end of the day, these are policies that are utterly decisive for the structuring of the family. These legal constraints explain the way in which nuclear families are dispersed throughout Europe into networks of extended families, and the reason why they do not tend to concentrate within neighborhoods typical of extended families, as in the case of the 1960s French *banlieues*. (A whole literature has focused on the standardization of the French peripheral neighborhood and research has been carried out on its alienated living conditions.) The nuclearization of the Moroccan family, the feminisation of migration flows, and the family ideology articulated within immigration policies in Europe are all definite factors that have led to a spatial configuration of Moroccan families in a diverse scenario that stretches across several countries.

The most important focus point is to see how family strategies fit in with migratory strategies: the choice of a mixed marriage, be it with a MRE (e.g., migrants in Europe marrying people from the countries' of origin, often referred to as *halal* partners in the marriage market) from the extended family or someone from the same neighborhood, the presence of polygamy structures divided between countries, and the impact of the rising divorce rates. All of these are considered factors that encourage departure, and they are, therefore, key elements through which people formulate their migration strategies. Marrying a foreign male is becoming more common now; it is the migration strategy which best represents the "Romeo and Juliette syndrome." It often means marrying not only without the parents' advice but also marrying a partner outside the *umma.*

What is usually depicted more openly is the connection between migration projects and wedding plans, as shown by Family 1. According to this perception, the possible candidates to travel to Spain are Iddah, the separated wife, and Sara, the factory worker. Emigration by either of them would represent a respite in the familial responsibilities of Ihsan, their mother. They even asked me openly if I could find a Spanish man to marry Iddah.

Ultimately then, three considerations should be made when considering family strategies. Firstly, there are some important elements to take into account, which have been established by law that govern the margin of movement for family strategies: divorces and refusals to pay child support (the *nafaqa*), and the religious restrictions on the regulation of mixed marriages. Morocco only recognizes religious marriages or, rather, if a Moroccan Muslim gets married in a registry office in Spain, the marriage is not valid in Moroccan eyes. Nevertheless, it should be mentioned that in recent years in Morocco, many more women have married non-Muslim men. In any case, the process is still quite a long one, as it has to go through complex administrative stages. In particular, the case of divorce is vitally important to an understanding of the dynamics of survival, especially in Family 1. When Meriem—the mother of Family 2—told me that she would be happy to have a daughter-in-law like me, the subject of "marrying for documents" came up again. What they all wanted was to go and live in Spain. As I was told once in a mobile phone shop, if they allowed all the Tangierines who feel a special attraction for Spain to leave the city, Tangier would be left deserted.

Secondly, I have tried to address the institution of marriage in order to examine how marriage strategies operate in relation to social class, ethnic community, religious belief, and in the formulation of migration projects. As always, it continued to surprise me that in many cases, social class does not seem to be an obstacle to marriage: one of the most important factors for the woman is whether the man has a job, though he does also need to have a house to live in. I do not know to what extent the basis for social class is stronger, within an urban social structure—such as in Casablanca—or in rural areas. Aboumalek's research (1994) is helpful in examining all these generalizations in greater detail in the context of a common social class. The choice of cousins as candidates and the people who are—to a greater or lesser extent—part of the family, whether through family ties or semi-family ties, are still effective, though "modernity" brings new interpretations.

Thirdly, there is an ethnic component that affects family strategies. I refer to the fact that the Rifians and the Soussis have managed to establish their family strategies in an endogamous manner within their community, and that this structure still persists. Other forms of ethnic affinity that also existed until recently include the Jebala/Aroubia divisions in the choice of candidates for migration. In Tangier, even young modern men are often not yet prepared to marry people who do not come from the north of Morocco.

Fourthly, marriage and marriage transactions constitute a key issue because they reveal the strategies of international unions within the context of the capitalist economy as well as in the context of the commodification of migration documents. Consequently, the centrality of marriage can be understood here in the embeddedment between migration and its relation with labor migration. On the marriage market, those who have relatives abroad or those who are already living there enjoy a higher status as future candidates. It is through these linkages that one can determine the family's wealth and its social prestige within the community.

Marriage strategies. The focus on marriage from the perspective of the ceremony, the ritual, and the impact on the Moroccan social order has been a classic in Moroccan ethnography. Before, marriage strategies were considered to be an object of study in and of themselves (Eickleman 2003: 245). The focus on marriage was a constant in my stays with the families; with the visits of Family 1, wedding celebrations were the main topic of their videotapes, they were seen as an indicator of the family own's image and an indication of social status. The wedding celebration marks an important rite of passage in Moroccan society and the videos make it clear to the family's hosts, the neighbors, and the rest of the community.

Endogamy still plays an important role in community tradition. Family reunion takes precedence over the policy of social integration. They influence each other; on the one hand, migration policies often provoke a long-term separation of the nuclear family in two or more countries, which often serves to delay or bring forward marriages and general changes in family planning. On the other hand, we have to understand marriage logics, the family formation, and the family system in general as a structure in which to understand the migratory dynamic. Families here can also work with their own agency against the agendas of migration policies in the EU countries. Therefore, it is through the accent on *agency* that we can unpack here the grassroots of globalization and the impact on locality.

The marriage institution plays a key role in the socialization of the adult, in the preservation of identity, and in the sense of belonging to the Muslim community. The idea of marriage is strongly embedded among the community; people often plan their marriage prospects before going out with a partner. The predominant model is still that of dominant marriage with the consent of both sets of parents, excluding all forms of negotiation that lie outside the family (Aboumalek 1994: 40). The idea of marriage brings with it the image of the ideal woman who takes care of her home and her children. Apart from the anti-bachelorhood-oriented traditions we should also add those that condemn women who have no children or those that have a large family. The latter are normally associated with the stereotypical image of the rural female, or those from peripheral areas such as Bir Chifa. It is the pressures against spinsterhood that make us understand a common saying in Tangier, "An umarried 25-year-old woman is a problem for the family." It is also important to note that among the people located at the bottom of the urban social hierarchy there is a greater tendency to marry partners from the same region, area or city; "it is a need of security to push to find a spouse in the country of origin, and if possible inside the same family." (Aboumalek, 1994: 195).

Hence, marriage strategies seem to emerge as the defining axis on which different social patterns take place: from the various negotiations by men and women in the rural and urban environments to the marriages of immigrants in Europe, who are, in turn, driven by the family reunion policies. Moreover, documentation procedures in Europe speed up marriage practices. The issue here is whether these new and old marriage strategies work in the space of international migration. These kinds of examples serve to show how in the articulation of globalization and migration, seen from a micro-level, new forms coexist with former established forms. They illustrate a way of understanding continuities and discontinuities. The new forms are built from reinterpretation and reaction; they are built of a complex dialogue with the cultural homogenizing trends.

Marriage, most clearly, is a vehicle of stability, in spite of being hampered by difficult socioeconomic conditions. In addition, marriage strategies in Tangier are very different from the marriage strategies based on nineteenth-century romantic love, which is the dominant contemporary schema in Europe. Marriage is often arranged quite quickly, as someone in Family 1 expressed: "marriage is quickly organized in order to avoid sexual relations outside marriage." In general terms, new forms of relations interplay with the old ones, thus, the concept of modern love, and often a very romantic one, intertwines with the old concept attached to the classical code of honor and male domination.

Another difference is that marriage and divorce contracts are signed and broken quite easily. In Morocco there is a much more flexible attitude toward marriage than in places like neighboring Spain, where it is still difficult to get divorced. In addition, for many women, marrying represents a kind of freedom to leave the family home. Women frequently use marriage as a means to an end. However, it is usually a short-term view, because later they tend to distance themselves from the relationship. It is then that the man turns into the "ghost" husband, to which Ángeles Ramírez refers in her book, *Gender and Islam* (1998).

The summer holidays are inundated with weddings, and much of what happens then in the sphere of social relations is directly connected with the arrival of the MREs. This results in a kind of commodification of marriage, in which decisions are made rather quickly. Therefore, maximum advantage is taken of the arrival of the MREs, and choosing a spouse fulfills a function of the migration project. The weddings take place in brightly lit houses that look like fairground constructions, or like a summer *fiesta*. In the small border town of Bel Yunech, Yasmine is the single woman in the family. Her father seems to be expecting her to get married, just as her sisters have. Weddings are the perennial subject of conversation, and the word "wedding" and any kind of joke about a possible wedding are constant elements in most families. It is as if the concept of local fiestas does not exist there, because the perfect party is always a wedding, and particularly in the summer. Weddings are most often the reason for family visits: "You have to marry off your daughter." This also is related to the women's limitations within the labor market, since they are often poorly educated.

Marriage is one of the central pillars of Moroccan social life. All men and women are expected to marry, and if they refuse it is frowned upon. When they reach a certain age, women become obsessed with being single and not having risen socially to the status of a married woman, and from there to the status of a mother. It is also understood that all Muslims should marry and produce descendents.

I previously mentioned that Mohammed Ad-dubbu was waiting for an opportunity to go to live in Belgium. However, in the end, his father advised him to wait for a couple more years, so he would be able to finance the trip, as the 3 million dirham that he had saved for his son was to be invested in something else: his father was marrying a girl of Mohammed's age near R'Milat. It seems clear that it was Mohammed's maternal grandmother who organized the marriage, as the girl is a neighbor of hers. And so, Mohammed now has no money "to pay for the visa," and he cannot leave. He has a secret girlfriend, while the girl they have planned for him to marry is a cousin of his age who lives in Madrid. In Mohammed's view, the solution to this situation is for him and his girlfriend to both find work in a factory. Nobody knows anything about their relationship except Mohammed's mother and his girlfriend's sister. For him, the image of independence and freedom is definitely that of factory work.

The factory-emigration hypothesis. What context relates the factory-family-emigration hypothesis in this case? The answer to this question, engaging many other links, can be found in at least four situations.

First of all, one can find an interesting answer through analyzing the context of the local market. In this sense, one of the most characteristic traits of the labor market in Spain in recent years has been the growing incorporation of women. According to Alós et al. (2001: 44), in Morocco the opposite would appear to be happening, as the de-ruralization of the population brings with it lower numbers of women entering paid employment (figures for female rural activity are twice that of female urban employment). A rise in paid employment would generally be expected to bring with it increasing numbers of women joining the labor market, partly due to the low remuneration rates for men. A significant fact is that although female labor activity rates in Morocco are low, unlike in Spain, those women who do join the labor market tend to remain in it, even after they have acquired family commitments (marriage or children).

Secondly, equally interesting is the answer found through reflecting on the family context interacting with the labor market. Considering the differences mentioned above, from which patterns does the hypothesis emerge? The above answer means that female participation in the labor market is lower yet more sustained (through extended family commitments) than in Spain, and is not restricted to the time prior to the formation of a family. This development can probably be attributed to low salaries and the need to meet the demands of the family, in a border context defined by labor inequality and in a family context related to international migration. Youth often desire to travel to Europe in order to accomplish a project of getting married and forming a family one day. Among working classes, when someone asks a young man when he plans to have a woman it is synonymous with the question of when he is going to form a household. However, changes in the family life not only question the geographical space and the circulation of people and family members, but how the transition of forms from vertical solidarity to horizontal solidarity of the family (peculiar to the Maghreb, as Adel notes, 2000: 140) is taking place.

Thirdly, there is the effect of foreign capital on building the labor force. It is interesting to note that industrial localization finds its most suitable actors in Tangier; they are illiterate woman as the docile labor force, which is even truer in the north of the country. Let us recall some data for this issue. If we compare the literacy rates of those over fifteen years of age in Spain and Morocco, we see that in Spain it stands at 97.4 percent, compared with 47.1 percent in Morocco. The breakdown according to gender is 98.4 percent and 60.3 percent, respectively, for men, and 96.5 percent and 34.5 percent for women (Alós et al. 2001: 37, based on figures for 1998). Another relationship between internal migration and industrialization can be noted in these "border families," in the high number of young women into the urban labor force.

Textile factories have been favored by the social discontinuities of the city marked here by the arrival of rural families encountering industrial capitalism in mechanized factories.

As Kwan Lee (1995: 385) points out, in Shenzhen factories, management normally uses the notion of "maiden worker," emphasizing young women's single status, immaturity, imminent marriage, possible short-term commitment to factory work, low job aspirations, and low motivation to acquire skills. Consequently, management judges that "maiden workers" worked only until they have saved enough for their dowries, a social construction opposed to the "matron workers."

Fourthly, we can consider textile production in relation to international migration. Women play a role in this area also because both strategies can be combined through the different phases of the family cycle. It is interesting to stress here the linkages between the processes of export-led industrialization and international migration. The difference between the gender conception implicit in these two processes is that production here has been relocated to a low-wage country, and when we refer to migrant women's jobs up north we note that they are really needed because social reproduction jobs are very much in demand in specific locations. Capital mobility, especially in the highly mobile garment industry, where production facilities and factories can be moved easily, leaves workers with little strength for labor organizing.

Other elements of interaction with the processes of export-led industrialization and international migration can be pointed out, namely in cases where the presence of foreign firms facilitates access to information and a sense of familiarity with the potential destination, as we will also see with some Italian firms in Albania. Futhermore, this underlined connection between industrial relocation and female migration is related to basic processes in the current phase of global capitalism. Regarding migration to Spain, foremen at the factories consider that this is a definite factor within their workers' future projects. There was the case of a man who went abroad, saying simply: "I have to travel," and the forewoman knew exactly what he meant. Even though it is a rather vague hypothesis, one of the most interesting theories that I have deduced from an analysis of family genograms is that if "the small family" does not have a member of the family working abroad, then one of them works in a factory. However, if this happens in the context of an extended family, it is not relevant, since in the end what is important is the income of the "small family."

Let's take here the example of Hesham. He is the third of six children; there are in total four sisters and two brothers. He has been living and working in the construction sector on the outskirts of Barcelona for two years. His father is fifty-five years old but he no longer works due to health conditions. The classic model of Mediterranean migration, the single male who has gone alone to help the family, functions here as the direct generator of remittances. He is the one who is economically supporting the whole remodeling and reconstruction of the family house, and this actually is what has become the clearest expression of success in the eyes of the neighborhood, together with the photographs of him and his friends, which he sends every now and again. Two of his sisters work in the textile factories in Tangier; the family uses this income for the everyday expenses. This is a way of responding to the double income earning typical of nuclear couples claiming this strategy as an intensification of their consumption trends. Whereas here is an extended family strategy, where sisters and not spouses tend to function as an aid more than a base for the family income.

This is the way the household income is organized when combining migration of a single male member in Spain and women's factory work in the city of origin. It is through this information that we can approximate the gender division of the different forms of circulation that take place in this border city. The example posits that there is a relation between international emigration and the feminization of wage-labor. In the absence of formal unemployment benefits, the reserve wage is set by the family household production unit to acquire the subsistence levels. This kind of strategy leads for waged labor-absorbing activities by the different members of the family. Families use then their major asset, labor, in order to pool different incomes, if possible with the manufacturing jobs or with international migration. Taken from this case, the male member is the primary provider and the working sisters are seen as bringing in an additional income to the family budget, usually temporarily, so for the sisters their entry into paid employment does not necessarily mean improving their position in the family.

Hesham's main group of reference in Barcelona is formed by the old peer groups he had earlier in Tangier, that is to say the network from his childhood, school, and neighborhood now form his reception network. He is now preparing the new documents to get other people from the same neighborhood; the only solution is to pay for them. In these days, family reunion or purchasing travel documents and contracts are the only ways to make a friend or relative cross the Strait. This also explains why there are so many pressures for the commodification of marriage, in the context of closed borders and lack of socioeconomic opportunities, and why social contacts can become highly instrumentalized. Therefore, it is in this context that we understand the different links taking place: industrial relocation and women's survival strategies, together with the enhancement of the reciprocity networks in a closed political structure (the reinterpretation of the solidarity networks disposed by a particular community). It is also the lack of socioeconomic opportunities that contextualized the family pressures and, consequently, the reinterpretation of family roles. Therefore, labor demands, be they in Tangier or in European cities, have a powerful effect on both migration patterns and household arrangements.

Tirana-Durrës

The Socio-Historical Context

Unlike other European countries, Italy had no colonies prior to the nineteenth century. The Italians referred to their own colonies as "Italian communities." Compared with European policy of maintaning colonies, Italian expansion took a different form since, more than a form of colonialism, it was the expression of Italian fascism in foreign lands. Colonialism and fascism therefore went hand-in-hand, and all those who were subjected to it were under Mussolini's rule. Later on, when fascism came to an end, so did Italy's colonialism—of Albania, Libya, Ethiopia, and the Dodecanese Islands. In this sense, it is interesting to note that some of Mussolini's arguments on the concept of race and colonialism can still be detected in Albania, as referred texts were translated from Italian into Albanian.

Albania has often been often considered as a place apart. Albania had always represented the closed border not only towards the Mediterranean but also towards the rest of the world. It followed a policy of extreme isolation, resulting from the fear of the big powers attacking small Albania. A common stereotype for the country was that of the only Stalinist and atheist country in the world, with non-productive and uncivilized people. Nevertheless, communism was not the only factor to blame—the isolation of the Albanian people had taken place before then, and partly as a result of the country's geography. Books on the country's history and geography make constant reference to the fact that Albania is isolated by mountains, and how for centuries these mountains have functioned as a natural border. However, the disconnection of Albanian people is often a myth. We can see, for instance, the tradition of the kurbet system in the nineteenth and twentieth centuries, or the particular position of the Albanians in the Ottoman Empire.[13]

Transformations occurring at different times have subsequently resulted in sudden leaps from one system to another: from feudalism to communism, and from communism to extreme capitalism. In this age of rampant capitalism, Albanians lament the loss of their community values, and some are even relatively nostalgic for the austere life they used to lead, and for the greater value that was placed on friendship in the time of communism.

The first decade after the collapse of communism led to the opening up of a globalized world, which has had dubious effects. As Fuga highlights, in the fields of technology, production methods, commercial exchange, social services, and cultural life the country is more traditional now than in the times of communism (Fuga 2000: 35). Nowadays, in contrast, the values of the individual prevail: "everyone looks out for himself"(informants repeat). It is also recently that burgeoning trafficking networks and new mafias have sprung up and proliferated, all deriving from the vigorous dismantling of the state (a fact that is repeatedly mentioned by many Albanians and foreigners living in Albania). Given this situation, conversations in the fieldwork concerning the migratory context criticize "the fact that the Albanians fell into the trap of desiring the capitalism they saw on the television, and assimilating an image of the West that was iconized into big cars and dancing girls." This is the constant idea behind their desire to reach the level the Italians have attained, without wanting to wait for development at Albania's own pace. This argument goes on to complain about people being obsessed with superficial appearances, a view that has been instilled by the spirit of capitalism.

According to the mayor of Tirana, in a transitional society, people wanted to experience the freedom to obtain land and property, and thus to reduce the size of their enemy's land. According to him, since communism, all the elements concerning a collective social identity have been destroyed, and attacking public space came to be considered as something democratic. According to his explanations, during the time of communism, the state had hijacked the people's whole sense of universal values. And as people had an inflated idea of these values, they later avenged themselves by destroying public spaces, thinking that by acting this way they were carrying out a democratic act. According to his words, there are two Albanias: the public one, which is full of problems, rubbish, a lack of infrastructure, and secondly, the "private space," the Albania that is now under control, and under law and order. For the current mayor, these ten years of transition have represented a continuous struggle between a weak state and the people's dreams of becoming some kind of Rambo. Some people even go so far as to say that the Albanians have acted like chained-up dogs that went crazy when they were set free. Many people had this view of the Albanians, the image of a country that longs for freedom.

History still provides all the signs from the past within the urban space. As the mayor points out, in Tirana city center you can trace back all the city's love affairs through its symbols: the love between the king and the fascists, the communists and the Russians, the communists and the Chinese, and between democrats and other democrats. Taking music as an example, many Albanians mention how under communism, the ideology was suffocating, but the quality of everything was better. In contrast, cultural life nowadays is low quality, as you can no longer find, for instance, those lovely old buildings and the *tcham*[14] music of the past. Rody (sociology teacher) calls the Tcham language a dialect of Albanian, and he adds that people have to be careful about saying things to the contrary because "nowadays everyone wants to throw mud on everything." According to Rody, the problem is that Albania is not a strong state, and he goes on to say that the history of Albania is a history of continuous destruction.

The position of the periphery was explained by Oti (from Family 4, an arts teacher), who maintained that Albania has always been on the periphery of everything—it was on the edge of the Roman Empire, for example. Albanians have constantly been looking towards the West, which for them means Italy, not Greece, as for Albanians, Italy is the true symbol of Europe. After spending ten months in Crete, Oti reached the conclusion that the Greeks have a Byzantine mentality. Sometimes I can see similarities between the Albanians and the Turks, but they always want to differentiate themselves from Turkey because they see it as a country that is rather backward. One can also deduce that their sense of modernity is anti-Turkish and, to a certain degree, anti-Muslim. When we speak of religion in Albania, I have in mind that it is always surprising to hear the church bells ringing and the call to prayer from the mosques taking place almost simultaneously, which also occurred in the period of international Tangier. There are some people who celebrate the festival of Bayram as well as Christmas. In Albania, the whole historical substratum of different religious customs serves to highlight the border sense of a cultural mix. At the same time, it is interesting to note that religious practices used to be concealed, and have only flourished since 1991, following the fall of the communist regime. In spite of the Muslim influence, many young people you meet today tend to identify more with the Christian faith. One of the social workers in Créche International emphasized that in Albania, religions have always been associated with foreign influences: orthodox religion with the Greeks, Catholicism with the Italians, and Islam with the Turks. But in the end, she points out, Albanians do not believe in anything. She comes originally from an orthodox family, but converted to Protestantism at an early age. However, she left the faith after hearing about serious cases of corruption in the church. This approach to religion also shows how people see everything from abroad as being better; as I have seen with some girls, it seems that being Christian and putting a cross round your neck is more trendy.

Oti hates his first name—Ostman—because it suggests a Muslim origin, or rather Turkish. In his view, like most young people in Albania, Islam and Turkishness imply something dark and oriental—the negation of modernity. However, many people do consider themselves to be Muslims, but they do not know how to pray. Furthermore, I also realized that they were ignorant of the rites for preparing Halal meat. They believe in God, but most are not practicing believers. Some even reckon that Albania has been punished for not believing in God. Young people say that only aged men go to the mosque, and mostly gypsies.

Oti claims that Albanians are not yet prepared to live under democracy, and that they still possess a transition mentality. This would explain why the people sometimes show a certain indifference or suspicion. Oti stresses his point that Albanians have managed to forget what they experienced during the time of communism. He also goes back to the argument about the poles between European and non-European, Muslim and non-Muslim. "Now we prefer Latin-based names because Ottoman names are old-fashioned." With respect to Muslims, he says, "Remember that two generations of our families have lived under communism. My mother was ten years old when Enver arrived—how would she know how to pray? We do not have a Cyrillic alphabet, we use Roman characters and we feel European." Through his discourse we see again the reproduction of the historical complexities, but also the social-psychological attempt to achieve modernity.

According to Tarkan (head of marketing for a Turkish company), as a consequence of this brain drain, the country is now comprised of two groups: the old communist elite who have now retired, and the middle-aged generation. The younger labor force has left the country, and the only ones remaining are either retired or the poorly qualified. The problem is that the money did not circulate; the *scafistas*—the traffickers—knew they were taking a risk, and that it was not totally safe, but they always thought that they would have time to get the money out.

The Tirana-Durrës axis. This axis is considered the major site playing a role in Albanian-EU cooperation. For instance, 35 percent of Albanian enterprises are located in the Tirana-Durrës region, and it is the destination for 60 percent of all foreign investment. Durrës is Albania's largest seaport, covering 85 percent of the maritime trade (IOER and GTZ 2002: 15).

Architecturally speaking, Durrës, which is the oldest city in the Balkans, maintains more vestiges from the Communist era than Tirana does. Since the fall of communism, the advantage this city offers with respect to internal migration is that it is surrounded by areas of ownerless land that can be easily occupied—areas that used to be marshland. Thus, Durrës has become the ideal setting for a post-industrial city scenario. Between 1989 and 1992, the city's economy suffered a significant setback, when factories began to close and production took a nose-dive. Nowadays, the forces of privatization have rallied a timid form of industrialization by foreign investors, which has been established in the "Korridori Tiranë-Durrës," along with the migrants from the rural exodus.

Tirana is certainly the center of, and for, every activity. It is not only the center of economic development and the cultural and political center, but also it represents the focal point of the social perception shared by Albanians of their own country. Furthermore, on a strategic-economic level, the rest of the country does not play a very important role, and this should be borne in mind when the limitations of this ethnographic case are considered. In my study, the Tirana-Durrës axis shapes the representation of the Mediterranean of the "East," even though Durrës will always be considered the ideal research site. Therefore, the analysis also takes into account the situation of the inhabitants coming in from the north who have settled next to the motorway and the old Durrës-Tirana main road. This whole axis symbolizes a great pole of attraction for the rural exodus, and which has been called the "Korridori Tirane-Durrës." This whole area has been usurped, as the migrants search for free sites to set up their homes near the sea, the airport, and the motorway. One might reasonably suppose that living conditions are better in these settlements, compared to the terrible conditions they had to put up with in their places of origin—which is something I saw for myself when I traveled to the north. Certainly, this translates as a great improvement for these people.

The city of Durrës. Durrës is an excellent case for illustrating the existence of Mediterranean circuits, because it marks a direct shipping line to the south and north of Italy and, subsequently, across to northern Europe. It is a basic transport route, especially given the construction of Paneuropean Corridor 8. The main road going east follows the Roman Via Egnatia. However, access into the former Yugoslavia is much more difficult, owing to the mountains. Nowadays Durrës is the second largest city in Albania. It has an estimated population of 246,500 inhabitants, and out of those, 40 percent are young people.

As the country's largest port, Durrës has had the misfortune of becoming one of the places most seriously affected by the trafficking of prostitution, especially in the rural areas around the city. Quite a lot of work on social intervention has been carried out to determine the social reasons for the trafficking. It is often argued that it is a consequence of a political system in transition, which is suffering from weak government institutions, and it has unleashed a renaissance of the old practices of corruption. In socioeconomic terms, one key explanation is the widespread unemployment and the spreading of pockets of poverty. These two factors serve as an excellent base for the development of organized crime. On a geographical scale, the city occupies a prominent position between the East and the West, which provides it with a major role in the scenario of international migration flows into Europe, as well as a good location for commercial activities at the port. Moreover, due to its strategic position as an international border, it also suffers from the impact of the restrictions on international migration. Lastly, on a socio-cultural level, we should note the significance of the large-scale changes that are taking place within one particular social institution in Albanian society: the family. In reality, it is the family structure that receives the main brunt of the changes taking place in the new relationships that are emerging within the bosom of the family itself. The resulting situation is also a consequence of the disappearance of Albania's old ancestral family values, especially those concerning the low status of women. Within this family context it is estimated that remittances from emigrants total around $400-$600 a year, most of which are sent from Greece and Italy. In addition, 30 percent of families live below the poverty threshold.

As for the coordination of social services, the most problematic areas of the city are those that are dominated by internal migration, particularly three neighborhoods located on the outskirts of Durrës: Porto Romano, Spitale, and Këneta, as well as the areas of Katundi i Ri, Sukth, and Rrashbull. Poverty within the city of Durrës is focused within the following areas (in a list which goes from the most to the least problematic): Këneta, Porto Romano, Spitallë,

Shkozet, and Plazh. As for the characteristics of the Këneta area, the population is made up of immigrants who arrived between 1990 and 1992. It is an area of high unemployment and has no infrastructure. The majority of the population are involved in casual work, and many of them can be seen daily waiting next to the hospital in the hope that somebody will offer them a job.

Floriana (from the Durrës municipality) explained in detail the current urban planning program for Durrës, which had previously been drafted by the Italians, though their planning regulations were maintained during the communist period. In spite of this conservationist spirit, communism represented a grey period for the city, the only positive point being the construction of a kind of official housing estate. Rody, a sociologist, explains that in the time of communism the buildings were all low-rise because the state decreed a maximum height of six stories. It was not until the 1980s that the construction of taller buildings was promoted. Nowadays, Albanians complain about having to put up with deliberate, direct, explicit, and conscious deterioration of the public space caused by those in charge in governmental offices, as well as with the indirect deterioration deriving from the absence of any maintenance of infrastructures.

In order to obtain a better profile for the configuration of Durrës, I asked Floriana for some specific points of comparison between the country's two main cities. The presence of the port in Durrës is what mainly differentiates it from Tirana. It is a transport center that receives both cargo and passenger ships, and is also quite a popular tourist attraction. With respect to the scale of urban planning, the great problem for the city's inhabitants are the beaches, owing to the fact that people are settling by the sea-front as part of the compensation program for resettling landowners. This negative aspect is, however, countered by some positive ones, and specifically a series of factors that favor the city's position: (1) the city's proximity to the Gulf of Lalz, which helps to encourage tourism, (2) the city's link with marine transport, and (3) the fact that Durrës is a strategic nucleus for transport, since its prefecture includes Rinas airport, the motorway, and the port. On the other side of the coin are the negative factors, such as: (1) problems related to the landowners law. Difficulties have come about because everyone wants to live by the sea; (2) problems concerning foundations, which are very costly in terms of construction; and (3) problems relating to infrastructure, such as the lack of water, particularly in spring and summer.

In contrast with Tirana, Durrës is not the capital city; it is a center that does not attract so much capital investment. Nevertheless, some positive characteristics are still manifested, such as a city development plan, and its great economic and intellectual potential. Even so, the law is often unclear, and this is the main stumbling point. The objective of the urban planning policy always used to be to conserve the city's ruins, though Floriana agrees that I am quite right when I point out that this policy is no longer respected. The reasons for this are the following:

1. Problems related to the land legislation.
2. A general difficulty in the application of the laws.
3. A lack of infrastructure.
4. Problems connected with a lack of electricity, water, and canalization problems. Durrës suffers from huge problems with its drinking water and canalization, and these affect the whole peripheral area.
5. The non-consolidation of a legal state. There is not enough money to pay for the works because taxes are not collected.
6. Widespread corruption.
7. The lack of economic resources and the lack of any budget for investment in general terms.

Within this context, what do internal migrations represent for the city? For migrants arriving in Durrës, the great advantage of this place is the abundance of ownerless land. For example, the entire expanse of land that used to be the old marsh still has no owner. In fact, this is the main reason why many people choose to live there. They travel from the far north, as well as from other cities such as Korçë, Berat, Kukës, Ballsh, and Skrapar. According to Floriana it is very likely that this phenomenon is not as widespread in Tirana. Durrës is also part of an area that is included in the agricultural compensation programs, which means that those who arrive in the city will receive as compensation a house and some land to till. The government formulated the plan so that it would be executed in this way. In addition, the law has set aside large areas for agricultural development. However, the negative side of all this is the illegal building that goes on.

Just as with the port of Tangier, the port of Durrës represents a specific site for the circuits of control. We find the real border, on one side physically represented by the port customs, and on the other, through the circulation of goods and passenger circuits.

The development strategy for Durrës can be summarized into two large projects. The first is called Area I, and covers the old quarter, which is focused on archaeological conservation and specific construction conditions, while the second covers Area II—the area that includes the beach, the port, and the station, a project funded by European Union programs.

According to Alexander (from the EU delegation), Durrës comprises three central development axes: (1) urban planning, (2) tourism, and (3) the port. Durrës' beach suffers from pollution problems, as it has degenerated into a garbage dump. Moreover, Albania has no waste incinerators, and so garbage tends to be dumped anywhere. In this plan of socioeconomic development, tourism plays a substantial role, a fact that is emphasized by Spanish cooperation. The third of these axes, the port of Durrës, represents the most important strategic point since it is the main entrance into the country, as well as the main route into Kosovo. The urban planning project is in the hands of the World Bank, which has offered loans at low interest, much lower than those offered by the EIB (European Investment Bank). However, we must remember that these organizations are not donors, they are money-lenders. Three institutions are participating in the port rehabilitation project: the World Bank, the EIB, and the European Union. This strategic entrance gate connects directly with Paneuropean Corridor 8, which runs from Durrës through Tirana, Elbassan, and Macedonia, and on to the port of Burgas in Bulgaria. This corridor is a strategic route for the economic development of the whole region. The port is currently underused, inefficient and in need of renovation, and it is the object of a transformation project, which is divided into three parts: the ferry terminal quays (European Union, participating as a supervisor through the CARDS program[15]), the cargo docks (World Bank), and the container docks, because at present there is no storage area. Prior to the works project, some 140 families—gypsies as well as non-gypsies—lived here in shacks. The slum dwellings were pulled down and the population re-housed in apartment blocks by the old Tirana road. It was the World Bank that supervised the project, and Alexander claims that they approached the matter from a perspective of social awareness. Basically, people were quite happy with their new accommodations, though some criticized the poor quality of the flats.

As for the connection between the port of Durrës and the migratory exodus of 1997, we can consider two large migratory waves: in 1991, the people who left the country were often the ones who had lost all hope; and in 1997, the people who emigrated extended to those with social capital and intellectuals.

Features of a Border City

The difficulty in supporting the border-city features is that they were not always so clear, which is why I was unable to reach a decision to select the specific area of Durrës as a border ethnography until I had spent some time in Albania, as I had also been considering other possible cases.

The first of these other possibilities was Vlorë. Vlorë has always been a place of passing and the center of operations for irregular migration. Until recently, that is, before these networks were broken up mainly as a result of Operation Eagle, organized by the Italian police to fight the trafficking networks. However, Vlorë was neither the beginning nor the end of these networks, it was merely a passing point halfway along the routes. People who arrived there had already paid to get there. Even the haulage companies had to pay a "sweetener" to get through the police road checkpoints. Emigrants often had to wait for several days until they could leave the country, and used to stay in houses near the port, waiting for a cloudy day with poor visibility. In 1997, a war almost broke out in Vlorë. During the 1990s, it was the base for the *scafistas* and the prostitution networks. I was told that in 1998, during the Kosovo war, some Kosovans paid traffickers to take them to Italy, but they dumped them on Sazan, an island off the Albanian coast, telling them that it was Italy.

Vlorë, as in the case of Durrës, portrayed that constant look towards Italy. Italy is the country of reference for Albanians, not so much due to cultural affinities but in terms of geographical proximity to a rich nation. Italy represents the *dolce vita* and fashion, the art of eating, the success of Mediterranean individualism; it is FIAT and Ferrari, Mulino Bianco and Benetton, "Lamerica," RAI and even Fininvest. Albania, which had been for Italians the "East next door" is now the "refugees next door," and for Albanians Italy is "Capitalism next door" (Morozzo della Rocca 1997: 5).

Secondly, another major factor in the selection of frontiers is the significance of the border with Greece, which is a borderland of extraordinary importance. To see for myself, I visited the southeast of Albania, as I wanted to verify that this control post was a major border pass for the influx of Greek products, and that it resulted in greater use of the Greek language, higher emigration into Greece, and the broadcasting of Greek television channels. Thus, I arrived at the city of Korçë, which lies huddled between snowy mountains. We stayed the night at the home of Erika's maternal aunt, who was about forty-five years old. She has four children; the two girls are already married, one lives in Greece, and the other in Italy. Each has two children who live with their maternal grandmother, and so the house is full of children—her two young offspring as well as her grandsons. The aunt and her husband used to work in Crete, he in the olive orchards, and she as a waitress. Erika tells me that they got tired of living there and came back. Her daughter in Italy will be coming back soon to live in Tirana with her husband and their daughters. They can speak a little Greek because they have lived in Athens and Crete, and they claim to like Greece a lot. The house is simple and old-style, with a few sofas and an Aga for heating and cooking purposes. In Erika's view, this is a poor people's house; she dislikes it and gave me the impression that she cannot "stand all these ignorant children." Erika told me that it was her grandfather who built the house, and I later found out that in the old days everyone built their own houses.

Erika described to me the second house (which belongs to her other cousins) which is in a border town, and is larger and better structured, but most importantly to her, it has a decent bathroom, as well as a large living room with long sofas. According to Erika, they are the rich people of the town. The parents live there with their twenty-year-old daughter and their son of nineteen. In the time of communism, the father had some kind of position in the party. It is interesting to break down the family's economic strategy: they have a building in the center of town that is divided into three parts; on the ground floor there is the hairdresser's where Meda, the daughter, works. Next to this there is a video rental shop, where they also sell music; the son, Toti, works there. Above the shops is a small hotel that is managed by their father. Frequent guests in this hotel include migrants returning from Greece and illegal emigrants preparing to cross the border and who pay three hundred leks (about two Euro, 1 = 139 leks.) to stay overnight at the hotel. To sum up, Korçë represented one of the Albanian borders with Europe: the use of the Greek language as a second language, the influence of the Greek TV channels, the Greek textile factories,[16] and a massive orientation towards migration to Greece.

Border of Fortress Europe. The construction of Fortress Europe, a term that was coined in the early 1990s, has had a decisive effect on Europe's borders throughout these years. That is to say, the process of strengthening and uniting Western Europe has consequently led to the creation of a peripheral Europe. This "new" Europe, in turn, excludes other populations, as part of a new process of restructuring of the walls and boundaries that define a different geography of center and periphery (Ribas-Mateos 2003a).

At present we are witnessing a time of closure and the impact it is having on everyday lives. This closure is based on agreements within what is called the Associative Stability Pact, which comprises part of the necessary requirements for European Integration, as well as being a response to bilateral agreements. Within this general framework, Albania has been given three conditions: it must stop the trafficking of illegal immigrants, put an end to smuggling, and strengthen the military and police forces. Closure has been directed by the political will of one particular person: Fatos Nano, the prime minister. Thus, the police force has now been strengthened, and that is the key factor for the real closure. The same developments can also be noted in Vlorë.

Given the presence of the European Union and the massive presence of international organizations and donors within the country, many people are wondering whether these bodies will end up taking the place of the state itself. It is easy enough to make broad generalizations about this foreign presence, but in reality the issue represents a contradiction. This is essentially the case since these organizations have absorbed a large amount of space within civil society, yet at the same time Albanian society would not have been able to achieve anything without them. It is a complex contradiction. In addition, the pressures being placed on Albania with regard the struggle against trafficking are very much subject to Albania's demand for future European integration. Since May 1, 2004, the following countries have already become part of the Union: Estonia, Latvia, Lithuania, Poland, Slovakia, the Czech Republic, Hungary, Malta, and Cyprus. In 2007, Bulgaria and Romania will enter. It is interesting to examine the criteria that govern the decision to allow countries into Europe. Are they political, economic cultural, or geographical criteria? How are the boundaries and borders of the European Union being transformed? How are the boundaries and their outlying areas being shifted? We should also be asking whether the adjoining spaces will be broken up or, on the contrary, can the Union develop close relationships with these peripheries.

It is not enough to merely regard the role of the European Union in Albania; it is also worth considering the role of the United States—within a political context—in much of the aid that is provided. I am referring specifically to the fact that the role that the American ambassador plays in Albania is an overly exaggerated one, to the extent that he has to be present at all official functions. All of this ties in with the role played by North Americans in the Balkans. I was able to verify this by going through the contents of the *Albanian Daily News*, the only newspaper in English in Albania.

Before attending the meeting I had requested with the members of the European Commission delegation, I looked through the European Union 2000-2006 strategy for Albania. What struck me was the discovery that the press would be unable to survive without the help of external financing. The foremost goal for the European Union is the reduction of poverty (GPRS, Growth and Poverty Reduction Strategy). A person is considered to be poor if he earns less than 6,500 leks a month (49). Everything clearly points to the ultimate objective of strengthening the border control and facilitating cross-border trade; this will be made possible through the effective administration of borders, anti-trafficking policies, an improvement in human and political values, border management by strengthening the police force, and the fight against organized crime.

At the European Delegation in Albania, they basically work on the level of macroeconomic and social policies. Albania is one step away from achieving integration with Europe. Migration issues are vitally important in terms of the Third Pillar and the Maastricht and Amsterdam treaties. Key documents for an understanding of this perspective include: (1) "Integrated Border Management" (CARDS program) in the control of borders that are deemed to be highly permeable, while the main ports and the airport are considered to be central axes; (2) "Communication from the Commission to the Council and the European Parliament. Integrating migration issues in the European Union's relations with third countries (COM 2002, Brussels, 3.12.2002, 703 final). This is divided into two sections: (1) migration and development and (2) financial resources of immigrants and rejected asylum-seekers for management of external borders and for the asylum and migration projects in Third World countries. I was especially interested in the view of the Mediterranean and in the funds being provided for controlling borders and for the fight against emigration in Albania and Morocco. In Albania, this is based on border and police administration, but in Morocco there is more diversity, as investments are made in business projects and the social development program of the north.

Polarization trends. It is interesting to note here how urban society is based on the antagonism characterized by segregation and how it becomes defined through segregation (Fuga 2000: 35). I take here polarization trends as part of the border city features.

My first impressions of the city of Tirana reminded me of the mixture of features that are also visible on the streets of Thrace (Greece), and particularly in the Muslim neighborhood of Komotini (see research in first part of the book), typical for its low-rise buildings, and which also bears a certain similarity to the center of Tirana. What really exemplifies the Balkan graphically is the ensemble of these physical associations that reveal the study's Balkan references. Moreover, they explain to a certain extent exactly what Eastern Mediterranean cultures are comprised of, and how those two parts of the Mediterranean fit together. In regards to the outskirts of the city, the open-work brick buildings reminded me of the Bir Chifa neighborhood in Tangier. In Tirana, different neighborhoods radiate outwards from the emblematic Skanderberg district: firstly, there is the Blloku, with its expensive shops, in sharp contrast with other central neighborhoods with their low-rise houses, where there is no electricity and the pavements are full of holes. The Sky Tower (or the "Vodafone Tower") in Tirana´s Blloku is the best reflection of this new city and the way it has become the home for the new powers that have been recently established in the country: Siemens, International Trade, the Greek Embassy, the Norwegian Embassy, the UNDP, and the Southeastern Economic Development Project, among others. Meanwhile, on the top floor of the skyscraper there is a deluxe café, which gives you an entire view of Tirana, standing between mountains. Sitting up there, you can even begin to forget about the poverty of some of the city's neighborhoods. Out of the city, the Tirana-Durrës train offers a clear view of the structure of the capital's peripheral area: for miles all you can see are houses that seem to be half villas, half country cottages. They all have an external staircase that leads up to the first floor and a small adjoining area of cultivated land, which is used to grow food for the family.

The mayor of Tirana states that the division between the center and the outskirts is a legacy from the past: "our friendly partner the World Bank has, in fact, failed us during our ten years of transition, because their aim was to fight against polarization." According to him, the World Bank had deemed it would be better to invest in more remote areas rather than in Tirana and Durrës, so as to fight against this polarization of the country. Consequently, Tirana had to resign itself to becoming a city surrounded by illegal settlements. The mayor made this point forcefully, stressing that in the end, the problem of polarization can be found in the heart of the cities following the arrival of a migrant population with a rural tradition. For country people, the concept of wealth under communism was strictly related to the state, but with the advent of capitalism, once the cooperatives and their crops had been destroyed, the country people looked to the city for a new life.

One powerful example of the polarization of urban life in the two main Albanian cities is the connection that exists between informal urban development and the informal economy, and the multiple intertwined phenomena that result from these processes. The tax system serves to illustrate this transformation. For ten years, everything was tax-free because there was no tradition of taxation. All family strategies are aimed at forms that are parallel to what is effectively a social welfare system; everything is based around the family system, because individually they cannot cover the expenses. Consequently, the elderly, with their meager pensions, have to live with their children. All in all, most people work in the informal market, as they have no incentive to enter the formal labor market. All this goes to show that given their extremely limited social capital resources, people are simply incapable of competing in the formal labor sector.

I will now attempt to describe the situation of several neighborhoods, which exemplify very accurately the city's tendency towards polarization: they are Bathore (Tirana), Kinostudio (Tirana), Këneta (Durrës), and Porto Romano (Durrës).

BATHORE. During the last ten years, the region of Tirana-Durrës-Kruja has almost doubled its population, though the increase was particularly felt in the city of Durrës. Bathore, on the outskirts of Tirana, represents a paradigmatic illustration of this growth, as well as overemphasizing the importance of the function of monetary remittances within the family economy. The infrastructure is in a wretched state—many streets have not been asphalted and the houses are without running water, and people have to draw water from a well. Even so, thanks to remittance money they have been able to build houses that look quite attractive from the outside. As I walked along the streets, I was told that each of the homes had relatives living abroad, in countries such as Germany and Italy.

This large neighborhood in the north of Tirana has a population of 60,000 people, who live in settlements on what used to be agricultural land. Bathore has come to represent the symbol par excellence of informal settlements in Albania. The main problems in this area are those of infrastructure. As the population was unregistered, this meant that they were illegible for loans, in addition to the problem that these internal migrants did not tend to integrate well into these communities. This situation, deriving from a lack of infrastructure or the use of a minimum infrastructure, has meant that people have ended up solving their problems through community projects, such as the case of the sewers.

From 1997 to 1999, the NGO B-plan conducted an urban land management project in Bathore, with the support of the Albanian government and the World Bank, aimed at carrying out a study of housing conditions and a process of settlement legalization. B-plan's activity in the area was based around a project that combines both physical and social aspects. Previously, in 1994, it had been decided that a model for land and services should be introduced, what was called the sites and services model. The first stage of this model was for the government to sell land to this population at a fairly low price, and the second stage involved them building their own houses. The project started with a process of negotiation with all the different communities, in an attempt to convince the population, in any way possible, of why they should pay the 20 percent, as well as helping the people to see the benefits it would bring them.

This project was carried out using a PACA method (Participatory Approach for Community Action). B-plan has tried employing participatory methods, and they point out that it is very difficult for them to work there, compared to the highly organized Roma community.

KINOSTUDIO. Pierre (from Créche International) works in Kinostudio, which is one of the poorest areas on the outskirts of Tirana. It contains 20 percent of the population of a whole district of Tirana, this population being comprised of internal migrations by rural families and gypsy families who were forced to sell their houses, and fell into poverty about seven years ago. The living conditions in this area are deplorable, and problems include a high infant mortality rate, child labor, children being forced to work, low rates of school attendance, a lack of hygiene, a great deal of shack-like dwellings, and a poor diet. The girls get married at around fourteen and soon after they start having children. The association *Créche International* is attempting to work on changing their habits, "as these people simply do not understand why they should have to get up every day at six in the morning to go to work." After a while they get tired of their jobs and leave them. During the communist period, the gypsies enjoyed better living conditions in many ways, but particularly because there was a greater link between school and work." All in all, the gypsies have been forced into marginalization, and have been set apart from the rest of the population. The problem with this situation is that under communism, gypsies had equal status with other citizens, and racism was generally more diffuse.

We visited a shantytown area in the *Créche International* jeep. The neighborhood is called 3700 and is in the Bregulimet area. What Bregulimet and the area we later visited have in common is the fact that these shantytowns began to grow in the 1990s along the river that descends from the mountains. The inhabitants have used diverse materials to build their homes, such as recycled metal and cardboard. Another common quality of these two areas is that they are new settlements in areas where nobody lived before. The population is comprised of two groups: the gypsies who lived in the mountains during the time of communism, and the migrants produced by the rural exodus.

One differentiating trait of this neighborhood is the ever-increasing number of gypsy beggar children who are mutilated in some way—most of them are missing a leg, though some just fake it. They manage to bend one leg back in such a way that the limb seems to be missing. Elvis, the social worker for the association, told me that some even mutilate themselves so they can work as beggars. This reminded me of the case of an adolescent who burned his leg and who bares it for passers-by, so they can see the raw flesh. Unlike the difficult case of a boy who was injecting heroin, his sisters—who had all been beggars—had been successfully rehabilitated and began studying in school. The entire situation here is based around a complex cycle of poverty that involves poor living conditions, begging, and emigration—although I believe that in the case of the Roma people, internal migration is not significant when compared to other populations. It seems that movements within the country are more the result of a patriarchal marriage strategy.

Elvis claims that after working with these families he has seen everything, and nothing surprises him anymore. He gives the example of cases of incest, which is a result of families living in one single space. Elvis is convinced that the only conception this population has of leisure activities is limited to two things: sex and *raki* (the typical Albanian *spirits*). Following his view, the hardest thing to achieve with the gypsy community is to change their mentality, as it would require a lot of funds and a large-scale project.

KËNETA. Just before the end of the Tirana-Durrës motorway, on the right, lies the former marshland of Këneta, now occupied by around 30,000 people *(Lagje 14, 16,* Neighborhoods 14 and 16). Këneta is an isolated, marginal neighborhood that has not been able to integrate properly into the context of the city. It has no relations with the city outside it, not even in terms of schools. For the first time, in September 2003, some improvements were to be introduced, such as providing services and building a school.

You need a jeep to get around this area. It is filled with small shacks, as well as little wooden houses that are sometimes quite pretty. The luckier ones have already managed to build a house. In any case, nothing yet has been legalized in this area, not even the premises rented by the associations. When people arrive here, they start off building wooden houses, but as soon as they have saved a little money, they rebuild them in cement. They have no sewers or legal electrical supply. It was the neighbors themselves who installed their own electricity cable posts and the water pipes that hook up to other pipes to bring in drinking water. Usually, settlements are built by family groups who have all come from the same origin. Once we enter the area, we pass more wooden houses. They have nine community leaders, and so they are self-organized. The population comes from many different parts of Albania, such as Tropoja, Burrel, and Peskopy. It is the men who do most of the casual work in the area. They have recently built a school and a small health center that can serve 3,000 people, though in fact it needs to be able to treat 30,000. There are only a few cafés and shops. However, in spite of these conditions, there is no crime in the area, which is quite incredible given the prevailing unemployment and poverty. It is not known exactly what percentage of the population is Roma—perhaps 20 percent. However, the Roma mainly live on other sites, such as by the train station or the stadium.

The strategy of the families combines the men's casual jobs in construction with various forms of emigration to Greece and Italy. Emigration in Këneta is normally conceived of as part of the project to build a house. However, the peculiarity of these migrations is that they only go for short periods—a few months abroad and then a couple of months back in Albania. As they do not have access to legal documents for traveling abroad, they try to get to Greece (which in itself is difficult for them) and then they attempt to regularize their situation. Since Italy opened up to family reunification during the previous year, this made it easier for many people to obtain the required documents.

As for the subject of illegal settlements, everyone there knows very well that they are not the lawful landowners. But the population believes that they do have some sort of right to the ownership of this land. They recognize that Albania is their country and that as a result they are entitled to live in this land. Moreover, they do not want to merely settle for their current temporary situation, they want to have enough space to be able to divide up the land in several parts and pass it on to their children, just like they used to do in the countryside. This entire topic is related to the land reforms that are still in process. These reforms will affect Këneta, in particular, as they will be offering a plot of 500 square meters of land to each family. Meanwhile, rumors are circulating that the port rehabilitation project is also going to affect this neighborhood, since the storage area for the port is going to be built there.

One of the women who visited the community center had settled there three years ago. She is twenty-five and is in the process of divorce. They have three small children, an eight-year-old girl, a six-year-old boy, and a one-year-old baby. She got married when she was only sixteen; her family decided that she had to, as they were very poor. She has separated from her husband because "he was always drunk, violent," and he did nothing to support his family. They took a while to separate, staying together for the children's sake. They moved to Këneta because her husband had some cousins who bought them—irregularly—some land. While he was in Këneta, the husband worked in construction. Two weeks ago she sent her smallest children to live with her parents because she is unable to support them, as she has no income whatsoever. She even buys food on account from shops. She chose Durrës because land is cheaper there, the same reason that has brought many people from very diverse origins. Both the first and the second woman visiting the center live in wooden houses. They have electricity, but no water or television. Neither of them has relatives abroad, though later I discovered that the second woman's sister-in-law had gone to Italy, but she cannot return there because she does not have any documents. In Italy she worked on a tobacco plantation and now she works pruning trees. With the money she earned in Italy she built a house and bought some furniture, but now she does not have enough money to process the documents to return and live in Italy. She would like to travel there, but she does not see it happening soon.

PORTO ROMANO. Within this ethnography, this site displays a key phenomenon of peripheralization at a border location. From an ethnographic viewpoint, it is the ideal convergence point for the following factors: the communist past, internal migrations, the formation of neo-urban nuclei, and the focus on Italy. It is a place of wide contrasts, ranging from the sea and colorful surroundings to a mountain pitted with bunkers. In Spitale, on the road to Porto Romano, there is also a Western Union office, just one of the many branches that can be found in the remotest corners of the country. Today, many of the economic transactions of international migrants are undertaken by global financial actors. This use of migrant remittances as a financial tool transacted by powerful global capitalist actors is becoming more and more powerful. See in Table 4.10 the weight of remittances.

When you enter Porto Romano, you once again find bunkers looking onto the Adriatic Sea. These are the signs and symbols of post-industrial processes in a transitional economy that is linked to new forms of agriculture and fisheries. Porto Romano presents great contradictions: on one hand, there is a large accumulation of urban waste (above all, plastic, with its resulting smell), and on the other, the beautiful shoreline and the sea, which is so calm that it makes the seventy kilometers that separate Albania from the bustling European Union seem much farther away.

Together with the area of Spitale, Porto Romano, the fifteenth neighborhood in region four of the Durrës prefecture, seems to be a paradigmatic case for the dynamics of internal migrations. The two areas contain 16,246 inhabitants, or 3,875 families, and it is estimated that 60 percent of the total population come from northeast Albania. According to the association's data (Center for Social Services), 40.59 percent come from the north (Dibra, Kukës, Tropoja, and Puka) and 39.79 percent from the south (Tepelene, Skrapar, Progradec, and Korçë).

The project reveals (see Ngjeci 2003) that the area is characterized by the following factors: (1) high unemployment and irregular and occasional male work (laborer's assistant, assistant electrician, assistant for hydro-electrical work). Women tend to remain at home and work to a lesser extent in the textile sector, in Belgian and German sweatshops; (2) rigid gender relationships, a mentality that maintains an early marrying age, above all for girls, and strong patriarchal attitudes; (3) poor educational conditions and a high percentage of school drop outs; (4) difficult ecological condi-

Table 4.10
Main Source of Income for Home Purchase in P. Romano and Spitalle

No.		Number	Percentage %
1.	From selling of properties in the previous residence	93	31.80%
2.	From work in international emigration	68	23.23%
3.	From son'(s') work in international emigration	19	6.50%
4.	From professional work	54	18.50%
5.	By working as a businessman	10	3.45%
6.	From son's(s') work as a businessman	2	0.70%
7.	Other	46	15.70%

Source: Ngjeci, E. (2003) "Evaluation of the Socio-economic and Cultural Situation of Immigrants in a Suburb Area of Durrës (Porto-Romano and Spitalle, Durrës)." Council of Associations offering social services.

tions (a high degree of water and land toxicity due to the existence of a chemical factory during communism).

An examination of the outside appearance of the housing reveals who has emigrant family members abroad and who does not. It is obvious how monetary remittances are used—they are spent directly on basic needs. Most families need these remittances to enable them to pay the loans on their houses, many of which are little more than hovels. The families in Porto Romano speak openly of the *Kanun*[17] law. They say that everything is structured around the gender divide, since only one person makes the decisions: the male with the most power. However, decision-making is not very complicated when income is so limited. Everybody agrees that basic needs must be covered, as the lucky ones receive poverty subsidy pensions of no more than twenty-five dollars a month.

At a seminar, Berta (association for social services) addresses some Porto Romano women, trying to persuade them that they should do away once and for all with the barrier that is created by different mentalities—the idea that southerners are different from northerners. I was impressed to see that all these women are literate, which means that this is quite a different situation compared to the illiteracy rates that NGOs have to work with in Morocco. One woman says that she does not think it is normal for a man to wash the dishes, and that she even considers it offensive. This problem, the question of *mentaliteite* (mentality) is something that requires endless work by the associations, in their fight against the ancestral mentality that governs gender relationships. This is one of the classic stereotypes regarding northerners. Curiously, I noted that while the associations question the workings of the closed mentality, this does not seem to be the case in Morocco, where everything tends to be justified by the Muslim culture. At the end of the meeting, I asked how many had family members abroad. Contrary to what I expected, only one of the families did—in Pescara, Italia. Berta explained to me that this is because these are all extremely poor families. At this point, I gave up on the idea I had of drawing a parallel between the situations in Bir Chifa, Tangier, and Porto Romano. The existence of this population, these neo-urbanites, showed a clear contrast, an accentuated polarization of social classes. There is great inequality between the marginalized, peripheral groups and those who consider themselves "the true citizens," that is to say, the urban elite.

One of the most serious problems in the area is toxicity. A UNEP (United Nations Environmental Program) study shows that in Porto Romano a great deal of pollution is caused by dangerous chemical waste from the old chemical plant, a rubbish dump, and an abandoned chemical storage center. All this has an impact on people's health, on the water, and on the marine habitat. Some ten hectares alone are polluted with chromium VI components. At the municipality, I reviewed the report entitled, "The main pollutants that cause ecological catastrophe in Porto Romano and the possible remedial options to get out of the situation."[18] UNEP made nine supervisory environmental inspections on different areas, five of which were declared hot-spots in Albania. One of these was Porto Romano, the worst place in the Balkan states and in Europe in terms of the environment. For instance, a sample of cow's milk showed a concentration of BETA HCT (isomer concentrations) that was a hundred times greater than that acceptable to European standards. Porto Romano has even been called the Chernobyl of Albania.

The general environmental picture for this location can be summed up as follows: (1) an area of several square kilometers polluted with dangerous chemicals, chemical waste, a rubbish dump, and an abandoned chemical storage center; (2) 30,000 people have arrived from other areas and live in the polluted vicinity; (3) serious health problems among the population, and pollution of water and the sea. The Durrës chemical factory, which was closed in 1990, is today an ecological disaster area. Some of the houses have been built using contaminated bricks taken from the factories. The pollution problems became worse in 1991-92, when the factory was destroyed. The impact of Lindane on health can cause blood and hormonal disorders and cancer, as well as affecting the liver and kidneys. It is particularly associated with liver cancer. As for chromium VI, it can poison people through respiration, in food or drinking water, and can cause bronchitis and genotoxicity. The ideal situation would be to close Porto Romano and to re-house the families as soon as possible. In addition, the population increase has exhausted the water supply and now people have an hour's walk to fetch water. The doctor for the area has detected skin infections, which in the future will become cancerous. It has also been shown that a greater number of miscarriages take place in this area than in other areas around Durrës.

Migrations

Peculiarities of Internal Migration. Fuga introduces the concept of ex-locality used by Oleg Stanek in the book, *L'Agriculture familiale,* to show how the peasant family in Albania has chosen a strategy of ex-locality, especially for family members under thirty. It assumes that young generations are supposed to leave the village and the region in order to settle in the cities or abroad through a wild rural exodus, produced as an immediate one, without previously considering any other option of social promotion (Fuga 2000: 130). He even refers to the "imaginarium of a rural escape" to the cities and abroad manifested by the youngsters, to countries they know nothing about except from television images and the symbol of the foreign car (Fuga 2000: 20).

In the old days, everybody knew each other in the city of Tirana and this is still the case, with the exception of the people who have originated from rural migration. That is how the processes of dualization are perceived: as far as the people of Tirana are concerned, the newcomers are a new, anonymous mass. In the area around Durrës and Tirana it is easy to pinpoint the emergence of an entire repopulation that until very recently did not exist: this is internal migration from, above all (though not exclusively) the rural areas in the north of the country. You can see houses everywhere, houses just finished or still being built. It is clear that many of them have only recently been inhabited, as they are festooned with their flag and hanging doll to ward off the evil eye. All these sites are self-built. These families work the land, growing cabbages and other horticultural products, and they also keep animals. From the train, I saw pigs, cows, and sheep. In fact, the piece of land worked by each house is larger than the land possessed by the mountain people from the north. This whole scenario opens up the debate about the existence and extension of these new spaces. They cannot be called periurban; it is more of a strategy that combines periurban and perirural. Nevertheless, people here have little access to commerce because the houses are isolated and there are no shops nearby. However, considering the climate and the distances they were used to when they lived in the mountains, they probably consider this mobility to be a step closer to an urban existence.

Then comes the second part of this transformation—what this scenario means for the citizens of Durrës, the more long-term residents of Durrës. They see the immigrants as radically different from them, differentiating them by their paler faces and blond hair, not to mention their more countrified appearance and clothing. In general, people do not appear to show much friendliness towards them. They claim that northerners only marry among themselves, and they speak another dialect that they do not understand. We keep coming across isolated houses with a continually greater number of cattle. There are also mountains of rubbish that are so colorful that they can even look quite picturesque. Entire families work in rubbish distribution, from children to the elderly. There is a rubbish incinerator there, and the families who work it live there as well. These families were originally from Mirdita, in the north, and are all related to one another. Social workers mentioned to me: "they live in a clan structure[19] and the young women already have a lot of children."

After that, I went on to the area of Shevenlash, where I saw more houses that have now merged into a village. I also saw abandoned factories bearing painted signs referring to Enver Hoxha, and warning that animals must not be brought into industrial warehouses. This was a typically Albanian scene: bunkers and large abandoned factories that are now used as stables for animals. Just another of the paradoxes of this transition which, in spatial terms, has led industrial processes back into semi-rural processes.

The north of Albania, origin of internal and external migration. Discourses based on the idea of the stereotype of a primitive North are common. De Rapper (1998) points out how those divisions are central for the discourse of Albanian differences and not the religious divisions.[20]

The NGO Osca Albania claims that it is a much better idea to invest in countries of origin than to strengthen borders. It confirmed that the majority of families with members abroad made a living from agriculture, and argued that investment should be directed towards infrastructure and agriculture. It justifies this approach by pointing out that 50 percent of the Albanian GNP is derived from agriculture and that, unfortunately, little investment is being made in this sector.

My visit to the north of Albania was organized around the activities of the nongovernmental organization, Osca, of the Rural Development Program in the isolated towns of Shllak and Dukagjina in the area of Shkoder, in the north of the country (see Table 4.11 for migrant percentages from Northern provinces). These are the poorest areas of Albania, and are badly affected by increasing illiteracy rates and worsening health conditions. Apart from the areas having the worst poverty indicators in the country, this mountainous region is also the land of the *Kanun*, the customary law. This is the historical substratum of custom and oral traditions in which the *besa*, the oath, the word given, is also embedded; the besa is rather the relations between the different families or between individuals who are not family related. This code is the rule that binds the internal family system together, covering gender relationships, manhood, courage, forms of marriage, relationships with other families, conflicts between them, and the forms of reprisal and *vendetta*.

The people live in isolated houses, which, no doubt, have been repaired thanks to remittances from recent migrations. Within the family unit, most migratory projects have been designed towards both Greece and England. Greece comes as the cheapest destination for Albanians, as it is attainable on foot, which makes it a reachable location given their migratory resources. It is used as a gateway and a springboard in the migratory projects of young men going off to other European countries. These are large Catholic families, and most of the homes I visited contained Catholic icons with figures of the Virgin Mary and Christ. These economies are totally dependent on foreign remit-

Table 4.11
Main Places of Origin of P. Romano and Spitalle Migrants

No.	Places of origin	No. of immigrants	Percentage
1.	Berat	24	8.19%
2.	Diber	28	1.70%
3.	Kavaje	21	7.16%
4.	Puke	49	16.72%
5.	Skrapar	25	6.52%
6.	Others	175	59.71%
	TOTAL	322	100%

Source: Ngjeci, E. (2003) "Evaluation of the Socio-economic and Cultural Situation of Immigrants in a Suburb Area of Durrës (Porto-Romano and Spitalle Durrës)." Council of Associations offering social services, 2.

tances, creating a phenomenon similar to that of remittance-dependent Caribbean societies. The families have a piece of land that provides them little by way of subsistence. For example, they combine vegetable-growing with raising livestock such as pigs, cows, and goats, though the former two animals are less popular because people say they eat too much.

In general, the families have little information about their emigrants, only a vague idea of the migratory routes and no knowledge about any of the details. When they talk about destinations they generalize so much that sometimes the researcher is not quite sure whether they are concealing something or not. The women never emigrate, except to marry, and autonomous female emigration is never considered and is simply out of the question. To reconstruct migration logics, we must observe the established dynamics in the family system, where it has been confirmed that male mobility is predominant and female mobility follows a logic that leads women towards the man's family in a European destination. As always, there are numerous cases of Albanians who try to pass as asylum-seekers (such as Kosovars) in the United Kingdom.

Families in the north of Albania normally receive an annual visit from their emigrant relatives, who stay at these country houses for a period of a month to a month and a half. The most frequent outgoing routes to northern Europe are from Greece to Italy and from there to Belgium, on lorries. They talk of the expense involved in the journey, because they can only enter Italy with a false passport. For instance, one family had to pay 300,000 Greek drachma for the fabricated documents. Apart from internal emigration and emigration abroad, the peasants in the north also mention other changes. People conceive migration as only one of many recent changes. One of the families I visited told me that before the 1990s there was no prostitution or drugs in Albania, and then suddenly both appeared.

Peculiarities of Albanian emigration abroad. Regarding the peculiarities of Albanian emigration abroad, we can highlight the following characteristics:

1. Albanian emigration as an explosion effect. This has been the main approach used to understand the first stage of Albanian migrations, which are only ten years old (much like the history of democracy in the country). Migrations always parallel crucial events, in this case a fledgling democracy. The outgoing migratory flows can be explained by two types of crises that were unleashed at two very specific moments: the opening of the borders in 1991, and the pyramid crisis of 1997 and the consequent popular revolts. The first group of emigrants left in March 1991, and this first exodus managed to settle, gradually, in Italy. The central thread to all these events points to another, totally different kind of rhythm compared to, for example, the more consolidated Moroccan emigrations. During these periods, I was told, the fact of leaving and wanting to escape, had become "a kind of sickness" for the Albanians. This explosion effect was

the counterpoint to the processes of destruction occurring within Albania. After communism, the population lashed out in fury, destroying their own country, above all from 1997-98 onwards. The answer was to emigrate, to accept the concept of emigration as an enforced exodus. Difficult living conditions resulting from a lack of infrastructure, water shortages, and power cuts are constants within the context of emigration, together with people's fears about safety and future uncertainty.

2. The influence of neighboring countries as the first stop-off point. In general, Albanians see "the country of the eagles" as if it were merely a bridge to Italy. The preeminent land border is the one with Greece, and the sea border, with Italy. In the early 1990s, people took the boat from Durrës to Ancona, and from there they traveled to Bologna. It seems that at the beginning of the 1990s this was the only ship that sailed as far as Trieste. Italy has always seemed the closest and most "Western" country to Albania, and many Albanians have learned Italian from the television.

3. The family and the network system. The family uses these structures to manage emigration channels. As for the articulation of the network, the contacts are responsible for dealing with the bureaucracy that leaving the country involves. Would-be migrants need someone to write them a letter of invitation, which is what they call a "guarantee" enabling them to travel abroad. In the articulation of the family network, documents tend to become the support stand for undocumented migrants. Starting from one person who has all their documents in order, a whole network system is generated, and this family member is used as the central pivot of the migratory chain. An illustration of the way this works is the case of Bart, a twenty-five-year-old unemployed social worker. Bart described his difficulties in finding a job after having finished his studies and living between Germany and Switzerland for two years. He now drives a large Mercedes that his brother brought from Germany. His brother is now documented, which is a key point, since many people do not have their official papers. The resulting hierarchy that is established within one single family is interesting to observe. This brings us to the question of whether hierarchies exist that are based on the fact of being documented, and which, consequently, establish the axis of reciprocal action and dependent relationships within a family.

4. Mixed migration destinations. Family destinations may diverge towards two locations abroad, or even three. Frequently, emigration to Greece and to Italy is combined within the scope of one single nuclear family. In this country, Albanian women are employed as care workers for the young and the elderly and as domestic helpers. However, I believe that in spite of their skill, other groups such as the Philippine community can withstand this kind of work better over the longer term. See in Table 4.13 the break-down of Albanian destinations.

5. The return. I was struck by the fact that, in contrast to other Mediterranean migrations, the phenomenon of the return is salient in Albania. I myself have encountered small businesses opened after someone has returned from Greece and Italy. When referring to the return, we should distinguish between a diversity of reasons: there are those who were unable to get

documents, and are thinking about returning. Meanwhile, others wish to return because they think they might find a job in Albania now that the situation is calmer. Others want to return home with the idea of opening a small business. And lastly, some returns are for family reasons, for example a temporary return owing to a death in the family.

6. Gender roles. For the separated woman, life is more bearable abroad. Thus, not only men must deal with the highly negative image of the Albanians, but also women. They have to cope with the stereotype of the prostitute or the uneducated peasant. It is interesting to observe, from the society of origin, the modernizing strategies that the Albanian woman employs. I have always noticed that Albanian women tend to be much more modern than their male counterparts (the opposite to the situation in Morocco). As a general rule, it is true that the women's situation has worsened since communism and that the phenomenon of female submissiveness has now returned in a new form. In this sense it is interesting to analyze what it means for an Albanian woman to have an Italian boyfriend, or to be able to marry an Italian, in her search for the participatory type of man. This can also act as an integration tool within the receiving society.

7. The brain drain. It is insistently repeated that this is an idiosyncrasy of Albanian emigration—that all the most intelligent people in the country have gone abroad. In any case, this would have to be compared with data from other locations to prove whether it is really an exaggerated phenomenon. For example, in Morocco, the figures for university graduates who went abroad were also significantly high.

8. A particular context of departure. For many people it was abroad that they were able to find their first job, and this is especially relevant since foreign countries signify their first employment, while others had previously worked in factories or in the countryside in Albania.

Table 4.12
Main Destinations of Albanian Emigration Abroad

Countries	Number
Greece	500,000
Italy	200,000
Germany	12,000
USA	12,000
Canada	5,000
Belgium	2,500
Turkey	2,000
France	2,000

Source: UNDP using Ministry of Labour and Social Affairs, 1999 data—UNDP(2000) "Albania Human Development Report 2000," Tirana: UNDP, 39.

Changes in migratory routes. In recent years, Albania has acquired an increasing role as a country of transit. According to sources from international organizations in Tirana, Albanian authorities are continually repatriating people without any type of procedure or without making any record of the fact. Where possible, these persons contact UNHCR (United Nations High Committee for Refugees) to request asylum, and while they wait they are given a temporary residence card. UNHCR's work is complicated because its target population is basically made up of economic migrants who are simply seeking the chance to gain access to Europe. These persons enter, for instance, through Rinas airport. UNHCR has a refugee center although little is known about it. Here, changes in migration seem to be less visible than in Tangier, though the government would currently prefer to deal with the whole subject of the fight against illegal immigration quite openly, as a form of publicity for the government. As a consequence, they have displayed images of how they have been burning the *gommoni* (motor dinghies).

In the 1990s, the arrival routes for illegal immigrants originated in Turkey, Greece, and Macedonia. The Montenegro route was the one most commonly used, but only by the prostitution networks. The most crucial ones were linked to Yugoslavia and Romania, the salient point of the former country being Tutze. When the emigrants reached Vlorë, they were kept in apartments that housed between ten and fifteen young women, who paid 1,500 marks each. In spite of the changes, Albania still plays the role of a stopover country, sometimes much more than it appears, although it is not a subject that is spoken about.

According to Rodríguez (UNHCR), "as far as our work is concerned, the most important job has been pre-screening, via the shared work of ACNUR, IMO, OSCE and the Albanian refugee office." This pre-screening works on the basis of an agreement between UNHCR and the Albanian government. If foreigners are detained inside their own country, they contact the committee to find out whether they can seek asylum, or whatever other alternative they have in a particular situation. The UNHCR processes the type of profile: request for asylum, return to country of origin, transfer to the IOM (who return economic emigrants) or expulsion to Greece (which is the country they have come from). Out of these different profiles, UNHCR data show that 25 percent request asylum, though we must take into account that the Albanian government does not possess the right to asylum, and it is Greece that possesses it for the entire region. Asylum requests also operate in the case of trafficking victims. According to their data, the following ethnic-national groups are most commonly affected: Kurdish Turks and Iraqi Arabs, Moldavian women and, lastly, groups from Bangladesh, Chad, and Sierra Leone. The aforementioned pre-screening system only operates within the country and is not applied to border detentions. They consider that any reinforcement and extension to the borders will require a new budget to cover the police, local authorities, interpreters, etc. So far, the pre-screening has been accepted as a good practice as well as a successful collaboration project between the IOM, organizations working for human rights and the OSCE.

Until recently, Vlorë was a key point of departure for migratory routes, and is the city that has best represented the illegal circuits. However, as a consequence of a large-scale police operation, the direction of trafficking has now been reversed. During the 1990s and early 2000, the following routes were identified: (1) Greece—Albania—Vlorë, (2) Turkey—Greece—Albania, and (3) Turkey—Balkan states (via Montenegro). With respect to the first route, Greece—Albania (for smuggling from the south), a stopover was made in Albania for one or two months, and if the crossing was not then possible, the route through Kosovo was used as far as Sarajevo and then on to Western Europe. Since 2002, the innovation has been the Macedonia route; this is a consequence of an improved security climate in the country, which was immersed in civil war until 2001. The second new route is through Romania. Not only have the routes changed, but also the phenomenon of trafficking. The prostitution networks only cover internal consumption; that is, they meet the demand from international military forces in Kosovo and Bosnia and, lastly, local consumption. Due to this change, the context of trafficking has also begun to change the programs. Such is the case for the IOM voluntary return program, which received very few applications, and, in fact, ended when the route dried up.

Recently arrived expatriates see the changes that have taken place in the control of the migratory routes in Albania and they wonder how such great success has been achieved. "It was because the police knew everything, they knew every route perfectly, and so it wasn't that difficult for them" (Rodríguez). At the moment the situation has calmed down, but there is still one dark area to be dealt with: the links between the forces of law and organized crime in Albania. These organizations consider, furthermore, that the smuggling of persons, drugs, and arms are all closely interlinked, although drugs and arms are much more lucrative. When they talk about drugs, they mean heroin from Afghanistan and the locally produced marijuana.

Mixed destinations. When considering the migratory routes of Albanians, Greece can be depicted as the golden key to Europe, while Italy is the main door. However, for many rural families from the Hellenic border provinces, it is Greece that is the gateway to Europe. In the north of the country many families recall the time when groups of men marched for nine days to arrive in Athens, constantly suffering violent attacks from the Greek police. Many walked through the mountains in groups during the 1997 riots. People's conversations also include constant references to Vlorë and to the "*gommoni* and *scafi*"[21] circuits.

It is important to stress the binomial nature of Greece and Italy in the selection of a migration destination. On one hand, it depends on the geographical route: for some places, Italy is most outstanding and in others Greece, depending on their physical proximity. Selection also depends on the social class of origin, the expansion of family networks, and the migratory resources available (i.e., access to visas, spending power capacity). It appears that for a person with limited migratory resources, the best option is Greece, since it is the most accessible pass, a place that can also act as a springboard to another country. In the case of Greece, circular migration and temporary work are very common amongst Albanians. In this sense, three types of migratory projects can be established: (1) circular or pendular mobilities: a few months in Albania and a few in Greece, (2) transitional: or short periods: a stay in Greece for one or two years and then return to one's country, and (3) definite: for a long period and for a definitive settling abroad.

Anila's research (from a religious NGO) showed, through the association's survey, that many people migrated for periods of only two or three months. In addition, everyone who was contacted in Greece reported that they all wanted to return home. This is significant because in many other places, there are very few return migrations. Moreover, Anila indicates that Albanians are not happy in Greece and feel angry with the treatment they receive, claiming that after ten years of residence in the country, they still cannot obtain documents. This facet of migration brings out a contradiction within the transition period: those who are here want to leave and those who have left want to return. Currently, a reorientation of the so-called illegal routes is being carried out. Now people can travel from Korçë and Girokaster to Patras, and from there to many other places.

Families frequently organize migration movement abroad using a triangular system: Greece, Italy, plus a new European country that could be Belgium, the UK, or France. They also use a two-destination system that includes Greece as the entry gateway or springboard and then another European country economically similiar to Greece. For the emigrants, Italy symbolizes the real door to Europe. For them it is also the channel, the springboard to the United Kingdom, the Netherlands, and Belgium. These latter two countries were significant because many girls could find work there (they also mention what they call "the shop window girls"). However, for some, the main attraction of Belgium is the existence of criminality and the easy access from there to the United Kingdom, while in the Netherlands, it is the trafficking. However, destinations are extremely mixed. This is illustrated in the case of a family from the north where the father worked as a technician on the once national hydroelectrical project. They have eleven children, three of whom are in Greece, one in Belgium, and another in England. Of the three who are in Greece, two are married and, as normally occurs in such cases, they send fewer remittances because they have to support a nuclear family in their destination country. Several families explain that their children left Greece because they maintained that the Greeks are racist. People tend to prefer England because of the better wages but also because they cannot cope with the racism in Greece. Unlike Italy, Greece offers no channels for family reunion. There are currently around 600,000 Albanians in Greece.

Most of the Albanians who reached the United Kingdom manage to pass themselves off as Kosovars. From conversations with families, I learned that most of those in the United Kingdom appear to be undocumented. In contrast with Greece, Italy as a destination represents legality and the chance of obtaining documents. In fact, when Italy crops up in conversation, the first thing that is mentioned is documents. This is the stereotype of Italy as far as migrants are concerned.

The influence of remittances. The system of how remittances operate corresponds to the ways people operate and think up ways to help their family economically. Therefore, to uncover remittance dynamics, one only needs to understand the underlying strategies that prioritize supporting the family, which means, in this case, the family in the country of origin. As an illustration of this mechanism we can cite the case of an Albanian family living in Porto Romano, in the peripheral area of Durrës. One of the children emigrated to Italy, but soon after traveled to England, where wages are thought to be better and, consequently, remittance values. In addition, he also felt free from the sensation of being under constant control, which is what immigrants experience in Italy. One of his objectives is to be able to furnish the house through his remittances, since his future project is to return to his city of origin to get married, start a family, and set up a construction company. This view of the future appears to be a long-term one, since this young man's intention—like that of most Albanian immigrants from this region—is not to return to the north. This is one of the reasons why he decided to buy a new washing machine, because the family machine was old and decrepit, in spite of the fact that the father, who has always worked in construction, wanted to spend this money on building a stable for the cow instead. So, it is clear that the person who sends the money is the one who decides how it will be used. The frequency of remittances depends on emigrants' current working situation. In this case, remittance channels coming from England are managed through Western Union (see Table 4.14 for the break-down of movements in Durrës),[22] while in the case of Greece, informal remittances—depending on migrant circumstances—are channeled through Alpha Bank (Hellenic bank) in Tirana. Remittances sent into Albania from emigration are considerable, and Fatos Nano, the current prime minister, calculates them as totaling around $800,000 annually, of which $450,000 come from Greece.

There are villages that depend on the remittances in both the north and the south of the country. Within a family it is understood that the youngest son has to remain in the family home. In the case of one of the families from the north of the country, supporting eleven children is much less difficult, given

Table 4.13
Weight of Remittances in Durrës Western Union

Branches of Western Union, Durrës	Incoming Remmittances	Outgoing Remittances
1. (Spitalle)	Italy 65% Greece 30% UK 5%	Italy 80% Greece 20%
2. Teuta 2000 Rr. Skenderbeg,	Italy 50% Greece 15% Uk and others 5%	Non available
3. Teuta office L.12, Blv. Deshmoret Nr. 411	Italy 80% Greece 15% Uk and others 5%	61% Italy 35% Greece 2% Netherlands 2% per annun in main Albanian cities
4. AGI Rr. Tregtare, Nr,3	59% Italy 31% Greece 10% UK and others	74% Italy 10% UK 12% other Albanian cities 4% Greece
5. AMA exchange Rr. Tregtare , Nr. 40	75-80% Italy Greece 25-30%	66% Italy 31% Greece 3% others
6. Western Union Shijak	90-95% Italy 5%-10% other Albanian cities	90% Italy 10% other Albanian cities

Source: Approximate percentages provided through interviewing Western Union staff. (May 2003). Precise data was unavailable because of privacy reasons.

that the size of land they till is quite small. Remittance money sent by one of the children from Greece has enabled them to install a running water supply to the family home, and then when the second son emigrated, they were able to build a bathroom. The remittances have also enabled them to marry off their four daughters. The husbands of two of the daughters are Albanian emigrants in Crete, although the women continue to live in Albania with their in-laws; the other two daughters live in mountainous areas. Each marriage involved paying a dowry of 3,000. The couples did not know each other previously, which suggests that marriages are arranged. Also thanks to the remittances, they have been able to buy all the furniture in the house, from the carpet to the television set.

Fabi (from Co-B association) mentions that nowadays the influence of remittances is beginning to decrease as a form of financing home-building in the urban peripheries. Therefore, choosing to invest in a house has greatly influenced the rhythm of remittances, because when building is finished, the remittances cease completely. In terms of migration, the family project cycle that is based on the relation between home-building and remittance income is completed once each of the brothers has succeeded in building a house. In Bathore, when they discuss the family building process, they refer to several phases. First, they mark out a site with stones to demarcate the ground plan of the new building. Secondly, if all goes well, they begin building a shack. And, thirdly, they build the house. In this initial stage, the family divides itself into several spaces: for instance, one brother stays in the house of origin, in the north; another works abroad, while a third occupies the land. Building these homes is carried out using the family's own labor, even to the point of making their own bricks. They use a type of gray cement brick that is manufactured in the underground economy in the same area in which they live. It is interesting to note that they use the same traditional method of building houses as they did in the old days.

Adaptation to the host society. In this regard, adaptation to the host society in the different European countries is highlighted by the following characteristics:

1. A gateway to labor flexibility. The immigrant worker is of value only due to the advantage offered by labor market flexibility. In the face of the dilemma of cheap labor sought by delocalization, or cheap labor from emigration, the employer if faced with the following question—Which is preferable, illegal work in Greece and Italy, or to buy a labor force directly in Eastern Europe?
2. Silent racism and the strategy of assimilation. In Greece and Italy, Albanians frequently use a strategy of assimilation. They can pass more easily unnoticed than other immigrant groups due to their physical appearance, and they adapt quite well to the new languages. However, they are often the victims of silent racism, which is closely linked to the social construction of criminality.
3. Forms of identification. The Albanians make a real effort to prevent their children forgetting their language, culture, and native folklore. Compared with the image that Albanians have of themselves, their view of Italians is that they are very talkative, but they do not keep their word. As a last resort, maintaining their Albanian identity always takes the form of national pride and nationalist feelings. Maintaining Albanian cultural values abroad is often reiterated, as well as honesty and above all, family values. As a consequence, it is the sense of family and a specific type of family ideology that gives the Albanian identity an articulated structure. Several elements become important in this conservation of family values: a strong sense of family union, the prevalence of young marriages, the absence of any tradition of spinsterhood and bachelorhood, the cult of fertility, and the preference for male newborn babies. Within the scope of the family, it is also essential to consider the condition of women, as it is their status that distinguishes the image of Tirana women from foreign women. The people working in the associations judge Tirana women to be more highly valued, better educated, and they can often drive.
4. The argument of criminality. An analysis of criminality is crucial, given that the image of the Albanian abroad is only understood through such arguments. This is apparent abroad, but it is also of primordial importance in the context of origin, as there is a constant reinforcing of all these topics

and a constant counter-criticism regarding construction of the stereotypes. The fact that this question is also a constant peculiarity in locations of origin is because the Balkans is often described as one of the main regions in the world for criminal networks. What seems peculiar about Albanian criminality is its widespread nature—for example, cases of homicides within the same family. With emigration, the just pay for the sinners, and the honest workers end up shouldering the blame for the huge network of terrorism and the mafias.

Forms of Control

Visas are the most obvious expression of border control management. At the Italian trade office based in Tiraha, they explained visa evolution in recent years and stressed that the increase in numbers of legal visas must be taken into account as well as the slight improvement in the socioeconomic situation, since economic opportunities have improved. They consider that the lack of investment in the country in relation to the migratory context is due mainly to three causes: infrastructure—above all a lack of energy; a lack of investment; and governance—that is to say, poor management and bureaucratic problems owing to corruption. The advantage now is that other economic sectors are opening up and there is an increase in skilled services, which will absorb the return migration.

My interview with the Italian consul helped me to analyze the data on visa applications during 1997, 1998, 2000, 2001, and 2002 (see Table 4.14). Throughout the year 2000, applications decreased owing to socioeconomic improvements in Albania and, consequently, in the living conditions of the population. In this same period, growth and development took place in sectors such as construction, leading to greater work opportunities. When analyzing the visas one should consider that a greater number of multiple-entry visas are currently being handed out, that is to say, visas lasting for ninety days within a half-year period. This leads to a reduction in job vacancies at the same time as it attracts people from a higher socioeconomic level (such as entrepreneurs, institutions, and associations) who will benefit from this type of visa. The district of Tirana is the most significant and the most representative example of these trends. This includes the Durrës population; and, furthermore, everybody ends up using the ferry that leaves from the city because it is the most economical form of travel. It should be pointed out that the Vlorë and Shkodër consulates were created in 1999 and 2001, respectively.

Irregular strategies implemented through transnational borders can be explained in terms of the difficulty that Albanians have in obtaining a visa. Even when they have a family member in Italy whom they want to visit, they find it hard, and thus it is even more difficult to obtain a multiple-entry visa. Furthermore, even people working in international organizations share this view, and

Table 4.14
Evolution of Issued Visas to Italy in Tirana

Type of visa	1997	1998	1999	2000	2001	2002
Family Reunion	4,383	9,024	7,697	6,661	8,000	6,157
Tourism	3,144	4,327	6,719	10,145	9,600	4,526
Work	86	1,376	1,276	2,275	3,841	1,602
Student	1,386	1,376	1,535	876	1,200	1,276
Total of visas	21,888	27,127	34,406	28,962	31,300	20,729
Total of requested visas	Not available	Not available	Not available	50,000	45,000	35,000

Source: Interview with the Italian Consul in Tirana (May 2003). Only for the Consulate of Italy in Tirana.

report that "the people who work with us suffer from all these problems, so it's easy to imagine that it would be harder for people from another social class" (John Bridge, World Bank). This led me to consider the relationship between positions in the social structure and the advantages or blockages in the granting of visas. At the end of the day, the alternative strategies for visas are a constant trait for all layers of the population: "We all have to pass through this system of corruption at the Italian and Greek embassies. In the end, they force us to behave like bastards, because they leave us no other option" (Berta). Berta believes that discrimination prevents Albanians from obtaining visas, despite the fact that "we are at the center of Europe."

In Albania, one noteworthy element when examining the types of control is the multiplicity of channels that exist for border control. Joachim, a police officer and member of PAMECA (Police Assistance Mission of the European Community to Albania) told me about the control methods that are used at the borders. Foreign police working in Albania are not operational; they work solely within police cooperation. A large number of international organizations carry out control operations in Albania, the most predominant being: (1) CAM-A, a customs organization devoted to financial matters; (2) PAMECA (European-wide), which deals with police control and law; (3) INTERFORCE, dealing with police cooperation and cross-border crime with Italy; (4) OSCE and EUMM, probably the main police control programs; the difference between them and other organizations such as PAMECA is that they are not solely European; (5) ICITAP (International Criminal Investigative Training Advisory Project), run by the United States and linked to the American embassy; and (6) NATO. This military organization has now an administrative base in Tirana and a military base in Durrës, although they are currently inactive.

After the serious crisis of 1997, the European Union established three types of police programs: public order, organized crime, and border management. According to one of the European organizations, PAMECA, Albania is the country in which they operate the most. When they started to work on the organization of the country, they began with public order structures and the police force, to ensure that the law would be obeyed and they would be respected, since the main problem they encountered at first in Albania was that there was simply no law and order. The population did not respect the police, and the police did not know what to do about it. This was the situation they found—in terms of police aid from the European Union—when they first arrived in the country, although on an international level, Italy provides the largest amount of police aid.

Definition of Circuits

Ultimately, by descending from theoretical research to empirical research, we have managed to create a model of understanding for the different circuits that exist within these border cities. We take into consideration a perspective capable of integrating simultaneously the different circuits of capital mobility and human mobility that are materialized in this type of city. We could point to several processes resulting from these circuits: the north-south relocalization of textile manufacturing (with its consequent proletarization and feminization of the labor force), we could even dare to say the south-north relocalization of prostitution (with its consequent feminization and internationalization of sexual services), the south-north relocalization of begging (with its consequent trafficking in children, especially Roma). In all, taking into account these three processes, it can be verified that capital and human mobility circuits have a specific impact on certain social groups present in these border spaces. Consequently, an examination of this impact effectively shows a transparent and often contradictory expression that the impact of globalization (economically speaking and regarding the complexity of mobility types) has upon the vulnerable social groups in particular geographies. Moreover, it is through this definition of circuits that one can clearly see how family dynamics function. Although I was sometimes quite distracted by the mixture of different elements that make up a border city, I concluded that the domestic strategy is a fundamental component of the study. However, the influence of the strategy analysis is diluted when one considers that many families use this kind of ability on a short-term basis. This means living day-to-day and never considering any sustained future projects, owing to a rational calculation based chiefly on effectiveness. However, the alternative option posed to international emigration becomes meaningful when one considers that it presupposes the first step for a long-term strategy among many families, since it is the one that most clearly enables them to build a house. Thus at this point, other topics become intertwined, some of which are worth consideration; these include property in Albania, the reproduction of organizational patterns of the rural family and the persistence of subsistence agriculture in the urban periphery. In short, the *patchwork economy,* as a formulation of all the different resources that come into the home (as seen in chapter 3), also portrays a formulation of global changes; it becomes the lens through which we can clearly see how these changes have materialized.

The context of the Albanian economy. The IMF (International Monetary Fund) opened its doors in Albania in 1992. Its basic objectives were to create stability through macro-economic policies, to attempt to reduce instability, to promote the ideal climate for private investment and economic growth, and to improve living conditions. Among other tasks, it carries out the function of monitoring economic policy, and thus has a close relationship with the Albanian government. These are the only objectives of the IMF, and it has no specific projects underway. In any case, it has been partially involved in the alleviation of poverty program initiated by the World Bank in June 2002, and which is currently functioning within infrastructure projects. Therefore, the IMF's mission in Albania is the same as in any other country: to prevent the economy from falling into decline. In addition, it acts as an advisory board to the government on policy execution. Its main interlocutors are the Ministry of Finance and the Central Bank.

The economic structure of the country could be compared to some regions of the Caribbean or Cabo Verde, as it is characterized by little exportation, mainly caused by the fact that Albania is so dependent on remittances. A large part of this income remains in the country, and is spent in the construction industry. As for the dynamics of the Albanian economy, on one hand there are the import of goods and the purchase of foreign services, and on the other, exports and the influx of international funds.

However, between these extremes there is a large vacuum that is filled by the reception of remittances. Data on remittances can be obtained from the Commercial Bank and Western Union offices. Even though the remittance inflows can be traced back via these entities, we should differentiate between legal incoming earnings and income deriving from a more illegal source, such as profits from crime, which would be difficult to investigate as they are also linked to migrations by undocumented workers. The Albanian people still do not entrust management of their savings to banks, as they still have a vivid memory of the events of 1997. Thus, nowadays, Albanian society only believes in using cash, hard currency that they keep at home. During 2003, renewed rumors about instability began to circulate from Greece, provoking great alarm.

Looking at an economic map of the country, three very differentiated sections can be distinguished: the northern mountains, the center, and the south. Elbassan is the industrial heart of Albania and the central region. The city contains three large industries: Elbassan Cement, Elbassan Steel, and Ferrocromum-Darfo. The strategic position of Durrës makes this city the main outgoing port, particularly to Italy. Consequently, Durrës is a border city and a key point for textiles and footwear for sale in Italy. According to Tarkan (head of marketing for a Turkish company), around 150,000 people in Albania work for Italians, either directly or indirectly, owing to the widespread sub-contracting that goes on. In the textile sector, these business strategies to reduce production costs involve farming out work to families.

This process also occurs with the Greeks in Korçë and in Girokaster. These two cases are based on the *outbound* production system, which in Albania is known as *façonnier*[23] and consists of a three-stage system: first, the material is imported, then the raw materials are transformed and, finally, the goods are exported. Simply by analyzing the data relating to imports and exports to and from Greece and Italy, one can see the importance of this economic system. From the different inquiries, I have deduced that geography plays a key role in the country's economy: geographical proximity and the possibility of access to neighboring countries are of fundamental importance to the population.

The passing of time and the change in the political regime have helped to create a climate in which Albanians now find greater work opportunities, and more peace within the society; these factors have led some emigrants to return to their country to open businesses. Even so, the importance of illegal activities still persists. The great failure of the financial pyramids, through which the country unexpectedly lost $3 billion, led to an increase in illegal activities. A total of $4 billion have entered the country as a result of these activities, a phenomenon that can be explained by the facts that the country's production figures are very low and the private sector is basically concentrated on trade and not on production. Rami (a journalist in Tirana) also mentioned the diffi-culties for, and reticence of foreign investors in Albania, owing chiefly to the weakness of the infrastructure when it comes to business development—prob-lems such as the lack of water and electricity and the poor state of the motorways. This problem is one of the main contradictions in the lives of Albanians to-day—on one hand, they are prepared for the future, yet on the other, their shoddy infrastructure always leaves them at a disadvantage. As Rami remarked: "Albanians have a mobile phone in one hand and a candle in the other."

In Albania, the influence of the informal economy is so great that it is estimated to be three times larger than the formal economy. According to Tarkan, of the different types of illegality, he considers prostitution networks to be the most lucrative in Albania. A Moldavian prostitute costs $700 while an Italian one costs $1,500. Consequently, all this profitmaking has been introduced into the economy, and as a result Albania is in the midst of rapid growth. The situation in Albania is unparalleled, and therefore cannot be compared to other places, because unique circumstances exist in this country, such as the fact that: (1) it has been isolated since 1978, (2) it was much more backward than other communist countries, and (3) it underwent three serious conflicts in 1991, 1997, and 1999.

To many foreign visitors, Albania today confirms certain aspects of a new form of colonialism. If this is true, as Kadaré claims, it would seem to be a protectorate of the European Union. In my work plan, I always prioritized the process of the intense internationalization of socioeconomic processes within the country. By this I mean the way that the main international donors set budgets and lines of action within local associations. Thus, this is a top-down approach affecting the internationalization of Albanian civil society. Eva (from the association, For Women) gave me the example of the IOM, which holds a monopoly over the local associations. However, her foundation has a totally different approach, since it believes that local women's associations are strong enough to work by themselves.

The different international institutions based in the center of the capital, such as the World Bank, IOM, WHO, and UNDP, began appearing in 1991, and brought with them a colony of expatriate workers. These expatriates often use the stereotype of "the others" when talking about local people, and their poor level of civilization and cleanliness, as well as the extent of disorganization, inefficiency, and corruption. Even those people who think that the socialist past is still fresh for Albanians keep using the stereotypes of "uncivilized natives."

Albania depends highly on the action of foreign countries for its dynamism: in 1997, the main aid donors were the European Union (35 percent), Italy (14 percent), Germany (10 percent), and the World Bank (10 percent) (see Table 4.15 for detailed external financing). The common question shared by most foreigners working in international organizations is: What will happen when foreign funding ceases? Contrary to what should normally happen, donors were the first to arrive in Albania, and then the NGOs were set up reactively. Normally the reverse happens—when something is already in progress, it begins to get funding, as might occur a little more in the case of Moroccan civil society. The presence of foreigners in Albania definitely plays a leading role in all fields: the presence of OSCE, PAMECA, KFOR and all the police cooperation between Italy, France, and other countries.

The clothing circuit. The key process by which we can understand the driving force of the clothing circuit is industrial relocalization, which is run by Italian and Greek entrepreneurs. I found that gaining access to the circuits connected with Greek delocalization in border provinces was virtually impossible, though this does not mean that they do not exist. There are large, well-known, Greek-owned factories that justify their subcontracting in Albania through the global changes in competition and the capital mobility in the market since 1995. They tend to set up intensive operations and use arguments that are based on the fight against female unemployment. See Table 4.17 for translation into the exports-imports balance.

The *façon* system—as they refer to it in Albania—represents the classic relationship of inequality between a developing country and a developed one. In this case, the Italians operate through small and medium-sized enterprises using the façon system; that is, the raw material is imported, the manufacturing process is carried out in Albania, and the product is then shipped back abroad for the finishing processes. This is how the Shoelace factory operates, to cite just one example.

Table 4.15
External Financing of the Albanian Public Investment Program

Financing agency	Before 1996	1996	1997	1998	1999	Total
Multilateral:						
European Union	501.5	52.3	56.7	56.4	119.3	786.2
European Investment bank	33.7	12.0		22.1	*	67.9
EBRD	31.4	0.27		0.18	45.5	77.4
The World Bank	217.8	57.3	26.9	51.9	106.0	460.0
Others	50.4	18.4	1.18	2.7	*	72.8
Total	834.1	140.2	84.7	133.3	270.8	1464.3
Bilateral						
Germany	111.4	48.2	4.19	24.3	9.01	197.2
Greece	15.1		38.3	42.2	1.18	96.9
Italy	206.9	25.4	25.9	63.4	43.8	365.6
Japan	41.6	26.5	1.09	2.2	3.6	75.1
USA	180.1			4.4	*	184.5
Others	98.3	12.7	1.9	5.6	15.8	134.5
Total	**653.4**	**112.8**	**71.3**	**142.1**	**73.3**	**1053.8**
Overall	1488.2	253.0	156.0	275.4	344.1	**2518.1**

* Non available.

UNDP using Ministry of Economic Co-operation and Trade data UNDP (2000) "Albania Human Development Report 2000," Tirana: UNDP, 13.

Italian entrepreneurs began to appear in Albania in 1991, though they suffered a serious setback in the 1997 disturbances. Factories and machinery were destroyed, not only in Vlorë but also in Tirana and Durrës. Some factories never recovered, and some companies left and never returned, though others continue to operate or have returned again. In 1998, over sixty new companies were registered.

However, in this specific area of industrial outsourcing (even though this is more or less present in border locations), Albania does not attract a great amount of foreign capital, as investors judge other locations such as Croatia and Macedonia to be preferable. In the case of Romania, wages are similar to Albania and there is also the problem of corruption. It is interesting to note how the *façonnier*, or outbound production system, ultimately combines with a customs system known as inward processing. This is a special system for importing temporary goods, and is a way of facilitating imports of raw materials and then quickly exporting the final product. This particular type reinforces a certain model of economic policy that encourages the country's economic growth. The most typical products are textiles and shoes, but other sectors are also involved, such as furniture. This system of inward processing has been around for a long time and is used throughout the world.

Table 4.16
Main Albanian Imports and Exports

Main exports	% of total	Main imports	% of total
Textiles & footwear	69.7	Textiles & footwear	14.5
Base metals	8.4	Machinery & equipment	13.8
Foodstuffs, beverages & tobacco	5.4	Mineral products	13.1
Vegetable products	4.7	Foodstuffs, beverages & tobacco	9.0
Leather & articles	3.2	Vegetable products	8.4

Source: Data provided by Economist Intelligence Unit—Economist Intelligence Unit (2002) Country Report January 2002 Albania. UK. *The Economist*, 5.

My conversations at the Italian trade office confirmed the dominant influence of the façonnier system as being the central point for an insight on the trade relationships between Italy and Albania. In Italy, the façonnier model originated in the late 1960s, which was a period of economic growth and the start of flexible production. While the façon system is still in expansion in Albania, it is already widespread in Romania because there delocalization began in the late 1970s. Furthermore, in Romania, it is much more traditional and deeply rooted. What advantages does Albania have over Romania? At the trade office they replied with the classic answer: "Labor is cheap here and we are geographically closer." However, what they also see as Albania's chief difference is the legal framework—tax laws, administrative operations, obtaining business permits—which is believed to be weaker in Albania. Therefore, Italians feel more protected in Romania, as the application of the law in Albania is still too discretionary. These are the main differences between the countries. Italians still hold strong negative preconceptions about Albania, and this has greatly influenced Italian entrepreneurs, even after 1997 when a campaign of image building was implemented.

In any case, even though the façon system used to be the dominant relationship, the Italian trade office is now seeking to diversify the type of investments. Specifically, they are trying to attract investors' attention to other sectors such as tourism and the materials industries, such as mineral mining, and the telecommunications sector. Currently, they are exploring strategies for attracting companies such as Telecom and Wind, which are businesses that would bring with them a whole range of important services, such as in banking. The attitude tends to be one of "Why ask for money or carry out transfers with Greeks or Turks when we can use an Italian banking service?"

According to their argument, the impact on development can be distinguished within the following sectors: firstly, textile—lower risk capital—typical of a first stage of introduction into the country, and secondly, telecommunications—high risk capital—with a need for a sense of trust and settling in the country. For the model of Italian investments in Albania, this distinction matches two economic development models: (1) one based on a form of low-cost industrialization, which is interested in the advantages of distance and low production costs. This represents a development impact only to the extent that it serves to alleviate pockets of poverty, in a place where a regular job is the privilege of a very few; (2) a second model is based on what is known as a strategic investment sector: this is technology-based; it can stimulate faster development in the information sector and requires more highly skilled labor. It seems that this second strategy has been adopted in an intelligent manner by the Greeks in Albania and throughout the Balkans. This depends, in turn, on the laws regulating investment in the Balkans. Apparently, these have worked better for the Greeks than for the Italians, as the Greeks have encountered greater stability. Giancarlo (Italian investment office) also specified the differences of an economic presence depending on the conception of a borderland or a maritime border: a borderland is more accessible and the Greeks have managed to enter it easily. Furthermore, they also have a more accurate perception of the country.

In real terms, Italian manufacturing in Albania is a sector that is in rapid expansion. A total of 350 Italian companies have been registered throughout all economic sectors, although we should bear in mind that these are just the ones that have agreed to appear publicly, as privacy laws are now very strict in Italy. Therefore, between 15 and 20 percent more should be added to this list.

This whole introduction of a façonnier system explains the significant role that factories play in internal migration, given that they create an attraction that promotes rural to urban migration. Furthermore, in these factories, a high percentage of the labor force is also female. Work in factories or textile workshops, created through foreign capital that is interested in the low cost of the female Albanian worker, does not change much in the sense of contributing to women's emancipation. In the case of young women, this kind of work provides a strategy of family survival for the main body of the family. The only advantage such a job can bring is to kill time while the woman is waiting to get married. And this waiting time may or may not lead to international emigration, especially to Italy. Whichever way you look at it, these women inevitably end up depending on Italy: either on Italian customers, on Italian employers, or on Italian laws concerning family reunion (in case someone has embarked on an international migratory project).

As far as the feminization of labor is concerned, it should be noted that it is very difficult to confirm this type of trend in certain areas such as Porto Romano and, even more, I believe it is often an inverse process by which women end up remaining at home following internal migration when they used to work in their places of origin, in the north of the country. In this case, then, one should not speak of the feminization of factories, but simply the feminization of trafficking. Women textile workers like Clara and Diana constantly complain about their working conditions, while they live with their original families in rented apartments. They normally come from highly feminized families, or rather, families with few male members.

In Tirana, the old textile factories are NVP, *Ndeumarrja Punimeva and Veshjeve* (the ancient communist name). The latter was also a textile factory in the Communist era. I have only visited Italba, a shirt factory. It was founded three years ago and the forewoman insists that working conditions are fully respected. She called my attention to the fact that the workers were aged between thirty and forty, though I had hoped to find a few young women. The forewoman explained that this is because they are the same workers that they started with years back. The factory is composed of two production lines in one room. Italba sells its products to Jet, and the latter use them for the Naples-based brand "Arte delle camise." One hundred and ten people work in this factory, with the highest earners taking home 20,000 leks a month, and the lowest only 14,000. Labor is organized in two rooms: one where they manufacture tailor-made shirts, and production. In this first room, the system runs as follows: a particular customer asks them to manufacture a tailor-made shirt, and they make it in just fifteen days. They have a Japanese sewing machine that even embroiders the customer's initials, and they also package the shirts into individual boxes in the same room. All the material is bought in Italy; in Albania they just provide the labor. The factory uses the outbound production system, and has clear connections with southern Italy. They claim that the system was already operating under communism, exporting to East Germany, Italy, and France. I asked why Tirana was chosen as a location and not Durrës, and the response was the same as from another forewoman: it is a question of labor. It seems that the Tirana workforce is more highly skilled. Furthermore, she mentioned that Tirana is safer, and that 40 km. distance from Durrës does not mean a lot. They have no electricity problems because the forewoman has good contacts. There is also a foreman who is from Bari, though he lives here. He told me that they start by offering a three-month contract, what they call a "test contract," as labor is highly mobile and does not last long.

In the Threeshirts factory, none of the workers are from Durrës. The Durrës women do not work, or if they do, they will only accept a good position in a factory. All the labor force has originated from internal emigration, from the migratory population flows that followed communism. When the economy was freed up, the population's mobility was also liberalized, in terms of both internal and external population flows. The workshop occupies the site of the former Communist textile factory. The structure of the factory is composed of a main room with four production lines: the oldest workers, who have an average age of forty, work in the first line, as they have the most experience. They use special sewing machines and work with the most delicate products, in this case, men's polo-neck sweaters. On another production line they add the finishing touches, ironing, and carrying out production control on a cheaper, less sophisticated garment designed for the southern Italian markets, and which has no specific brand. They also produce a more expensive, more refined garment designed for northern Italy, which carries the well known Invicta brand. They told me they would soon begin to work for Armani. The manufactured products are designed for two main customer types, with much of production being of children's wear and ladies' wear, while they also manufacture smaller quantities of men's wear. They told me they need to diversify their customer type to reduce risks.

This visit was based around the arguments of two people: Bruno, the owner, and Eritiana, the factory manager. Bruno moved to Durrës in 1997, just after the period of disturbances. He decided to remain there, even though most Italians preferred Romania or other Eastern European countries. Bruno's discourse is a good illustration of the typical arguments of industrial relocalization agents. He repeated that he was not a *mafioso* and that one should not confuse people. He prefers younger workers because the older women still have a communist-style mentality and are very closed-minded. He also stated that women are very good workers. On several occasions he claimed that the country is not prepared for democracy, since people are very "stubborn, are unable to discuss issues and are very closed-minded." He stated that now the Albanians constitute the labor force but in ten years' time they will become the new consumers. He believes people should learn to respect authority more, particularly authority in the factory. He admits that he never talks to the workers; he just watches them and through his gaze, makes them feel afraid. His next project is to recruit a greater number of women, "because the business has got to grow to be successful." "The rag trade is a jungle," he says, and within it, he has no friends, just competitors. He went on talking about the restructuring of the factory that took place last year. A bad atmosphere had developed and he sacked a hundred female workers. He recruited Eritiana for that operation, and his plan was "to mould her so she would learn how to be harder on the worker," to which she agreed with a nod.

The subject of the feminization of the textile factories and sweatshops is also present in the footwear sector. However, in the furniture factories (which basically use the same production model as the textile sector) most workers are male. Shoelace is a leather footwear manufacturer with two factories in Albania, one in Tirana and another in Durrës, each with around 550 workers, of which 80 percent are women. On one side of the factory, there are seven production lines, and on the other, nine. It is beyond any doubt the largest factory I visited. The most common manufacturing system here is to first produce the leather uppers, after which the sole is added in Italy. However, they are now introducing one part of the sole into the manufacturing process in place, and in the future they aim to carry out the whole process. Roberto (the Italian administrator) confirmed that there was an absolute link between the people working in factories and emigration to Italy, given that many people working with them were planning a trip abroad—in fact, even the manageress of the company had gone. As for the female workers, he told me that they would all prefer to marry an Italian man.

I conducted thirteen brief interviews with the workers in this factory. The interviews covered three topics: (1) the nature of the work in the factory (duration, future labor prospects, and previous employment); (2) internal migration dynamics (where from and why); (3) migration abroad (where to, how many in the family, length of migration, type of employment abroad, migrant status, and weight of remittances). Summarizing the results, I discovered the following.

1. *Regarding the nature of work.* For many women, working for Shoelace represents the first experience of paid work. In the case of female workers who are still single, they tend to originate from families where there are more sisters than brothers. Frequently, several sisters from the same family work in the factory. When they are married, the husband tends to hold casual jobs, usually related to construction work, loading and unloading and miscellaneous repair work.

2. *Regarding internal migration dynamics.* Most employees come from the north of the country. In contrast, the women from the Durrës area have greater access to more highly skilled jobs. We should point out that a system of discrimination is present against women from the north; this is fairly well-concealed, as few people mention it, but it is expressed through the constantly mentioned stereotype of the peasant woman.

3. *Regarding migration abroad.* Italian cities are cited as the main destinations, particularly Brescia, Modena, and Bologna. A model emerged for the first stage of Albanian emigration of young males who had left in the early 1990s, that started off a kind of typical Mediterranean migration. This basically involved them first going abroad alone, after which they would bring over an Albanian woman or else marry an Italian one. A better understanding of remittances can be obtained by examining the model of extensive relationship, while bearing in mind two criteria: (1) that the male migrant is single because, when he marries, the dynamics of remittances are completely altered; (2) remittance regularity is closely related to the rhythm of house construction. When the works are finished, the transfers also come to an end. Thus, building a house shapes the whole migratory project. Typical jobs for emigrants in Italy are, for a man, working in construction, and for a woman, working as a domestic helper and care-giver, though on principle, no woman travels abroad alone. Generally speaking, single women tend to be very preoccupied with the subject of marriage.

Following are some of the most notable cases.

One of Eda's sisters is married to an Italian and lives in Brescia, as does another brother who is also married. He is employed in public works and his brother-in-law is a construction worker, though Eda's sister does not work. Her brother helps her economically through Western Union transfers. With this money, they have been able to finish building their house. They want to go to Italy, but they have not been granted documents yet. They have also tried to obtain an invitation letter through her sister, but they are still waiting. Eda states that she is not happy in Albania and that "life is better there, it's another life."

This is Edlira's first job and she tells me she will keep it if she gets a good offer from Shoelace, otherwise she will leave the job if she finds a good husband. The administrator, Roberto, comments jokingly that Shoelace has to compete with the good prospect that a potential husband typifies. Edlira adds that this is really the way things operate in Albania, although now women are more independent, above all in the cities. The whole family is from Shijak. She has a brother in Modena, who left in March 1991 on the big boats that sailed from Albania.

There are nine members in Evis's family. Four of them are in Brussels, including the whole of her brother's family; he is married and has two children. He does not send money home, except sporadically. He has been in Belgium for a year and a half, but he recently returned to Albania for one month. Just yesterday he went off again on the boat, without documents, and his family are very worried because they still haven't heard from him. Vali (one of the interviewers) comments that many people leave the country in this way. Evis complains of having had a high temperature for two days, but she cannot ask for permission to leave work. She has been engaged to a young man from Driba for a month; they met on a chance encounter on the street and later went to speak to her father to ask for her hand. Vali mentions that it is important to understand the value that is placed on virginity. According to tradition, girls cannot sleep in the groom's house even though they are engaged, though in contrast, this tradition does not exist in southern Albania. Furthermore, mobility is only available to women with an educational plan or a skilled work project. Otherwise, they are totally de-legitimized in terms of movement. Another way is marriage, though with the institution of marriage, the woman exchanges one form of control for another, contrary to the commonly held idea that marriage means passing from a means of control into a form of freedom. At the end of the day, female workers are divided by the north-south distinction, which results in women from the north being more excluded and discriminated against. As I mentioned above, they are commonly referred to as peasant women (*malok*).

The spaces of trafficking. For a long time, Vlorë was the emblematic connection for trafficking in Albania. The city has two beaches from which the boats sailed for Italy: the old beach and the new one, and it was from the latter that the dinghies used to leave for Italy. The name for these dinghies—*gommoni*—is the same in Italian as in Albanian, and is also the name the smugglers call them. Yet for some time now, the boats have been unable to leave from there, and so boats now tend to sail from Aradim and Porto Palermo. Since the gommone cannot leave from Vlorë any more, the only way of transporting smuggled goods is by fishing or passenger boats. Another reason that has complicated the business in this area is the fact that the dinghies could not remain more than fifteen minutes on the beach.

Paradoxical though it may seem, in the city of Vlorë there has been a transformation from a criminal economy to a more formal one. The most obvious example is Foam beer: the man who used to smuggle in this beer has now opened a warehouse for the brand in Vlorë. At present, it is just a warehouse for imported beers, but he is soon going to open a brewery. During the 1990s, the families of Vlorë lived off the trafficking economy, from selling boat fuel to providing lodging for emigrants in transit. All these forms of income were interlinked with migrants' remittances and from petty trade profits. Most consumer goods tend to be Italian, even more so than in other parts of the country, and this Italianization of products is due to the excellent connections between Brindisi and Vlorë, two cities that are only seventy kilometers away by sea. In the city, most people watch Italian television. Furthermore, in the port of Brindisi you can buy Albanian tobacco and many Albanians live there.

The city of Vlorë was, until recently, a key site on the smuggling circuits for at least a decade; it was the location for all kinds of petty crime, such as video cameras stolen in Albania, as well as trafficking in drugs and illegal immigrants. During this period, the entire city lived off smuggling, since everybody was involved in these economic networks. One excellent example is a person who sold bread, and who did a better business when the weather was bad, since the customers were the irregular migrants waiting to cross the border. Thus. we can see that climatic changes affected everyone, and that small businesses were highly vulnerable to the dynamics of the smuggling circuit. The money the scafistas made was not invested in banks; over time they have realized that tourism is a profitable enterprise and they have started investing in building hotels. However, due to the lack of any regulatory plan for the city, they purchase the building permits without any previous plans. Thus, most investment is in small-scale tourism, though it is rather hesitant in nature, as they know they have bought the permits illegally and they may run into problems in the near future. Currently, the city is going through a period of change, because people are now looking for other means of making a living, ways of working with a clearer vision of the future, that is to say, searching for a way to obtain legal employment.

Elton (a scafista´s son) explained well how traffickers find the amount of remittances that emigrants send their families to be simply laughable. For example, one scafista would make 7,500 million leks in a single night (1 = 139 leks). This money is shared as follows: 550,000 for the sailor, 1 million for the pilot, and the rest for the scafista. Therefore, in relation to mobility two types of family exist in Vlorë: those living off remittances, and the scafista families. The amounts mentioned should be compared with those in Tangier. In comparison, prices for crossing in a dinghy from Tangier to Spain range from 400 to 1000 per head. In Albania, with the pyramids, money increased its value at a rate of 24 percent a month. Of course the scafistas knew that they were taking a risk, and that it was not completely safe, but they always thought they would get their money out in time.

The first gommone were brought in from Greece and Italy, but soon they went on sale in Albania, too. The boats cost around 70,000 leks, and have two 250cc outboard engines. Around twenty gommone would leave the beach every night, knowing that the police would chase two or three of them and that the others would escape, if they were lucky. This procedure was like an unwritten rule of gommone trafficking. The price of a passage depended on meteorological conditions. This was not only regarded as the route to Italy for most Albanians, but also for other groups such as Chinese and Kurds. Gommone lore is filled with fabulous tales. Elton's father was one of the first in the whole of Albania to have a gommone. The main characters in the history of these boats were men who were familiar with life on the sea, men who knew about weather and how it could undergo sudden changes. His father's first boat had a motor of between 150-200 cc and he used it as if it was a taxi. He had his license and his Albanian flag, and everything was shipshape, except for the passengers. During that period, three of his gommone were confiscated by the police. He got into the trafficking network through contact with some friends of his who knew an Italian in Bari, who sold stolen vehicles. Elton´s father bought his third boat in Greece, and with his three gommone, he would make up to three journeys a night, until they were seized. Elton remembers that it was his father who made gommone fashionable in Vlorë. In the early 1990s, the system was very simple, since only one pilot was needed. Later on, the crew expanded to include a pilot, a sailor, and a companion. Weighing the pros and cons of trafficking, it can be deduced that the stricter the police control, the greater the number of intermediaries needed to get around the controls. Before they set sail, photographs were taken of all the irregular migrants. These photos were kept as guarantee that would grant them either a refund or a second try at crossing, within a margin of three days.

One of my most surprising discoveries in Albania was the degree of collaboration between the Albanians and the Italian police, something which is generally absent on the Spanish-Moroccan border, where an island (Parsley Island) has become a symbol of occupation during July 2002. Gianpietro[24] explains it in terms of political agreements. He told me the tale of a case that occurred some time ago in Vlorë: one night, ten scafi or gommone left Vlorë. However, only a few of the boats were able to pass the filter established by the police, and the filter control depended on the type of merchandise they were carrying.

At first three types of launches were used, depending on the product being transported: arms, drugs, or human beings. Nevertheless, as time went on, business started to get mixed together. If the police spotted bags and sacks from their helicopter, they opened fire, as long as there was nobody close by. Several characters were involved on this circuit, such as the smuggler (or scafista) and his companion (*acompaniatore*), among others. As I mentioned, migrants were entitled to repeat the trip thanks to the photos that had been taken of them beforehand. Another strategy was to leave the future prostitutes in a house in Vlorë for a month to give them a sort of training seminar. Moldavian women tended to be more costly than Albanians since, due to the linguistic problem, it took longer to teach them. In these types of sexual work seminars they also recruited sixteen-year-old male youths as clients in order to be able to experiment with them freely. Tobacco trafficking was not carried out from Vlorë, it tended to follow the Montenegro route to Bari. Other products transported by boat included arms from Albania, cocaine from Colombia, and heroin from Turkey. Once they reached Lecce, an Italian taxi network would take the merchandise to the city, which was situated around forty kilometers from the arrival point. They usually stopped off in a wooded area, changed clothes, and took the emigrants to the station at Lecce or Brindisi.

Elton described in detail everything that took place in this illegal circulation through Vlorë, though only two months ago all the trafficking was stopped. However, Elton claims that it actually came to an end between six months and a year ago. Beforehand, you had to pay three intermediaries: the police, the customs, and the police in the destination country. Commonly smuggled goods included coffee, and above all, beer. In those days, they used to transport up to three hundred people in a night, while now the most common method for illegal emigrants who have managed to pay for false documents is a passenger ship, so the number of people has dropped to four or five. Beforehand, the price of a passage was a complete package, even including a visa issued by the Italian consulate. Now, in contrast, migrants cross using a false visa stating the person's true name. This whole area of document falsification takes many different forms, for instance, using your real passport and then making a false visa using your real name. If you have a false visa, you can also match it up to a false passport. Falsification is based on a system of corruption that is encouraged by the consulates, especially the lower echelons of consulate staff that seem to be more easily corruptible.

As has been shown, Vlorë has also experienced the transit of emigrants traveling to the European Union. At IOM (International Organization for Migration), I learned that the Albanian authorities are continually repatriating persons with no evidence of origin, and without keeping a record of them. Where possible, these persons are referred to UNHCR (United Nations High Committee for Refugees) to request asylum. In the meantime, while they are waiting, they kill time and are given a temporary residence permit. Consequently, the population that UNHCR works with in Albania is largely made up of economic migrants who are simply waiting for their chance to make the jump into Europe. Sometimes these people enter through Rinas airport, and are then kept in a refugee center. In any case, there is very little information available on this issue. On the other hand, the government wants to deal with the whole subject of the fight against illegal immigration very openly, with maximum publicity. This is why they have broadcast television footage of the gommone being burnt.

The woman as a trafficable object. The underlying social relations that create the body as a product in border places are here emphasized, particularly by showing how the woman's body becomes an economic commodity and a market is created, including its specific transport routes.

Between 1997 and 1998, there was a substantial growth in the problem following the conflict in Kosovo. Now, IOM offers social services to the most vulnerable segments of the population. It targets mainly three groups: (1) women victims of trafficking, (2) students abroad, and (3) workers abroad. Its main objective is to achieve harmony within mobility. The IOM's more specific objectives are (1) to fight against the trafficking of human beings, to bring about reintegration, and to offer support to police bodies; (2) to improve border management, specifically the control and management of both incoming and outgoing migrations in Albania; and (3) to develop the organization as a service provider. In short, to improve the local capabilities for the fight against trafficking, in addition to creating an advisory body to the government. The IOM has an information center for emigration abroad in Tirana, called the Migrant Assistance Center.

On the other hand, we should also mention the work of associations related to immigration in Italy. One of them criticized the IOM program against trafficking citing that it only offers a return channel and not a way forward for social integration in Italy. This point has been harshly criticized by associations in Rome.

In recent years, the most striking feature of the trafficking issue has been a boom in projects and research into the trafficking of women on an international level. Bibliographies are not only referenced for trafficking, but also for the phenomenon of trans-national prostitution, as indicated by the metaphor of *Open borders, open bodies.* Women turn to prostitution as a hidden survival strategy, an opportunity to increase their income.[25] For these women, prostitution becomes a deliberate survival strategy. The Vatra association reveals that during the period 2002-2003, figures have decreased considerably due to a strategy against the trafficking of human beings by the Albanian government (Tables 4.17, 4.18, and 4.19 provide a short summary of the characteristics of this trafficking). This association has been working for seven years in prevention and rehabilitation. It has also come across cases of young women who have freely chosen this work, although one peculiarity of the Albanian system is that these young women always work with a protector, never independently. These traffickers then use the money to invest in property. In addition, this phenomenon is the result of a context that directly results from a patriarchal mentality. That is to say, the existence of such a mentality stigmatizes the prostitute to the extent that she cannot reintegrate into the family and community; this same mentality also limits women's rights and exploits them in the home environment. At this point, some Albanian associations have had to ask themselves the question, where are women most exploited, in their own family or on Italian streets? They are referring here to the working of a market system where the emphasis is only placed on the supply inside—Albania—without considering the demand side—their Italian customers.

With respect to the trafficking of women, after more than a decade of open borders, one could expect that young Albanian women are better informed than before, but does the same apply to foreign women? The spreading of trafficking networks raises significant questions as to the reason why this has happened in Albania and nowhere else, and also why these networks have employed such cruel methods with women. Gianpietro believes it is simply a way of earning quick money, and should be studied from the basis of the condition of women in Albania, as they are extremely repressed. However, this situation is also changing considerably. Nowadays a new profile is emerging, one where women are obtaining university degrees, which means they can dress well and carry mobile phones. This phenomenon is similar to that of the *jineteras* (non-professional prostitutes) in Cuba and the young women in Tangier nightclubs. There is also the Vatra (local association) study, based on the city of Vlorë. The association documents several cases of trafficked women in villages close to Lushnja. It appears they did want to return home, but were not successful due to the villagers' mentality. As for forms of prevention, many people do not allow their daughters to go to school because of the fear they may be kidnapped.

With reference to women repatriated from trafficking, apparently 50 percent are from Roma families (information from Joana Hume, Catholic association). In my fieldwork, out of all the visited families, the Roma community and Kinostudio in Tirana stand out in terms of emigration to Greece rather than to

Table 4.17
Trafficking of Women in Albania from East European Countries

Nationality	N. of cases	Percentage
Romanian	30	46%
Moldavian	27	40%
Ukrainian	4	6%
Bulgarian	4	6%
Serbian	1	1%
Russian	1	1%

Source: Data provided by results of questionnaires in the Puka district. Renton, Daniel (2001), Save the children, Tirana, 65

Table 4.18
Trafficking of Women. Means of Trafficking in the Durrës District*

Means of trafficking	Number of girls	Percentage of girls
Cheated	75	61.9%
Abduction	31	25.6%
Free will	3	2.4%
Revenge	2	1.7%
Economic reason	2	1.7%
Others	113	6.7%

* Trafficking cases for six villages of Durrës (Manze, Sukth, Shijak, Xhafzotaj, Katund i Ri)

Source: Data provided by results of 500 questionnaires in the Durrës District. Çeveli B,. Elezi M., Mukaj.A., Ngjeci.E. (2002) "Be careful and protect yourself," Durrës: Council associations offering social services, 28-33.

Table 4.19
Destination Country of Trafficked Victims

Country trafficked to	Number of cases
Italy	20
Albania	16
Greece	5
Kosovo	3
Netherlands	2
Belgium	1
England	1
Germany	1
Total	49

Source: IOM 2002 "Interim Report on Reintegration Assistance to Albanian Victims of Trafficking through the Capacity Building of a National Reintegration Support Network" (RTA), Tirana: IOM, 7.

Italy, as this is a migration destination that is related to migration patterns for Albanians with fewer economic resources. On the same grounds, we can affirm that begging in migration is also more present in Greece. On balance, all this comprises a theme that has caught my attention: the existence of a particular pattern in these migration circuits, since Joana Hume told me that 50 percent of repatriated prostitutes were Roma. What this boils down to is a widespread situation that is defined by a complex circle of poverty where scarcity, deceit and emigration are all intertwined.

Children as trafficable objects. During the 1990s, thousands of Albanian children were working in the streets (begging, selling small items) in all the major cities of Greece (Athens and Salonica, but also Petras, Larissa, Ioannina, Kavala, and Heraklion). Integration into criminal networks happens not only in Greece but also in Third World countries. Normally, the child grows up within these networks until he himself becomes a leader of children or is used in other illegal networks. However, the so-called "traffic-light children" suddenly disappeared from Greek crossroads and streets when the police began to make large numbers of arrests from 1998 onwards. These badly dressed children, intended to induce pity in the Greek population, have given way to other children who are well-dressed and sell merchandise on café terraces (Terre des hommes 2003: 19). According to the statistics of the juvenile branch of the Athens police data indicate that of the 300 children on average arrested every year for begging, 90 percent are Albanian (Terre des hommes 2003: 9), whereas in Italy, 9,000 Albanian children have been placed in orphanages (idem).

In the prostitution milieu in Greece, according to Professor Lazos, there are 20,000 prostitutes, of whom 10 percent are minors. It appears that out of these minors 75 percent are Albanian. Some information collected confirms the sexual exploitation of girls from the age of 12 (idem). Death is a constant in this milieu: they are either murdered (in Italy, the Ministry of the Interior reported 168 murders of foreign prostitutes in 2000, of whom the majority were Albanian) or die in accidents (at crossroads; children have been accidentally injured or killed while working) (idem). In regard to border crossing, in Thessaloniki, the number of deportations of Albanian minors at the border increased from 213 in 1997 to 983 in 1998 (idem: 17).

Walking through the streets of the capital, you can see many child beggars, exhibiting their amputated legs and other physical defects. They work by showing exaggerated wounds that normally people tend to hide; here they become valorized through begging, a different presentation of the self, creating the image of someone in need. Frequently, it is these children who later become child migrants. Clarisse (from a children's NGO) clearly laid out the different stages in the fight against trafficking and stressed that her own focus of intervention was centered on prevention programs. She described Albania as being a double-faced map, with one side looking towards Greece and the other facing towards Italy, adding that it is this duality that stimulates traffic in one direction or the other. To her, Durrës is significant within any kind of circuit in the trafficking world, since all kinds of merchandise pass through this port, and it is through this city where legal and illegal trade are interwoven.

Clarisse is opposed to the programs of accompanying and repatriating children, and to support her view gives the example of a friendly gypsy boy who was being held at a center in Greece. He was considered a genius in Greece, but then agreed to be repatriated and has now been returned to his parents, who originally sold him because of their deplorable living conditions. She also described the daily route many of the street children of Durrës follow: at night they normally wait for the boats from Italy to arrive (there are even whole families who sleep in the port). The children have certain planned hours with their protector, who is generally an ex-street-child. At a specific time, they go to the post office, and at another to the market. In spite of being street children, they always sleep with their family or with their protector. They are not like the groups of children you can find in Brazil, by which she means the *meninos da Rua*. In contrast, Albanian street children maintain a vestige of family cohesion. In the end, she adds that what is most striking about Albanian child emigrants, compared to those from other countries, is that they are very young. Finally, Clarisse returns to the subject of the associations and explains that they are all run from abroad and have their local counterpart until, in time, they become autonomous.

In addressing child trafficking, Unicef states that first the concept of sexual work undertaken must be clarified to determine if it an act of free will or a form of trafficking and sexual exploitation. Under *kanun* law, daughters have a price, and this sale facilitates the commodification of women necessary for prostitution. Following interviews carried out by Unicef with Albanian traffickers, it was deduced that they consider the traffic of wives and brides to be a private matter. Interpol has 107 registered cases of lost women and in 1997, the police closed down forty-eight apartments that were being used for prostitution.

Gialla, a representative for the Emilia-Romagna region (Italy) in Albania, presented the results of a study on unaccompanied minors in her country. Between the years 2000 and 2002, the percentages for Puglia stand out: 18.7 percent, followed by Lombardy (14.9 percent) and Lazio (14.2 percent). For the same period, the study indicates the three leading countries of origin: Albania, 9,047 (57.9 percent), Morocco, 1,833 (11.3 percent), and Romania, 1,184 (7.3 percent), out of a total of 16,239 (the source for all these figures is the "Comitato per i minori stranieri"). In terms of age groups: 0-6 years old (1.5 percent), 7-14 (7.6 percent), 15 (5.9 percent), 16 (11.5 percent), 17 (22.2 percent), and those who are legally of age (51.2 percent). If we carry out a classification by sex, we can see that 84.2 percent are males and 15.8 percent females, bearing in mind that girls are underrepresented because they have been sheltered under residence permits for social protection. These are permits similar to those for social support given to minors on leaving prison. Going into greater detail, this study reflects the situation in the municipality of Modena. In fact, unaccompanied minors became very expensive for local councils, as around 500,000 are spent on hostels for minors. This is why they believe that it would be better to encourage occupational training in the country of origin. Table 4.20 provides an overview of the means of trafficking children.

Table 4.20
**Trafficking of Children: Means of Trafficking Children in the
Durrës District**

Means of trafficking	Number of children	Percentage of children
Organ's transplantation	4	44.4%
Economic reasons	2	22.2%
Abduction	1	11.1%
Violence	1	11.1%
As beggar	1	11.1%

Source: Data provided by results of 800 questionnaires in the Durrës District. Çeveli B., Elezi M., Mukaj. A, Ngjeci. E. (2002). "Be careful and protect yourself," Durrës: Council associations offering social services, 28-33.

The Family's World

All the families I visited fulfilled the rules of hospitality, offering me sweets as soon as I had sat down in the dining room and seeing me off at the door. These visits have once again pinpointed the significance of the family ideology as a form of structuring the social and economic life in capitalist Albania. The family continues to wield a strong influence and, as Elvis's father said, "the family is very strong in the Balkans" and it is in this environment that we can detect microscopic changes in society. Families in the Balkans are known to be different not only to those of the Western world but also to Eastern Europe. De Rapper[26] points out that in the absence of the state and civil society, the Albanian family plays a crucial role, that of the family as an economic and moral unit. In contrast, people of the villages often tend to use evolutionist models of families. They have the image of a Western family as a unit where love and solidarity are excluded (De Rapper 1998: 526).

At the same time, the family is the unit where patriarchy, virilocality, exogamy, and patrilineality are best embodied and most clearly expressed. Albanians constantly praise the importance of the family and familial values, even calling the family the regulator of the people. It is on these grounds that we have focused our attention on such relationships in migratory contexts. The strategies surrounding domestic economies provide enlightening examples of change in the country: factors such as globalization, privatization (setting property at the heart of the family dynamic), the speed of migration dynamics, the sudden urbanization, and the social construction of borders with Europe. To understand the nature of the family in Albania, its conception, its values, the occupational insertion of its members, its marriage strategies and its logic of geographical dispersion, one must remember that the rules of patrilineality and virilocality govern the ways the family adjusts to a new social reality. One strong example of this came up in the fieldwork, where it turned out that married women with children said that their children always took precedence, that they were always judged to be more important to them than the husband was.

The theme of marriage is a common topic in all the family visits. Marriage is definitely a recurring theme in conversation, a point that invites reflection. The average marrying age for a man from the mountain region is around twenty-five, while for a woman it is normally between eighteen and twenty. Marrying age varies according to whether one is in a rural or urban environment. One of the families with whom I worked explained that their sons went to Italy and married at thirty-five, which their father considers too late. The northern Albanian tradition is to have a large family so as not to be left childless, given the high mortality rate traditionally caused by *vendetta* and disease.

The patchwork economy. Eva (from the association, For Women) gave a brilliant interpretation of how the logic of the patchwork economy functions. The families live with a base, with a single wage that is more or less stable. They obtain extra income through other activities. In this way, the strategy is expressed by combining each type of income. Eva believes it is essential to realize how families suffer from a squandering mentality—as soon as they get a little money, they spend it. Once they are paid, they consume in large quantities. As a consequence of all this it follows that the underlying rationale of the patchwork economy is based around short-term projects with few plans for future savings.

Fabi (Association Co-B) considers that the woman's influence is vital to the decision-making process in the homes in urban Albanian peripheries. Theoretically, the family works according to the pattern that the wife remains at home to do all the domestic tasks, separated from the outside community, while the husband is her link to it, not only in abstract terms but also in terms of public participation. It is Fabi´s opinion that NGOs tend to assume that the female adult is weak and the male adult is strong. Consequently, in areas of community participation and home decision-making, the man is supposedly dominant. However, through NGO projects they have learned that decisions in the home are heavily influenced by women, though it is then the man who formulates these demands to the outside world. This was apparent in the management of the water supply in Bathore, Tirana: it was the women who knew more on the subject, since it is the women who are responsible for fetching the water. Therefore, in the end, both men and women share the same decision-making power. On reflection, according to Fabi, it seems that women's conditions are not as oppressive as the NGOs based in Albania would have people believe. Albanian women do not identify with the stereotype of the oppressed woman, since it is they who decide how to administrate and manage the family economy, as well as having greater knowledge than their husbands in questions of local infrastructures. Also, though women work just as hard as men in the area of agriculture, they are unable to conceive of it as work for two reasons: firstly, because they do not receive any kind of economic remuneration in exchange for it and it is done in the home space; and, secondly, because it does not fall into their mental idea of labor.

The wide contrast in consumer practices can easily be seen in the different categories of restaurants and bars in the capital. Some are extremely luxurious, while others look quite poor. In this country there is always this divide between the *chic* and the rest of the population, and these two Tiranas are immediately visible from the moment the visitor arrives. There is the juxtaposition of the streets and buildings of the *Blloku* (that enclosed city ruled by the Communist leader that was depicted so well by Bashkim Shehu in *Tiran(i)a* [Tyranny] (2002) with the popular streets of the moneychangers around Skanderberg square. There are the luxurious cafés and the spacious pizzerias on one hand and the plastic market stalls on the other. It leads to an overmagnified contrast of spaces that virtually border on one another, giving the effect of a striking proximity of spaces that can be compared to an African-style peripheralization. Furthermore, the dual-type of business location involves a dual pricing system where the high-status product is always the globalized one, for example, the Italian *cappuccino*. In any case, most products are imported. This Italian question is a constantly recurring one and deserves special consideration. Italian imports are the dominant consumer products, which implies that a process of assimilation is taking place that Italianizes the product, giving it its "Made in Italy" status. The working-class household economy, naturally, is more modest and is based on recycling and on the consumption of fresh produce. On this side of the city, in the Blloku, the shops are better maintained and the atmosphere is more middle-class. It is full of young women wearing coats costing almost 100 . Here lies the key to how the patchwork economy works. How do these consumer patterns interplay with European prices and such low wages? Other questions still to be resolved include the remittance strategies, moonlighting jobs, irregular and illegal benefits, and the articulation of different family earnings.

On the subject of food consumption, the market is dominated by fruit imported from Greece. In contrast, packaged products are basically all Italian. Again, it seems to be the same phenomenon as the merchandise from Sebta that arrives at the Moroccan borders. Since the transition period, one of the major changes has been the advent of foreign television, and whereas previously there was only a single official channel, now there are around twenty. The films are mainly in Italian (even though they are USA-made) and are often subtitled in English.

Due to harsh living conditions in Albania, and above all to the frequent power cuts, families have to manage complex daily strategies in regard to the use of water and electricity. Winter in the capital differs according to one's social class. One difference in the living conditions is the electricity supply, which marks a clear division between households. Who has it and who does not? Who has a generator and who does not? This is the great paradox that Albanians face today, when providing electricity to the country had been one of the symbols of socialist figurativeness.

As has already been observed, consumer practices reproduce the strong contrasts between social classes in Albania. On one hand, there is poverty and on the other, expensive clothes, expensive cars, and the latest-generation mobile phones. Everyone agrees that the traffickers are in the latter group. People observe how students are normally well dressed, since they spend most of their money on clothes, however, in contrast, at home they live in poor conditions. There are many shops selling Italian cookers, as well as furniture shops, fueling people's desires of having a new bathroom. The importance of one's image even extends to cars and clothes as the most directly visible status symbols. Apart from American music and the modern and traditional folklore of the country, the music of Italian singers is also very popular.

The case-study of Elena's family reveals three interesting elements in their patchwork economy, since they articulate three types of strategy at once: (1) the bar, which is open the maximum number of hours possible, previously run by her husband and now by Elena herself. In theory, Oti helps her in the mornings, but he does not do much; (2) the strategy of the classic Mediterranean type of remittance reception, from a single man who is not highly skilled; (3) the strategy of sacrificing oneself for the children's education, sending them where their parents believe they can obtain the best educational opportunities. They know that Germany offers a better standard of living than Italy.

Family strategies and mobility limits. It is in situations similar to that of Fani's family where we have seen households transformed due to youth emigration abroad, such as when the parents are relatively young, and afterwards the couple falls victim to a kind of "empty nest" syndrome. This also occurred with Berta, whose two daughters are still studying in Scotland. As Amira's family explained to me, they pulled down the old house and built a new one last summer. It is clear that most people tend do use the remittance money in a similar way. In other words, international emigration allows families to pull down the old one and start anew, setting up another house with a modern, functional bathroom and kitchen. In turn, families then begin to delve through the Italian furniture on show in the stores of the outermost suburbs.

It is interesting to see how the phenomenon of trafficking functions specifically within the context of traditional values. How can something which, at first sight, represents a schizophrenia of values possibly operate? In the process of communist modernization, the traditional function of honor was completely deregulated, pride was progressively substituted with a type of imprecise, vague, and weak culpability. Orwell's doublethink, common to all totalitarian regimes, could here be translated into a principle of double honor which implies a modality of honor for the public space and another for the private sphere (Ditchev 1996: 30). This public-private contrast is a reflection of what Enver Hoxha referred to as backwards: "patriarchal leftovers," of clannishness, attachment to private property, feeling of kinship and preservation. The dictator instead wished to promote the productive capacity of women in the economy as a form of emancipation (Hoxha 1987: 704). So lied implicitly and explicitly—under the project of the "New Albania" and the ideals related to the "Albanian people,"—the discourse on the Albanian emancipation of women.

This dissonance is a question of double values, in which the private family space has always been a space that conserves ancestral values, and was preserved throughout the communist period, while it is the public space where people see transition taking place. The family functions under an Albanian-style patriarchal system, which implies a specific code of behavior for women, particularly related to physical mobility more so than to access to employment. Going out at night and traveling abroad are the two classic restrictions in terms of placing limits on women's mobility. However, these limitations have also been fostered within a context of family nuclearization. Placed against this are the values that have deteriorated in the public sphere, where communist universalism gave way to an individualism lacking in any collective ethics. These are the values one judges others by, and it is here where the move towards individualism has left its mark. Nobody is concerned about the community values demanded by communism, and community practices and beliefs are theoretically no longer important. Furthermore, community morale in the widest sense is understood from the context of marketing in trafficking practices within the transition economies. All this has been produced by the erosion of civil society. It is only by rigorous observation and analysis that we can understand the double moral standards that structure the context of trafficking practices. On one hand, the regime brought extraordinary improvements in educational levels, given the stark contrasts in literacy rates since the beginning of the century. This improvement also involved women, an obviously positive point. However, the negative point is the existence of trafficking in women and children.

It is extremely worthwhile analyzing the subject of the prostitution networks in relation to what this signifies for freedom or restriction of female mobility. Albanians often mention the fact that nowadays gypsy women tend to be the prostitutes in Albania, and that they also were in the past when prostitution was forbidden during communism. On one hand, Albanian women appear to be fairly liberated in terms of their incorporation into the labor market, as well as in their way of dressing and of communicating with men. On the other hand, the family continues to exert strict control on women's mobility, since they are not free to go out at night and cannot travel except when accompanied by a family member. In this sense, it is understandable how autonomous emigration for women has consequently been prohibited. What this boils down to is that women do not feel safe enough to emigrate alone and if they do leave, they follow their fiancée. From that point onward, social relation connections involve the spouse's integration into a family-style network governed by the husband's place of origin.

And so, with regard to gender relationships, it is clear that extreme discrimination exists against women, something that is not perceptible at first sight, and international prostitution networks are justified and legitimized on the basis of this discrimination system. Paradoxically, during the socialist period, women managed to achieve a relatively high proportion of political power, reflected in the fact that there were fifty women in the Parliament. However, people often counter that point by arguing that gender relations only changed in the public sphere, and not inside Albanian homes. This both poses the problem and provides the basic explanation for the persistence of specific gender relationships in Albania: the traditional family system is considered by many to be immutable. When Elton was asked about the question of the underlying morality in the existence of the prostitution networks, he explained that the people of Vlorë accepted the fact of such networks by simply justifying them as a source of income. It is again a purely economic reason; in a way, the same rationale as under communism. All this goes to show that Elton appears to be in agreement with the continuation of this moral double standard: "I would not allow my daughter to do it because it is dishonorable, but I don't care if other girls do, because it makes them money." Nil (an Italian sociologist) adds that all this is explained by the collective micro-order, a typical product of the transition period. Nor does the question of undocumented migrants create problems among families with respect to economic profits.

The underlying ethics seem to be a self-justification of rampant capitalism. The great majority of people use all the stereotypes of Albanian sexuality to deny the existence of typical vehicles of sexually transmitted diseases, and they do the same with respect to other areas such as homosexuality. On the contrary—and I saw that most international organizations also believe this to be true—they think diseases come from abroad, from European emigrants. However, the fact is that data on trafficked women reveal low rates of AIDS infection, a point that surprised both Marta (a United Nations volunteer) and myself. In addition, the rate is also shown to be very low among drug addicts. Marta did not seem to be totally convinced by this data, as it contrasts sharply with the increase shown in other countries in transition for those particular categories.

Nora's family: Life on the periphery of a border city. I drafted Nora's family genogram (see Figure 4.3), including criteria of origin, external migration, and occupational category, during and after communism, for all family members. Adult males almost always left the place of origin before women did, and therefore, what can be observed from this mobility in terms of gender is that the first movement comes from a mobility of the male family members. Alhough, on the other hand, within the context of reception, female integration plays an important role. In terms of the depth of relationships, this family represents a replica of Ihsan's family in Tangier.

Nora's family comes from Lushnja. In Albania, it is very important to ask about one's family origins, even though someone may have been settled in another location for generations. She claimed that those who came here from the north are still different from them. Seventy years ago, Nora's father came to Porto Romano from Lushnja. He traveled along with another 150 families in order to work in a petrol refinery. Of these 150 families, only twenty-eight remain. In the 1990s most of them had left when they became aware of the risk they were running from the high toxicity levels in the area. The great majority moved to the center of Durrës. Porto Romano had previously been a significant industrial center of Durrës, along with Shijak.

Outside Nora's house there is a plot of land with almond trees, a potato and an onion patch, as well as a chicken coop. It is curious to see how this area mixes post-industrial features with agricultural culture. The family lives in a relatively large, particularly well-kept house. On the living room wall there is a large poster of Mecca. They insist that they are Muslims, that they believe in God, but that they do not know how to pray; this is the typical comment made by most people.

In this family, the reverse to what normally happens in other parts of the world has occurred: during communism all women worked, but now they have all become housewives. Cora, one of Nora's sisters, remarked that she studied accounting but has ended up working as a peasant. Her sisters said, scornfully, that they did not live in Porto Romano they lived in Durrës. On one of my visits I discovered that Nora worked for an hour in a dentist's surgery as a cleaner, though she did not acknowledge that she was actually working.

Nora has two brothers in Italy who left during the exodus of 1991. One is in Rimini and works as a construction worker, although he is now a foreman. He is married and has two children. Her sister is also married, has children, and lives in Pescara. Both send money and help out their parents as much as they can. They send money through friends or through Western Union, and they also help Nora; for instance, they bought her a mobile phone.

Nora has two children. Altin, Nora's son, and his cousin Martin are both fifteen; neither are active in any way—they do not go to school or work. Altin is decisive on the subject of work, saying it is just not worth working here. He plans to wait until he can be better paid, or rather, until he finds work in Italy. Altin showed me the Albanian passport that has just been issued. Martin, unlike Altin, has a different project: to stay in Albania and become a minibus driver.

On one of my visits, two interpreters came along—a girl of fourteen and a boy of twelve. They were siblings who had lived for a while in Birmingham, England. Their father washed cars there, since he was undocumented and

Figure 4.3
Genograme Nora

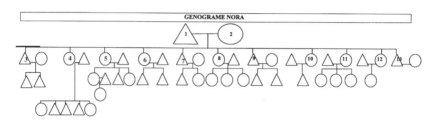

1: **MAN**, Aged 80,:Origin: Lushnje; Place of residence: Durrës; War veteran against the Germans; Now retired (agriculture).

2: **WOMAN**, Aged 70; Origin: Lushnje; Residence: Durrës; Worked during 35 years in agriculture.

3: **Man**: Aged 52; Builder in Durrës; During Communism: tractor driver. / **Woman**: Housewife; During Communism: farmer/ **Children**: Aged 22 and 27; Fishermen in Porto Romano.

4: **Woman**: Aged 48; During Communism: doctor's helper in hospital/ **Man**: Aged 50; Mechanic in Lushnje; During Communism: same job/ **Girl**: Aged 27; Works in the water company. Lives in Durres, married and with child.

5: **Woman**: Aged 45; Works in hospital; During Communism: same job/ **Man**: Aged 50; builder in a hospital; During Communism: same job/**Girl**: Aged 22; Spent 3 years in Acula, near Pescara, Italy. Her husband has been working as a builder for 10 years. She has a baby aged 6 months. / **Girl**: Aged 18; Student in Durrës. **Son**: Aged 16; Student.

6: **NORA**. **Woman**: Aged 43; Housewife; During Communism: brigadiere/ **Man**: Aged 45; Builder; During Communism: miner/ **Children**: Aged 18/ Aged 16; wishes to go to Italy.

7: **Man**: Aged 41; Farmer/Woman: Aged 37; Housewife; During Communism: fishing-factory in Italy /**Children**: Aged 15: Does not do anything, does not wish to emigrate.

8: **Woman**: Aged 38; Housewife; During Communism: a cook / **Man**: Aged 50; Business in a house; During Communism: a military mechanic. He is orthodox/ **Children**: Aged 17, Aged 15 and Aged 14; Students.

9: **Man**: Aged 36; Road builder during 7 years in Italy. He went first alone and after followed by his wife; During Communism: he used to be a loader in Porto Romano. / **Woman**: housewife.

10: **Woman**: Aged 34; Has worked for 4 years in a furniture factory in Pisa, Italy/ **Man**: Aged 35; Has been working for 4 years in Pisa, Italy, in a nail factory; During Communism: he was a funereal sculptor. / **Children**: Aged 10.

11: **Woman**: Aged 32; Housewife in Durrës/ **Man**: Aged 35; Has been working for 2 years in building in Brescia, Italy/ Children: Aged 15, Aged 13 and Aged 7; Students.

12: **Woman**: Aged 30; Housewife; pregnant (5 months)/ **Man**: Aged 30; Fisherman in Porto Romano.

13: **Man**: Aged 25; Waiter. / **Woman**: Aged 22; Worker in cosmetic factory (Spitalle, Durrës).

Figure 4.4
Structure of a Home in Durrës

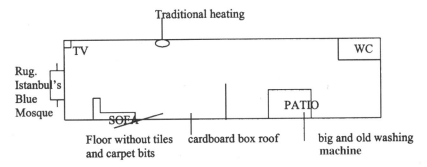

could not get regular work. The police finally repatriated the entire family to Kosovo. I suppose he must have requested asylum as a Kosovar, the common ploy used by Albanians in the UK. Since the father saw that there were more job opportunities in Kosovo than in Albania, he stayed there to work for a while repairing cars, assisted by his son. When they returned to Albania, they bought a very small house from Nora in Porto Romano. The children do not go to school because they do not know how to write in Albanian, and because they consider that school is not safe for a girl. The boy says it is because other boys might bother her. The subject of safety is very important to them. Six months ago, the father returned to England, though he is currently unemployed, and their mother works in a bakery. The skin on the girl's hands is in shreds from doing domestic work. The children explained that when they returned to Albania, it seemed like the end of the world to them; it was a terrible shock. The youngest daughter was born in England and her mother asked me if she had the right to British nationality, although it seems she is not registered anywhere. They think their daughter might be able to return one day to England and live there. For these people, being repatriated to a place where there are no occupational prospects was a terrible misfortune.

Clara's Story: Her youth trapped in a factory. Doriana is Nora's sister-in-law. She turned up one day at Nora's, accompanied by her two daughters, Clara, who is seventeen, and Claudia. Doriana and Claudia work in the plastics factory. Clara and her family situation meet all the specifications I have been looking for to examine the combination of strategies in a border location: emigration to border countries (Greece and Italy), internal migration, female labor in the Italian-owned textile workshops, and a candidate for emigration to Italy with some knowledge of the prostitution trafficking networks. As far as emigration is concerned, finding the combination of Italy and Greece in one single family is quite common. In this sense, further research would be needed in order to better articulate the existence of this binomial feature of migratory strategies inside the nuclear family. It is particularly interesting that this is also reflected in Moroccan migration, shaping a familiar double destination in European geographies. I wonder why the family cannot carry out the full strategy in one single destination, but it is clear that all of this depends on documents related to migration policies, the contacts available, and the proximity or distance with the kin family member.

For many years, Clara's father worked as a farmer in Greek agriculture, while the rest of the family remained in Albania. Clara and her mother decided that that situation could not go on forever, and that they should all go to live in Greece. However, her father always came up with excuses and tried to get the idea out of their heads. Finally, their mother managed to find enough money to go over, thanks to her husband's brothers. They traveled undocumented to Greece, but when they arrived, they discovered that her father had a Greek wife. They then spent two very difficult years, because her mother refused to leave since she thought her role was to stay next to her husband. In any case, she had married him under duress, and had not wanted to. She complains about her father since he has never behaved like one. Meanwhile in Greece, Clara lived with her twenty-four-year-old sister, who is married to an Albanian with whom she has a two-year-old daughter. Apparently the husband beat her, and Clara could not cope with seeing her sister living in such conditions in Greece. However, her sister has not left her husband because she sees the situation as being normal. In the end, they decided to return to Albania and moved to the city of Korçë. From the age of twelve to fourteen, Clara lived in Korinthos, Greece, with her mother. Both of them say it is very beautiful, although they did not have time to look around it much.

A short while after she returned, Clara began work in the textile workshop. Her mother has now separated from her father, but she has not made the news public because it would be frowned upon. Her father does not send them any money, and as a result all three remaining family members in Albania have to work. Clara gives most of her wages to her mother and keeps only a small part for herself. When she first began working at the sweatshop, she did not even know how to sew.

Clara also explained that it was her uncle who told her she had to get married and looked for a husband for her. At first, she agreed to this idea and was engaged to a man for six months. She told the fiancé that her dream was to go to Italy and he promised her they would go together one day. She often had doubts about that because she had heard of the cases of boyfriends forcing their partners to work as prostitutes in Italy. Finally, she left him, explaining that she did not feel anything for him. Apparently he is now in prison, but she did not explain why he had been convicted.

Clara views Albania as a beautiful country, though it has been neglected and is now in need of a strong state. Many interlocutors repeated this description; and, in fact, Albania is much prettier than foreigners realize. Yet many people (and especially expatriates) also reiterate the perceived lack of a state, the anarchic state of the country, and the image of a lawless place. Clara also speaks of a need for emancipation and freedom, and strongly condemns the situation of women in the country. She thinks she will eventually find the freedom she is searching for in Italy, and she confesses that this is her real dream. She criticizes the behavior of Albanian men. Thus, the best way of summing up Clara´s arguments is that she is clearly a candidate for emigration. It should be noted here that one type of women's emigration is explicitly marked by the women's emancipation project.

Clara is now working in an Italian sweatshop, where around 200 people work manufacturing clothes. Clara mentioned all the negative aspects of her job, above all the strain on her eyesight, though she thinks it is less difficult than working in the plastics factory. Furthermore, with time she is now used to it because she has worked there since she was fifteen. Clara explained that the place pays overtime, but she complains that nobody can refuse to work extra hours. She informs us that girls under sixteen are also recruited to work in the factory. For her, the advantage of this job is that for two hours every day there is a doctor present who, if she deems it necessary, can send the worker to the hospital. They have hardly any holidays over Christmas, and the duration of the summer holidays always depends on the factory orders. When we broached the subject of the previous year's restructuring of the factory, she said that this restructuring depended on the function of the production line and not on the individual workers.

Diana is Clara's friend, a girl from the north of the country who has only been working in the factory for two years. In spite of being an excellent student, she was forced to leave school at fourteen, as was Clara. Diana's father works as a builder, and she says that it is difficult to find any other kind of work. Her mother, who is forty, is ill. She has a married sister with a young daughter whose husband has been working as a mechanic in Italy for the last year. In the meantime, the sister lives in her in-laws' house because tradition dictates that a wife has to live with the husband's family. Diana also has two small brothers. I believe that, in this case, the youngest always has to work because the father's wages do not cover all their needs.

Clara and Diana maintain that their lives are limited to the daily trips from home to the factory and back again. Clara explains this is the situation of the factory girls who lead dull lives and never go out together because there is always some relative or other they have to visit. According to her, every one of them follows the same routine, and they feel depressed to be stuck in such a dead-end situation. They expect a similar future: to work at the factory until they can get married. Garment employment serves as a waiting period, as a shock absorber to the marriage market for young people. Diana's parents do not let her visit Clara's house; she does not know why, although Diana suggests that it could be because there are all women at Clara's house, and not having a man in the house is frowned upon.

On one of our walks, Clara and Diana informed me that for the first time they had been offered a work contract at the factory. The management had tried to force them to sign their contracts, but the girls refused because they wanted to read them first. The modifications in the contract stipulated that on Saturdays they would have to work for eight hours instead of five, and they must be prepared to work on Sundays when it is deemed necessary, depending on the orders coming in from Italy. The great dependence of these factories on outside orders is surprising. In general terms, the new contract ensures a greater dependency on work ordered by external purchasers. Clara and Diana are absolutely sick of so many conditions, and they feel unsatisfied and unmotivated because they do not believe that a negotiating space exists for them to obtain better working conditions.

Dora's case: The gypsy girl who dreams of Greece. Dora, a fourteen-year-old gypsy girl, is the clearest example of this complicated circle involving scarcity, child labor, begging, and migration. When I went to Dora's house in Kinostudio (Tirana), the first thing I saw was that the entrance was comprised of chunks of iron and a recycled door. After two months I saw that they had torn down the room they lived in and built another on the other side of the patio, which is now much more cheerful. It is constructed of a gray brick that gives it a more elegant appearance. However, there are still gaps between the ceiling and walls, but at least it has a splendid view of the river and the Dajti mountain.

We were welcomed by the fifty-year-old mother, whose hands looked as if she had been working on the land. Her grandchildren, two boys aged three and six, also live with her. The house consists of one single, shack-type room, in which the father was currently sleeping. When he woke up, he explained that he suffered from heart problems and needed to get better. However, his meager pension from the Albanian army did not provide him with enough to do so. He then told an incredible story in his stumbling Italian. He left Albania in 1947 for a period of eight years, and traveled to Italy (to Naples and Turin, among other towns). He remembers Naples at that time as being in terrible condition. It appears he worked for the Albanian *segurimi* (the former communist state police), and one of his tasks was to check up on an Albanian who had married an Italian woman. Elvis (the social worker) added that during this period, the regime jailed people just for leaving the country. He also added that Dora's father may have been imprisoned during the Hoxha period. The mother told us that during the communist period she used to clean the streets of Tirana on the nightshift. With the fall of communism, they decided to sell the house on the Dajti mountain to come down to Tirana. At first they wanted to swap it with someone, but they thought it would be too complicated. The mother said that during communism they lived better because at least everybody had a job.

This couple has four children. One of the daughters is divorced with three children, two live in the household, and the third, a boy, lives with his father.

Another of her sons is twenty and is a heroin addict. He steals the small amount of money they have to buy heroin, and even stole the television set to sell it. The mother tells us that she is going to report him to the police because she thinks it would be better if he is under control than leading such an uncontrolled life. Another of her daughters is sixteen.

The most surprising case in the family is fourteen-year-old Dora. She was a street child who used to clean car windshields at the traffic lights by the Pyramid, in the center of Tirana. Créche International took her in for several months, where she learned to read. However, she can no longer continue there because there are no places available, so now she just wants to work or else to go to Greece. She is constantly asking Elvis for work. Between the two of us, we tried to encourage her to be patient, because she is still too young to work. Her mother stated that she, too, is unemployed and wants to find a job. I asked Elvis why she could not work as a cleaner and he said it is because of discrimination against the Roma. Dora wants to go to Greece and also has a friend with the same idea in mind; she later tells us there is the chance they could go to Greece accompanied by a man.

In our second visit to Dora's house, she was out, as she had gone to work again at the traffic lights by the Pyramid in the city center. Today the Ireland-Albania match is being played, so there will be a lot of traffic, and we imagine she will have a lot of customers. Thus, Dora broke her promise to Elvis not to go back on the street to wash windshields. Her mother told me Dora was forced to go because her heroin addict son had stolen her jacket. We went to the city center, but once we found her, Dora did not tell us this part of the story, only her side of it, and that they needed the money.

On a third visit, Dora explained that it was five days since she had last been to the traffic lights, because the family had finally received some money from her sister in Greece. In addition, the sister is coming home next September for the first time in five years. The jumper Dora was wearing was also a present from her sister Afroditi, which is the Greek name she now uses in Greece. Albanian children in Greek streets are normally registered under false Greek-sounding names, on the advice of their bosses and institutions. Elvis told me that everyone takes a Greek name there, and that it is one of the forms of assimilation used by Albanians in Greece.

Placing Borders, Circuits, and Control

This second part has framed the conceptual and empirical development of border cities in order to find a possible border-city model. It was a theoretical as well as an ethnographic search—through *petit* narratives—to find elements of the border city, in which I reviewed the concept of the global, the border city, and the patchwork economy, starting with the general conditions of "the global," for example, as having an impact on the conditions of the migratory departure.

This was followed by a look at how the border city has not only border features but also creates peculiar conditions to examine the global-local, for example, in the way the informal economy serves as a pooling tool in border economies.

Industrial delocalization seems to have found in Tangier and Durrës a suitable field, especially in the way it benefits from a cheap labor force—in Tangier illiterate women—and in general, in both places, its use of the internal female migration. Industrial delocalization in these border cities strongly reproduces the typical gender values translated into the need for low status jobs.

On the patchwork economy. The premeditated obstinacy of my work on the patchwork economy found its direct point of reference in the work of Kibria (1993). Translating it into my fieldwork I understood the patchwork strategy as a response, as an answer, as a tool that conveys the unplanned quality of the household living under globally defined impacts. The patchwork strategy is not so much a concept as it is a strategical tool, the pooling of resources, by tackling the type of resources, that is, the different assets. It is through them that I have tried to make clear the different assets contributed by family member´s contributions. This was possible by bearing in mind the determining influence of the familist ideology.

Migration strategies are part of these assets, for example in organizing transnational reciprocity networks in European extended families, like Moroccan families settling in Spain. This happens when there is also a process of nuclearization of the family and feminization of migration flows. Reciprocity networks do become strengthened by passing over the nuclear family, for example, in organizing family networks in internal migration. We have seen how the strategy of ex-locality in rural Albania (Fuga 2000: 20) responds to a family project that links one member in the north of the country, one member in Tirana´s outskirsts, and another member abroad; together they do find a way of building a home in the growing outskirts of urban Albania. Hence, international migration becomes meaningful when one considers that it is the step to enable a longer-term project, such as being the first investment for a family project. Whereas in Morocco people become somewhat dependent on migration policies that add pressures to the wedding rhythms; even religious practices then become embedded in the migration policies guidelines.

Irregular migration is also a part of these assets, by combining informality and irregularity as acts of resistance in places where people seem to be living a certain kind of imprisonment, such as youngsters in Tangier. Border smuggling is another part of these assets, which can be seen, for example, in the importing of European brand products. Informalities, too, are part of these assets, for example, in textile factory work.

The so-called factory-emigration hypothesis has been in both ethnographies a complex way to try to verify household strategies. Grasping the factory-emigration hypothesis pretended to be the culmination of such strategies. There are several aspects to the problem of understanding how the hypothesis of factory-emigration works, though it is centered around the question of whether there is a coincidence between families who have daughters in factories and simultaneously have emigrant members abroad.

And it is true for the Durrës ethnography: there definitely are cases where both conditions occur at the same time, and I even know of working mothers and daughters who have a husband in Italy. Different possibilities must be discussed to explain this situation: it may result from the fact that the man does not have a good job in Italy, or has no documents, and as a consequence the women have to continue working. One case in point is Clara and other workers, as she and her sisters tell us that even though they are dreaming about marrying an Italian they have to carry on at the factories. This case met all the idiosyncrasies I had looked to find in household strategies in a border location: emigration to border countries (Greece and Italy), internal migration, feminization of labor in the Italian-owned textile workshops, a candidate for emigration to Italy and some knowledge of the prostitution trafficking networks. Under this situation, Clara feels unmotivated in her work and thinks, like the rest of her co-workers that they totally lack negotiating power.

Ultimately, what emerges with respect to the family is the hypothesis that we have been searching for from the beginning of this ethnography, one that we have not succeeded in refining. We are not at all sure whether there is a correspondence between the families of the women working in the factories and those families with emigrants abroad. We do not have enough cases to be able to corroborate this. Therefore, we are lacking in reliable data.

It can be also said that in Morocco there is also little evidence for this correspondence and that in Albania when such matches occur, they do so in the heart of the external family, and that both strategies tend to coincide less in the same nuclear environment. When comparing data on female work in Morocco and Spain, it was interesting to see that Moroccan women remain more active in the labor market, even after they have acquired family commitments (children). This explains how extended family commitments can still be helpful to the women there, making a difference in the care responsibilities on one side or the other of the Mediterranean.

On migration issues in borders. The border city and its relation to the dynamics of internal-external migration has enabled me to point out the migration features in both ethnographies. In this sense, remittances seem to be the underlying structure in those dynamics, for example, explaining how foreign remittances help families building a house in the internal migration settlement in Durrës. It also translates as the underlying project of families who move to Tangier to be able to combine the project with international migration or to make the exit abroad easier. It also explains the settlement of people from the south in border villages where people can find an easier way to establish a transborder business.

Moroccan emigration abroad is a result of a long period of international migrations that do conform now to stable phases, while Albanian emigration is still young and has resulted from an "explosion effect."

Moroccan emigration abroad has diversified destinations towards Southern Europe (Spain and Italy) and at the same time has become more transeuropean, while Albanian emigration uses neighboring countries as strong references and has just now started to diversify towards Northern Europe. In both places, it is common to find families that combine diverse destinations.

Moroccan emigration abroad uses settled communities as a context in which to develop reciprocity networks, while Albanian emigration uses new contexts where there is no colony. In both places, the invitation from a family member who is already documented is the key to understanding chain migrations.

For both types of migrations, sending labor force serves as a gateway to labor flexibility in Southern Europe. However, culturally speaking, a stronger strategy of assimilation is presented by the Albanians abroad in comparison with Moroccans. Assimilation strategies are stronger, in fact, as a result of Albanians' intentions to avoid the criminalized stereotypes, which are placed more often on them than on the Moroccans. Furthermore, emigrants abroad do follow diverse forms of identification; in the case of Albania they are in particular attached to the idea of the Albanian people, whereas in the case of Morocco they are primarily based on an identification with "Muslim Morocco."

Identifying people in circuits. The different circuits that exist within these strategic places cities are intensely bounded places with Southern Europe, generating flows of capital as well as migration flows. In this second and last part of the book, by going from theoretical research to empirical research, we have managed to create a model of understanding for the different circuits that exist within these border cities. The definition of circuits will be graphically shown in the last part of the conclusion (see the different figures as well as their corresponding explanations).

We have identified the circuits through their different natures: textile manufacturing (with its consequently high rate of female workers), the south-north delocalization of begging (with its consequent trafficking in children, especially Roma), the delocalization of prostitution (and internationalization of sexual services). In this second circuit it is intriguing to see how the phenomenon of trafficking relates in a complex fashion with traditional family values. A doublethink strategy could be assumed here for a principle of double honor, which implies a model of honor for the public space and another for the private sphere (Ditchev 1996).

Finally, we have introduced the idea of social vulnerability in such places, in other words, identifying how capital and human mobility circuits have a specific impact on certain social groups in particular geographies. We have mainly outlined the situation of women and minors, not to stigmatize the weakest, but because in these border zones it becomes very clear that such people are the hardest hit by socioeconomic changes related to border restrictions.

Mediterranean youth. Just as in Tangier, the young men working in NGOs in Albania are the ones who are about to go or who have already gone abroad. It is precisely with these perspectives of the interrelation between labor-migration projects and living projects that youngsters from these eastern and western borders of the Mediterranean fully converge.

Elvis is fed up and unmotivated by his work, which is why he has a negative view of Albanians. He lists the country's attractions: it has rivers, mountains, the sea…it has everything, but the trouble is the people. Elvis reckons that this is a very difficult period for Albanians, given the fact that they are living through such "wild capitalism." He makes the distinction between conditions in his own job and those of groups of foreigners who come to work here. He argues that foreigners generally come to Albania with a temporary project and an idealistic idea of what it means to work in the country. He also complains about ex-pats, because they always criticize the Albanians' poor working habits.

In general, from what I have been able to discern, it is significant to understand the concept of work, and the value this has in the enormous transformations Albanian people are going through. On the one side, there are those whose work rhythm is too slow, and on the other, those who work unceasingly. I have seen this type of intensive work on several occasions. In terms of wages, the waiters in Tirana and Durrës, for instance, earn a hundred dollars a month, while the cost of living is very high. Neighboring countries such as Italy and Greece offer wages that are absolutely incomparable to Albania's, and a lifestyle that offers the younger generations wider opportunities for the future, both short term and long term. Furthermore, the youth live their everyday lives embedded in the migration realities, those of their relatives and friends for whom mobility is a way of life.

Notes

1. The wilaya is a regional entity corresponding to a delegation of the central government.
2. However, it is difficult to know to what extent the different communities where really mixed, as it does not seem the case through reading Vázquez's novel *La vida perra de Juanita Narboni*. It relates the story of a woman born in Tangier of a false English father from Gibraltar and an Andalusian mother, involved in the Sefardi community (Jewish Spanish speakers). The context is her life in a no man's land, the Tangier of the international zone, where people from Polish, French, and Andalusian backgrounds seemed to have a common lifestyle different from the Moroccan Muslims, being portrayed only as servants.
3. The Sultan of Morocco retained his power over Muslims and Jews within the population of Tangier, and his representative in the city was the *Mendoub*.

4. It is a treaty between Morocco and Spain, "Tratado de Amistad, Buena Vecindad y Cooperación entre España y Marruecos" (4 July 1991), which makes it possible.
5. For instance, to discover, paradoxically enough, that female emigration of Moroccans to Europe can result in an ambivalent situation, often combining on the one hand, a emancipatory strategy for some women (Ribas-Mateos 2001b), as well as a cloistered situation for others, I refer here to the situation of those women who stay in European homes isolated from the traditional women's network they used to enjoy in their zones of origin.
6. A simple wooden boat used by fishermen. This colloquial Spanish word has been absorbed into the Moroccan dialect.
7. Data showing the population of Tangier depending on birthplace provide us with the following results: Tangier (77.58 percent), other towns (22.42 percent). Considering the outside geographic origin: Tetouan (16.7 percent), Larache (11.7 percent), other (9.7 percent), rural areas from Tangier (5.4 percent), Chaouen (5.2 percent), Fes (5.1 percent), Hoceima (4.8 percent), Nador (4.5 percent), Casablanca (4.5 percent), Ksar Kbir (4.4 percent), Rabat (2.9 percent), Agadir (2.9 percent), Asilah (2.8 percent), Meknes (2.4 percent), Sahara (1.8 percent), Ouazzane (1.3 percent), Sidi Kacem (1.1 percent), Europe (1 percent) (Plan d'aménagement de la Commune Urbaine de Tanger, Rapport enqûete ménages, Cabinet d'Architecture et d'Urbanisme, January 1999).
8. Data showing reasons to immigrate to the city of Tangier provide us with the following results: family (62.87 percent), work (33.21 percent), other (2.19 percent), lack of social infrastructure (0.75 percent), poverty (0.50 percent), and studies (0.48 percent) (Plan d'aménagement de la Commune Urbaine de Tanger, Rapport enqûete ménages, Cabinet d'Architecture et d'Urbanisme, January 1999).
9. The concept of *hawma* does not exactly correspond to the notion of an administrative neighborhood, it has a relational sense more than an administrative one. In the north of the country, *hawma* is used while the rest of the country uses the term of *darb*, adding a "b" to the home, *dar*.
10. Al Sayrafi lives in Tangier. He has worked with a taxi driver in Fndek, Castillejos, transporting smuggled goods from Fndek to Tangier and on to all the regions in Morocco. He explained various aspects of smuggling to me: the route, the type of goods, the rules at the checkpoints (taxes, police), the seasonal changes, and the changes through the years.
11. Minor is here conceptualized according to the Convention of Children´s Rights, where a minor's age is between 0 and 18 years. However, in Morocco—which has also ratified the convention—they refer to different ages according to: age to marriage (18), right to vote (21), penal responsibility (16), right to work (15). Adult age is 20 years old, according to article 137 of the Mudawana (family law).
12. The increase of single parenthood in most of the Western world has opened up the debate on the new family formations, its sociological conceptualization as well as its relation to welfare benefits and market wages. Among the new indicators, one can find the increase of single parenthood independent of marital and child status. Single (lone) motherhood statistics in most of the Western world reveal the decline of the married mother and a wide typology of options concerning the increasing lone motherhood household.

    A considerable part of U.S. and European literature in particular has evolved concerning the association between the incidence of lone female headship and family with children and welfare policy. In most countries of the world a child is a person below the age of 18, and a single mother is one whose marital status is either never married or previously married (i.e., divorced, repudiated, separated or widowed).

This includes women who may be cohabiting. In some cultures the term "single mother" is often negatively stereotyped, thus, some areas of sociological work tend to use the term "lone mother." The lone mother term stresses parenthood status rather than marital status—in short, this term specifically responds to the type of "single parent family headed by a woman."

13. I would like to thank Gilles de Rapper for this comment.

14. *Tcham* is how they refer to the Arvanites from Greece. However, not all Arvanites are called Tcham. Tchams live or used to live in present-day Thesprotia and in Albania, south of the river Pavla (Konispol and some villages around it). Of those, only Christians are likely to be identified with Arvanites, but not Muslims.

15. One of the immediate objects of the program for 2001 was to develop an Integrated Border Management Strategy, including training of the border control staff for the identification of falsified documents, in particular staff operating at the Tirana International Airport and at the main seaports. The objective of the budget for the Cards program in Albania responds to the training of the Ministry of Public Order and to renovating a reception center as making specific provision for the Albanian program for Asylum and Migration.

16. This has been referred to, for example, in an article concerning the recent experience of rural industrial growth occurring in Peonia, near Salonica, a garment case that exemplifies the form that flexible specialization can take in the European periphery. However, the authors note, "the relocation of production to nearby sources of cheap and adaptable labour is only one of the challenges confronting Peonia. Further dangers are involved in the return of tens of thousands of migrants from the former socialist countries, particularly Albania and Poland...the employment of legal and illegal newcomers in the industry seems to have been another means of driving down production costs" (Simmons and Kalantaridis 1994: 669).

17. The Code of Leke Dukajini was a body of oral customary laws by which the northern clans of Albania were ruled from about the fifteenth to the beginning of the twentieth century, affecting people's rights and obligations. In no other part of the world were people to be found with the sign of death revenge on their clothing. The reality of the north of the country as seen through Kadaré's novel "Broken April" is represented through the life of the mountaineer, who becomes valued or undervalued depending on his relation with death (Kadaré 2001:74). According to this law, the death of a man must be avenged in blood (*gjak/marrje*) by a male family member. Death debits among families and clans could be extended through generations.

Following the very same novel, the Rrafsh is shown as the only region of Europe that in spite of forming part of a modern state and not being a region "of primitive tribes" has overlooked laws, police, judges, in short the whole state machinery. It has rejected them in order to substitute their own moral laws, which obliged foreign administrations and then the independent the Albanian state to recognize them, to leave the Rrash, nearly half of the kingdom, out of its control (idem. 75). Today, after the impasse of communism, the *kanun* has in a way been reborn, with a new style in the north of the country as well as in the big urban peripheries.

18. The three main elements are: lindane, hexachlorocyclohexane (HCH), and CR YI2. Lindane was prohibited in Austria in 1998 by a European decision, but there are vast quantities in Porto Romano. There are also 10 tons of sodium dichromate and 20,000 tons of CrVI products.

19. By this clanic structure they refer to the traditional home base of the extended family from mountainous areas, which contains a common origin, name, and social status in the area in question. They relate in a system of family cooperation formed by diverse married couples. Within this patrilocal and strictly gendered tradition male descen-

dents are highly valued as giving strength to the family, in properties, labor force, social status.

20. De Rapper does not that religion is not important, rather that it is central for the representation of the local society concerned. When it comes to the whole nation, the North-South division becomes central, but it often functions the same way as the Muslim-Christian division does.

21. *Scafista* comes from *scafa*, boat in Italian, and from *scafo*, a boat hull, since they are those who pilot the boats.

22. Western Union is the main world service agency for monetary transfer. It is divided into two sections: North American section: (Canada and the United States), and the international section: (Western Europe and South-Eastern Europe).

23. "Façonnier" is understood by intervieews to mean a company specialized in subcontracting their customers' work.

24. Gianpietro was working with the Arcobaleno Mission in 1998, when a Kosovar camp was established in Vlorë.

25. The anti-trafficking program covers the following number of villages in the following districts of Durrës: Shijak 4, Mamimas 7, Sukth 6, Manez 8, Xhafzotjaj 8, Katunidiri 7.

26. De Rapper through his research in the border village of Bilisht, in southern Albania, gives a full account of the centrality of the family: "If the situation of a family member improves, all the rest have to take advantage of it. In the old times it could have been extended until third cousins" (De Rapper: 1998).

Conclusion: The Global in One Sea

Looking for a Space

This final chapter also represents a final period of analysis focused on Mediterranean migration. Years ago, my interest was centered on Morocco, especially on Moroccan migration towards Spain. However, the difficulty in finding funding caused me to transfer my focus to Mediterranean Europe. After a number of years, my interest in border cities of Southern Europe offered the possibility of returning to Morocco, which extended my research to my last trip covered in this volume, the Albanian site. The theme finale moved me to search out a space where there were substantial unresolved demands concerning the space of the Mediterranean in contemporary social sciences.

The itinerary of the book follows the trip itself. Therefore, I combine in this conclusion a fusion of my own research trips in conjunction with the theoretical questions. It passes from the descriptive phase of the first part and the development of the ethnographies in the second part, to a final question which requires more profound reflection: what do all those descriptions, evaluation, and interpretation of cases mean for the analysis of a Mediterranean space?

The answer is that they present two sides of the same coin, therefore linking in a circular manner with the introduction. Firstly, in both sections we see how the city emerges as a strategic explanatory site, through the importance of large cities of the Northern, Southern and Eastern Mediterranean. The study of the city has used the nation-state context but has not assumed that it is coterminous with it. Nevertheless, the state holds a key role in defining sharp border controls and managing the welfare state restructuring, all of which shows that the notion of space has become central for the volume. The basic idea underlying it can at least be depicted as two-fold in a territorialized space (each one of the case studies) and a deterritorialized one, related to the intrinsic movements driven by neo-liberal globalization in the Mediterranean Sea. Those spaces will be fully displayed through different levels of analysis in the final two sections. Secondly, we also find a continuum of deconstruction tendencies in both parts of the book: the first part set on the conditions that have promoted the demand for migrant labor in Southern European cities in the shift to a service economy; the second part, on the conditions that have promoted informalization in the demand for manufacturing labor at European borders.

Thirdly, in both parts we have underlined the role of the family as the *axis mundi* of migration: the family's world simultaneously reveals the variations in migratory practices and the constrictions for family reunion policies in the host countries. The family reveals itself as the critical institution where all of these changes and re-adaptations can be seen, not only through the continuity of old migratory practices but also by challenging the introduction of new forms. It is through them that we can also understand the articulation of family reunion processes, patterns of welfare mix variations, and the local response of the household strategy. As Perulli notes it, "the subsequent development of the question of the family in post-welfare societies is part of the renewed and general interest in self-help and volunteer networks, often the response to welfare crises" (Perulli 1992: 34).

Let us consider here two interesting examples concerning the family changes directly. First, particular roles for migrant women have recently emerged from the household needs in Southern Europe or else from the increasing recruitment of a female work force in factories located in border cities. These situations illustrate the complex color of the global care chain. Secondly, unaccompanied minors in international migrations provide us with another example. Minors are to be found trapped between the contradictions of North-South borders as well between the contradictions of the developmentalist states and those of European welfare systems.

In contemporary Southern Europe, the normative family model tends to refer to a nuclear family structure based on two children, where half reluctantly use the foreign labor force for the care of the family. In border cities, the model is based on the nuclear family embedded in horizontally extended family relations, where half reluctantly send the female labor force to factories and to Europe. The scenario is that of a peripheral economy dependent on EU outproduction and a household economy left to find alternative circuits of international migration. For instance, this is the situation in Albanian postindustrial cities that marks paradoxical spaces in the transition to capitalism.

On the European side of the Mediterranean, such one-sided reciprocal arrangements, whereby one household contributes with work and time to ensure the survival of the other, lead to the consolidation of the reproduction pattern of the receiver rather than the provider. The latter is forced by its weak bargaining power in the labor market and the host society to make its own household and care arrangements. Ironically, this situation can be replicated in the country of origin where migrants' children and elderly relatives may, in turn, be looked after by paid or unpaid local care-givers, giving rise to a complex global care chain.

However, the true interdependent relation between the first part and second part of the book is the asymmetrical nature of the relationship between receiver societies and provider societies, which is based on two general perspectives. This is by no means new, but it is a symptom of continuity. On the one hand, the connection is related to the relevance of each of the selected cases in the context of the Mediterranean space. Indeed, each of them has something to say about the Western Mediterranean today, especially concerning the different interpretations about the region. Yet on the other hand, it is also related to the fractures of globalization in those particular spaces, namely, the gaps in the welfare system on one side of the Mediterranean and, the contradiction of border cities on the other.

Mediterranean differences and unity must here be considered together. The reference to an area of circulation and exchange provides unity. Differences, in the manifestations of conflict, can be attributed today to the global space and the reinforcement of borders. It is only in this sense that this idea of the Mediterranean can be thought of as a paradigmatic case of international migration in the age of globalization, even though this is an inherent feature of general neo-liberal globalization trends.

The study of this critical site is not that of a unique place, which was common to classical sociological methods. The extended fieldwork uses seven cases in the first part of the book and two in the second: case studies through interviews and two border ethnographies provide descriptions of the ground transformations. What all those places show is that they all can be wrapped up in a general theoretical category of neo-liberal restructuring. Moreover, the richness of the empirical work sets a serious question mark against the complexity of surveys in such varied places. This seems to be the strongest point of such an over ambitious piece of research. The book entails dealing with a vast amount of evidence that had to be constantly disaggregated in order to capture the different analytical dimensions; it often happened through the ethnographic method implied. A single, but striking example of such complexity can be seen, for example, when describing the area of Porto Romano in Durrës. It is too arduous to take into account the narrative of the family, the perception of the family members about their own history and their own position, without making the effort of a constant rereading.

A number of issues arise from this conclusion. After considering the research space of the Mediterranean, I suggest a model for other scholars who might be interested in working with it. In order to clear the ground I first comment on the conclusions related to globalization and afterward to the role of international migration. Finally, I present the conceptual model by using a combination of figures and explanations of those figures: operationalizing a new space in Southern Europe and operationalizing a new space in border cities.

In the Age of Globalization

Certainly, globalization is, from my point of view, one of the most interesting debates in the social sciences today, and the young bibliography on it provided the general framework in which to set our debate for this book. Changes related to globalization and scale (especially the regional and subnational, notably cities and regions) made me think about the challenges of theoretical and methodological questions in order to find the empirical way in which strategic economic and political processes territorialize in peripheral Europe and in its southern borders, zones separated by semi-closed borders with a lightly functional porosity.

One of my starting points was to criticize the opinions of those who believe that the consequences of globalization are limited to a rhetorical construction; or of those who insist that the concept of globalization is empty and incapable of withstanding even a merely historical perspective; or those who believe that opening up the globalization debate is simply joining the bandwagon of fashionably bland scientific concepts (see the general debate in Held and McGrew 2000 and Ribas-Mateos 2002a). New goals in research methodology naturally lead to new forms of research, awakening our curiosity regarding new empirical fields that attempt to confirm which social forms are or are not being adopted.

I knew that historically there had been long cross-border economic processes—flows of capital, labor, goods, raw materials, and tourists that shaped the relational geography of the Mediterranean. However, this has changed dramatically as a result of privatization, deregulation, digitalization, the opening up of national economies to foreign firms, and the growing participation of national economic actors in global markets. Now, labor costs and economies of scale make an international division of labor cost-effective. One of the aspects of the mobility of capital is the transnationalization in ownership, not only through foreign direct investment but also through mergers, acquisitions, and joint ventures, which raises anew the issue of the nationality of capital (Sassen 2001: 23). Through this reading and by following in part the way Sassen articulates the global city, I conceptually framed my border cities. It is worth highlighting how I previously considered the place-ness of the global city as a crucial theoretical and methodological issue.

When focusing on economic globalization I have put the accent on the global commodity chain framework. By emphasizing the relation of the foreign producers and the local labor force I have tried to bridge the global-local divide by locating it in the space of female factory workers and their strategies at the household level. Globalization was firstly conceived as the freedom of foreign investments. This was empirically translated into free trade in relation to textile commodities. I ended up considering the manufacturing of clothing as one of the clearest examples of international subcontracting, which, in the ethnography, was later translated into appealing to the conditions of intensive low-skilled female work, low skilled and geographical separation. In the case of the EU, the geographical pair corresponds to North African and Eastern European countries.

Secondly, globalization also means limiting circulation as well as repressing clandestine practices in border zones in an era of zero immigration policies, when labor continues to be controlled and often penalized for mobility, in particular, the restriction to certain types of labor mobility, the limitation to mobility of non-skilled workers. Yet, within structural restrictions, people find ways to be able to buy the right to migrate, facing not only a physical border in the Mediterranean Sea but also a technological one—the one articulated by databases controlling the movement of people.

Globalization also enhances segregation as we have seen through the matching of space, welfare, and racism in Southern European cities. Degraded jobs on the labor market correspond to degraded housing: Omonia in Athens, Porta Palazzo in Turin, Stazione Centrale in Naples. Expressions of racism can be seen as a result of insecurities on the labor market characterized by the hard mismatch between demand and supply. I refer to labor markets with a high degree of precariousness due to an extended underground economy, which makes a migratory project in Southern Europe more profitable. Globalization also enhances segregation through polarization trends led by internal migration in two selected border cities, Durrës and Tangier. Polarization is evidenced by the impoverishment of the urban poor in all cities of the world, seen as a destabilizing force and suffering. This was detected through ethnographic work but it was due to the structural adjustment programs inspired by the World Bank and the International Monetary Fund. When examining this polarization there were also important dynamics related to the connection between internal and international migration.

The Role of Mediterranean Migration

The main goal of this volume is to look for a way to find a space of analysis in which to articulate present and future research into globalization in a certain part of the world, into the meaning of Mediterranean migration, in particular its circulation and its restrictions. Limiting the scope to the western part of the Mediterranean is a proposal to dwarf the scope of future research in the age of globalization.

The Mediterranean is instructive as it sits at the axis of two major fault lines of a global economic and political geography. The first line divides the global North from the global South, which face each other on opposite shores of the Mediterranean "Río Grande" (King 1998). The second is the rejuvenated frontier between East and West, which weaves a tricky course through the Balkans, Adriatic, and eastern Alps, affecting particularly Italy and Greece. Hence, Southern Europe faces two migration pressure routes in the contemporary global geography of international migration: from the South (from North Africa, particularly Morocco, and beyond) and from the East (from Eastern Europe, particularly Albania, and beyond) (King and Ribas-Mateos 2004). There, two general types of border city can be envisaged: introverted and extroverted. The former, from outside to inside of European Schengen, forms places of arrival, mixes and distributes (cities such as Lisbon, Barcelona, the historical migration in Marseilles, and Genoa). The latter, extruded towards, but out of Western Europe (such as Tangier, Tunis, Istanbul), includes cities that gather migrants from the greater hinterlands of the South and East, and launches them on the often short, perilous journey towards "Eldorado" (King 2000). This Mediterranean Eldorado is closer to the image of the U.S. western frontier—frontier as land and journey and not as a border.

Andalzúa's border is "*una herida abierta*" (an open wound) where the Third World grates the first and bleeds (Aldalzúa 1999: 25). The bleeding can also be said to apply to Mediterranean population contrasts in the region, which seem for some to be a curse on Southern Europe, another way of winding between the North-South relations. Two geographical points appeared to me as perfectly clear, the 14 km distance separating the Moroccan coast from Spain and the 70 km distance separating Albania from Italy.

Nevertheless, there could have been many other borders of Europe, such as that of the German-Polish frontier, or that between the Adriatic coast and the Aegean coast. There could have been abandoned borders such as the Portbou/Cerbère border (between Spain and France), or borders that were starting to play a new role in refugee issues such as Sangatte, especially when they talk about Calais as the European Tijuana.

We began with a double face of borders and we end up by discovering multiple border relations, in a way reproducing the division Peraldi indicates: "we are culturally globalized and politically sendentary" (Peraldi 2003:28). Generally, the border seems to be a topologic boundary that separates an exterior and interior territory, where the "confine" is the limit of a space where there is no movement between the exterior and the interior. For some, borders function in co-spatiality, in superposed places like Sebta and Melilla. For others, borders are the paradigm of crossing (historically, the Strait of Gibraltar), material mixing (cultural and others), resistance (against blocking).

For others yet, borders are paradigmatic concentrators of control, namely the new wall of Berlin (which separated the then worlds of the Cold War) that is now placed in contemporary Southern Europe. In practice, problematization is seen through the examples of the difficulties experienced in family visits for people who live in the South and have family who live in the North (Peraldi 2003:26). It is also seen in the right to hospitality, meaning the right of the foreigner, when he/she arrives into somebody else's territory; he/she should not be treated as an enemy, because the perception of foreigner is susceptible to the Kantian reciprocity in hospitality (Peraldi 2003: 26). Finally, borders can be a synthesized mix, combining compassion and brutality, humanitarian and discretionary aspects (Peraldi 2002). Not only have our case studies of border cities served as a valuable scale of research, but even small-scale visions have helped us to see micro-examples of these border relations, as in the villages of Bel Yunech (in Morocco) and Bilisht (in Albania).

Morocco and Albania are seen through European eyes as the key doors for Southern European migration. They are at the front-line, the first to suffer from the closure of Fortress Europe. Furthermore, Albanians and Moroccans are the most criminalized groups in Southern Europe. Morocco and Albania seem to conform to the characteristic role of the European periphery.

Changes in international migration related to feminization, the construction of new routes, higher forms of circulation (both elite circulation and the increase of circulation among lower classes) have been noted in the relation of those places to Southern Europe. Through interviews and ethnography we have seen how migrants often live and plan their lives in transnational circuits (woven by peer-groups, relatives, friends, and neighbors). Therefore, they are living in the same dynamics as those organized by the global flows of capital but using reciprocity scales instead of transnational companies e-mails. Notwithstanding, if population flows of capital have not been at a pace comparable to those capital flows of trade in goods and services (as noted by Tapinos and Delaunay 2000), it may be because migrants are intensively involved in underground practices or in grassroots forms of globalization.

Albanian and Moroccan migrants provide a dual incorporation onto the global as well as onto the European state they seem to choose. And the fact that families are now following global patterns of mobility is a sharp difference for Southern Europe. For example, 63 percent of Moroccans in Valencia have close relatives in European countries whereas in France this figure is only 3 percent (Tarrius 2002a). This opens up the question of how to look at a form of transnationalism that challenges the rupture between emigration conditions and the social integration paradigm, and consequently has posed and still poses new questions to the perspective of international migration.

The borders to Southern Europe were exemplified by two selected cities, where financial movements, capital investment, and transnational companies were highlighted, as well as the actors' social agency (the expressed creativity against the closed doors). This meant looking at how household members generate alternative production and consumption patterns to ensure survival in a time of closed borders; it is through them that we learn how barriers are circumvented. I have demonstrated how repression of border control encourages, paradoxically, the reconstruction and the strengthening of reciprocity networks, where networks are normally articulated through hierarchical solidarities.

The interest in the narratives on borders responded to a particular focus on gray zones or fuzzy borders, in which the national is being transgressed. This is what happens in border zones, cities and spaces where North meets South, an open floor where borderlife is caught in the contradiction between border processes and state ideology, which creates the conditions of crossing. It also challenges a regional scale. This is often a pattern characterized by migration, twin plants, pollution and urban growth, which explains why the U.S.-Mexican border region has become one of the most rapidly urbanizing regions in the world. Whereas in European border zones, these issues put forward many questions regarding national spaces especially on the type of police-state or welfare state, or on the role of the Europeanization process, which means strengthening the role of nation-states[1] towards migration while cities have to deal with the local impact. Therefore, showing the variability between the national and the global was also a common element of both parts of the research.

I began this book by referring to the often constructed monolithic image of the Southern European model. In it, I have given international migration a key interpretative role, playing with changes and continuities at once. It is the sign of changing times. In other words, just when the traditional worker´s unions get weaker, international migrations are intensified. I began by trying to identify the theoretical convergence in Southern European immigration in terms of a triangular context defined by labor market features (especially in the informal sector), the welfare state (especially in the local forms of the welfare state, as a way to test the local capability of globalization in relation to migration), and in the role of family changes. Southern Europe was at that time showing particular cases of problematization regarding comparative research as well as anticipating the hypothesis of a conception of welfare based on the family structure. The book has used short monographs of diverse cities. Notwithstanding, the reader will often need to reference other literature in case he/she is interested in a more precise local background.

The local focus in Southern European cases has helped us to see the weight of local differences when dealing with the global impact, for example, by resetting the Italian North-South division as differences in the port of entry role and type of welfare mix maturity. The division in Spain was set through the differences in the general-specific debate as well as on the role of social racism. In Portugal, the case of Lisbon showed a distinct historical background and the specific impact of poverty and rehousing projects as well as a different participation of the female labor force. In Greece, the specificity of a Balkan context was reflected by regional exclusion, low associationism, and deregulated policies.

The local focus on border cities has provided us with a micro-view of the contradictions of globalization. In spite of different socio-historical contexts the role of migration seems to be similar in Durrës and in Tangier, as well as the definition of circuits in the globalized scenario. And again, family ideology seems to play a key role in all those border city conditions where the earnings of the household are thought to be in constant readaptation to global conditions in a Mediterranean space that means closing, passage, transit or waiting place.

Operationalizing a New Space in Southern Europe

Finally, I will present the theoretical and empirical articulation of the conceptual landscape, portraying a synthetic inside of the book's conceptual inquiry and of the developed applied research. This section gives an account of the eight different figures attached. We can distinguish here the conceptual framework related to the spaces of migration discourses and the spaces of the global-border site.

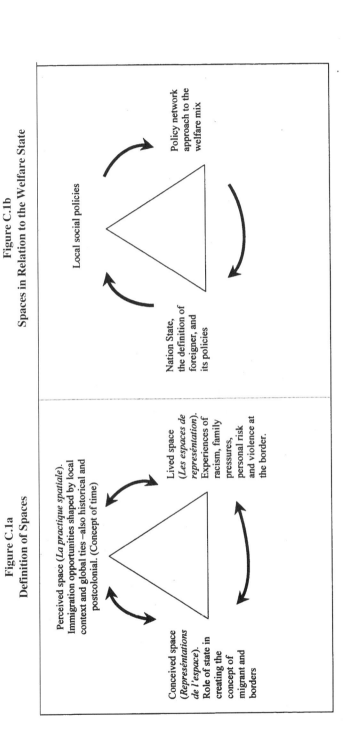

Figure C.1a
Definition of Spaces

Perceived space (*La practique spatiale*).
Immigration opportunities shaped by local
context and global ties –also historical and
postcolonial. (Concept of time)

Lived space
(*Les espaces de
représéntation*).
Experiences of
racism, family
pressures,
personal risk
and violence at
the border.

Conceived space
(*Representations
de l'espace*).
Role of state in
creating the
concept of
migrant and
borders

Figure C.1b
Spaces in Relation to the Welfare State

Local social policies

Policy network
approach to the
welfare mix

Nation State,
the definition of
foreigner, and
its policies

Definition of Spaces (Figure 6.1a)

The most relevant ideas are here related to the creation of analytical and research spaces. In order to frame the different spaces of migration, I use a spatial analysis found in the work of Henri Lefebvre (Lefebvre 1991) to clarify the spatiality of migration through a rich study of everyday life, which can recognize its various components. Through a triplicity of the space, Lefebvre distinguishes the social practices (which take into account production and reproduction), the representation of the space (linked to the relations of production), and the spaces of representation (linked to the complexity of symbolism). It is not an abstract model of the *"perçu-conçu-vécu"* (perceived-conceived-lived) but an understanding of the social space through empirical examples. For our purpose, this thesis can be broken down into three components:

1. *The experienced* (the social practices), which refers to the discourses on migration policies: the framing of immigrant opportunities, documents and employment abroad are all shaped by the local context and global ties (also historical, the legacy/image of colonial and communism being the most significant). Time is taken also as a coordinate: "in the specific case of the study of spatial mobility, these variables (space and time) are not simply reference points that allow us to locate a social event, but are actually intrinsic elements that define its very existence" (Pascual de Sans 2001: 3). In a broad sense, migration can be here understood as the different processes hallmarked by mobilities that people experience in the social organization of space and time.

   Within this perceived space there are also some resonances between the first part and the second part of the book. Take as an example the problems of health as the most exaggerated lack of universal migrants´ rights and the commodification of the body in border areas, constituting an allegory of extreme vulnerability provoked by global capitalism.

2. *The conceived space* (linked to relation of production). We consider different elements of the research, such as the question of scale in migration and the position of the nation-state. I refer to the role of the state in creating the concepts of the "immigrant," the "irregular/undocumented," "the illegal," and the "border." Under this context, I have tried to conceptualize the migrant through an operational definition adaptable to the new mobilities of the circular migration, transnational networks, and return migration as characteristic of human mobility in the Mediterranean region. The state creates the borders, militarizes them, and ties them to the national project, as it also creates the poor and uses the immigrant as workforce.

   We can also consider here the contradiction of immigrant perception: between the crisis and the revision of the welfare state and the re-emergence of the underground economy, which is highly racialized, as we saw in the last section of chapter three. There is a tendency to use migrants in

Southern Europe to lower the cost of production and to raise the organizational flexibility, as also happens with the garment industry in border-cities. However, while services are kept to core economies, the manufacturing of garments is placed at the borders.

3. *Lived spaces* (linked to symbolism). The concepts presented in this volume (both in part 1 and part 2) emerge from the ethnography of everyday life, the family's world. They comprise the experiences of racism, family pressure, obligations and responsibility, personal risk and the violence of the border, and include the use and framing of the body in stimulating the migrant, as well as the identification of the immigrant as "other." Most of the conceptual categories used in the first part regarding globalization, the informal economy, subcontracting, and the feminization of migrant flows and its impact on the family are to be found again in the second part. They link the book to the conceptual side of the border city and become articulated in the lived space of the ethnographies.

Moreover, the welfare mix dynamics have some interesting parallels with the patchwork economy of the border ethnographies; they all function according to causality. In it, through the lived experience of migration, from the everyday life either of the migrant or in the context of the family, the concept of the patchwork economy emerges along with its ties/relations to the welfare mix.

Spaces in Relation to the Welfare State (Figure C.1b)

Migration discourses are defined by the above mentioned perceived, conceived, and lived spaces to be found through discourse repertoires. Spaces can be also defined in relation to the welfare state in order to see the intertwining of local social policies, the nation-state and the definition of the foreigner and the policy network approach to welfare mix . Thus, the project of the first part of the book was to find a specific research topos for the understanding of immigration and welfare mix.

*Spaces in Relation to a Common Southern European Model (*Figure C.2a)

Spaces can also be defined in relation to a Southern European model of immigration, built on restricted-control borders and a lack of social integration policies. A number of key issues arise from this construction (see Figure C.2a). First, the global migration/local labor market (especially the informal sector) contexts address the figure of the migrant as the provider of services. Second, the welfare state conceived as clientelist in a period of neo-liberal restructuring of the state (especially in the local forms of welfare), addresses the figure of the migrant as a user of services. Third, the persistent deficit in the system of social protection stimulates the development of irregular work in two important forms: a peculiar symbiosis between the private and the public sphere (in a privatization tendency) and the role of the families and kinship structures

Figure C.2a
Spaces in Relation to a Common Southern European Model

Figure C.2b
Spaces in Relation to Case Typology in Southern Europe

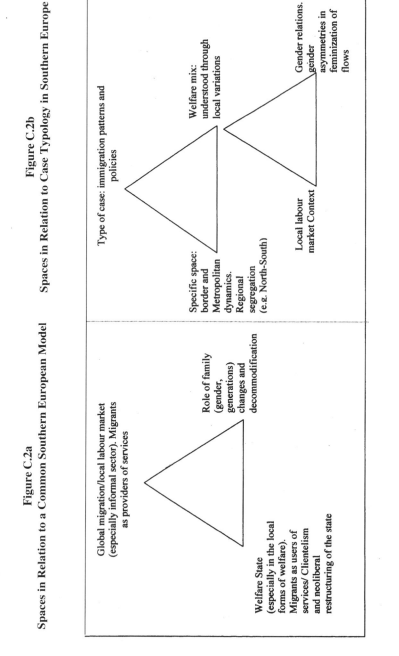

as "shock absorbers." On the other hand, immigrant women are not only supposed to complement welfare services but also to replace autochthonous female roles within the reproduction of a specific, often traditional, family model.

All these points are reinforced by evidence from field case studies. What we search for is the specificity of each case in relation to an ideal-case typology. In order to achieve it we have explored the specific space (enlightened by border and metropolitan dynamics, regional segregation) of migrants in specific related cities. Take the case of Italy, where the concentration effect of the underclass can be set in the representation of territorial dualism.

Spaces in Relation to a Case Typology in Southern Europe (Figure C.2b)

A leading argument in the first part of the book is how case studies set in the local context show a high diversity of welfare mix variations, in spite of the Southern European immigration model. Additionally, there is the consideration of space in relation to types of social policies that impact differently based on the health and the human rights gap, on the education and cultural model and on a specific spatialization of community relations.

Specific Spatialization in Relation to Types of Policies (Figure C.3)

There is the related problem of how to explain this specific spatialization (through the polarization trends, the articulation of the dual welfare, and the expressions of conflict through social racism). This figure may help to make clear that spatialization is diverse according to the local context. Even if we are concluding here, we can still illustrate it with a question: Why in some Catalan towns and villages does the construction of mosques pose a problem to one neighborhood and not to others?

A further complication to take into account is the matching of the migration discourse with the different contexts. I have sought to find the answer through "the local" in the informal economy and in the racialized and gendered system, through the role that historical links and historical images play. It seeks to explain historically, for instance, Greek nationality and the construction of the foreigner; Spain as the Latin-American motherland; Portugal and the Lusophone affiliation in Africa; and lastly, the repeated discourse focusing on the regularization axis (all covered in chapter 2).

Operationalizing a New Space in Border Cities

It is in the first part of the book that I have advanced the thesis on the complexity of the Southern European model of immigration. This line of thinking on the Southern European model has brought us to another side of the question: How do we define its border spaces? The answer was to be found by reflection on the work of spaces of transit and spaces of settlement, emergency

Figure C.3
Specific Spatialization in Relation to Type of Social Policies in Southern Europe

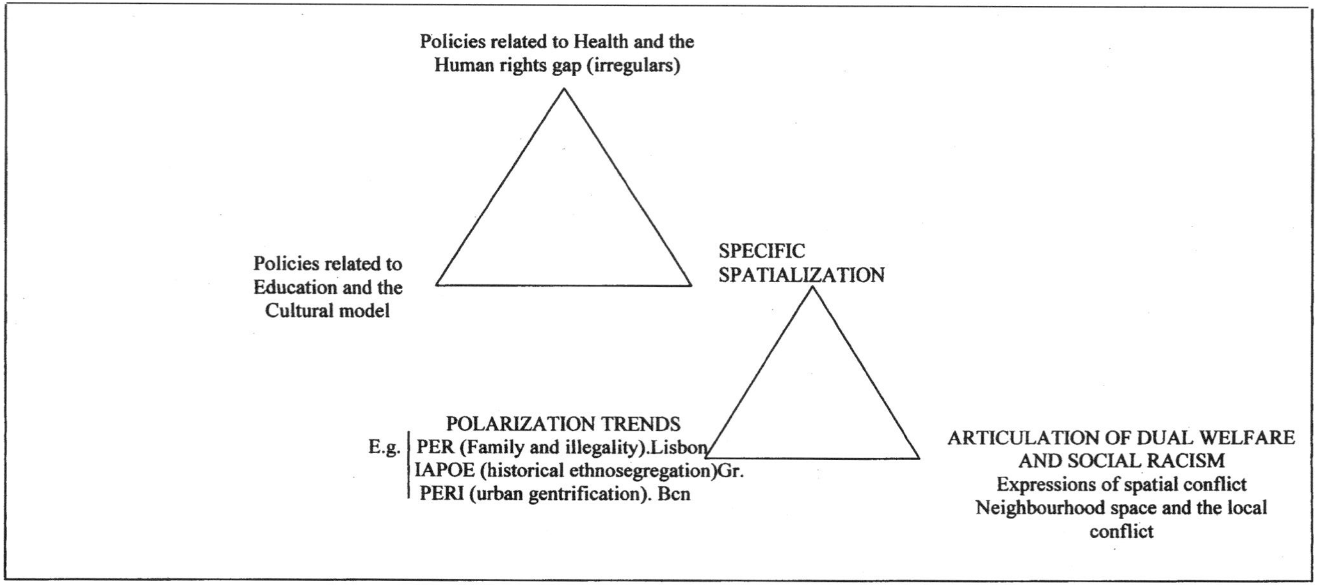

Policies related to Health and the
Human rights gap (irregulars)

Policies related to
Education and the
Cultural model

SPECIFIC
SPATIALIZATION

POLARIZATION TRENDS

E.g. PER (Family and illegality).Lisbon
IAPOE (historical ethnosegregation)Gr.
PERI (urban gentrification). Bcn

ARTICULATION OF DUAL WELFARE
AND SOCIAL RACISM
Expressions of spatial conflict
Neighbourhood space and the local
conflict

and border restrictions in Southern European cities, as developed in the first part to the narrative on the concept of border—Mediterranean border cities to Southern Europe, as developed in the second part. In this task, the spaces of the global border-site were defined, elucidating its conditions, features, and dynamics.

Spaces of the Global-Border Sites (Figure C.4)

The focus on the global-border site has served several purposes. First, it provides an empirical referent for identifying specific modes of integration of cases in migration systems and in globalization dynamics (Figure C.4). Secondly, it allows us to comprehend the global-local divide (Figure C.5), which I deconstructed by locating economic globalization (restrictions to human spatial mobility, foreign investment, etc.) and which deserves special consideration because of the high complexity in its problems. The argument in support of this approach was to refer to the household as an institution of the global economy, where household strategies are open to the contested terrain of contradictory agency, within a strategy of patchwork economy that merges structure and agency. Nevertheless, a disaggregation effort was made to distinguish carefully between the homogenization forces of globalization and the heterogeneization forces (specific cultural and historical processes, regional differences, kinship and family ideology). Within them household practices were considered. It is worth noting here the relation of the pooling system of survival strategies to informalization in the global economy: housework and the female role of survival, remittance dependent economies, privatization, subcontracting (foreign investment), smuggling, and the closing of borders (new forms of trafficking).

Spaces of the Global-Local Divide (Figure C.5)

I wish to focus my attention next on how to articulate all the different actors in the space of the global-local divide (see Figure C.5). For this we need to discuss in more detail, the effects of the global (the mobility of labor, capital, information), the role of the state (in how the notion of the state has become a critical issue in its neo-liberal restructuring and in the forms of transgression of the national state), and the role of international migration (e.g., in circularities as a post-Fordist expression) and as an explicit form of the contradiction of globalization. We identify on one hand, the open door, the metaphor of mixing communities and the free circulation of goods; on the other, borders as physical fences of the Europeanized nation-state. Finally, we identify the core notion of the border, be it as a border enforcement or as a form of resistance to itself.

The Circuits between Border-Cities and Southern Europe (Figure C.6)

The true and materialized relations in the global-local divide can be considered in the light of the circuits' space between border cities (in Albania and

Figure C.4
Spaces of the Global-Border Site

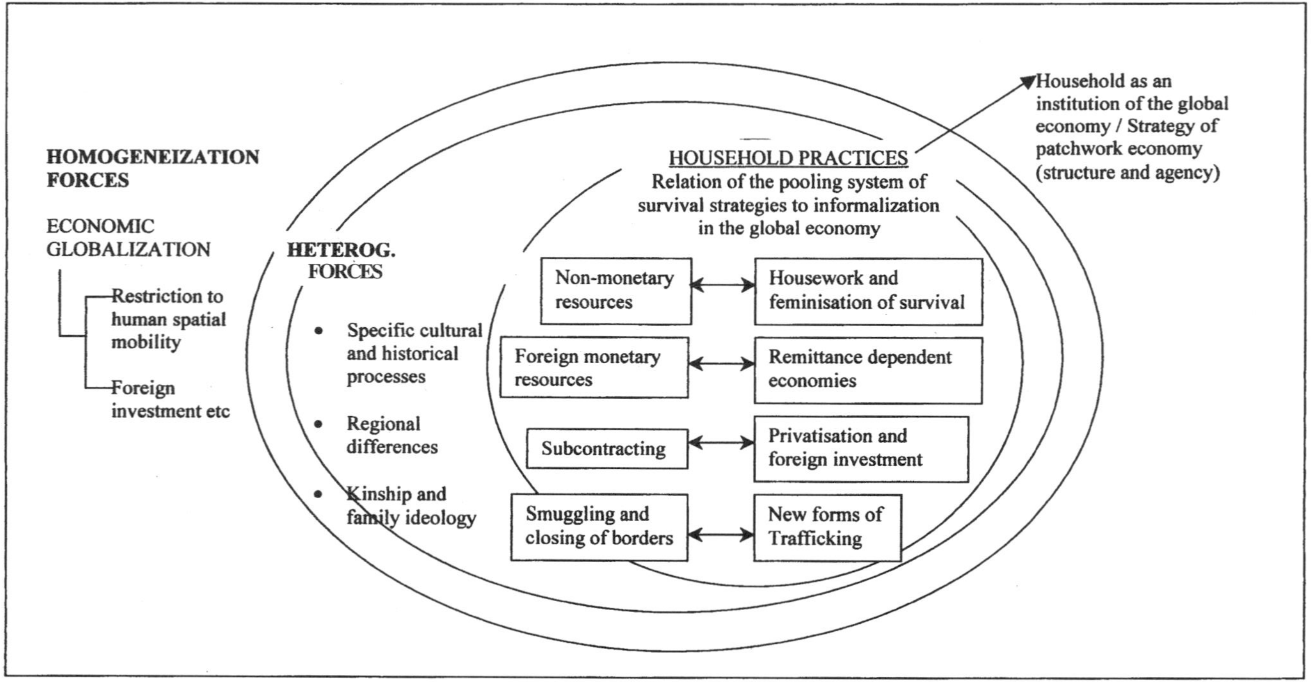

HOMOGENEIZATION FORCES

ECONOMIC GLOBALIZATION

- Restriction to human spatial mobility
- Foreign investment etc

HETEROG. FORCES

- Specific cultural and historical processes
- Regional differences
- Kinship and family ideology

HOUSEHOLD PRACTICES
Relation of the pooling system of survival strategies to informalization in the global economy

Non-monetary resources	↔	Housework and feminisation of survival
Foreign monetary resources	↔	Remittance dependent economies
Subcontracting	↔	Privatisation and foreign investment
Smuggling and closing of borders	↔	New forms of Trafficking

Household as an institution of the global economy / Strategy of patchwork economy (structure and agency)

Figure C.5
Spaces of the Global-Local Divide

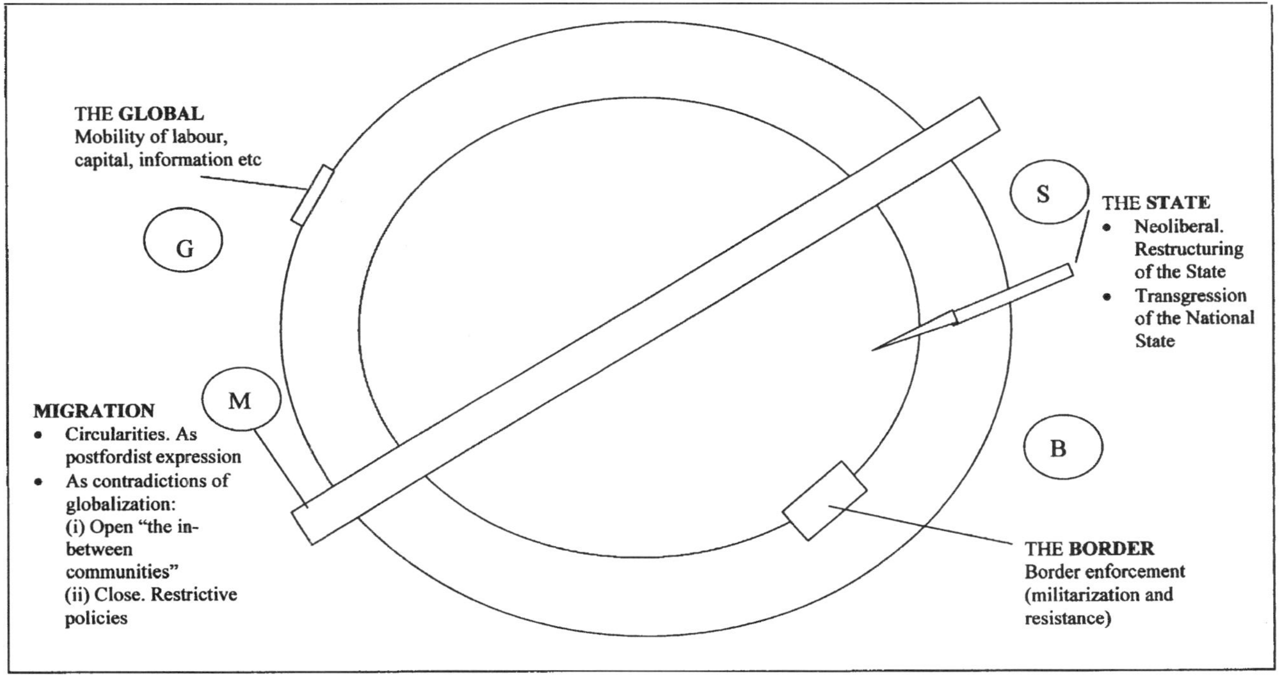

THE STATE
- Neoliberal. Restructuring of the State
- Transgression of the National State

S

B

THE BORDER
Border enforcement (militarization and resistance)

THE GLOBAL
Mobility of labour, capital, information etc

G

M

MIGRATION
- Circularities. As postfordist expression
- As contradictions of globalization:
  (i) Open "the in-between communities"
  (ii) Close. Restrictive policies

Figure C.6
The Circuits between Border Cities and Southern Europe

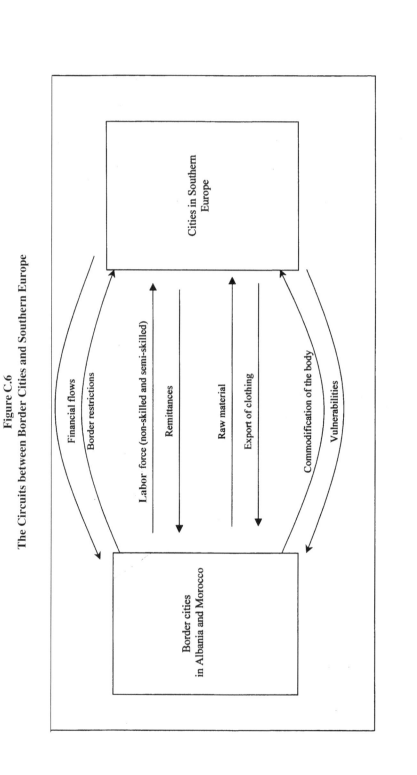

Morocco) and in Southern Europe. Through them we can discover a wide diversity of contemporary counterparts: namely, financial flows and border restrictions, the labor force with its associated remittances, raw material/clothing export, and the commodification of the body/social vulnerabilities. The underlying social relations that create the body in border places are to be emphasized particularly by showing how the woman´s body becomes a product and a market is created, including transport routes, in an economic logic largely imposed from the outside, and that ends up by reducing and problematizing women's agency.

Spaces of the Border City: Its Elements (Figure C.7a)

One of the main purposes of the book is to put forward the notion of the "border city" as an analytical tool to dissect the concepts of migration and border within the context of globalization, and also from a particular research methodology that focuses on the countries of emigration and not only those of immigration. The activity of naming the elements of the border city is part of the conceptual task in the second part of the book. Those elements were to be found in a definition that was both quantitative and qualitative as embodied in terms of specific data and dynamics obtained from the city of emigration. Instead of neutralizing distance and place, I found through the notion of the border city how I could focus on nodal points, a very specific type of place, that serve a border function to Fortress Southern Europe, first, in relation to circulation, transit, waiting place, and restriction; secondly, in relation to a socio-historical context, communism, colonialism, Islam; and thirdly, in relation to a global commodity chain framework (border economy, clothing manufacturing and international subcontracting, telecom circuits, commodification of the body), which is deeply articulated with processes present in the global economy.

The City Polarized Space (Figure C.7b)

Global transformations assume the form of increased social and economic polarization. We have reviewed the different forms that shape the polarized place in Southern European cities as well as in border cities. In border cities we have distinguished the core of the city, as a center (the place of migration from one urban place to another, jobs with more stable income, previous socio-historical infrastructure) and the periphery (the belt of the informal economy, where the informalizing production and distribution activities are ways of surviving under the conditions of the global economy). The periphery is featured by its cheaper land, its weight of internal migration, urban inequality, the location of remittance dependent neighborhoods, and more intense patchwork practices. I offer here the examples of Bathore (Durrës) and Bir Chifa

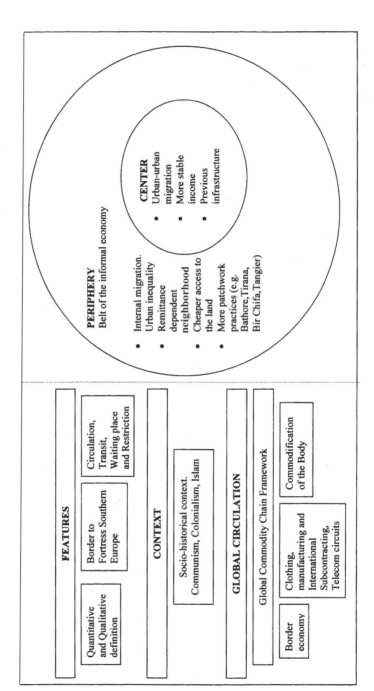

Figure C.7a
Spaces of the Border City: Its Elements

FEATURES

| Quantitative and Qualitative definition | Border to Fortress Southern Europe | Circulation, Transit, Waiting place and Restriction |

CONTEXT

Socio-historical context.
Communism, Colonialism, Islam

GLOBAL CIRCULATION

Global Commodity Chain Framework

| Border economy | Clothing, manufacturing and International Subcontracting, Telecom circuits | Commodification of the Body |

Figure C.7b
The City Polarized Space

PERIPHERY
Belt of the informal economy

- Internal migration.
- Urban inequality
- Remittance dependent neighborhood
- Cheaper access to the land
- More patchwork practices (e.g. Bathore, Tirana, Bir Chifa, Tangier)

CENTER

- Urban-urban migration
- More stable income
- Previous infrastructure

Figure C.8
The Family Space as Axis Mundi

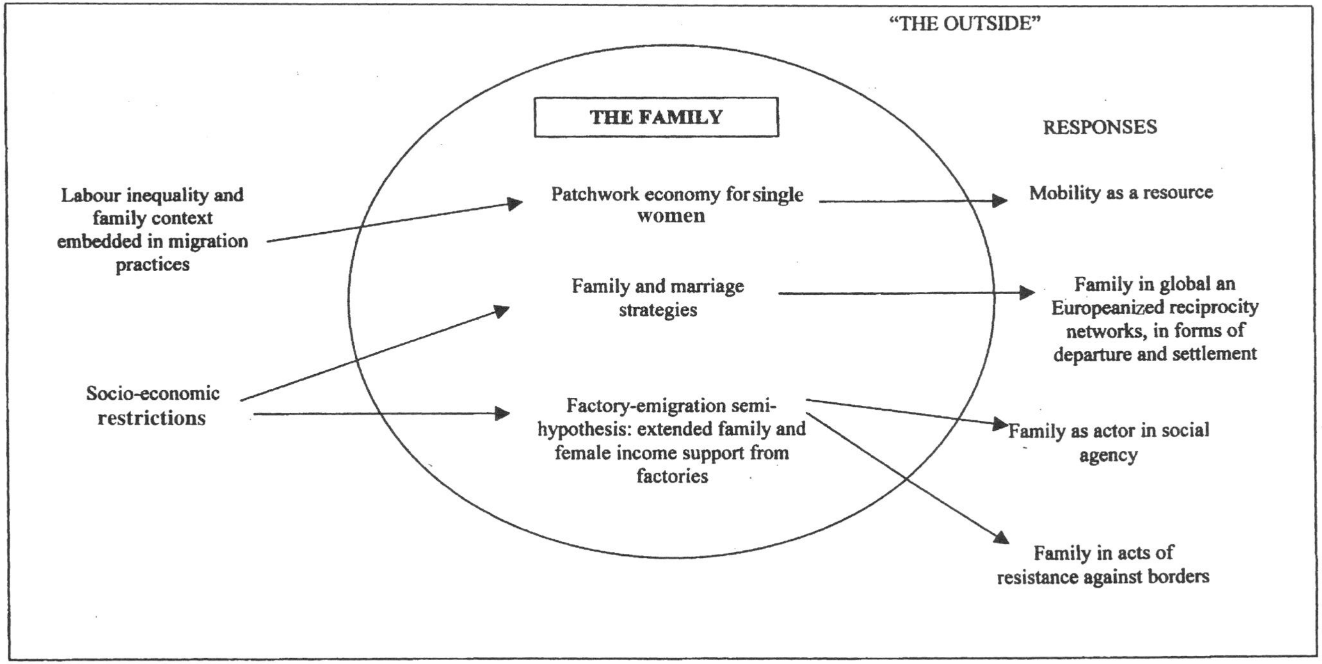

"THE OUTSIDE"

RESPONSES

Mobility as a resource

Family in global an Europeanized reciprocity networks, in forms of departure and settlement

Family as actor in social agency

Family in acts of resistance against borders

THE FAMILY

Patchwork economy for single women

Family and marriage strategies

Factory-emigration semi-hypothesis: extended family and female income support from factories

Labour inequality and family context embedded in migration practices

Socio-economic restrictions

(Tangier). Within the Albanian ethnography, we have mapped out cases of peripheralization at a border location. From an ethnographic viewpoint, they fit the ideal convergence point for the following factors: the communist history, internal migrations, the formation of neo-urban nuclei, and the focus on Italy. In fact, these are important components that constitute a border city.

The Family Space as Axis Mundi (Figure C.8)

Lastly, the family space has emerged as the axis mundi of the conceptualized framework. There, we can practically locate the feedback from the global economy towards the most intimate worlds of everyday life. Firstly, from the outside the family inherits a context of labor inequality, a context closely tied to international migration, and, in interesting cases of a patchwork economy, to lone women. In the case of Tangier, this development can probably be attributed to low salaries and the need to meet the demands of the family in a border context defined by sharp inequality. It is there where the patchwork economy emerges as a crucial concept not only through theoretical categorization of the data but also through empirical descriptive detail. The place-ness of a border zone creates peculiar conditions for the examination of the informal economy as a pooling tool as well as acts of resistance against a globally determined context. Apparently submissive to socioeconomic restrictions, family strategies respond to innovative forms of marriage strategies and to interesting forms of balancing family and work life as we have seen through the development of the factory-emigration hypothesis. This was found as a method families used to combine the extended kin and family resources with factories' income.

Hence, the family reacts towards the outside using mobility as a resource, knitting family in a global and European extended reciprocity network, not only in shaping ways of departure but also of settlement. Therefore, families try to move beyond the structural conditions of the global economy and the sealed borders, stimulating the family as a main actor for social agency on the border city and on migrant transnational strategies.

Note

1.   Actually, we should diffferentiate clearly between the scope of the political state and the welfare state. If we refer to the welfare state benefits, thus the welfare state itself is clearly based on nationality than the political state. Social rights are less national than political rights.

References

Abdelhak, K., and El Kamouni, R. (2001). "Monographie et développement socio-économique de Tanger." Mémoire pour l'obtention de licence en sciences économiques. Tangier: Université Abdelmalek Essaadi. Faculté des Sciences Juridiques Economiques et Sociales.

Abouhani, A. (1999). "Le rôle des amicales dans le fonctionnement et la restructuration des quartiers d'habitat clandestin au Maroc." In Signoles, P., El Kadi, G., and Sidi Boumedine, R., *L'urbain dans le monde arabe. Politiques, instruments et acteurs*, 355-373. Paris: CNRS Editions.

Aboumalek, M. (1994). *Qui épouse qui? Le mariage en milieu urbain.* Casablanca: Afrique Orient.

Abrahamson, P. (1995). "Regímenes europeos de bienestar y políticas sociales europeas: ¿convergencia de solidaridades?" In Sarasa, S., and Moreno, L. (eds.), *El Estado de Bienestar en la Europa del Sur*, 113-153. Madrid: CSIC (Consejo Superior de Investigaciones Científicas).

Abu-Lughod, J. L. (1999). *Sociology for the Twenty-First Century. Continuities and Cutting Edges.* Chicago: The University of Chicago Press.

Abu-Lughod, J. (1980). *Rabat: Urban Apartheid in Morocco.* Princeton, NJ: Princeton University Press.

Addi, L. (1999). *Les mutations de la société algérienne, famille et lien social dans l'Algérie contemporaine.* Paris: Éditions la Découverte.

Adel, F. (2000). "Formation du lieu conjugal et noveaux modeles familiaux en Algérie." In Bourquia, R., Charrad, M., Gallagher, N., *Femmes, Culture et société au Maghreb. I. Culture, femmes et famille*, 139-155. Casablanca: Afrique Orient.

Akalay, L. (1996). "Tanger au miroir d'elle-même." In *Horizons Maghrébins. Le droit à la mémoire,* 31-32, 202-210. Toulouse: Université de Toulouse-Le Mirail.

Akkar, A. (1982). "Le développement urbain de l'agglomération tangéroise: facteurs, problèmes et politique urbaine." Thèse de Doctorat de troisième cycle, Université de Paris IV.

Albanian Center for Economic Research (ACER). (2002). *Common Country Assessment Albania 2002.* Tirana: UN Resident Coordinator.

Albera, D., Blok, A., and Bromberger, C. (2001). *L'anthropologie de la Méditerranée. Anthropology of the Mediterranean.* Paris: Maisonneuve et Larose, Maison méditerranéenne des sciences de l'homme.

Albera, D., and Blok, A. (2001). "The Mediterranean as a Field of Ethnological Study. A Retrospective." In Albera, D., Blok, A., Bromberger, C. (dirs.), *L'anthropologie de la Méditerranée. Anthropology of the Mediterranean*, 15-37. Paris: Maisonneuve et Larose.

Alburquerque, R., Ferreira, L. E, and Viegas, T. (2000). *O Fenómeno Asociativo em Contexto Migratório.* Oeiras: Celta Editora.

Aliaj, B., Lulo, K., and Myftiu, G. (2003). *Tirana. The Challenge of Urban Development.* Tirana: Cetis.

Almeda, E. (2002). "Familias monoparentales y rupturas matrimoniales en Cataluña: apuntes para un debate." In Flaquer, L. (ed.) *Políticas familiares en la Unión Europea.* (88-13) Barcelona: Institut de Ciències Polítiques i Socials.

Alós, R., Kaioua, A., Benbada, O. (2001). *La inversión industrial española en Marruecos. Una aproximación desde las dos orillas del Mediterráneo.* CDT-FPS (Confederación Democrática del Trabajo, Fundació Pau i Solidaritat), Casablanca (Marruecos). Barcelona: Fons Català de Cooperació al Desenvolupament.

Aman, A. C. (1996). "Introduction: Feminism and Globalization: The Impact of the Global Economy on Women and Feminist Theory." *Indiana Journal of Global Legal Studies* (4), 1-49.

Amaturo, E., Gambardella, D., Morlicchio, E., Orientale Caputo, G. (1998). "Politiche per i minori e profili di povertà a Napoli." In E. Mingione (1999) *Le sfide dell'esclusione: metodi, luoghi, soggetti.* Bologna: Il Mulino.

Ammor, M. F., Chaker, A., Balenghien, A., Abzahd, M., Mejjati, R., Zouiten, M. R (2001). "Le secteur informel." In *Bulletin économique du Maroc.* Rabat: Editions Okad (59-82).

Andalzúa, G. (1987). *Borderlands/La Frontera: The New Mestiza.* San Francisco: Aunt Lute Books.

Anderson, B. (1996). "Living and Working Conditions of Overseas Domestic Workers in the European Union." A report for *Stichting Tegen Vrouwenhandel.* July.

Anderson, M., Bechhofer, F., and Gershuny, J. (eds.). (1994a). *The Social and Political Economy of the Household.* Oxford: Oxford Univesity Press, 19-67.

Anderson, M., Bechhofer, F., and Kendrick, S. (1994b). "Individual and Household Strategies." In Anderson, M., Bechhofer, F., and Gershuny, J. (eds.), *The Social and Political Economy of the Household.* Oxford: Oxford Univesity Press.

Anderson, N. (1975). *The American Hobo. An Autobiography.* Leiden: E. J. Brill.

Andrade Ramos, A. (1991). "Attitudes e comportamentos no realojamento no Alto da Loba-Payo d'Arnos." *Dissertaçâo.* Lisboa: ISCTE.

Antonnen, A. (1998). "Families and Social Services." *TMR Workshop on Families and Social Services.* University of Tampere, Finland, 27 August.

Antonnen, A., and Spilä, J. (1996). "European Social Care Services: Is It Possible to Identify Models? *Journal of European Social Policy*, 6 (22), 87-100.

Appadurai, A. (2000). "Disjuncture and Difference in the Global Cultural Economy." In Held, D., and McGrew, A. (2000). *The Global Transformation Reader. An Introduction to the Globalization Debate*, 230-237. Cambridge: Polity Press.

Arbaci, S. (2002). "Patterns of Ethnic and Socio-Spatial Segregation in European Cities: Are Welfare Regimes Making a Difference?" In Fonseca, M. L. et al. (eds.), *Immigration and Place in Mediterranean Metropolises*, 83-115. Lisbon: Luso-American Development Foundation.

Armvruster-Sandoval, R. (1999). "Globalization and Cross-Border Labor Organizing: The Guatemalan Maquiladora Industry and the Phillips Van Heusen Worker's Movement." *Latin American Perspectives* 26 (2), 108-128.

Arrighi, G. (ed.) (1985). *Semiperipheral Development. The Politics of Southern Europe in the Twentieth Century.* Beverly Hills, New Delhi: Sage Publications.

Ascoli, U., and Pasquinelli, S. (1993). *Il welfare mix. Stato sociale e terzo settore.* Milan: Franco Angeli.

Asociación Pro Derechos de la Infancia (2002). "Informe sobre las expulsiones sumarias de menores no acompañados a la frontera marroquí efectuadas desde el mes de Julio del año 2001 en Melilla." Melilla: Asociación Pro Derechos de la Infancia.

Aubarell, G. (2003). *Perspectivas de la inmigración en España. Una aproximación desde el territorio.* Barcelona: Icaria Antrazyt.

Augé, M. (1998). *Hacia una antropología de los mundos contemporáneos*. Barcelona: Editorial Edisa.

Augé, M. (1992). *Non-lieux. Introduction à une anthropologie de la surmodernité*. Paris: Éditions du Seuil.

Baganha, M. I., and Peixoto, J. (1996). "O Estudo das Migrações Nacionais: Ponto de Intersecção Disciplinar." In Carvalho Ferreira, J. M. Marques, R., Peixoto, J., and Raposo, R. (org.), *Entre a Economia e a Sociologia*. Oeiras: Celta Editora.

Baganha, M. I., and Góis, P. (1999). "Migrações internacionais de e para Portugal: o que sabemos e para onde vamos?" *Revista Crítica de Ciencias Sociais*," 52-53 (November 1998/ Februrary 1999), 229-280.

Bagnasco, A. (1977). *La problematica territoriale dello sviluppo economico italiano*. Bologna: Il Mulino.

Bair, J., and Jereffi, G. (2001). "Local Clusters in Global Chains: The Causes and the Consequences." *World Development Industry* 29 (II), 1885-1903.

Balbo, L. (1991). *Tempi di vita*. Milan: Feltrinelli.

Balbo, L. (1978). "La doppia presenza." *Inchiesta* 32, 3-6.

Baldwin-Edwards, M. (2002). "Semi-Reluctant Hosts: Southern Europe's Ambivalent Response to Immigration." *Studi Emigrazione*, 145: 27–48.

Baldwin-Edwards, M. (1998). "The Social Protection of Third Country Nationals in the European Union." in Arango, J. et al. (eds.), *International Migration at Century's End: Trends and Issues*. Oxford: Clarendon Press

Baldwin-Edwards, M. (1997). "The Emerging European Immigration Regime: Some Reflections on Implications for Southern Europe." *Journal of Common Market Studies*, 35 (4), 497-498.

Baldwin-Edwards, M., and Schain, M. A. (1994). "Introduction," in Baldwin-Edwards, M.; Schain, M.A. (eds.), *The Politics of Immigration in Western Europe*. London: Cass.

Balland, N., Duroyaume, P., and Salenson, I. (2000). "La medina de Tanger: élements de diagnostic urbain." Rapport d´enquêtes ménages. Institut Français d´urbanisme. D.E.S.S Urbanisme et Aménagement. Paris: Institut Français d´Urbanisme.

Barbagli, M. (1998). *Immigrazione e criminalità in Italia. Una coraggiosa indagine empirica su un tema che ci divide*. Il Mulino: Bologna.

Barjaba, K. (2002). *Ondate senza Ritorno. Scritti e saggi sull'emigrazione albanese*. Roma: OIM.

Barret, M., and McIntosh, M. (1982). *The Antisocial Family*. London: Verso.

Barros, L. Lahlou, M., Escouffier, C., Pumares, P. and Ruspini, P. (et al.) (2002). "La inmigración irregular subsahariana a través y hacia Marruecos." *Estudios sobre migraciones internacionales*. N 54. Geneva: Oficina Internacional del Trabajo.

Bastenier, A., and Dasseto, F. (eds.) (1990). *Italia, Europa e nuove immigrazioni*. Turin: Fondazione Giovanni Agnelli.

Baübock, R. (1998). "The Crossing and Blurring of Boundaries in International Migration. Challenges for Social and Political Theory." In R. Baubock and J. Rundell (eds.) *Blurred Boundaries: Migration, Ethnicity, Citizenship*. Aldershot: Ashgate.

Bauman, Z. (1998). *Globalization: The Human Consequences*. New York: Columbia University Press.

Beck, U. (2000). "What is Globalization?" In Held, D. and McGrew, A., *The Global Transformation Reader*. Cambridge: Polity Press.

Benería, L., and Feldman, S. (1992). *Unequal Burden. Economic Crisis, Persistent Poverty and Women's Work*. Boulder and Oxford: Westview Press.

Berger, S., and Piore, M. J. (1989). *Dualism and Discontinuity in Industrial Societies*. Cambridge: Cambridge University Press

Bernard V. (1981). "Représentation mythique du monde et domination masculine chez les Pomakes grecs." In *The Greek Review of Social Research. Numéro Spécial. Aspects du changement social dans la campagne grecque.* EKKE, 121-142.

Bernard, C. (dir.). (1991). *Nouvelles logiques marchandes au Maghreb. L'informel dans les années 80.* Paris: Editions du CNRS.

Bethemont, J. (2000). *Géographie de la Méditerranée.* Paris: Armand Colin.

Biberaj, E. (1998). *Albania in Transition.* Oxford: Westview Press.

Blanc, F. P., and Zeidguy, R. (2000). *Moudawana. Code de Statut Personnel et des Successions.* Casablanca: Sochepress.

Bolaffi, G. (1996). *Una politica per gli immigrati.* Bologna: Il Mulino.

Bonte, P. (1994). *Épouser au plus proche. Inceste, prohibitions et strategies matrimoniales autour de la Méditerranée.* Paris: Éditions de l'École des Hautes Études en Sciences sociales.

Boria, E., and Rivera-Ramos, J. C. (2002). "Rethinking Space and Practice in Globalization: Conceptualizing the Production of Space for Transnational Practices." Prepared for the Globalization Conference at the University of Chicago, 8 April.

Boughali, M. (1974). *La représentation de l'espace chez le marocain illettré.* Casablanca: Editions Anthropos.

Bouillon, F. (2001). "Des acteurs et des lieux: les économies de la rue à Marseille." In M. Peraldi (dir.) *Cabas et containers. Activités marchandes informelles et réseaux migrants transfrontaliers. Séries Frontières, villes; lieux de passage,* 237-267. Paris: Maisonneuve & Larose.

Boulifa, A. (1986). *Mutations et organisation d'un espace peri-urbain: le Fahs de Tanger et ses bordures (Le Tangerois).* Études Méditerranéennes. Fascicule 10. Poitiers: Centre Universitaire d'études méditerranéennes.

Bourdieu, P. (2002). *Le bal des célibataires. Crise de la société paysanne en Béarn.* Paris: Éditions Du Seuil.

Bourdieu, P. (2001). *Science de la science et réflexivité.* Paris: Éditions Raisons d´Agir.

Bourdieu, P. (2000). *Les structures sociales de l'économie.* Paris: Éditions du Seuil

Bourdieu, P. (1998). Appendix, "The Family Spirit" Practical Reasons. In Bourdieu, P., *On the theory of action.* Cambridge: University Press.

Bourdieu, P. (1994). *Raisons pratiques. Sur la théorie de l'action.* Paris: Éditions du Seuil.

Bourdieu, P. (1972). "Les strategies matrimoniales dans le système de reproduction." *Annales Economies sociétés civilisations,* 1105-1125.

Bourdieu, P., and Sayad, A. (1964). *Le déracinement. La crise de l'agriculture traditionnelle en Algérie.* Paris: Les Éditions de Minuit.

Bourquia, R., Charrad, M., and Gallagher, N. (2000a). *Femmes, culture et société au Maghreb. I Culture, femmes et famille.* Casablanca: Afrique Orient.

Bourquia, R., Charrad, M., and Gallagher, N. (2000b). *Femmes, culture et société au Maghreb. II Femmes, Pouvoir politique et Développement.* Casablanca: Afrique Orient.

Brachimi, A. (1983). "La famille marocaine en milieu urbain: étude démographique d'après des enquêtes dans des villes du Nord-Ouest du Maroc." Thèse de Doctorat d'Etat, Université de Paris V.

Braudel, F. (1990a). *La Méditerranée et le monde méditerranéen à l'époque de Philippe II. 1. La part du milieu.* Paris: Armand Colin.

Braudel, F. (1990b). *La Méditerranée et le monde méditerranéen à l'époque de Philippe II. 2. Destins collectifs et mouvements d'ensemble.* Paris: Armand Colin.

Braudel, F. (1993). "Una prueba esencial: la frontera." In Braudel, F., *La identidad de Francia. El espacio y la historia.* Barcelona: Editorial Edisa.

Braudel, F. (1976). *El Mediterráneo y el Mundo Mediterráneo en la época de Felipe II.* Madrid: Fondo de cultura económica. Sección de obras de Historia.

Bravo Nieto, A. (2000). *Arquitectura y urbanismo español en el Norte de Marruecos.* Sevilla: Junta de Andalucía, Consejería de Obras Públicas y Transportes.

Brejon de Lavergnee, N., and Quitot, A. (1991). *L´aménagement rural dans la région Nord-Ouest: onze ans d´expérience.* Paris: Éditions L´Harmattan.

Brettel, C. (1986). *Men Who Migrate Women Who Wait.* Princeton NJ: Princeton University Press.

Bromberger, C. (2001). "Aux trois sources de l'ethnologie du monde méditerranéen dans la tradition française." In Albera, D., Blok, A., Bromberger, C. (dirs.), *L'anthropologie de la Méditerranée. Anthropology of the Mediterranean*, 65-83. Paris: Maisonneuve Larose.

Bromberger, C., and Durand, J. Y. (2001). "Faut-il jeter la Méditerranée avec du bain?" In Albera, D., Blok, A., Bromberger, C. (dirs.), *L'anthropologie de la Méditerranée. Anthropology of the Mediterranean*, 733-756. Paris: Maison et Larose.

Burke, P. (2001). "Passing through Three Crises." In Albera, D., Blok, A., Bromberger, C. (dirs.), *L'anthropologie de la Méditerranée. Anthropology of the Mediterranean*, 99-103. Paris: Maison et Larose.

Cabinet d´Architecture et d´Urbanisme (1999). *Plan d´aménagement de la Commune Urbaine de Tanger. Rapport enquête ménages.* Tanger: Ministeré de l´Interieur, Wilaya de Tanger, Préfecture de Tanger Asilah, Commune urbaine de Tanger.

Capdevila, M., and Ferrer, M. (2003). "Els menors estrangers indocumentats no acompanyats (MEINA)." Documents de treball. Formació i investigació social i criminològica. Generalitat de Catalunya. Centre d'Esudis Jurídics i Formació Especialitzada.

Caponio, T. (2000). *Models of integration and social policies for immigrants in Italy. The contradictory mid-path approach.* Département de science politique. Université de Genève. (mimeo).

Caponio, T. (1996). *Associazionismo e integrazione politica degli immigrati. Un´analisi comparata.* Tesi di Laurea. Turin: Facoltà di Lettere e Filosofia.

Caponio, T., Dilesen, A, and Ribas, N. (2000). "The Policy Mirror Mechanism: The Case of Turin." *Papers: revista de Sociologia*, 60, 67-83, Universidad Autónoma de Barcelona. Monographic "Inmigración femenina en el Sur de Europa."

Carchedi, F., Piccolini, A., Mottura, G. (eds.) (2000). *I colori della notte. Migrazioni, sfruttamento sessuale, experienze di intervento sociale* Milan: Franco Angeli.

Cardelús, J., and Pascual, À. (1982). "Processes of Migration and Capitalist Integration in Catalonia." In Rex, J., and Solomos, J., *Migrant Workers in Metropolitan Cities.* Strasbourg: European Science Foundation.

Caritas (2002). *Immigrazione. Dossier Statistico 2002. II Rapporto sull'immigrazione Caritas-Migrantes.* Rome: Nuova Anterem.

Carrasco, C. (1991). *Trabajo doméstico y reproducción social.* Madrid: Instituto de la Mujer.

Cassey, J. (1997). "El papel de las organizaciones no gubernamentales en la elaboración de políticas públicas. El caso de la integración de inmigrantes extranjeros en Cataluña." *Dossiers Barcelona Associacions*, 20. Barcelona: Ajuntament de Barcelona.

Castells, M. (1996). *The Rise of the Network Society.* Cambridge, MA: Blackwell Publishers.

Castells, M. (2000). *La era de la información. Vol. 1. La sociedad red.* Segunda edición. Madrid: Alianza Editorial.

Castells, M., and Portes, A. (1989). "World underneath: The Origins, Dynamics, and Effects of the Informal Economy." In Portes, A., Castells, M., and Benton, L. A., *The Informal Economy. Studies in Advanced and Less-Developed Countries*, 11-37. Baltimore: The John Hopkins University Press.

Castles, F. G,. and Ferrera, M. (1996). "Casa e welfare state. Le contraddizioni dei paesi sud-europei." *Stato e Mercato*, 48, 409-431.

Castles, S. (2000). *Ethnicity and Globalization*. London, Thousand Oaks, New Delhi: SAGE Publications.

Castles, S., and Davidson, A. (2000). *Citizenship and Migration. Globalization and the Politics of Belonging*. New York: Routledge.

Castles, S., and Miller, M. J. (1998). *The Age of Migration. International Population Movements in the Modern World*. New York: The Guilford Press.

Castronovo, R. (1997). "Compromised Narratives along the Border. The Mason-Dixon Line, Resistance and Hegemony." In Michaelsen, S., and Johnson, D. E. (eds.), *The Limits of Cultural Politics*. Minneapolis: University of Minessota Press.

Castronuo, E. (1996). *L'inserimento dei bambini immigrati nella scuola elementare a Napoli*. Tesi di Laurea in Sociologia del Lavoro. Università Degli Studi di Napoli Federico III. Facoltà di Sociologia.

Center for Refugee and Migration Studies (2001). *Internal Displacement in Albania. Seminar Report*, Tirana, 4 June.

Çeveli B., Elezi, M., Mukaj, A., Ngjeci, E. (2002). *Be Careful and Protect Yourself*. Durrës: Council of Associations Offering Social Services.

Chebel, M. (1993). *L'imaginaire arabo-musulman*. Paris: Presses Universitaires de France.

Checa, F. (dir.). (2001). *El Ejido: la ciudad-cortijo. Claves socioeconómicas del conflicto étnico*. Barcelona: Icaria Antrazyt.

Cheng, L. K., Kierkowski H., and Fung W. (eds.). (2001). *Global Production and Trade in East Asia*. Boston, MA: Kluwer Academic Press.

Chickering, A. L., and Salahdine, M. (1991). *The Silent Revolution. The Informal Sector in Five Asian and near Eastern Countries*. San Francisco: ICS Press.

Choukri, M. (2000). *For Bread Alone*. New York: Saqi Books.

Clarke, S. (1999). *New Forms of Employment and Household Survival Strategies in Russia*. Coventry and Moscow: ISITO/CCLS.

Colombo, A. (1998). *Etnografia di un´economia clandestina. Immigrati algerini a Milano*. Bologna: Il Mulino.

Comas d´Argemir, D., and Pujadas Muñoz, J. J. (1991). "Familias migrantes: reproducción de la identidad y sentimiento de pertenencia." *Papers: Revista de Sociologia*, 36, 35-56.Universitat Autònoma de Barcelona.

Combe, S. (1996). "Après le 'tournant': l'Albanie à l'épreuve de la démocratie." In Combe, S., and Ditchev, I. (dirs.), *Albanie Utopie. Huis clos dans les Balkans*, 13-27. Paris: Éditions Autrement.

Combe, S., and Ditchev, I. (dirs.). (1996). *Albanie Utopie. Huis clos dans les Balkans*. Paris: Éditions Autrement.

Comisión Europea. (1994). *Libro Blanco de la Políticas Sociales Europeas*. Brussells: European Commision.

Commaile, J. (1993). *Les stratégies des femmes. Travail, famille et politique*. Paris: Édition La Découverte.

Commission of the European Communities. (2002). "Communication from the Commission to the Council and the European Parliament. Integrating Migration Issues in the European Union´s Relation with Third countries." Brussels, 3.12.2002 703 final.

Commune Urbaine de Tanger (1999). Plan d'Aménagement de la Commune Urbaine de Tanger. "Rapport Enquête Ménages," Janvier. Tangier : Ministère de l'Intérieur. Wilaya de Tanger, Préfecture de Tanger Asilah, Commune Urbaine de Tanger.

Comune di Modena, Assessorato alle Politiche Sociali (2003). *"La prospettiva di tornare a casa..." Ricerca-azione sulla relata dei minori immigrati non accompagnati nel Comune di Modena*. Modena: Regione Emilia Romagna.

Courbage, Y., and Fargues, P. (1992). *Chrétiens et Juifs dans l'islam arabe et turc*. Paris: Éditions Payot & Rivages.

Culpitt, I. (1992). *Welfare and Citizen—Beyond the Crisis of the Welfare State?* London: Sage Publications.

Damianakos, S., Handman, M. E., Pitt-Rivers, J. J., and Ravis-Giordani, G. (coords.). (1995). *Les amis et les autres. Mélanges en l'honneur de John Peristiany. Brothers and Others. Essays in Honor of Jonh Peristiany*. Athens: E.K.K.E.

Davis, J. (1983). *Antropología de las sociedades mediterráneas*. Barcelona: Editorial Anagrama.

De Filippo, E. (ed.) (1996a). *Condizioni di vita e di lavoro delle donne africane nelle provincia di Napoli*. Naples: Dedalus.

De Filippo, E. (1996b). "I Rom nella provincia di Napoli." In P. Brunello (ed.), *L'urbanistica del disprezzo. I campi Rom e società italiana*. Roma: Manifestolibri.

De Filippo, E., and Morniroli, A. (1998). "L'immigrazione straniera a Napoli: il sistema dei servizi." Rapporto di ricerca: *For the Project "Lire, Escire, S'inserer*. Iniziativa Comunitaria Occupazione. Horizon. Naples, April 1998.

De la Verone, C. (1972). *Tanger sous l'occupation anglaise d'après une description anonyme de 1674*. Publication du Centre d'Etudes islamiques et orientales d'histoire comparée. Paris : Libraire orientaliste Paul Geuthner.

De Sousa Santos, B. (1995). "Relationships among Perceptions that We Call Identity: Doing Research in Rio's Squatter Settlements." In De Sousa Santos, B. (1995) *Toward a New common Sense: Law, Science and Politics in the Paradigmatic Transition*. New York: Routledge.

Decimo, F. (1996). "Reti di solidarietà e strategie economiche di donne somale immigrate a Napoli." *Studi Emigrazione*, 123.

Délégation Provinciale de l'Habitat de Tanger. (1992). *Projet de restructuration des Quartiers Sous-Equipés*. Tanger.

De Rapper, G. (1998). *La frontière albanaise: famille, société et identité collective en Albanie du sud*. thése de doctorat, Université de Paris X, Nanterre.

Direction de la Statistique. (2000). *Annuaire statistique du Maroc 2000*. Rabat: Direction de la Statistique.

Direction de la Statistique. Royaume du Maroc. Premier Ministre. Ministere chargé de la population. (1994). *Caracteristiques démographiques et socio-économiques de la population des communes du royaume*. Recensement Général de la population et de l'habitat de 1994, volume IV. Chefchaouen, Khemisset, Rabat, Sidi Kacem, Tanger, Kenitra, Larache, Sale, Skhirate-Temara, Tetouan.

Ditchev, I. (1996). "D'Oncle Enver à Oncle Sam: les ruines de l'utopie." In Combe, S., and Ditchev, I. (dirs.), *Albanie Utopie. Huis clos dans les Balkans*, 28-39. Paris: Éditions Autrement.

Doja, A. (2000). *Naître et grandir chez les Albanais. La construction culturelle de la personne*. Paris and Montreal: l'Harmattan.

Dore-Cabral, C. (1995). "Introducción." In Portes, A., *En torno a la informalidad: ensayos sobre teoría y medición de la economía no regulada*. México: Grupo Editorial Miguel Ángel Porrua.

Dowding, K. (2001). "Explaining Urban Regimes." *International Journal of Urban and Regional Research*, 25 (1), 7-19.

Driessen, H. (1994). "La puerta trasera de Europa. Notas etnográficas sobre la frontera húmeda entre España y Marruecos" *Historia y fuente oral*, 12, 59-69.

Dumon, W. A. (1993). "Famiglia e movimenti migratori." In Scabini, E., and Pierpalo, D. (eds.). *La famiglia in una società multietnica*, 12, 27-53. Milan: Vita e Pensiero. Pubblicazioni dell'Università Cattolica.

Dumon, W. A. (1979). "The Situation of Children of Migrants and Their Adpatation and Integration in the Host Society, and Their Situation in the Country of Origin." *International Migration*, 17, 59-65.

Dunay, J., Hernández, L., and Rey, C. A. (1995). *El barrio Gandul: economía subterránea y migración indocumentada en Puerto Rico*. Caracas: Editorial Nueva Sociedad.

Dunford, D., and King, R. (2001). "Mediterranean Economic Geography." In King, R., de Mas, P., and Beck, M. (eds.). *Geography, Environment and Development of the Mediterranean*, 1-25. Brighton and Portland: Sussex Academic Press.

Ech-Channa, A. (2000). *Miseria*. Témoignages. Casablanca: Editions Le Fennec.

Economist Intelligence Unit. (2002). *Country Report January 2002 Albania*. UK: *The Economist* (www.store.eiu.com).

Eickelman, D. F. (2001). "Patrons and Clients in the 'New' Muslim Politics." In Albera, D., Blok, A., Bromberger, C. (dirs.), *L'anthropologie de la Méditerranée. Anthropology of the Mediterranean*, 331-349. Paris: Maisonneuve et Larose.

Eickelman, D. F. (2003). *Antropología del mundo islámico*. Barcelona: Bellaterra.

Eickelman, D. F. (1976). *Moroccan Islam. Tradition and Society in a Pilgrimage Center*. Modern Middle East Series, N 1. Austin and London: University of Texas Press.

Elías, N., and Scotson, J. L. (1994). *The Established and the Outsiders*. London, Thousand Oaks, and New Delhi: Sage.

Erman, T. (1998). "The Impact of Migration on Turkish Rural Women: Four Emergent Patterns." *Gender and Society*, 12 (2), 146-167.

Escallier, R. (1996). *Élites, pouvoirs et villes dans le monde arabe: Éléments d'analyse de la Citadinité*. Collection Sciences de la Ville. N. 13. Fascicule de Recherches n 29 d'Urbama. Tours: Urbama and MSV.

Eschbach, K. H., Rodríguez, N.P., Hernández-León, R., Bailey, S. (1999). "Death at the Border." *International Migration Review*, 33 (2), 430-454.

Escrivá, A. (2000). "¿Empleadas de por vida? Peruanas en el servicio doméstico de Barcelona." In *Papers*, monographic Female Immigration in Southern Europe. N. 60, 327-342.

Esping-Andersen, G. (1990). *The Three Worlds of Welfare Capitalism*. Cambridge: Polity Press.

Eurostat. (1995). *Les femmes et les hommes dans l'Union européene. Portrait statistique*. Luxemburg: European Commission.

Fakiolas, R. (1994). "Migration from and to Greece." *1994 SOPEMI Report*. Paris: OECD-SOPEMI.

Fakiolas, R. (1993). "Migration from and to Greece." *1993 SOPEMI Report*. Paris: OECD-SOPEMI.

Feldman, S. (1992). "Crisis, Poverty and Gender Inequality: Current Themes and Issues." In Beneriá, L., and Feldman, S. (eds). *Unequal Burden. Economic Crises, Persistent Poverty and Women's Work*. Boulder, CO, and Oxford: Westview Press.

Fernández-Kelly, M. P. (1983). *For We Are Sold, I and My People. Women and Industry in Mexico's Frontier*. New York: State of New York Press.

Ferreira, V. (1999). "Os paradoxos da situação das mulheres em Portugal." *Revista Crítica de Ciencias Sociais*, 52-53 (November 1998-February 1999), 199-227.

Ferrera, M. (1995). "Los estados del bienestar del sur en la Europa Social." In Sarasa, S., and Moreno, L. (eds.), *El Estado de Bienestar en la Europa del Sur*, 85-111. Madrid: CSIC (Consejo superior de investigaciones científicas).

Ferrera, M. (1984). *Il Welfare state in Italia. Sviluppo e crisi in prospettiva comparata*. Bologna: Il Mulino.

Flaquer, L., and Brullet, C. (1998). *Polítiques familiars a Catalunya: una primera aproximació*. Estudi encarregat per la Fundació Jaume Bofill. Barcelona, September.

Folgheraiter, F. (1998). *Teoria e metodologia del servizio sociale. La prospettiva direte.* Milan: Angelli.

Fuga, A. (2000). *Identités périphériques en Albanie. La recomposition du milieu rural et les nouveaux types de rationalité politique.* Paris: l'Harmattan.

Garland, D. (2001). *The Culture of Control. Crime and Social Order in Contemporary Society.* Chicago: The University of Chicago Press.

Garnsey, E., and Pauket, L. (1987). *Industrial Change and Women's Employment: Trends in the New International Division of Labour.* Geneva: ILO.

Geertz, C. (1992 [1972]). "The Bazaar Economy: Information and Search in Peasant Marketing." In Granovetter, M., and Swedberg, R. (eds.), *The Sociology of Economic Life*, 225-32. Boulder, CO, and Oxford: Westview Press.

Geertz, C. (1996). *Tras los hechos.* Barcelona: Paidós.

Gellner, E. (1981). *Muslim Society.* Cambridge, New York, and Melbourne: Cambridge University Press.

Ghezzi, S. (1995). "Le reti sociali primarie: la famiglia e gli eventi critici." In Kazepov, Y. (ed.), I nuovi poveri in Lombardia. Sistemi di welfare e traiettorie di esclusione sociale, Regione Lombardia, *Quaderni Regionali di Ricerca* n.1.

Giner, S. (1995). "La modernización de la Europa meridional: una interpretación sociológica." In Sarasa, S., and Moreno, L. (eds.) *El Estado de Bienestar en la Europa del Sur*, 9-59. Madrid: CSIC (Consejo superior de investigaciones científicas).

Giner, S. (1994). "Ciudad y politeya en la Europa Meridional. Algunas reflexiones históricas y sociológicas." In Alabart, A., García, S., and Giner, S. (eds.), *Clase, poder y ciudadanía*, 17-60. Madrid: Siglo XXI de España Editores.

Ginsburg, N. (1992). *Divisions of Welfare. A Critical Introduction to Comparative Social Policy.* London: Sage Publications.

Gjeçovi, S. (trans.Christian Gut). (2001). *Le Kanun de Lekë Dukagjini.* Pejë: Dukagjini Publishing House.

Goody, J. (2001). "The Great and Little Traditions in the Mediterranean." In Albera, D., Blok, A.,Bromberger, C. (dirs.), *L'anthropologie de la Méditerranée. Anthropology of the Mediterranean*, 473-489. Paris: Maison et Larose.

Gomà, R., and Subirats, M. (coords.). (1998). *Políticas publicas en España.Contenidos, Redes de actores y niveles de gobierno.* Barcelona: Ariel Ciencia Política.

González, M. J., Jurado, T., and Naldini, M. (1999). "Introduction: Interpreting the Transformation of Gender Inequalities in Southern Europe." In González, M. J, Jurado, T., Naldini, M., *South European Society & Politics*, 4 (2), 4-34.

González Calleja, E. (2000). Les différentes utilisations de la *Mare Nostrum*: représentations de la Méditerranée dans L'Espagne contemporaine. In Vázquez Montalban, M. and González Calleja, E. *La Méditerranée espangole*. Collection edited by T. Fabre and R. Ilbert. Paris: Maisonneuve et Larose (33-135).

Goytisolo, J. (1990). *Reivindicación del Conde Don Julián.* Madrid: Alianza Editorial.

Goytisolo, J. (2004). Metáforas de la migración. Opening speech at the World Congress of Human Movements and Immigration. Barcelona, September 2004.

Graeme, H. (1994). "Migration and the Family." *United Nations Occasional Papers series* no. 12, Vienna, U.N. Secretariat.

Gramsci, A. (1952). *La questione meridionale.* Rome: Rinascita.

Granovetter, M. (1992 **[1985]).** "Economic Action and Scoial Structure: The Problem of Embeddedness." In Granovetter, M., and Swedberg, R. (eds.), *The Sociology of Economic Life*, 30-53. Boulder, CO, and Oxford: Westview Press.

Granovetter, M., and Swedberg, R. (1992). *The Sociology of Economic Life.* Boulder, CO, Oxford: Westview Press.

Granovetter, M. (1974). *Getting a Job.* Cambridge, MA: Harvard University Press.

Greek Helsinki Monitor and Minority Rights Group. Web page, 21-1- 98. http://www.greekhelsinki.gr.

Green, N. L. (1996). "Women and Immigrants in the Sweatshop: Categories of Labor Segmentation Revisited." Vol., Issue 3 (July 1996): 411-433.

Gregorio, C., and Ramírez, A. (2000). "¿Es España diferente?" In *Papers n.60*, 257-273. Monographic Female Immigration in Southern Europe.

Groppe Compass Maroc. (1999). *The Best of Morocco. Morocco's Economy and Its Leading Companies*. Casablanca: Edicom.

Guarnizo, L. E., and Smith, M. P. (eds.). (1998). "Introduction." In Smith, M. P., and Guarnizo, L. E. (eds.), *Transnationalism from Below*, 3-34. New Brunswick, NJ: Transaction Publishers.

Guiguet-Bologne, P. (1996). *Un Guide de Tanger et de sa région*. Tangier: Philippe Guiguet-Bologne Editeur.

Habermas, J. (1996). "Civil Society and the Political Public Sphere." In *Between Facts and Norms Contribution to a Discourse Theory of Law and Democracy*. Oxford: Polity Press.

Habermas, J. (1994). *The New Obscurity: The Case of the Welfare State and the Exhaustion of Utopian Energies*. Oxford: Polity Press.

Hall, P. (1996). *Cities of Tomorrow. An Intellectual History of Urban Planning and Design in the Twentieth Century*. Oxford and Malden: Blackwell Publishers.

Hamilton, B. (1992). *Albania Who Cares?* Grantham: Autumn House.

Hart, D. M. (1957). "Notes on the Rifian Community of Tangier." *Middle East Journal* (Spring): 153-160.

Held, D., and McGrew, A. (eds.). (2000). *The Global Transformations Reader. An Introduction to the Globalization Debate*. Cambridge: Polity Press.

Herzog, L. A. (1990). *Where North Meets South. Cities, Space and Politics on the U.S.-Mexico Border*. Austin: Center for Mexican American Studies, University of Texas at Austin.

Hirst, P., and Thompson, G. (1999). *Globalization in Question*. Cambridge: Polity Press.

Hoxha, E. (1987). "We Must Involve the Woman Actively in the Problems of Society." In Hoxha, E., *Selected Works. Vol VI*, 688-706. Tirana: 8 Nëntori Publishing House.

Hochschild, A. (2000). "The Nanny Chain." *The American Prospect*, 41 (4) (January).

Human Development Promotion Center (HDPC). (2002a). *The Albanian Response to the Millennium Development Goals*. Tirana: UN Resident Coordinator.

Human Development Promotion Center (HPDC). (2002b). *Human Development Report, Challenges of Local Governance and Regional Development*. Tirana: HDPC.

H.R.W. Human Rights Watch. (1998). "Greece. The Turks of Western Thrace." *A Human Rights Watch Report*. 11 (1(D).

Ilbert, R. (2003). L'échelle du monde. Séminaire commun: La Méditerranée, un système relationnel? Maison Méditerranéenne des Sciences de l´Homme, Aix-en-Provence, 19 June 2003.

ICMC and IOM. (2002). "II Research Report on Third Country National Trafficking Victims in Albania in Inter-Agency Referral System (IARS)." Project for Return and Reintegration Assistance to Victims of Trafficking. Tirana: IOM.

IDRA/DPA. (2002). *Albania Business Guide*. Tirana: Institute for Development Research and Alternatives (IDRA)/ DPA Consulting Ltd.

IMF. (2001). *International Monetary Fund Country Report No. 01/118*. Washington DC: IMF.

INSTAT. (2002). *The Population of Albania in 2001. Main Results of the Population and Housing Census*. Tirana: INSTAT.

Institut Français d´Urbanisme. (2000). *La medina de Tanger: élements de diagnostic urbain. Les enjeux commerciaux et artisanaux*. Paris: Institut Français d´Urbanisme.

Institute of Ecological and Regional Development (IOER) and Deutsche Gesellschaft für Technische Zusammentarbeit (GTZ). (2002). *Towards a Sustainable Development Study for the Tirana-Durres Region. Regional Development Study for the Tirana-Durres Region: Development Concept.* Tirana: IOER and GTZ.

IOM. (2002a). *Report on the Nationwide Survey Conducted on the Attitude of Albanian Teenagers on Migration and Trafficking in Human Beings.* Tirana: IOM.

IOM. (2002b). *Interim Report on Reintegration Assistance to Albanian Victims of Trafficking through the Capacity. Building of a National Reintegration Support Network (RTA).* Tirana: IOM.

IOM/ICMC. (2002). "II Research Report on Third Country National Trafficking Victims in Albania. Inte-Agency Referral System (IARS)." Project for Return and Reintegration Assistance to Victims of Trafficking. Tirana: ICMC, IOM.

IRES (Istituto di Richerche Economico Sociali), Morosini, L. (dir.). (1998). *Le leggi, i servizi, la rete. La presenza degli immigrati extracomunitari a Torino.* Relazione del grupo di ricerca di Torino. Progetto Horizon "Ecrire, lire, s´inserer."

IRES, Morosini. (1997). *Il mondo dei minori stranieri a Torino.* Torino: Provincia di Torino. Assessorato alla Solidarietà e Politiche per i giovani.

IRES, Morosini. (1994). *Le chiavi della città. Politiche per gli immigrati a Torino e Lione.* Turin: Rosenberg & Sellier.

Jiménez Álvarez, M. (2003). *Buscarse la vida. Análisis transnacional de los procesos migatorios de los menores marroquíes en Andalucía. Cuadernos de la Fundación Santa María.* Madrid: SM Ediciones.

Jiménez Álvarez, M. (2001). "La emigración irregular de menores marroquíes no acompañados a España: el contexto migratorio en Tánger y su área urbana." *Agencia Española de Cooperación Internacional.*Tangier, July.

Jiménez, M., and Trichot, C. (2001). "Condiciones Laborales de las empresas marroquíes de confección textil subcontratadas por empresas españolas: el fenómeno de la internacionalización." Fundación Jaume Bofill. Barcelona, June.

Kadaré, I. (2001). *Abril quebrado.* Madrid: Alianza Editorial.

Kadaré, I. (1995). *Dialogue avec Alain Bosquet.* Paris: Libraire Arthème Fayard.

Kagitçibasi, C. (1992). *Evoluzione della famiglia nelle società islamiche e oltre,* relazione al Convegno "Famiglie musulmane immigrate fra pratiche e diritto." Fondazione Giovanni Agnelli, Turin, 5-6 October 1992.

Karidis, V. (1993). "Migrants as a Political Enterprise: The Greek-Albanian Case." *Chroniques* 8, 93-96.

Khatibi, A. (dir.) (2001). *Rapport du Social 2001, Bulletin Économique et Social du Maroc,* Rabat: OKAD.

Kibria, N. (1993). *Family Tightrope. The Changing Lives of Vietnamese Americans.* Princeton, NJ: Princeton University Press.

King, R. (1997). "Southern Europe in the Changing Global Map of Migration." International Conference: "Non-military Aspects of Security in Southern Europe: Migration, Employment and the Labour Market." Santorini (Greece), 19-21 September.

King, R. (1998). "The Mediterranean—Europe's Rio Grande." In Anderson, M., and Bort, E. (eds.), *The Frontiers of Europe,* 19-34. London: Pinter.

King, R. (ed.). (2000). "Introduction." In King, R., Lazaridis, G., and Tsardanidis, C. (eds). *Eldorado or Fortress? Migration in Southern Europe,* 3-26. Basingstoke: Macmillan Press Ltd.

King, R. (ed.) (2001). *The Mediterranean Passage. Migration and New Cultural Encounters in Southern Europe.* Liverpool: Liverpool University Press.

King, R., and Ribas-Mateos, N. (2004). International Migration and Globalisation in the Mediterranean: The "Southern European model" (in press).

King, R., Mai, N., and Dalipaj, M. (2003). *Exploding the Migration Myths.* London: The Fabian Society/Oxfam.

King, R., and Ribas-Mateos, N. (2002). *"Towards a Diversity of Migratory Types and Contexts in Southern Europe."* Studi Emigrazione, *145: 5-25.*

King, R., Cori, B., and Vallega, A. (2001). "Unity, Diversity and the Challenge of Sustainable Development: An Introduction to the Mediterranean." In King, R., de Mas, P., and Beck, M. (eds.), *Geography, Environment and Development of the Mediterranean*, 1-17. Brighton and Portland: Sussex Academic Press.

King, R., and Zontini, E. (2000). "The Role of Gender in the South European Immigration Model." In *Papers*, N. 60, 35-52, Monographic Female Immigration in Southern Europe.

King, R., Fielding, A., and Black, R. (1997). "The International Migration Turnaround in Southern Europe." In King, R., and Black, R. (eds.), *Southern Europe and the New Immigrations*, 1-25. Brighton: Sussex Academic Press.

Knox, P. L., and Taylor, P. (eds.). (1995). *World Cities in a World-system.* Cambridge: Cambridge University Press.

Kuhnle, S., and Selle, P. (1993). "Enti pubblici e organizzazioni volontarie: un approccio relazionale." In Ascoli, U., and Pasquinelli, S. (eds.), Il welfare mix. Stato sociale e terzo settore. Milan: Franco Angeli.

Kwan Lee, Ch. (1995). "Engendering the Worlds of Labor: Women Workers, Labor Markets and Prodution Politics in the South China Economic Miracle." *American Sociological Review*, 60 (3), 378-397.

La Cava, G., and Nannetti, R. (2000). *Albania. Filling the Vulnerability Gap.* World Bank Technical Paper n. 460. Washington DC: The International Sustainable Development Series.

Lahlou, M. (2002). "¿Por qué emigrans?" In Barros, L. (et al.), La inmigración irregular subsahariana a través y hacia Marruecos. *Estudios sobre migraciones internacionales.* N 54, 1-15. Geneva: Oficina Internacional del Trabajo.

Lahlou, M. (2001). "Activité, emploi et chômage (1999-2000)." *Bulletin économique du Maroc*, 51-58. Rabat: Editions Okad.

Lefebvre, H. (1991). *The Production of Space.* Oxford: Blackwell.

Lee, C. (1995). "Engendering the Worlds of Labor: Women Workers, Labor Markets and Production Politics in the South China Economic Miracle." *American sociological Review*, 60, 378-397.

Leiken, R. S. (2000). *The Melting Border. Mexico and Mexican Communities in the United States.* Washington, DC: Center for Equal Opportunity.

Lenclud, G. (2001). "Le patronage politique. Du contexte aux raisons." In Albera, D., Blok, A., Bromberger, C. (dirs.), *L'anthropologie de la Méditerranée. Anthropology of the Mediterranean*, 277-306. Paris: Maison et Larose.

Leuthardt, B. (2002). *Aux marges de l'Europe. Reportages.* Lausanne: Éditions d'en bas.

Lewis, J. (ed.) (1999). *Gender, Social Care and Welfare Restructuring in Europe.* Aldershot: Ashgate Publishing Company.

Lewis, J. (1993). *Women and Social Policies in Europe: Work, Family and the State.* Aldershot: Edward Elgar Publishing.

Lewis, J. (1983). "Introduction." In Lewis, J. (ed.) *Women's Welfare, Women's Rights.* London and Sydney: Croom Helm.

Lewis, J., and Hobson, B. (1997). "Introduction." In Lewis, J. (ed.), *Lone Mothers in European Welfare Regimes. Shifting Policy Logics*, 50-70. London: Jessica Kingsley Publishers.

Lianos, T. P., Sarris, A. H., and Katseli, L. (1996). "Illegal immigration and Local Labour Markets: The Case of Northern Greece." *International Migration Review* 34 (3).

Lin, N. (1998). *Reconstructing China Town. Ethnic Enclave, Global Change.* Minnneapolis and London: University of Minnesota Press.

Lloyd, C. (1995). "International Comparisons in the Field of Ethnic Relations." In Hargreaves, A. G., and Leaman, J. (eds.) *Racism, Ethnicity, and Politics in Contemporary Europe.* Aldershot: Edward Elgar Publishing Limited.

Lomnitz, L. (1977a). *The Social and Economic Organization of a Mexican Shanty-Town.* Oxford: Oxford University Press.

Lomnitz, L. (1977b). *Networks and Marginality. Life in a Mexican Shanty-Town.* London: Academic Press.

Lostia, A., and Tomaino, G. (1994). "Diritti sociali e differenze territoriali." In Zincone, G., *Uno schermo contro il razzismo. Per una politica deu diritti utili.* Roma: Donzelli editore.

Lussault, M., and Signoles, P. (1996). "La citadinité en questions." Collection Sciences de la Ville. *URBAMA*, n. 13, Fascicule de Recherches n. 29. Tours: Centre d´Etudes et de Recherches URBAMA. "Urbanisation du Monde Arabe" et MSV, Maison des sciences de la ville.

Lynch, K. (1960). "The City Image and Its Elements," from the Image of the City. Extract in LeGates, R. T., and Stout, E. (eds.), *The City Reader*, 1996, 2nd ed., 2000. Routledge: London and New York.

Machado, F. L., and Firmino da Costa, A. (1998). "Processo de uma mordernidade inacabada. Mudanças estruturais e mobilidade social." In Leite Viegas, M., and Firmino da Costa, A. (orgs.), *Portugal, que Modernidade?* 17-44. Oeiras: Celta.

Maher, V. (1994). "La famiglia immigrata." In Reginato, M. (ed.), *La famiglia immigrata: interpretazioni socio-demografiche di una realtà in crescita.* Turin: Cicsene.

Mai, N. (2003). "The Cultural Construction of Italy in Albania and Vice Versa: Migration Dynamics, Strategies of Resistance and Politics of Mutual Self-destination across Colonialism and Post-colonialism." *Modern Italy*, 8 (1), 77-93.

Mai, N. (2002). *Between Losing and Finding Oneself: The Role of Italian Television in the Albanian Migration to Italy.* Dphil Thesis in Media and Cultural Studies Graduate Centre in Culture and Communication, University of Sussex.

Makhija, M., Kim, K., and Williamson, S. (1997). "Measuring Globalization of Industries Using a National Industry Approach: Empirical Evidence across Five Countries and over Time." *Journal of International Business Studies*, 28 (4), 679-710.

Malheiros, J. (2001). "Arquipélagos Migratorios: transnacionalismo e Inovação." Ph,D, diss., Universidade de Lisboa, Faculdade de Letras, Lisbon.

Malheiros, J., and Ribas-Mateos, N. (2002). "Immigration and Place in Northern Mediterranean Cities: Issues for Debate." In Fonseca et al. (dirs.), *Immigration and Place in Mediterranean Metropolises*, 293-308. Lisbon: Luso-American Foundation.

Manry, V. (2001). "Être en affaire Compétences relationnelles, éthique de la performance et ordre social au marché aux Puces." In Peraldi, M. (dir.), *Cabas et containers. Activités marchandes informelles et réseaux migrants transfrontaliers.* Séries Frontières, villes: lieux de passage. Paris: Maisoneuve et Larose/Maison méditerranéenne des sciences de l´homme.

Marcus, G. E. (1998). *Ethnography through Thick and Thin.* Princeton, NJ: Princeton University Press.

Marcus, G. E. (1995). "Ethnography in the World System: The Emergence of Multi-Sited Ethnograpny." *Annual Review of Anthropology*, 25, 95-117.

Marques, M. M., Santos, R., Ralha, T., and Cordeiro, A.R. (1998). "Oeiras City Template. Multicultural Policies and Modes of Citizenship." *SOCINOVA Working Papers*, no. 6, FCSH-UNL.

Marshall, T. H. (1950). *Citizenship and Social Class.* Cambridge: Cambridge University Press.

Martín Corrales, E. (2000). *La imagen del magrebí en España. Una perspectiva histórica siglos XVI-XX.* Barcelona: Edicions Bellaterra.

Martin, C. (1997). "Protection sociale et protection par la famille en Europe du Sud: quelles spécificités?" In MIRE (ed.), *Comparer les systèmes de protection sociale en Europe du Sud,* 341-362. Actes des rencontres de Florence, Institut universitaire européen, Imprimerie nationale, Ministère des Affaires sociales, July.

Martin-Hilali, F. (1996). "Images du centre ville de Tanger: pratique et perception de l'espace." In Samrakandi, M. H., and El Kouche, B., *Tangier au miroir d'elle-meme.* No. 31-32 (Spring), 49-57.

Martínez, O. J. (1994). *Border People. Life and Society in the US-Mexico Borderlands.* Tucson: The University of Arizona Press.

Martínez Veiga, U. (1999). *Pobreza, segregación y exclusión espacial. La vivienda de los inmigrantes extranjeros en España.* Barcelona: Icària-Institut Català d'Antropologia.

Mauss, M. (1990). *The Gift.* London and New York: Routledge Classics.

Mcfate, K., Lawson, R., Wilson, W. J. (eds.). (1995). *Poverty, Inequality and the Future of Social Policy.* New York: Russel Sage Foundation.

Menjot, D. (1996). "La ville frontière: un modèle original d'urbanisation?" In Menjot, D. (ed.), *Les villes frontière (Moyen Age-Epoque Moderne).* Paris and Montreal: L'Harmattan.

Merton, R. K. (1987). "Three Fragments from a Sociologist's Notebook: Establishing the Phenomenon, Specified Ignorance, and Strategic Research Materials." *Annual Review of Sociology* 13, 1-28.

Messina, A. (1992). *Albania.* Turin: Clup-Guide.

Millet, K. (1970). *Sexual Politics.* New York: Doubleday and Cia.

Minardi, E. (1997). "Lavoratori in Italia, imprenditori in patria. E'possibile un circolo virtuoso per l'immigrazione?" In Convegno Internazionale *Migrazione, interazioni e conflitti nella construzioni di una democrazia Europea.* Bologna, 17 December.

Mingione, E. (1996a). "Youth Unemployment and Informal Work: Is there a Model for Southern Europe?" *Inchiesta,* 21 (113), (July-September), 65-73.

Mingione, E. (1996b). "Urban Poverty in the Advanced Industrial World: Concepts, Analysis and Debates." In Mingione, E. (ed.), *The Conditions of Urban Poverty.* Oxford: Blackwell.

Mingione, E. (1995). "Labour Market Segmentation and Informal Work in Southern Europe." *European Urban and Regional Studies* 2 (2), 121-143.

Mingione, E. (1994). "Life Strategies and Social Economies in the Postfordist Age." *International Journal of Urban and Regional Research* 18 (1), 24-45.

Mingione, E. (1991). *Fragmented Societies. A Sociology of Economic Life Beyond the Market Paradigm.* Oxford: Basil Blackwell. (Spanish edition of 1994 used).

Mingione, E. (1986). "La povertà familiare nelle città meridionali." *Inchiesta,* Anno XVI, Luglio-Settembre. Bari: Dedalo, no.73, 53-71.

Mingione, E., Miguélez, F., and Alois, W. (1990). *Programme for Research and Action on the Development of the Labour Market. Underground Economy and Irregular Forms of Employment* (Travail au noir). Luxembourg: Commission of the EC.

Mingione, E., and Quassoli, F. (2000). "The Participation of Immigrants in the Underground Economy in Italy." In King, R., Lazaridis, G., and Tsardanidis, C. (eds.), *Eldorado or Fortress? Migration in Southern Europe,* 27–56. London: Macmillan.

Ministère de la Prévision Economique et du Plan. (2000). "Plan De Développement Economique et Social: La Valorisation des Ressources Humaines et le Développement Social." Rabat: Ministére de la Prévision Economique et du Plan.

Ministerio del Interior. (2000). *Estadísitica general de población penitenciaria. Administración General y total nacional.* Madrid: Gabinete técnico. Servicio de Planificación y Seguimiento.

Ministerio de Trabajo y Asuntos Sociales. (2002). *Anuario de Migraciones 2002*. Madrid: Subdirección General de Publicaciones.

Mittelman, J. (2000). *The Globalization Syndrome. Transformation and Resistance*. Princeton, NJ: Princeton University Press.

Mittelman, J. (1996). *The Dynamics of Globalization: Critical Reflections*. International Political Economy Yearbook, vol. 9. Boulder, CO: Lynne Reinner.

Montagut, T. (1994). *Democràcia i serveis socials*. Barcelona: ed. Hace.

Montenay, Y. (2001). "Méditerranée: Les contrastes démographiques." *Population & Avenir*, 655, 4-6.

Moreno, L. (1984). *Il Welfare state in Italia. Sviluppo e crisi in prospettiva comparata*. Bologna: Il Mulino.

Morlichio, E. (1996a). *Povertà, Disoccupazione ed Esclusione Sociale*. Naples: Libreria Dante & Descartes.

Morlichio, E. (1996b). "Exclusion from Work and the Impoversihment Processes in Naples," In Mingione, E. (ed.), *Urban Poverty and the Underclass: A Reader*. Cambridge, MA: Blackwell.

Morozzo della Rocca, R. (1997*). Albania. Le radici della crisi*. Milan: Guerini e Associati.

Moser, C., and Peake, L. (1995). *Seeing the Invisible: Women, Gender and Urban Development. In Perspectives on the City*. Edited by R. Stren with J. Kjellberg Bell. Toronto: Centre for Urban and Community Studies.

Muka, E. (2002). "Caiguda lliure en el trànsit albanès." In Shehu, B. (coord.), *Tiran[í]a*, 145-158. Barcelona: CCCB and Diputació de Barcelona.

Muss, P., and Van Dam, W. (1996). *Comparative Research on International Migration and International Migration Policy. Migration from the Maghreb and Turkey to the European Union, and from Mexico, Guatemala and El Salvador to the United States*. European Commission. Luxembourg: Office for Official Publications of the European Communities.

Nash, J. (2001). "Global Integration and Subsistence Insecurity." In Rees, M. W., and Smar, J. (ed.), *Plural Globalities in Multiple Localities. New World Borders. Monographs in Economic Anthropology*, 12. Boston: University Press of America.

Nee, V., and Matthews, R. (1996). "Market Transition and Societal Transformation in Reforming State Socialism." *Annual Review of Sociology*, 22, 401-435.

Negri, N., and Saraceno, C. (1996). *Le politiche contra la povertà in Italia*. Bologna: Il Mulino.

Ngjeci, E. (2003). *Evaluation of the Socio-economic and Cultural Situation of Migrants in a Suburb Area of Durres (Porto-Romano and Spitalle, Durres)*. Council of Associations offering social services.

NNUU. (1999). *Informe sobre sobre el desarrollo humano 1999*. Madrid: Ediciones Mundi-Prensa.

Norris, H.T. (1993). *Islam in the Balkans. Religion and Society between Europe and the Arab World*. London: Hurts & Company.

Nunes de Almeida, A. (1984). *Do campo a cidade: impacto do processo de migraçâo na organizaçâo interna da familia*. Lisbon: Comissâo da Condiçâo Feminina.

Nunes de Almeida, A., Guerreiro, M. D., Lobo, C. Torres, A., Wall, K. (1998). "Relaçôes familiares: mudança e diversidade." In Leite Viegas, M., and Firmino da Costa, A. (orgs.), *Portugal, que Modernidade?* 45-78. Oeiras: Celta.

OECD. (1994). *Women and Structural Change. New perspectives*. Paris: OECD.

OECD (2001). *Trends in International Migration. Continuous Reporting System on Migration*. Paris: OECD.

OSCE. (2002). *Country Report Submitted to the Informal Group on Gender Equality and Anti-Trafficking in Human Beings*. OSCE Human Dimension Implementation Meeting, Tirana.

Oso, L. (1998). *La inmigración a España de las mujeres jefas de hogar.* Madrid: Instituto de la Mujer.

Papantoniou, A. K. (1996). *Migrant Insertion in the Informal Economy, Deviant Behaviour and the Impact on Receiving Societies.* Greek Report for the Commission of the European Community. MIGRINF Project.

Pardo, I. (1996). *Managing Existence in Naples. Morality, Action and Structure.* Cambridge: Cambridge University Press.

Pascual de Sans, A. (2001). "Sense of Place and Migratory Histories. Idiotopy and idiotope." Paper presented at the World Population Conference, Brazil, June.

Peraldi, M. (2003). "Droit de visite et principe d´humanité." *La pensée de midi.* n. 10 (Summer), 21-30.

Peraldi, M. (2001). "Introduction." In M. Peraldi (dir.), *Cabas et containers. Activités marchandes informelles et réseaux migrants transfrontaliers. Séries Frontiéres, villes: lieux de passage,* 7-31. Paris: Maisoneuve et Larose, Maison méditerranéenne des sciences de l´homme.

Peraldi, M., and Perrin, E. (1996). *Réseaux Productifs et Territoires Urbains.* Toulouse: Presses Universitaires du Mirail.

Peristiany, J., and Handman, M. E. (1989). *Le prix de l'alliance en Méditerranée.* Paris: Editions du CNRS.

Perulli, P. (1992). *Atlas metropolitano. El cambio en las grandes ciudades.* Bologna: Il Mulino.

Petmesidou, M. (1996). "Social Protection in Southern Europe: Trends and Prospects." *Journal of Area Studies. Southern Europe in Transition* 9 (Autumm), 95-125.

Petmesidou, M., and Tsoulovis, L. (1994). "Aspects of the Changing Political Economy of Europe: Welfare State, Class Segmentation and Planning in the Postmodern Era." *Sociology,* 28 (2), 99-519.

Petropolous, N. (1996). 1996 *SOPEMI Report on Greece.* Athens: OECD.

Pinson, D. (1992). *Modèles d´Habitat et contre-types domestiques au Maroc. Fascicule de Recherches* no. 23. Tours: Centre d´Etudes et de Recherches URBAMA. "Urbanisation du Monde Arabe."

Plasari, A. (1998). *La linea di Teodosio. Torna a dividere.* Bari: BESA Editrice.

PNUD (Programme des Nations Unies pour le Developpement). (1999). *Diagnostic de la Pauvrete à Tanger.* Programme pilote de lutte contre la pauvreté en milieu urbain et peri-urbain. Rabat: PNUD/Ministère du Developpement Social, de la Solidarité, de l´Emploi et de la Formation Professionnelle, Royaume du Maroc.

Portes, A. (1999). "La mondialisation par le bas. L´émergence des communautés transnationales." *Actes de la Recherche en Sciences Sociales.* "Délits d´immigration," 15-25. September.

Portes, A. (1997). "Immigration Theory for a New Century: Some Problems and Opportunities" *International Migration Review* 31 (4) (Winter), 799-825.

Portes, A. (1995). "Economic Sociology and the Sociology of Immigration: A Conceptual Overview." In Portes, A. (ed.), *The Economic Sociology of Immigration: Essay on Networks, Ethnicity, and Enterpreneurship,* 1-41. New York: Russell Sage Foundation.

Portes, A. (1995). *En torno a la informalidad: Ensayos sobre teoría y medición de la economía no regulada.* México: Grupo Editorial Miguel Ángel Porrua.

Portes, A., and Rumbaut, R. G. (1990). *Immigrant America. A Portrait.* Berkeley and Los Angeles: University of California Press.

Portes, A., Castells, M., and Benton, L.A. (1989a). "Introduction." In Portes, A., Castells, M., and Benton, L. A. (eds.), *The Informal Economy. Studies in Advanced and Less-Developed Countries,* 1-7. Baltimore: The John Hopkins University Press.

Portes, A., Castells, M., and Benton, L.A. (1989b). *The Informal Economy. Studies in Advanced and Less Developed Countries*. Baltimore and London: The Johns Hopkins University Press.

Poulton, H. (1997a). "Islam, Ethnicity and State in Contemporary Balkans." In Poulton, H., and Taji-Faourki, S. (eds.), *Muslim Identity and the Balkan State*. New York: New York University Press.

Poulton, H. (1997b). "Changing Notions of National Identity among Muslims in Thrace and Macedonia: Turks, Pomaks and Roma." In Poulton, H., and Taji-Faourki, S. (eds.), *Muslim Identity and the Balkan State*, 82-102. New York: New York University Press.

Prencipe, L. (1994). "Famiglia-Migrazioni-Europa: quali agganci possibili?" *Servizio Migranti,* Serie Migrantes, IV, 1, (January-February).

Psycho-Social Center "Vatra." (2002). "The Girls and the Trafficking. Research on the Trafficking in Human Beings for the Year 2002." Vlora: Vatra Center.

Pteroudis, E. (1996). "Émigrations et immigrations en Grèce: évolutions récentes et questions politiques." *Revue Européene des Migrations Internationales* 12 (1), 159-187.

Pugliese, E. (1997). "Immigration in Southern Europe." Paper presented at the conference: "Migration, Social Exclusion and the Globalisation of Urban Populations." International conference organized by "Migrants in European Cities Network." Scarman House Conference Centre. University of Warwick, United Kingdon, 29-31 May.

Pugliese, E. (1996). "L´immigrazione." In various authors, *Storia dell´Italia Repubblicana*. Turin: Einaudi, III/1.

Pumares, P. (2003). "La inmigración en España: perspectivas desde el territorio." In Aubarell, G. (dir.), *Perspectivas de la inmigración en España*, 177-200. Barcelona: Icaria-Antrazyt.

Pumares, P. (1996). *La integración delos inmigrantes marroquíes. Familias marroquies en la Comunidad de Madrid*. Barcelona: Fundación "la Caixa."

Rabinow, P. (1988 [1977]) *Un ethnologue au Maroc. Réflexion sur une enquête de terrain*. Paris: Hachette.

Ragin, C. C., and Becker, H. S. (1992). *What is a Case? Exploring the Foundations of Social Inquiry*. Cambridge: Cambridge University Press.

Ram, M., Abbas, A., Sanghera, B., Barlow, G., and Jones, T. (2001). "Making the Link: Households and Small Business Activity in a Multi-Ethnic Context." *Community, Work and Family* (3), 327-348.

Ramírez, A. (1998). *Migraciones, género e Islam. Mujeres marroquíes en España*. Madrid: Agencia Española de Cooperación Internacional.

Ramírez, A., and López García, B. (eds.). (2002). *Antropología y antropólogos en Marruecos*. Barcelona: Edicions Bellaterra.

Ranci, C. (1998). "El papel del tercer sector en las políticas de bienestar en Italia." In Sarasa, S., and Moreno, L. (eds.), *El Estado de Bienestar en la Europa del Sur*, 187-214. Madrid: CSIC (Consejo superior de investigaciones científicas).

Rees, M. W., and Smart, J. (2001). *Plural Globalities in Multiple Localities. New World Borders. Monographs in Economic Anthropology*. Lanham: University Press of America.

Refass, M. (1993). "Réflexion sur le tourisme et l'emploi touristique à Tangier." *Espace, économie et societé*. Tangier: Université Mohammed V. Faculté des Lettres et des Sciences humaines and Université Abdelmalek Es-Saadi. Ecole Supérieure Roi Fah de Traduction.

Reffas, M. (1996). *L´organisation urbaine de la péninsule tingitane*. Rabat: Faculté des Lettres et des Sciences Humaines.

Reher, D. S. (1998). "Family Ties in Western Europe: Persistent Contrasts." *Population and Development Review* 24 (2) (June) 203-234.

Renton, D. (2001). "Results of Questionnaires in the Puka district." In *Child Trafficking in Albania.* Save the Children. Tirana.

Renton, D., and Capra, S. (2002). *Bambine in vendita. Un'indagine sul traffico dei minori dall'Albania.* Milan: Associazione Culturale Mimesis.

Reyneri, E. (ed.). (2001). *Migrants in Irregular Employment in the Mediterranean Countries of the European Union.* International Migration Papers, 41. Geneva: International Labour Office.

Ribas-Mateos, N. (2003a). "Tanger & Durrës: sur les marches de l´Europe Méditerranéenne." *La pensée de midi.* n. 10,(Summer), 52-63.

Ribas-Mateos, N. (2003b). "Redes y espacios. Formación de redes sociales en la movilidad." In Aubarell, G. (dir.), *Perspectivas de la inmigración en España*, 205-226. Barcelona: Icaria Antrazyt Mediterráneo.

Ribas-Mateos, N. (2002a). *El debate sobre la globalización.* Colección Biblioteca del ciudadano. Barcelona: Edicions Bellaterra.

Ribas-Mateos, N. *(2002b). "Migrant Women in Southern European Cities." In Fonseca, M. L. et al.,* Immigration and Place in Mediterranean Metropolises*, 53–65. Lisbon: Luso-American Foundation.*

Ribas-Mateos, N. (2001a). "Revising Migratory Contexts: The Mediterranean Caravanserai." In King, R. (ed.), *The Mediterranean Paṣṣage. Migration and New Cultural Encounters in Southern Europe*, 22-40. Liverpool: Liverpool University Press.

Ribas-Mateos, N. (2001b). "¿Estrategias trasnacionales? Una pregunta acerca de las migraciones femeninas en España." *Revista Arxius de Ciències Socials*, 5, (November), 69-92.

Ribas-Mateos, N. (2000). "Old Communities, Excluded Women and Change in Western Thrace." Monographic "Inmigración femenina en el Sur de Europa" *Revista, Papers*, 60.

Ribas-Mateos, N. (1999a). "Female Birds of Passage, Leaving and Settling in Spain." In Floya, A., and Lazaridis, G., *Women in the Diaspora: Gender and Migration in Southern Europe*, 173-197. Oxford: Berg Publishers.

Ribas-Mateos, N. (1999b). *Las presencias de la inmigración femenina. Un recorrido por Filipinas, Gambia y Marruecos en Cataluña.* Colección Icaria Antracyd. Barcelona: Editorial Icaria.

Ribas-Mateos, N. (1998). "Les ciutats i els immigrants: cinc casos de gestió municipal a Europa." Barcelona: Ajuntament de Barcelona (internal report).

Ribas-Mateos, N. (1997). "Greek Immigration Policies: The Impact on Immigrants and Their Families." *Laboratorio de Estudios Interculturales.* Facultad de Educacion. Universidad de Granada. September (unpublished).

Ribas-Mateos, N., Almeda, E., and Bodelón, E. (2005). *Rastreando lo invisible. Mujeres inmigrantes en las cárceles españolas.* Barcelona: Anthropos.

Ring, H. (1995). "Refugees in Sweden: Inclusion and Exclusion in the Welfare State." In Miles, R., and Thränhardt, D. (eds.), *Migration and European Integration. The Dynamics of Inclusion and Exclusión.* London and Madison: Pinter Publishers and Fairleigh Dickinson University Press.

Rodríguez Cabrero, G. (1998). "El Estado de Bienestar en España: pautas evolutivas y reestructuración institucional." In Gomà, R.; Subirats, J. (coords.), *Políticas publicas en España. Contenidos, Redes de actores y niveles de gobierno*, 61-84. Barcelona: Ariel Ciencia Política.

Romano, O. (1999). *L´Albania nell´era televisiva. Le vie della demodernizzazione.* Turin: L´Harmattan Italia. Collana "Logiche Sociali."

Roque, M. A. (dir.). (1999). *L´espai mediterrani llatí*. Barcelona: Institut Català de la Mediterrània.

Roque, M. A. (dir.). (2002). *La sociedad civil en Marruecos. La emergencia de nuevos actores*. Barcelona: Icaria Antrazyt/Iemed.

Rosenau, J. N. (1997). *Along the Domestic-Foreign Frontier: Exploring Governance in a Turbulent World*. Cambridge: Cambridge University Press.

Royaume du Maroc. (2000). *Anuaire Statistique Régional Tanger-Tetovan*. Rabat: Ministére de la Prévision Economique et du Plan.

Royaume du Maroc. (1998). *Diagnostic de la pauvreté en milieu urbain et peri-urbain a Tanger*. Ministére du Developpement social, de la Solidarité, de l'Emploi et de la Formation Professionnelle and Programme des Nations Unies pour le Développement (PNUD). Tangier: Programme Pilote de Lutte contre la pauvreté en milieu urbain et peri-urbain.

S.D.A.U. (Schéma Directeur d'Aménagement Urbain de Tanger). (1997). *Plan de ordenación urbana de Tánger*. Final Report. Ministére de l´Interieur, Royaume du Maroc and Ministerio de Asuntos Exteriores.

Sahlins, P. (1989). *The Making of France and Spain in the Pyrenees*. Berkeley: University of California Press.

Said, E. W. (1995). *Orientalism*. London: Penguin.

Sainsbury, D. (ed.). (1994). *Gendering Welfare States*. London: Sage.

Saint-Blancat, C. (1995). *L´Islam della diaspora*. Rome: Edizioni Lavoro Roma.

Salzinger, L. (2003). *Genders in Production. Making Workers in Mexico's Global Factories*. Berkeley: University of California Press.

Samrakandi, M., and El Kouche, B. (1996). "Tanger au miroir d´elle-même." *Horizons Maghrébins*, 31-32. Toulouse: Université de Toulouse-Le Mirail.

Samuel, N. (1989). "A quoi sert la recherche comparative internationale." *Comparaisons Internationales*, numéro special. IRESCO (Institut de recherce sur les sociétés contemporaines). September, 1-7.

SAPS (Seminari D´Anàlisi de Polítiques Socials), UAB. (1998). "Las relaciones entre política social y estructura social: una propuesta teórica." TMR Workshop on *The Institutionalisation of Family Policies*. Barcelona.

Saraceno, C. (ed.). (2003). *Social Assistance Dynamics in Europe. National and Local Welfare Regimes*. Cambridge: Polity Press.

Saraceno, C. (1998). *Mutamenti della famiglia e politiche sociali in Italia*. Bologna: Il Mulino.

Saraceno, C. (1997). "La politiche per la famiglia." In Barbagli, M., and Saraceno, C. (eds.), *Lo stato delle famiglie in Italia*. Bologna: Il Mulino.

Saraceno, C. (1995). "Familismo ambivalente y clientelismo categórico en el estado del bienestar italiano." In Sarasa, S., and Moreno, L. (eds.), *El Estado de Bienestar en la Europa del Sur*, 261-286. Madrid: CSIC (Consejo superior de investigaciones científicas).

Sarasa, S. (1995). "La sociedad civil en la Europa del sur. Una perspectiva comparada de las relaciones entre estado y asociaciones altruistas." In Sarasa, S., and Moreno, L. (eds.), *El Estado de Bienestar en la Europa del Sur*, 157-186. Madrid: CSIC (Consejo superior de investigaciones científicas).

Sassen, S. (2001). *The Global City: New York, London, Tokyo*. Princeton, NJ, and Oxford: Princeton University Press.

Sassen, S. (2000). *Cities in a World Economy*. Thousand Oaks, CA: Pine Forge Press.

Sassen, S. (2000a). "Regulating Immigration in a Global Age: A New Policy Landscape." *AAPSS*, 570, 65-77.

Sassen, S. (2000b). "The Global City: Strategic Site/New Frontier." *American Studies* 42 (2/3), 79-95.

Sassen, S. (2000c). "Women's Burden: Counter-Geographies of Globalization and the Feminization of Survival." *Journal of International Affairs*. 53 (2), 503-524.

Sassen, S. (1999). "Beyond Sovereignty: De-Facto Transnationalism in Immigration Policy." *European Journal of Migration and Law* 1, 177-198.

Sassen, S. (1999a). *Guests and Aliens*. New York: The New Press.

Sassen, S. (1998). *Globalization and Its Discontents. Essays on the New Mobility of People and Money.* New York: The New York Press.

Sassen, S. (1996). *Losing Control? Sovereignty in an Age of Globalization*. New York: Columbia University Press.

Sassen, S. (1995). "Immigration and Local Labor Markets." In Portes, A. (ed.), *The Economic Sociology of Immigration*, 87-127. New York: Russell Sage Foundation.

Sassen, S. (1988). *The Mobility of Labor and Capital. A Study in International Investment and Labor Flow*. Cambridge: Cambridge University Press.

Sassen-Koob, S. (1984). "Notes on the Incorporation of Third World Women into Wage-Labor through Immigration and Off-shore Production." *International Migration Review*, 18 (4), 1144-1167.

Scanbini, E., and Regalia, C. (1993). "La famiglia degli extracomunitari nella percezione della prima generazione di immigrati." In Scanini, E., and Donati, P. (eds.), *La famiglia in una società multietnica*. Milan: Vita e Pensiero.

Schnapper, D. (1992). *L'Europe des Immigrés*, Paris: Francois Bourin.

Schwander-Sievers, S. (1999). "Humiliation and Reconciliation in Northern Albania. The Logics of Feuding in Symbolic and Diachronic Perspectives." In Elwert, G., Feuchtwang, S., and Neubert, D. (eds.), *Dynamics of Violence: Processes of Escalation and De-escalation in Violent Group Conflicts*. Sociologus, supplement 1, 133-152. Berlin: Dunker and Humbolt.

Seabrook, J. (1996). *In the Cities of the South. Scenes from a Developing World.* London and New York: Verso.

Shehu, B. (coord.). (2002). *Tiran[i]a.* Barcelona: CCCB and Diputació de Barcelona.

Signoles, P. (1999). "Acteurs publics et acteurs privés dans le développement des villes du monde arabe." In Signoles, P., El Kadi, G., and Sidi Boumedine, R. *L'urbain dans le monde arabe. Politiques, instruments et acteurs*, 19-53. Paris: CNRS Editions.

Signoles, P., El Kadi, G., and Sidi Boumedine, R. (1999a). *L'urbain dans le monde arabe. Politiques, instruments et acteurs*. Paris: CNRS Editions.

Signoles, P., El Kadi, G., and Sidi Boumedine, R. (1999b). "Introduction." In Signoles, P., El Kadi, G,. and Sidi Boumedine, R., *L'urbain dans le monde arabe. Politiques, instruments et acteurs*, 1-16. Paris: CNRS Editions.

Simmons, C. P., and Kalantaridis, C. (1994). "Flexible Specialization in the Southern European Periphery: The Growth of Garment Manufacturing in Peonia County, Greece." *Comparative Studies in Society and History* 36 (4), 649-675.

Simon, G. (1987). "La façade Sud de l'Union Européenne: de nouveaux espaces d'immigration" In Simon, G., *Géodynamique des migrations internationales dans le monde*. Paris: Presses Universitaires de France.

Smith, J., and Wallerstein, I. (1992). *Creating and Transforming Households. The Constraints of the World Economy*. Cambridge and Paris: Cambridge University Press and Editions de la Maison de l'Homme.

Smith, J., Wallerstein, I., and Evers, H. D. (eds.). (1984). *Households and the World Economy*. Beverly Hills, London, and New Delhi: Sage Publications.

Smith, M. P. (1992). "Postmodernism, Urban Ethnography and the New Social Space of Ethnic Identity." *Theory and Society*, 21 (4), 493-531.

Solé, C., and Ribas-Mateos, N. (eds.). (2004). "Migration and the European South." Monographic. *Journal of Ethnic and Migration Studies.*

Solé C., Ribas, N., Bergalli, V., Parella, N. (1998). "Irregular Employment amongst Migrants in Spanish Cities." *JEMS*, 24 (2), 333-346.

Solomos, J. (1982). "Urban Policies, Migrant Workers and Political Authority Processes of Migration and Capitalist Integration in Catalonia." In Rex, J., and Solomos, J. (eds.). *Migrant Workers in Metropolitan Cities.* Strasbourg: European Science Foundation.

Solsona, M., Houle, R., and Simó, C. (1999). "Separation and Divorce in Spain." In González, M. J., Jurado, T,. and Naldini, M., "Introduction: Interpreting the Transformation of Gender Inequalities in Southern Europe," in González, M. J., Jurado, T., Naldini, M. *South European Society & Politics,* 4, (2), 195-222.

SOS Racismo. (2001). *Informe anual 2001 sobre el racismo en el Estado español.* Barcelona: Icaria.

Soulis, S. (1987). "L´immigration illégale en Grèce." *L´avenir des migrations.* Paris: OCDE.

Soysal Nuhoglu, Y. (1994). *Limits of Citizenship: Migrants and Postnational Membership in Europe.* Chicago: University the Chicago Press.

Stame, N. (1990). *Strategie familiari e teorie dell´azione sociale.* Milan: Franco Angeli.

Staud, K. (1998). *Free trade? Informal Economies at the US-Mexico Border.* Philadephia: Temple University Press.

Stewart, A. (1998). *The Ethnographers's Method.* Thousand Oaks, CA: Sage Publications.

Subirats, J. (1998). "Contexto e instrumental de análisis." In Gomà, R., and Subirats, J. (eds.), *Políticas publicas en España. Contenidos, Redes de actores y niveles de gobierno.* Barcelona: Ariel Ciencia Política.

Subirats, J., and Gomà, R. (1998). "Democratización: dimensiones de conflicto y políticas públicas en España." In Gomà, R., and Subirats, J. (eds.). *Políticas publicas en España. Contenidos, Redes de actores y niveles de gobierno.* Barcelona: Ariel Ciencia Política.

Taji-Faoruki, S., and Poulton, H. (1997). "Introduction." In Poulton, H., and Taji-Faourki, S. (eds.). *Muslim Identity and the Balkan State*, 1-12. New York: New York University Press.

Tapinos, G. P. (2000). "Globalisation, Regional Integration, International Migration." *International Social Science Journal*, 52, 3 (165), 297-306.

Tapinos, G., and Delaunay, D. (2000). *Can One Really Talk of the Globalization Migration Flows? Globalization, Migration and Development.* Paris: OECD.

Tarrius, M. (2002). "Au-delà des Etats-Nations: réseaux et sociétés de migrants en Méditerrannée Occidentale." Colloque Economie de bazar dans les métropoles euroméditerranéenes. Aix-en-Provence, 29-31 May 2002. Maison Méditerranéene des Sciences de l´Homme.

Tarrius, A. (2000). *Les nouveaux cosmopolitismes. Mobilités, identités, territoires.* La Tour d´Aigues: Editions de l´Aube.

Terre des hommes. (2003). *The Trafficking of Albanian Children in Greece.* Tirana: Terre des hommes.

Tersigni, S. (2001). "Honneur maghrébin" différence culturelle et intégration. Variations sur quelques mots/maux des sciences sociales." *Confluences Méditerranée*, 29, (Autumn), 55-65.

Torns, T. (1995). "Los nuevos empleos, cualificación y valoración." Paper presented at the Séminaire IRIS: Une vision plus large, Brussels. June.

Trifiletti, R. (1998). "Southern European Welfare Regimes and the Worsening Position of Women." TMR Conference *Family and Family Policies in Southern Europe*, Turin, 19-21 November.

UNDP. (2000). *Albania Human Development Report 2000.* Tirana: UNDP.

United Nations Centre for Human Settlements (Habitat). (2001). *Cities in a Globalizing World. Global Report on Human Settlements 2001*. London and Sterling : Earthscan.

Urry, J. (2000). *Sociology beyond Societies. Mobilities for theTwenty-First Century*. London: Routledge.

USAID, Vitosha Research. (2002). *Corruption Indexes. Regional Corruption Monitoring in Albania, Bosnia and Herzekovina, Bulgaria, Croatia, Macedonia, Romania, and Yugoslavia, April 2002*.

Various authors. (1994). *La salute straniera. Epidemiologia, culture, diritti*. Naples: Edizioni Scientifiche Italiane.

Vázquez, A. (1990 [1976]). *La vida perra de Juanita Narboni*. Barcelona: Seix Barral.

Vellante, S., and Consiglio P. (1990). "Il lavoro extra-comunitario in un´area del Mezzogiorno." *La questione agraria*, 39, 147-188.

Vernier, B. (1981). "Représentation mythique du monde et domination masculine chez les Pomakes grecs." *The Greek Review of Social Research*. Numéro Spécial. Aspects du changement social dans la campagne grecque. EKKE, 121-142.

Vernier, V. (1955). *La Singulière Zone de Tanger. Ses différents aspects et ce qu´elle pourrait devenir si...* Paris: Editions surafricanes.

Vertovec, S. (1997). "Minority Association, Networks and Public Policies: Re-assessing Relationships." MIGCITIES Conference *Migration, Social Exclusion and the Globalisation of Urban Populations*, Warwick, 29-31 May.

Vickers, M. (1995). *The Albanians. A Modern History*. New York: St. Martin Press.

Vila, P. (ed.). (2003a). *Ethnography at the Border. Cultural Studies of the Americas*, 13. Minneapolis and London: University of Minnesota Press.

Vila, P. (ed.). (2003b). "Introduction: Border Ethnographies." In Vila, P. (ed.), *Ethnography at the Border. Cultural Studies of the Americas*, 13, xi-xxxv. Minneapolis and London: University of Minnesota Press.

Vila, P. (ed.). (2003c). "Conclusion: The Limits of American Border Theory." In Vila, P. (ed.),*Ethnography at the Border. Cultural Studies of the Americas*, 13, 306-341. Minneapolis and London: University of Minnesota Press.

Vila, P. (2001). "Border Ethnographies. Cultural Studies and the Limits of Border Theory." Paper presented at the American Sociological Association Annual Conference, Annaheim. August.

Wall, K. (1998). "Portugal: Issues Concerning the Family in 1996." *European Observatory on National Family Policies, Developments in National Family Policies in 1996*, 213-249. Keighley: European Commission.

Wall, K. (1982). *A outra face da emigraçâo; estudos sobre a situaçâo das mulheres que ficam no pais de origem*. Comisissâo para a igualdade e para diretos das mulheres. Lisbon.

Wallerstein, I. (1985). "The Relevance of the Concept of Semiperiphery to Southern Europe." In Arrighi, G., *Semiperipheral Development. The Politics of Southern Europe in the Twentieth Century*, 31-39. Beverly Hills, New Delhi: Sage Publications.

Wallerstein, I. (1984). "Household Structures and Labour Force Formation in the Capitalist World-Economy." In Smith, J., Wallenstein, I., and Evers, H. D. (eds.), *Households and the World Economy*, 17-22. Beverly Hills, London and New Delhi: Sage Publications.

Wallerstein, I., and Smith, J. (1992). "Core-periphery and Household Structures." In Smith, J., and Wallerstein, I. (eds.). *Creating and Transforming Households. The Constraints of the World Economy*. Cambridge and Paris: Cambridge University Press and Editions de la Maison des Sciences de l´Homme.

Walton, J. (1982). "International Economy and Peripheral Urbanization." In Fainstein, I., and Fainstein, S., *Urban Poverty under Capitalism*, 119-135. Beverly Hills, London, and New Delhi: Sage Publications.

Wellman, B., Carrington, P.J., and Hall, A. (1998). "Networks as Personal Communities." In B. Wellman, B., and Berkomta, S. P. (eds.), *Social Structures: A network approach*, 61-80. Cambridge: Cambridge University Press.

Werth, M., and Körner, H. (1991). "Immigration of Citizens from Third Countries into the Southern Member States of the EEC." *Social Europe*, Supplement 1/91.

Wijers, M., and Lap-Chew, L. (1997). *Trafficking in Women, Forced Labour and Slavery-like Practices in Marriage Domestic Labour and Prostitution*. Utrecht: STV.

Wilkinson, F. (et al.) (edS.). (1981). *The Dynamics of Labour Market Segmentation*. London: Academic Press.

Wilson, F. (1989). *Social Policy: A Critical Introduction. Issues of Race, Gender and Class*. Oxford and New York: Polity Press and Basil Blackwell.

Wilson, W. J. (1996). *When Work Disappears. The World of the New Urban Poor*. New York: Alfred A. Knopf.

Wilson, W. J. (ed.). (1993). *The Ghetto Underclass. Social Science Perspectives*. London: Sage.

Wilson, W. J. (1987). *The Truly Disadvantaged: The Inner City, the Underclass, and Public Policy* Chicago: University of Chicago Press.

World Bank. (2003). *World Bank Financing to Albania*. Tirana: ILAR.

World Bank. (2000a). *Urban and Local Government Strategy*. Washington DC: World Bank.

World Bank. (2000b). *Albania: Filling the Vulnerability Gap*. Washington DC: World Bank.

World Bank (2000c). *Cities in Transition. World Bank Urban and Local Government Strategy*. Washington, DC: World Bank.

Yue-Man Yeung. (1995). "Globalization and Cities in Developing Countries." In Stren, R., and Kjellberg Bell, J. (eds.), *Perspectives on the City*. Toronto: Centre for Urban and Community Studies.

Zincone, G. (ed.). (2001). *Secondo rapporto sull'integrazione degli immigrati in Italia*. Bologna: Il Mulino.

Zincone, G. (1994a). *Uno schermo contro il razzismo. Per una politica dei diritti utili*. Rome: Donzelli editore.

Zincone, G. (1994b). "Immigration to Italy: Data and Policies." In Heckmann, F., and Bosswick, W. (eds.), *Migration Policies: a Comparative Perspective*. Bamberg: European Forum for Migration Studies.

Zontini, E. (2001). "Family Formation in Gendered Migrations: Moroccan and Filipino Women in Bologna." In King, R., *The Mediterranean Passage: Migration and the New Cultural Encounters in Southern Europe*, 231-257. Liverpool: Liverpool University Press.

Index